WANT TO LEARN MORE?

Scan the QR code below or visit **cpm.org/cpminfo.** Watch the video to see CPM in action and **sign up for a free two-week preview of our eBooks!** A group of experienced CPM classroom teachers, rather than a sales team, serves as the Regional Coordinators for the schools and teachers in their local areas. Contact your Regional Coordinator to set up a presentation or workshop for your school or district. **Visit our website at CPM.ORG.**

CPM CPM EDUCATIONAL PROGRAM
an educational 501(c)(3) nonprofit

Core Connections Geometry
Second Edition*, Version 5.0

Managing Editors / Authors

Leslie Dietiker, Ph.D., Director of Curriculum (First Edition)
Boston University
Boston, MA

Michael Kassarjian (2nd Edition)
CPM Educational Program
Kensington, CA

Contributing Authors

Elizabeth Coyner
Christian Brothers High School
Sacramento, CA

Scott Coyner
Christian Brothers High School
Sacramento, CA

Lew Douglas
The College Preparatory School
Oakland, CA

David Gulick
Phillips Exeter Academy
Exeter, NH

Judy Kysh
San Francisco State University
San Francisco, CA

Lara Lomac
Phillip and Sala Burton Academic
High School, San Francisco, CA

Sarah Maile
CPM Educational Program
Sacramento, CA

Damian Molinari
Phillip and Sala Burton Academic
High School, San Francisco, CA

Jason Murphy-Thomas
George Washington High School
San Francisco, CA

Chris Mikles
Post Falls Middle School
Post Falls, ID

Leslie Nielsen
Isaaquah High School
Issaquah, WA

Misty Nikula
CPM Educational Program
Bellingham, WA

Karen O'Connell
San Lorenzo High School
San Lorenzo, CA

Bob Petersen
Rosemont High School
Sacramento, CA

Ward Quincey
Gideon Hausner Jewish Day School
Palo Alto, CA

Tom Sallee
University of California, Davis
Davis, CA

Barbara Shreve
San Lorenzo High School
San Lorenzo, CA

Michael Titelbaum
University of California
Berkeley, CA

Technical Manager

Sarah Maile
Sacramento, CA

Program Directors

Elizabeth Coyner
CPM Educational Program
Sacramento, CA

Leslie Dietiker, Ph.D.
Boston University
Boston, MA

Lori Hamada
CPM Educational Program
Fresno, CA

Brian Hoey
CPM Educational Program
Sacramento, CA

Michael Kassarjian
CPM Educational Program
Kensington, CA

Judy Kysh, Ph.D.
Departments of Education and
Mathematics San Francisco
State University, CA

Tom Sallee, Ph.D.
Department of Mathematics
University of California, Davis

Karen Wootton
CPM Educational Program
Odenton, MD

*Based on *Geometry Connections*

e-book Manager
Carol Cho
Director of Technology
Martinez, CA

e-book Programmers
Rakesh Khanna
Daniel Kleinsinger
Kevin Stein

e-book Assistants
Stephanie Achondo
Debbie Dodd
Shirley Paulsen
Wendy Papciak
Anna Poehlmann

Assessment Manager
Karen Wootton
Director of Assessment
Odenton, MD

Assessment Contributors
John Cooper
Leslie Dietiker, Ph.D.
Damian Molinari

Laura Lomac
Barbara Shreve

Assessment Website
Elizabeth Fong
Michael Huang
Daniel Kleinsinger

Illustration
Kevin Coffey
San Francisco, CA

Homework Help Manager
Bob Petersen
CPM Educational Program

Homework Help Website
Carol Cho
Director of Technology

Parent Guide with Extra Practice
Karen Wootton
CPM Educational Program
Odenton, MD

Elizabeth Coyner
Christian Brothers High School
Sacramento, CA

Bob Petersen
CPM Educational Program
Sacramento, CA

Technical Manager
Rebecca Harlow

Technical Assistants
Stephanie Achondo
Carrie Cai
Elizabeth Fong
Thomas Leong
Marcos Rojas

Erica Andrews
Daniel Cohen
Rebecca Harlow
Aubrie Maize
Susan Ryan

Elizabeth Burke
Carmen de la Cruz
Michael Leong
Anna Poehlmann

5 6   18 17 16 15
Printed in the United States of America

Version 5.0
ISBN: 978-1-60328-108-9

A Note to Students:

Welcome to a new year of math! In this course, you will learn to use new models and methods to think about problems as well as solve them. You will be developing powerful mathematical tools and learning new ways of thinking about and investigating situations. You will be making connections, discovering relationships, figuring out what strategies can be used to solve problems, and explaining your thinking. Learning to think in these ways and communicate about your thinking is useful in mathematical contexts, other subjects in school, and situations outside the classroom. The mathematics you have learned in the past will be valuable for learning in this course. That work, and what you learn in this course, will prepare you for future courses.

In meeting the challenges of this course, you will not be learning alone. You will cooperate with other students as a member of a study team. Being a part of a team means speaking up and interacting with other people. You will explain your ideas, listen to what others have to say, and ask questions if there is something you do not understand. In this course, a single problem can often be solved several ways. You will see problems in different ways than your teammates do. Each of you has something to contribute while you work on the lessons in this course.

Together, your team will complete problems and activities that will help you discover mathematical ideas and develop solution methods. Your teacher will support you as you work, but will not take away your opportunity to think and investigate for yourself. Each topic will be revisited many times and will connect to other topics. If something is not clear to you the first time you work on it, you will have more chances to build your understanding as the course continues.

Learning math this way has an advantage: as long as you actively participate, make sure everyone in your study team is involved, and ask good questions, you will find yourself understanding mathematics at a deeper level than ever before. By the end of this course, you will have a powerful set of mathematical tools to use to solve new problems. With your teammates you will meet mathematical challenges you would not have known how to approach before.

In addition to the support provided by your teacher and your study team, CPM has also created online resources to help you, including help with homework, and a parent guide with extra practice. You will find these resources and more at www.cpm.org.

We wish you well and are confident that you will enjoy this next year of learning!

Sincerely,

The CPM Team

Core Connections Geometry
Student Edition

CHAPTER 1   Shapes and Transformations

Welcome to Geometry! *Geo* means Earth (*geo*graphy is mapping the Earth, for example) and *metry* means measurement. Geometry applies the arithmetic, algebra and reasoning skills you have learned to the objects you see all around you. During this course, you will ask and answer questions such as "How can I describe this shape?", "How can I measure this shape?", "Is this shape symmetrical?", and "How can I convince others that what I think about this shape is true?"

This chapter begins with some activities that will introduce you to the big ideas of the course. Then you will apply motions to triangles and learn how to specify a particular motion. Finally, you will explore attributes of shapes that can be used to categorize and name them and find the probabilities of selecting shapes with certain properties from a "shape bucket."

In this chapter, you will:

➢ Become familiar with basic geometric shapes and learn how to describe each one using its attributes, such as parallel sides or rotation symmetry.

➢ Investigate three basic rigid transformations: reflection (flip), rotation (turn), and translation (slide).

Chapter Outline

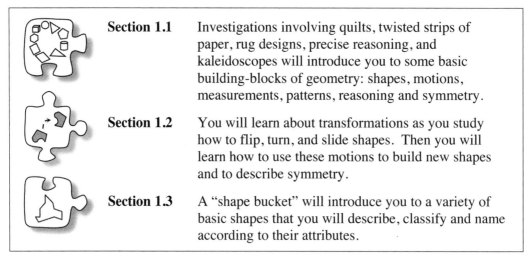

	Section 1.1	Investigations involving quilts, twisted strips of paper, rug designs, precise reasoning, and kaleidoscopes will introduce you to some basic building-blocks of geometry: shapes, motions, measurements, patterns, reasoning and symmetry.
	Section 1.2	You will learn about transformations as you study how to flip, turn, and slide shapes. Then you will learn how to use these motions to build new shapes and to describe symmetry.
	Section 1.3	A "shape bucket" will introduce you to a variety of basic shapes that you will describe, classify and name according to their attributes.

1.1.1 How can I design it?

. . . .

Creating a Quilt Using Symmetry

Welcome to Geometry! But what is geometry? At the end of this chapter you will have a better understanding of what geometry is. To start, you will focus on several activities that will hopefully challenge you and introduce you to important concepts in geometry that you will study in this course. While all of the problems are solvable with your current math skills, some will be revisited later in the course so that you may apply new geometric tools to solve and extend them.

Today you will consider an example of how geometry is applied in the world around you. A very popular American tradition is to create quilts by sewing together remnants of cloth in intricate geometric designs. These quilts often integrate geometric shapes in repeated patterns that show symmetry. For centuries, quilts have been designed to tell stories, document special occasions, or decorate homes.

1-1.   DESIGNING A QUILT, Part One

How can you use symmetry to design a quilt? Today you will work with your team to design a patch that will be combined with other team patches to make a class quilt. Before you start, review the Team Roles, which are outlined following this problem.

a.   Each team member will receive four small squares. With a colored pencil or marker, shade in *half* of each square (one triangle) as shown at right. Each team member should use a different color.

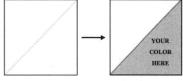

b.   Next arrange your squares to make a larger 2-by-2 square (as shown at right) with a design that has **reflection symmetry**. A design has reflection symmetry if it can be folded in half so that both sides match perfectly. Make sure that you have arranged your pieces into a different symmetrical pattern than the rest of your team.

Problem continues on next page →

1-1.   *Problem continued from previous page.*

    c.   Next, create a 4-by-4 square using the designs created by each team member as shown on the Lesson 1.1.1B Resource Page. Ask your teacher to verify that your designs are all symmetrical and unique. Then glue (or tape) all sixteen pieces carefully to the resource page and cut along the surrounding dashed square so that you have a blank border around your 4-by-4 square.

    d.   Finally, discuss with your team what all of you personally have in common. Come up with a team sentence that captures the most interesting facts. Write your names and this sentence in the border so they wrap around your 4-by-4 design.

To help you work together today, each member of your team has a specific job, assigned by your first name (or last name if team members have the same first name).

Team Roles

Resource Manager – If your name comes first alphabetically:

- Make sure the team has all of the necessary materials, such as colored pencils or markers and the Lesson 1.1.1A and 1.1.B Resource Pages.

- Ask the teacher when the *entire* team has a question. You might ask, *"No one has an idea? Should I ask the teacher?"*

- Make sure your team cleans up by delegating tasks. You could say, *"I will put away the _____ while you _____ ."*

Facilitator – If your name comes second alphabetically:

- Start the team's discussion by asking, *"What are some possible designs?"* or *"How can we make sure that all of our designs are symmetrical?"* or *"Are all of our designs different?"*

- Make sure that all of the team members get any necessary help. You don't have to answer all the questions yourself. A good facilitator regularly asks, *"Do you understand what you are supposed to do?"* and *"Who can answer _____'s question?"*

Recorder/Reporter – If your name comes third alphabetically:

- Coordinate the taping or gluing of the quilt pieces together onto the resource page in the orientation everyone agreed to.

- Take notes for the team. The notes should include phrases like, *"We found that we all had in common …"* and explanations like, *"Each of our designs was found to be unique and symmetrical because …"*

- Help the team agree on a team sentence: *"What do we all have in common?"* and *"How can I write that on our quilt?"*

Task Manager – If your name comes fourth alphabetically:

- Remind the team to stay on task and not to talk to students in other teams. You can suggest, *"Let's try coming up with different symmetrical patterns."*

- Keep track of time. Give your team reminders, such as *"I think we need to decide now so that we will have enough time to …"*

1-2.   DESIGNING A QUILT, Part Two

Your teacher will ask the Recorder/Reporters from each team to bring their finished quilt patches up to the board one at a time and tape them to the other patches. Be prepared to explain how you came up with your unique designs and interesting ideas about symmetry. Also be prepared to read your team sentence to the class. As you listen to the presentations, look for relationships between your designs and the other team designs.

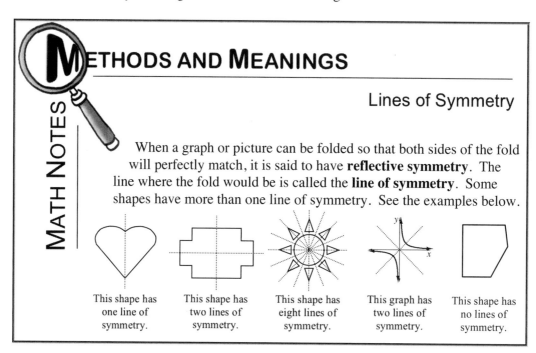

MATH NOTES

METHODS AND MEANINGS

Lines of Symmetry

When a graph or picture can be folded so that both sides of the fold will perfectly match, it is said to have **reflective symmetry**. The line where the fold would be is called the **line of symmetry**. Some shapes have more than one line of symmetry. See the examples below.

This shape has one line of symmetry.

This shape has two lines of symmetry.

This shape has eight lines of symmetry.

This graph has two lines of symmetry.

This shape has no lines of symmetry.

Review & Preview

1-3.   One focus of this Geometry course is to help you recognize and accurately identify a shape. For example, a **rectangle** is a four-sided shape with four right angles. Which of the shapes below can be called a rectangle? More than one answer is possible.

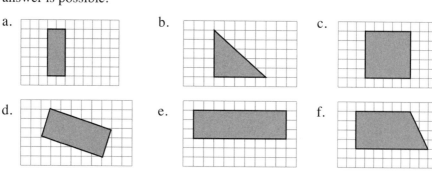

Core Connections Geometry

1-4.   Calculate the values of the expressions below. Show all steps in your process.
        The answers are provided for you to check your result. If you miss two or more
        of these and cannot find your errors, be sure to seek help from your team or
        teacher.

        a. $2 \cdot (3(5+2)-1)$ **[40]**   b. $6-2(4+5)+6$ **[–6]**

        c. $3 \cdot 8 \div 2^2 +1$ **[7]**   d. $5-2 \cdot 3+6(3^2+1)$ **[59]**

1-5.   Match each table of data on the left with its equation on the right and briefly
        explain why it matches the data.

        a.
x	1	0	–4	2	–2	–1
y	4	3	–1	5	1	2

        b.
x	–1	3	1	0	–2	2
y	–1	–9	–1	0	–4	–4

        c.
x	3	–2	1	0	2	–3
y	12	7	4	3	7	12

        d.
x	–3	4	2	–2	0	–10
y	–10	11	5	–7	–1	–31

        (1) $y = x$

        (2) $y = 3x - 1$

        (3) $y = x + 3$

        (4) $y = x^2$

        (5) $y = -x^2$

        (6) $y = x^2 + 3$

1-6.   Simplify the expressions below as much as possible.

        a. $2a + 4(7 + 5a)$ b. $4(3x + 2) - 5(7x + 5)$

        c. $x(x + 5)$ d. $2x + x(x + 6)$

1-7.   Examine the graph at right. Then, in a sentence
        or two, suggest reasons why the graph rises at
        11:00 a.m. and then drops at 1:15 p.m.

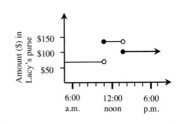

1.1.2 Can you predict the results?

· ·

Making Predictions and Investigating Results

Today you will investigate what happens when you change the attributes of a Möbius strip. As you investigate, you will record data in a table. You will then analyze this data and use your results to brainstorm further experiments. As you look back at your data, you may start to consider other related questions that can help you understand a pattern and learn more about what is happening. This way of thinking, called investigating, includes not only generating new questions, but also rethinking when the results are not what you expected.

1-8.   Working effectively with your study team will be an important part of the learning process throughout this course. Choose a member of your team to read aloud these Study Team Expectations:

STUDY TEAM EXPECTATIONS

Throughout this course you will regularly work with a team of students. This collaboration will allow you to develop new ways of thinking about mathematics, increase your ability to communicate with others about math, and help you strengthen your understanding by having you explain your thinking to someone else. As you work together,

- You are expected to share your ideas and contribute to the team's work.

- You are expected to ask your teammates questions and to offer help to your teammates. Questions can move your team's thinking forward and help others to understand ideas more clearly.

- Remember that a team that functions well works on the same problem together and discusses the problem while it works.

- Remember that one student on the team should not dominate the discussion and thinking process.

- Your team should regularly stop and verify that everyone on the team agrees with a suggestion or a solution.

- Everyone on your team should be consulted before calling on the teacher to answer a question.

1-9. On a piece of paper provided by your teacher, make a "bracelet" by taping the two ends securely together. Putting tape on both sides of the bracelet will help to make sure the bracelet is secure. In the diagram of the rectangular strip shown at right, you would tape the ends together so that point *A* would attach to point *C*, and point *B* would attach to point *D*.

Now predict what you think would happen if you were to cut the bracelet down the middle, as shown in the diagram at right. Record your prediction in a table like the one shown below or on your Lesson 1.1.2 Resource Page.

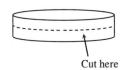

Cut here

	Experiment	Prediction	Result
1-9	Cut bracelet in half as shown in the diagram.		
1-10			
1-11			
1-12a			
1-12b			
1-12c			
1-12d			

Now cut your strip as described above and record your result in the first row of your table. Make sure to include a short description of your result.

1-10. On a second strip of paper, label a point X in the center of the strip at least one inch away from one end.

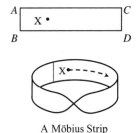

A Möbius Strip

Now turn this strip into a **Möbius strip** by attaching the ends together securely after making one twist. For the strip shown in the diagram at right, the paper would be twisted once so that point *A* would attach to point *D*. The result should look like the diagram at right.

Predict what would happen if you were to draw a line down the center of the strip from point X until you ran out of paper. Record your prediction, conduct the experiment, and record your result.

1-11.   What do you think would happen if you were to cut your Möbius strip along the central line you drew in problem 1-10? Record your prediction in your table.

Cut just one of your team's Möbius strips. Record your result in your table. Consider the original strip of paper drawn in problem 1-9 to help you explain why cutting the Möbius strip had this result.

1-12.   What else can you learn about Möbius strips? For each experiment below, first record your expectation. Then record your result in your table after conducting the experiment. Use a new Möbius strip for each experiment.

a.   What if the result from problem 1-11 is cut in half down the middle again?

b.   What would happen if the Möbius strip is cut one-third of the way from one of the sides of the strip? Be sure to cut a constant distance from the side of the strip.

c.   What if a strip is formed by 2 twists instead of one? What would happen if it were cut down the middle?

d.   If time allows, make up your own experiment. You might change how many twists you make, where you make your cuts, etc. Try to generalize your findings as you conduct your experiment. Be prepared to share your results with the class.

1-13.   LEARNING REFLECTION

Think over how you and your study team worked today, and what you learned about Möbius strips. What questions did you or your teammates ask that helped move the team forward? What questions do you still have about Möbius strips? What would you like to know more about?

METHODS AND **M**EANINGS

The Investigative Process

The **investigative process** is a way to study and learn new mathematical ideas. Mathematicians have used this process for many years to make sense of new concepts and to broaden their understanding of older ideas.

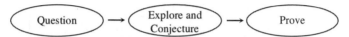

In general, this process begins with a **question** that helps you frame what you are looking for. For example, a question such as, "*What if the Möbius strip has 2 half-twists? What will happen when that strip is cut in half down the middle?*" can help start an investigation to find out what happens when the Möbius strip is slightly altered.

Once a question is asked, you can make an educated guess, called a **conjecture**. This is a mathematical statement that has not yet been proven.

Next, **exploration** begins. This part of the process may last awhile as you gather more information about the mathematical concept. For example, you may first have an idea about the diagonals of a rectangle, but as you draw and measure a rectangle on graph paper, you find out that your conjecture was incorrect. When this happens, you just experiment some more until you have a new conjecture to test.

When a conjecture seems to be true, the final step is to **prove** that the conjecture is always true. A proof is a convincing logical argument that uses definitions and previously proven conjectures in an organized sequence.

1-14. A major focus of this course is learning the **investigative process**, a process you used during the Möbius Strip activity in problems 1-9 through 1-12. One part of this process is asking mathematical questions.

Assume your teacher is thinking of a shape and wants you to figure out what shape it is. Write down three questions you could ask your teacher to determine more about his or her shape.

1-15.   The shapes at right are examples of **equilateral triangles**. How can you describe an equilateral triangle? Examine them and make at least two statements that seem true for all equilateral triangles. Then trace these equilateral triangles on your paper and draw one more in a different orientation.

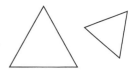

Examples of Equilateral Triangles

1-16.   Match each table of data below with the most appropriate graph and briefly explain why it matches the data.

   a.   Boiling water cooling down.

Time (min)	0	5	10	15	20	25
Temp (˚C)	100	89	80	72	65	59

   b.   Cost of a phone call.

Time (min)	1	2	2.5	3	4	5	5.3	6
Cost (cents)	55	75	75	95	115	135	135	155

   c.   Growth of a baby in the womb.

Age (months)	1	2	3	4	5	6	7	8	9
Length (inches)	0.75	1.5	3	6.4	9.6	12	13.6	15.2	16.8

Graph 1   Graph 2   Graph 3   Graph 4   Graph 5

1-17.   Solve for the given variable. Show the steps leading to your solution. Check your solution.

   a. $-11x = 77$ b. $5c + 1 = 7c - 8$

   c. $\frac{x}{8} = 2$ d. $-12 = 3k + 9$

1-18.   Calculate the values of the expressions below. Show all steps in your process.

   a. $\frac{3(2+6)}{2}$ b. $\frac{1}{2}(14)(5)$

   c. $7^2 - 5^2$ d. $17 - 6 \cdot 2 + 4 \div 2$

1.1.3 How can I predict the area?

• •

Perimeter and Area of Enlarging Tile Patterns

One of the core ideas of geometry is the measurement of shapes. Often in this course it will be important to find the areas and perimeters of shapes. How these measurements change as a shape is enlarged or reduced in size is especially interesting. Today your team will apply algebraic skills as you investigate the areas and perimeters of similar shapes.

1-19.   CARPETMART

Your friend Alonzo has come to
your team for help. His family owns
a rug manufacturing company,
which is famous for its unique and
versatile designs. One of their most
popular designs is shown at right.
Each rug design has an "original"
size as well as enlargements that are
exactly the same shape.

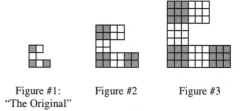

Figure #1:   Figure #2   Figure #3
"The Original"

Alonzo is excited because his family
found out that the king of a far-away
land is going to order an extremely large
rug for one of his immense banquet
halls. Unfortunately, the king is fickle
and won't decide which rug he will order
until the very last minute. The day
before the banquet, the king will tell
Alonzo which rug he wants and how big
it will need to be. The king's palace is
huge, so the rug will be VERY big!

Since the rugs are different sizes, and since each rug requires wool for the interior and fringe to wrap around the outside, Alonzo will need to quickly find the area and perimeter of each rug in order to obtain the correct quantities of wool and fringe.

Your Task: Your teacher will assign your team one of the rug designs to investigate (labeled (a) through (f) below). The "original" rug is shown in Figure 1, while Figures 2 and 3 are the next enlarged rugs of the series. With your team, create a table, graph, and equation for both the area and perimeter of your rug design. Then decide which representation will best help Alonzo find the area and perimeter for *any* figure number.

Problem continues on next page →

1-19.   *Problem continued from previous page.*

Be ready to share your analysis with the rest of the class. Your work must include the following:

- Diagrams for the rugs of the next two sizes (Figures 4 and 5) following the pattern shown in Figures 1, 2, and 3.

- A description of Figure 20. What will it look like? What are its area and perimeter?

- A table, graph, and equation representing the perimeter of your rug design.

- A table, graph, and equation representing the area of your rug design.

Rug Designs:

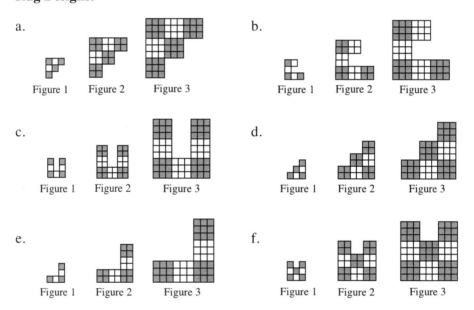

a.

Figure 1   Figure 2   Figure 3

b.

Figure 1   Figure 2   Figure 3

c.

Figure 1   Figure 2   Figure 3

d.

Figure 1   Figure 2   Figure 3

e.

Figure 1   Figure 2   Figure 3

f.

Figure 1   Figure 2   Figure 3

Further Guidance

1-20.   To start problem 1-19, first analyze the pattern your team has been assigned on graph paper, draw diagrams of Figures 4 and 5 for your rug design. Remember to shade Figures 4 and 5 the same way Figures 1 through 3 are shaded.

1-21.   Describe Figure 20 of your design. Give as much information as you can. What will it look like? How will the squares be arranged? How will it be shaded?

1-22.   A table can help you learn more about how the perimeter changes as the rugs
         get bigger.

   a.   Organize your perimeter data in a table like the one shown below.

Figure number	1	2	3	4	5	20
Perimeter (in units)						

   b.   Graph the perimeter data for Figures 1 through 5. (You do not need to
         include Figure 20.) What shape is the graph?

   c.   How does the perimeter grow? Examine your table and graph and
         describe how the perimeter changes as the rugs get bigger.

   d.   Generalize the patterns you have found by writing an equation that will
         find the perimeter of any size rug in your design. That is, what is the
         perimeter of Figure n? Show how you got your answer.

1-23.   Now analyze how the area changes with a table and graph.

   a.   Make a new table, like the one below, to organize information about the
         area of each rug in your design.

Figure number	1	2	3	4	5	20
Area (in square units)						

   b.   On a new set of axes, graph the area data for Figures 1 through 5. (You do
         not need to include Figure 20.) What shape is the graph?

   c.   How does the area grow? Does it grow the same way as the perimeter?
         Examine your table and graph and describe how the area changes as the
         rugs get bigger.

   d.   Write an equation that will find the area of Figure n. How did you find
         your equation? Be ready to share your strategy with the class.

                    _____   *Further Guidance*   _____
                              section ends here.

1-24.   The King has arrived! He demands a Rug #100, which is
         Figure 100 in your design. What will its perimeter be?
         Its area? Justify your answer.

METHODS AND MEANINGS

The Perimeter and Area of a Figure

The **perimeter** of a two-dimensional figure is the distance around its exterior (outside) on a flat surface. It is the total length of the boundary that encloses the interior (inside) region. See the example at right.

Perimeter $= 5 + 8 + 4 + 6 = 23$ units

The **area** indicates the number of square units needed to fill up a region on a flat surface. For a rectangle, the area is computed by multiplying its length and width. The rectangle at right has a length of 5 units and a width of 3 units, so the area of the rectangle is 15 square units.

Area $= 5 \cdot 3 = 15$ square units

Review & Preview

1-25. Read the Math Notes box for this lesson, which describes how to find the area and perimeter of a shape. Then examine the rectangle at right. If the perimeter of this shape is 120 cm, which equation below represents this fact? Once you have selected the appropriate equation, solve for x.

$2x + 5$

$6x - 1$

a. $2x + 5 + 6x - 1 = 120$

b. $4(6x - 1) = 120$

c. $2(6x - 1) + 2(2x + 5) = 120$

d. $(2x + 5)(6x - 1) = 120$

1-26. Delilah drew 3 points on her paper. When she connects these points, must they form a triangle? Why or why not? Draw an example on your paper to support your reasoning.

1-27. Copy the table below onto your paper. Complete it and then write an equation that relates x and y.

x	3	−1	0	2	−5	−2	1
y	0			−1			−2

1-28. Rebecca placed a transparent grid of square units over each of the shapes she was measuring below. Using her grid, determine the area of each shape.

a.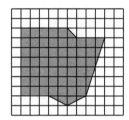

b.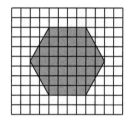

1-29. Evaluate each expression below if $a = -2$ and $b = 3$.

a. $3a^2 - 5b + 8$ b. $\frac{2}{3}b - 5a$ c. $\frac{a+2b}{4} + 4a$

1.1.4 Are you convinced?

Logical Arguments

"I don't have my homework today because…" Is your teacher going to be convinced? Will it make a difference whether you say that the dog ate your homework or whether you bring in a note from the doctor? Imagine your friend says, "I know that shape is a square because it has four right angles." Did your friend tell you enough to convince you?

Many jobs depend on your ability to convince other people that your ideas are correct. For instance, a defense lawyer must be able to form logical arguments to persuade the jury or judge that his or her client is innocent.

1-30.   TRIAL OF THE CENTURY

The musical group Apple Core has accused your math teacher, Mr. Bosky, of stealing its newest pop CD, "Rotten Gala." According to the police, someone stole the CD from the BigCD Store last Saturday at some time between 6:00 p.m. and 7:00 p.m. Because your class is so well known for only reaching conclusions when sufficient evidence is presented, the judge has made you the jury! You are responsible for determining whether or not there is enough evidence to convict Mr. Bosky.

Carefully listen to the evidence that is presented. As each statement is read, decide:

- *Does the statement convince you? Why or why not?*

- *What could be changed or added to the statement to make it more convincing?*

Problem continues on next page →

1-30.   *Problem continued from previous page.*

Testimony

Mr. Bosky: *"But I don't like that CD! I wouldn't take it even if you paid me."*

Mr. Bosky: *"I don't have the CD. Search me."*

Mr. Bosky: *"I was at home having dinner Saturday."*

Casey: *"There were several of us having dinner with Mr. Bosky at his house. He made us a wonderful lasagna."*

Mrs. Thomas: *"All of us at dinner with Mr. Bosky left his house at 6:10 p.m."*

Police Officer Yates: *"Driving as quickly as I could, it took me 30 minutes to go from Mr. Bosky's house to the BigCD store."*

Coach Teller: *"Mr. Bosky made a wonderful goal right at the beginning of our soccer game, which started at 7:00 p.m. You can check the score in the local paper."*

Police Officer Yates: *"I also drove from the BigCD store to the field where the soccer game was. It would take him at least 40 minutes to get there."*

1-31.   THE FAMILY FORTUNE

You are at home when the phone rings. It is a good friend of yours who says, "Hey, your last name is Marston. Any chance you have a grandmother named Molly Marston who was REALLY wealthy? Check out today's paper." You glance at the front page:

Family Fortune Unclaimed

City officials are amazed that the county's largest family fortune may go unclaimed. Molly "Ol' Granny" Marston died earlier this week and it appears that she was survived by no living relatives. According to her last will and testament, "Upon my death, my entire fortune is to be divided among my children and grandchildren." Family members have until noon tomorrow to come forward with a written statement giving evidence that they are related to Ms. Marston or the money will be turned over to the city.

You're amazed – Molly is your grandmother, so your friend is right! However, you may not be able to collect your inheritance unless you can convince city officials that you are a relative. You rush into your attic where you keep a trunk full of family memorabilia.

a.   You find several items that you think might be important in an old trunk in the attic. With your team, decide which of the items listed below will help prove that Ol' Molly was your grandmother.

> **Family Portrait** — a photo showing three young children. On the back you see the date 1968.

> **Newspaper Clipping** — an article from 1972 titled "Triplets Make Music History." The first sentence catches your eye: "Jake, Judy, and Jeremiah Marston, all eight years old, were the first triplets ever to perform a six-handed piano piece at Carnegie Hall."

> **Jake Marston's Birth Certificate** — showing that Jake was born in 1964, and identifying his parents as Phillip and Molly Marston.

> **Your Learner's Permit** — signed by your father, Jeremiah Marston.

> **Wilbert Marston's Passport** — issued when Wilbert was fifteen.

b.   Your team will now write a statement that will convince the city official (played by your faithful teacher!) that Ol' Molly was your grandmother. Be sure to support any claims that you make with appropriate evidence. Sometimes it pays to be convincing!

ETHODS AND MEANINGS

Solving Linear Equations

MATH NOTES

In Algebra, you learned how to solve a linear equation. This course will help you apply your algebra skills to solve geometric problems. Review how to solve equations by reading the example below.

- **Simplify.** Combine like terms on each side of the equation whenever possible.

- **Keep equations balanced.** The equal sign in an equation tells you that the expressions on the left and right are balanced. Anything done to the equation must keep that balance.

$$3x - 2 + 4 = x - 6 \quad \text{Combine like terms}$$
$$3x + 2 = x - 6$$
$$-x = -x \quad \text{Subtract } x \text{ on both sides}$$
$$2x + 2 = -6$$
$$-2 = -2 \quad \text{Subtract 2 on both sides}$$
$$\frac{2x}{2} = \frac{-8}{2} \quad \text{Divide both sides by 2}$$
$$x = -4$$

- **Move your *x*-terms to one side of the equation.** Isolate all variables on one side of the equation and the constants on the other.

- **Undo operations.** Use the fact that addition is the opposite of subtraction and that multiplication is the opposite of division to solve for *x*. For example, in the equation $2x = -8$, since the 2 and the *x* are multiplied, then dividing both sides by 2 will get *x* alone.

1-32.   One goal of this course will be to review and enhance your algebra skills. Read the Math Notes box for this lesson. Then solve for *x* in each equation below, show all steps leading to your solution, and check your answer.

   a. $34x - 18 = 10x - 9$ b. $4x - 5 = 4x + 10$

   c. $3(x - 5) + 2(3x + 1) = 45$ d. $-2(x + 4) + 6 = -3$

1-33. The day before Gerardo returned from a two-week trip, he wondered if he left his plants inside his apartment or outside on his deck. He knows these facts:

- If his plants are indoors, he must water them at least once a week or they will die.

- If he leaves his plants outdoors and it rains, then he does not have to water them. Otherwise, he must water them at least once a week or they will die.

- It has not rained in his town for 2 weeks.

When Gerardo returns, will his plants be dead? Explain your reasoning.

1-34. For each of the equations below, solve for y in terms of x.

a. $2x - 3y = 12$ b. $5x + 2y = 7$

1-35. Examine the rectangle at right.

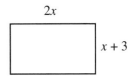

a. What is the perimeter in terms of x? In other words, find the perimeter.

b. If the perimeter is 78 cm, find the dimensions of the rectangle. Show all your work.

c. Verify that the area of this rectangle is 360 sq. cm. Explain how you know this.

1-36. The **slope** of a line is a measure of its steepness and indicates whether it goes up or down from left to right. For example, the slope of the line segment A at right is $\frac{1}{2}$, while the slope of the line segment B is $-\frac{3}{4}$.

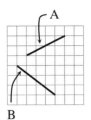

For each line segment below, find the slope. You may want to copy each line segment on graph paper in order to draw slope triangles.

a. 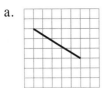 b.  c.  d.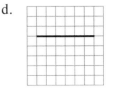

1.1.5 What shapes can you find?

Building a Kaleidoscope

Today you will learn about angles and shapes as you study how a kaleidoscope works.

1-37.   BUILDING A KALEIDOSCOPE

How does a kaleidoscope create the complicated, colorful images you see when you look inside? A hinged mirror and a piece of colored paper can demonstrate how a simple kaleidoscope creates its beautiful repeating designs.

Your Task: Place a hinged mirror on a piece of colored, unlined paper so that its sides extend beyond the edge of the paper as shown at right. Explore what shapes you see when you look directly at the mirror, and how those shapes change when you change the angle of the mirror. Discuss the questions below with your team. Be ready to share your responses with the rest of the class.

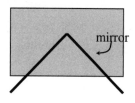

Discussion Points

What do you notice?

What happens when you change the angle (opening)
formed by the sides of the mirror?

How can you describe the shapes you see in the mirror?

1-38.   To complete your exploration, answer these questions together as a team.

a.   What happens to the shape you see as the angle formed by the mirror gets bigger (wider)? What happens as the angle gets smaller?

b.   What is the smallest number of sides the shape you see in the mirror can have? What is the largest?

c.   With your team, find a way to form a **regular hexagon** (a shape with six equal sides and equal angles).

d.   How might you describe to another team how you set the mirrors to form a hexagon? What types of information would be useful to have?

1-39.   A good way to describe an angle is by measuring how *wide* or *spread apart* the angle is. For this course, you can think of the **measure of an angle** as the measure of rotation of the two sides of the mirror from a closed position. The largest angle you can represent with a hinged mirror is 360°. This is formed when you open a mirror all the way so that the backs of the mirror touch. This is a called a **circular angle** and is represented by the diagram at right.

360°

a.   Other angles may be familiar to you. For example, an angle that forms a perfect "L" or a quarter turn is a 90° angle, called a **right angle** (shown at right). Four right angles can together form a circular angle.

90°

What if the two mirrors are opened to form a straight line? What measure would that angle have? Draw this angle and label its degrees. How is this angle related to a circular angle?

b.   Based on the examples above, estimate the measures of the angles shown below. Then confirm your answer using a **protractor**, a tool that measures angles.

i.   *ii.*   *iii.*

1-40.   Now use your understanding of angle measurement to create some specific shapes using your hinged mirror. Be sure that both mirrors have the same length on the paper, as shown in the diagram at right.

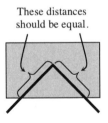
These distances should be equal.

a.   Antonio says he can form an **equilateral triangle** (a triangle with three equal sides and three equal angles) using his hinged mirror. How did he do this? Once you can see the triangle in your mirror, place the protractor on top of the mirror. What is the measure of the angle formed by the sides of the mirror?

Problem continues on next page →

1-40.   *Problem continued from previous page.*

   b.   Use your protractor to set your mirror so that the angle formed is 90°. Be sure that the sides of the mirror intersect the edge of the paper at equal lengths. What is this shape called? Draw and label a picture of the shape on your paper.

   c.   Carmen's mirror shows the image at right, called a **regular pentagon**. She noticed that the five triangles in this design all meet at the hinge of her mirrors. She also noticed that the triangles must all be the same size and shape, because they are reflections of the triangle formed by the mirrors and the paper.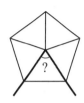

        What must the sum of these five angles at the hinge be? And what is the angle formed by Carmen's mirrors? Test your conclusion with your mirror.

   d.   Discuss with your team and predict how many sides a shape would have if the angle that the mirror forms measures 40°. Explain how you made your prediction. Then check your prediction using the mirror and a protractor. Describe the shape you see with as much detail as possible.

1-41.   Reflect on what you learned during today's activity.

   a.   Based on this activity, what are some things that you think you will be studying in Geometry?

   b.   This activity was based on the question, *"What shapes can be created using reflections?"* What ideas from this activity would you want to learn more about? Write a question that could prompt a different, but related, future investigation.

METHODS AND MEANINGS

MATH NOTES

Types of Angles

When trying to describe shapes, it is convenient to classify types of angles. An angle is formed by two rays joined at a common endpoint. The measure of an angle represents the number of degrees of rotation from one ray to the other about the vertex. This course will use the following terms to refer to angles:

ACUTE: Any angle with measure *between* (but not including) 0° and 90°.

Less than 90°.

RIGHT: Any angle that measures 90°.

90°

OBTUSE: Any angle with measure *between* (but not including) 90° and 180°.

More than 90° and less than 180°.

STRAIGHT: Straight angles have a measure of 180° and are formed when the sides of the angle form a straight line.

180°

360°

CIRCULAR: Any angle that measures 360°.

Review & Preview

1-42.   Estimate the size of each angle below to the nearest 10°. A right angle is shown for reference so you should not need a protractor.

a.

b.

c.

26   *Core Connections Geometry*

1-43.   Rosalinda examined the angles at right and wrote the
        equation below.

$$(2x+1°)+(x-10°)=90°$$

a.   Does her equation make sense? If so, explain why her equation must be
      true. If it is not correct, determine what is incorrect and write the equation.

b.   If you have not already done so, solve her equation, clearly showing all
      your steps. What are the measures of the two angles?

c.   Verify that your answer is correct.

1-44.   Angela had a rectangular piece of paper
        and then cut a rectangle out of a corner
        as shown at right. Find the area and
        perimeter of the resulting shape.

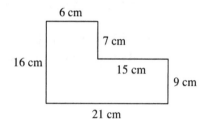

1-45.   For each equation below, solve for the given variable. If necessary, refer to the
        Math Notes box in Lesson 1.1.4 for guidance. Show the steps leading to your
        solution and check your answer.

a. $75=14y+5$ b. $-7r+13=-71$

c. $3a+11=7a-13$ d. $2m+m-8=7$

1-46.   On graph paper, draw four different rectangles that each have an area of 24
        square units. Then find the perimeter of each one.

1.2.1 How do you see it?

Spatial Visualization and Reflections

Were you surprised when you looked into the hinged mirror during the Kaleidoscope Investigation of Lesson 1.1.5? Reflection can create many beautiful and interesting shapes and can help you learn more about the characteristics of other shapes. However, one reason you may have been surprised is because it is sometimes difficult to predict what a reflection will be. This is where spatial visualization plays an important role. Visualizing, the act of "picturing" something in your mind, is often helpful when working with shapes. In order to be able to investigate and describe a geometric concept, it is first useful to visualize a shape or action.

Today you will be visualizing in a variety of ways and will develop the ability to find reflections. As you work today, keep the following focus questions in mind:

How do I see it?

How can I verify my answer?

How can I describe it?

1-47.   BUILDING BOXES

Which of the nets (diagrams) below would form a box with a lid if folded along the interior lines? Be prepared to defend your answer.

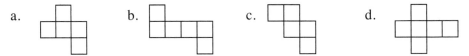

a.   b.   c.   d.

1-48.   Have you ever noticed what happens when you look in a mirror? Have you ever tried to read words while looking in a mirror? What happens? Discuss this with your team. Then re-write the following words as they would look if you held this book up to a mirror. Do you notice anything interesting?

a.   GEO   b.   STAR   c.   WOW

1-49.   When Kenji spun the flag shown at right very quickly about its pole, he noticed a three-dimensional shape emerge.

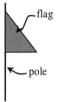

a.   What shape did he see? Draw a picture of the three-dimensional shape on your paper and be prepared to defend your answer.

b.   What would the flag need to look like so that a **sphere** (the shape of a basketball) is formed when the flag is rotated about its pole? Draw an example.

1-50.   REFLECTIONS

The shapes created in the Kaleidoscope Investigation in Lesson 1.1.5 were the result of reflecting a triangle several times in a hinged mirror. However, other shapes can also be created by a reflection. For example, the diagram at right shows the result of reflecting a snowman across a line.

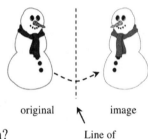

a.   Why do you think the image is called a reflection? How is the image different from the original?

b.   On the Lesson 1.2.1 Resource Page provided by your teacher, use your visualization skills to predict the reflection of each figure across the given line of refection. Then draw the reflection. Check your work by folding the paper along the line of reflection.

1-51.   Sometimes, a motion appears to be a reflection when it really isn't. How can you tell if a motion is a reflection? Consider each pair of objects below. Which diagrams represent reflections across the given lines of reflection? Study each situation carefully and be ready to explain your thinking.

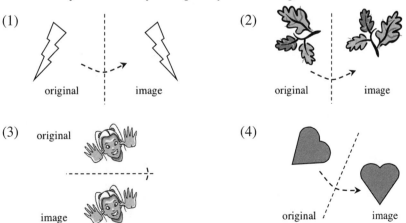

1-52.   CONNECTIONS WITH ALGEBRA

What other ways can you use reflections? Consider how to reflect a graph as you answer the questions below.

a.   On your Lesson 1.2.1 Resource Page, graph the parabola $y = x^2 + 3$ and the line $y = x$ for $x = -3, -2, -1, 0, 1, 2, 3$ on the same set of axes.

b.   Now reflect the parabola over the line $y = x$. What do you observe? What happens to the x- and y-values of the original parabola?

1-53.   LEARNING LOG

Throughout this course, you will be asked to reflect on your understanding of mathematical concepts in a Learning Log. Your Learning Log will contain explanations and examples to help you remember what you have learned throughout the course. It is important to write each entry of the Learning Log in your own words so that later you can use your Learning Log as a resource to refresh your memory. Your teacher will tell you where to write your Learning Log entries and how to structure or label them. Remember to label each entry with a title and a date so that it can be referred to later.

In this first Learning Log entry, describe what you learned today. For example, is it possible to reflect any shape? Is it possible to have a shape that, when reflected, doesn't change? How does reflection work? If it helps you to explain, sketch and label pictures to illustrate what you write. Title this entry "Reflections" and include today's date.

ETHODS AND MEANINGS

MATH NOTES

Probability Vocabulary and Definitions

Event: Any outcome, or set of outcomes, from a probabilistic situation. A **successful event** is the set of all outcomes that are of interest in a given situation. For example, rolling a die is a probabilistic situation. Rolling a 5 is an event. If you win a prize for rolling an even number, you can consider the set of three outcomes {2, 4, 6} a successful event.

Sample space: All possible outcomes from a probabilistic situation. For example, the sample space for flipping a coin is heads and tails; rolling a die has a sample space of {1, 2, 3, 4, 5, 6}.

Probability: The likelihood that an event will occur. Probabilities may be written as ratios (fractions), decimals, or percents. An event that is certain to happen has a probability of 1, or 100%. An event that has no chance of happening has a probability of 0, or 0%. Events that "might happen" have probabilities between 0 and 1, or between 0% and 100%. The more likely an event is to happen, the greater its probability.

Experimental probability: The probability based on data collected in experiments.

$$\text{experimental probability} = \frac{\text{number of successful outcomes in the experiment}}{\text{total number of outcomes in the experiment}}$$

Theoretical probability: Probability that is mathematically calculated. When each of the outcomes in the sample space has an *equally likely chance* of occurring, then

$$\text{theoretical probability} = \frac{\text{number of successful outcomes}}{\text{total number of possible outcomes}}.$$

For example, to calculate the probability of rolling an even number on a die, first figure out how many possible (equally likely) outcomes there are. Since there are six faces on the number cube, the total number of possible outcomes is 6. Of the six faces, three of the faces are even numbers—there are three successful outcomes. Thus, to find the probability of rolling an even number, you would write:

$$P(\text{even}) = \frac{\text{number of ways to roll an even number}}{\text{number of faces on a number cube}} = \frac{3}{6} = 0.5 = 50\%$$

1-54. Graph each line below on the same set of axes.

a. $y = 3x - 3$ b. $y = -\frac{2}{3}x + 3$ c. $y = -4x + 5$

1-55. **Probability** is used to make predictions. See the Math Notes in this lesson for more details. Whenever the outcomes are *equally likely*, the probability in general is:

$$P(\text{success}) = \frac{\text{number of successes}}{\text{total number of possible outcomes}}$$

For example, if you were to reach into a bag with 16 total shapes, four of which have right angles, and randomly pull out a shape, you could use probability to predict the chances of the shape having a right angle.

$$P(\text{right angle}) = \frac{\text{number of successes}}{\text{total number of possible outcomes}} = \frac{4 \text{ shapes with right angles}}{16 \text{ total shapes}}$$

$$= \frac{4}{16} = \frac{1}{4} = 0.25 = 25\%$$

The example above shows all forms of writing probability: $\frac{4}{16}$ (read "4 out of 16") is the probability as a ratio, 0.25 is its decimal form, and 25% is its equivalent percent. What else can probability be used to predict? Analyze each of the situations below:

a. The historic carousel at the park has 4 giraffes, 4 lions, 2 elephants, 18 horses, 1 monkey, 6 unicorns, 3 ostriches, 3 zebras, 6 gazelles, and even 1 dinosaur. Eric's niece wants for Eric to randomly pick an animal to ride. What is the probability (expressed as a percent) that Eric picks a horse, a unicorn, or a zebra?

b. Eduardo has in his pocket $1 in pennies, $1 in nickels, and $1 in dimes. If he randomly pulls out just one coin, what is the probability that he will pull out a dime?

c. P(rolling an 8) with one regular die if you roll the die just once.

d. P(dart hitting a shaded region) if the dart is randomly thrown and hits the target at right.

target

1-56.   The distance along a straight road is measured as shown in the diagram below. If the distance between towns A and C is 67 miles, find the distance between towns A and B.

$$5x - 2 \qquad 2x + 6$$

A   B   C

1-57.   For each equation below, solve for x. Show all work. The answers are provided so that you can check them. If you are having trouble with any solutions and cannot find your errors, you may need to see your teacher for extra help (you can ask your team as well).

a. $5x - 2x + x = 15$ $[\ x = 3.75\ ]$

b. $3x - 2 - x = 7 - x$ $[\ x = 3\ ]$

c. $3(x - 1) = 2x - 3 + 3x$ $[\ x = 0\ ]$

d. $3(2 - x) = 5(2x - 7) + 2$ $[\ x = 3\ ]$

e. $\frac{26}{57} = \frac{849}{5x}$ $[\ x \approx 372.25\ ]$

f. $\frac{4x+1}{3} = \frac{x-5}{2}$ $[\ x = -3.4\ ]$

1-58.   The three-dimensional shape at right is called a **cylinder**. Its bottom and top bases are both circles, and its side is perpendicular to the bases. What would the shape of a flag need to be in order to generate a cylinder when it rotates about its pole? (You may want to refer to problem 1-49 to review how flags work.)

1.2.2 What if it is reflected more than once?

Rigid Transformations: Rotations and Translations

In Lesson 1.2.1, you learned how to change a shape by reflecting it across a line, like the ice cream cones shown at right. Today you will learn more about reflections and learn about two new types of transformations: rotations and translations.

original   image

1-59. As Amanda was finding reflections, she wondered, *"What if I reflect a shape twice over parallel lines?"* Investigate her question as you answer the questions below.

a. On the Lesson 1.2.2 Resource Page, find △*ABC* and lines *n* and *p* (shown below). What happens when △*ABC* is reflected across line *n* to form △*A′B′C′* and then △*A′B′C′* is reflected across line *p* to form △*A″B″C″*? First visualize the reflections to predict the result. Then test your idea of the result by drawing both reflections.

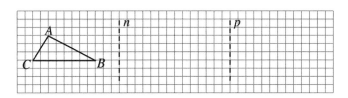

b. Examine your result from part (a). Compare the original triangle △*ABC* with the final result, △*A″B″C″*. What single motion would change △*ABC* to △*A″B″C″*?

c. Amanda analyzed her results from part (a). *"It looks like I could have just slid △ABC over!"* Sliding a shape from its original position to a new position is called **translating**. For example, the ice cream cone at right has been translated. Notice that the image of the ice cream cone has the same *orientation* as the original (that is, it is not turned or flipped). What words can you use to describe a translation?

original   image

d. The words "transformation" and "translation" sound alike and can easily be confused. Discuss in your team what these words mean and how they are related to each other.

1-60.   After answering Amanda's question in problem 1-59, her teammate asks, "*What if the lines of reflection are not parallel? Is the result still a translation?*" Find ΔEFG and lines *v* and *w* on the Lesson 1.2.2 Resource Page.

a.   First visualize the result when ΔEFG is reflected over *v* to form $\Delta E'F'G'$, and then $\Delta E'F'G'$ is reflected over *w* to form $\Delta E''F''G''$. Then draw the resulting reflections on the resource page. Is the final image a translation of the original triangle? If not, describe the result.

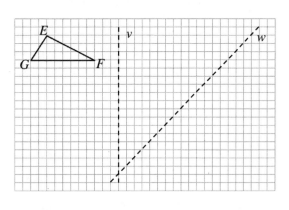

b.   Amanda noticed that when the reflecting lines are not parallel, the original shape is rotated, or turned, to get the new image. For example, the diagram at right shows the result when an ice cream cone is rotated about a point.

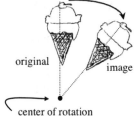

In part (a), the center of rotation is at point *P*, the point of intersection of the lines of reflection. Use a piece of tracing paper to test that $\Delta E''F''G''$ can be obtained by rotating ΔEFG about point *P*. To do this, first trace ΔEFG and point *P* on the tracing paper. While the tracing paper and resource page are aligned, apply pressure on *P* so that the tracing paper can rotate about this point. Then turn your tracing paper until ΔEFG rests atop $\Delta E''F''G''$.

c.   The rotation of ΔEFG in part (a) is an example of a 90° clockwise rotation. The term "clockwise" refers to a rotation that follows the direction of the hands of a clock, namely ↻. A rotation in the opposite direction (↺) is called "counter-clockwise."

On your resource page, rotate the "block L" 90° counter-clockwise (↺) about point *Q*.

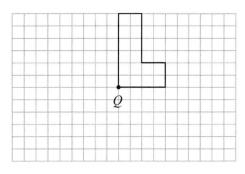

1-61.   NOTATION FOR TRANSFORMATIONS

Notice that the figure labels can help you
recognize what transformations are
involved. For example, in the diagram at
right, the original square *ABCD* on the
left was *translated* to the image square on
the right. The image location is different
from the original, so different letters are used to label its vertices (corners).

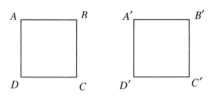

To keep track of how the vertices correspond, we call the image *A′B′C′D′*. The
′ symbol is read as "prime," so the shape on the right is called, "*A* prime *B*
prime *C* prime *D* prime." *A′* is the image of *A*, *B′* is the image of *B*, etc. This
notation tells you which vertices correspond.

a.   The diagram at right shows a
different transformation of *ABCD*.
Look carefully at the correspondence
between the vertices. Can you rotate
or reflect the original square to make
the letters correspond as shown? If you can reflect, where would the line
of reflection be? If you can rotate, where would the point of rotation be?

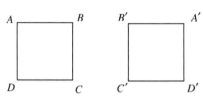

b.   This time, *ABCD* is rotated 180° about
the point as shown. Copy the diagram
(both squares and the point) and label
the vertices of the image square on the
right. If you have trouble, ask your
teacher for tracing paper.

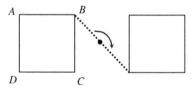

1-62.   What if you have the original figure and its image
after a sequence of transformations? Examine
Δ*ABC* and Δ*A′B′C′* in the graph at right.

a.   With your team, describe at least two
different ways to move Δ*ABC* onto Δ*A′B′C′*.

b.   Are there always multiple ways to describe
any transformation that does not change the
shape or size of the figure? Discuss this
question with your team and be prepared to
share your reasons with the class.

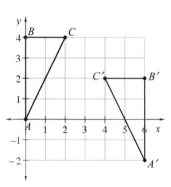

METHODS AND MEANINGS

Rigid Transformations

A **rigid transformation** maps each point of a figure to a new point, so that the resulting image has the same size and shape of the original. There are three types of rigid transformations, described below.

A transformation that preserves the size, shape, and orientation of a figure while *sliding* it to a new location is called a **translation**.

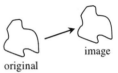

original   image

A transformation that preserves the size and shape of a figure across a line to form a mirror image is called a **reflection**. The mirror line is a **line of reflection**. One way to find a reflection is to *flip* a figure over the line of reflection.

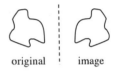

original   image

A transformation that preserves the size and shape while *turning* an entire figure about a fixed point is called a **rotation**. Figures can be rotated either clockwise (↻) or counterclockwise (↺).

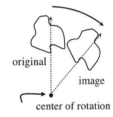

original

image

center of rotation

When labeling a transformation, the new figure (image) is often labeled with **prime notation**. For example, if $\triangle ABC$ is reflected across the vertical dashed line, its image can be labeled $\triangle A'B'C'$ to show exactly how the new points correspond to the points in the original shape. We also say that $\triangle ABC$ is **mapped** to $\triangle A'B'C'$.

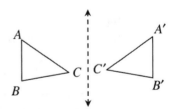

1-63.   The diagram at right shows a flat surface containing a line and a circle with no points in common. Can you visualize moving the line and/or circle so that they intersect at exactly one point? Two points? Three points? Explain each answer and illustrate each with an example when possible.

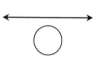

1-64.   Decide which transformation was used on each pair of shapes below. Some may have undergone more than one transformation, but try to name a single transformation, if possible.

a. 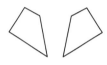   b.    c.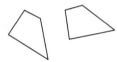

d.    e.    f.

1-65.   The perimeter of the triangle at right is 52 units. Write and solve an equation based on the information in the diagram. Use your solution for x to find the measures of each side of the triangle. Be sure to confirm that your answer is correct.

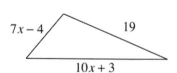

1-66.   Bertie placed a transparent grid made up of unit squares over each of the shapes she was measuring below. Using her grid, approximate the area of each region.

a. 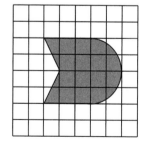   b.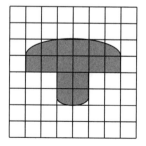

1-67.   For each equation below, find y if $x = -3$.

a. $y = -\frac{1}{3}x - 5$ b. $y = 2x^2 - 3x - 2$ c. $2x - 5y = 4$

1.2.3 What is the relationship?

Slopes of Parallel and Perpendicular Lines

In Lesson 1.2.2, you learned how to label vertices in an image to show how those vertices correspond to vertices in the original figure. Today, you will learn about relationships between an object and its image that will help you to predict the image's position. These relationships are described using algebra and are just one example of a connection between the new concepts you are studying in geometry and the math you learned in previous courses.

1-68. At right, $\triangle PQR$ was reflected across line l to form $\triangle P'Q'R'$. Describe the relationship of the original triangle and its image to the line of reflection. Specifically, how far away is each triangle from the line of reflection? What do you notice about the location of the image relative to the angle of reflection and the original triangle?

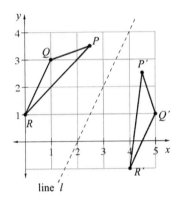

1-69. **CONNECTIONS WITH ALGEBRA**

In problem 1-68, you made some observations about reflections. Slope can help reveal more about transformations such as reflections.

a. Begin by graphing the equation $y = \frac{3}{5}x - 4$. Use tracing paper to translate the graph of $y = \frac{3}{5}x - 4$ up 5 units. Write the equation of the resulting image. What is the relationship between $y = \frac{3}{5}x - 4$ and its image? How do their slopes compare?

b. Now use tracing paper to rotate $y = \frac{3}{5}x - 4$ 90° clockwise ($\circlearrowright$) about $(0, 0)$. Write the equation of the result. Describe the relationship between $y = \frac{3}{5}x - 4$ and this new image.

c. The original line and the rotated line in part (b) are **perpendicular** because they form a 90° angle where they intersect. Look at the slopes of the original line and the rotated line and make any observations you can about the relationship between the slopes.

Perpendicular lines form a right angle.

1-70.   INVESTIGATING SLOPES

Do you think that all perpendicular slopes are related in the way you observed in problem 1-69? Investigate this idea by drawing three different lines with slope triangles on graph paper. Use slopes 1, $\frac{1}{3}$, and $\frac{-3}{4}$.

a.   Use tracing paper to rotate each line with its slope triangle 90°, either counterclockwise (↺) or clockwise (↻). Find the slope of each new line.

b.   How does the slope of each rotated line compare to the slope of its original line? Share any patterns you find with your teammates.

c.   Use patterns from the work you have done to describe the general relationship of the slopes of perpendicular lines. That is, if you have two perpendicular lines and know the slope of one, how can you find the slope of the other?

1-71.   SLOPES OF PERPENDICULAR LINES

Two lines are perpendicular whenever one line can be rotated 90° onto the other. However, a rotation does not only move the points on the line – it moves all the points on the graph! Therefore, the relationship of the slopes of perpendicular lines can be demonstrated as true by rotating a non-special line along with its slope triangle.

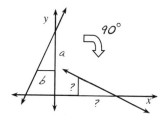

However, to prove something mathematically, you must be able to explain why it is true in all cases, and not just for particular numbers. To prove the relationship between perpendicular slopes, Sabrina drew the picture above.

a.   Use Sabrina's drawing to explain why the slope of the perpendicular line must always be $-\frac{b}{a}$ if neither a nor b is zero.

b.   What if the original line has a slope of 0? Explain what happens to a line with slope of 0 if it is rotated 90°, and what the slope of the perpendicular line would be.

1-72.   Now that you know more about the slope of
parallel and perpendicular lines, revisit the
reflection from problem 1-68 and confirm the
relationships using slope.

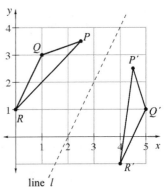

a.   Graph the triangles onto graph paper so
that $P(2.5, 3.5)$, $Q(1, 3)$, $R(0, 1)$ and
$P'(4.5, 2.5)$, $Q'(5, 1)$, $R'(4, -1)$. Then use
your ruler to draw three dashed lines: $\overleftrightarrow{PP'}$,
$\overleftrightarrow{QQ'}$, and $\overleftrightarrow{RR'}$. What is the relationship of
these dashed lines? Use your knowledge
of slope to verify your observations.

b.   Now focus on the relationship between the line of reflection and each of
the segments connecting a point with its image. What do you notice about
the lengths and angles? Be as specific as you can. Use what you know
about reflections to explain why your observations must be true.

c.   Use slope to confirm that the line of reflection is perpendicular to the line
segments connecting each original point and its image.

1-73.   Evan has graphed the point $(5, 7)$ and he wants to
reflect it over the line $y = -\frac{2}{5}x + 6$. He predicts that
the reflected point will have coordinates $(2, 2)$.
Without graphing, can you confirm his answer or
show that he cannot be correct?

1-74.   EXTENSION

Suppose the equation for line A is $y = \frac{6}{5}x - 10$. Line A is parallel to line B,
which is perpendicular to line C. If line D is perpendicular to line C and
perpendicular to line E, what is the slope of line E? Justify your conclusion.

1-75.   LEARNING LOG

In your Learning Log, summarize what you have learned
today. Be sure to explain the relationship between the
slopes of perpendicular lines and describe how to get the
slope of one line when you know the slope of a line perpendicular to it. Title
this entry "Slopes of Perpendicular Lines" and include today's date.

1-76. TOP OF THE CHARTS

Renae's MP3 player can be programmed to randomly play songs from her playlist without repeating a single song. Currently, Renae's MP3 player has 5 songs loaded on it, which are listed at right. As she walks between class, she only has time to listen to one song.

a. Is each song equally likely to be chosen as the first song?

b. What is the probability that her MP3 player will select a country song?

c. What is the probability that Renae will listen to a song with "Mama" in the title?

d. What is the probability she listens to a duet with Hank Tumbleweed?

e. What is the probability she listens to a song that is not R & B?

PLAYLIST

I Love My Mama (country)
by the Strings of Heaven

Don't Call Me Mama (country)
Duet by Sapphire and Hank Tumbleweed

Carefree and Blue (R & B)
by Sapphire and Prism Escape

Go Back To Mama (Rock)
Duet by Bjorn Free and Sapphire

Smashing Lollipops (Rock)
by Sapphire

1-77. Use what you learned about the slopes of parallel and perpendicular lines to find the equation of a line that would meet the criteria given below.

a. Find the equation of the line that goes through the point $(0, -3)$ and is perpendicular to the line $y = -\frac{2}{5}x + 6$.

b. Find the equation of the line that is parallel to the line $-3x + 2y = 10$ and goes through the point $(0, 7)$.

1-78. Examine the diagram at right. Which angle below is another name for $\angle ABC$? Note: More than one solution is possible.

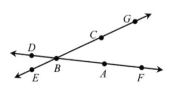

a. $\angle ABE$

b. $\angle GBD$

c. $\angle FBG$

d. $\angle EBC$

e. None of these

Core Connections Geometry

1-79.   Solve for the variable in each equation below. Show your steps and check your answer.

a. $4p+8p+12=-48$

b. $9w+33=12w-27$

c. $-2x+7=-21$

d. $25=10y+8$

1-80.   Copy the table below, complete it, and write an equation relating x and y.

x	-3	-2	-1	0	1	2	3	4
y	-7			2	5			14

1.2.4 How can I move it?

Defining Transformations

In Lesson 1.1.1, your class made a quilt using designs based on a geometric shape. Similarly, throughout American history, quilters have created quilts that use transformations to create intricate geometric designs. For example, the quilt at right is an example of a design based on rotation and reflection, while the quilt at left contains translation, rotation, and reflection.

Sue Sales. *Balance From Within.*

Sue Sales, *Hearts.*

In Lesson 1.2.3, you found ways to locate the image of a shape after it is reflected. Today, you will work with your team to develop ways to describe the image of a shape after it is rotated or translated.

1-81.   ROTATIONS ON A GRID

Consider what you know about rotation, a motion that turns a shape about a point. Does it make any difference if a rotation is clockwise (↻) versus counterclockwise (↺)? If so, when does it matter? Are there any circumstances when it does not matter? And are there any situations when the rotated image lies exactly on the original shape?

Investigate these questions as you rotate the shapes below about the given point on the Lesson 1.2.4 Resource Page. Use tracing paper if needed. Be prepared to share your answers to the questions posed above.

a.   180° ↺

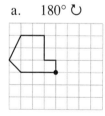

b.   180° ↻

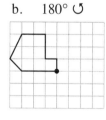

c.   90° ↺

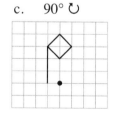

d.   90° ↻

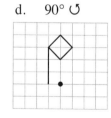

e.   270° ↺

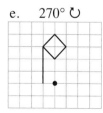

f.   360° ↺

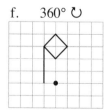

g.   180°

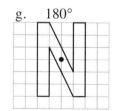

h.   90°

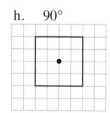

1-82.   So what exactly is a rotation? If a figure is rotated, how can you describe it?
Investigate this question below.

a.   On graph paper, graph $\overline{AB}$ with coordinates $A(4,1)$ and $B(2,5)$. Then use
tracing paper to rotate $\overline{AB}$ 90° counterclockwise (↺) about the point
$O(0,0)$ to graph $\overline{A'B'}$.

b.   Compare the lengths of and angles formed by the line segments that
connect points A, B, A' and B' to the point of rotation O. Which lengths
are equal? Which angle measures are equal? Be specific. To help, you
may want to draw the line segments connecting each point with O.

c.   Why does it make sense that for all points P in the graph, a rotation about
a point O moves it to a new point P' so that $OP = OP'$ and $m\angle POP'$
equals the measure of rotation? Use tracing paper to make sense of this
relationship.

d.   Use tracing paper to help explain why a rotation does not change any
angles or lengths of a figure.

1-83.   TRANSLATIONS ON A GRID

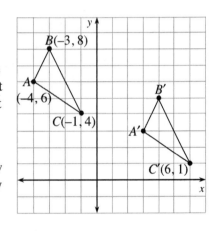

So what is a translation? The formal name
for a slide is a translation. (Remember that
translation and transformation are different
words.) $\triangle A'B'C'$ at right is the result of
translating $\triangle ABC$.

a.   Describe the translation. That is, how
many units to the right and how many
units down does the translation move
the triangle?

b.   On graph paper, plot $\triangle EFG$ with coordinates $E(4, 2)$, $F(1, 7)$, and $G(2, 0)$.
Find the coordinates of $\triangle E'F'G'$ if $\triangle E'F'G'$ is translated the same way as
$\triangle ABC$ was in part (a).

c.   For the translated triangle in part (b), draw a line segment connecting each
vertex to its translated image. What do you notice these line segments?
What does this tell you about how a translation moves each point of the
graph?

d.   Use the tracing paper to help explain how you know that a translation does
not change any angles or lengths of a figure.

1-84.   FACTS ABOUT ISOSCELES TRIANGLES

How can transformations such as reflections help us to learn
more about familiar shapes? Consider reflecting a **line segment**
(the portion of a line between two points) across a line that
passes through one of its endpoints. An example of this would
be reflecting $\overline{AB}$ across $\overrightarrow{BC}$ in the picture at right.

a.   Copy $\overline{AB}$ and $\overrightarrow{BC}$ and draw $\overline{A'B}$, the reflection of $\overline{AB}$.
When points A and A' are connected, what figure is
formed by points A, B, and A'?

b.   Use what you know about reflection to make as many statements as you
can about the shape from part (a). For example, are there any sides that
must be the same length? Are there any angles that must be equal? Is
there anything else special about this shape?

c.   LEARNING LOG

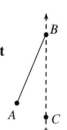

When two sides of a triangle have the same length, that
triangle is called **isosceles**. In your Learning Log,
describe all the facts you know about isosceles
triangles based on the reflection. Be sure to include a
diagram. Title this entry "Isosceles Triangles" and include today's date.

Core Connections Geometry

MᴇᴛʜODS AND Mᴇᴀɴɪɴɢs

Formal Definitions of Rigid Transformations

In algebra, you learned that a function is an equation that assigns each input a unique output. Most of these functions involved expressions and numbers such as $f(x) = 3x - 5$, so $f(2) = 1$.

In this course, you are now studying functions that assign each point in the plane to a unique point in the plane. These functions are called **rigid transformations (or motions)** because they move the entire plane with any figures you have drawn so that all of the figures remain unchanged. Therefore, angles and distances are preserved. There are three basic rigid motions that we will consider: reflections, translations, and rotations. All rigid motions can be seen as a combination of them.

Reflections: When a figure is reflected across a line of reflection, such as the figure at right, it appears that the figure is "flipped" over the line. However, formally, a reflection across a line of reflection is defined as a function of each point (such as A) to a point (such as A') so that the line of reflection is the perpendicular bisector of the segments connecting the points and their images (such as $\overline{AA'}$). Therefore, $AP = A'P$.

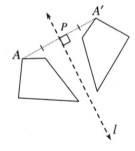

Rotations: Formally, a rotation about a point O is a function that assigns each point (P) in the plane a unique point (P') so that all angles of rotation $\angle POP'$ have the same measure (which is the angle of rotation) and $OP = OP'$.

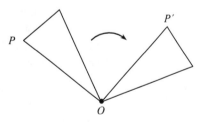

Translations: Formally, a translation is a function that assigns each point (Q) in the plane a unique point (Q') so that all line segments connecting an original point with its image have equal length and are parallel.

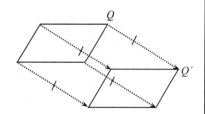

1-85.   Plot the following points on another sheet of graph paper and connect them in the order given. Then connect points A and D.

$$A(-3,4),\ B(1,6),\ C(5,-2),\ \text{and}\ D(1,-4)$$

   a.   A rectangle is a four-sided polygon with four right angles. Does the shape you graphed appear to be a rectangle? Use slope to justify your answer.

   b.   If $ABCD$ is rotated $90°$ clockwise ($\circlearrowright$) about the origin to form $A'B'C'D'$, what are the coordinates of the vertices of $A'B'C'D'$?

1-86.   Solve for the variable in each equation below. Show the steps leading to your answer.

   a. $8x - 22 = -60$ b. $\frac{1}{2}x - 37 = -84$

   c. $\frac{3x}{4} = \frac{6}{7}$ d. $9a + 15 = 10a - 7$

1-87.   While waiting for a bus after school, Renae programmed her MP3 player to randomly play two songs from her playlist, at right. Assume that the MP3 player will not play the same song twice.

   a.   A **sample space** is a list of all possible outcomes for a probabilistic situation. List the sample space for all the combinations of two songs that Renae could select. The order that she hears the songs does not matter for your list. How can you be sure that you listed all of the song combinations?

   b.   Are each of the combinations of two songs equally likely? Why is that important?

   c.   Find the probability that Renae will listen to two songs with the name "Mama" in the title.

> **PLAYLIST**
>
> a. **I Love My Mama** (country) by the Strings of Heaven
>
> b. **Don't Call Me Mama** (country) Duet by Sapphire and Hank Tumbleweed
>
> c. **Carefree and Blue** (R & B) by Sapphire and Prism Escape
>
> d. **Go Back To Mama** (Rock) Duet by Bjorn Free and Sapphire
>
> e. **Smashing Lollipops** (Rock) by Sapphire

   d.   What is the probability that at least one of the songs will have the name "Mama" in the title?

   e.   Why does it make sense that the probability in part (d) is higher than the probability in part (c)?

1-88.   On graph paper, graph the line through the point $(0, -2)$ with slope $\frac{4}{3}$.

a.   Write the equation of the line.

b.   Translate the graph of the line up 4 and to the right 3 units. What is the result? Write the equation for the resulting line.

c.   Now translate the original graph down 5 units. What is the result? Write the equation for the resulting line.

d.   How are the three lines you graphed related to each other? Justify your conclusion.

e.   Write the equation of a line that is perpendicular to these lines and passes through point $(12, 7)$.

1-89.   Evaluate the expression $\frac{1}{4}k^5 - 3k^3 + k^2 - k$ for $k = 2$.

1.2.5 What shapes can I create with triangles?

Using Transformations to Create Shapes

In Lesson 1.2.4, you practiced reflecting, rotating and translating figures. Since these are rigid transformations, the image always had the same size and shape as the original. In this lesson, you will combine the image with the original to make new, larger shapes from four basic "building-block" shapes.

As you create new shapes, consider what information the transformation gives you about the resulting new shape. By the end of this lesson, you will have generated most of the shapes that will be the focus of this course.

1-90. THE SHAPE FACTORY

The Shape Factory, an innovative new company, has decided to branch out to include new shapes. As Product Developers, your team is responsible for finding exciting new shapes to offer your customers. The current company catalog is shown at right.

Since your boss is concerned about production costs, you want to avoid buying new machines and instead want to reprogram your current machines.

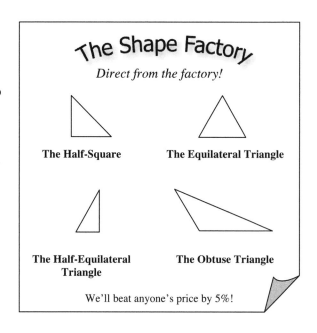

The Shape Factory

Direct from the factory!

The Half-Square   The Equilateral Triangle

The Half-Equilateral   The Obtuse Triangle
Triangle

We'll beat anyone's price by 5%!

The factory machines not only make all the shapes shown in the catalog, but they also are able to rotate or reflect a shape. For example, if the half-equilateral triangle is rotated 180° about the **midpoint** (the point in the middle) of its longest side, as shown at right, the result is a rectangle.

Your Task: Your boss has given your team until the end of this lesson to find as many new shapes as you can. Your team's reputation, which has suffered recently from a series of blunders, could really benefit by an impressive new line of shapes formed by a triangle and its transformations. For each triangle in the catalog, determine which new shapes are created when it is rotated or reflected so that the image shares a side with the original triangle. Be sure to make as many new shapes as possible. Use tracing paper or any other reflection tool to help.

1-91.   Since there are so many possibilities to test, it is useful to start by considering the shapes that can be generated just from one triangle. For example:

    a.   Test what happens when the half-square is reflected across each side. For each result (original plus image), draw a diagram and describe the shape that you get. If you know a name for the result, state it.

    b.   The point in the middle of each side is called its middle point, or **midpoint** for short. Try rotating the half-square 180° about the midpoint of each side to make a new shape. For each result, draw a diagram. If you know its name, write it near your new shape.

    c.   Repeat parts (a) and (b) with each of the other triangles offered by the Shape Factory.

——————— *Further Guidance* ———————
section ends here.

1-92.   EXTENSION

What other shapes can be created by reflection and rotation? Explore this as you answer the questions below. You can investigate these questions in any order. Remember that the resulting shape includes the original shape and all of its images. Remember to record and name each result.

- What if you reflect an equilateral triangle twice, once across one side and another time across a different side?

- What if an equilateral triangle is repeatedly rotated about one vertex so that each resulting triangle shares one side with another until new triangles are no longer possible? Describe the resulting shape.

- What if you rotate a trapezoid 180° around the midpoint of one if its non-parallel sides?

1-93.   BUILDING A CATALOG

Your boss now needs you to create a catalog page that includes your shapes. Each entry should include a diagram, a name, and a description of the shape. List any special features of the shape, such as if any sides are the same length or if any angles must be equal. Use color and arrows to highlight these attributes in the diagram.

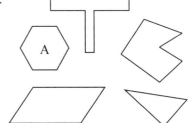 ETHODS AND MEANINGS

Polygons

A **polygon** is defined as a two-dimensional closed figure made up of straight line segments connected end-to-end. These segments may not cross (intersect) at any other points.

At right are some examples of polygons.

Shape A at right is an example of a **regular polygon** because its sides are all the same length and its angles have equal measure.

Polygons are named according to the number of sides that they have. Polygons that have 3 sides are **triangles**, those with 4 sides are **quadrilaterals**, polygons with 5 sides are **pentagons**, polygons with 6 sides are **hexagons**, polygons with 8 sides are **octagons**, polygons with 10 sides are **decagons**. For most other polygons, people simply name the number of sides, such as "11-gon" to indicate a polygon with 11 sides.

Review & Preview

1-94.   Augustin is in line to choose a new locker at school. The locker coordinator has each student reach into a bin and pull out a locker number. There is one locker at the school that all the kids dread! This locker, # 831, is supposed to be haunted, and anyone who has used it has had strange things happen to him or her! When it is Augustin's turn to reach into the bin and select a locker number, he is very nervous. He knows that there are 535 lockers left and locker # 831 is one of them. What is the probability that Augustin reaches in and pulls out the dreaded locker # 831? Should he be worried? Explain.

1-95.   Lourdes has created the following challenge for you: She has given you three of the four points necessary to determine a rectangle on a graph. She wants you to find the points that "complete" each of the rectangles below.

a. $(-1, 3), (-1, 2), (9, 2)$

b. $(3, 7), (5, 7), (5, -3)$

c. $(-5, -5), (1, 4), (4, 2)$

d. $(-52, 73), (96, 73), (96, 1483)$

1-96.   Find the area of the rectangles formed in parts (a), (b), and (d) of problem 1-95.

1-97.   Copy the diagrams below on graph paper. Then find the result when each indicated transformation is performed.

a.   Reflect Figure A across line *l*.

b.   Rotate Figure B 90° clockwise (↻) about point P.

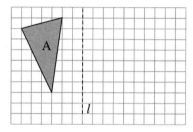 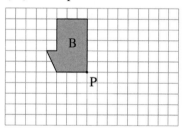

c.   Reflect Figure C across line *m*.

d.   Rotate Figure D 180° about point Q.

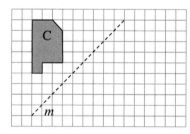 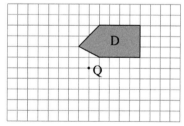

1-98.   At right is a diagram of a **regular hexagon** with center C.
          A polygon is regular if all sides are equal and all angles
          are equal. Copy this figure on your paper, then answer the
          questions below.

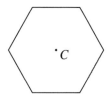

   a.   Draw the result of rotating the hexagon about
        its center 180°. Explain what happened. When
        this happens, the shape has **rotation symmetry**.

   b.   What is the result when the original hexagon is
        reflected across line n, as shown at right? A
        shape with this quality is said to have **reflection**
        symmetry and line n is a **line of symmetry** of
        the hexagon (not of the reflection).

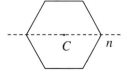

   c.   Does a regular hexagon have any other lines of symmetry? That is, are
        there any other lines you could fold across so that both halves of the
        hexagon will match up? Find as many as you can.

1.2.6 What shapes have symmetry?

Symmetry

You have encountered symmetry several times in this chapter. For instance, the quilt your class created in Lesson 1.1.1 contained symmetry. The shapes you saw in the hinged mirrors during the kaleidoscope investigation (Lesson 1.1.5) were also symmetric. But so far, you have not developed a test for determining whether a polygon is symmetric. And since symmetry is related to transformations, how can you use transformations to describe this relationship? This lesson is designed to deepen your understanding of symmetry.

By the end of this lesson, you should be able to answer these target questions:

What is symmetry?

How can I determine whether or not a polygon has symmetry?

What types of symmetry can a shape have?

1-99.   REFLECTION SYMMETRY

In problem 1-1, you created a quilt panel that had **reflection symmetry** because if the design were reflected across the line of symmetry, the image would be exactly the same as the original design. That is, a figure has reflection symmetry if a reflection carries it onto itself. See an example of a quilt design that has reflection symmetry at right.

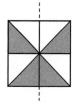

Obtain the Lesson 1.2.6 Resource Page. On it, examine the many shapes that will be our focus of study in this course. Which of these shapes have reflection symmetry? Consider this as you answer the questions below.

a.   For each figure on the resource page, draw all the possible lines of symmetry. If you are not sure if a figure has reflection symmetry, use tracing paper or a reflective tool to explore.

b.   Which types of triangles have reflection symmetry?

c.   Which types of **quadrilaterals** (polygons with four sides) have reflection symmetry?

d.   Which figures on your resource page have more than three lines of symmetry?

1-100.   ROTATION SYMMETRY

In problem 1-99, you learned that many shapes have reflection symmetry. These shapes remain unaffected when they are reflected across a line of symmetry. Similarly, some figures can also be rotated onto themselves so that they remain unchanged.

a.   Examine the diagram at right. Can this figure be rotated onto itself? Trace this shape on tracing paper and test your conclusion. If it is possible, where is the point of rotation?

b.   Jessica claims that she can rotate <u>all</u> figures in such a way that they will not change. How does she do it?

c.   Since all figures can be rotated 360° without change, that is not a very special quality. However, the shape in part (a) above was special because it could be rotated less than 360° and still remain unchanged. A shape with this quality is said to have **rotation symmetry**.

But what shapes have rotation symmetry? Examine the figures on your Lesson 1.2.6 Resource Page and identify those that have rotation symmetry.

d.   Which shapes on the resource page have 90° rotation symmetry? That is, which can be rotated about a point 90° and remain unchanged?

1-101.   TRANSLATION SYMMETRY

In problems 1-99 and 1-100, you identified shapes that have reflection and rotation symmetry. What about translation symmetry? Is there an object that can be translated so that its end result is exactly the same as the original object? If so, draw an example and explain why it has **translation symmetry**.

Core Connections Geometry

1-102.   DESCRIBING SYMMETRY

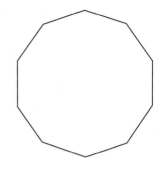

Now describe all types of symmetry for the same
figure if possible. For example, assume you have a
regular polygon with 10 sides (called a **decagon**).

a.   What reflections carry this decagon onto itself?
That is, describe its lines of reflections. If this
polygon has no reflection symmetry, explain
how you know.

b.   What rotations carry this polygon onto itself? That is, describe a point of
rotation and angles for which this polygon has rotation symmetry. If this
polygon has no rotation symmetry, explain how you know.

c.   What translations carry this decagon onto itself? That is, describe a
translation for which this polygon has translation symmetry. If this
polygon has no translation symmetry, explain how you know.

1-103.   CONNECTIONS WITH ALGEBRA

During this lesson, you have focused on the types of symmetry that can exist in
geometric objects. But what about shapes that are created on graphs? What
types of graphs have symmetry?

a.   Examine the graphs below. Decide which have reflection symmetry,
rotation symmetry, translation symmetry, or a combination of these.

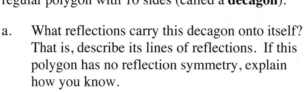

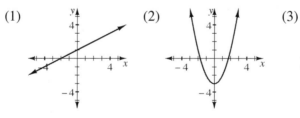

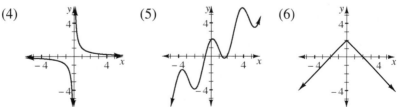

b.   If the y-axis is a line of symmetry of a graph, then its function is referred
to as **even**. Which of the graphs in part (a) are even functions?

c.   If the graph has rotation symmetry about the origin $(0, 0)$, its function is
called **odd**. Which of the graphs in part (a) are odd functions?

1-104.   LEARNING LOG

Reflect on what you have learned during this lesson. In
your Learning Log, answer the questions posed at the
beginning of this lesson, reprinted below. When helpful,
give examples and draw a diagram. Title this entry
"Symmetry" and include today's date.

What is symmetry?

How can I determine whether or not a polygon has symmetry?

What types of symmetry can a shape have?

Core Connections Geometry

ⓂETHODS AND MEANINGS

Slope of a Line and Parallel and Perpendicular Slopes

During this course, you will use your algebra tools to learn more about shapes. One of your algebraic tools that can be used to learn about the relationship of lines is slope. Review what you know about slope below.

The **slope** of a line is the ratio of the change in y (Δy) to the change in x (Δx) between any two points on the line. It indicates both how steep the line is and its direction, upward or downward, left to right.

$$\text{slope} = \frac{\text{vertical change}}{\text{horizontal change}} = \frac{\Delta y}{\Delta x}$$

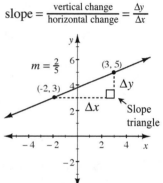

Lines that point upward from left to right have positive slope, while lines that point downward from left to right have negative slope. A horizontal line has zero slope, while a vertical line has undefined slope. The slope of a line is denoted by the letter m when using the $y = mx + b$ equation of a line.

One way to calculate the slope of a line is to pick two points on the line, draw a slope triangle (as shown in the example above), determine Δy and Δx, and then write the slope ratio. Be sure to verify that your slope correctly resulted in a negative or positive value based on its direction.

Parallel lines are lines that lie in the same plane (a flat surface) and never intersect. Lines l and n at right are examples of parallel lines.

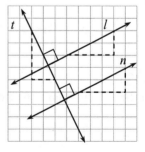

On the other hand, **perpendicular lines** are lines that intersect at a right angle. For example, lines t and n at right are perpendicular, as are lines t and l. Note that the small square drawn at the point of intersection indicates a right angle.

The **slopes of parallel lines** are the same. In general, the slope of a line parallel to a line with slope m is also m.

The **slopes of perpendicular lines** are opposite reciprocals. For example, if one line has slope $\frac{4}{5}$, then any line perpendicular to it has slope $-\frac{5}{4}$. If a line has slope -3, then any line perpendicular to it has slope $\frac{1}{3}$. In general, the slope of a line perpendicular to a line with slope m is $-\frac{1}{m}$.

1-105.   On graph paper, graph each of the lines below on the same set of axes. What is the relationship between lines (a) and (b)? What about between (b) and (c)?

a. $y = \frac{1}{3}x + 4$ b. $y = -3x + 4$ c. $y = -3x - 2$

1-106.   The length of a side of a square is $5x + 2$ units. If the perimeter is 48 units, complete the following.

a.   Write an equation to represent this information.

b.   Solve for x.

c.   What is the area of the square?

1-107.   What is the probability of drawing each of the following cards from a standard playing deck? See the entry "playing cards" in the glossary to learn what playing cards are included in a deck.

a.   P(Jack)

b.   P(spade)

c.   P(Jack of spades)

d.   P(not spade)

1-108.   Examine the figure graphed on the axes at right.

a.   What happens when you rotate this figure about the origin 90°? 45°? 180°?

b.   What other angle could the figure at right be rotated so that the shape does not appear to change?

c.   What shape will stay the same no matter how many degrees it is rotated?

1-109. Copy the diagrams below on graph paper. Then find each result when each indicated transformation is performed.

a. Reflect A across line *l*.

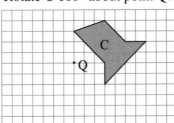

b. Rotate B 90° counterclockwise (↺) about point P.

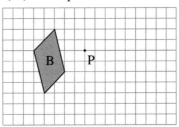

c. Rotate C 180° about point Q.

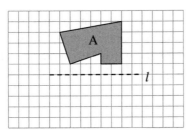

d. Reflect D across line *m*.

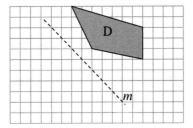

1.3.1 How can I classify this shape?

• •

Attributes and Characteristics of Shapes

In Lesson 1.2.5, you generated a list of shapes formed by triangles and in Lesson 1.2.6, you studied the different types of symmetries that a shape can have. In Section 1.3, you will continue working with shapes to learn more about their attributes and characteristics. For example, which shapes have sides that are parallel? And which basic shapes are equilateral?

By the end of this lesson you should have a greater understanding about the attributes that make shapes alike and different. Throughout the rest of this course you will study these qualities that set shapes apart as well as learn how shapes are related.

1-110.   INTRODUCTION TO THE SHAPE BUCKET

Obtain a Shape Bucket and a Lesson 1.3.1B Resource Page from your teacher. The Shape Bucket contains most of the basic geometric shapes you will study in this course. Count the items and verify that you have all 16 shapes. Take the shapes out and notice the differences between them. Are any alike? Are any strangely different?

Once you have examined the shapes in your bucket, work as a team to build the composite figures below (also shown on the resource page). Composite figures are made by combining two or more shapes to make a new figure. On the Lesson 1.3.1B Resource Page, show the shapes you used to build the composite shapes by filling in their outlines within each composite shape.

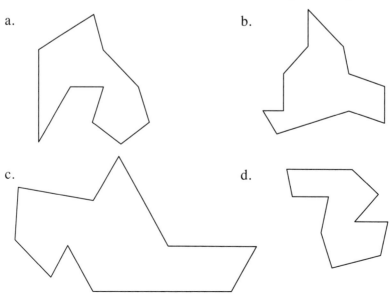

a.

b.

c.

d.

1-111. **VENN DIAGRAMS**

Obtain a Venn diagram (Lesson 1.3.1C Resource Page) from your teacher.

a. The *left* circle of the Venn diagram, Circle #1, will represent the attribute "has at least one pair of parallel sides" and the *right* side, Circle #2, will represent the attribute "has at least two sides of equal length" as shown below. Sort through the shapes in the Shape Bucket and decide as a team where each shape belongs. Be sure to record your solution on paper. As you discuss this problem with your teammates, justify your statements with reasons such as, "I think this shape goes here because…"

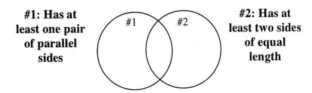

#1: Has at least one pair of parallel sides #1 #2 **#2: Has at least two sides of equal length**

b. Next, reclassify the shapes for the new Venn diagram shown below. Describe each region in a sentence.

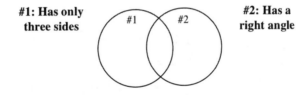

#1: Has only three sides #1 #2 **#2: Has a right angle**

c. Finally, reclassify the shapes for the new Venn diagram shown below. Describe each region in a sentence

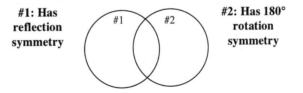

#1: Has reflection symmetry #1 #2 **#2: Has 180° rotation symmetry**

METHODS AND MEANINGS

Venn Diagrams

A Venn diagram is a tool used to classify objects. It is usually composed of two or more circles that represent different conditions. An item is placed or represented in the Venn diagram in the appropriate position based on the conditions it meets. See the example below:

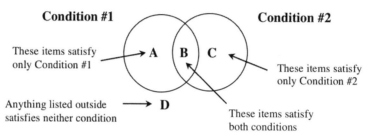

Condition #1

These items satisfy only Condition #1 → **A** **B** **C** ← These items satisfy only Condition #2

Anything listed outside satisfies neither condition → **D**

These items satisfy both conditions

Condition #2

Review & Preview

1-112.   Copy the Venn diagram below on your paper. Then show where each person described should be represented in the diagram. If a portion of the Venn diagram remains empty, describe the qualities a person would need to belong there.

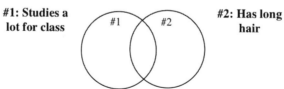

#1: Studies a lot for class   #1   #2   **#2: Has long hair**

a.   Carol: "*I rarely study and enjoy braiding my long hair.*"

b.   Bob: "*I never do homework and have a crew cut.*"

c.   Pedro: "*I love joining after school study teams to prepare for tests and I like being bald!*"

1-113.   Sandy has a square, equilateral triangle, rhombus, and regular hexagon in her Shape Bucket, while Robert has a scalene triangle, kite, isosceles trapezoid, non-special quadrilateral, and obtuse isosceles triangle in his. Sandy will randomly select a shape from her Shape Bucket, while Robert will randomly select a shape from his.

   a.   Who has a greater probability of selecting a quadrilateral? Justify your conclusion.

   b.   Who has a greater probability of selecting an equilateral shape? Justify your conclusion.

   c.   What is more likely to happen: Sandy selecting a shape with at least two sides that are parallel or Robert selecting a shape with at least two sides that are equal?

1-114.   Solve the equations below for *x*, if possible. Be sure to check your solution.

   a. $\frac{3x-1}{4} = -\frac{5}{11}$

   b. $(5-x)(2x+3) = 0$

   c. $6 - 5(2x-3) = 4x + 7$

   d. $\frac{3x}{4} + 2 = 4x - 1$

1-115.   When the shapes below are reflected across the given line of reflection, the original shape and the image (reflection) create a new shape. For each reflection below, name the new shape that is created.

   a.

   b.

   c.

   d.   Use this method to create your own shape that has reflection symmetry. Add additional lines of symmetry. Note that the dashed lines of reflection in the figures above become lines of symmetry in the new shape.

1-116.   Copy △*ABC* at right on graph paper.

   a.   Rotate △*ABC* 90° counter-clockwise (↺) about the origin to create △*A'B'C'*. Name the coordinates of *C'*.

   b.   Reflect △*ABC* across the vertical line *x* = 1 to create △*A"B"C"*. Name the coordinates of the vertices.

   c.   Translate △*ABC* so that *A'''* is at (4, −5). Name the coordinates of *B'''*.

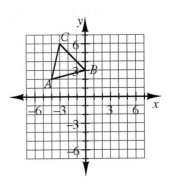

1.3.2 How can I describe it?

....

More Characteristics of Shapes

In Lesson 1.3.1, you used shapes to build new, unique, composite shapes. You also started to analyze the attributes (qualities) of shapes. Today you will continue to look at their attributes as you learn new vocabulary.

1-117.   Using your Venn diagram Resource Page from Lesson 1.3.1, categorize the shapes from the Shape Bucket in the Venn diagram as shown below. Record your results on paper.

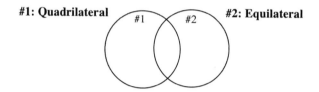

#1: Quadrilateral   #1   #2   **#2: Equilateral**

1-118.   DESCRIBING A SHAPE

How can you describe a square? With your class, find a way to describe a square using its attributes (special qualities) so that anyone could draw a square based on your description. Be as complete as possible. You may not use the word "square" in the description.

Square

1-119.   Each shape in the bucket is unique; that is, it differs from the others. You will be assigned a few shapes to describe as completely as possible for the class. But what is a complete description? As you work with your team to create a complete description, consider the questions below.

   • What do you notice about your shape?

   • What makes it different from other shapes?

   • If you wanted to describe your shape to a friend on the telephone who cannot see it, what would you need to include in the description?

1-120.   SHAPES TOOLKIT

Obtain the Lesson 1.3.2A Resource Page entitled "Shapes Toolkit".

a.   In the space provided, describe the shape based on the descriptions generated from problem 1-119. Leave space so that later observations can be added for each shape. Note that the description for "rectangle" has been provided as an example.

b.   On the diagram for each shape, mark sides that must have equal length or that must be parallel. Also mark any angles that measure 90°. See the descriptions for how to do this below.

- To show that two sides have the same length, use "tick marks" on the sides. However, to show that one pair of equal sides may not be the same length as the other pair of equal sides, you should use one tick mark on each of the two opposite, equal sides and two tick marks on each of the other two opposite, equal sides, as shown below.

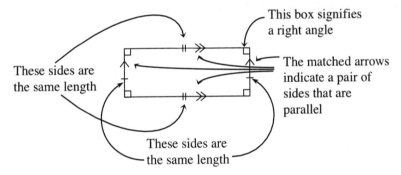

- To show that the rectangle has two pairs of parallel sides, use one ">" mark on each of one pair of parallel sides and two ">>" marks on each of the other two parallel sides, as shown above.

- Also mark any right angles by placing a small square at the right angle vertex (the corner). See the example above.

c.   The Shapes Toolkit Resource Page is the first page of a special information organizer, called your Geometry Toolkit, which you will be using for this course. It is a reference tool that you can use when you need to remember the name or description of a shape. Find a safe place in your Geometry binder to keep your Toolkit.

1-121.   Examine the Venn diagram at right.

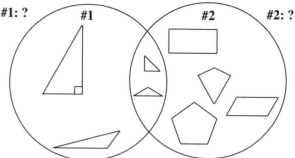

a.   What attribute does each circle represent? How can you tell?

b.   Where would the regular hexagon from your Shape Bucket go in this Venn diagram? What about the trapezoid? Justify your reasoning.

c.   Create another shape that would belong outside both circles. Does your shape have a name that you have studied so far? If not, give it a new name.

1-122.   Elizabeth has a Venn diagram that she started at right. It turns out that the only shape in the Shape Bucket that could go in the intersection (where the two circles overlap) is a square! What are the possible attributes that her circles could represent? Discuss this with your team and be ready to share your ideas with the class.

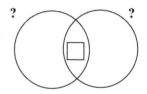

1-123.   If no sides of a triangle have the same length, the triangle is called **scalene** (pronounced SCALE-een). And, as you might remember, if the triangle has two sides that are the same length, the triangle is called isosceles. Use the markings in each diagram below to decide if △ABC is isosceles or scalene. Assume the diagrams are not drawn to scale.

a.

b.

c.   ABDC is a square

1-124.   Find the probabilities of randomly selecting the following shapes from a Shape Bucket that contains all 16 basic shapes.

a.   P(quadrilateral)

b.   P(shape with an obtuse angle)

c.   P(equilateral triangle)

d.   P(shape with parallel sides)

1-125.   Without referring to your Shapes Toolkit, see if you can recall the names of each
         of the shapes below. Then check your answers with definitions from your
         Shapes Toolkit. How did you do?

a.   b.   c.

d.   e.   f.

1-126.   Copy the Venn diagram at
         right onto your paper. Then
         carefully place each
         capitalized letter of the
         alphabet below into your Venn
         diagram based on its type
         of symmetry.

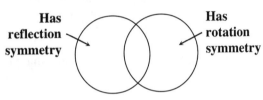

         A, B, C, D, E, F, G, H, I, J, K, L, M, N, O, P, Q, R, S, T, U, V, W, X, Y, Z

1-127.   Throughout this book, key problems have been selected as "checkpoints." Each
         checkpoint problem is marked with an icon like the one at left. These
         checkpoint problems are provided so that you can check to be sure you are
         building skills at the expected level. When you have trouble with checkpoint
         problems, refer to the review materials and practice problems that are available
         in the "Checkpoint Materials" section at the back of your book.

         This problem is a checkpoint for solving linear equations. It will be referred to
         as Checkpoint 1.

         a. $3x + 7 = -x - 1$ b. $1 - 2x + 5 = 4x - 3$

         c. $-2x - 6 = 2 - 4x - (x - 1)$ d. $3x - 4 + 1 = -2x + 5 + 5x$

         Check your answers by referring to the Checkpoint 1 materials located at the
         back of your book.

         Ideally, at this point you are comfortable working with these types of problems
         and can solve them correctly. If you feel that you need more confidence when
         solving these types of problems, then review the Checkpoint 1 materials and try
         the practice problems provided. From this point on, you will be expected to do
         problems like these correctly and with confidence.

Chapter 1 Closure What have I learned?

Reflection and Synthesis

The activities below offer you a chance to reflect about what
you have learned during this chapter. As you work, look for
concepts that you feel very comfortable with, ideas that you
would like to learn more about, and topics you need more
help with. Look for connections between ideas as well as
connections with material you learned previously.

①   TEAM BRAINSTORM

What have you studied in this chapter? What ideas were important in what you
learned? With your team, brainstorm a list. Be as detailed as you can. To help
get you started, lists of Learning Log entries, Toolkit Entries, and Math Notes
boxes are below.

What topics, ideas, and words that you learned *before* this chapter are connected
to the new ideas in this chapter? Again, be as detailed as you can.

How long can you make your list? Challenge yourselves. Be prepared to share
your team's ideas with the class.

Learning Log Entries
- Lesson 1.2.1 – Reflections
- Lesson 1.2.3 – Slopes of Perpendicular Lines
- Lesson 1.2.4 – Isosceles Triangles
- Lesson 1.2.6 – Symmetry

Toolkit Entries
- Shapes Toolkit (Lesson 1.3.2A Resource Page and problem 1-120)

Math Notes
- Lesson 1.1.1 – Lines of Symmetry
- Lesson 1.1.2 – The Investigative Process
- Lesson 1.1.3 – The Perimeter and Area of a Figure
- Lesson 1.1.4 – Solving Linear Equations
- Lesson 1.1.5 – Types of Angles
- Lesson 1.2.1 – Probability Vocabulary and Definitions
- Lesson 1.2.2 – Rigid Transformations
- Lesson 1.2.4 – Formal Definitions of Rigid Transformations
- Lesson 1.2.5 – Polygons
- Lesson 1.2.6 – Slope of a Line and Parallel and Perpendicular Slopes
- Lesson 1.3.1 – Venn Diagrams

MAKING CONNECTIONS

Below is a list of the vocabulary used in this chapter. Make sure that you are familiar with all of these words and know what they mean. Refer to the glossary or index for any words that you do not yet understand.

acute	angle	area
conjecture	equilateral	graph
image	isosceles	line segment
obtuse	midpoint	parallel
perimeter	perpendicular	polygon
probability	protractor	prove
random	ratio	reflection
regular polygon	right angle	rotation
scalene	slope	solve
straight angle	symmetry	rigid transformation
translation	triangle	Venn diagram
vertex (vertices)		

Make a concept map showing all of the connections you can find among the key words and ideas listed above. To show a connection between two words, draw a line between them and explain the connection, as shown in the model below. A word can be connected to any other word as long as you can justify the connection. For each key word or idea, provide an example or sketch that shows the idea.

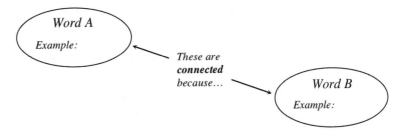

Your teacher may provide you with vocabulary cards to help you get started. If you use the cards to plan your concept map, be sure either to re-draw your concept map on your paper or to glue the vocabulary cards to a poster with all of the connections explained for others to see and understand.

While you are making your map, your team may think of related words or ideas that are not listed here. Be sure to include these ideas on your concept map.

③ PORTFOLIO: EVIDENCE OF MATHEMATICAL PROFICIENCY

In the Shape Factory, you investigated what shapes you could create with four basic triangles. But what if you had started with quadrilaterals instead? Showcase what you know about rotating and reflecting by finding all shapes that could be made by rotating or reflecting the four quadrilaterals below. Remember that once rotated or reflected, the image should share a side with the original shape. Use tracing paper to help generate the new shapes. If you know the name of the new figure, state it.

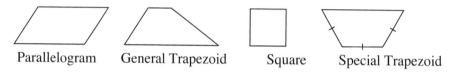

Parallelogram   General Trapezoid   Square   Special Trapezoid

Now write three "What if ...?" questions that would extend your investigation above.

Choose one of your questions to investigate. Decide how you will investigate your question. For example, will you need tracing paper? Do you need to make a table and record information?

After you have answered your question, write the results of your investigation clearly so that someone else can understand what question you selected, how you investigated your question, and any conclusions you made.

Your teacher may give you the Chapter 1 Closure Resource Page: Transformation Graphic Organizer to work on (or you can download these three pages from www.cpm.org). A Graphic Organizer is a tool you can use to organize your thoughts, showcase your knowledge, and communicate your ideas clearly.

④   WHAT HAVE I LEARNED?

Most of the problems in this section represent
typical problems found in this chapter. They
serve as a gauge for you. You can use them to
determine which types of problems you can do
well and which types of problems require further
study and practice. Even if your teacher does
not assign this section, it is a good idea to try
these problems and find out for yourself what
you know and what you still need to work on.

Solve each problem as completely as you can. The table at the end of the
closure section has answers to these problems. It also tells you where you
can find additional help and practice with problems like these.

CL 1-128.   Trace the figures in parts (a) and (b) onto your paper and perform the
indicated transformations. Copy the figure from part (c) onto graph paper
and perform the indicated transformation. Label each image with prime
notation $(A \rightarrow A')$.

a.   Rotate *EFGHI*   b.   Reflect *JKLMN*   c.   Translate *ABCD*
90° clockwise ↻   over line *t*   down 5 units and
about point *Z*   right 3 units

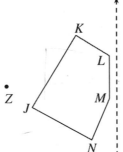

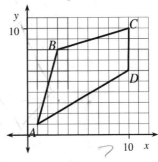

CL 1-129.   Assume that all angles in the diagram at right are
right angles and that all the measurements are in
centimeters. Find the perimeter of the figure.

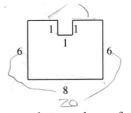

CL 1-130.   Estimate the measures of the angles below. Are there any that you know for
sure?

a.   b.   c.   d.

CL 1-131.   Examine the angles in problem CL 1-130. If these four angles are placed in a bag, what is the probability of randomly selecting:

a.   An acute angle

b.   An angle greater than 60°

c.   A 90° angle

d.   An angle less than or equal to 180°

CL 1-132.   Examine the shapes at right.

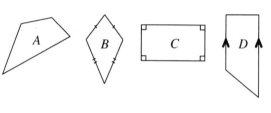

a.   Describe what you know about each shape based on the information provided in the diagram. Then name the shape.

b.   Decide where each shape would be placed in the Venn diagram at right.

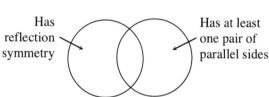

Has reflection symmetry

Has at least one pair of parallel sides

CL 1-133.   Solve the equations below. Check your solutions.

a. $3x - 12 + 10 = 8 - 2x$
  $+2x$ $+2x$
  $5x - 2 + 10 = 8$ $5x + 10 = 20$
  $5x - 2 + 10 = 8$ $-10 \ -10$

b. $\frac{x}{7} = \frac{3}{2}$ $2 \cdot y = 2x$ $x = 10.5$

c. $5 - (x + 7) + 4x = 7(x - 1)$
  $5 + 3x + 7 = 7x - 1$
  $-3x \qquad -3x + 1$
  $5 + 7 = 4x$
  $b = 4x \quad x = 3$

  $5 - x + 7 + 4x = 7x - 1$ $5x = 10$
                                   $\frac{3}{3} \ \frac{5}{5}$
                                   $x = 2$

d. $x^2 + 11 = 36$
  -36
  $x^2 + 11 - 36$ $(x.$ $(x\ )$

CL 1-134.   Find the value of y for each equation twice: first for $x = 8$, then for $x = -3$.

a. $y = x^2 + 13x + 8$
  $y = 9 - 39 + 8$

b. $y = 6x - 2$

CL 1-135.   Graph and connect the points in the table below. Then graph the equation in part (b) on the same set of axes. Also, find the equation for the data in the table.

a.

x	−4	−3	−2	−1	0	1	2	3	4
y	−5	−3	−1	1	3	5	7	9	11

b. $y = x^2 + x - 2$
  $4 \ 12$ $y = 4$
  $y = 1 + x -$

CL 1-136. $\triangle ABC$ at right is equilateral. Use what you know about an equilateral triangle to write and solve an equation for x. Then find the perimeter of $\triangle ABC$.

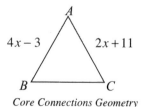

$4x - 3$ $2x + 11$

CL 1-137. Check your answers using the table at the end of this section. Which problems do you feel confident about? Which problems were hard? Have you worked on problems like these in math classes you have taken before? Use the table to make a list of topics you need help on and a list of topics you need to practice more.

Answers and Support for Closure Activity #4
What Have I Learned?

MN = Math Note, LL = Learning Log

Problem	Solutions	Need Help?	More Practice
CL 1-128. a. b. c.		Lessons 1.2.2 and 1.2.4 MN: 1.2.2 and 1.2.4	Problems 1-64, 1-97, 1-109, and 1-116
CL 1-129. Perimeter = 30 centimeters		MN: 1.1.3	Problems 1-25, 1-35, 1-44, 1-46, 1-65, and 1-106
CL 1-130. a. 90° b. ≈ 100° c. 180° d. ≈ 30°		Lesson 1.1.5 MN: 1.1.5	Problems 1-39 and 1-42
CL 1-131. a. $\frac{1}{4}$ b. $\frac{3}{4}$ c. $\frac{1}{4}$ d. 1		MN: 1.2.1	Problems 1-55, 1-76, 1-87, 1-94, 1-107, and 1-113

Problem	Solutions	Need Help?	More Practice
CL 1-132.	a. A: Four sides make it a generic quadrilateral. B: Two pairs of equal sides make it a kite. C: Four right angles and a pair of parallel sides make it a rectangle. D: A quadrilateral with two parallel sides is a trapezoid. b.	Lesson 1.3.2 MN: 1.3.1 Shapes Toolkit	Problems 1-112, 1-125, and 1-126

b.

Has reflection symmetry

Has at least one pair of parallel sides

B (C) D

A

Problem	Solutions	Need Help?	More Practice
CL 1-133.	a. $x = 2$ b. $x = \frac{21}{2}$ c. $x = \frac{5}{4}$ d. $x = \pm 5$	MN: 1.1.4	Problems 1-17, 1-32, 1-45, 1-57, 1-79, 1-114, and 1-127
CL 1-134.	a. $y = 176$ and $y = -22$ b. $y = 46$ and $y = -20$	Review from a previous course.	Problems 1-29, 1-67, and 1-89
CL 1-135.	a. $y = 2x + 3$ b.	Review from a previous course.	Problems 1-5, 1-27, 1-54, 1-80, and 1-105

Problem	Solutions	Need Help?	More Practice
CL 1-136.	$4x - 3 = 2x + 11$, so $x = 7$. Therefore, each side is $4(7) - 3 = 25$ units long, and the perimeter is 75 units.	Lesson 1.1.3 MN: 1.1.3 Shapes Toolkit	Problems 1-15, 1-25, 1-43, 1-56, 1-65, and 1-106

Core Connections Geometry

CHAPTER 2   Angles and Measurement

In Chapter 1, you studied many common geometric shapes and learned ways to describe a figure using its attributes. In this chapter, you will further investigate how to describe a complex figure by developing ways to accurately determine its angles, area, and perimeter. You will also use transformations from Chapter 1 to uncover special relationships between angles within a figure.

Throughout this chapter you will be asked to solve problems, such as those involving area or angles, in more than one way. This will require you to "see" shapes in multiple ways and to gain a broader understanding of problem solving.

Guiding Question

Mathematically proficient students construct viable arguments and critique the reasoning of others.

As you work through this chapter, ask yourself:

How can I justify my conclusions?

In this chapter, you will deepen your understanding of:

➢ The relationships between pairs of angles formed by transversals and the angles in a triangle.

➢ How to find the area and perimeter of triangles, parallelograms, and trapezoids.

➢ The relationship among the three side lengths of a right triangle (the Pythagorean Theorem).

➢ How to determine when the lengths of three segments can and cannot form a triangle.

Chapter Outline

Section 2.1 You will broaden your understanding of angle to include relationships between angles, such as those formed by intersecting lines or those inside a triangle.

Section 2.2 You will develop methods to find the areas of triangles, parallelograms, and trapezoids as well as more complicated shapes.

Section 2.3 You will review the relationship among the sides of a right triangle called the Pythagorean Theorem. This will allow you to find the perimeter of triangles, parallelograms, and trapezoids, and to find the distance between two points on a graph.

2.1.1 What is the relationship?

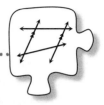

Complementary, Supplementary, and Vertical Angles

In Chapter 1, you compared shapes by looking at similarities between their parts. For example, two shapes might have sides of the same length or equal angles. In this chapter you will examine relationships between parts within a *single* figure or diagram. Today you will start by looking at angles to identify relationships in a diagram that make angle measures equal. As you examine angle relationships today, keep the following questions in mind to guide your discussion:

How can I name the angle?

What is the relationship?

How do I know?

2-1. SOMEBODY'S WATCHING ME

In order to see yourself in a small mirror, you usually have to be looking directly into it — if you move off to the side, you cannot see your image any more. But Mr. Douglas knows a neat trick. He claims that if he makes a right angle with a hinged mirror, he can see himself in the mirror no matter from which direction he looks into it.

a. By forming a right angle with a hinged mirror, test Mr. Douglas's trick for yourself. Look into the place where the sides of the mirror meet. Can you see yourself? What if you look in the mirror from a different angle?

b. Does the trick work for *any* angle between the sides of the mirror? Change the angle between the sides of the mirror until you can no longer see your reflection where the sides meet.

c. At right is a diagram of a student trying out the mirror trick. What appears to be true about the lines of sight? Can you explain why Mr. Douglas's trick works? Talk about this with your team and be ready to share your ideas with the class.

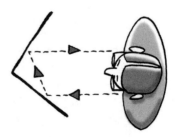

2-2. To completely understand how Mr. Douglas's reflection trick works, you need to learn more about the relationships between angles. But in order to clearly describe relationships between angles, you will need a convenient way to refer to and name them. Examine the diagram of equilateral $\triangle ABC$ at right.

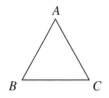

a. The "top" of this triangle is usually referred to as "angle A," written $\angle A$. Point A is called the **vertex** of this angle. The measure of $\angle A$ (the number of degrees in angle A) is written $m\angle A$. Since $\triangle ABC$ is equilateral, write an equation showing the relationship between its angles.

b. Audrey rotated $\triangle ABC$ around point A to form $\triangle AB'C'$. She told her teammate Maria, "*I think the two angles at A have equal measure.*" Maria did not know which angles she was referring to. How many angles can you find at A? Are there more than three?

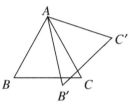

c. Maria asked Audrey to be more specific. She explained, "*One of my angles is $\angle BAB'$.*" At the same time, she marked her two angles with the same marking at right to indicate that they have the same measure.

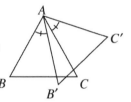

Name her other angle. Be sure to use three letters so there is no confusion about which angle you mean.

2-3. ANGLE RELATIONSHIPS

When you know two angles have a certain relationship, learning something about one of them tells you something about the other. Certain angle relationships come up often enough in geometry that they are given special names.

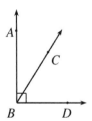

a. Two angles whose measures have a sum of 90° are called **complementary angles**. Since $\angle ABD$ is a right angle in the diagram at right, angles $\angle ABC$ and $\angle CBD$ are complementary. If $m\angle CBD = 76°$, what is $m\angle ABC$? Show how you got your answer.

b. Another special angle is a straight angle or one that is 180°. If the sum of the measures of two angles is 180°, they are called **supplementary angles**. In the diagram at right, $\angle LMN$ is a straight angle. If $m\angle LMP = 62°$, what is $m\angle PMN$?

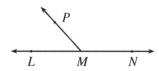

Problem continues on next page →

2-3.   *Problem continued from previous page.*

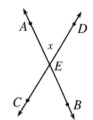

c.   Now consider the diagram at right, which shows $\overleftrightarrow{AB}$ and $\overleftrightarrow{CD}$ intersecting at E. If $x = 23°$, find $m\angle AEC$, $m\angle DEB$, and $m\angle CEB$. Show all work.

d.   Based on your work in part (c), which angle has the same measure as $\angle AED$?

e.   When two lines intersect, the angles that lie on opposite sides of the intersection point are called **vertical angles**. For example, in the diagram above, $\angle AED$ and $\angle CEB$ are vertical angles. Find another pair of vertical angles in the diagram.

2-4.   Travis noticed that the vertical angles in parts (c) and (d) of problem 2-3 have equal measure and wondered if other pairs of vertical angles also have equal measure.

a.   Return to the diagram above and find $m\angle CEB$ if $x = 54°$. Show all work.

b.   Based on your observations, write a **conjecture** (a statement based on an educated guess that is unproven). Start with, *"Vertical angles …"*

2-5.   In the problems below, you will use geometric relationships to find angle measures. Start by finding a special relationship between some of the sides or angles, and use that relationship to write an equation. Solve the equation for the variable, then use that variable value to answer the original question.

a.   Find $m\angle MNP$.

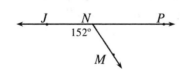

b.   Find $m\angle FGH$.

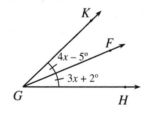

c.   Find $m\angle DBC$.

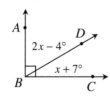

d.   Find $m\angle LPQ$ and $m\angle LPN$.

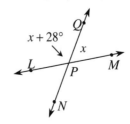

2-6.   PROOF OF VERTICAL ANGLE RELATIONSHIP

When Jacob answered part (b) of problem 2-4, he wrote the conjecture: "*Vertical angles have equal measure.*" (Remember that a conjecture is an educated guess that has not yet been proven.)

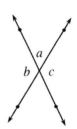

a. Do you think Jacob's vertical angle conjecture holds for *any* pair of vertical angles? Be prepared to convince the rest of the class.

b. Jacob's explanation included the diagram showing intersecting lines. He then wrote that $a + b = 180°$ and $a + c = 180°$. Are these statements true? Why?

c. How can you use Jacob's statements in part (b) to prove that vertical angles always have equal measure?

d. Once a conjecture is proven to be true, it is referred to as a **theorem**. Proving that vertical angles are always congruent in part (c) changed this conjecture into a theorem that can now be used in later problems without needing to reprove it again. Discuss with your team the difference between a conjecture and a theorem and write down your ideas about the difference.

2-7.   LEARNING LOG

Describe each of the angle relationships you learned about today in an entry in your Learning Log. Include a diagram, a description of the angles, and what you know about the relationship. For example, are the angles always equal? Do they have a special sum? Title this entry "Angle Relationships" and include today's date.

Methods and Meanings

Angle Relationships

MATH NOTES

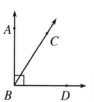

If two angles have measures that add up to 90°, they are called **complementary angles**. For example, in the diagram at right, ∠ABC and ∠CBD are complementary because together they form a right angle.

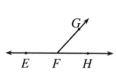

If two angles have measures that add up to 180°, they are called **supplementary angles**. For example, in the diagram at right, ∠EFG and ∠GFH are supplementary because together they form a straight angle.

Two angles do not have to share a vertex to be complementary or supplementary. The first pair of angles at right are supplementary; the second pair of angles are complementary.

Supplementary   **Complementary**

---

*Review &
Preview*

2-8.   Find the area of each rectangle below.

a.   b.   c.

11
cm

3 cm

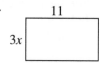

11

3x

3x   −4

11x

−2

2-9.   Mei puts the shapes at right into a bucket and asks Brian to pick one out.

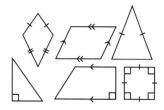

a.   What is the probability that he pulls out a quadrilateral with parallel sides?

b.   What is the probability that he pulls out a shape with rotation symmetry?

2-10.   Camille loves guessing games. She is going to
tell you a fact about her shape to see if you can
guess what it is.

   a.   "My triangle has only one line of
symmetry. What is it?"

   b.   "My triangle has three lines of symmetry.
What is it?"

   c.   "My quadrilateral has no lines of symmetry but it does have rotation
symmetry. What is it?"

2-11.   Jerry has an idea. Since he knows that an isosceles
trapezoid has reflection symmetry, he reasons, *That means
that it must have two pairs of angles with equal measure.*
He marks this relationship on his diagram at right.

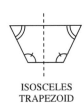

ISOSCELES
TRAPEZOID

Copy the shapes below onto your paper. Similarly mark which angles
must have equal measure due to reflection symmetry.

   a.   b.   c.   d.

KITE   ISOSCELES TRIANGLE   REGULAR HEXAGON   RHOMBUS

2-12.   Larry saw Javon's incomplete Venn diagram at
right, and he wants to finish it. However, he
does not know the condition that each circle
represents. Find a possible label for each circle,
and place two more shapes into the diagram.

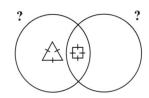

Core Connections Geometry

2.1.2 What is the relationship?

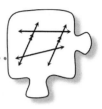

Angles Formed by Transversals

In Lesson 2.1.1, you examined vertical angles and found that vertical angles are always equal. Today you will look at another special relationship that guarantees angles have equal measure.

2-13. Examine the diagrams below. For each pair of angles marked on the diagram, quickly decide what relationship their measures have. Your responses should be limited to one of three relationships: same (equal measures), complementary (have a sum of 90°), and supplementary (have a sum of 180°).

a.   b.   c.   d.

2-14.   Marcos was walking home after school thinking about special angle relationships when he happened to notice a pattern of parallelogram tiles on the wall of a building. Marcos saw lots of special angle relationships in this pattern, so he decided to copy the pattern into his notebook.

The beginning of Marcos's diagram is shown at right and provided on the Lesson 2.1.2 Resource Page. This type of pattern is sometimes called a **tiling**. In this tiling, a parallelogram is copied and translated to fill an entire page without gaps or overlaps.

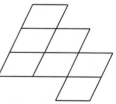

a. Since each parallelogram is a translation of another, what can be stated about the angles in the rest of Marcos' tiling? Use a technology tool or tracing paper to determine which angles must have the same measure. Color all angles that must be equal the same color.

Problem continues on next page →

2-14.   *Problem continued from previous page.*

b.   Consider the angles inside a single parallelogram. Which angles must have equal measure? How can you justify your claim?

c.   What about relationships between lines? Can you identify any lines that must be parallel? Mark all the lines on your diagram with the same number of arrows to show which lines are parallel.

2-15.   Julia wants to learn more about the angles in Marcos's diagram and has decided to focus on just a part of his tiling. An enlarged view of that section is shown in the image below right, with some points and angles labeled.

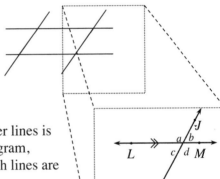

a.   A line that crosses two or more other lines is called a **transversal**. In Julia's diagram, which line is the transversal? Which lines are parallel?

b.   Trace $\angle x$ on tracing paper and shade its interior. Then translate $\angle x$ by sliding the tracing paper along the transversal until it lies on top of another angle and matches it exactly. Which angle in the diagram corresponds with $\angle x$?

c.   In this diagram, $\angle x$ and $\angle b$ are called **corresponding angles** because they are in the same position at two different intersections of the transversal. What is the relationship between the measures of angles x and b? Must one be greater than the other, or must they be equal? Explain how you know.

2-16.   CORRESPONDING ANGLES FORMED BY PARALLEL LINES

The corresponding angles in Julia's diagram in problem 2-15 have equal measure because they were formed by translating a parallelogram.

a.   Name all the other pairs of corresponding angles you can find in Julia's diagram from problem 2-15.

b.   Suppose $b = 60°$. Use what you know about vertical, supplementary, and corresponding angle relationships to find the measures of all the other angles in Julia's diagram.

2-17. Frank wonders whether corresponding angles *always* have equal measure. For parts (a) through (d) below, use tracing paper to decide if corresponding angles have the same measure. Then determine if you have enough information to find the measures of x and y. If you do, find the angle measures and state the relationship.

a.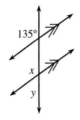

b.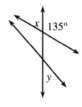

c.

d.

e. Answer Frank's question: Do corresponding angles always have equal measure? If not, when are their measures equal?

f. Conjectures are often written in the form, "*If…, then…*". A statement in if-then form is called a **conditional statement**. Make a conjecture about corresponding angles by completing this conditional statement: "*If …, then corresponding angles have equal measure.*"

g. Prove that your conjecture in part (f) is always true. That is, explain why this conjecture is a theorem.

2-18. For each diagram below, find the value of x, *if possible*. If it is not possible, explain how you know. State the relationships you use. Be prepared to justify every measurement you find to other members of your team.

a.

b.

c.

METHODS AND MEANINGS

Naming Parts of Shapes

Part of geometry is the study of parts of shapes, such as points, line segments, and angles. To avoid confusion, standard notation is used to name these parts.

A **point** is named using a single capital letter. For example, the vertices (corners) of the triangle at right are named A, B, and C.

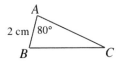

If a shape is transformed, the image shape is often named using **prime notation**. The image of point A is labeled A' (read as "A prime"), the image of B is labeled B' (read as "B prime"), etc. At right, $\triangle A'B'C'$ is the image of $\triangle ABC$.

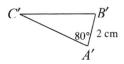

The side of a polygon is a line segment. A **line segment** is a portion of a line between two points and is named by naming its endpoints and placing a bar above them. For example, one side of the first triangle above is named $\overline{AB}$. When referring to the length of a segment, the bar is omitted. In $\triangle ABC$ above, $AB = 2$ cm.

A **line**, which differs from a segment in that it extends infinitely in either direction, is named by using two points on the line and placing a bar with arrows above them. For example, the line below is named $\overleftrightarrow{DE}$. When naming a segment or line, the order of the letters is unimportant. The line below could also be named $\overleftrightarrow{ED}$.

$$\overleftrightarrow{D \quad E}$$

An **angle** can be named by putting an angle symbol in front of the name of the angle's vertex. For example, the angle measuring 80° in $\triangle ABC$ above is named $\angle A$. Sometimes using a single letter makes it unclear which angle is being referenced. For example, in the diagram at right, it is unclear which angle is referred to by $\angle G$. When this happens, the angle is named with three letters. For example, the angle measuring 10° is called $\angle HGI$ or $\angle IGH$. Note that the name of the vertex must be the second letter in the name; the order of the other two letters is unimportant.

To refer to an angle's measure, an m is placed in front of the angle's name. For example, $m\angle HGI = 10°$ means "the measure of $\angle HGI$ is 10°."

2-19.   Examine the diagrams below. What is the geometric relationship between the labeled angles? What is the relationship of their measures? Then, use the relationship to write an equation and solve for *x*.

a.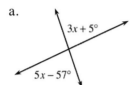

b.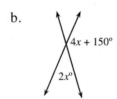

2-20.   In problem 2-11, you determined that because an isosceles triangle has reflection symmetry, then it must have two angles that have equal measure.

a.   How can you tell which angles have equal measure? For example, in the diagram at right, which angles must have equal measure? Name the angles and explain how you know.

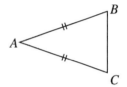

b.   Examine the diagram for part (a). If you know that $m\angle B + m\angle C = 124°$, then what is the measure of $\angle B$? Explain how you know.

c.   Use this idea to find the value of *x* in the diagram at right. Be sure to show all work.

2-21.   On graph paper, draw the quadrilateral with vertices $(-1, 3), (4, 3), (-1, -2)$, and $(4, -2)$.

a.   What kind of quadrilateral is this?

b.   Translate the quadrilateral 3 units to the left and 2 units up. What are the new coordinates of the vertices?

2-22.   Find the equation for the line that passes through $(-1, -2)$ and $(4, 3)$. Is the point $(3, 1)$ on this line? Be sure to justify your answer.

2-23.   Juan decided to test what would happen if he rotated an angle.

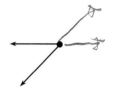

a.   He copied the angle at right on tracing paper and rotated it 180° about its vertex. What type of angle pair did he create? What is the relationship of these angles?

b.   Juan then rotated the same angle 180° through a different point (see the diagram at right). On your paper, draw Juan's angle and the rotated image. Describe the overall shape formed by the two angles.

Core Connections Geometry

2.1.3 What is the relationship?

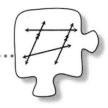

More Angles Formed by Transversals

In Lesson 2.1.2, you looked at corresponding angles formed when a transversal intersects two parallel lines. Today you will investigate other special angle relationships formed in this situation.

2-24.   Whenever one geometric figure can be translated, rotated, or reflected (or a combination of these) so that it lies on top of another, the figures must have the same shape and size. When this is possible, the figures are said to be **congruent** and the symbol ≅ is used to represent the relationship.

    a.   Review the angle relationships you have studied so far. Which types of angles must be congruent?

    b.   Angles are not the only type of figure that can be congruent. For example, sides of a figure can be congruent to another side. Also, a complex shape (such as a trapezoid) can be congruent to another if there is a sequence of rigid transformations that carry it onto the other.

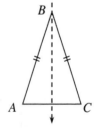

        Consider an isosceles triangle, like the one shown at right. Because of its reflection symmetry, which parts must be congruent? State each relationship using symbols.

2-25.   Suppose ∠a in the diagram at right measures 48°.

    a.   Use what you know about vertical, corresponding, and supplementary angle relationships to find the measure of ∠b.

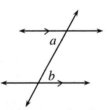

    b.   Julia is still having trouble seeing the angle relationships clearly in this diagram. Her teammate, Althea explains, *"When I translate one of the angles along the transversal, I notice its image and the other given angle are a pair of vertical angles. That way, I know that angles a and b must be congruent."*

Problem continues on next page →

2-25.   *Problem continued from previous page.*

Use Althea's method and tracing paper to determine if the following angle pairs are congruent or supplementary. Be sure to state whether the pair of angles created after the translation is a vertical pair or forms a straight angle. Be ready to justify your answer for the class.

(1)   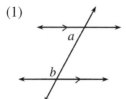   (2)   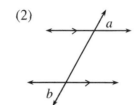   (3)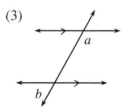

2-26.   ALTERNATE INTERIOR ANGLE RELATIONSHIP

In problem 2-25, Althea showed that the shaded angles in the diagram are congruent. However, these angles also have a name for their geometric relationship (their relative positions on the diagram). These angles are called **alternate interior** angles. They are called "alternate" because they are on opposite sides of the transversal, and "interior" because they are both inside (that is, between) the parallel lines.

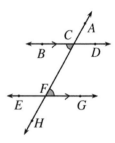

a.   Find another pair of alternate interior angles in this diagram.

b.   Think about the relationship between the measures of alternate interior angles. If the lines are parallel, are they always congruent? Are they always supplementary? Complete the conjecture, "*If lines are parallel, then alternate interior angles are…*".

c.   Instead of writing conditional statements, Roxie likes to write **arrow diagrams** to express her conjectures. She expresses the conjecture from part (b) as:

Lines are parallel → *alternate interior angles are congruent.*

This arrow diagram says the same thing as the conditional statement you wrote in part (c). How is it different from your conditional statement? What does the arrow mean?

d.   Prove that alternate interior angles are congruent. That is, how can you use rigid transformations to move ∠CFG so that it lands on ∠BFC? Explain. Be sure your team agrees.

2-27.   The shaded angles in the diagram at right have another
         special angle relationship. They are called **same-side
         interior** angles.

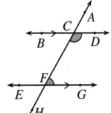

   a.   Why do you think they have this name?

   b.   What is the relationship between the angle
         measures of same-side interior angles? Are they
         always congruent? Supplementary? Talk about
         this with your team. Then write a conjecture about the relationship of the
         angle measures. Your conjecture can be in the form of a conditional
         statement or an arrow diagram. If you write a conditional statement, it
         should begin, "*If lines are parallel, then same-side interior angles are…*"

   c.   Claudio decided to prove this theorem this way. He
         used letters in his diagram to represent the measures
         of the angles. Then, he wrote $a + b = 180°$ and
         $a = c$. Is he correct? Explain why or why not.

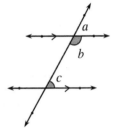

   d.   Finish Claudio's proof to explain why same-side
         interior angles are always supplementary whenever
         lines are parallel.

2-28.   THE REFLECTION OF LIGHT

         You know enough about angle relationships now to start analyzing how light
         bounces off mirrors. Examine the two diagrams below. Diagram A shows a
         beam of light emitted from a light source at A. In Diagram B, someone has
         placed a mirror across the light beam. The light beam hits the mirror and is
         reflected from its original path.

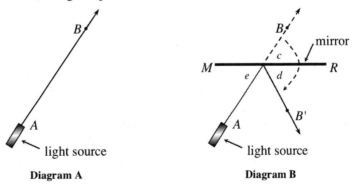

Diagram A   Diagram B

   a.   What is the relationship between angles *c* and *d*? Why?

   b.   What is the relationship between angles *c* and *e*? How do you know?

Problem continues on next page →

2-28.   *Problem continued from previous page.*

   c.   What is the relationship between angles *e* and *d*? How do you know?

   d.   Use your conclusions from parts (a) through (c) to prove that the measure
         of the angle at which light hits a mirror equals the measure of the angle at
         which it bounces off the mirror.

2-29.   A DVD player (or a CD-ROM
         reader) works by bouncing a laser
         off the surface of the DVD, which
         acts like a mirror. An emitter sends
         out the light, which bounces off the
         DVD and then is detected by a
         sensor. The diagram below shows a
         DVD held parallel to the surface of
         the DVD player, on which an
         emitter and a sensor are mounted.

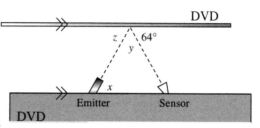

   a.   The laser is supposed to bounce off the DVD at a 64° angle as shown in
         the diagram above. For the laser to go directly into the sensor, at what
         angle does the emitter need to send the laser beam? In other words, what
         does the measure of angle *x* have to be? Justify your conclusion.

   b.   The diagram above shows two parts of the laser beam: the one coming out
         of the emitter and the one that has bounced off the DVD. What is the
         angle ($\angle y$) between these beams? How do you know?

2-30.   ANGLE RELATIONSHIPS TOOLKIT

         Obtain a Lesson 2.1.3 Resource Page ("Angle
         Relationships Toolkit") from your teacher. This will be a
         continuation of the Geometry Toolkit you started in
         Chapter 1. Think about the new angle relationships you
         have studied so far in Chapter 2. Then, in the space
         provided, add a diagram and a description of the
         relationship for each special angle relationship you know.

         Be sure to specify any relationship between the measures of the angles (such as
         whether or not they are always congruent). In later lessons, you will continue to
         add relationships to this toolkit, so be sure to keep this resource page in a safe
         place. At this point, your Toolkit should include:

   •   Vertical angles   •   Straight angles

   •   Corresponding angles   •   Alternate interior angles

   •   Same-side interior angles

METHODS AND MEANINGS

Systems of Linear Equations

In a previous course, you learned that a **system of linear equations** is a set of two or more linear equations that are given together, such as the example at right. In a system, each variable represents the same quantity in both equations. For example, y represents the same quantity in *both* equations at right.

$$y = 2x$$
$$y = -3x + 5$$

To represent a system of equations graphically, you can simply graph each equation on the same set of axes. The graph may or may not have a **point of intersection**, as shown circled at right.

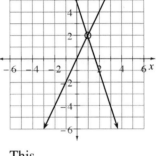

Sometimes two lines have *no* points of intersection. This happens when the two lines are parallel. It is also possible for two lines to have an *infinite* number of intersections. This happens when the graphs of two lines lie on top of each other. Such lines are said to **coincide**.

$$x = -3y + 1$$
$$4x - 3y = -11$$

The **Substitution Method** is a way to change two equations with two variables into one equation with one variable. It is convenient to use when only one equation is solved for a variable. For example, to solve the system at right:

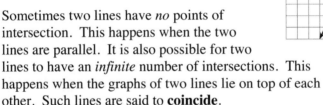

- Use substitution to rewrite the two equations as one. In other words, replace x with $(-3y+1)$ to get $4(-3y+1) - 3y = -11$. This equation can then be solved to find y. In this case, $y = 1$.

$$4(-3y+1) - 3y = -11$$
$$-12y + 4 - 3y = -11$$
$$-15y + 4 = -11$$
$$-15y = -15$$
$$y = 1$$

- To find the point of intersection, substitute to find the other value.

- Substitute $y = 1$ into $x = -3y + 1$ and write the answer for x and y as an ordered pair.

$$x = -3(1) + 1 = -2$$
$$(-2, 1)$$

- To test the solution, substitute $x = -2$ and $y = 1$ into $4x - 3y = -11$ to verify that it makes the equation true. Since $4(-2) - 3(1) = -11$, the solution $(-2, 1)$ must be correct.

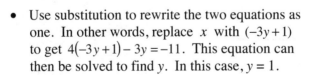
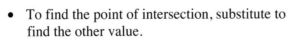

2-31. The set of equations at right is an example of a **system of equations**. Read the Math Notes box for this lesson on how to solve systems of equations. Then answer the questions below.

$$y = -x + 1$$
$$y = 2x + 7$$

a. Graph the system on graph paper. Then write its solution (the point of intersection) in (x, y) form.

b. Now solve the system using an algebraic method of your choice. Did your solution match your result from part (a)? If not, check your work carefully and look for any mistakes in your algebraic process or on your graph.

2-32. On graph paper, graph the rectangle with vertices at $(2, 1), (2, 5), (7, 1)$, and $(7, 5)$.

a. What is the area of this rectangle?

b. Shirley was given the following points and asked to find the area, but her graph paper is not big enough. Find the area of Shirley's rectangle, and explain to her how she can find the area without graphing the points.

Shirley's points: $(352, 150), (352, 175), (456, 150)$, and $(456, 175)$

2-33. Looking at the diagram below, John says that $m\angle BCF = m\angle EFH$.

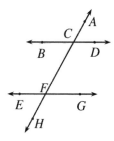

Note: This stoplight icon will appear periodically throughout the text. Problems with this icon display common errors that can be made. Be sure not to make the same mistakes yourself!

a. Do you agree with John? Why or why not?

b. Jim says, "*You can't be sure those angles are equal. An important piece of information is missing from the diagram!*" What is Jim talking about?

2-34.   Use your knowledge of angle relationships to solve for x in the diagrams below. Justify your solutions by naming the geometric relationship.

a.

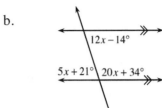

$5x + 7°$ $9x - 63°$

b.

$12x - 14°$

$5x + 21°$ $20x + 34°$

2-35.   When Ms. Shreve randomly selects a student in her class, she has a $\frac{1}{3}$ probability of selecting a boy.

a.   If her class has 36 students, how many boys are in Ms. Shreve's class?

b.   If there are 11 boys in her class, how many girls are in her class?

c.   What is the probability that she will select a girl?

d.   Assume that Ms. Shreve's class has a total of 24 students. She selected one student (who was a boy) to attend a fieldtrip and then was told she needed to select one more student to attend. What is the probability that the second randomly selected student will also be a boy?

2-36.   On graph paper, draw line segment $\overline{AB}$ if $A(6, 2)$ and $B(3, 5)$.

a.   Reflect $\overline{AB}$ across the line $x = 3$ and connect points A and A'. What shape is created by this reflection? Be as specific as possible.

b.   What polygon is created when $\overline{AB}$ is reflected across the line $y = -x + 6$ and all endpoints are connected to form a polygon?

2.1.4 How can I use it?

Angles in a Triangle

So far in this chapter, you have investigated the angle relationships created when two lines intersect, forming vertical angles. You have also investigated the relationships created when a transversal intersects two parallel lines. Today you will study the angle relationships that result when three non-parallel lines intersect, forming a triangle.

2-37. Marcos decided to change his tiling from problem 2-14 by drawing diagonals in each of the parallelograms. Find his pattern, shown at right, on the Lesson 2.1.4 Resource Page.

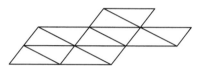

a. Copy one of Marcos's triangles onto tracing paper. Use a colored pen or pencil to shade one of the triangle's angles on the tracing paper. Then use the same color to shade every angle on the resource page that is equal to the shaded angle.

b. Repeat this process for the other two angles of the triangle, using a different color for each angle in the triangle. When you are done, every angle in your tiling should be shaded with one of the three colors.

c. Now examine your colored tiling. What relationship can you find between the three different-colored angles? You may want to focus on the angles that form a straight angle. What does this tell you about the angles in a triangle? Write a conjecture in the form of a conditional statement or an arrow diagram. If you write a conditional statement, it should begin, "*If a polygon is a triangle, then the measure of its angles…*".

d. How can you convince yourself that your conjecture is true for all triangles? That is, given parallel lines (since the tiling was generated by translating parallelograms), why does $a = d$ and $c = e$ in the diagram at right? If technology is available, use it to test many different angle measures.

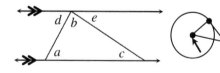

Then add this angle relationship to your Angle Relationships Toolkit from Lesson 2.1.3. This will be referred to as the **Triangle Angle Sum Theorem**. (A theorem is a statement that has been proven.)

Core Connections Geometry

2-38.   Use your theorem from problem 2-37 about the angles in a triangle to find *x* in each diagram below. Show all work.

a.

b.
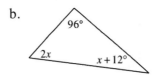

2-39.   What can the Triangle Angle Sum Theorem help you learn about special triangles?

a.   Find the measure of each angle in an equilateral triangle. Justify your conclusion.

b.   Consider the isosceles right triangle (also sometimes referred to as a "half-square") at right. Find the measures of all the angles in a half-square.

c.   What if you only know one angle of an isosceles triangle? For example, if $m\angle A = 34°$, what are the measures of the other two angles?

2-40.   TEAM REASONING CHALLENGE

How much can you figure out about the figure at right using your knowledge of angle relationships? Work with your team to find the measures of all the labeled angles in the diagram at right. Justify solutions with the name of the angle relationship you used. Carefully record your work as you go and be prepared to share your reasoning with the rest of the class.

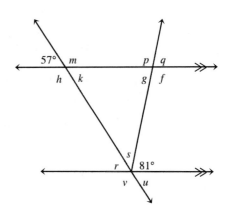

METHODS AND MEANINGS

More Angle Pair Relationships

Vertical angles are the two opposite (that is, non-adjacent) angles formed by two intersecting lines, such as angles $\angle c$ and $\angle g$ in the diagram at right. $\angle c$ by itself is not a vertical angle, nor is $\angle g$, although $\angle c$ and $\angle g$ together are a pair of vertical angles. Vertical angles always have equal measure.

Corresponding angles lie in the same position but at different points of intersection of the transversal. For example, in the diagram at right, $\angle m$ and $\angle d$ form a pair of corresponding angles, since both of them are to the right of the transversal and above the intersecting line. Corresponding angles are congruent when the lines intersected by the transversal are parallel.

$\angle f$ and $\angle m$ are **alternate interior angles** because one is to the left of the transversal, one is to the right, and both are between (inside) the pair of lines. Alternate interior angles are congruent when the lines intersected by the transversal are parallel.

$\angle g$ and $\angle m$ are **same-side interior angles** because both are on the same side of the transversal and both are between the pair of lines. Same-side interior angles are supplementary when the lines intersected by the transversal are parallel.

Review & Preview

2-41.   Find all missing angles in the diagrams below.

a.
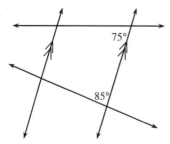
75°
85°

b.
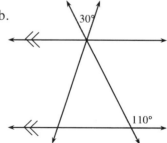
30°
110°

2-42.   Robert believes the lines graphed at right are perpendicular, but Mario is not convinced. Find the slope of each line, and explain how you know whether or not the lines are perpendicular.

2-43.   The diagram at right represents only half of a shape that has the graph of $y = 1$ as a line of symmetry. Draw the completed shape on your paper, and label the coordinates of the missing vertices.

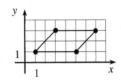

2-44.   Janine measured the sides of a rectangle and found that the sides were 12 inches and 24 inches. Howard measured the same rectangle and found that the sides were 1 foot and 2 feet. When their math teacher asked them for the area, Janine said 288, and Howard said 2. Why did they get two different numbers for the area of the same rectangle?

2-45.   Solve the system of equations at right using the method of your choice. Then state the solution to the system. If there is not a solution, explain why.

$$y = -\tfrac{2}{5}x + 1$$

$$y = -\tfrac{2}{5}x - 2$$

2.1.5 What is the relationship?

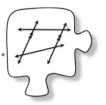

Applying Angle Relationships

During Section 2.1, you have been learning about various special angle relationships that are created by intersecting lines. Today you will investigate those relationships a bit further, then apply what you know to explain how Mr. Douglas's hinged mirror trick (from problem 2-1) works. As you work in your teams today, keep the following questions in mind to guide your discussion:

What is the relationship?

Are the angles equal? Are they supplementary?

How can I be sure?

2-46. Use your knowledge of angle relationships to answer the questions below.

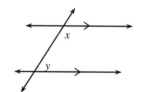

a. In the diagram at right, what is the sum of angles *x* and *y*? How do you know?

b. While looking at the diagram at right, Rianna exclaimed, "*I think something is wrong with this diagram.*" What do you think she is referring to? Be prepared to share your thinking with the class.

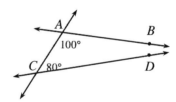

2-47. Maria is not convinced that the lines in part (b) of problem 2-46 *must* be parallel. She decides to assume that they are not parallel and draws the diagram at right.

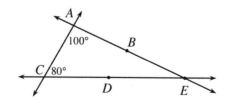

a. Why must lines $\overleftrightarrow{AB}$ and $\overleftrightarrow{CD}$ intersect in Maria's diagram?

b. What is $m\angle BED$? Discuss this question with your team and explain what it tells you about $\overleftrightarrow{AB}$ and $\overleftrightarrow{CD}$.

c. If the angle measures at points *A* and *C* are as marked, could $\overleftrightarrow{AB}$ and $\overleftrightarrow{CD}$ intersect at a point on the other side of $\overleftrightarrow{AC}$? Why or why not?

2-48.   Examine the diagram at right.

   a.   In this diagram, must $\overrightarrow{FG}$ and $\overrightarrow{HI}$ be
        parallel? Explain how you know.

   b.   Write a theorem based on your conclusion
        to this problem.

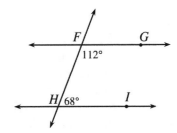

2-49.   Use your theorem from problem 2-48 to explain why lines must be parallel in
         the diagrams below.

   a.   b.

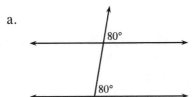

   c.   Looking back at the diagrams in parts (a) and (b), write two new theorems
        that begin, "*If corresponding angles are congruent, …*" and "*If the
        measures of alternate interior angles are congruent, …*".

2-50.   SOMEBODY'S WATCHING ME, Part Two

         Remember Mr. Douglas' trick from problem 2-1? You now know enough
         about angle and line relationships to analyze why a hinged mirror set so the
         angle between the mirrors is 90° will reflect your image back to you from any
         angle. Since your reflection is actually light that travels from your face to the
         mirror, you will need to study the path of the
         light. Remember that a mirror reflects light, and
         that the angle the light hits the mirror will equal
         the angle it bounces off the mirror.

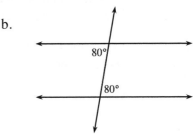

         Your Task: Explain why the mirror bounces your image
         back to you from any angle. Include in your analysis:

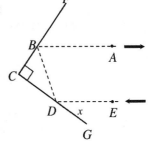

         •   Use angle relationships to find the measures of
             all the angles in the figure. (Each team member
             should choose a different *x*-value and calculate
             all of the other angle measures using his or her
             selected value of *x*.)

         •   What do you know about the paths the light takes
             as it leaves you and as it returns to you? That is,
             what is the relationship between $\overrightarrow{BA}$ and $\overrightarrow{DE}$?

         •   Does Mr. Douglas' trick work if the angle between the mirrors is not 90°?

Further Guidance

2-51. Since you are trying to show that the trick works for *any* angle at which the light could hit the mirror, each team will work with a different angle measure for *x* in this problem. Your teacher will tell you what angle *x* your team should use in the diagram at right.

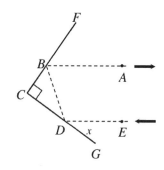

a. Using angle relationships and what you know about how light bounces off mirrors, find the measure of every other angle in the diagram.

b. What is the relationship between $\angle ABD$ and $\angle EDB$? What does this tell you about the relationship between $\overline{BA}$ and $\overline{DE}$?

c. What if $m\angle C = 89°$? Does the trick still work?

2-52. Explain why the 90° hinged mirror always sends your image back to you, no matter which angle you look into it from.

*Further Guidance
section ends here.*

2-53. Use what you have learned in Section 2.1 to find the measures of *x*, *y*, and *z* at right. Justify each conclusion with the name of a geometric relationship from your Angle Relationships Toolkit.

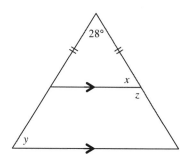

2-54. EXTENSION

Hold a 90° hinged mirror at arm's length and find your own image. Now close your right eye. Which eye closes in the mirror? Look back at the diagram from problem 2-50. Can you explain why this eye is the one that closes?

METHODS AND MEANINGS

Proof by Contradiction

The kind of argument you used in Lesson 2.1.5 to justify "If same-side interior angles are supplementary, then lines are parallel" is sometimes called a **proof by contradiction**. In a proof by contradiction, you prove a claim by thinking about what the consequences would be if it were false. If the claim's being false would lead to an impossibility, this shows that the claim must be true.

For example, suppose you know Mary's brother is seven years younger than Mary. Can you argue that Mary is at least five years old? A proof by contradiction of this claim would go:

Suppose Mary is less than five years old.

Then her brother's age is negative!

But this is impossible, so Mary must be at least five years old.

To show that lines $\overleftrightarrow{AB}$ and $\overleftrightarrow{CD}$ must be parallel in the diagram at right, you used a proof by contradiction. You argued:

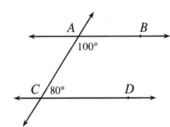

Suppose $\overleftrightarrow{AB}$ and $\overleftrightarrow{CD}$ intersect at some point E.

Then the angles in $\triangle AEC$ add up to more than 180°.

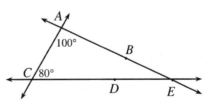

But this is impossible, so $\overleftrightarrow{AB}$ and $\overleftrightarrow{CD}$ must be parallel.

This is true no matter on which side of $\overleftrightarrow{AC}$ point E is assumed to be.

2-55.   Solve for x in the diagram at right.

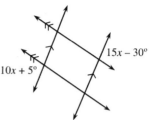

2-56.   For each diagram below, set up an equation and solve for x.

a. Perimeter = 76 units

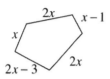

b.

c.

d.

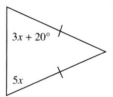

2-57.   Solve each system of equations below. Then verify that your solution makes each equation true. You may want to refer to the Math Notes box in Lesson 2.1.3.

a. $y = 5x - 2$
       $y = 2x + 10$

b. $x = -2y - 1$
       $2x + y = -20$

2-58.   Graph the line $y = \frac{3}{4}x$ on graph paper.

a.   Draw a slope triangle.

b.   Rotate your slope triangle 90° around the origin to get a new slope triangle. What is the new slope?

c.   Find the equation of a line perpendicular to $y = \frac{4}{3}x$.

2-59.   Mario has 6 shapes in a bucket. He tells you that the probability of pulling an isosceles triangle out of the bucket is $\frac{1}{3}$. How many isosceles triangles are in his bucket?

2.2.1 How can I measure an object?

Units of Measure

How tall are you? How large is the United States? How much water does your bathtub at home hold? All of these questions ask about the size of objects around you. How can you answer these questions more specifically than saying "big" or "small"? Today you will be investigating ways to answer these and other questions like them.

2-60.   Your teacher will describe with words a figure he or she has drawn. Your job is to try to draw the *exact same figure* on your paper so that if you placed your drawing on top of your teacher's, the figures would match perfectly. Redraw your figure as many times as necessary.

2-61.   Length often provides a direct way to answer the question, "How big?" In this activity, your teacher will give your team rulers with a unit of length to use to measure distances. For instance, if you have an object that has the same length as three of your units placed next to one another, then the object's length is "3 units."

    a.   Common units you may have used before are inches or meters. However, your unit does not match any of the familiar units. Give your unit of measure a unique name. Then continue marking and labeling units on your ruler as accurately as possible.

    b.   The **dimensions** of a figure are its measurements of length. For example, the measurements in each figure below describe the relative size of each object.

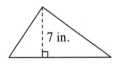

Dimensions can describe how long, wide, or tall the object is by measuring the lengths of the edges.

Or, dimensions can be found by measuring a length that is not a side.

Find the dimensions of the shape on the Lesson 2.2.1A Resource Page using your unit of length. That is, how wide is the shape? How tall? Compare your results with those of other teams. What happened?

Problem continues on next page →

2-61.   *Problem continued from previous page.*

c.   The local baseball club is planning to make a mural that is the same general shape as the one you measured in part (b) (but fortunately a much larger version!). The club plans to frame the mural with neon tubes. Approximately how many units of neon tube will they need to do this?

2-62.   To paint the mural, the wall must first be covered with a coat of primer. How much surface will need to be painted with the primer? Remember that the measurement of the region inside a shape is called the **area** of the shape.

a.   Just as you were able to use your unit of length to measure distance, you need a unit of area to measure a surface. Use your team's ruler to make unit squares that are 1 unit long on each side. The area that your square unit covers is called "one square unit" and can be abbreviated as 1 sq. unit or 1 un^2. What would you call this unit of measure, given the name you chose in problem 2-61?

b.   What is the approximate area of the mural? That is, how many of your square units fit within your shape?

2-63.   Use your unit of measure to make a rectangle that has dimensions 3 units by 5 units.

a.   What is the area of your rectangle? (That is, how many unit squares are there in your rectangle?)

b.   When you answered part (a), did you count the squares? Did your team use a shortcut? If so, why does the shortcut work?

c.   Compare your rectangle to rectangles that other teams made. What is the same about the rectangles and what is different?

2-64.   If you found out that your gym teacher is going to make you run 31,680 inches next period, how useful is this information? Or, if you knew that you were 0.00030977 miles long at birth, do you have any idea how long that is?

An important part of measurement is choosing an appropriate unit of measurement. With your team, suggest a unit of measurement that can best measure (and describe) each of these situations.

a.   The distance you travel from home to get to school.

b.   The surface of the school's soccer field.

c.   The width of a strand of hair.

d.   The length of your nose.

e.   The amount of room in your locker.

METHODS AND MEANINGS

Triangle Angle Sum Theorem

The **Triangle Angle Sum Theorem** states that the measures of the angles in a triangle add up to 180°. For example, in $\triangle ABC$ at right:

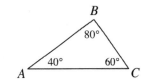

$$m\angle A + m\angle B + m\angle C = 180°$$

The Triangle Angle Sum Theorem can be verified by using a tiling of the given triangle (shaded at right). Because the tiling produces parallel lines, the alternate interior angles must be congruent. As seen in the diagram at right, the three angles of a triangle form a straight angle. Therefore, the sum of the angles of a triangle must be 180°.

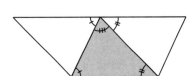

2-65.   Examine the shapes in your Shape Toolkit. Then name all of the shapes in the Shape Toolkit that share both of the following qualities.

- They have only one line of symmetry.

- They have fewer than four sides.

2-66.   Examine the diagram at right. Then use the information provided in the diagram to find the measures of angles $a, b, c,$ and d. For each angle, name the relationship from your Angle Relationships Toolkit that helped justify your conclusion. For example, did you use vertical angles? If not, what type of angle did you use?

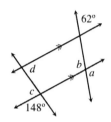

2-67.   Examine the triangle at right.

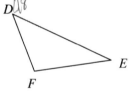

a.   If $m\angle D = 48°$ and $m\angle F = 117°$, then what is $m\angle E$?

b.   Solve for x if $m\angle D = 4x + 2°, m\angle F = 7x - 8°,$ and $m\angle E = 4x + 6°$. Then find $m\angle D$.

c.   If $m\angle D = m\angle F = m\angle E$, what type of triangle is $\triangle FED$?

2-68.   Plot $\triangle ABC$ on graph paper if $A(6, 3), B(2, 1),$ and $C(5, 7)$.

a. $\triangle ABC$ is rotated about the origin 180° to become $\triangle A'B'C'$. Name the coordinates of $A', B',$ and C'.

b.   This time $\triangle ABC$ is rotated 180° about point C to form $\triangle A''B''C''$. Name the coordinates of B''.

c.   If $\triangle ABC$ is rotated 90° clockwise (↻) about the origin to form $\triangle A'''B'''C'''$, what are the coordinates of point A'''?

2-69.   Examine the graph at right.

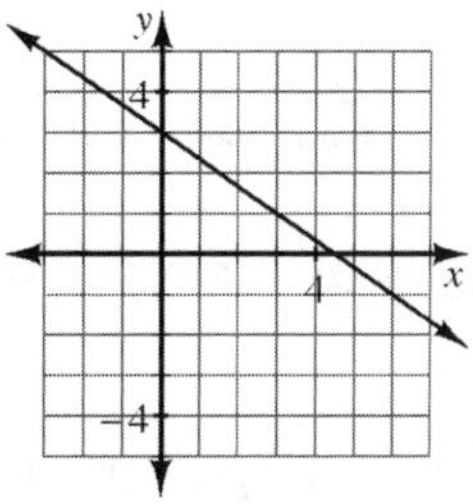

    a.   Find the equation of the line.

    b.   Is the line $y = \frac{3}{2}x + 1$ perpendicular to this line? How do you know?

    c.   On graph paper, graph $\overrightarrow{AB}$ if $A(-2, 4)$ and $B(4, 7)$. Then find the equation of $\overrightarrow{AB}$.

    d.   Find an equation of $\overrightarrow{AC}$ if $\overrightarrow{AC} \perp \overrightarrow{AB}$ from part (c).

2.2.2 How can I find the area?

Areas of Triangles and Composite Shapes

How much grass would it take to cover a football field? How much paint would it take to cover a stop sign? How many sequins does it take to cover a dress? Finding the area of different types of shapes enables us to answer many questions. However, different people will see a shape differently. Therefore, during this lesson, be especially careful to look for different strategies that can be used to find area.

As you solve these problems, ask yourself the following focus questions:

What shapes do I see in the diagram?

Does this problem remind me of one I have seen before?

Is there another way to find the area?

2-70.   STRATEGIES TO MEASURE AREA

In Lesson 2.2.1 you used a grid to measure area. But what if a grid is not available? Or what if you want an exact measurement?

Examine the variety of shapes below. Work with your team to find the area of each one. If a shape has shading, then find the area of the shaded region. Be sure to listen to your teammates carefully and look for different strategies. Be prepared to share your team's method with the class.

a.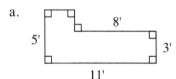

b.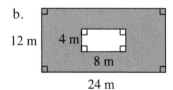

c.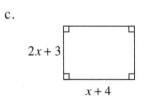

d.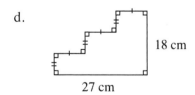

e.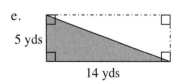

f.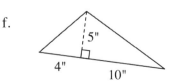

2-71.   Ismael claimed that he did not need to calculate the area for part (f) in problem
2-70 because it must be the same as the area for the triangle in part (e).

a.   Is Ismael's claim correct? How do you know? Draw diagrams that show
your thinking.

b.   Do all triangles with the same bases and heights have the
same areas? Use your technology tool to investigate. If no
technology is available, obtain the Lesson 2.2.2 Resource
Page and compare the areas of the given triangles.

c.   Explain why the area of any triangle is half the area of a rectangle that has
the same base and height. That is, show that the area of a triangle must be
$\frac{1}{2}bh$.

2-72.   How do you know which dimensions to use when finding the area of a triangle?

a.   Copy each triangle below onto your paper. Then find the area of each
triangle. Draw any lines on the diagram that will help. Turning the
triangles may help you discover a way to find their areas.

(1)   (2)   (3)

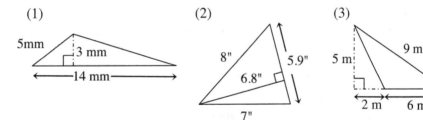

b.   Look back at your work from part (a). Which numbers from each triangle
did you use to find the area? For instance, in the center triangle, you
probably used only the 6.8" and 5.9". Write an explanation and/or draw a
diagram that would help another student understand how to choose which
lengths to use when calculating the area.

c.   Mario, Raquel, and Jocelyn
are arguing about where the
height is for the triangle at
right. The three have written
their names along the part they
think should be the height.
Determine which person is correct. Explain why the one you
chose is correct and why the other two are incorrect.

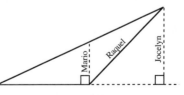

2-73.   LEARNING LOG

In a Learning Log entry, describe at least two different
strategies that were used today to find the area of irregular
shapes. For each method, be sure to include an example.
Title this entry "Areas of Composite Figures" and include today's date.

Mᴇᴛʜᴏᴅꜱ ᴀɴᴅ Mᴇᴀɴɪɴɢꜱ

Multiplying Binomials

One method for multiplying binomials is to
use a generic rectangle. That is, use each
factor of the product as a dimension of a
rectangle and find its area. If $(2x + 5)$ is the
base of a rectangle and $(3x - 1)$ is the height,
then the expression $(2x + 5)(3x - 1)$ is the
area of the rectangle. See the example below.

	$2x$	$+5$	
-1	$-2x$	-5	-1
$3x$	$6x^2$	$15x$	$3x$
	$2x$	$+5$	

Multiply: $(2x+5)(3x-1)$ $=$ $6x^2 - 2x + 15x - 5$
$=$ $6x^2 + 13x - 5$

2-74.   Review how to multiply binomials by reading the Math Notes box for this
lesson. Then rewrite each of the expressions below by multiplying binomials
and simplifying the resulting expression.

a. $(4x+1)(2x-7)$ b. $(5x-2)(2x+7)$

c. $(4x-3)(x-11)$ d. $(-3x+1)(2x-5)$

2-75.   The shaded triangle at right is surrounded by a
rectangle. Find the area of the triangle.

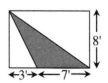

2-76.   For each diagram below, solve for x. Explain what relationship(s) from your Angle Relationships Toolkit you used for each problem.

a.
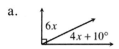
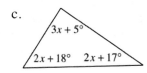

b.
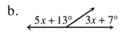

c.
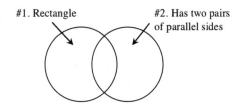

d.

2-77.   Daniel and Mike were having an argument about where to place a square in the Venn diagram at right. Daniel wants to put the square in the intersection (the region where the two circles overlap).

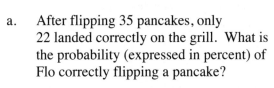

Mike doesn't think that's right. "*I think it should go in the right region because it is a square, not a rectangle.*"

"*But a square IS a rectangle!*" protests Daniel. Who is right? Explain your thinking.

2-78.   Flo thinks she may be able to increase sales if she makes a big show of flipping pancakes at her diner. But flipping pancakes high in the air takes a lot of practice!

a.   After flipping 35 pancakes, only 22 landed correctly on the grill. What is the probability (expressed in percent) of Flo correctly flipping a pancake?

b.   Flo needs 42 pancakes for a large hungry group that just arrived. How many pancakes should she attempt to flip so that 42 flip correctly?

c.   A customer orders a side of "Flo's grab bag of flapjacks" in which a customer gets one randomly chosen pancake. Flo has prepared a pan of 12 sourdough pancakes and 15 buttermilk pancakes. How many banana pancakes should Flo add to the pan if she wants the probability of randomly grabbing one banana pancake to be $\frac{1}{10}$?

2.2.3 What is the area?

Areas of Parallelograms and Trapezoids

In Lesson 2.2.2, you used your knowledge of the area of a rectangle to develop a method to find the exact area of a triangle that works for all triangles. How can your understanding of the area of triangles and rectangles help with the study of other shapes? As you work today, ask yourself and your team members these focus questions:

What do you see?

What shapes make up the composite figure?

Is there another way?

2-79.   Find the areas of the figures below. Can you find more than one method for each shape?

a.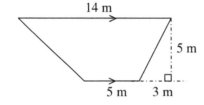

b.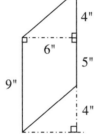

2-80.   FINDING THE AREA OF A PARALLELOGRAM

One of the shapes in your Shape Bucket is shown at right. It is called a **parallelogram**: a four-sided shape with two pairs of parallel sides. How can you find the area of a parallelogram? Consider this question as you answer the questions below.

a.   Kenisha thinks that the rectangle and parallelogram below have the same area. Her teammate Shaundra disagrees. Who is correct? Justify your conclusion.

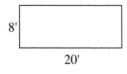 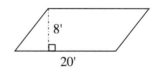

Rectangle   **Parallelogram**

Problem continues on next page →

2-80.   *Problem continued from previous page.*

    b.   In the parallelogram shown in part (a), the two lengths that you were given are often called the **base** and **height**. Several more parallelograms are shown below. In each case, find a related rectangle for which you know both the base and height. Rotating your book might help. Use what you know about rectangles to find the area of each parallelogram.

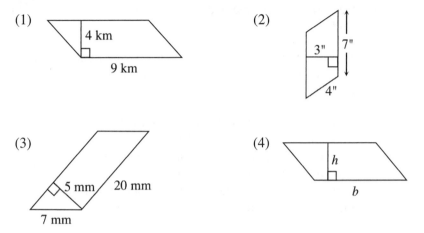

(1)   4 km   9 km

(2)   3"   7"   4"

(3)   5 mm   20 mm   7 mm

(4)   h   b

    c.   Describe how to find the area of a parallelogram when given its base and height.

    d.   Does the angle at which the parallelogram slants matter? Does every parallelogram have a related rectangle with equal area? Why or why not? Explain how you know.

2-81.   Shaundra claims that the area of a parallelogram can be found by *only* using triangles.

    a.   Do you agree? Trace the parallelogram at right onto your paper. Then divide it into two triangles. (Do you see more than one way to do this? If you do, ask some team members to divide the parallelogram one way, and the others a second way.)

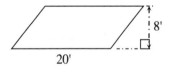

8'

20'

    b.   Use what you know about calculating the area of a triangle to find the area of the parallelogram. It may help to trace each triangle separately onto tracing paper so that you can rotate them and label any lengths that you know.

    c.   How does the answer to part (b) compare to the area you found in part (a) of problem 2-80?

2-82.   FINDING THE AREA OF A TRAPEZOID

Another shape you will study from the Shape
Bucket is a **trapezoid**: a four-sided shape that has
at least one pair of parallel sides. The sides that
are parallel are called **bases**, as shown in the
diagram at right. Answer the questions below with
your team to develop a method to find the area of a
trapezoid.

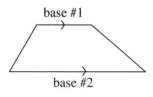

base #1

base #2

Trapezoid

a.   While playing with the shapes in her Shape Bucket, Shaundra noticed that
two identical trapezoids could be arranged to form a parallelogram. Is she
correct?

Trace the trapezoid shown at right onto a piece
of tracing paper. Be sure to label its bases and
height as shown in the diagram. Work with a
team member to move and rearrange the
trapezoid on each piece of tracing paper so that
they create a parallelogram.

b_1

h

b_2

b.   Since you built a parallelogram from two trapezoids, you can use what you
know about finding the area of a parallelogram to find the area of the
trapezoid. If the bases of each trapezoid are b_1 and b_2 and the height of
each is h, then find the area of the parallelogram. Then use this area to
find the area of the original trapezoid.

c.   Kenisha sees it differently. She sees two
triangles inside the trapezoid. If she divides a
trapezoid into two triangles, what area will she
get? Again assume that the bases of the
trapezoid are b_1 and b_2 and the height is h.

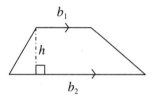

d.   Are the area expressions you created in parts (b) and (c)
equivalent? That is, will they calculate the same area?
Use your algebra skills to demonstrate that they are equivalent.

Core Connections Geometry

2-83.   Calculate the exact areas of the shapes below.

a.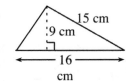

b.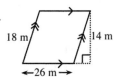

c.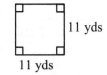

d.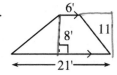

2-84.   EXTENSION

Examine the diagram of the kite at right. Work with your team
to find a way to show that its area must be half of the product of
the diagonals. That is, if the length of the diagonals are a and b,
provide a diagram or explanation of why the area of the kite must
be $\frac{1}{2}ab$.

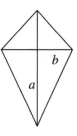

MᴇᴛHODS AND MᴇᴀNINGS

Conditional Statements

MATH NOTES

A **conditional statement** is written in the form "**If …, then ….**"
Here are some examples of conditional statements:

If a shape is a rhombus, then it has four sides of equal length.

If it is February 14th, then it is Valentine's Day.

If a shape is a parallelogram, then its area is $A = bh$.

2-85.   Berti is the Shape Factory's top
        employee. She has received
        awards every month for having the
        top sales figures so far for the year.
        If she stays on top, she will receive
        a $5000 bonus for excellence. She
        currently has sold 16,250 shapes
        and continues to sell 340 per
        month.

        Since there are eight months left in
        the sales year, Sarita is working
        hard to catch up. While she has only sold 8,830 shapes, she is working
        overtime and on weekends so that she can sell 1,082 per month. Will Sarita
        catch up with Berti before the end of the sales year? If so, when?

2-86.   Calculate the area of the shaded region at
        right. Use the appropriate units.

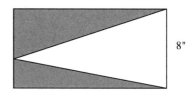

        8"

        17"

2-87.   How tall are you? How do you
        measure your height? Consider
        these questions as you answer
        the questions below.

        a.   Why do you stand up
             straight to measure your
             height?

        b.   Which diagram best
             represents how you
             would measure your
             height? Why?

        Diagram 1   **Diagram 2**

        c.   When you measure your height, do you measure up to your chin? Down
             to your knees? Explain.

2-88.   Read the Math Notes box for this lesson. Then rewrite each of the following statements as a conditional statement.

    a.   Mr. Spelling is always unhappy when it rains.

    b.   The sum of two even numbers is always even.

    c.   Marla has a piano lesson every Tuesday.

2-89.   Simplify the following expressions.

    a. $2x + 8 + 6x + 5$ b. $15 + 3(2x - 4) - 4x$

    c. $(x - 3)(3x + 4)$ d. $5x(2x + 7) + x(3x - 5)$

2.2.4 How can I find the height?

···

Heights and Areas

In Lesson 2.2.2, you learned that triangles with the same base and height must have the same area. But what if multiple dimensions of a shape are labeled? How can you determine which dimension is the height?

2-90. Candice missed the lesson about finding the area of the triangle. Not knowing where to start, she drew a triangle and measured its sides, as shown at right. After drawing her triangle, Candice said, *"Well, I've measured all of the sides. I must be ready to find the area!"*

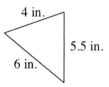

If you think she is correct, write a description of how to use the side lengths to find the area. If you think she needs to measure anything else, copy the figure on your paper and add a line segment to represent a measurement she needs.

2-91. HEIGHT LAB

What is the height of a triangle? Is it like standing at the highest point and looking straight down? Or is it like walking up a side of the triangle? Today your team will build triangles with string and consider different ways height can be seen for triangles of various shapes.

a. Use the materials given to you by your teacher to make a triangle like the one in the diagram below.

(1) Tie one end of the short string to the weight and the other to the end of a pencil (or pen).

(2) Tape a 15 cm section of the long string along the edge of a desk or table. Be sure to leave long ends of string hanging off each side.

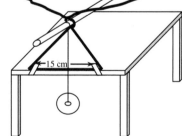

(3) Bring the loose ends of string up from the table and cross them as shown in the diagram. Then put the pencil with the weight over the crossing of the string. Cross the strings again on top of the pencil.

Problem continues on next page →

2-91.   *Problem continued from previous page.*

   b.   Now, with your team, build and
        sketch triangles that meet the three
        conditions below. To organize your
        work, assign each team member one
        of the jobs described at right.

        (1) The height of the triangle is inside
             the triangle.

        (2) The height of the triangle is a side
             of the triangle.

        (3) The height of the triangle is outside of the triangle.

   c.   Now make sure that everyone in your team has sketches of the triangles
        that you made.

Student jobs:
• Hold the pencil (or pen) with the weight.
• Make sure that the weight hangs freely.
• Draw accurate sketches.
• Obtain and return materials as directed by the teacher.

2-92.   How can you find the height of a triangle if it is not a right triangle?

   a.   On the Lesson 2.2.4 Resource Page there are four triangles labeled (1)
        through (4). Assume you know the length of the side labeled "base." For
        each triangle, draw in the height that would enable you to find the area of
        the triangle. Note: You do not need to find the area.

   b.   Find the triangle for part (b) at the bottom of the same resource page. For
        this triangle, draw all three possible heights. First choose one side to be
        the base and draw in the corresponding height. Then repeat the process of
        drawing in the height for the other two sides, one at a time.

   c.   You drew in three pairs of bases and heights for the triangle in part (b).
        Using centimeters, measure the length of all three sides and all three
        heights. Find the area three times using all three pairs of bases and heights.
        Since the triangle remains the same size, your answers should match.

2-93.   AREA TOOLKIT

   Over the past several days, you have explored how to find
   the areas of triangles, parallelograms, and trapezoids. Obtain
   the Lesson 2.2.4B Resource Page from your teacher. Today
   you will start a new page of your Geometry Toolkit, called
   the Area Toolkit. Keep this Toolkit in a safe place. You
   will want it for reference in class and when doing homework.

   At this time, describe what you know about finding the areas of triangles,
   rectangles, parallelograms, and trapezoids. Be sure to include an example for
   each shape.

Ⓜ ETHODS AND MEANINGS

Areas of Triangles, Parallelograms, and Trapezoids

The area of a triangle is half the area of a rectangle with the same base and height. If the base of the triangle is length b and the height length h, then the area of the triangle is:

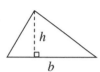

$$A = \tfrac{1}{2}bh \ .$$

The area of a parallelogram is equal to the area of a rectangle with the same base and height. If the base of the parallelogram is length b and the height length h, then the area of the parallelogram is:

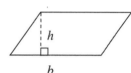

$$A = bh \ .$$

Finally, the area of a trapezoid is found by averaging the lengths of the two bases and multiplying by the height. If the trapezoid has bases b_1 and b_2 and height h, then the area is:

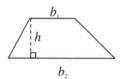

$$A = \tfrac{1}{2}(b_1 + b_2)h \ .$$

2-94.   Find the area of each figure below. Show all work. Remember to include units in your answer.

a.   a square:

7 cm

b.

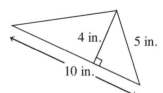

4 in.   5 in.

10 in.

c.

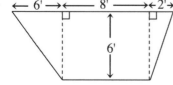

← 6' → ← 8' → ← 2' →

6'

2-95.   Multiply the expressions below. Then simplify the result, if possible.

a. $3x(5x + 7)$ b. $(x + 2)(x + 3)$

c. $(3x + 5)(x - 2)$ d. $(2x + 1)(5x - 4)$

2-96.   Graph the following equations on the same set of axes. Label each line or curve with its equation. Where do the two curves intersect?

$$y = -x - 3 \qquad\qquad y = x^2 + 2x - 3$$

2-97.   On graph paper, plot quadrilateral $ABCD$.

$$A(2, 7), B(4, 8), C(4, 2), D(2, 3)$$

a.   What is the best name for this shape? Justify your conclusion.

b.   Quadrilateral $A'B'C'D'$ is formed by rotating $ABCD$ 90° clockwise about the origin. Name the coordinates of the vertices.

c.   Find the area of $ABCD$. Show all work.

2-98.   What is the probability of drawing each of the following cards from a standard playing deck? Refer to the glossary entry "playing cards" if you need information about a deck of cards.

a.   P(face card)   b.   P(card printed with an even number)

c.   P(red ace)   d.   P(purple card)

2.3.1 Is the answer reasonable?

Triangle Inequality

You now have several tools for describing triangles (lengths, areas, and angle measures), but can *any* three line segments create a triangle? Or are there restrictions on the side lengths of a triangle? And how can you know that the length you found for the side of a triangle is accurate? Today you will investigate the relationship between the side lengths of a triangle.

2-99. Roiri (pronounced "ROAR-ree") loves right triangles and has provided the one at right to analyze. He wants your team to find the length of the **hypotenuse** (the longest side: $\overline{AC}$).

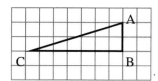

a. Estimate the length of $\overline{AC}$.

b. Roiri decided to repeatedly rotate the triangle on graph paper as shown at right. He says the quadrilateral constructed on $\overline{AC}$ is a square. Do you agree? Justify your answer.

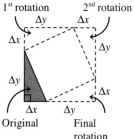

c. With your team, find a strategy to determine the area of the central square. Then use the area of the central square to find the length of the hypotenuse (the longest side of the right triangle). Was your result for the hypotenuse close to your estimate? Why or why not?

d. Will Roiri's strategy of rotating the triangle and finding the areas always work to find the longest length of a right triangle? Explain.

2-100. For a different triangle $\triangle ABC$ where $AB = 3$ units and $BC = 4$ units, Roiri found that $AC = 25$ units. Donna is not sure that is possible. What do you think? Visualize this triangle and explain if you think this triangle is possible or not.

2-101.   PINK SLIP

Oh no! During your last shift at the
Shape Factory everything seemed to be
going fine--until the machine that was
producing triangles made a huge
CLUNK and then stopped. Since your
team was on duty, all of you will be held
responsible for the machine's
breakdown.

Luckily, your boss has informed you that
if you can figure out what happened and
how to make sure it will not happen
again, you will keep your job. The last
order the machine was processing was for a
triangle with sides 3 cm, 5 cm, and 10 cm.

a.   Use the manipulative (such as a technology tool or pasta)
     provided by your teacher to investigate what happened
     today at the factory. Can a triangle be made with *any* three
     side lengths? If not, what condition(s) would make it
     impossible to build a triangle? Try building triangles with
     the side lengths listed below:

     (1) 3 cm, 5 cm, and 10 cm   (2) 4 cm, 9 cm, and 12 cm

     (3) 2 cm, 4 cm, and 5 cm   (4) 3 cm, 5 cm, and 8 cm

b.   For those triangles that could not be built, what happened? Why were they
     impossible?

c.   Use your technology tool (or dry pasta) to investigate the restrictions on
     the three side lengths that can form a triangle. For example, if two sides of
     a triangle are 5 cm and 12 cm long, respectively, what is the longest side
     that could join these two sides to form a triangle? (Could the third side be
     12 cm long? 19 cm long?) What is the shortest possible length that could
     be used to form a triangle? (Does 5 cm work? 9 cm?)

d.   Write a memo to your boss explaining what happened. If you can
     convince your boss that the machine's breakdown was not your fault *and*
     show the company how to fix the machine so that this does not happen
     again, you might earn a promotion!

2-102. The values you found in parts (a) and (c) of problem 2-101 were the *minimum* and *maximum* limits for the length of the third side of any triangle with two sides of lengths 5 cm and 12 cm. The fact that there are restrictions on the side lengths that may be used to create a triangle is referred to as the **Triangle Inequality**.

Determine the minimum and maximum limits for each missing side length in the triangles below.

a.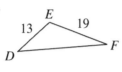

b.

c.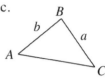

2-103. LEARNING LOG

In a Learning Log entry, explain how you can tell if three sides will form a triangle or not. Draw diagrams to support your statements. Title this entry, "Triangle Inequality" and include today's date.

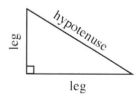

2-104. Draw a right triangle with legs of length 6 and 8 units, respectively, onto graph paper. Construct a square on the hypotenuse and use the square's area to find the length of the hypotenuse.

2-105. One of the algebra topics you have reviewed during this chapter is solving systems of equations. Assess what you know about solving systems as you answer the questions below.

a. Find the points of intersection of the lines below using any method. Write your solutions as a point (x, y).

(1) $y = -x + 8$
        $y = x - 2$

(2) $2x - y = 10$
        $y = -4x + 2$

b. Find the equation for each line on the graph at right. Remember, the general form of any line in the **slope-intercept form** is $y = mx + b$.

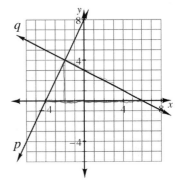

c. What is the relationship between the two lines in part (b)? How do you know?

d. Solve the system of equations you found in part (b) algebraically. Verify that your solution matches the one shown in the graph at right.

2-106. Lines p and q graphed in problem 2-105 form a triangle with the x-axis.

a. How can you describe this triangle? In other words, what is the most appropriate name for this triangle? How do you know?

b. Find the area of the triangle.

c. What is the perimeter?

2-107.   Examine the diagram at right. Based on the
information in the diagram, which angles can
you determine? Copy the diagram on your
paper and find *only* those angles that you can
justify.

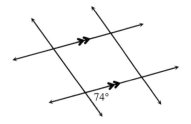

2-108.   On graph paper, plot *ABCD* if *A*(–1, 2), *B*(0, 5), *C*(2, 5), and *D*(6, 2).

    a.   What type of shape is *ABCD*? Justify your answer.

    b.   If *ABCD* is rotated 90° counterclockwise (↺) about the origin, name the
coordinates of the image *A′B′C′D′*.

    c.   On your graph, reflect *ABCD* across the *y*-axis to find *A″B″C″D″*. Name
the coordinates of *A″* and *C″*.

    d.   Find the area of *ABCD*. Show all work.

2.3.2 Is there a shortcut?

. . . .

The Pythagorean Theorem

In Lesson 2.3.1, you learned a method to find the length of a
hypotenuse of a right triangle by finding the area of the square built
on the hypotenuse, as shown in the diagram at right. However, what
if the sides of the triangle make it difficult to draw (such as very large
numbers or decimal values)? Or what if you do not even know the
lengths of one of the legs?

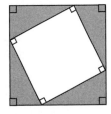

Today, you will work with your team to find the relationship between the legs and
hypotenuse of a right triangle. By the end of this lesson, you should be able to find the
side of *any* right triangle, when given the lengths of the other two sides.

2-109. Roiri complained that while his
method from problem 2-99 works, it
seems like too much work! He
remembers that rearranging a shape
does not change its area and thinks he
can find a shortcut. Obtain a Lesson
2.3.2 Resource Page for your team and
cut out the shaded triangles. Note that
the lengths of the sides of the triangles
are a, b, and c units respectively.

a. First, arrange the triangles to look like Roiri's in
the diagram at right. Draw this diagram on your
paper. What is the area of the unshaded square?

b. Roiri claims that moving the triangles within the
outer square won't change the area of the
unshaded square. Is Roiri correct? Why or why
not?

c. Move the shaded triangles to match the diagram
at right. In this configuration, what is the total
area that is unshaded?

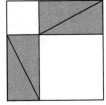

d. Write an equation that relates the two ways
that you found to represent the unshaded area
in the figure.

2-110.   The relationship between the square of the lengths of the legs and the square of the length of the hypotenuse in a right triangle that you found in problem 2-109 is known as the **Pythagorean Theorem**. This relationship is a powerful tool because once you know the lengths of any two sides of a right triangle, you can find the length of the third side.

   a.   Use a technology tool to examine how the square of the hypotenuse always equals the sum of the squares of the legs of a right triangle. Think about it until it makes sense and you can explain it to someone else so that it will make sense to him or her.

   b.   LEARNING LOG

         Add an entry in your Learning Log for the Pythagorean Theorem, explaining what it is and how to use it. Be sure to include a diagram. Title this entry, "Pythagorean Theorem" and include today's date.

2-111.   Apply the Pythagorean Theorem to answer the questions below.

   a.   For each triangle below, find the value of the variable.

   i. 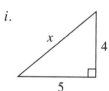   *ii.*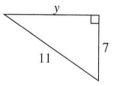

   b.   Examine the rectangle shown at right. Find its perimeter and area.

   c.   On graph paper, draw $\overline{AC}$ with coordinates $A(2, 6)$ and $C(5, -1)$. Then draw a slope triangle. Use the slope triangle to find the length of $\overline{AC}$.

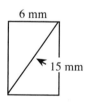

2-112.   The Garcia family took a day trip from Cowpoke Gulch. Their online directions told them to drive four miles north, six miles east, three miles north, and then one mile east to Big Horn Flat. Draw a diagram and calculate the direct distance (straight) from Cowpoke Gulch to Big Horn Flat.

Ⓜ ETHODS AND MEANINGS

The Pythagorean Theorem

The **Pythagorean Theorem** states that in a right triangle,

$$(\text{length of leg } \#1)^2 + (\text{length of leg } \#2)^2 = (\text{length of hypotenuse})^2$$

The Pythagorean Theorem can be used to find a missing side length in a right triangle. See the example below.

$$5^2 + x^2 = 8^2$$
$$25 + x^2 = 64$$
$$x^2 = 39$$
$$x = \sqrt{39} \approx 6.24$$

In the example above, $\sqrt{39}$ is an example of an **exact** answer, while 6.24 is an **approximate** answer.

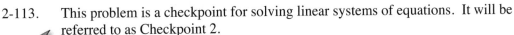

2-113.   This problem is a checkpoint for solving linear systems of equations. It will be referred to as Checkpoint 2.

Solve each system of equations.

a. $y = 3x + 11$
    $x + y = 3$

b. $y = 2x + 3$
    $x - y = -4$

c. $x + 2y = 16$
    $x + y = 2$

d. $2x + 3y = 10$
    $3x - 4y = -2$

Ideally, at this point you are comfortable working with these types of problems and can solve them correctly. If you feel that you need more confidence when solving these types of problems, then review the Checkpoint 2 materials and try the practice problems provided. From this point on, you will be expected to do problems like these correctly and with confidence.

2-114. Hannah's shape bucket contains an equilateral triangle, an isosceles right triangle, a regular hexagon, a non-isosceles trapezoid, a rhombus, a kite, a parallelogram and a rectangle. If she reaches in and selects a shape at random, what is the probability that the shape will meet the criterion described below?

   a.   At least two sides congruent.

   b.   Two pairs of parallel sides.

   c.   At least one pair of parallel sides.

2-115. Find the area of the trapezoid at right. What strategies did you use?

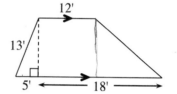

2-116. Use the relationships in the diagrams below to solve for x, if possible. If it is not possible, state how you know. If it is possible, justify your solution by stating which geometric relationships you use.

   a.

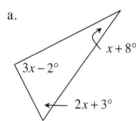

   b.

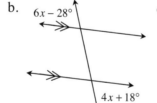

   c.

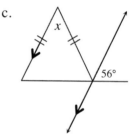

2-117. Find the minimum and maximum limits for the length of a third side of a triangle if the other two sides are 8" and 13".

Chapter 2 Closure   What have I learned?

Reflection and Synthesis

The activities below offer you a chance to reflect about what
you have learned during this chapter. As you work, look for
concepts that you feel very comfortable with, ideas that you
would like to learn more about, and topics you need more
help with. Look for connections between ideas as well as
connections with material you learned previously.

①   TEAM BRAINSTORM

What have you studied in this chapter? What ideas were important in what you
learned? With your team, brainstorm a list. Be as detailed as you can. To help
get you started, lists of Learning Log entries, Toolkit entries, and Math Notes
boxes are below.

What topics, ideas, and words that you learned *before* this chapter are connected
to the new ideas in this chapter? Again, be as detailed as you can.

How long can you make your list? Challenge yourselves. Be prepared to share
your team's ideas with the class.

Learning Log Entries
- Lesson 2.1.1 – Angle Relationships
- Lesson 2.2.2 – Areas of Composite Figures
- Lesson 2.3.1 – Triangle Inequality
- Lesson 2.3.2 – Pythagorean Theorem

Toolkit Entries
- Angle Relationships Toolkit (Lesson 2.1.3 Resource Page and problems
  2-30 and 2-37)
- Area Toolkit (Lesson 2.2.4B Resource Page and problem 2-93)

Math Notes
- Lesson 2.1.1 – Angle Relationships
- Lesson 2.1.2 – Naming Parts of Shapes
- Lesson 2.1.3 – Systems of Linear Equations
- Lesson 2.1.4 – More Angle Pair Relationships
- Lesson 2.1.5 – Proof by Contradiction
- Lesson 2.2.1 – Triangle Angle Sum Theorem
- Lesson 2.2.2 – Multiplying Binomials
- Lesson 2.2.3 – Conditional Statements
- Lesson 2.2.4 – Areas of Triangles, Parallelograms, and Trapezoids
- Lesson 2.3.1 – Right Triangle Vocabulary
- Lesson 2.3.2 – The Pythagorean Theorem

②   MAKING CONNECTIONS

Below is a list of the vocabulary used in this chapter. Make sure that you are familiar with all of these words and know what they mean. Refer to the glossary or index for any words that you do not yet understand.

alternate interior angles	area	arrow diagram
base	complementary angles	conditional statement
congruent	conjecture	corresponding angles
dimension	height	hypotenuse
leg	parallelogram	perimeter
proof by contradiction	prove	Pythagorean Theorem
rectangle	rhombus	right angle
right triangle	same-side interior angles	square
square root	straight angle	supplementary angles
theorem	transversal	trapezoid
unit of measure	vertical angles	

Make a concept map showing all of the connections you can find among the key words and ideas listed above. To show a connection between two words, draw a line between them and explain the connection, as shown in the model below. A word can be connected to any other word as long as you can justify the connection. For each key word or idea, provide an example or sketch that shows the idea.

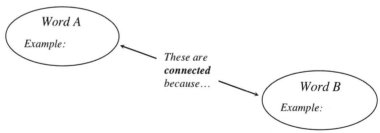

Your teacher may provide you with vocabulary cards to help you get started. If you use the cards to plan your concept map, be sure either to re-draw your concept map on your paper or to glue the vocabulary cards to a poster with all of the connections explained for others to see and understand.

While you are making your map, your team may think of related words or ideas that are not listed here. Be sure to include these ideas on your concept map.

Think about the diagrams that you have looked at or drawn during this chapter. When have you had to understand information from a diagram or picture? What helps you to see what is in the diagram? What diagrams or parts of diagrams have you seen in a previous math class? You may want to flip through the chapter to refresh your memory about the problems that you have worked on. Discuss any of the methods you have developed to examine the problem in order to identify what is important or what information is conveyed in a diagram.

Once your discussion is complete, think about the way you think as you answer the following problems.

a. Sometimes, examining a shape means you have to disregard how it *looks* and concentrate on the information provided by the markings. For example, examine the shape at right. This shape looks like a square, but is it? Make as many statements as you can about this shape based on the markings. What shape is *ABCD?* Which statements are obvious from the diagram and which ones did you have to think about?

b. At other times, examining a diagram suggests that you notice different parts that contribute to the entire diagram. For example, look at the diagram at right. Assuming that the diagram is drawn to scale, what shapes can you find in the diagram?

c. In part (a), you looked for attributes of a shape, while in part (b), you looked for shapes within a shape. However, another aspect of examining a diagram is to look for relationships between parts of the diagram. For example, examine the diagram at right. What relationships do you see between the angles in the diagram? What relationships can you find between the lines and/or line segments? List as many relationships as you can based on the information in the diagram.

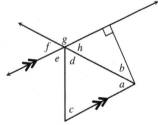

d. Consider the relationships you saw in part (c) above. Which relationships are always true, and which are true only under certain conditions?

WHAT HAVE I LEARNED?

Most of the problems in this section represent typical problems found in this chapter. They serve as a gauge for you. You can use them to determine which types of problems you can do well and which types of problems require further study and practice. Even if your teacher does not assign this section, it is a good idea to try these problems and find out for yourself what you know and what you still need to work on.

Solve each problem as completely as you can. The table at the end of the closure section has answers to these problems. It also tells you where you can find additional help and practice with problems like these.

CL 2-118.   As Sandra drives, her music player randomly selects music from her playlist. Sandra's playlist contains:

> 3 traditional country songs
>
> 6 traditional rock songs
>
> 4 hip-hop rap songs
>
> 5 contemporary country songs
>
> 1 Latin rap song
>
> 3 traditional pop songs

a.   What is the probability that the player will select some rap music next?

b.   Find P(traditional), that is, the probability that the player will randomly select traditional music of any kind.

c.   Find P(traditional pop).

d.   Find P(not country), the probability that the next song is *not* country music.

CL 2-119.   Find the area of each figure.

a.
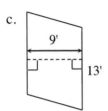
12"   10"
8"
15"

b.
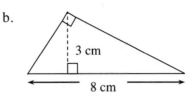
3 cm
8 cm

c.

9'
13'

d.
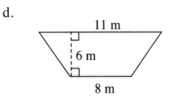
11 m
6 m
8 m

CL 2-120.   Name each of the following shapes.

a.
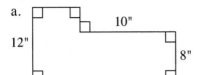

b.

c.

d.

e.

f.   Graph the following points and then name the shape that is created when you connect the points in the given order.

$N(-2,6)$, $A(-4,6)$, $M(-4,3)$, $E(-2,3)$

CL 2-121.   Graph the segment that connects the points $A(-4,8)$ and $B(6,3)$.

a.   What is the slope of $\overline{AB}$?

b.   Write an equation for the line that connects points A and B.

c.   Write an equation for a line that is parallel to $\overline{AB}$.

d.   Write an equation for a line that is perpendicular to $\overline{AB}$.

CL 2-122. Identify the geometric angle relationship(s) in each diagram. Use what you know about those relationships to write an equation and solve for *x*.

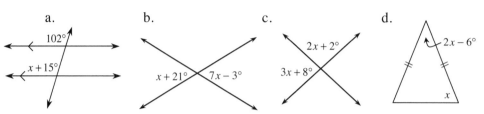

a.
102°
x + 15°

b.
x + 21°   7*x* − 3°

c.
2*x* + 2°
3*x* + 8°

d.
2*x* − 6°
x

CL 2-123. Examine the system of equations at right.

$$y = -2x + 6$$
$$y = \tfrac{1}{2}x - 9$$

a. Solve the system below *twice*: graphically and algebraically. Verify that your solutions from the different methods are the same.

b. What is the relationship between the two lines? How can you tell?

c. Solve the system at right using your method of choice.

$$2x + 3y = 18$$
$$4x - 3y = 6$$

CL 2-124. Charlotte was transforming the hexagon *ABCDEF*.

a. What single transformation did she perform in Diagram #1?

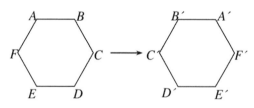

Diagram #1

b. What single transformation did she perform in Diagram #2?

c. What transformation didn't she do? Write directions for this type of transformation for hexagon *ABCDEF* and perform it.

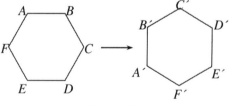

Diagram #2

CL 2-125. Explain what you are doing when you find the perimeter of a flat shape. How is that different than finding its area?

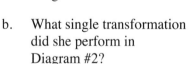

CL 2-126.   Check your answers using the table at the end of this section. Which
             problems do you feel confident about? Which problems were hard? Have
             you worked on problems like these in math classes you have taken before?
             Use the table to make a list of topics you need help on and a list of topics
             you need to practice more.

Answers and Support for Closure Activity #4
What Have I Learned?

MN = Math Notes, LL = Learning Logs

Problem	Solutions	Need Help?	More Practice
CL 2-118.	a. $\frac{5}{22} \approx 0.23$ b. $\frac{12}{22} \approx 0.55$ c. $\frac{3}{22} \approx 0.14$ d. $\frac{14}{22} \approx 0.64$	MN: 1.2.1	Problems CL 1-131, 2-9, 2-35, 2-78, 2-98, and 2-114
CL 2-119.	a. 140 sq. in. b. 12 sq. cm c. 117 sq. ft d. 57 sq. m	Section 2.2 MN: 2.2.4 LL: 2.2.2	Problems 2-75, 2-86, 2-94, 2-97, and 2-115
CL 2-120.	a. parallelogram b. trapezoid c. rhombus d. right triangle e. equilateral triangle f. rectangle	MN: 1.3.1 Shapes Toolkit	Problems CL 1-130, 2-21, 2-36, 2-65, 2-97, 2-106 (a), and 2-108 (a)
CL 2-121.	a. $m = -\frac{1}{2}$ b. $y = -\frac{1}{2}x + 6$ c. Answers will vary, but will have a slope of $m = -\frac{1}{2}$. d. Answers will vary, but will have a slope of $m = 2$.	MN: 1.2.6	Problems 2-22, 2-42, 2-58, 2-69, and 2-105

Problem	Solutions	Need Help?	More Practice
CL 2-122.	a. $x + 15° = 102°$; $x = 87°$; corresponding angles b. $7x - 3° = x + 21°$; $x = 4°$; vertical angles c. $2x + 2° + 3x + 8° = 180°$; $x = 34°$; supplementary angles d. $x + x + 2x - 6° = 180°$; $x = 46.5°$; sum of angles in a triangle is $180°$	Section 2.1 MN: 2.1.1, 2.1.4, and 2.2.1 LL: 2.1.1	Problems 2-34, 2-55, 2-56, 2-66, 2-67, 2-76, 2-107, and 2-116
CL 2-123.	a. $(6, -6)$ b. They are perpendicular because the slopes are opposite reciprocals. c. $(4, \frac{10}{3})$	Checkpoint 2 MN: 1.2.6 and 2.1.3	Problems 2-31, 2-45, 2-57, 2-58, 2-69, 2-96, and 2-105
CL 2-124.	a. Reflection (flip) across the vertical line of symmetry b. Rotation (turn counterclockwise $90°$) c. Translation (slide). Answers will vary, an example is provided below.	Lessons 1.2.2 and 1.2.4 MN: 1.2.2 and 1.2.4 LL: 1.2.1	Problems CL 1-128, 2-11, 2-21, 2-36, 2-68, and 2-108
CL 2-125.	The perimeter of a flat shape is the length of that shape's boundary. While the area measures the region (the number of squares) *inside* the boundary.	Lesson 2.2.1 MN: 1.1.3	Problems CL 1-129 and 2-106

CHAPTER 3   Justification and Similarity

Measuring, describing, and transforming: these are three major skills in geometry that you have been developing. In this chapter, you will focus on comparing; you will explore ways to determine if two figures have the same shape (that is, they are **similar**). You will also develop ways to use the information about one figure to learn more about another that has the same shape.

Making logical and convincing arguments that support specific ideas about the shapes you are studying is another important skill. In this chapter you will learn how you can document facts to support a conclusion in a flowchart.

Guiding Question

Mathematically proficient students model with mathematics.

As you work through this chapter, ask yourself:

Can I apply the mathematics that I know to problems in everyday life?

In this chapter, you will learn:

➢ How to support a mathematical statement using flowcharts and conditional statements.

➢ About the special relationships between shapes that are similar or congruent.

➢ How to determine if triangles are similar or congruent.

Chapter Outline

Section 3.1 Through an exploration with rubber bands, students will generate similar figures, which will launch a focus on similarity for Sections 3.1 and 3.2. During these lessons, students will determine the common qualities that similar figures have.

Section 3.2 As students discover the conditions that cause triangles to be similar or congruent, they will learn about using a flowchart to organize facts and support their conclusions.

3.1.1 What do these shapes have in common?

Dilations

In Section 1.3, you organized shapes into groups based on their size, angles, sides, and other characteristics. You identified shapes using their characteristics and investigated relationships between different kinds of shapes, so that now you can tell if two figures are both parallelograms or trapezoids, for example. But what makes two figures look alike?

Today you will be introduced to a new transformation that enlarges a figure while maintaining its shape, called a **dilation**. After creating new enlarged figures, you and your team will explore the interesting relationships that exist between figures that have the same shape.

3-1.   WARM-UP STRETCH

Before computers and copy machines existed, it sometimes took hours to enlarge documents or to shrink text on items such as jewelry. A pantograph device (like the one shown below) was often used to duplicate written documents and artistic drawings. You will now employ the same geometric principles by using rubber bands to draw enlarged copies of a design. Your teacher will show you how to do this.

During this activity, discuss the following questions:

What do the figures have in common?

What do you predict?

What specifically is different about the figures?

3-2.	Stretching a figure as you did in problem 3-1 is another transformation called a dilation. When a figure is dilated from a point, the result is a **similar** figure. How are dilated figures related to their original figures? That is, what do similar figures have in common? To answer these questions and to develop a definition of "similar," your team will need to create dilations that you can measure and compare.

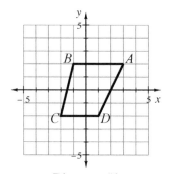

Diagram #1

a.	Obtain a Lesson 3.1.1 Resource Page from your teacher. On it, find the quadrilateral shown in Diagram #1 at right.

Dilate (stretch) the quadrilateral from the origin by a factor of 2, 3, 4, or 5 to form $A'B'C'D'$. Each team member should pick a different enlargement factor. You may want to imagine that your rubber band chain is stretched from the origin so that the knot traces the perimeter of the original figure.

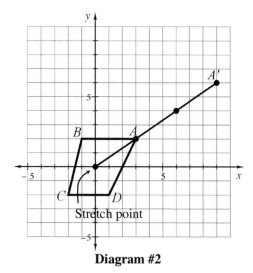

Diagram #2

For example, if your job is to stretch *ABCD* by a factor of 3, then A' would be located as shown in Diagram #2 at right.

b.	Carefully cut out your enlarged figure and compare it to your teammates' figures. How are the four enlargements different? How are they the same? As you investigate, make sure you compare both angles and side lengths of the similar figures. Be ready to report your conclusions to the class.

3-3. WHICH SHAPE IS THE EXCEPTION?

Sometimes figures look the same and
sometimes they look very different.
What characteristics make figures alike
so that you can say that they are the
same shape? How are figures that look
the same but are different sizes related
to each other? Understanding these
relationships will allow us to know if
figures that appear to have the same
shape actually do have the same shape.

Your Task: For each set of figures below, three are **similar** (meaning that they
are related through a sequence of transformations including dilation), and one is
an exception. Find the exception in each set of figures.

Use tracing paper to answer each of these questions for both sets of shapes
below:

- Which figure appears to be the exception? What makes that shape
  different from the others?

- What do the other three shapes have in common?

- Are there commonalities in the angles? Are there differences?

- Are there commonalities in the sides? Are there differences?

a. 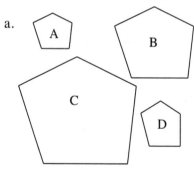   b.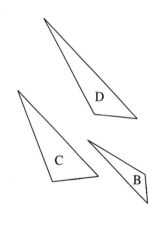

3-4. LEARNING LOG

Write an entry in your Learning Log about the
characteristics that figures with different sizes need to
have in order to maintain the same shape. Add your own
diagrams to illustrate the description. Title this entry
"Same Shape, Different Size" and include today's date.

METHODS AND MEANINGS

MATH NOTES

Dilations

The transformations you studied in Chapter 1 (translations, rotations, and reflections) are called rigid transformations because they all maintain the size and shape of the original figure.

However, a **dilation** is a transformation that maintains the shape of a figure but multiplies its lengths by a chosen factor. In a dilation, a figure is stretched proportionally from a particular point, called the **point of dilation** or **stretch point**. For example, in the diagram at right, $\triangle ABC$ is dilated to form $\triangle A'B'C'$. Notice that while a dilation changes the size and location of the original figure, it does not rotate or reflect the original. While lengths can change, angles do not change under a dilation.

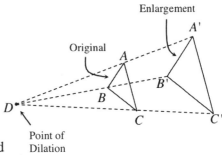

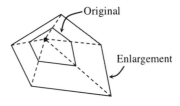

Note that if the point of dilation is located inside a shape, the enlargement encloses the original, as shown at right.

Review & Preview

3-5.   Plot triangle ABC formed with the points $A(0, 0)$, $B(3, 4)$, and $C(3, 0)$, on graph paper. Use the method used in problem 3-2 to enlarge it from the origin by a factor of 2 (using two "rubber bands"). Label this new triangle $A'B'C'$.

a.   What are the side lengths of the original triangle, $\triangle ABC$?

b.   What are the side lengths of the enlarged triangle, $\triangle A'B'C'$?

c.   Find the area and the perimeter of $\triangle A'B'C'$.

Core Connections Geometry

3-6.   Solve each equation below for x. Show all work and check your answer by substituting it back into the equation and verifying that it makes the equation true.

   a. $\frac{x}{3} = 6$ b. $\frac{5x+9}{2} = 12$ c. $\frac{x}{4} = \frac{9}{6}$ d. $\frac{5}{x} = \frac{20}{8}$

3-7.   Examine the triangle at right.

   a.   Estimate the measure of each angle of the triangle at right.

   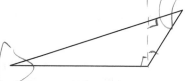

   b.   Given only its shape, what is the best name for this triangle?

3-8.   On graph paper, graph line $\overleftrightarrow{MU}$ if $M(-1, 1)$ and $U(4, 5)$.

   a.   Find the slope of $\overleftrightarrow{MU}$ and write an equation for the line.

   b.   Find MU (the distance from M to U).

   c.   Are there any similarities to the calculations used in parts (a) and (b)? Any differences?

3-9.   Examine each diagram below. Identify the error in each diagram.

   a.   b.   c.

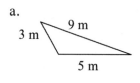   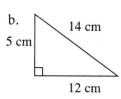   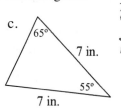

3-10.   Rewrite the statements below into conditional ("If …, then …") form.

   a.   All equilateral triangles have 120° rotation symmetry.

   b.   A rectangle is a parallelogram.

3.1.2 How can I maintain the shape?

Similarity

So far you have studied several figures that appear to have exactly the same shape but not necessarily the same size. But how can you know for sure that two figures have the same shape? Today you will focus on the relationship between the lengths of sides of dilations by enlarging and reducing figures and looking for patterns.

3-11. Find your work from problem 3-5. The shapes that you created should resemble those on the graph at right.

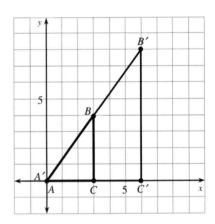

a. In problem 3-5, you dilated (stretched) $\triangle ABC$ to create $\triangle A'B'C'$. Which side of $\triangle A'B'C'$ corresponds to $\overline{CB}$? Which side corresponds to $\overline{AB}$?

b. What is the relationship of the corresponding sides? Write down all of your observations. How could you get the lengths of $\triangle A'B'C'$ from the lengths of $\triangle ABC$?

c. Why does $\overline{A'B'}$ lie directly on $\overline{AB}$ and $\overline{A'C'}$ lie directly on $\overline{AC}$, but $\overline{B'C'}$ does not lie directly on $\overline{BC}$?

d. Could you get the side lengths of $\triangle A'B'C'$ by adding the same amount to each side of $\triangle ABC$? Try this and explain what happened.

e. Monica dilated $\triangle ABC$ to get a different triangle. She knows that $\overline{A''B''}$ is 20 units long. How many times larger than $\triangle ABC$ is $\triangle A''B''C''$? (That is, how many "rubber bands" did she use?) And how long is $\overline{B''C''}$? Show how you know.

3-12.   SIMILARITY

An important aspect of dilation is that the shape of a figure does not change even though its size may change. This is because dilations do not affect angles while they change lengths proportionally.

a.   If Monica rotated $\triangle A''B''C''$ about a point, would it still remain the same shape as $\triangle ABC$? Why or why not? What if she translated it or reflected it?

b.   When two figures are related by a series of transformations (including dilation), they are called **similar**. Similar figures have the same shape but not necessarily the same size. Similar figures can be created by multiplying each side length by the same number. This number is called the **zoom factor**.

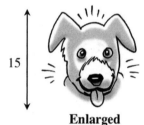

5
Original

You may have used a zoom factor before when using a copy machine. For example, if you set the zoom factor on a copier to 50%, the machine shrinks the image in half (that is, multiplies it by 0.5) but keeps the shape the same. In this course, the zoom factor will be used to describe the ratio of the new figure to the original figure.

15
Enlarged

What zoom factor was used to enlarge the puppy shown at right?

3-13.   Casey decided to enlarge her favorite letter: C, of course! Your team is going to help her out. Have each member of your team choose a different zoom factor below. Then on graph paper, enlarge (or reduce) the block "C" at right by your zoom factor.

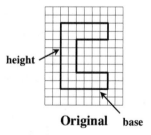

height

a.   3   b.   2

c.   1   d. $\frac{1}{2}$

Original   base

3-14.   Look at the different "C's" that were created in problem 3-13.

   a.   What happened when the zoom factor was 1?

   b.   When there is a sequence of rigid transformations that carries one figure
         onto another, then the two figures are the same shape *and* the same size
         (that is, the zoom factor is 1) and they are called **congruent**. Compare the
         shapes below with tracing paper and determine which shapes are
         congruent.

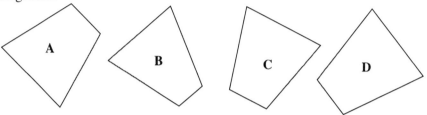

3-15.   EQUAL RATIOS OF SIMILARITY

         Casey wants to learn more about her enlarged "C"s. Return to your work from
         problem 3-13.

   a.   Since the zoom factor
         multiplies each part of the
         original shape, then the ratio of
         the widths must equal the ratio
         of the lengths.

         Casey decided to show these
         ratios in the diagram at right.
         Verify that her ratios are equal.

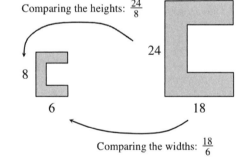

Comparing the heights: $\frac{24}{8}$

Comparing the widths: $\frac{18}{6}$

   b.   When looking at Casey's work, her
         brother wrote the equation $\frac{8}{6} = \frac{24}{18}$. Are
         his ratios, in fact, equal? And how
         could he show his work on his
         diagram? Copy his diagram at right
         and add arrows to show what sides
         Casey's brother compared.

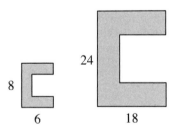

   c.   She has decided to create an enlarged "C"
         for the door of her bedroom. To fit, it
         needs to be 20 units tall. If *x* is the width
         of this "C", write and solve an equation to
         find out how wide the "C" on Casey's
         door must be. Be ready to share your
         equation and solution with the class.

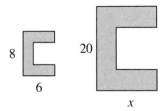

Core Connections Geometry

3-16.   Use your observations about ratios between similar figures to answer the
following questions.

  a.   Assume one triangle has side lengths 6, 7, and 10 units while another has
side lengths 3, 4, and 5 units. Are these triangles similar? How do you
know?

  b.   If the pentagons at right are similar,
what are the values of *x* and *y*?

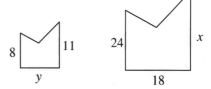

3-17.   LEARNING LOG

In a new entry of your Learning Log, explain what you know
about the side lengths and angle measures of similar figures.
If you know the dimensions of one triangle, how can you
find the dimensions of another triangle that is similar to it?
Also, how can you decide, when given side lengths, if the two triangles are
similar? Title this entry, "Similar Figures" and include today's date.

Methods and Meanings

Ratio of Similarity and Zoom Factor

The term ratio was introduced in Chapter 1 in the context of probability. But ratios are very important when comparing two similar figures. Review what you know about ratios below.

A comparison of two quantities (numbers or measures) is called a **ratio**. A ratio can be written as:

$$a{:}b \quad \text{or} \quad \frac{a}{b} \quad \text{or} \quad a \text{ to } b$$

Each ratio has a numeric value that can be expressed as a fraction or a decimal. For the two similar right triangles below, the ratio of the small triangle's hypotenuse to the large triangle's hypotenuse is $\frac{6}{10}$ or $\frac{3}{5}$. This means that for every three units of length in the small triangle's hypotenuse, there are five units of length in the large triangle's hypotenuse.

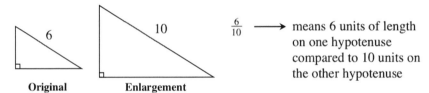

$\frac{6}{10} \longrightarrow$ means 6 units of length on one hypotenuse compared to 10 units on the other hypotenuse

Original   Enlargement

The ratio between any pair of corresponding sides in similar figures is called the **ratio of similarity**.

When a figure is enlarged or reduced, each side is multiplied (or divided) by the same number. While there are several names for this number, this text will refer to this number as the **zoom factor**. Note that "scale factor" is another commonly used term. To help indicate if the figure was enlarged or reduced, the zoom factor is written as the ratio of the new figure to the original figure. For the two triangles above, the zoom factor is $\frac{10}{6}$ or $\frac{5}{3}$.

3-18.   Use the method from problem 3-2 to enlarge the shape at right from the origin by a zoom factor of 4.

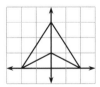

3-19.   The ratios Casey wrote from part (a) of problem 3-15 are common ratios
         between **corresponding sides** of the two shapes. That is, they are ratios
         between the matching sides of two shapes.

    a.   Look at the two similar shapes below. Which sides correspond? Write
         common ratios with the names of sides and lengths.

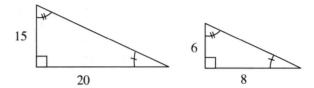

    b.   Find the hypotenuse of each triangle above. Is the ratio of the hypotenuses
         equal to the ratios you found in part (a)?

3-20.   Are the lines represented by the equations at right parallel?
         Support your reasoning with convincing evidence.

$$y = -\frac{3}{5}x + 2$$
$$y = -\frac{3}{5}x - 3$$

3-21.   Multiply the expressions below. Then simplify if possible.

    a. $2x(3x - 4)$ b. $(x + 3)(2x - 5)$

    c. $(2x + 5)(2x - 5)$ d. $x(2x + 1)(x - 3)$

3-22.   Examine the relationships in the diagram at right.
         Then solve for x and y, if possible. Justify your work
         using angle relationships.

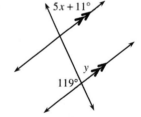

3-23.   Read the following statements and decide if, when combined, they present a
         convincing argument. You may need to refer back to your Shape Toolkit as you
         consider the following statements and decide if the conclusion is correct. Be
         sure to justify your reasoning.

         Fact #1: A square has four sides of equal length.

         Fact #2: A square is a rectangle because it has four right angles.

         Fact #3: A rhombus also has four sides of equal length

         Conclusion: Therefore, a rhombus is a rectangle.

3.1.3 How are the figures related?

Using Ratios of Similarity

You have learned that when you enlarge or reduce a shape so that it remains similar (that is, it maintains the same shape), each of the side lengths have been multiplied by a common zoom factor. You can also set up ratios within shapes and make comparisons to other similar shapes. Today you will learn about how changing the size of an object affects its perimeter. You will also learn how ratios can help solve similarity problems when drawing the figures is not practical.

3-24. Trace the rectangles below onto your paper.

a. Show that there is a sequence of one or more transformations that can carry one rectangle onto the other.

b. Use ratios to show that these rectangles are similar (figures that have the same shape, but not necessarily the same size).

c. What other ratios could you use?

d. Linh claims that these figures are not similar. When she compared the heights, she wrote $\frac{2}{7}$. Then she compared the bases and got $\frac{21}{6}$. Why is Linh having trouble? Explain completely.

3-25. Each pair of figures below is similar. Review what you have learned so far about similarity as you solve for x.

a.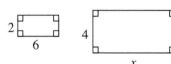

b.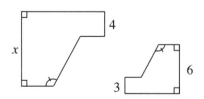

c.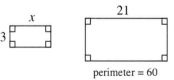

3-26.   Casey's back at it! Now she wants you to enlarge the block "U" for her spirit
         flag.

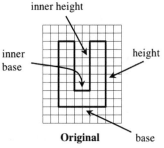

   a.   Copy her "U" onto graph paper.

   b.   Now draw a larger "U" with a zoom
         factor of $\frac{3}{2} = 1.5$. What is the height of
         the new "U"?

   c.   Find the ratio of the perimeters. That is,
         find $\frac{\text{perimeter new}}{\text{perimeter original}}$. What do you notice?

   d.   Casey enlarged "U" proportionally so that it has a
         height of 10. What was her zoom factor? What is
         the base of this new "U"? Justify your conclusion.

3-27.   After enlarging his "U" in problem
         3-26, Al has an idea. He drew a
         60° angle, as shown in Diagram
         #1 at right. Then, he extended the
         sides of the angle so that they are
         twice as long, as shown in
         Diagram #2. *"Therefore, the new
         angle must have measure 120°,"*
         he explained. Do you agree?
         Discuss this with your team and write
         a response to Al.

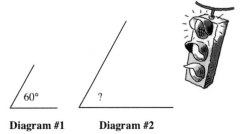

   Diagram #1   Diagram #2

3-28.   Al noticed that the ratio of the perimeters of two
         similar figures is equal to the ratio of the side
         lengths. *"What about the area? Does it grow the
         same way?"* he wondered.

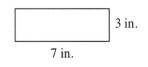

   a.   Find the area and perimeter of the rectangle above.

   b.   Test Al's question by enlarging the rectangle by a zoom factor of 2. Then
         find the new area and perimeter.

   c.   Answer Al's question: Does the perimeter double? Does the area double?
         Explain what happened.

METHODS AND **M**EANINGS

Proportional Equations

A **proportional equation** is one that compares two or more ratios. Proportional equations can compare two pairs of corresponding parts (sides) of similar shapes, or can compare two parts of one shape to the corresponding parts of another shape.

For example, the following equations can be written for the similar triangles at right:

$$\frac{a}{c} = \frac{b}{d} \quad \text{or} \quad \frac{a}{b} = \frac{c}{d}$$

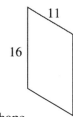

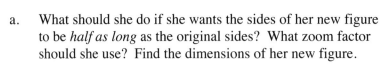

3-29.   Rakisha is puzzled. She is working with the parallelogram drawn at right and wants to make it smaller instead of bigger.

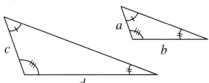

a.   What should she do if she wants the sides of her new figure to be *half as long* as the original sides? What zoom factor should she use? Find the dimensions of her new figure.

b.   While drawing some other shapes, Rakisha ended up with a shape congruent to the original parallelogram. What is the common ratio between pairs of corresponding sides?

3-30.   Enlarge the shape at right on graph paper using a zoom factor of 2. Then find the perimeter and area of both shapes. What do you notice when you compare the perimeters? The areas?

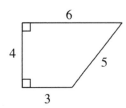

3-31.   Solve each equation below. Show all work and check your answer.

a. $\frac{14}{5} = \frac{x}{3}$ b. $\frac{10}{m} = \frac{5}{11}$ c. $\frac{t-2}{12} = \frac{7}{8}$ d. $\frac{x+1}{5} = \frac{x}{3}$

3-32.   Examine the graph of line $\overleftrightarrow{AB}$ at right.

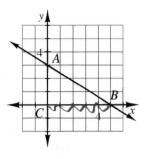

a.   Find the equation of $\overrightarrow{AB}$.

b.   Find the area and perimeter of $\triangle ABC$.

c.   Write an equation of the line through A that is perpendicular to $\overleftrightarrow{AB}$.

3-33.   Rewrite the statements below into conditional ("If …, then …") form.

a.   Lines with the same slope are parallel.

b.   A vertical line has undefined slope.

c.   The lines with slopes $\frac{2}{3}$ and $-\frac{3}{2}$ are perpendicular.

3-34.   Examine the diagram at right. Name the geometric relationships of the angles below.

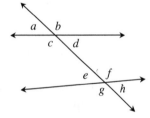

a. d and e b. e and h

c. a and e d. c and d

3.1.4 How can I use equivalent ratios?

Applications and Notation

Now that you have a good understanding of how to use ratios in similar figures to solve problems, how can you extend these ideas to situations outside the classroom? You will start by considering a situation for which you want to find the length of something that would be difficult to physically measure.

3-35.   GEORGE WASHINGTON'S NOSE

On her way to visit Horace Mann University, Casey stopped by Mount Rushmore in South Dakota. The park ranger gave a talk that described the history of the monument and provided some interesting facts. Casey could not believe that the carving of George Washington's face is 60 feet tall from his chin to the top of his head!

However, when a tourist asked about the length of Washington's nose, the ranger was stumped! Casey came to her rescue by measuring, calculating and getting an answer. How did Casey get an answer?

Your Task: Figure out the length of George Washington's nose on the monument. Work with your team to come up with a strategy. Show all measurements and calculations on your paper with clear labels so anyone could understand your work.

Discussion Points

What is this question asking you to find?

How can you use similarity to solve this problem?

Is there something in this room that you can use to compare to the monument?

What parts do you need to compare?

Do you have any math tools that can help you gather information?

3-36.   When solving problem 3-35, you may have written a proportional equation like the one below. When solving proportional situations, it is very important that parts be labeled to help you follow your work.

$$\frac{\text{Length of George's Nose}}{\text{Length of George's Head}} = \frac{\text{Length of Student's Nose}}{\text{Length of Student's Head}}$$

Likewise, when working with geometric shapes such as the similar triangles below, it is easier to explain which sides you are comparing by using notation that everyone understands.

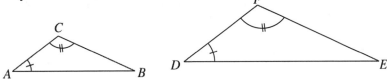

a.   One possible proportional equation for these triangles is $\frac{AC}{AB} = \frac{DF}{DE}$. Write at least three more proportional equations based on the similar triangles above.

b.   Jeb noticed that $m\angle A = m\angle D$ and $m\angle C = m\angle F$. But what about $m\angle B$ and $m\angle E$? Do these angles have the same measure? Or is there not enough information? Justify your conclusions.

3-37.   The two triangles at right are similar. Read the Math Notes box for this lesson to learn about how to write a statement to show that two shapes are similar.

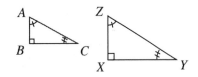

Then examine the two triangles below.

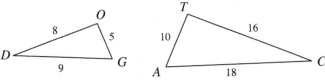

a.   Describe a sequence of transformations that carries one triangle onto the other. Use tracing paper to help.

b.   Which of the following statements are correctly written and which are not? Note that more than one statement may be correct. Discuss your answers with your team.

    i. $\Delta DOG \sim \Delta CAT$ ii. $\Delta DOG \sim \Delta CTA$

    iii. $\Delta OGD \sim \Delta ATC$ iv. $\Delta DGO \sim \Delta CAT$

3-38. Find the value of the variable in each pair of similar figures below. You may want to set up tables to help you write equations.

a. ABCD ~ JKLM

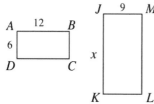

b. ΔNOP ~ ΔXYZ

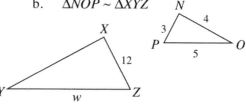

c. ΔGHI ~ ΔPQR

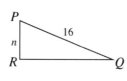

d. ΔABC ~ ΔXYZ

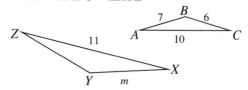

3-39. Rochida drew ΔABC at right and then dilated it to create ΔAB′C′.

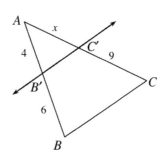

a. Why are the two triangles similar?

b. What is the relationship of the lengths $\overline{AB'}$ and $\overline{AB}$? What about between $\overline{AC'}$ and $\overline{AC}$? Justify your answer.

c. Rochida decides to redraw the shape as two separate triangles, as shown at right. Write and solve a proportional equation to find x using the corresponding sides.

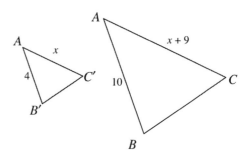

d. How long is $\overline{AC}$? How long is $\overline{AC'}$?

e. What must the ratio of the original segment $\overline{BC}$ to its image $\overline{B'C'}$ be? Explain.

f. What is the relationship between $\overleftrightarrow{B'C'}$ and $\overleftrightarrow{BC}$?

3-40.   LEARNING LOG

Write a Learning Log entry describing the different ways
you can compare two similar objects or quantities with
equivalent ratios. Title this entry "Comparing With Ratios"
and include today's date.

 METHODS AND **M**EANINGS

MATH NOTES

Writing a Similarity Statement

A **similarity transformation** is a sequence of transformations
that can include rigid transformations, dilations, or both. Two figures
are **similar** if there is a similarity transformation that takes one shape
onto the other. Similarity transformations preserve angles, parallelism
of two lines, and ratios of side lengths.

To represent the fact that two shapes are similar, use the symbol "~".
For example, if there is a similarity transformation that takes $\triangle ABC$
onto $\triangle DEF$, then you know they are similar and this can be stated as
$\triangle ABC \sim \triangle DEF$. The order of the letters in the name of each triangle
determines which sides and angles correspond. For example, in the
statement $\triangle ABC \sim \triangle DEF$, you can determine that $\angle A$ corresponds to
$\angle D$ and that $\overline{BC}$ corresponds to $\overline{EF}$.

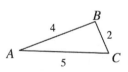

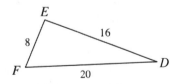

3-41.   Solve for the missing lengths in the sets of similar figures below.

a.   △ABC ~ △OPQ

 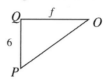

b.   EFGHI ~ STUVW

 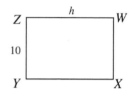

c.   JKLM ~ WXYZ

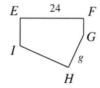 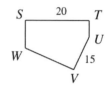

3-42.   In recent lessons, you have learned that similar triangles have equal
corresponding angles. Is it possible to have equal corresponding angles when
the triangles do not appear to match? What if you are not given all three angle
measures? Consider the two cases below.

a.   Find the measure of the third angle in the first
pair of triangles at right. Compare the two
triangles. What do you notice?

b.   Examine the second pair of triangles at right.
Without calculating, do you know that the
unmarked angles must be equal? Why or
why not?

3-43.   Frank and Alice are penguins. At birth,
         Frank's beak was 1.95 inches long, while
         Alice's was 1.50 inches long.

   a.   Frank's beak grows by 0.25 inches
         per year and Alice's grows by
         0.40 inches per year. Write an
         equation to represent the length of
         each penguin's beak in x years.

   b.   How old will they be when their beaks are the same length?

3-44.   Rewrite the statements below into conditional ("If …, then …") form.

   a.   The area of a rectangle with base x and height $2x$ is $2x^2$.

   b.   The perimeter of a rectangle with base x and height $3y$ is $2x + 6y$.

   c.   A rectangle with base 2 feet and height 3 feet has an area of 864 square
         inches.

3-45.   Misty is building a triangular planting bed. Two of the sides have lengths of
         eight feet and five feet. What are the possible lengths for the third side?

3-46.   Plot $ABCDE$ formed with the points $A(-3, -2)$, $B(5, -2)$, $C(5, 3)$, $D(1, 6)$, and
         $E(-3, 3)$ onto graph paper.

   a.   Use the method from problem 3-2 to enlarge it from the origin by a factor
         of 2. Label this new shape $A'B'C'D'E'$.

   b.   Find the area and the perimeter of both figures.

3.2.1 What information do I need?

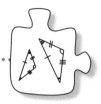

••

Conditions for Triangle Similarity

Now that you know what similar shapes have in common, you are ready to turn to a related question: How much information do I need to conclude that two triangles are similar? As you work through today's lesson, remember that similar polygons have corresponding angles that are congruent and corresponding sides that are proportional.

3-47.   ARE THEY SIMILAR?

Erica thinks the triangles below might be similar. However, she knows not to trust the way figures look in a diagram, so she asks for your help.

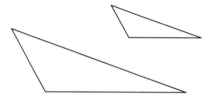

a.   If two shapes are similar, what must be true about their angles and sides?

b.   Obtain the Lesson 3.2.1 Resource Page from your teacher. Measure the angles and sides of Erica's triangles and help her decide if the triangles are similar or not.

c.   Assuming that the corresponding sides of these similar triangles are parallel, demonstrate that there is a dilation that carries one onto the other by finding the point of dilation (the stretch point) for the two triangles on the resource page.

3-48.   HOW MUCH IS ENOUGH?

Jovan is tired of measuring all the angles and sides to determine
if two triangles are similar. *"There must be an easier way,"* he
thinks. *"What if I know that all of the angles are congruent?
Does that mean that the triangles are similar?"*

a.   Before experimenting, make a prediction. Do you think that the triangles
have to be similar if all three corresponding angles are congruent?

b.   Experiment with Jovan's idea. To do this, use a technology tool or straws
with protractors, to make a triangle with angles 38°, 62°, and 80°. Can
you make another triangle, with the same angles, that is *not* similar to your
original triangle? Can you create any two triangles with the same three
angle measures that are *not* similar? Investigate, sketch your shapes, and
write down your conclusion.

c.   Describe a sequence of transformations to show that two triangles that
have the same three angles are similar.

3-49.   Scott is looking at the set of shapes at
right. He thinks that ΔEFG ~ ΔHIJ but
he is not sure that the shapes are drawn
to scale.

a.   Are the corresponding angles equal?
Convince Scott that these triangles
are similar.

b.   How many pairs of angles need to be
congruent to be sure that triangles are
similar? How could you abbreviate
this similarity condition?

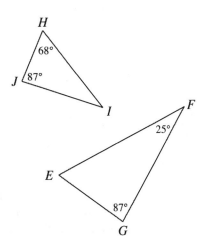

3-50. Carlos then asks, *"What if we only know that one angle is congruent, but the two pairs of corresponding sides that make the angle are proportional? Does that mean the triangles are similar?"*

a. Use a technology tool (or straws and protractors) to test triangles with two pairs of corresponding sides that are proportional, with the included angles congruent as follows.

Create a triangle with side lengths 4 cm and 5 cm and an angle of 20° between these two sides, as shown at right. If a second triangle has an angle of 20°, and the two sides that make the angle share a common ratio with 4 cm and 5 cm (such as 8 cm and 10 cm), is the second triangle always similar to the first triangle? That is, is it possible to make a second triangle with two sides proportional to 4 cm and 5 cm, and an included angle of 20° that is *not* similar?

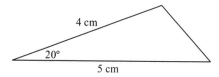

b. Test your ideas from part (a) on the additional triangles below. Is it possible to make a second triangle with two of the sides proportional to the given triangle and with the same included angle that is *not* similar?

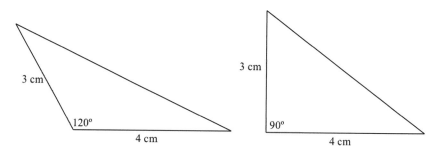

c. Based on your investigations from parts (a) and (b), what can you conclude about triangles with SAS similarity (SAS ~)? Justify your response with transformations.

3-51.   Based on your conclusions from problems 3-49 and 3-50, decide if each pair of triangles below is similar. If they are similar, describe a sequence of transformations that carries one onto the other. Explain your reasoning.

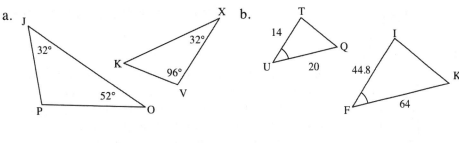

a.

b.

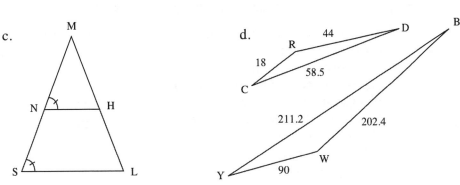

c.

d.

3-52.   LEARNING LOG

Read the Math Notes box for this lesson, which introduces new names for the observations you made in problems 3-49 and 3-50. Then write a Learning Log entry about what you learned today. Be sure to address the question: *How much information do I need about a pair of triangles in order to be sure that they are similar?* Title this entry "AA ~ and SAS ~" and include today's date.

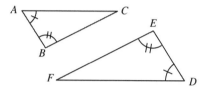 ETHODS AND MEANINGS

MATH NOTES

Conditions for Triangle Similarity

When two figures are similar, there is a similarity transformation that takes one onto the other. Since both dilations and rigid motions preserve angles, the corresponding angles must have equal measure. In the same way, since every similarity transformation preserves ratios of lengths, you know that corresponding sides must be proportional.

These relationships can also help you decide if two figures are similar. When two pairs of corresponding angles have equal measures, the two triangles must be similar. This is because the third pair of angles must also be equal. This is known as the **AA Triangle Similarity** condition (which can be abbreviated as "AA Similarity" or "AA ~" for short).

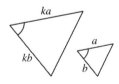

AA ~ : If two pairs of angles have equal measures, then the triangles are similar.

To prove that AA ~ is true for a pair of triangles with two pairs of congruent angles (like $\triangle ABC$ and $\triangle DEF$ at right), use rigid transformations to move the image A' to point D, the image B' to $\overrightarrow{DE}$ and C' to $\overrightarrow{DF}$. Then you know that $\overleftrightarrow{B'C'}$ and $\overleftrightarrow{EF}$ are parallel because corresponding angles are congruent. This means that the dilation of triangle $\triangle A'B'C'$ from point D to take the image B' to point E will also carry C' to point F. Therefore, $\triangle A'B'C'$ will move onto $\triangle DEF$ and you have found a similarity transformation taking $\triangle ABC$ to $\triangle DEF$.

Another condition that guarantees similarity is referred to as the **SAS Triangle Similarity** condition (which can be abbreviated as "SAS Similarity" or "SAS ~" for short.) The "A" is placed between the two "S"s because the angle is *between* the two sides. Its proof is very similar to the proof for AA ~ above.

3-53.   Assume that all trees are green.

a.   Does this statement mean that an oak tree
must be green? Explain why or why not.

b.   Does this statement mean that anything green
must be a tree? Explain why or why not.

c.   Are the statements "*All trees are green*" and "*All green things are trees*"
saying the same thing? Explain why or why not.

3-54.   Decide if each pair of triangles below is similar. If the triangles are similar,
justify your conclusion by stating the similarity condition you used. Also
describe a possible sequence of transformations that would carry one onto the
other. If the triangles are not similar, explain how you know.

a.

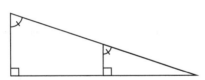

b.

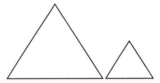

Equilateral Triangles

c.

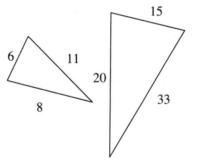

d.

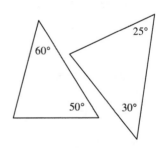

3-55.   Remember that two figures are similar whenever there is a sequence of
transformations (including dilation) that carries one onto the other.

a.   Explain why all circles must be similar. That is, describe a sequence of
transformations that will always carries one circle onto another.

b.   Can you think of any other shapes that are always similar? If you can,
draw an example and explain why they are always similar.

3-56.   When you list *all* of the possible outcomes in a
         sample space by following an organized system
         (an orderly process), it is called a **systematic list**.
         There are different strategies that may help you
         make a systematic list, but what is most important
         is that you methodically follow your system until
         it is complete.

         To get home, Renae can take one of four buses:
         #41, #28, #55, or #81. Once she is on a bus, she
         will randomly select one of the following equally likely activities:
         listening to her MP3 player, writing a letter, or reading a book.

   a.   Create the sample space of all the possible ways Renae can get home and
         do one activity by making a systematic list.

   b.   Use your sample space to find the following probabilities:

         i.   P(Renae takes an odd-numbered bus)

         ii.   P(Renae does not write a letter)

         iii. P(Renae catches the #28 bus and then reads a book)

   c.   Does her activity depend on which bus she takes? Explain why or why
         not.

3-57.   Graph the following points and then connect them in the order given. Then find
         the area and perimeter of the shape. Show all work.

         $A(-2, -3), B(-6, 5), C(11, 5), D(7, 2), E(7, -3)$

3-58.   Assume that each pair of figures below is similar. Write a similarity statement
         to illustrate which parts of each shape correspond. Remember, letter order is
         important!

   a.   *ABCD ~ ?*   b.   *RIGHT ~ ?*

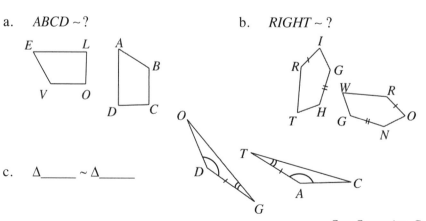

   c.   Δ_____ ~ Δ_____

3.2.2 How can I organize my information?

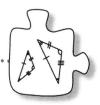

Creating a Flowchart

In Lesson 3.2.1, you developed the AA ~ and SAS ~ conditions to help confirm that triangles are similar. Today you will continue working with similarity and will learn how to use flowcharts to organize your reasoning.

3-59. Examine the triangles at right.

a. Are these triangles similar? Use full sentences to explain your reasoning.

b. Julio decided to use a diagram (called a **flowchart**) to explain his reasoning.

Compare your explanation to Julio's flowchart. Did Julio use the same reasoning you used?

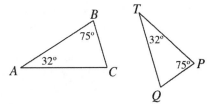

JULIO'S FLOWCHART

$m\angle A = m\angle T$ $m\angle B = m\angle P$

$\triangle CAB \sim \triangle QTP$

AA ~

3-60. Besides showing your reasoning, a flowchart can be used to organize your work as you determine whether or not triangles are similar.

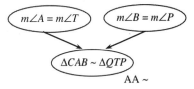

a. Are these triangles similar? Which triangle similarity condition can you use?

b. What facts must you know to use the triangle similarity condition you chose? Julio started to list the facts in a flowchart at right. Copy them on your paper and complete the third oval.

Facts:

$\frac{12}{3} = 4$ $\frac{8}{2} = 4$

c. Once you have the needed facts in place, you can conclude that you have similar triangles. Add to your flowchart by making an oval and filling in your conclusion.

Conclusion:

d. Finally, draw arrows to show the flow of the facts that lead to your conclusion and record the similarity condition you used, following Julio's example from problem 3-59.

3-61.   Now examine the triangles at right.

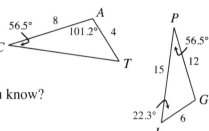

a.   Are these triangles similar? Justify
       your conclusion using a flowchart.

b.   What is the length of *CT*? How do you know?

3-62.   Lindsay was solving a math problem and drew the
         flowchart below right:

a.   Draw and label two triangles that
      could represent Lindsay's
      problem. What question did the
      problem ask her? How can you
      tell?

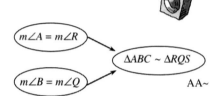

b.   Lindsay's teammate was working
      on the same problem and made a
      mistake in his flowchart:

      How is this flowchart different from
      Lindsay's? Why is this the wrong
      way to explain the reasoning in
      Lindsay's problem?

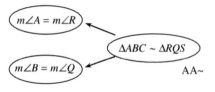

3-63.   Ramon is examining
         the triangles at right.
         He suspects they may
         be similar by SAS ~.

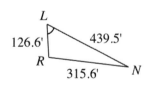

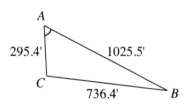

a.   Which pair of corresponding sides
      do you think Ramon is relying on? Why?

b.   Set up ovals for the facts you need to know to show that the triangles are
      similar. Complete any necessary calculations and fill in the ovals.

c.   Are the triangles similar? If so, complete your flowchart and name an
      appropriate similarity condition. If not, explain how you know.

3-64. LEARNING LOG

In your Learning Log, explain how to set up a flowchart.
For example, how do you know how many ovals you
should use? How do you know what to put inside the
ovals? Provide an example. Title this entry "Using
Flowcharts" and include today's date.

Methods and Meanings

Congruent Shapes

If two figures have the same shape and are
the same size, they are **congruent**. Since the
figures must have the same shape, they must
be similar.

Two figures are congruent if they meet both of the
following conditions:

- The two figures are similar, and

- Their side lengths have a common ratio of 1.

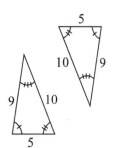

Another way to prove that two shapes are congruent is to show that there
is a rigid motion that takes one exactly onto the other.

3-65.   Solve for the missing lengths in the sets of similar figures below. You may
want to set up tables to help you write equations.

a. $ABCD \sim JKLM$

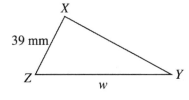

b. $\triangle NOP \sim \triangle XYZ$

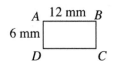

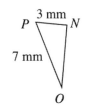

3-66.   Examine each diagram below. Which diagrams are possible? Which are impossible? Justify each conclusion.

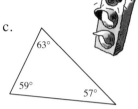

a.
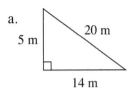
20 m
5 m
14 m

b.
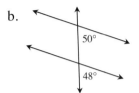
50°
48°

c.
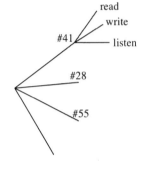
63°
59°   57°

3-67.   Recall from problem 3-56 that Renae can take one of four buses to get home: #41, #28, #55, or #81. Once she is on a bus, she will randomly select one of the following equally likely activities: listening to her MP3 player, writing a letter, or reading a book.

read
write
#41   listen

#28

#55

Creating a **tree diagram**, like the one started at right, is one way to organize all the outcomes of a sample space. This structure organizes the list by connecting each bus with each activity.

In this tree, the first set of branches represents the bus options. At the end of each of these branches are branches representing the activities. For example, if you follow the bold branches, Renae will take the #41 bus and will listen to her MP3 player.

a.   On your paper, complete this tree diagram to show all of the different travel options that Renae could take. What is the probability that Renae does not read on the way home?

b.   Renae's cousin, Greg, can get home using the #101 bus or by going with his older brother. On the way home, Greg can listen to his MP3 player, play video games on his MP3 player, read his novel for English, or talk to the person next to him. Make a tree diagram for all the possible outcomes. What is the probability Greg uses his MP3 player?

3-68.   Determine whether or not the reasoning in the flowchart at right is correct. If it is wrong, redo the flowchart below to make it correct.

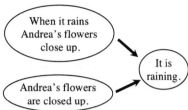

3-69.   Describe a sequence of transformations that can show the figures below are similar. Remember that there can be more than one way.

a.

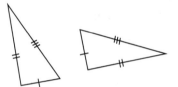

b.

c.

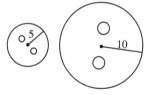

d.

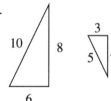

3-70.   Sketch each triangle if possible. If not possible, explain why not.

a.   Right isosceles triangles

b.   Right obtuse triangles

c.   Scalene equilateral triangles

d.   Acute scalene triangles

3.2.3 How can I use equivalent ratios?

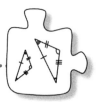

Triangle Similarity and Congruence

By examining and testing side ratios and angles, you are now able to determine whether two figures are similar. But how can you tell if two shapes are the same shape *and* the same size? In this lesson you will examine properties that guarantee that shapes are exact replicas of one another. Note that some figures in this lesson and throughout the course may not be drawn to scale. Always use the factual information stated about or marked on the figure(s) to make decisions.

3-71. Decide if each pair of triangles below is similar. Use a flowchart to organize your facts and conclusion for each pair of triangles.

a.

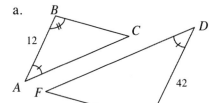

b.

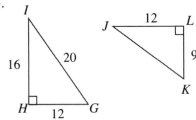

c.

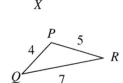

d.

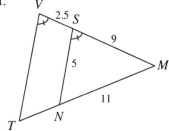

3-72. For the diagrams in problem 3-71, find the lengths of the segments listed below, if possible. If it is not possible, explain why not.

a. $\overline{BC}$ b. $\overline{AC}$ c. $\overline{VT}$ d. $\overline{TN}$

3-73.   Kamraan offers you a challenge.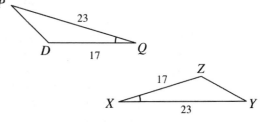
Are the triangles at right
similar? How do you know?
Examine the triangles at right.

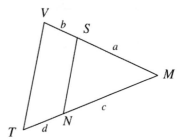

   a.   Use a flowchart to organize
         your explanation.

   b.   Kamraan says, *"These triangles aren't just similar—they're congruent!"*
         Is Kamraan correct? What special value in your flowchart indicates that
         the triangles are congruent?

   c.   Write a conjecture (in "If…, then…" form) for your observation in
         part (b). Then prove that it is true by justifying the conclusion.

3-74.   Kamraan has a new challenge. He drew
triangle *VTM* at right and $\overleftrightarrow{SN}$ which
intersects the sides so that the subdivided
lengths are proportional, that is, so that
$\frac{b}{a} = \frac{d}{c}$. He asks, *"Is $\overrightarrow{VT}$ parallel to $\overleftrightarrow{SN}$?
How do you know?"* Think about this
question as you answer the questions below.

   a.   Kamraan's figure looks like two
         triangles on top of each other.
         Separate the triangles, label the
         vertices and all the side lengths you can.

   b.   How can you prove that $\frac{a+b}{a} = \frac{c+d}{c}$? Talk about this with your team and be
         ready to share your reasoning with the class.

   c.   Are the triangles similar? How do you know?

   d.   Address Kamraan's challenge: Prove that $\overrightarrow{VT}$ is parallel to $\overleftrightarrow{SN}$. Record
         your reasoning.

3-75. Flowcharts can also be used to represent real-life situations. For example, yesterday Joe found out that three people in his family (including Joe) wanted to see a movie, so he went to the theater and bought three tickets. Unfortunately, while he was gone, three more family members decided to go. When everyone arrived at the theater, Joe did not have enough tickets.

Joe sat down later that night and tried to create a flowchart to describe what had happened. Here are the three possibilities he came up with:

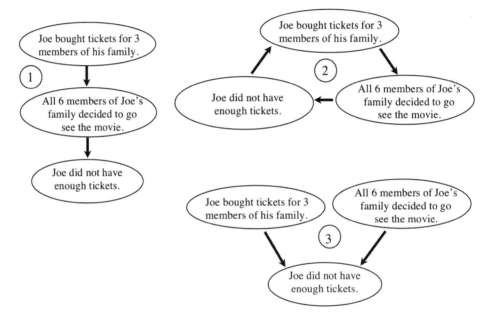

a. Which of these flowcharts best captures the situation that happened on Saturday? Why?

b. What is wrong with the other two flowcharts as descriptions of this situation?

3-76.   On graph paper, plot *ABCD* if *A*(0, 3), *B*(2, 5), *C*(6, 3), and *D*(4, 1).

   a.   Rotate *ABCD* 90° clockwise (↻) about the origin to form *A′B′C′D′* .
         Name the coordinates of *B′* .

   b.   Translate *A′B′C′D′* up 8 units and left 7 units to form *A″B″C″D″* . Name
         the coordinates of *C″* .

   c.   After rotating *ABCD* 180° to form *A‴B‴C‴D‴* , Arah noticed that its
         position and orientation was the same as *ABCD*. What was the point of
         rotation? How did you find it?

3-77.   Examine the graph of line $\overleftrightarrow{CM}$ at right.

   a.   Find the equation of $\overleftrightarrow{CM}$.

   b.   Find the area and perimeter of Δ*CPM*.

   c.   Write an equation of the line through point *M*
         that is perpendicular to $\overleftrightarrow{CM}$.

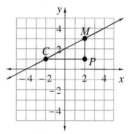

3-78.   Use the relationships in each diagram below to solve for *x*. Justify your solution
         by stating which geometry relationships you used.

   a.
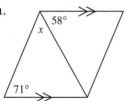

   b.
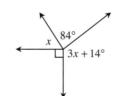

   c.
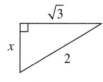

3-79.   Congratulations! You are going to be a
contestant on a new game show with a chance
to win some money. You will spin the two
spinners shown below to see how much money
you will win.

a.   Make a tree diagram of all the possible outcomes of spinning the two
spinners. At the ends of the branches, on the far right, write the amount
you would win for each combination of spins.

b.   Are each of the outcomes in the sample space equally likely?

c.   What is the probability that you will take home $200? What is the
probability that you will take home more than $500?

d.   What is the probability that you will double your winnings? Does the
probability that you will double your winnings depend on the result of the
first spinner?

e.   What if the amounts on the first spinner were $100, $200, and $1500?
What is the probability that you would take home $200? Justify your
conclusion.

3-80.   Solve for the indicated side lengths. Show all work.

a. $\triangle GHI \sim \triangle PQR$ b. $\triangle ABC \sim \triangle XYZ$

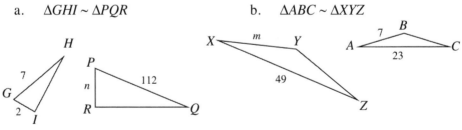

3-81.   Explain why the shapes at right are similar.

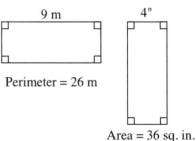

Perimeter = 26 m

Area = 36 sq. in.

$3.2.4$ What information do I need?

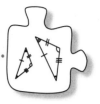

More Conditions for Triangle Similarity

So far, you have worked with two methods for determining that triangles are similar: the AA ~ and the SAS ~ conditions. Are these the only ways to determine if two triangles are similar? Today you will investigate similar triangles and complete your list of triangle similarity conditions.

Keep the following questions in mind as you work together today:

How much information is needed?

Are the triangles similar? How can you tell?

Can I find a triangle with this information that is not similar?

3-82. Robel's team is using the SAS ~ condition to show that two triangles are similar. *"This is too much work,"* Robel says. *"When we're using the AA ~ condition, we only need to look at two pairs of corresponding parts. Let's just calculate the ratios for two pairs of corresponding sides to determine that triangles are similar."*

If two pairs of corresponding side lengths share a common ratio, must the triangles be similar? If not, what additional information is needed? Investigate these questions by completing parts (a) and (b) below.

a. Robel has a triangle with side lengths 4 cm and 5 cm. If your triangle has two sides that share a common ratio with Robel's, does your triangle have to be similar to his? Is SS ~ a valid similarity condition? Explain how you know.

b. Kashi asks, *"I want to test ASA~, which means I start with two pairs of congruent angles and the lengths of the sides connecting these angles are proportional. Would that be enough to know the triangles are similar?"* Discuss this with your team and write Kashi an explanation.

3-83.   What other triangle similarity conditions involving sides and angles might there be? List the names of every other possible triangle similarity condition you can think of that involve corresponding side lengths and angles.

3-84.   In problem 3-82, Robel discovered that SS ~ was not a valid similarity condition. But Kendall wondered if SSS ~ was valid.

   a.   Before experimenting, make a prediction. Do you think that the triangles have to be similar if all three of the corresponding sides share a common ratio?

   b.   Experiment with Kendall's idea. To do this, use a technology tool to test triangles with proportional side lengths. Begin with those listed below, then try some others. If you do not have access to a technology tool, cut straws into the lengths below and create two triangles. Can you create two triangles with proportional sides that are *not* similar? Investigate, sketch your shapes, and write down your conclusion.

   Triangle #1: side lengths 3, 5, and 7; Triangle #2: side lengths 6, 10, and 14

   Triangle #1: side lengths 3, 4, and 5; Triangle #2: side lengths 6, 8, and 10

3-85.   SSS SIMILARITY?

Kendall observes that whenever she builds triangles with the same three lengths, the triangles always end up congruent.

a.   Are two triangles with the same three side lengths always congruent?

b.   Kendall now wants to figure out if three pairs of corresponding proportional side lengths (SSS ~) can be used to determine if triangles are similar. She decides to test triangles with side lengths 4, 6, and 8 units and 6, 9, and 12 units shown at right.

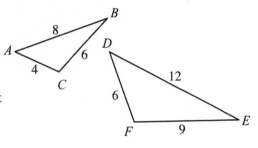

Start by drawing ΔDEF on your paper. Then mark the point G at the place 4 units away from point D on $\overline{DF}$. Then 8 units away from point D on $\overline{DE}$, mark the point J. Connect points G and J.

c.   Your diagram looks like two triangles on top of each other. Draw the two triangles side by side and label the vertices on both triangles. Rename vertex D on the smaller triangle as vertex H.

d.   Now label the lengths of the sides of both triangles. Use the concepts of dilation and similarity to find $\overline{GJ}$. Justify your answer.

e.   Knowing the dimensions of ΔGHJ, what can you conclude about ΔDEF and ΔABC?

f.   Can you extend this reasoning to other pairs of triangles with three pairs of proportional sides? Discuss this with your team and explain why or why not.

3-86.   TESTING MORE SIMILARITY CONDITIONS

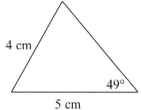

Cori's team put "SSA ~" on their list of possible
triangle similarity conditions. To test their idea,
Cori started by drawing the triangle at right.

4 cm

5 cm

49°

a.   Use a technology tool, or straws and a
protractor to investigate whether SSA ~ is a
valid triangle similarity condition. If a triangle has two sides
sharing a common ratio with Cori's, and has the same angle
that is not in between those sides, must it be similar to Cori's
triangle? In other words, can you create a triangle that is *not*
similar to Cori's?

If you determine SSA ~ is not a valid similarity condition, cross it off your
list!

b.   Go through your list of possible triangle similarity conditions, crossing off
all of the invalid ones and the ones that contain unnecessary information.
How many valid triangle similarity conditions (without extra information)
are there? List them.

3-87.   LEARNING LOG

Reflect on what you have learned today. In your Learning
Log, write down the triangle similarity conditions that help
to determine if triangles are similar. You can write these
conditions as conditional statements (in "If…, then…"
form) or as arrow diagrams. Title this entry "Triangle
Similarity Conditions" and include today's date.

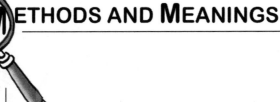

METHODS AND MEANINGS

Writing a Flowchart

A **flowchart** helps to organize facts and indicate which facts lead to a conclusion. The bubbles contain facts, while the arrows point to a conclusion that can be made from a fact or multiple facts.

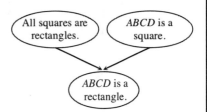

For example, in the flowchart at right, two independent (unconnected) facts are stated: *"All squares are rectangles"* and *"ABCD is a square."* These facts together lead to the conclusion that *ABCD* must be a rectangle. Note that the arrows point toward the conclusion.

3-88. If possible, draw a triangle that has exactly the following number of lines of symmetry. Then name the kind of triangle drawn.

 a. 0 b. 1 c. 2 d. 3

3-89. Do two lines always intersect? Consider this as you answer the questions below.

 a. Write a system of linear equations that does not have a solution. Write each equation in your system in **slope-intercept form** ($y = mx + b$). Graph your system on graph paper and explain why it does not have a solution.

 b. How can you tell algebraically that a system of linear equations has no solution? Solve your system of equations from part (a) algebraically and demonstrate how you know that the system has no solution.

3-90.   Determine which of the following pairs of triangles are similar. Justify your
         answer.

a.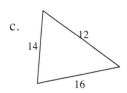

b.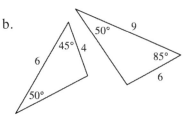

c.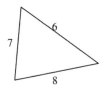

3-91.   The dashed line at right represents the line of
         symmetry of the shaded figure. Find the area and
         perimeter of the shaded region. Show all work.

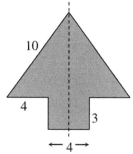

3-92.   Determine whether or not
         the reasoning in the
         flowchart at right is correct.
         If it is wrong, redo the
         flowchart to make it correct.

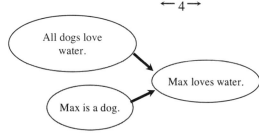

3-93.   Examine the diagrams below. For each one, write and solve an equation to find
         x. Show all work.

a.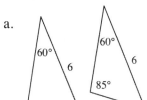

b.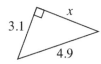

c.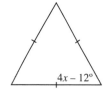

d.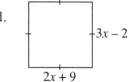

3.2.5 Are the triangles similar?

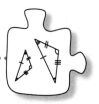

Determining Similarity

You now have a complete list of the three triangle similarity conditions (AA ~, SAS ~, and SSS ~) that can be used to verify that two triangles are similar. Today you will continue to practice applying these conditions and using flowcharts to organize your reasoning.

3-94. Lynn wants to show that the triangles at right are similar.

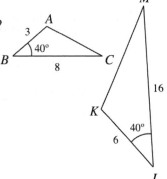

a. What similarity condition should Lynn use?

b. Make a flowchart showing that these triangles are similar.

3-95. Below are six triangles, none of which is drawn to scale. Among the six triangles are three pairs of similar triangles. Identify the similar triangles, then for each pair make a flowchart justifying the similarity.

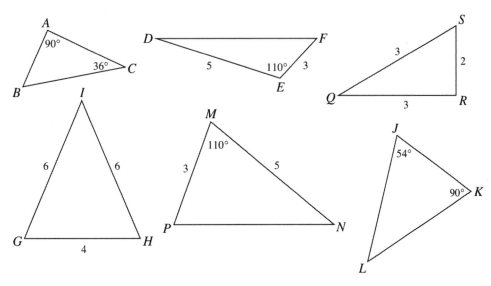

Chapter 3: Justification and Similarity

189

3-96.   Revisit the similar triangles from problem 3-95.

    a.   Which pair of triangles are congruent? How do you know?

    b.   Suppose that in problem 3-95, $AB = 3$ cm, $AC = 4$ cm, and $KJ = 12$ cm. Find all the other side lengths in $\triangle ABC$ and $\triangle JKL$.

3-97.   Examine the triangles at right.

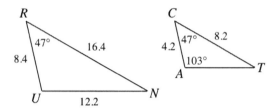

    a.   Are these triangles similar? If so, make a flowchart justifying their similarity.

    b.   Charles has $\triangle CAT \sim \triangle RUN$ as the conclusion of his flowchart. Leesa has $\triangle NRU \sim \triangle TCA$ as her conclusion. Who is correct? Why?

    c.   Are $\triangle CAT$ and $\triangle RUN$ congruent? Explain how you know.

    d.   Find all the missing side lengths and all the angle measures of $\triangle CAT$ and $\triangle RUN$.

3-98.   THE FAMILY FORTUNE, Part Two

In Lesson 1.1.4, you had to convince city officials that you were a relative of Molly "Ol' Granny" Marston, who had just passed away leaving a sizable inheritance. Below is the evidence you had available:

> **Family Portrait** — a photo showing three young children. On the back you see the date 1968.

> **Newspaper Clipping** — from 1972 titled "Triplets Make Music History." The first sentence catches your eye: "Jake, Judy, and Jeremiah Marston, all eight years old, were the first triplets ever to perform a six-handed piano piece at Carnegie Hall."

> **Jake Marston's Birth Certificate** — showing that Jake was born in 1964, and identifying his parents as Phillip and Molly Marston.

> **Your Learner's Permit** — signed by your father, Jeremiah Marston.

> **Wilbert Marston's Passport** — issued when Wilbert was fifteen.

As their answer to this problem, one team wrote the following argument for the city officials:

> *The birth certificate shows that Jake Marston was Molly Marston's son. The newspaper clipping shows that Jeremiah Marston was Jake Marston's brother. Therefore, Jeremiah Marston was Molly Marston's son. The learner's permit shows that Jeremiah Marston is my father. Therefore, I am Molly Marston's grandchild.*

Your Task: Make a flowchart showing the reasoning in this team's argument. This flowchart will have more levels than the ones you have made in the past, because certain conclusions will be used as facts to support other conclusions. So plan carefully before you start to draw your chart.

ETHODS AND MEANINGS

Complete Conditions for Triangle Similarity

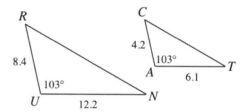

There are exactly three valid, non-redundant triangle similarity conditions that use only sides and angles. (A similarity condition is "redundant" if it includes more information than is necessary to establish triangle similarity.) They are abbreviated as: SSS ~, AA ~, and SAS ~. In the SAS~ condition, the "A" is placed between the two "S"s to indicate that the angle must be *between* the two sides used.

For example, $\triangle RUN$ and $\triangle CAT$ at right are similar by SAS ~. $\frac{RU}{CA} = 2$ and $\frac{UN}{AT} = 2$, so the ratios of the side lengths of the two pairs of corresponding sides are equal. The measure of the angle between $\overline{RU}$ and $\overline{UN}$, $\angle U$, equals the measure of the angle between $\overline{CA}$ and $\overline{AT}$, $\angle A$, so the conditions for SAS ~ are met.

3-99.   Determine which similarity conditions (AA ~, SSS ~, or SAS ~) could be used to establish that the following pairs of triangles are similar. List as many as you can.

a.

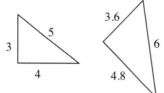

b.

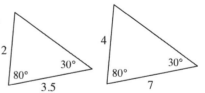

c.

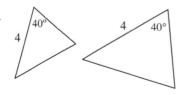

3-100.   You are feeling kind of crazy, so you are going
         to have the owner of the pet store randomly
         pick a fish for your aquarium at home.

   a.   A tank at the pet store contains 9 spotted
        guppies, 14 red barbs, 10 red tetras, and
        7 golden platys. What is the probability
        (expressed as a percent) of getting a red-
        colored fish from this tank?

   b.   In a different tank that contains only golden platys, the probability of
        getting a female fish is 30%. If there are 18 female fish in the tank, how
        many total fish are in the tank?

3-101.   Multiply the expressions in parts (a) and (b). Solve the equations in parts (c)
         and (d).

   a. $(3x+2)(4x-5)$ b. $(4x-1)^2$

   c. $2x(x+3)=(x+1)(2x-5)$ d. $3^2+(x+1)^2=(x+2)^2$

3-102.   A laser light is pointed at a mirror as shown at
         right. If $\angle x$ measures 48°, what are the measures
         of $\angle y$ and $\angle z$. Justify your reasons.

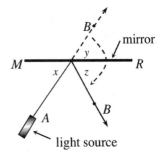

3-103.   On graph paper, graph line $\overleftrightarrow{LD}$ if
         $L(-2, 1)$ and $D(4, -4)$.

   a.   Find the slope of $\overleftrightarrow{LD}$.

   b.   Find LD (the distance from L to D).

   c.   Describe how you might determine the lengths of the sides of the slope
        triangle without using graph paper.

3-104.   On graph paper, sketch a rectangle with side lengths of 15 units and 9 units.
         Shrink the rectangle by a zoom factor of $\frac{1}{3}$. Make a table showing the area and
         perimeter of both rectangles.

3.2.6 What can I do with similar triangles?

Applying Similarity

In previous lessons, you have learned methods for finding similar triangles. Once you find triangles are similar, how can that help you? Today you will apply similar triangles to analyze situations and solve new applications. As you work on today's problems, ask the following questions in your team:

What is the relationship?

Are any triangles similar? What similarity condition can you use?

3-105. YOU ARE GETTING SLEEPY...

Legend has it that if you stare into a person's eyes in a special way, you can hypnotize them into squawking like a chicken. Here's how it works.

Place a mirror on the floor. Your subject has to stand exactly 200 cm away from the mirror and stare into it. The only tricky part is that you need to figure out where you have to stand so that when you stare into the mirror, you are also staring into your subject's eyes.

If your calculations are correct and you stand at the *exact* distance, your subject will squawk like a chicken!

a. Choose a member of your team to hypnotize. Before heading to the mirror, first analyze this situation. Draw a diagram showing you and your subject standing on opposite sides of a mirror. Measure the heights of both yourself and your subject (heights to the eyes, of course), and label all the lengths you can on the diagram. (Remember, your subject will need to stand 200 cm from the mirror.)

b. Are there similar triangles in your diagram? Justify your conclusion. (Hint: Remember what you know about how light reflects off mirrors.) Then calculate how far you will need to stand from the mirror to hypnotize your subject.

c. Now for the moment of truth! Have your teammate stand 200 cm away from the mirror, while you stand at your calculated distance from the mirror. Do you make eye contact? If not, check your measurements and calculations and try again.

3-106.   LESSONS FROM ABROAD

Latoya was trying to take a picture of her family in front of the Big Ben clock tower in London. However, after she snapped the photo, she realized that the top of her father's head exactly blocked the top of the clock tower!

While disappointed with the picture, Latoya thought she might be able to estimate the height of the tower using her math knowledge. Since Latoya took the picture while kneeling, the camera was 2 feet above the ground. The camera was also 12 feet from her 6-foot tall father, and he was standing about 930 feet from the base of the tower.

a.   Sketch the diagram above on your paper and locate as many triangles as you can. Can you find any triangles that must be similar? If so, explain how you know they are similar.

b.   Use the similar triangles to determine the height of the Big Ben clock tower.

3-107.   REVISITING THE PYTHAGOREAN THEOREM WITH SIMILARITY

In Lesson 2.3.2, you proved the Pythagorean Theorem using a proof involving the area of triangles and squares. Did you know that you can also prove the Pythagorean Theorem using triangle similarity? For example, in triangle ABC with right angle at A below, how can similarity be used to prove that $(AB)^2 + (AC)^2 = (BC)^2$? In this problem, you will support this proof by providing reasons for each part of the justification.

a.   Find three different triangles in the diagram. Why are all of these triangles similar?

b.   Carol argues that $\frac{DB}{AB} = \frac{AB}{CB}$ and $\frac{DC}{AC} = \frac{AC}{BC}$. Do you agree? Why or why not?

c.   How can you use Carol's equations to show that $(AB)^2 = (CB)(DB)$ and $(AC)^2 = (BC)(DC)$?

d.   Why does $(AB)^2 + (AC)^2 = (CB)(DB) + (BC)(DC)$?

e.   Why does $(CB)(DB) + (BC)(DC) = BC(DB + DC) = (BC)^2$?

f.   Finish the proof: Why does $(AB)^2 + (AC)^2 = (BC)^2$?

3-108. Use the relationships in the diagram at right to solve for x and y. Justify your solutions.

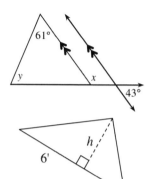

3-109. The area of the triangle at right is 25 square feet. Find the value of h. Then find the perimeter of the entire triangle. Show all work.

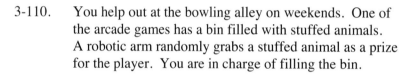

3-110. You help out at the bowling alley on weekends. One of the arcade games has a bin filled with stuffed animals. A robotic arm randomly grabs a stuffed animal as a prize for the player. You are in charge of filling the bin.

a. You are told that the probability of getting a stuffed giraffe today is $\frac{2}{5}$. If there are 28 giraffes in the bin, what is the total number of stuffed animals in the bin?

b. The next weekend, you arrive to find the bin contains 22 unicorns, 8 gorillas, 13 striped fish, and 15 elephants. A shipment of stuffed whales arrives. What is the probability of getting a sea animal (whale or fish) if you add 17 whales to the bin? Express the probability as a percent.

c. You are told that the probability of selecting a stuffed alligator needs to be 5%. One weekend you arrive to find there are exactly 3 alligators left. How many total animals should be in the bin to maintain the probability of 5% for an alligator?

3-111. This problem is a checkpoint for writing linear equations from multiple representations. It will be referred to as Checkpoint 3.

Write a linear equation that represents each situation.

a. An equation for the line at right.

b. An equation for a line perpendicular to the line at right and passing through the point $(-1, -3)$.

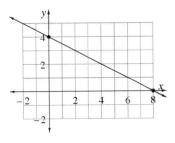

c. An equation of the line passing through the points $(4, 3)$ and $(-1, 1)$.

d. At the concert, Elite Parking charges $15 for the first hour and $7 for each additional hour of parking. Write an equation to represent the cost (C) for parking (t) hours.

Check your answers by referring to the Checkpoint 3 materials located at the back of your book.

Ideally, at this point you are comfortable working with these types of problems and can solve them correctly. If you feel that you need more confidence when solving these types of problems, then review the Checkpoint 3 materials and try the practice problems provided. From this point on, you will be expected to do problems like these correctly and with confidence.

3-112. Patti lives 20 miles northeast of Matt. Simone lives 15 miles due south of Patti. If Matt lives due west of Simone, approximately how many miles does he live from Simone? Draw a diagram and show all work.

3-113. List a sequence of transformations that demonstrates $ABCD \sim WXYZ$, then find y and z.

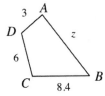

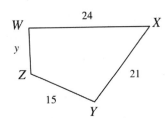

Chapter 3 Closure   What have I learned?

Reflection and Synthesis

The activities below offer you a chance to reflect about what you have learned during this chapter. As you work, look for concepts that you feel very comfortable with, ideas that you would like to learn more about, and topics you need more help with. Look for connections between ideas as well as connections with material you learned previously.

①   TEAM BRAINSTORM

What have you studied in this chapter? What ideas were important in what you learned? With your team, brainstorm a list. Be as detailed as you can. To help get you started, lists of Learning Log entries and Math Notes boxes from this chapter are below.

What topics, ideas, and words that you learned *before* this chapter are connected to the new ideas in this chapter? Again, be as detailed as you can.

Next consider the Standards for Mathematical Practice that follow Activity ③: Portfolio. What Mathematical Practices did you use in this chapter? When did you use them? Give specific examples.

How long can you make your lists? Challenge yourselves. Be prepared to share your team's ideas with the class.

Learning Log Entries
- Lesson 3.1.1 – Same Shape, Different Size
- Lesson 3.1.2 – Similar Figures
- Lesson 3.1.4 – Comparing with Ratios
- Lesson 3.2.1 – AA ~ and SAS ~
- Lesson 3.2.2 – Using Flowcharts
- Lesson 3.2.4 – Triangle Similarity Conditions

Math Notes
- Lesson 3.1.1 – Dilations
- Lesson 3.1.2 – Ratio of Similarity and Zoom Factor
- Lesson 3.1.3 – Proportional Equations
- Lesson 3.1.4 – Writing a Similarity Statement
- Lesson 3.2.1 – Conditions for Triangle Similarity
- Lesson 3.2.2 – Congruent Shapes
- Lesson 3.2.4 – Writing a Flowchart
- Lesson 3.2.5 – Complete Conditions for Triangle Similarity

②   MAKING CONNECTIONS

Below is a list of the vocabulary used in this chapter. Make sure that you are familiar with all of these words and know what they mean. Refer to the glossary or index for any words that you do not yet understand.

AA ~	angle	conditional
congruent	corresponding sides	dilation
enlarge	flowchart	hypotenuse
logical argument	original	perimeter
proportional equation	ratio	relationship
SAS ~	sides	similar
similarity statement	similarity transformation	SSS ~
translate	vertex	zoom factor

Make a concept map showing all of the connections you can find among the key words and ideas listed above. To show a connection between two words, draw a line between them and explain the connection, as shown in the model below. A word can be connected to any other word as long as you can justify the connection. For each key word or idea, provide an example or sketch that shows the idea.

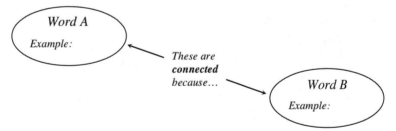

Your teacher may provide you with vocabulary cards to help you get started. If you use the cards to plan your concept map, be sure either to re-draw your concept map on your paper or to glue the vocabulary cards to a poster with all of the connections explained for others to see and understand.

While you are making your map, your team may think of related words or ideas that are not listed here. Be sure to include these ideas on your concept map.

③ PORTFOLIO: EVIDENCE OF MATHEMATICAL
PROFICIENCY

Think about the way you think, as you answer the
questions below. When did you need to make sense
out of multiple pieces of information? What helps you
to determine what makes sense? Were there times
when you made assumptions instead of relying on
facts? How have you used reasoning in a previous
math class?

a. At right is a crossword puzzle and a
list of words that fit within the
puzzle. Do you know where all of
the words MUST go or is there more
than one possible solution? Write an
argument that will convince your
teacher of your answer.

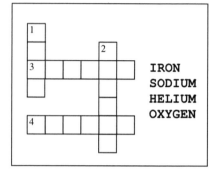

b. Examine the Venn
diagram at right.
What shape(s) can go
in the intersection?
Justify your
statements so that they
are convincing.

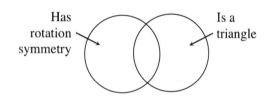

c. Being able to justify your thinking is especially important when you are
working in a team. While you may have a correct idea, if you cannot
convince your team that your ideas are valid, your teammates may not
agree.

Consider the diagram at right. Assume that
your teammates think angles *a* and *b* must
be congruent. Do you agree? How can you
explain your reasoning so that your team is
convinced? Use a diagram to support your
argument.

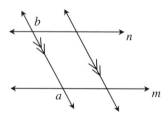

Activity continues on next page →

③   *Activity continued from previous page.*

d.   What if someone else is trying to convince you of something? How do you think as you follow someone else's argument? Consider this as you read Lila's reasoning below. Then decide if you agree with her statement or not. If you agree, what helped convince you?

I know that the sum of the angles of a triangle is 180°, but I don't think that is true for a quadrilateral. If I draw a diagonal, I split my quadrilateral into two triangles. I know that the angles of each of these triangles add up to 180°. Therefore, I think the angles of the quadrilateral must add up to 360°.

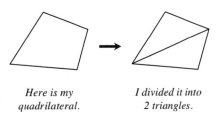

Here is my quadrilateral.   *I divided it into 2 triangles.*

Your teacher may give you the Chapter 3 Closure Resource Page: Similarity Graphics Organizer to work on (or you can download this page from www.cpm.org). A Graphic Organizer is a tool you can use to organize your thoughts, showcase your knowledge, and communicate your ideas clearly.

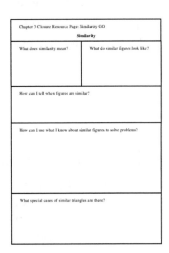

Now consider the Standards for Mathematical Practice that follow. What Mathematical Practices did you use in this chapter? When did you use them? Give specific examples.

BECOMING MATHEMATICALLY PROFICIENT
The Common Core State Standards for Mathematical Practice

This book focuses on helping you use some very specific Mathematical Practices. The Mathematical Practices describe ways in which mathematically proficient students engage with mathematics everyday.

Make sense of problems and persevere in solving them:

Making sense of problems and persevering in solving them means that you can solve problems that are full of different kinds of mathematics. These types of problems are not routine, simple, or typical. Instead, they combine lots of math ideas and everyday situations. You have to stick with challenging problems, try different strategies, use multiple representations, and use a different method to check your results.

Reason abstractly and quantitatively:

Throughout this course, everyday situations are used to introduce you to new math ideas. Seeing mathematical ideas within a context helps you make sense of the ideas. Once you learn about a math idea in a practical way, you can "**reason abstractly**" by thinking about the concept more generally, representing it with symbols, and manipulating the symbols. **Reasoning quantitatively** is using numbers and symbols to represent an everyday situation, taking into account the units involved, and considering the meaning of the quantities as you compute them.

Construct viable arguments and critique the reasoning of others:

To **construct a viable argument** is to present your solution steps in a logical sequence and to justify your steps with conclusions, relying on number sense, facts and definitions, and previously established results. You communicate clearly, consider the real-life context, and provide clarification when others ask. In this course, you regularly share information, opinions, and expertise with your study team. You **critique the reasoning of others** when you analyze the approach of others, build on each other's ideas, compare the effectiveness of two strategies, and decide what makes sense and under what conditions.

Model with mathematics:

When you **model with mathematics**, you take a complex situation and use mathematics to represent it, often by making assumptions and approximations to simplify the situation. Modeling allows you to analyze and describe the situation and to make predictions. For example, to find the density of your body, you might model your body with a more familiar shape, say, a cylinder of the same diameter and height. Although a model may not be perfect, it can still be very useful for describing situations and making predictions. When you interpret the results, you may need to go back and improve your model by revising your assumptions and approximations.

Use appropriate tools strategically:

To **use appropriate tools strategically** means that you analyze the task and decide which tools may help you model the situation or find a solution. Some of the tools available to you include diagrams, graph paper, calculators, computer software, databases, and websites. You understand the limitations of various tools. A result can be checked or estimated by strategically choosing a different tool.

Attend to precision:

To **attend to precision** means that when solving problems, you need to pay close attention to the details. For example, you need to be aware of the units, or how many digits your answer requires, or how to choose a scale and label your graph. You may need to convert the units to be consistent. At times, you need to go back and check whether a numerical solution makes sense in the context of the problem.

You need to **attend to precision** when you communicate your ideas to others. Using the appropriate vocabulary and mathematical language can help make your ideas and reasoning more understandable to others.

Look for and make use of structure:

To **look for and making use of structure** is a guiding principle of this course. When you are involved in analyzing the structure and in the actual development of mathematical concepts, you gain a deeper, more conceptual understanding than when you are simply told what the structure is and how to do problems. You often use this practice to bring closure to an investigation.

There are many concepts that you learn by looking at the underlying structure of a mathematical idea and thinking about how it connects to other ideas you have already learned. For example, geometry theorems are developed from the structure of repeated translations.

Look for and express regularity in repeated reasoning:

To **look for and express regularity in repeated reasoning** means that when you are investigating a new mathematical concept, you notice if calculations are repeated in a pattern. Then you look for a way to generalize the method for use in other situations, or you look for shortcuts. For example, repeated reasoning allows for increasingly complex geometric proofs to be developed from simpler ones.

④ WHAT HAVE I LEARNED?

Most of the problems in this section represent typical problems found in this chapter. They serve as a gauge for you. You can use them to determine which types of problems you can do well and which types of problems require further study and practice. Even if your teacher does not assign this section, it is a good idea to try these problems and find out for yourself what you know and what you still need to work on.

Solve each problem as completely as you can. The table at the end of the closure section has answers to these problems. It also tells you where you can find additional help and practice with problems like these.

CL 3-114. Examine the shape at right.

a. Using the technique from problem 3-2, enlarge this shape from the origin by a factor of 3.

b. Now redraw the enlarged shape from part (a) using a zoom factor of $\frac{1}{2}$.

CL 3-115. Jermaine has a triangle with sides 8, 14, and 20. Sadie and Aisha both think that they have triangles that are similar to Jermaine's triangle. The sides of Sadie's triangle are 2, 3.5, and 5. The sides of Aisha's triangle are 4, 10, and 16. Decide who, if anyone, has a triangle similar to Jermaine's triangle. Be sure to explain how you know.

CL 3-116. For the points R $(-2, 7)$ and P $(2, 1)$ determine each of the following:

a. The slope of the line through the points.

b. The distance between the points.

c. An equation of the line $\overleftrightarrow{RP}$.

d. An equation of the line perpendicular to line $\overleftrightarrow{RP}$ and passing through point P.

CL 3-117.　For each given set of numbers, determine if a triangle with those side lengths can be made or not. If a triangle can be made, determine if the triangle is a right triangle. Justify all answers.

　　　a.　8, 15, 17　　　　　　　　　　　b.　8, 12, 4

CL 3-118.　Each pair of figures below is similar. Find the lengths of the unknown sides that are marked with a variable.

　　　a.

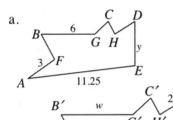
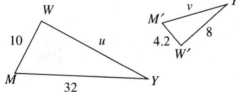

　　　b.

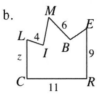
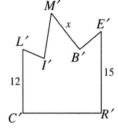

　　　c.

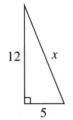
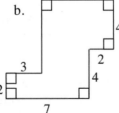

CL 3-119.　Find the perimeter and area of each figure.

　　　a.

　　　b.

　　　c.

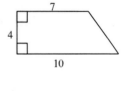

CL 3-120.　Solve each equation.

　　　a.　$x(3x-2)=(3x+1)(x-2)$　　　　b.　$(x+1)(x+2)=(x+3)(x-1)$

　　　c.　$\frac{x+1}{3}=\frac{x}{6}$　　　　　　　　d.　$\frac{3}{x}=\frac{2}{5}$

CL 3-121.   Create a flowchart that represents the following story.

Marcelle and Harpo live at Apt. I, 8 Logic St. Marcelle took his guitar to band practice across town and isn't back yet. Harpo hears guitar music in the hallway. He decides that someone else in the building also plays guitar.

CL 3-122.   Among the triangles below are pairs of similar triangles. Find the pairs of similar triangles and state the triangle similarity condition that you used to determine that the triangles are similar.

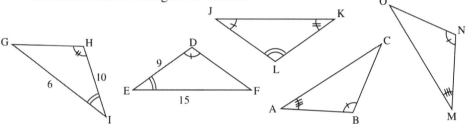

CL 3-123.   To help boost their healthy eating habits, Alyse and Haley are getting creative making juices. They are going to put fruits and vegetables in an ice chest, and then close their eyes to randomly pick fruits and vegetables to blend into juice. They hope to create something new and delicious!

a.   The ice chest can hold 18 pieces of fruit or vegetables. For their first drink, Alyse and Haley want the probability of picking a carrot to be about 40%. How many carrots should they put in the ice chest?

b.   For their second drink, there are 2 red apples, 5 apricots, 1 mango, 2 red tomatoes, 1 red grapefruit, 4 bananas, 2 nectarines, and 1 peach in the ice chest. What is the probability (expressed as a percent) that the first piece they pick is red?

c.   Haley *loves* pomegranates. So she adds 7 pomegranates to the bin in in part (b). What is the probability (expressed as a percent) that the first fruit picked will be a pomegranate?

CL 3-124.   Check your answers using the table at the end of this section. Which problems do you feel confident about? Which problems were hard? Have you worked on problems like these in math classes you have taken before? Use the table to make a list of topics you need help on and a list of topics you need to practice more.

Answers and Support for Closure Activity #4
What Have I Learned?

Note: MN = Math Notes, LL = Learning Log

Problem	Solutions	Need Help?	More Practice
CL 3-114.	a. b.	Lessons 3.1.1 and 3.1.2 MN: 3.1.1 and 3.1.2 LL: 3.1.1 and 3.1.2	Problems 3-29, 3-30, 3-46, and 3-104
CL 3-115.	Sadie's triangle is similar to Jermaine by SSS ~; The ratio of the corresponding sides is $\frac{1}{4}$. The sides of Aisha's triangle do not have the same ratio to the sides of Jermaine's triangle.	Section 3.2 MN: 3.2.1 and 3.2.5 LL: 3.1.2 and 3.2.4	Problems 3-54, 3-81, 3-90, and 3-99
CL 3-116.	a. $-\frac{3}{2}$ b. $\sqrt{52} = 2\sqrt{13} \approx 7.21$ c. $y = -\frac{3}{2}x + 4$ d. $y = \frac{2}{3}x - \frac{1}{3}$	Checkpoint 3 MN: 1.2.6 and 2.3.2	Problems CL 2-121, 3-8, 3-32, 3-43, 3-77, 3-103, and 3-111
CL 3-117.	a. right triangle b. no triangle possible	Lesson 2.3.1 LL: 2.3.1	Problems 2-117, 3-9, 3-45, and 3-66
CL 3-118.	a. $w = 8$, $y = \frac{21}{4} = 5.25$ b. $x = 10$, $z = \frac{36}{5} = 7.2$ c. $u \approx 19.05$, $v = 13.44$	Section 3.1 MN: 3.1.2 and 3.1.3 LL: 3.1.4	Problems 3-41, 3-65, 3-80, and 3-113

Problem	Solutions	Need Help?	More Practice
CL 3-119.	a. $x = 13$ unit, P = 30 units, A = 30 units^2 b. P = 34 units, A = 46 units^2 c. P = 26 units, Area = 34 units^2	Section 2.2 MN: 1.1.3, 2.2.4, and 2.3.2 LL: 2.2.2	Problems CL 1-129, CL 2-119, 3-91, and 3-109
CL 3-120.	a. $x = -\frac{2}{3}$ b. $x = -5$ c. $x = -2$ d. $x = 7\frac{1}{2}$	Checkpoint 1 MN: 1.1.4 and 2.2.2	Problems CL 1-133, 3-6, 3-31, and 3-101
CL 3-121.	Harpo hears guitar music in the hallway. / Marcelle took his guitar to band practice across town and isn't back yet. / Harpo decides that someone else in the building also plays guitar.	Lesson 3.2.2 MN: 3.2.4 LL: 3.2.2	Problems 3-68 and 3-92
CL 3-122.	$\triangle ABC \sim \triangle MNO$, by AA ~ $\triangle EDF \sim \triangle IGH$, by SAS ~ $\triangle EDF \sim \triangle LJK$, by AA ~ $\triangle IGH \sim \triangle LJK$, by AA ~	Section 3.2 MN: 3.2.1 and 3.2.5 LL: 3.2.4	Problems 3-54, 3-58, 3-90, and 3-99
CL 3-123.	a. $\frac{?}{18} = \frac{40}{100}$; 7 carrots b. $\frac{2+2+1}{18} = \frac{5}{18} \approx 27.8\%$ c. $\frac{7}{25} = 28\%$	MN 1.2.1	Problems CL 1-131, CL 2-118, 3-67, 3-79, 3-100, and 3-110

CHAPTER 4   Trigonometry and Probability

In Chapter 3, you investigated similarity and discovered that similar triangles have special relationships. In this chapter, you will discover that the side ratios in a right triangle can serve as a powerful mathematical tool that allows you to find missing side lengths and missing angle measures for any right triangle. You will also learn how these ratios (called trigonometric ratios) can be used in solving problems.

You will also develop additional prediction skills as you extend your understanding of probability. You will examine different models to represent possibilities and to assist you in calculating probabilities.

Guiding Question

Mathematically proficient students will use appropriate tools strategically.

As you work through this chapter, ask yourself:

Can I use the available tools to solve problems and decide which tool might be the most helpful?

In this chapter, you will learn:

➢ The trigonometric ratio of tangent.

➢ How the tangent ratio is connected to the slope of a line.

➢ How to apply trigonometric ratios to find missing measurements in right triangles.

➢ How to model real world situations with right triangles and use trigonometric ratios to solve problems.

➢ Several ways to model probability situations, such as tree diagrams and area models.

➢ How to formalize methods for computing probabilities of unions, intersections, and complements of events.

➢ How to find expected value in games of chance.

Chapter Outline

Section 4.1 Students will investigate the relationship between the slope of a line and the slope angle. The slope ratio will be used to find missing measurements of a right triangle and to solve real world problems.

Section 4.2 Students will continue their study of probability by using tree diagrams and area models to calculate probabilities of events that are not equally likely. Students will calculate expected values and probabilities of unions, intersections, and complements of events.

         Core Connections Geometry

4.1.1 What patterns can I use?

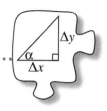

Constant Ratios in Right Triangles

In Chapter 3, you looked for relationships between triangles and ways to determine if they are similar or congruent. Now you are going to focus your attention on slope triangles, which were used in algebra to describe linear change. Are there geometric patterns within slope triangles themselves that you can use to answer other questions? In this lesson, you will look closely at slope triangles on different lines to explore their patterns.

4-1.   LEANING TOWER OF PISA

For centuries, people have marveled at the Leaning Tower of Pisa due to its slant and beauty. Ever since construction of the tower started in the 1100s, the tower has slowly tilted south and has increasingly been at risk of falling over. It is feared that if the angle of slant ever falls below 83°, the tower will collapse.

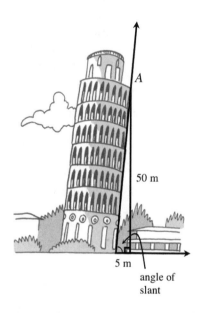

Engineers closely monitor the angle at which the tower leans. With careful measuring, they know that the point labeled *A* in the diagram at right is now 50 meters off the ground. Also, they determined that when a weight is dropped from point *A*, it lands 5 meters from the base of the tower, as shown in the diagram.

a.   With the measurements provided above, what can you determine?

b.   Can you determine the angle at which the tower leans? Why or why not?

c.   At the end of Section 4.1, you will know how to find the angle for this situation and many others. However, at this point, how else can you describe the "lean" of the leaning tower?

4-2.   PATTERNS IN SLOPE TRIANGLES

In order to find an angle (such as the angle at which the Leaning Tower of Pisa leans), you need to investigate the relationship between the angles and the sides of a right triangle. You will start by studying slope triangles. Obtain the Lesson 4.1.1 Resource Pages from your teacher and find the graph shown below. Notice that one slope triangle has been drawn for you. Note: For the next several lessons angle measures will be rounded to the nearest degree.

a. Draw three new slope triangles on the line. Each should be a different size. Label each triangle with as much information 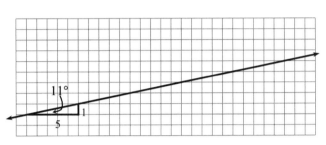 as you can, such as its horizontal and vertical lengths and its angle measures.

b. Explain why all of the slope triangles on this line must be similar.

c. Since the triangles are similar, what does that tell you about the slope ratios?

d. Confirm your conclusion by writing the slope ratio for each triangle as a fraction, such as $\frac{\Delta y}{\Delta x}$. (Note: Δy represents the vertical change or "rise," while Δx represents the horizontal change or "run.") Then change the slope ratio into decimal form and compare.

4-3.   Tara thinks she sees a pattern in these slope triangles, so she decides to make some changes in order to investigate whether or not the patterns remain true.

a. She asks, "*What if I draw a slope triangle on this line with $\Delta y = 6$? What would be the Δx of my triangle?*" Answer her question and explain how you figured it out.

b. "*What if Δx is 40?*" she wonders. "*Then what is Δy?*" Find Δy, and explain your reasoning.

c. Tara wonders, "*What if I draw a slope triangle on a different line? Can I still use the same ratio to find a missing Δx- or Δy-value?*" Discuss this question with your team and explain to Tara what she could expect.

4-4.   CHANGING LINES

In part (c) of problem 4-3, Tara asked, *"What if I draw my triangle on a different line?"* With your team, investigate what happens to the slope ratio and slope angle when the line is different. Use the grids provided on your Lesson 4.1.1 Resource Pages to graph the lines described below. Use the graphs and your answers to the questions below to respond to Tara's question.

a.   On graph A, graph the line $y = \frac{2}{5}x$. What is the slope ratio for this line? What does the slope angle appear to be? Does the information about this line support or change your conclusion from part (c) of problem 4-3? Explain.

b.   On graph B, you are going to create $\angle QPR$ so that it measures 18°. First, place your protractor so that point P is the vertex. Then find 18° and mark and label a new point, R. Draw ray $\overrightarrow{PR}$ to form $\angle QPR$. Find an approximate slope ratio for this line.

c.   Graph the line $y = x + 4$ on graph C. Draw a slope triangle and label its horizontal and vertical lengths. What is $\frac{\Delta y}{\Delta x}$ (the slope ratio)? What is the slope angle?

4-5.   TESTING CONJECTURES

The students in Ms. Coyner's class are writing conjectures based on their work today. As a team, decide if you agree or disagree with each of the conjectures below. Explain your reasoning.

- All slope triangles have a ratio $\frac{1}{5}$.

- If the slope ratio is $\frac{1}{5}$, then the slope angle is approximately 11°.

- If the line has an 11° slope angle, then the slope ratio is approximately $\frac{1}{5}$.

- Different lines will have different slope angles and different slope ratios.

METHODS AND MEANINGS

Slope and Angle Notation

MATH NOTES

The slope of a line is the ratio of the vertical distance to the horizontal distance in a slope triangle formed by two points on a line. The vertical part of the triangle is called Δy, (read "change in y"), while the horizontal part of the triangle is called Δx (read "change in x"). Slope can then be written as $\frac{\Delta y}{\Delta x}$. Slope indicates both how steep the line is and its direction, upward or downward, left to right.

When a side length in a triangle is missing, that length is often assigned a variable from the English alphabet such as x, y, or z. However, sometimes you need to distinguish between an unknown side length and an unknown angle measure. With that in mind, mathematicians sometimes use Greek letters as variables for angle measurement. The most common variable for an angle is the Greek letter θ (*theta*), pronounced "THAY-tah." Two other Greek letters commonly used include α (*alpha*), and β (*beta*), pronounced "BAY-tah."

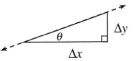

When a right triangle is oriented like a slope triangle, such as the one in the diagram above, the angle the line makes with the horizontal side of the triangle is called a **slope angle**.

4-6. Use what you know about the angles of a triangle to find the value of x and the angles in each triangle below.

a.
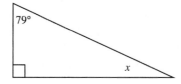
79°

b.

x
x

c.
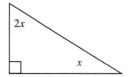
$2x$
x

d.
22°
x

4-7. Use the triangles at right to answer the following questions.

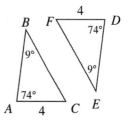

a. Are the triangles at right similar? How do you know? Show your reasoning in a flowchart.

b. Examine your work from part (a). Are the triangles also congruent? Explain why or why not.

4-8. As Randi started to solve for x in the diagram at right, she wrote the equation $7^2 + x^2 = (x+1)^2$.

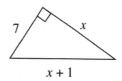

a. Is Randi's equation valid? Explain your thinking.

b. To solve her equation, first rewrite $(x+1)^2$ by multiplying $(x+1)(x+1)$. You may want to review the Math Notes box in Lesson 2.2.2.

c. Now solve your equation for x.

d. What is the perimeter of Randi's triangle?

4-9.   Assume that the shapes at right are similar. Find the values of x, y, and z.

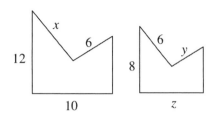

4-10.   ROLL AND WIN

You begin the game *Roll and Win* by picking a number. Then you roll two regular dice, each numbered 1 through 6, and *add* the numbers that come up together. If the sum is the number you chose, you win a point. For example, if you choose "11," and a 6 and a 5 are rolled, you win!

a.   What is the sample space, which can be thought of as the set of all the possible outcomes, when two dice are rolled and their numbers added?

b.   One way to analyze this situation is to make a model of all the possible outcomes like the one at right. Copy and complete this table of sums on your paper. Are each of the outcomes in this table equally likely?

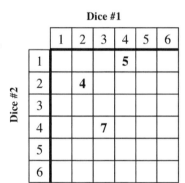

c.   What is P(even)? P(10)? P(15)?

d.   Which sum is the most likely result? What is the probability of rolling that sum?

4-11.   The temperature in San Antonio, Texas is currently 77°F and is increasing by 3° per hour. The current temperature in Bombay, India is 92°F and the temperature is dropping by 2° per hour. When will it be as hot in San Antonio as it is in Bombay? What will the temperature be?

4.1.2 How important is the angle?

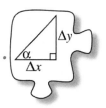

Connecting Slope Ratios to Specific Angles

In Lesson 4.1.1, you started **trigonometry**, the study of the measures of triangles. As you continue to investigate right triangles with your team today, use the following questions to guide your discussion:

What do I know about this triangle?

How does this triangle relate to other triangles?

Which part is Δx? Which part is Δy?

4-12.   What do you know about this triangle? To what other triangles does it relate? Use any information you have to solve for y.

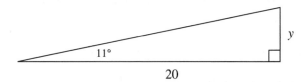

4-13.   For each triangle below, find the missing angle or side length. Use your work from Lesson 4.1.1 to help you.

a.

b.
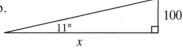

c.
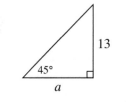

d.

e.
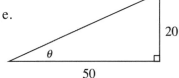

f.
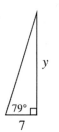

4-14. Sheila says the triangle in part (f) of problem 4-13 is the same as her drawing at right.

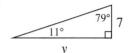

a. Do you agree? Use tracing paper to convince yourself of your conclusion.

b. Use what you know about the slope ratio of 11° to find the slope ratio for 79°.

c. What is the relationship of 11° and 79°? What is the relationship between their slope ratios?

4-15. For what other angles can you find the slope ratios based on the work you did in Lesson 4.1.1?

a. For example, since you know the slope ratio for 22°, what other angle do you know the slope ratio for? Use tracing paper to find a slope ratio for the complement of each slope angle you know. Use tracing paper to help re-orient the triangle if necessary.

b. Use this information to find x in the diagram at right.

c. Write a conjecture about the relationship of the slope ratios for complementary angles. You may want to start with, "*If one angle of a right triangle has the slope ratio $\frac{a}{b}$, then …*"

4-16. BUILDING A TRIGONOMETRY TABLE TOOLKIT

So far you have looked at several similar slope triangles and their corresponding slope ratios. These relationships will be very useful for finding missing side lengths or angle measures of right triangles for the rest of this chapter.

Before you forget this valuable information, organize information about the triangles and ratios you have discovered so far in the table on the Lesson 4.1.2 ("Trig Table Toolkit") Resource Page provided by your teacher. Keep it in a safe place for future reference. Include all of the angles you have studied up to this point. An example for 11° is filled in on the table to get you started.

METHODS AND MEANINGS

Slope Ratios and Angles

In Lesson 4.1.1, you discovered that certain slope angles produce slope triangles with special ratios. Below are the triangles you have studied so far. Note that the angles below are rounded to the nearest degree.

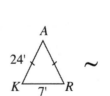

4-17. Use your Trig Table Toolkit from problem 4-16 to help you find the value of each variable below.

a.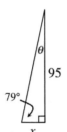

b.

c.

4-18. The triangles shown at right are similar.

a. What is the ratio of side length *NE* to side length *AK*?

b. Use a ratio to compare the perimeters of △*ENC* and △*KAR*. How is the perimeter ratio related to the side length ratio?

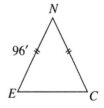

c. If you have not already done so, find the length of $\overline{EC}$.

4-19.   Examine each pair of figures below. Are they similar? Explain how you know.

a.

b.
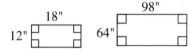

c.
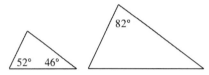

4-20.   Find the area and perimeter of the triangle at right.

4-21.   Examine the figure at right, which is not drawn to scale. Which is longer, $\overline{AB}$ or $\overline{BC}$? Explain your answer.

4-22.   Joan and Jim are planning a dinner menu including a main dish and dessert. They have 4 main dish choices (steak, vegetable-cheese casserole, turkey burgers, and vegetarian lasagna) and 3 dessert choices (chocolate brownies, strawberry ice cream, and chocolate chip cookies.)
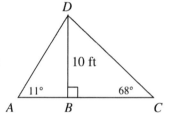

a.   Joan and Jim would like to know how many different dinner menus they have to choose from. One way to make sure you have considered the entire sample space – all the possible menu outcomes – is to make a table like the one at right. How many different menus are there?

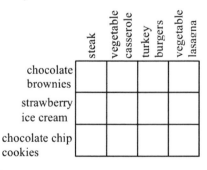

b.   Assume the main dish choice and the dessert choice are both chosen randomly. Are all the menus equally likely?

c.   What is the probability they pick a menu without meat? What is the probability they pick a menu with chocolate?

Core Connections Geometry

4.1.3 What if the angle changes?

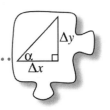

Expanding the Trig Table

In the last few lessons, you found the slope ratios for several angles. However, so far you are limited to using the slope angles that are currently in your Trig Table. How can you find the ratios for other angles? And how are the angles related to the ratio?

Today your goal is to determine ratios for more angles and to find patterns. As you work today, keep the following questions in mind:

What happens to the slope ratio when the angle increases? Decreases?

What happens to the slope ratio when the angle is 0°? 90°?

When is a slope ratio more than 1? When is it less than 1?

4-23.   On your paper, draw a slope triangle with a slope angle of 45°.

a.   Now visualize what would happen to the triangle if the slope angle increased to 55°. Which would be longer? Δy or Δx? Explain your reasoning.

b.   Using your technology tool (or the Lesson 4.1.3 Resource Page), create a triangle with a slope angle measuring 55°. Then use the resulting slope ratio to solve for x in the triangle at right. (Note: The triangle at right is not drawn to scale.)

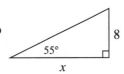

4-24.   Copy each of the following triangles onto your paper. Decide whether or not the given measurements are possible. If the triangle is possible, find the value of x, y, or θ. Use the technology tool to find the appropriate slope angles or ratios needed. If technology is not available, your teacher will provide a Lesson 4.1.3 Resource Page with the needed ratios. Round angle measures to the nearest degree. If a triangle's indicated measurement is not possible, explain why.

a.

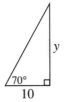

b.

c.

Problem continues on next page →

4-24.   *Problem continued from previous page.*

d.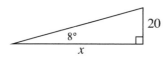

e.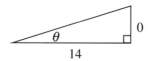

f.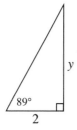

g.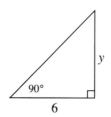

4-25.   If you have not already, add these new slope ratios with their corresponding angles to your Trig Table Toolkit. Be sure to draw and label the triangle for each new angle. Summarize your findings—which slope triangles did not work? Do you see any patterns?

4-26.   What statements can you make about the connections between slope angle and slope ratio? In your Learning Log, write down all of your observations from this lesson. Be sure to answer the questions given at the beginning of the lesson (reprinted below). Title this entry, "Slope Angles and Slope Ratios" and include today's date.

What happens to the slope ratio when the angle increases? Decreases?

What happens to the slope ratio when the angle is 0°? 90°?

When is a slope ratio more than 1? When is it less than 1?

MΕΤHODS AND MEANINGS

Sequences

A sequence is a function in which the independent variable is a positive integer (usually called the "term number") and the dependent value is the term value. A sequence is usually written as a list of numbers.

Arithmetic Sequences

In an arithmetic sequence, the **common difference** between terms is constant. For example, in the arithmetic sequence $4, 7, 10, 13, \ldots$, the common difference is 3.

The equation for an arithmetic sequence is: $t(n) = mn + b$ or $a_n = mn + a_0$ where n is the term number, m is the common difference, and b or a_0 is the zeroth term. Compare these equations to a continuous linear function $f(x) = mx + b$ where m is the growth (slope) and b is the starting value (y-intercept).

For example, the arithmetic sequence $4, 7, 10, 13, \ldots$ could be represented by $t(n) = 3n + 1$ or by $a_n = 3n + 1$. (Note that "4" is the first term of this sequence, so "1" is the zeroth term.)

Another way to write the equation of an arithmetic sequence is by using the first term in the equation, as in $a_n = m(n - 1) + a_1$, where a_1 is the first term. The sequence in the example could be represented by $a_n = 3(n - 1) + 4$.

You could even write an equation using any other term in the sequence. The equation using the fourth term in the example would be $a_n = 3(n - 4) + 13$.

Geometric Sequences

In a geometric sequence, the **common ratio** or **multiplier** between terms is constant. For example, in the geometric sequence $6, 18, 54, \ldots$, the multiplier is 3. In the geometric sequence $32, 8, 2, \frac{1}{2}, \ldots$, the common multiplier is $\frac{1}{4}$.

The equation for a geometric sequence is: $t(n) = ab^n$ or $a_n = a_0 \cdot b^n$ where n is the term number, b is the sequence generator (the multiplier or common ratio), and a or a_0 is the zeroth term. Compare these equations to a continuous exponential function $f(x) = ab^x$ where b is the growth (multiplier) and a is the starting value (y-intercept).

For example, the geometric sequence $6, 18, 54, \ldots$ could be represented by $t(n) = 2 \cdot 3^n$ or by $a_n = 2 \cdot 3^n$.

You can write a first term form of the equation for a geometric sequence as well: $a_n = a_1 \cdot b^{n-1}$. For the example, first term form would be $a_n = 6 \cdot 3^{n-1}$.

4-27. Ben thinks that the slope ratio for this triangle is $\frac{7}{10}$.
Carlissa thinks the ratio is $\frac{10}{7}$. Who is correct?
Explain your thinking fully.

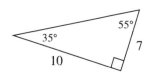

4-28. Use your observations from problem 4-26 to answer the following
questions:

a. Thalia did not have a tool to help her find the
slope angle in the triangle at right. However,
she claims that the slope angle has to be more
than 45°. Do you agree with Thalia? Why?

b. Lyra was trying to find the slope ratio for the triangle at
right, and she says the answer is $\frac{\Delta y}{\Delta x} = 2.675$. Isiah claims
that cannot be correct. Who is right? How do you know?

c. Without finding the actual value, what information
do you know about x in the diagram at right?

4-29. Examine each sequence below. State whether it is arithmetic, geometric, or
neither. For the sequences that are arithmetic or geometric, find the equation
for $t(n)$ or a_n. Refer to the Math Notes box in this lesson if you need additional
help.

a. $1, 4, 7, 10, 13, \ldots$ b. $0, 5, 12, 21, 32, \ldots$

c. $2, 4, 8, 16, 32, \ldots$ d. $5, 12, 19, 26, \ldots$

4-30. Edwina has created her own Shape Bucket and has provided the clues below
about her shapes. List one possible group of shapes that could be in her bucket.

$$P(\text{equilateral}) = 1$$

$$P(\text{triangle}) = \frac{1}{3}$$

4-31. Renae has programmed her music player
to play all five songs in her playlist in a
random order without repeating songs.

PLAYLIST

a. **I Love My Mama** (country)
by the Strings of Heaven

b. **Don't Call Me Mama** (country)
Duet by Sapphire and Hank
Tumbleweed

c. **Carefree and Blue** (R & B)
by Sapphire and Prism Escape

d. **Go Back To Mama** (Rock)
Duet by Bjorn Free and Sapphire

e. **Smashing Lollipops** (Rock)
by Sapphire

a. What is the probability that the first
song is a country song?

b. If the first song is a country song,
does that affect the probability that
the second song is a country song?
Explain your thinking.

c. As songs are playing, the number of
songs left to play decreases.
Therefore, the probability of playing each of the
remaining songs depends on which songs that
have played before it. This is an example of
events that are **not independent**. If Renae has
already listened to "Don't Call Me Mama,"
"Carefree and Blue," and "Smashing
Lollipops," what is the probability that one of
the singers of the fourth song will be Sapphire?
Explain your reasoning.

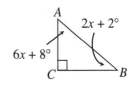

d. To get home, Renae can take one of four buses: #41, #28, #55, or #81.
Once she is on a bus, she will randomly select one of the following equally
likely activities: listening to her music player, writing a letter, or reading a
book. Her choice of bus and choice of entertainment are **independent
events**, because the bus that Renae took did not affect which activity she
chose. For example, what is the probability that Renae writes a letter if
she takes the #41 bus? What is the probability that Renae writes a letter if
she takes the #55 bus?

4-32. Use what you know about the sum of the angles
of a triangle to find $m\angle ABC$ and $m\angle BAC$. Are
these angles acute or obtuse? Find the sum of
these two angles. How can you describe the
relationship of these two angles?

A

$2x + 2°$

$6x + 8°$

C   *B*

4.1.4 What about other right triangles?

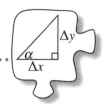

The Tangent Ratio

In Lesson 4.1.2 you started a Trig Table Toolkit of angles and their related slope ratios. Unfortunately, you only have information for a few angles. How can you quickly find the ratios for other angles when a computer is not available or when an angle is not on your Trig Table? Do you have to draw each angle to get its slope ratio? Or is there another way?

4-33. **WILL IT TOPPLE?**

In problem 4-1, you learned that the Leaning Tower of Pisa is expected to collapse once its angle of slant is less than 83°. Currently, the top of the seventh story (point A in the diagram at right) is 50 meters above the ground. In addition, when a weight is dropped from point A, it lands 5 meters from the base of the tower, as shown in the diagram.

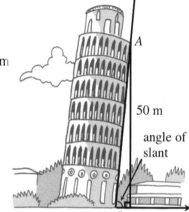

a. What is the slope ratio for the tower?

b. Use your Trig Table Toolkit to determine the angle at which the Leaning Tower of Pisa slants. Is it in immediate danger of collapse?

4-34. Solve for the variables in the triangles below. It may be helpful to first orient the triangle (by rotating your paper or by using tracing paper) so that the triangle resembles a slope triangle. Use your Trig Table for reference.

a.
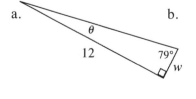

b.

c.
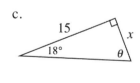

4-35.   MULTIPLE METHODS

Tiana, Mae Lin, Eddie, and Amy are looking at the triangle at right and trying to find the missing side length.

a.   Tiana declares, "*Hey! We can rotate the triangle so that 18° looks like a slope angle, and then Δy = 4.*" Will her method work? If so, use her method to solve for *a*. If not, explain why not.

b.   Mae Lin says, "*I see it differently. I can tell Δy = 4 without turning the triangle.*" How can she tell? Explain one way she could know.

c.   Eddie replies, "*What if we use 72° as our slope angle? Then Δx = 4.*" What is he talking about? Discuss with your team and explain using pictures and words.

d.   Use Eddie's observation in part (c) to confirm your answer to part (a).

4-36.   USING A SCIENTIFIC CALCULATOR

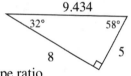

Examine the triangle at right.

a.   According to the triangle at right, what is the slope ratio for 32°? Explain how you decided to set up the ratio. Write the ratio in both fraction and decimal form.

b.   What is the slope ratio for the 58° angle? How do you know?

c.   Scientific calculators have a button that will give the slope ratio when the slope angle is entered. In part (a), you calculated the slope ratio for 32° as 0.625. Use the "tan" button on your calculator to verify that you get approximately 0.625 when you enter 32°. Does that button give you approximately 1.600 when you enter 58°? Be ready to help your teammates find and use the button on their calculators.

d.   The ratio in a right triangle that you have been studying is referred to as the **tangent ratio**. When you want to find the slope ratio of an angle, such as 32°, it is written "tan 32°." So, an equation for this triangle can be written as $\tan 32° = \frac{5}{8}$. Read more about the tangent ratio in the Math Notes box for this lesson.

4-37.   For each triangle below, trace the triangle on tracing paper. Label its legs Δy
         and Δx based on the given slope angle. Then write an equation (such as
         $\tan 14° = \frac{x}{5}$), use your scientific calculator to find a slope ratio for the given
         angle, and solve for x.

a.

b.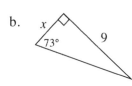

c.

4-38.   How do you set up a tangent ratio equation? How do you
         know which side of the triangle is Δy? How can you use
         your scientific calculator to find a slope ratio? Write a
         Learning Log entry about what you learned today. Be sure
         to include examples or refer to your work from today.
         Title this entry "The Tangent Ratio" and include today's date.

Ⓜ ETHODS AND MEANINGS

MATH NOTES

The Tangent Ratio

For any slope angle in a slope triangle, the ratio that compares
the Δy to Δx is called the **tangent ratio**. The ratio for any angle
is constant, regardless of the size of the triangle. It is written:

$$\tan \text{(slope angle)} = \frac{\Delta y}{\Delta x}$$

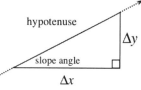

One way to identify which side is Δy and Δx
is to first reorient the triangle so that it looks
like a slope triangle, as shown at right.

For example, when the triangle at right is rotated,
the resulting slope triangle helps to show that the
tangent of θ is $\frac{p}{r}$, since θ is the slope angle, p is
Δy and r is Δx. This is written:

$$\tan \theta = \frac{p}{r}$$

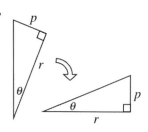

Whether the triangle is oriented as a slope
triangle or not, you can identify Δy as the leg
that is always opposite (across the triangle
from) the angle, while Δx is the leg closest to
the angle.

$$\tan \theta = \frac{\text{opposite leg}}{\text{adjacent leg}} = \frac{p}{r}$$

4-39.   Find the missing side length for each triangle. Use the tangent button on your calculator to help.

a.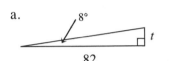

b.

c.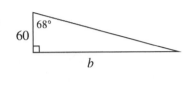

4-40.   Use the relationships in the diagrams below to write an equation and solve for x.

a.

b.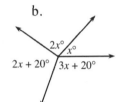

c.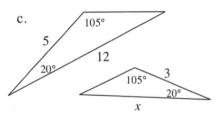

4-41.   What is the relationship of the triangles at right? Justify your conclusion using rigid transformations.

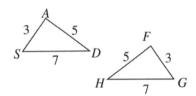

4-42.   Alexis, Bart, Chuck, and Dariah all called in to a radio show to get free tickets to a concert. List all the possible orders in which their calls could have been received.

4-43.   When she was younger, Mary had to look up at
a 68° angle to see into her father's eyes
whenever she was standing 15 inches away.
How high above the flat ground were her
father's eyes if Mary's eyes were 32 inches
above the ground?

4-44.   This problem is a checkpoint for finding areas and perimeters of complex
shapes. It will be referred to as Checkpoint 4.

For each figure below, find the area and the perimeter.

a.   Parallelogram

b.   Trapezoid

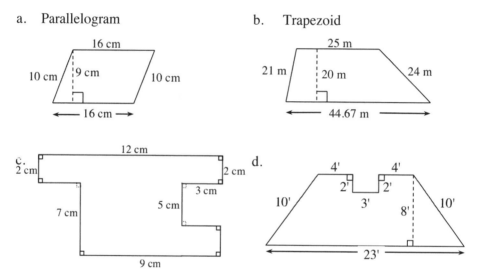

Check your answers by referring to the Checkpoint 4 materials located at the
back of your book.

Ideally, at this point you are comfortable working with these types of problems
and can solve them correctly. If you feel that you need more confidence when
solving these types of problems, then review the Checkpoint 4 materials and try
the practice problems provided. From this point on, you will be expected to do
problems like these correctly and with confidence.

4.1.5 What if I can't measure it?

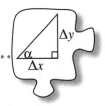

- -

Applying the Tangent Ratio

In this section so far, you have learned how to find the legs of a right triangle using an angle. But how can you use this information? Today you and your team will use the tangent ratio to solve problems and answer questions.

4-45.   STATUE OF LIBERTY

Lindy gets nosebleeds whenever she is more than 300 feet above the ground. During a class fieldtrip, her teacher asked if she wanted to climb to the top of the Statue of Liberty. Since she does not want to get a nosebleed, she decided to take some measurements to figure out the height of the torch of the statue. She found a spot directly under the torch and then measured 42 feet away and determined that the angle up to the torch was 82°. Her eyes are 5 feet above the ground.

Should she climb to the top or will she get a nosebleed? Draw a diagram that fits this situation. Justify your conclusion.

4-46.   HOW TALL IS IT?

How tall is Mount Everest? How tall is the White House? Often you want to know a measurement of something you cannot easily measure with a ruler or tape measure. Today you will work with your team to measure the height of something inside your classroom or on your school's campus in order to apply your new tangent tool.

Your Task: Get a **clinometer** (a tool that measures a slope angle) and a meter stick (or tape measure) from your teacher. As a team, decide how you will use these tools to find the height of the object selected by your teacher. Be sure to record all measurements carefully on your Lesson 4.1.5A Resource Page and include a diagram of the situation.

Discussion Points

What should the diagram look like?

What measurements would be useful?

How can you use your tools effectively to get accurate measurements?

METHODS AND MEANINGS

Independent Events

Two events are **independent** if knowing that one event occurred does not affect the probability of the other event occurring. For example, one probabilistic situation might be about a vocabulary quiz in science class today with possible outcomes {have a quiz, do not have a quiz}. Another probabilistic situation might be the outcome of this weekend's football game with the possibilities {win, lose, tie}. If you know that a quiz occurred today, it does not change the probability of the football team winning this weekend. The two events are independent.

A box contains three red chips and three black chips. If you get a red chip on the first try (and put it back in the box), the probability of getting a red chip on the second try is $\frac{3}{6}$. If you did not get a red chip on the first try, the probability of getting a red chip on the second try is still $\frac{3}{6}$. The probability of getting a red chip on the second try was not changed by knowing whether you got a red chip on the first try or not. When you return the chips to the box, the events {red on first try} and {red on second try} are independent.

However, if an event that occurred changes the probability of another event, the two events are **not independent**. Since getting up late this morning changes the probability that you will eat breakfast, these two events would not be independent.

If you get a red chip on the first try, and *do not put the first chip back in the box*, the probability of a red chip on the second try is $\frac{2}{5}$. If you did not get a red chip on the first try, the probability of getting a red chip on the second try is $\frac{3}{5}$. The probability of getting a red chip on the second try was changed by whether you got a red chip on the first try or not. When you do not replace the chips between draws, the events {red on first try} and {red on second try} are not independent.

Review & Preview

4-47.   The trapezoids at right are
          similar.

a.   What is the ratio
     of the heights?

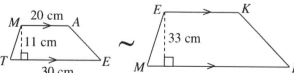

b.   Compare the areas. What is the ratio of the areas?

4-48.   For each diagram below, write an equation and solve for x, if possible.

a.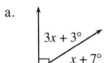

$3x + 3°$

$x + 7°$

b.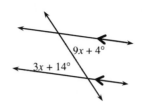

$9x + 4°$

$3x + 14°$

4-49.   Which of the following events are independent? Refer to the Math Notes in this lesson.

a.   Flipping a head, after flipping 5 heads in a row.

b.   Drawing an Ace from a deck of playing cards, after two Aces were just drawn (and not returned to the deck).

c.   Having blue eyes, if you have blonde hair.

d.   The probability of rain this weekend, if the debate team from North City High School wins the state championship.

e.   Randomly selecting a diet soda from a cooler filled with both diet and regular soda, after the person before you just selected a diet soda and drank it.

4-50.   Leon is standing 60 feet from a telephone pole. As he looks up, a red-tailed hawk lands on the top of the pole. Leon's angle of sight up to the bird is 22° and his eyes are 5.2 feet above the ground.

a.   Draw a detailed picture of this situation. Label it with all of the given information.

b.   How tall is the pole? Show all of your work.

4-51.   Examine each sequence below. State whether it is arithmetic, geometric, or neither. For the sequences that are arithmetic or geometric, find the equation for $t(n)$ or a_n.

a. $\frac{1}{2}, \frac{1}{4}, \frac{1}{8}, \ldots$

b. $-7.5, -9.5, -11.5, \ldots$

4-52.   Find the value of x in the triangle at right. Refer to problem 4-8 for help. Show all work.

$x + 3$

26

10

4.2.1 How can I represent it?

Using an Area Model

In previous courses you studied probability, which is a measure of the chance that a particular event will occur. In the next few lessons you will encounter a variety of situations that require probability calculations. You will develop new probability tools to help you analyze these situations. The next two lessons focus on tools for listing *all* the possible outcomes of a probability situation, called a **sample space**.

In homework, you have practiced determining probabilities in situations where each outcome you listed had an equal probability of occurring. But what if a game is biased so that some outcomes are more likely than others? How can you represent biased games? Today you will learn a new tool to analyze more complicated situations of chance, called an area model.

4-53.   IT'S IN THE GENES

Can you bend your thumb backwards at the middle joint to make an angle, like the example at right? Or does your thumb remain straight? The ability to bend your thumb back is thought to rely on a single gene.

Example of a thumb that can bend backwards at the joint.

What about your tongue? If you can roll your tongue into a "U" shape, you probably have a special gene that enables you to do this.

Assume that half of the U.S. population can bend their thumbs backwards and that half can roll their tongues. Also assume that these genes are independent (in other words, having one gene does not affect whether or not you have the other) and randomly distributed (spread out) throughout the population. Then the sample space of these genetic traits can be organized in a table like the one below.

a.   According to this table, what is the probability that a random person from the U.S. has both special traits? That is, what is the chance that he or she can roll his or her tongue *and* bend his or her thumb back?

b.   According to this table, what is the probability that a random person has only one of these special traits? Justify your conclusion.

Problem continues on next page →

234   *Core Connections Geometry*

4-53. *Problem continued from previous page.*

    c.   This table is useful because every cell in the table is equally likely. Therefore, each possible outcome, such as being able to bend your thumb but not roll your tongue, has a $\frac{1}{4}$ probability.

        However, this table assumes that half the population can bend their thumbs backwards, but in reality only about $\frac{1}{4}$ of the U.S. population can bend their thumbs backwards and $\frac{3}{4}$ cannot. It also turns out that a lot more (about $\frac{7}{10}$) of the population can roll their tongues. How can this table be adjusted to represent these percentages? Discuss this with your team and be prepared to share your ideas with the class.

4-54.   USING AN AREA MODEL

    One way to represent a sample space that has outcomes that are not equally likely is by using a **probability area model**. An area model uses a large square with an area of 1. The square is subdivided into smaller pieces to represent all possible outcomes in the sample space. The area of each outcome is the probability that the outcome will occur.

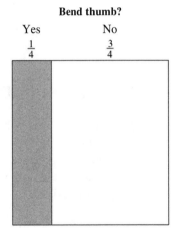

    For example, if $\frac{1}{4}$ of the U.S. population can bend their thumbs back, then the column representing this ability should take only one-fourth of the square's width, as shown at right.

    a.   How should the diagram be altered to show that $\frac{7}{10}$ of the U.S. can roll their tongues? Copy this diagram on your paper and add two rows to represent this probability.

    b.   The relative probabilities for different outcomes are represented by the areas of the regions. For example, the portion of the probability area model representing people with both special traits is a rectangle with a width of $\frac{1}{4}$ and a height of $\frac{7}{10}$. What is the area of this rectangle? This area tells you the probability that a random person in the U.S. has both traits.

    c.   What is the probability that a randomly selected person can roll his or her tongue but not bend his or her thumb back? Show how you got this probability.

4-55. PROBABILITIES IN VEIN

You and your best friend may not only look different, you may also have different types of blood! For instance, members of the American Navajo population can be classified into two groups: 73% percent (73 out of 100) of the Navajo population has type "O" blood, while 27% (27 out of 100) has type "A" blood. (Blood types describe certain chemicals, called "antigens," that are found in a person's blood.)

Navajo Person #1

	O $\frac{73}{100}$	A $\frac{27}{100}$
O $\frac{73}{100}$		
A $\frac{27}{100}$		

(Navajo Person #2)

a. Suppose you select two Navajo individuals at random. What is the probability that both individuals have type "A" blood? This time, drawing an area model that is exactly to scale would be challenging. A probability area model (like the one above) is still useful because it will still allow you to calculate the individual areas, even without drawing it to scale. Copy and complete this "generic" probability area model.

b. What is the probability that two Navajo individuals selected at random have the same blood type?

4-56. SHIPWRECKED!

Zack and Nick (both from the U.S.) are shipwrecked on a desert island! Zack has been injured and is losing blood rapidly, and Nick is the only person around to give him a transfusion.

Unlike the Navajo you learned of in problem 4-55, most populations are classified into four blood types: O, A, B, and AB. For example, in the U.S., 45% of people have type O blood, 40% have type A, 11% have type B, and 4% have type AB (according to the American Red Cross, 2004). While there are other ways in which people's blood can differ, this problem will only take into account these four blood types.

Problem continues on next page →

4-56.   *Problem continued from previous page.*

    a.   Make a probability area model representing the blood types in this problem. List Nick's possible blood types along the top of the model and Zack's possible blood types along the side.

    b.   What is the probability that Zack and Nick have the same blood type?

    c.   Luckily, two people do not have to have the same blood type for the receiver of blood to survive a transfusion. Other combinations will also work, as shown in the diagram at right. Assuming that their blood is compatible in other ways, a donor with type O blood can donate to receivers with type O, A, B, or AB, while a donor with type A blood can donate to a receiver with A or AB. A donor with type B blood can donate to a receiver with B or AB, and a donor with type AB blood can donate only to AB receivers.

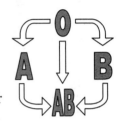

       Assuming that Nick's blood is compatible with Zack's in other ways, determine the probability that he has a type of blood that can save Zack's life!

4-57.   You made a critical assumption in problem 4-56 when you made a probability area model and multiplied the probabilities.

    a.   Blood type is affected by genetic inheritance. What if Zack and Nick were related to each other? What if they were brothers or father and son? How could that affect the possible outcomes?

    b.   What has to be true in order to assume a probability area model will give an accurate theoretical probability?

Solving a Quadratic Equation

In a previous course, you learned how to solve **quadratic equations** (equations that can be written in the form $ax^2 + bx + c = 0$). Review two methods for solving quadratic equations below.

Some quadratic equations can be solved by **factoring** and using the **Zero Product Property**. For example, because $x^2 - 3x - 10 = (x - 5)(x + 2)$, the quadratic equation $x^2 - 3x - 10 = 0$ can be rewritten as $(x - 5)(x + 2) = 0$. The Zero Product Property states that if $ab = 0$, then $a = 0$ or $b = 0$. So, if $(x - 5)(x + 2) = 0$, then $x - 5 = 0$ or $x + 2 = 0$. Therefore, $x = 5$ or $x = -2$.

Another method for solving quadratic equations is the **Quadratic Formula**. This method is particularly helpful for solving quadratic equations that are difficult or impossible to factor. Before using the Quadratic Formula, the quadratic equation you want to solve must be in standard form, that is, written as $ax^2 + bx + c = 0$.

In this form, a is the coefficient of the x^2 term, b is the coefficient of the x term, and c is the constant term. The Quadratic Formula states:

$$x = \frac{-b \pm \sqrt{b^2 - 4ac}}{2a}$$

This formula gives two possible answers due to the "$\pm$" symbol. This symbol (read as "plus or minus") is shorthand notation that tells us to calculate the formula twice: once using addition and once using subtraction. Therefore, every Quadratic Formula problem must be simplified twice to give:

$$x = \frac{-b + \sqrt{b^2 - 4ac}}{2a} \quad \text{or} \quad x = \frac{-b - \sqrt{b^2 - 4ac}}{2a}$$

To solve $x^2 - 3x - 10 = 0$ using the Quadratic Formula, substitute $a = 1$, $b = -3$, and $c = -10$ into the formula, as shown below.

$$x = \frac{-(-3) \pm \sqrt{(-3)^2 - 4(1)(-10)}}{2(1)} \implies \frac{3 \pm \sqrt{49}}{2} \implies \frac{3 + 7}{2} \text{ or } \frac{3 - 7}{2} \implies x = 5 \text{ or } x = -2$$

4-58.   Out of the 20 contestants in the state math championships, 10 are girls. For this round, each contestant gets asked one question. The first question goes to a randomly chosen contestant.

     a.   What is the probability the first contestant is a girl?

     b.   If the first contestant is a girl, what is the probability that the second contestant is a girl?

     c.   Is the probability that the second contestant is a girl independent of the first contestant being a girl? Refer to the Math Notes box at the end of Lesson 4.1.5.

4-59.   On graph paper, graph the parabola $y = 2x^2 - 5x - 3$.

     a.   What are the roots (x-intercepts) of the parabola?

     b.   Read the Math Notes box for this lesson. Then solve the equation $2x^2 - 5x - 3 = 0$ algebraically. Did your solutions match your roots from part (a)?

4-60.   Examine the graph at right with slope triangles A, B, and C.

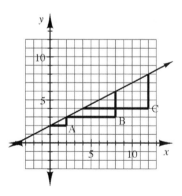

     a.   Find the slope of the line using slope triangle A, slope triangle B, and then slope triangle C.

     b.   Hernisha's slope triangle has a slope of $\frac{1}{2}$. What do you know about her line?

4-61.   Francis and John are racing. Francis is 2 meters in front of the starting line at time $t = 0$ and he runs at a constant rate of 1 meter per second. John is 5 meters in front of the starting line and he runs at a constant rate of 0.75 meters per second. After how long will Francis catch up to John?

4-62.   Solve each equation to find the value of x. Leave your answers in decimal form accurate to the thousandths place.

   a. $\frac{3.2}{x} = \frac{7.5}{x^2}$

   b. $4(x-2) + 3(-x+4) = -2(x-3)$

   c. $2x^2 + 7x - 15 = 0$

   d. $3x^2 - 2x = -1$

4-63.   Find the perimeter of the shape at right. Clearly show all your steps.

9 cm

17°

4.2.2 How can I represent it?

Using a Tree Diagram

In Lesson 4.2.1, you used a probability area model to represent probability situations where some outcomes were more likely than others. Today you will consider how to represent these types of situations using tree diagrams.

4-64.   Your teacher challenges you to a spinner game. You spin the two spinners with the probabilities listed at right. The first letter comes from Spinner #1 and the second letter from Spinner #2. If the letters can form a two-letter English word, you win. Otherwise, your teacher wins.

Spinner #1

I, U, A

$P(I) = \frac{1}{2}$
$P(U) = \frac{1}{6}$
$P(A) = \frac{1}{3}$

Spinner #2

T, F

$P(T) = \frac{1}{4}$
$P(F) = \frac{3}{4}$

a.   Are the outcomes for spinner #2 independent of the outcomes on spinner #1?

b.   Make a probability area model of the sample space, and find the probability that you will win this game.

c.   Is this game fair? If you played the game 100 times, who do you think would win more often, you or your teacher? Can you be sure this will happen?

4-65.   Sinclair wonders how to model the spinner game in problem 4-64 using a tree diagram. He draws the tree diagram at right.

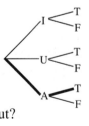

a.   Sabrina says, *"That can't be right. This diagram makes it look like all the words are equally likely."* What is Sabrina talking about? Why is this tree diagram misleading?

b.   To make the tree diagram reflect the true probabilities in this game, Sabrina writes numbers on each branch showing the probability that the letter will occur. So she writes a "$\frac{1}{3}$" on the branch for "A," a "$\frac{1}{4}$" on the branch for each "T," etc. Following Sabrina's method, label the tree diagram with probabilities on each branch.

Problem continues on next page →

4-65.   *Problem continued from previous page.*

    c.   According to the probability area model that you made in problem 4-64, what is the probability that you will spin the word "AT"? Now examine the bolded branch on the tree diagram shown above. How could the numbers you have written on the tree diagram be used to find the probability of spinning "AT"?

    d.   Does this method work for the other combinations of letters? Similarly calculate the probabilities for each of the paths of the tree diagram. At the end of each branch, write its probability. (For example, write "$\frac{1}{12}$" at the end of the "AT" branch.) Do your answers match those from problem 4-64?

    e.   Find all the branches with letter combinations that make words. Use the numbers written at the end of each branch to compute the total probability that you will spin a word. Does this probability match the probability you found with your area model?

4-66.   THE RAT RACE

Ryan has a pet rat Romeo that he boasts is the smartest rat in the county. Sammy overheard Ryan at the county fair claiming that Romeo could learn to run a particular maze and find the cheese at the end.

"I don't think Romeo is that smart!" Sammy declares, *"I think the rat just chooses a random path through the maze."*

Ryan has built a maze with the floor plan shown at right. In addition, he has placed some cheese in an airtight container (so Romeo can't smell the cheese!) in room A.

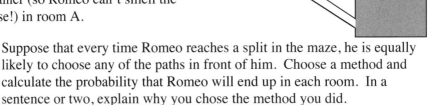

    a.   Suppose that every time Romeo reaches a split in the maze, he is equally likely to choose any of the paths in front of him. Choose a method and calculate the probability that Romeo will end up in each room. In a sentence or two, explain why you chose the method you did.

Problem continues on next page →

                  Core Connections Geometry

4-66.   *Problem continued from previous page.*

    b.   If the rat moves through the maze randomly, how many out of 100 attempts would you expect Romeo to end up in room A? How many times would you expect him to end up in room B? Explain.

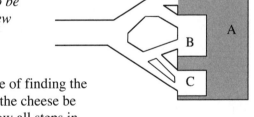

    c.   After 100 attempts, Romeo has found the cheese 66 times. Ryan says, "*See how smart Romeo is? He clearly learned something and got better at the maze as he went along.*" Sammy is not so sure.

        Do you think Romeo learned and improved his ability to return to the same room over time? Or could he just have been moving randomly? Discuss this question with your team. Then, write an argument that would convince Ryan or Sammy.

4-67.   Always skeptical, Sammy says, "*If Romeo really can learn, he ought to be able to figure out how to run this new maze I've designed.*" Examine Sammy's maze at right.

    a.   To give Romeo the best chance of finding the cheese, in which room should the cheese be placed? Choose a method, show all steps in your solution process, and justify your answer.

    b.   If the cheese is in room C and Romeo finds the cheese 6 times out of every 10 tries, does he seem to be learning? Explain your conclusion.

4-68.   Make an entry in your Learning Log describing the various ways of representing complete sample spaces. For each method, indicate how you compute probabilities using the method. Which method seems easiest to use so far? Label this entry "Creating Sample Spaces" and include today's date. Set this Learning Log aside in a safe place. You will need it in the next lesson.

4-69.   Eddie is arguing with Tana about the
probability of flipping three coins. They
decided to flip a penny, nickel, and a dime.

a.   Which would be better for determining
the sample space, a tree diagram or an
area model? Justify your answer.

b.   Make a sample space that shows all the
possible outcomes. How many outcomes are there?

c.   Find the probability of each of the following events occurring. Be sure to
show your thinking clearly:

i.   Three heads   *ii.*   One head and two tails

iii.   At least one tail   *iv.*   Exactly two tails

d.   Which is more likely, flipping at least 2 heads or at least 2 tails? Explain.

e.   How would the probabilities change if Tana found out that Eddie was
using weighted coins (coins that were not fair) so that the probability of
getting heads for each coin was $\frac{4}{5}$ instead of $\frac{1}{2}$? Would this change the
sample space? Recalculate the probabilities in part (c) based on the new
information.

4-70.   Are the triangles at right similar? If so, write
a flowchart that justifies your conclusion. If
not, explain how you know.

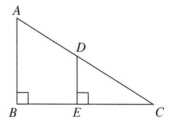

4-71.   You roll a die and it comes up a "6" three times in a row. What is the
probability of rolling a "6" on the next toss?

4-72.   Mr. Singer made the flowchart at right about a student named Brian.

   a.   What is wrong with Mr. Singer's flowchart?

   b.   Rearrange the ovals so the flowchart makes more sense.

4-73.   Write the first four terms of each of the following sequences.

   a. $a_n = 3 \cdot 5^{n-1}$

   b. $a_1 = 10$, $a_{n+1} = -5a_n$

4-74.   Find x and y in the diagram at right. Show all of the steps leading to your answer.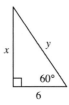

4.2.3 What model should I use?

Probability Models

In this lesson you will review ideas of probability as you use systematic lists, tree diagrams, and area models to account for all of the elements in a sample space, account for equally likely outcomes, and identify events. You will find that certain tools may work better for particular situations. In one problem a tree diagram or list might be most efficient, while in another problem an area model may be the best choice. As you work with your team, keep the following questions in mind:

> What are the possible outcomes?
>
> Are the outcomes equally likely?
>
> Will a tree diagram, list, or area model help?
>
> What is the probability for this event?

4-75.   ROCK, PAPER, SCISSORS

Your team will play a variation of "Rock, Paper, Scissors" (sometimes called "Rochambeau") and record points. You will need to work in a team of four. Have one person act as recorder while the other three play the game.

a.   List the names of the people in your team alphabetically. The first person on the list is Player A, the next is Player B, the third is Player C, and the fourth is the recorder. Write down who has each role.

b.   Without playing the game, discuss with your team which player you think will receive the most points by the end of the game. Assign points as follows:

   • Player A gets a point each time all three players match.

   • Player B gets a point each time two of the three players match.

   • Player C gets a point each time none of the players match.

c.   Now play "Rock, Paper, Scissors" with your team at least 20 times. The recorder should record the winner for each round. Does this game seem fair?

d.   Calculate the theoretical probability for each outcome (Player A, Player B, or Player C winning). Discuss this with your team and be prepared to share your results with the class.

e.   Devise a plan to make this game fair.

4-76. There is a new game at the school fair called "Pick a Tile," in which the player reaches into two bags and chooses one square tile and one circular tile. The bag with squares contains three yellow, one blue, and two red squares. The bag with circles has one yellow and two red circles. In order to win the game (and a large stuffed animal), a player must choose one blue square and one red circle.

Since it costs $2 to play the game, Marty and Gerri decided to calculate the probability of winning before deciding whether to play.

Gerri suggested making a systematic list of all the possible color combinations in the sample space, listing squares first then circles:

RY   *BY*   *YY*

RR   *BR*   *YR*

"So," says Gerri, *"the answer is $\frac{1}{6}$."*

"That doesn't seem quite right," says Marty. *"There are more yellow squares than blue ones. I don't think the chance of getting a yellow square and a red circle should be the same as getting a blue square and a red circle."*

a. Make a tree diagram for this situation. Remember to take into account the duplicate tiles in the bags.

b. Find the probability of a player choosing the winning blue square-red circle combination.

c. Should Gerri and Marty play this game? Would you? Why or why not?

4-77. Now draw a probability area model for the "Pick a Tile" game in problem 4-76.

a. Use the probability area model to calculate the probability of each possible color combination of a square and a circular tile.

b. Explain to Marty and Gerri why the probability area model is called an *area* model.

c. Discuss which model you preferred using to solve the "Pick a Tile" problem with your team. What are your reasons for your preference?

d. Could you have used the area model for the "Rock, Paper, Scissors" problem? Explain why or why not.

4-78.   BASKETBALL: Shooting One-and-One Free Throws

Rimshot McGee has a 70% free throw average. The
opposing team is ahead by one point. Rimshot is at the foul
line in a one-and-one situation with just seconds left in the
game. (A one-and-one situation means that the player
shoots a free throw. If they make the shot, they are allowed
to shoot another. If they miss the first shot, they get no
second shot. Each shot made is worth one point.)

a.   First, take a guess. What do you think is the most likely outcome for
      Rimshot: zero points, one point, or two points?

b.   Draw a tree diagram to represent this situation.

c.   Jeremy is working on the problem with Jenna
      and he remembers that area models are
      sometimes useful for solving problems related
      to probability. They set up the probability area
      model at right. Discuss this model with your
      team. Which part of the model represents
      Rimshot getting one point? How can you use
      the model to help calculate the probability that
      Rimshot will get exactly one point?

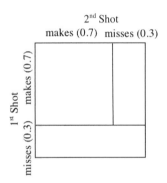

d.   Use either your tree diagram or the area model to help you calculate the
      probabilities that Rimshot will get either 0 or 2 points. What is the most
      likely of the three outcomes?

4-79.   With your team, examine the probability area model from problem 4-78.

a.   What are the dimensions of the large rectangle? Explain why these
      dimensions make sense.

b.   What is the total area of the model? Express the area as a product of the
      dimensions and as a sum of the parts.

c.   What events are represented by the entire area model?

4-80.   This Learning Log extends the entry that you made in
      problem 4-68. In that entry you described the various ways
      of representing complete sample spaces and showed how to
      use each method to find probabilities.

Expand upon your entry. Are there any conditions under which certain methods
to represent the sample space can or cannot be used? Which methods seem
most versatile? Why? Title this entry "Conditions For Using Probability
Methods" and include today's date.

METHODS AND MEANINGS

Probability Models

When all the possible outcomes of a probabilistic event are *equally likely*, you can calculate probabilities as follows:

$$\text{Theoretical probability} = \frac{\text{number of successful outcomes}}{\text{total number of possible outcomes}}$$

But suppose you spin the two spinners shown to the right. These outcomes are not all equally likely so another model is needed to calculate probabilities of outcomes.

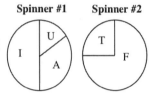

Spinner #1   **Spinner #2**

Spinner #1

	I $\left(\frac{1}{2}\right)$	**A** $\left(\frac{1}{3}\right)$	**U** $\left(\frac{1}{6}\right)$
T $\left(\frac{1}{4}\right)$	IT $\left(\frac{1}{8}\right)$	AT $\left(\frac{1}{12}\right)$	UT $\left(\frac{1}{24}\right)$
F $\left(\frac{3}{4}\right)$	IF $\left(\frac{3}{8}\right)$	AF $\left(\frac{1}{4}\right)$	UF $\left(\frac{1}{8}\right)$

Spinner #2

A **probability area model** is practical if there are exactly two probabilistic situations and they are independent. The outcomes of one probabilistic situation are across the top of the table, and the outcomes of the other are on the left. The smaller rectangles are the sample space. Then the probability for an outcome is the area of the rectangle. For example, the probability of spinning "UT" is $\frac{1}{6} \cdot \frac{1}{4} = \frac{1}{24}$. Notice that the area (the probability) of the large overall square is 1.

A **tree diagram** can be used even if there are more than two probabilistic situations, and the events can be independent or not. In this model, the ends of the branches indicate outcomes of probabilistic situations, and the branches show the probability of each event. For example, in the tree diagram at right the first branching point represents Spinner #1 with outcomes "I" "A" or "U". The numbers on the branch represent the probability that a letter occurs.

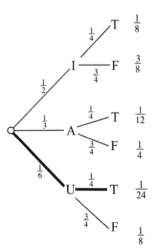

The numbers at the far right of the table represent the probabilities of various outcomes. For example, the probability of spinning "U" and "T" can be found at the end of the bold branch of the tree. This probability, $\frac{1}{24}$, can be found by multiplying the fractions that appear on the bold branches.

4-81. Eddie told Alfred, *"I'll bet if I flip three coins I can get exactly two heads."* Alfred replied, *"I'll bet I can get exactly two heads if I flip four coins!"* Eddie scoffed, *"Well, so what? That's easier."* Alfred argued, *"No, it's not. It's harder."* Who is correct? Show all of your work and be prepared to defend your conclusion.

4-82. Find the equation of the line with a slope of $\frac{1}{3}$ that goes through the point $(0, 9)$.

4-83. An airplane takes off and climbs at an angle of 11°. If the plane must fly over a 120-foot tower with at least 50 feet of clearance, what is the minimum distance between the point where the plane leaves the ground and the base of the tower?

a. Draw and label a diagram for this situation.

b. What is the minimum distance between the point where the plane leaves the ground and the tower? Explain completely.

4-84. Solve each equation below for the given variable. Show all work and check your answer.

a. $\sqrt{x} - 5 = 2$

b. $-4(-2 - x) = 5x + 6$

c. $\frac{5}{x-2} = \frac{3}{2}$

d. $x^2 + 4x - 5 = 0$

4-85. Can a triangle be made with sides of length 7, 10, and 20 units? Justify your answer.

4-86. According to the graph at right, how much money would it cost to speak to an attorney for 2 hours and 25 minutes?

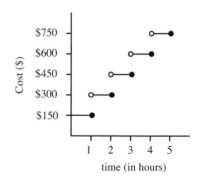

4.2.4 What if both events happen?

Unions, Intersections, and Complements

In the mid 1600's, a French nobleman, the Chevalier de Mere, was wondering why he was losing money on a bet that he thought was a sure winner. He asked the mathematician Blaise Pascal, who consulted with another mathematician, Pierre de Fermat. Together they solved the problem, and this work provided a beginning for the development of probability theory. Since argument over the analysis of a dice game provided a basis for the study of this important area of mathematics, casino games are a reasonable place to continue to investigate and clarify the ideas and language of probability.

As one of the simplest casino games to analyze, roulette is a good place to start. In American roulette the bettor places a bet, the croupier (game manager) spins the wheel and drops the ball and then everyone waits for the ball to land in one of 38 slots. The 38 slots on the wheel are numbered $00, 0, 1, 2, 3, \ldots$, 36. Eighteen of the numbers are red and eighteen are black; 0 and 00 are green. (In French roulette, also known as Monte Carlo, there is no 00, so there are only 37 slots on the wheel.)

Before the ball is dropped, players place their chips on the roulette layout, shown at right. Bets can be placed on:

- A single number;
- Two numbers by placing the chip on the line between them;
- Three numbers by placing a chip on the line at the edge of a row of three;
- Four numbers by placing the chip where the four corners meet;
- Five numbers $(0, 00, 1, 2, 3)$;
- Six numbers by placing the bet at an intersection at the edge;
- A column, the 1st twelve, 2nd twelve, or 3rd twelve;
- Even numbers;
- Odd numbers;
- 1-18;
- 19-36;
- Red numbers; or,
- Black numbers

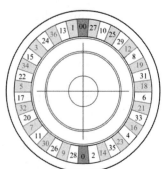

Note: The lightly shaded numbers, $1, 3, 5, 7, 9, 12, 14,$ $16, 18, 19, 21, 23, 25, 27, 30, 32, 34,$ and 36 are red.

4-87.   Obtain a Lesson 4.2.4A Resource Page from your teacher. On the resource
page, the "chips" A through K represent possible bets that could be made.

    a.   What is the sample space for one spin of the roulette wheel?

    b.   Are the outcomes equally likely?

    c.   A subset (smaller set) of outcomes from the sample space is called an
event. For example, chip A represents the event {30}, and chip B
represents the event {22, 23}. Make a list of events and their probabilities
for Chips A-K.

4-88.   Some roulette players like to make two (or more) bets
at the same time. A bettor places a chip on the event
{7, 8, 10, 11} and then another chip on the event
{10, 11, 12, 13, 14, 15}. What numbers will allow the
bettor to win both bets? Next find the bettor's chances
of winning the bet of the first chip *and* winning the bet
of the second chip on a single drop of the roulette ball.
This is called the probability of the ball landing on a
number that is in the **intersection** of the two events.

4-89.   When placing two different bets, most players are just hoping that they will win
on one *or* the other of the two events. The player is betting on the **union** of two
events.

    a.   Calculate the probability of winning either the bet on the event
{7, 8, 10, 11} *or* the bet on the event {10, 11, 12, 13, 14, 15}. Think about
the set of outcomes that will allow the bettor to win either of the bets. This
set of outcomes is the union of the two events.

    b.   Calculate the probability of the union of {numbers in first column} and
{"2nd 12" numbers 13 through 24}.

    c.   One bettor's chip is on the event {13, 14, 15, 16, 17, 18} and another on
{Reds}. What is the probability of the union of these events?

    d.   Explain your method for finding the probabilities in parts (a) through (c).

Core Connections Geometry

4-90.   Viola described the following method for finding the probability for part (a) of problem 4-89:

"When I looked at the probability of either of two events, I knew that would include all of the numbers in both events, but sometimes some numbers might be counted twice. So, instead of just counting up all of the outcomes, I added the two probabilities together and then subtracted the probability of the overlapping events or numbers. So it's just $\frac{4}{38} + \frac{6}{38} - \frac{2}{38} = \frac{8}{38}$."

Does Viola's method always work? Why or why not? Is this the method that you used to do problem 4-89? If not show how to use Viola's method on one of the other parts of problem 4-89.

4-91.   Viola's method of "adding the two probabilities and subtracting the probability of the overlapping event" is called the **Addition Rule** and can be written:

$P(A \ or \ B) = P(A) + P(B) - P(A \ and \ B)$

You have already seen that any event that includes event A *or* event B can be called a union, and is said "A union B." The event where both events A *and* B occur together is called an intersection. So the Addition Rule can also be written:

$P(A \ union \ B) = P(A) + P(B) - P(A \ intersection \ B)$

Use these ideas to do the following: A player places a chip on the event {1-18} and another on the event {Reds}. Consider the event {1-18} as event "A", and the event {Reds} as event "B." Clearly show two different ways to figure out the probability of the player winning one of the two bets.

4-92.   On the Lesson 4.2.4A Resource Page, consider a player who puts a chip on both events "G" and "I."

a.   How does the event {G *or* I} differ from the event {G *and* I}?

b.   List the set of outcomes for the intersection of events G and I, and the set of outcomes for the union of events G or I.

c.   Is the player who puts a chip on both G and I betting on the "or" or the "and?" Use both the counting method and the Addition Rule to find the probability that this player will win.

4-93.   Wyatt places a bet on event G.

    a.   What is the probability that he will lose?

    b.   How did you calculate the probability of {not event G}?

    c.   Show another method for calculating the probability of the bettor losing on event G.

4-94.   Sometimes it is easier to figure out the probability that something will *not* happen than the probability that it *will*. When finding the probability that something will not happen, you are looking at the **complement** of an event. The complement is the set of all outcomes in the sample space that are not included in the event.

Show two ways to solve the problem below, then decide which way you prefer and explain why.

    a.   Crystal is spinning the spinner at right and claims she has a good chance of having the spinner land on red at least once in three tries. What is the probability that the spinner will land on red at least once in three tries?

    b.   If the probability of an event A is represented symbolically as P(A), how can you symbolically represent the probability of the complement of event A?

METHODS AND MEANINGS

Unions, Intersections, and Complements

MATH NOTES

A smaller set of outcomes from a sample space is called an **event**. For example, if you draw one card from a standard deck of 52 cards, the sample space would be {A♠, A♣, A♥, A♦, 2♠, 2♣, 2♥, 2♦, … , K♠, K♣, K♥, K♦}. An event might be {drawing a spade}, which would be set {A♠, 2♠, 3♠, … , Q♠, K♠}. The event {drawing a face card} is the set {J♠, J♣, J♥, J♦, Q♠, Q♣, Q♥, Q♦, K♠, K♣, K♥, K♦}.

The **complement** of an event is all the outcomes in the sample space that are not in the original event. For example, the complement of {drawing a spade} would be all the hearts, diamonds, and clubs, represented as the complement of {drawing a spade} = {A♥, 2♥, 3♥, …, Q♥, K♥, A♦, 2♦, 3♦, … , Q♦, K♦, A♣, 2♣, 3♣, … , Q♣, K♣}.

The **intersection** of two events is the event in which *both* the first event *and* the second event occur. The intersection of the events {drawing a spade} and {face card} would be {J♠, Q♠, K♠} because these three cards are in both the event {drawing a spade} *and* the event {face card}.

The **union** of two events is the event in which the first event *or* the second event (or both) occur. The union of the events {drawing a spade} or a {face card} is {A♠, 2♠, 3♠, 4♠, 5♠, 6♠, 7♠, 8♠, 9♠, 10♠, J♠, Q♠, K♠, J♣, J♥, J♦, Q♣, Q♥, Q♦, K♣, K♥, K♦}. This event has 22 outcomes.

The probability of *equally likely* events can be found by:

$$P(\text{event}) = \frac{\text{number of successful outcomes}}{\text{total number of possible outcomes}}$$

The probability of {drawing a spade} or {drawing a face card} is $\frac{22}{52}$ because there are 22 cards in the union and 52 cards in the sample space.

Math Notes box continues on next page →

METHODS AND MEANINGS

Unions, Intersections, and Complements

Alternatively, the probability of the union of two events can be found by using the **Addition Rule**:

$$P(A \text{ or } B) = P(A) + P(B) - P(A \text{ and } B)$$

or

$$P(A \text{ union } B) = P(A) + P(B) - P(A \text{ intersection } B)$$

If you let event A be {drawing a spade} and event B be {drawing a face card}, $P(A) = P(\text{spade}) = \frac{13}{52}$, $P(B) = P(\text{face card}) = \frac{12}{52}$, $P(A \text{ and } B) = P(\text{spade and face card}) = \frac{3}{52}$.

Then, the probability of drawing a spade *or* a face card is:

$$P(A \text{ or } B) = P(A) + P(B) - P(A \text{ and } B) = \frac{13}{52} + \frac{12}{52} - \frac{3}{52} = \frac{22}{52}.$$

4-95.   Use an area model, a tree diagram, or refer to the table you created in problem 4-10 that represents the sample space for the sum of the numbers when rolling two standard six-sided dice.

a.   In a standard casino dice game the roller wins on the first roll if he rolls a sum of 7 or 11. What is the probability of winning on the first roll?

b.   The player loses on the first roll if he rolls a sum of 2, 3, or 12. What is the probability of losing on the first roll?

c.   If the player rolls any other sum, he continues to roll the dice until the first sum he rolled comes up again or until he rolls a 7, whichever happens sooner. What is the probability that the game continues after the first roll?

256   *Core Connections Geometry*

4-96.   A player in the casino dice game described in problem 4-10 rolled a sum of 6 on his first roll. He will win if he rolls a sum of six on the second roll but lose if he rolls a sum of seven. If anything else happens they ignore the result and he gets to roll again.

   a.   How many ways are there to get a sum of six?

   b.   How many ways are there to get a sum of seven?

   c.   How many possible outcomes are important in this problem?

   d.   What is the probability of getting a sum of six before a sum of seven?

4-97.   For each diagram below, solve for x. Name the relationship(s) you used. Show all work.

   a.

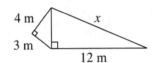

   b.

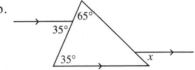

4-98.   The area of the rectangle shown at right is 40 square units. Write and solve an equation to find x. Then find the dimensions of the rectangle.

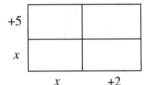

4-99.   Based on the measurements provided for each triangle below, decide if the angle θ must be more than, less than, or equal to 45°. Assume the diagram is not drawn to scale. Show how you know.

   a.

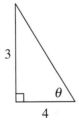

   b.

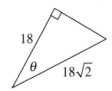

   c.

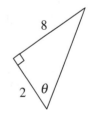

4-100.   Find the slope of the line through the points $(-5, 86)$ and $(95, 16)$. Then find at least one more point on the line.

4.2.5 How much can I expect to win?

Expected Value

Different cultures have developed creative forms of games of chance. For example, native Hawaiians play a game called Konane, which uses markers and a board and is similar to checkers. Native Americans play a game called To-pe-di, in which tossed sticks determine how many points a player receives.

When designing a game of chance, attention must be given to make sure the game is fair. If the game is not fair, or if there is not a reasonable chance that someone can win, no one will play the game. In addition, if the game has prizes involved, care needs to be taken so that prizes will be distributed based on their availability. In other words, if you only want to give away one grand prize, you want to make sure the game is not set up so that 10 people win the grand prize!

Today your team will analyze different games to learn about expected value, which helps to predict the result of a game of chance.

4-101.   TAKE A SPIN

Consider the following game: After you spin the wheel at right, you win the amount spun.

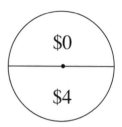

a.   If you play the game 10 times, how much money would you expect to win? What if you played the game 30 times? 100 times? Explain your process.

b.   What if you played the game *n* times? Write an equation for how much money someone can expect to win after playing the game *n* times.

c.   If you were to play only once, what would you expect to earn according to your equation in part (b)? Is it actually possible to win that amount? Explain why or why not.

4-102.   What if the spinner looks like the one at right instead?

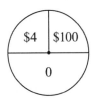

a.   If you win the amount that comes up on each spin, how much would you expect to win after 4 spins? What about after 100 spins?

b.   Find this spinner's **expected value**. That is, what is the expected amount you will win for each spin? Be ready to justify your answer.

c.   Gustavo describes his thinking this way: *"Half the time, I'll earn nothing. One-fourth the time, I'll earn $4 and the other one-fourth of the time I'll earn $100. So, for one spin, I can expect to win* $\frac{1}{2}(0)+\frac{1}{4}(\$4)+\frac{1}{4}(\$100)$." Calculate Gustavo's expression. Does his result match your result from part (b)?

4-103.   Jesse has created the spinner at right. This time, if you land on a positive number, you win that amount of money. However, if you land on a negative number, you lose that amount of money! Want to try it?

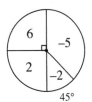

a.   Before analyzing the spinner, predict whether a person would win money or lose money after many spins.

b.   Now calculate the actual expected value. How does the result compare to your estimate from part (a)?

c.   What would the expected value be if this spinner were fair? Discuss this with your team. What does it mean for a spinner to be fair?

d.   How could you change the spinner to make it fair? Draw your new spinner and show why it is fair.

4-104.   DOUBLE SPIN

"Double Spin" is a new game. The player gets to spin a spinner
twice, but wins only if the same amount comes up both times.
The $100 sector is $\frac{1}{8}$ of the circle.

a.   Use an area model or tree diagram to show the sample space and
      probability of each outcome of two spins and then answer the following
      questions.

b.   What is the expected value when playing this game? That is, what is the
      average amount of money the carnival should expect to pay to players each
      turn over a long period of time?

c.   If it costs $3.00 for you to play this game, should you expect to break even
      in the long run?

d.   Is this game fair?

4-105.   BASKETBALL: Shooting One-and-One Free Throws Revisited

Recall the One-and-One situation from problem 4-78.
In this problem, Dunkin' Delilah Jones has a 60% free
throw average.

a.   Use an appropriate model to represent the sample
      space and then find what would be the most likely
      result when she shoots a one-and-one.

b.   Is it more likely that Delilah would make no
      points or that she would score some points?
      Explain.

c.   On average, how many points would you expect Dunkin' Delilah to make
      in a one and one free throw situation? That is, what is the expected value?

d.   Repeat part (a) for at least three other possible free throw percentages,
      making a note of the most likely outcome for each one.

e.   Is there a free throw percentage that would make two points and zero
      points equally likely outcomes? If so, find this percentage.

f.   If you did not already do so, draw an area model or tree diagram for
      part (e) using x as the percentage and write an equation to represent the
      problem. Write the solution to the equation in simplest radical form.

4-106.   Janine's teacher has presented her with an opportunity to raise her grade: She can roll a special die and possibly gain points. If a positive number is rolled, Janine gains the number of points indicated on the die. However, if a negative roll occurs, then Janine loses that many points.

Janine does not know what to do! The die, formed when the net at right is folded, offers four sides that will increase her number of points and only two sides that will decrease her grade. She needs your help to determine if this die is fair.

a.   What are the qualities of a fair game? How can you tell if a game is fair? Discuss this with your team and be ready to share your ideas with the class.

b.   What is the expected value of one roll of this die? Show how you got your answer. Is this die fair?

c.   Change only one side of the die in order to make the expected value 0.

d.   What does it mean if a die or spinner has an expected value of 0?

4-107.   Examine the spinner at right. If the central angle of Region A is 7°, find the expected value of one spin two different ways. Be ready to share your methods with the class.

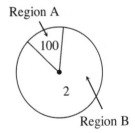

4-108.   Now reverse the process. For each spinner below, find x so that the expected value of the spinner is 3. Be prepared to explain your method to the class.

a.

b.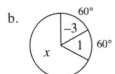

c.

4-109.   Revisit your work from part (c) of problem 4-108.

a.   To solve for x, Julia wrote the equation:

$$\tfrac{140}{360}(9)+\tfrac{40}{360}(18)+\tfrac{90}{360}(-3)+\tfrac{90}{360}\,x=3$$

Explain how her equation works.

b.   She is not sure how to solve her equation. She would like to rewrite the equation so that it does not have any fractions. What could she do to both sides of the equation to eliminate the fractions? Rewrite her equation and solve for x.

c.   If you have not done so already, write an equation and solve for x for parts (a) and (b) of problem 4-108. Did your answers match those you found in problem 4-108?

4-110.   When he was in first grade, Harvey played games with spinners. One game he especially liked had two spinners and several markers that you moved around a board. You were only allowed to move if your color came up on *both* spinners.

a.   Harvey always chose purple because that was his favorite color. What was the probability that Harvey could move his marker?

b.   Is the event that Harvey wins a union or an intersection of events?

c.   Was purple the best color choice? Explain.

d.   If both spinners are spun, what is the probability that no one gets to move because the two colors are not the same?

e.   There are at least two ways to figure out part (d). Discuss your solution method with your team and show a second way to solve part (d).

4-111.   Consider the sequence $2, 8, 3y + 5, \ldots$

a.   Find the value of y if the sequence is arithmetic.

b.   Find the value of y if the sequence is geometric.

Core Connections Geometry

4-112.   What is wrong with the
          argument shown in the
          flow chart at right?
          What assumption does
          the argument make?

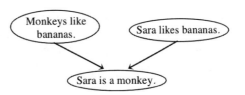

4-113.   Kamillah decided to find the height of the Empire State Building. She walked
          1 mile away (5280 feet) from the tower and found that she had to look up 15.5°
          to see the top. Assuming Manhattan is flat, if Kamillah's eyes are 5 feet above
          the ground how tall is the Empire State Building?

4-114.   What are the possible lengths for side $\overline{ML}$ in the
          triangle at right? Show how you know.

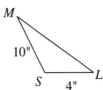

4-115.   Find the values of θ and α in the
          diagram at right. State the
          relationships you used.

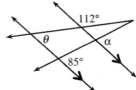

4-116.   Avery has been learning to play some new card
          games and is curious about the probabilities of
          being dealt different cards from a standard 52-card
          deck. Help him figure out the probabilities listed
          below.

          a.   What are P(king), P(queen), and P(club)?

          b.   What is P(king or club)? How does your
                answer relate to the probabilities you
                calculated in part (a)?

          c.   What is P(king or queen)? Again, how does your answer relate to the
                probabilities you calculated in part (a)?

          d.   What is the probability of not getting a face card? Jacks, queens, and kings
                are face cards.

4-117.   Woottonville currently has a population of 1532 people and is growing at a rate of approximately 15 people per year. Nearby, Coynertown has a population of 2740 people but is decreasing at a rate of approximately 32 people per year. In how many years will the towns have the same population?

4-118.   Examine the diagram at right. If $\overline{AC}$ passes through point B, then answer the questions below.

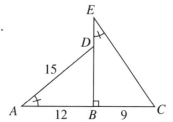

a.   Are the triangles similar? If so, make a flowchart justifying your answer.

b.   Are the triangles congruent? Explain how you know.

4-119.   Examine pentagon *SMILE* at right. Do any of its sides have equal length? How do you know? Be sure to provide convincing evidence. You might want to copy the figure onto graph paper.

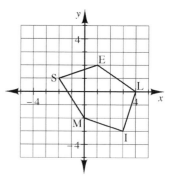

4-120.   Find the area of the triangle at right. Show all work.

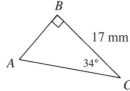

4-121.   On graph paper, plot $\triangle ABC$ if $A(-1,-1)$, $B(3,-1)$, and $C(-1,-2)$.

a.   Enlarge (dilate) $\triangle ABC$ from the origin so that the ratio of the side lengths is 3. Name this new triangle $\triangle A'B'C'$. List the coordinates of $\triangle A'B'C'$.

b.   Rotate $\triangle A'B'C'$ 90° clockwise (↻) about the origin to find $\triangle A''B''C''$. List the coordinates of $\triangle A''B''C''$.

c.   If $\triangle ABC$ is translated so that the image of point A is located at $(5, 3)$, where would the image of point B lie?

Chapter 4 Closure   What have I learned?

Reflection and Synthesis

The activities below offer you a chance to reflect about what you have learned during this chapter. As you work, look for concepts that you feel very comfortable with, ideas that you would like to learn more about, and topics you need more help with. Look for connections between ideas as well as connections with material you learned previously.

① TEAM BRAINSTORM

What have you studied in this chapter? What ideas were important in what you learned? With your team, brainstorm a list. Be as detailed as you can. To help get you started, lists of Learning Log entries, Toolkit entries, and Math Notes boxes are below.

What topics, ideas, and words that you learned *before* this chapter are connected to the new ideas in this chapter? Again, be as detailed as you can.

How long can you make your list? Challenge yourselves. Be prepared to share your team's ideas with the class.

Learning Log Entries
- Lesson 4.1.3 – Slope Angles and Slope Ratios
- Lesson 4.1.4 – The Tangent Ratio
- Lesson 4.2.2 – Creating Sample Spaces
- Lesson 4.2.3 – Conditions for Using Probability Methods

Toolkit Entries
- Trig Table Toolkit (Lesson 4.1.2 or 4.1.3 Resource Page and problems 4-16 and 4-25)

Math Notes
- Lesson 4.1.1 – Slope and Angle Notation
- Lesson 4.1.2 – Slope Ratios and Angles
- Lesson 4.1.3 – Sequences
- Lesson 4.1.4 – Tangent Ratio
- Lesson 4.1.5 – Independent Events
- Lesson 4.2.1 – Solving a Quadratic Equation
- Lesson 4.2.3 – Probability Models
- Lesson 4.2.4 – Intersections, Unions, and Complements

②   MAKING CONNECTIONS

Below is a list of the vocabulary used in this chapter. Make sure that you are familiar with all of these words and know what they mean. Refer to the glossary or index for any words that you do not yet understand.

α (alpha)	Addition Rule	angle
arithmetic sequence	clinometer	common difference
common ratio/multiplier	complement	conjecture
equally likely	expected value	fair game
geometric sequence	hypotenuse	independent events
intersection of two events	leg	non-independent events
orientation	probability	probability area model
random	ratio	sample space
slope angle	slope ratio	slope triangle
systematic list	tangent ratio	θ (theta)
tree diagram	trigonometry	union
Δx	Δy	

Make a concept map showing all of the connections you can find among the key words and ideas listed above. To show a connection between two words, draw a line between them and explain the connection, as shown in the model below. A word can be connected to any other word as long as you can justify the connection. For each key word or idea, provide an example or sketch that shows the idea.

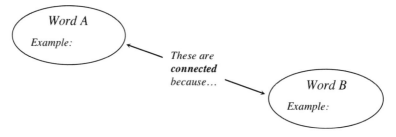

Your teacher may provide you with vocabulary cards to help you get started. If you use the cards to plan your concept map, be sure either to re-draw your concept map on your paper or to glue the vocabulary cards to a poster with all of the connections explained for others to see and understand.

While you are making your map, your team may think of related words or ideas that are not listed here. Be sure to include these ideas on your concept map.

        Core Connections Geometry

Visualization is required when you imagine a situation and want to draw a diagram to represent it. Read the descriptions below and visualize what each situation looks like. Then draw a diagram for each. Label your diagrams appropriately with any given measurements.

a.   Karen is flying a kite on a windy day. Her kite is 80 feet above ground and her string is 100 feet long. Karen is holding the kite 3 feet above ground.

b.   The bow of a rowboat (which is 1 foot above water level) is tied to a point on a dock that is 6 feet above the water level. The length of the rope between the dock and the boat is 8 feet.

Sometimes, visualization requires you to think about how an object can move in relation to others. For example, consider equilateral $\triangle ABC$ at right.

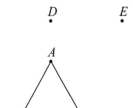

c.   Visualize changing $\triangle ABC$ by stretching vertex A to point D, which is directly above point A. What does the new triangle look like? Do you have a name for it?

d.   What happened to $m\angle A$ as you stretched the triangle in part (1)? What happened to $m\angle B$ and $m\angle C$?

e.   Now visualize the result after vertex A is stretched to point E. What type of triangle is the result? What happens to $m\angle B$ as the triangle is stretched? What happens to $m\angle C$?

An important use of visualization is to re-orient a right triangle to help you identify which leg is Δx and which leg is Δy. For each triangle below, visualize the triangle by rotating and/or reflecting it so that it is a slope triangle. Draw the result and label the appropriate legs Δx or Δy.

f. 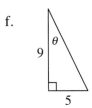   g. 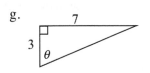   h.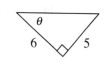

Activity continues on next page →

③ *Activity continued from previous page.*

Finally, visualization can help you view an object from different perspectives. For example, consider the square-based pyramid at right. Visualize what you would see if you looked down at the pyramid from a point directly above the top vertex. Draw this view on your paper.

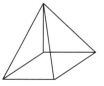

Next, showcase your understanding of probability by solving these problems. Explain your thinking in detail.

i. Harold sorted his jellybeans into two jars. He likes purple ones best and the black ones next best, so they are both in one jar. His next favorites are yellow, orange, and white, and they are in another jar. He gave all the rest to his little sister. Harold allows himself to eat only one jellybean from each jar per day. He wears a blindfold when he selects his jellybeans so he cannot choose his favorites first. Show a complete sample space. What is the probability that Harold gets one black jellybean and one orange jellybean, if the first jar has 60% black and 40% purple jellybeans and the second jar has 30% yellow, 50% orange, and 20% white jellybeans?

j. A game is set up so that a person randomly selects a shape from the shape bucket shown at right. If the person selects a triangle, he or she wins $5. If the person selects a circle, he or she loses $3. If any other shape is selected, the person does not win or lose money. If a person plays 100 times, how much money should the person expect to win or lose? If you play this game many times, what can you expect to win (what is the expected value)? Is this game fair?

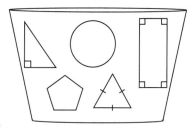

Your teacher may give you the Chapter 4 Closure Resource Page: Tangent Graphics Organizer to work on (or you can download this page from www.cpm.org). A Graphic Organizer is a tool you can use to organize your thoughts, showcase your knowledge, and communicate your ideas clearly.

④   WHAT HAVE I LEARNED?

Most of the problems in this section
represent typical problems found in
this chapter. They serve as a gauge
for you. You can use them to
determine which types of problems
you can do well and which types of
problems require further study and
practice. Even if your teacher does
not assign this section, it is a good
idea to try these problems and find
out for yourself what you know and what you still need to work on.

Solve each problem as completely as you can. The table at the end of the
closure section has answers to these problems. It also tells you where you
can find additional help and practice with problems like these.

CL 4-122.   Solve for the missing side length or angle below.

a.
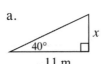

b.

c.

CL 4-123.   Use a flowchart to show how you know the triangles are similar. Then find
the value of each variable.

a.
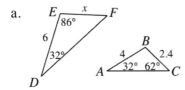

b.
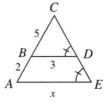

CL 4-124.   Salvador has a hot dog stand 58 meters from the base of the Space Needle in
Seattle. He prefers to work in the shade and knows that he can calculate
when his hotdog stand will be in the shade if he knows the height of the
Space Needle. To measure its height, Salvador stands at the hotdog stand,
gets out his clinometer, and measures the angle to the top of the Space
Needle to be 80°. Salvador's eyes are 1.5 meters above the ground.
Assuming that the ground is level between the hotdog stand and the Space
Needle, how tall is the Space Needle?

CL 4-125. Use the diagram at right to answer the questions below.

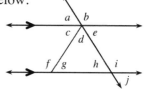

a.   State the name of the geometric relationship between the angles below. Also describe the relationship between the angle measures, if one exists.

   i. $\angle a$ and $\angle h$ ii. $\angle b$ and $\angle e$

   iii. $\angle c$ and $\angle g$ iv. $\angle g$, $\angle d$, and $\angle h$

b.   Find the measure of each angle listed below and justify your answer. Let $m\angle c = 32°$ and $m\angle e = 55°$ in the figure above.

   i. $m\angle j$ ii. $m\angle d$ iii. $m\angle a$ iv. $m\angle g$

CL 4-126. Draw a pair of axes in the center of a half sheet of graph paper. Then draw the figure at right and perform the indicated transformations. For each transformation, label the resulting image $A'B'C'D'E'$.

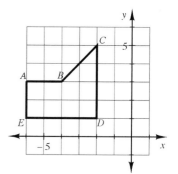

a.   Rotate $ABCDE$ 180° ↻ around the origin.

b.   Rotate $ABCDE$ 90° ↻ around the origin.

c.   Reflect $ABCDE$ across the y-axis.

d.   Translate $ABCDE$ up 5, left 7.

CL 4-127. Kiyomi has 4 pairs of pants (black, peach, gray, and cream), and she has 5 shirts (white, red, teal, black, and lavender).

a.   If any shirt can be worn with any pair of pants, represent the sample space of all possible outfits with both a probability area model and a tree diagram. How many outfits does she own?

b.   The closet light is burned out, so Kiyomi must randomly select a pair of pants and a shirt. What is the probability that she will wear something black?

CL 4-128.   In a certain town, 45% of the population has dimples and 70% has a widow's peak (a condition where the hairline above the forehead makes a "V" shape). Assuming that these physical traits are independently distributed, what is the probability that a randomly selected person has both dimples and a widow's peak? What is the probability that he or she will have neither? Use a probability area model or a tree diagram to represent this situation.

CL 4-129.   Trace each figure onto your paper and label the sides with the given measurements.

  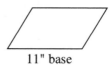 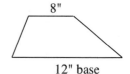

3" base   10" base   11" base   12" base

a.   On your paper, draw a height that corresponds to the labeled base for each figure.

b.   Assume that the height for each figure above is 7 inches. Add this information to your diagrams and find the area of each figure.

CL 4-130.   Find the perimeter of each shape below. Assume the diagram in part (b) is a parallelogram.

a.   b. 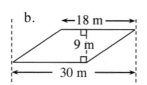   c.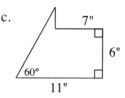

CL 4-131.   For each equation below, solve for x.

a. $\frac{x}{23} = \frac{15}{7}$

b. $(x+2)(x-5) = 6x + x^2 - 5$

c. $x^2 + 2x - 15 = 0$

d. $2x^2 - 11x = -3$

CL 4-132.   Check your answers using the table at the end of this section. Which problems do you feel confident about? Which problems were hard? Have you worked on problems like these in math classes you have taken before? Use the table to make a list of topics you need help on and a list of topics you need to practice more.

Answers and Support for Closure Activity #4
What Have I Learned?

MN = Math Notes, LL = Learning Logs

Problem	Solution	Need Help?	More Practice
CL 4-122.	a. $x \approx 9.23$ b. $x \approx 5.47$ c. $\theta = 45°$	Section 4.1 MN: 4.1.2 and 4.1.4 LL: 4.1.3 and 4.1.4	Problems 4-39, 4-63, and 4-74
CL 4-123.	a. $x \approx 3.6$ $m\angle EDF = m\angle BAC$ $m\angle DEF = m\angle ABC$ $\Delta EDF \sim \Delta BAC$ b. $x = 4.2$ $m\angle CDB = m\angle CEA$ $m\angle BCD = m\angle ACE$ $\Delta BCD \sim \Delta ACE$	Section 3.2 MN: 3.2.1, 3.2.4, and 3.2.5 LL: 3.2.2 and 3.2.4	Problems CL 3-121, 4-7, 4-41, 4-70, 4-42, and 4-118
CL 4-124.	Total height ≈ 330.4 m 80° 58 m 1.5 m not to scale	Lesson 4.1.5 MN: 4.1.4 LL: 4.1.4	Problems 4-43, 4-50, 4-83, and 4-113

Problem	Solution	Need Help?	More Practice
CL 4-125.	a. *i.* corresponding angles, congruent *ii.* straight angle pair, supplementary *iii.* alternate interior angles, congruent *iv.* triangle angle sum is 180° b. *i.* 55°: corresponding to $\angle e$ *ii.* 93°: straight angle with $\angle e$ and $\angle c$ *iii.* 55°: vertical to $\angle e$ *iv.* 32°: alternate interior to $\angle c$	Section 2.1 MN: 2.1.1, 2.1.4, and 2.2.1 LL: 2.1.1	Problems CL 2-122, 4-48, and 4-115
CL 4-126.	a. $A'(6, -3)$, $B'(4, -3)$, $C'(2, -5)$, $D'(2, -1)$, $E'(6, -1)$ b. $A'(-3, -6)$, $B'(-3, -4)$, $C'(-5, -2)$, $D'(-1, -2)$, $E'(-1, -6)$ c. $A'(6, 3)$, $B'(4, 3)$, $C'(2, 5)$, $D'(2, 1)$, $E'(6, 1)$ d. $A'(-13, 8)$, $B'(-11, 8)$, $C'(-9, 10)$, $D'(-9, 6)$, $E'(-13, 6)$	Lessons 1.2.2 and 1.2.4 MN: 1.2.2 and 1.2.4	Problems CL 1-128, CL 2-124, 3-76, and 4-121

Problem	Solution	Need Help?	More Practice
CL 4-127.	a. See diagrams below. 20 outfits b. 8 of the outcomes in the sample space contain a black item out of 20 possible outfits. $\frac{8}{20} = \frac{2}{5}$	Lessons 4.2.1, 4.2.2, and 4.2.3 MN: 4.2.3 LL: 4.2.2 and 4.2.3	Problems 4-69, 4-81, 4-95, and 4-96

shirts

pants		white	red	teal	black	lavender
	black	white shirt, black pants	red shirt, black pants	teal shirt, black pants	black shirt, black pants	lavender shirt, black pants
	peach	white shirt, peach pants	red shirt, peach pants	teal shirt, peach pants	black shirt, peach pants	lavender shirt, peach pants
	gray	white shirt, gray pants	red shirt, gray pants	teal shirt, gray pants	black shirt, gray pants	lavender shirt, gray pants
	cream	white shirt, cream pants	red shirt, cream pants	teal shirt, cream pants	black shirt, cream pants	lavender shirt, cream pants

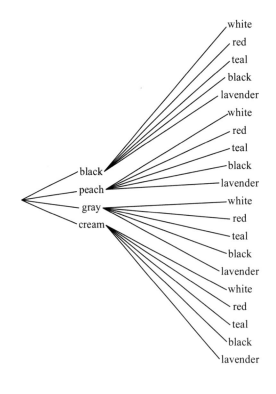

Problem	Solution		Need Help?	More Practice
CL 4-128.	P(both) = 31.5% P(neither) = 16.5%		Section 4.2 MN: 4.2.3 and 4.2.4 LL: 4.2.3	Problems 4-69, 4-81, 4-95, and 4-96
CL 4-129.	a. All heights should be 7 inches. b. 10.5", 70", 77", 70"		Section 2.2 MN: 1.1.3 and 2.2.4 Area Toolkit	Problems 4-20, 4-44, and 4-120
CL 4-130.	a. ≈ 23.899 mm b. $= 66$ m c. ≈ 32.93 inches		Lesson 4.1.3 MN: 1.1.3 and 4.1.4 LL: 2.2.2	Problems 4-20, 4-39, 4-44, 4-63, and 4-74
CL 4-131.	a. $x = 49.286$ b. $x = -\frac{5}{9}$ c. $x = 3$ or $x = -5$ d. $x = \frac{11 \pm \sqrt{97}}{4} \approx 5.21$ or 0.29		MN: 1.1.4, 2.2.2, and 4.2.1	Problems CL 1-133, CL 3-120, 4-62, and 4-84

For CL 4-128, the two-way table shows:

	Dimples? Yes	Dimples? No
Widow's Peak? Yes $\frac{70}{100}$	31.5%	38.5%
Widow's Peak? No $\frac{30}{100}$	13.5%	16.5%
	$\frac{45}{100}$	$\frac{55}{100}$

CHAPTER 5 Completing the Triangle Toolkit

In Chapter 4, you investigated the powerful similarity and side ratio relationships in right triangles. In this chapter, you will learn about other side ratio relationships using the hypotenuse that will allow you to find missing side lengths and missing angle measures for any right triangle.

In addition, you will develop tools to complete your triangle toolkit so that you can find the missing angle measures and side lengths for any triangle, provided that enough information is given. You will then explore ways to choose an appropriate tool to solve new problems in unfamiliar contexts.

Guiding Question

Mathematically proficient students use appropriate tools strategically.

As you work through this chapter ask yourself:

Which tool should I use to find missing parts of triangles?

In this chapter, you will learn:

➢ How to recognize and use special right triangles.

➢ The trigonometric ratios of sine and cosine as well as the inverses of these functions.

➢ How to apply trigonometric ratios to find missing measurements in right triangles.

➢ New triangle tools called the Law of Sines and the Law of Cosines.

➢ How to recognize when the information provided is not enough to determine a unique triangle.

Chapter Outline

Section 5.1 Students will extend their understanding of trigonometric ratios to include sine, cosine, and inverse trigonometric functions and will use these tools to find missing measurements in right triangles.

Section 5.2 Students will apply the Pythagorean Theorem and similar triangles to find patterns in special right triangles, such as 30°- 60°- 90° and 45°- 45°- 90° triangles and those with side lengths that are Pythagorean Triples.

Section 5.3 Once students investigate all of the types of information that can be given about a triangle (Lesson 5.3.1), they will focus on developing tools to find missing side lengths and angle measures in non-right triangles.

5.1.1 What if I know the hypotenuse?

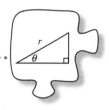

Sine and Cosine Ratios

In the previous chapter, you used the idea of similarity in right triangles to find a relationship between the acute angles and the lengths of the legs of a right triangle. However, you do not always work just with the legs of a right triangle – sometimes you only know the length of the hypotenuse. By the end of today's lesson, you will be able to use two new trigonometric ratios that involve the hypotenuse of right triangles.

5-1.   THE STREETS OF SAN FRANCISCO

While traveling around the beautiful city of San Francisco, Juanisha climbed several steep streets. One of the steepest, Filbert Street, has a slope angle of 31.5° according to her guidebook.

Once Juanisha finished walking 100 feet up the hill, she decided to figure out how high she had climbed. Juanisha drew the diagram below to represent this situation.

Can a tangent ratio be used to find Δy? Why or why not? Be prepared to share your thinking with the rest of the class.

Juanisha's Drawing

5-2.   In order to find out how high Juanisha climbed in problem 5-1, you need to know more about the relationship between the ratios of the sides of a right triangle and the slope angle.

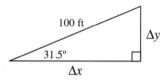

a.   Use two different strategies to find Δy for the slope triangles shown in the diagram at right.

b.   Find the ratio $\frac{\Delta x}{\text{hypotenuse}}$ for each triangle. Why must these ratios be equal?

c.   Find BC and AC in the triangle at right. Show all work.

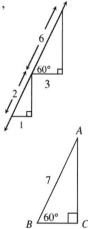

5-3.   NEW TRIG RATIOS

In problem 5-2, you used a ratio that included the
hypotenuse of $\triangle ABC$. There are several ratios that
you might have used. One of those ratios is
known as the **sine ratio** (pronounced "sign").
This is the ratio of the length of the side opposite
the acute angle to the length of the hypotenuse.

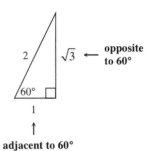

For the triangle shown at right, the sine of
$60°$ is $\frac{\sqrt{3}}{2} \approx 0.866$. This is written:

$$\sin 60° = \frac{\sqrt{3}}{2}$$

Another ratio comparing the length of the side adjacent to (which means "next
to") the angle to the length of the hypotenuse, is called the **cosine ratio**
(pronounced "co-sign"). For the triangle above, the cosine of $60°$ is $\frac{1}{2} = 0.5$.
This is written:

$$\cos 60° = \frac{1}{2}$$

a.   Like the tangent ratio, your calculator can give you both the sine and
cosine ratios for any angle. Locate the "sin" and "cos" buttons on your
calculator and use them to find the sine and cosine of $60°$. Does your
calculator give you the correct ratios?

b.   Use a trig ratio to write an equation and solve for
a in the diagram at right. Does this require the
sine ratio or the cosine ratio?

c.   Likewise, write an equation and solve for b for
the triangle at right.

5-4.   Return to the diagram from Juanisha's climb
in problem 5-1. Juanisha still wants to know
how many feet she climbed vertically when
she walked up Filbert Street. Use one of your
new trig ratios to find how high she climbed.

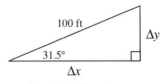

Juanisha's Drawing

5-5. For each triangle below, decide which side is *opposite* and which is *adjacent* to the given acute angle. Then determine which of the three trig ratios will help you find x. Finally, write and solve an equation.

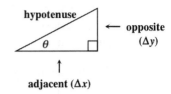

a.

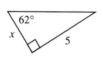

b.

c.

d.

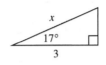

e.

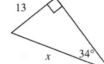

f.

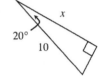

5-6. TRIANGLE TOOLKIT

Obtain a Lesson 5.1.1 Resource Page ("Triangle Toolkit") from your teacher. This will be a continuation of the Geometry Toolkit you started in Chapter 1. Think about the tools you have developed so far to solve for the measure of sides and angles of a triangle. Then, in the space provided, add a diagram and a description of each tool you know. In later lessons, you will continue to add new triangle tools to this toolkit, so be sure to keep this resource page in a safe place. At this point, your toolkit should include:

- Pythagorean Theorem
- Sine

- Tangent
- Cosine

5-7. You now have multiple trig tools to find missing side lengths of triangles. For the triangle at right, find the values of x and y. Your Triangle Toolkit might help. Which tools did you use?

5-8.   Lori has written the conjectures below. For each one, decide if it is true or not. If you believe it is not true, find a **counterexample** (an example that proves that the statement is false).

   a.   If a shape has four equal sides, it cannot be a parallelogram.

   b.   If $\tan\theta$ is more than 1, then θ must be more than 45°.

   c.   If two angles formed when two lines are cut by a transversal are corresponding, then the angles are congruent.

5-9.   **Multiple Choice:** In the triangle at right, x must be:

   a.   42°   b.   69°   c.   21°

   d.   138°   e.   none of these

5-10.   Susannah is drawing a card from a standard 52-card deck. See the entry "playing cards" in the glossary to learn what playing cards are included a deck.

   a.   What is the probability that she draws a card that is less than 5?

   b.   What is the probability that the card she draws is 5 or more? Use a complement.

   c.   What is the probability that the card she draws is a red card or a face card? Show how you can use the Addition Rule to determine this probability.

5-11.   Copy the trapezoid at right on your paper. Then find its area and perimeter. Keep your work organized so that you can later explain how you solved it. (Note: The diagram is not drawn to scale.)

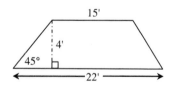

5-12.   Solve each of the equations below for the given variable. Be sure to check your answers.

   a. $4(2x+5)-11 = 4x-3$ b. $\frac{2m-1}{19} = \frac{m}{10}$

   c. $3p^2 +10p-8 = 0$ d. $\sqrt{x+2} = 5$

Core Connections Geometry

5.1.2 Which tool should I use?

Selecting a Trig Tool

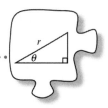

You now have several tools that will help you find the length of a side of a right triangle when given any acute angle and any side length. But how do you know which tool to use? And how can you identify the relationships between the sides and the given angle?

Today you will work with your team to develop strategies that will help you identify if the cosine, sine, or tangent ratio can be used to solve for a side of a right triangle. As you work, be sure to share any shortcuts you find that can help others identify which tool to use. Keep the focus questions below in mind.

> Is this triangle familiar? Is there something special about this triangle?
>
> Which side is opposite the given angle? Which is adjacent?
>
> Which tool should I use?

5-13.   Obtain the Lesson 5.1.2 Resource Page from your teacher. On it, find the triangles shown below. Note: the diagrams are not drawn to scale.

$$\cos \theta = \frac{\text{adj}}{\text{hyp}}$$

$$\sin \theta = \frac{\text{opp}}{\text{hyp}}$$

$$\tan \theta = \frac{\text{opp}}{\text{adj}}$$

With your study team:

- Look through all the triangles first and see if any look familiar or are ones that you know how to answer right away without using a trigonometric tool.

- Then, for all the other triangles, identify which tool you should use based on where the **reference angle** (the given acute angle) is located and which side lengths are involved.

- Write and solve an equation to find the missing side length.

a.

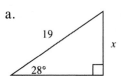

b.

c.

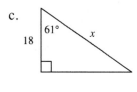

Problem continues on next page →

5-13.   *Problem continued from previous page.*

d.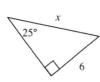

e.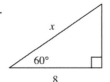

f.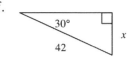

g.

h.

i.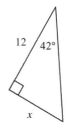

5-14.   Marta arrived for her geometry test only to find that she forgot her calculator. She decided to complete as much of each problem as possible.

a.   In the first problem on the test, Marta was asked to find the length x in the triangle shown at right. Using her algebra skills, she wrote and solved an equation. Her work is shown below. Explain what she did in each step.

$$\sin 25° = \frac{29}{x}$$
$$x(\sin 25°) = 29$$
$$x = \frac{29}{\sin 25°}$$

b.   Marta's answer in part (a) is called an exact answer. Now use your calculator to help Marta find the approximate length of x.

c.   Marta's teammate, Ziv, said he solved it differently but still got the same answer. He started with the equation $\cos(65°) = \frac{29}{x}$. Explain why this equation must give the same answer.

d.   Solve for y in the diagram at right two ways, using both sine and cosine ratios. Make sure both strategies result in the same answer.

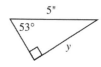

Core Connections Geometry

5-15.   In problem 5-13, you used trigonometric tools to find a side length. But do you
         have a way to find an angle? Examine the triangles below. Do any of them
         look familiar? How can you use information about the side lengths to help you
         figure out the reference angle (θ)? Your Trig Table Toolkit from Chapter 4
         may be useful.

a.

b.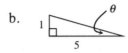

c.

5-16.   LEARNING LOG

         Write a Learning Log entry explaining how you know
         which trigonometric tool to use. Be sure to include
         examples with diagrams and anything else that would be
         useful to refer to later. Title this entry, "Choosing a Trig
         Tool" and label it with today's date.

METHODS AND **M**EANINGS

Trigonometric Ratios

MATH NOTES

You now have three **trigonometric ratios** you can use to solve
for the missing side lengths and angle measurements in any right
triangle. In the triangle below, when the sides are described
relative to the angle θ, the opposite leg is y and the adjacent leg
is x. The hypotenuse is h regardless of which acute angle is used.

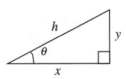

$$\tan \theta = \frac{\text{opposite leg}}{\text{adjacent leg}} = \frac{y}{x}$$

$$\sin \theta = \frac{\text{opposite leg}}{\text{hypotenuse}} = \frac{y}{h}$$

$$\cos \theta = \frac{\text{adjacent leg}}{\text{hypotenuse}} = \frac{x}{h}$$

In some cases, you may want to rotate the triangle so
that it looks like a slope triangle in order to easily
identify the reference angle θ, the opposite leg y, the
adjacent leg x, and the hypotenuse h. Instead of
rotating the triangle, some people identify the opposite
leg as the leg that is always opposite (not touching)
the angle. For example, in the diagram at right, y is
the leg opposite angle θ.

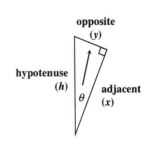

5-17.   For each triangle below, write an equation relating the reference angle (the given acute angle) with the two side lengths of the right triangle. Then solve your equation for x.

a.
22°
17
x

b.
x 49°
7

c.
6
60°
x

5-18.   While shopping at his local home improvement store, Chen noticed that the directions for an extension ladder state, "*This ladder is most stable when used at a 75° angle with the ground.*" He wants to buy a ladder to paint a two-story house that is 26 feet high. How long does his ladder need to be? Draw a diagram and set up an equation for this situation. Show all work.

5-19.   Examine each sequence below. State whether it is arithmetic, geometric, or neither. For the sequences that are arithmetic or geometric, find the formula for $t(n)$ or a_n.

a. $100, 10, 1, 0.1, \ldots$ b. $0, -50, -100, \ldots$

5-20.   The spinner at right has three regions: A, B, and C. To play the game, you must spin it *twice*. If the game were played 80 times, how many times would you expect to get A on both spins? Use a tree diagram or area model to help you answer the question.

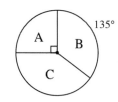

5-21.   Lori has written the conjectures below. For each one, decide if it is true or not. If you believe it is not true, find a counterexample (an example that proves that the statement is false).

   a.   If a triangle has a 60° angle, it must be an equilateral triangle.

   b.   To find the area of a shape, you always multiply the length of the base by the height.

   c.   All shapes have 360° rotation symmetry.

5-22.   Multiply each polynomial. That is, change each product to a sum.

   a. $(2x+1)(3x-2)$ b. $(2x+1)(3x^2-2x-5)$

   c. $(3y-8)(-x+y)$ d. $(x-3y)(x+3y)$

5-23.   Examine the triangles at right. Are the triangles similar? If so, show how you know with a flowchart. If not, explain how you know they cannot be similar.

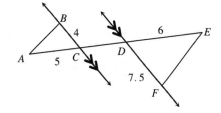

5.1.3 How can I find the angle?

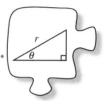

Inverse Trigonometry

You now know how to find the missing side lengths in a right triangle given an acute angle and the length of any side. But what if you want to find the measure of an angle? If you are given the lengths of two sides of a right triangle, can you work backwards to find the measurements of the unknown angles? Today you will work on "undoing" the different trigonometric ratios to find the angles that correspond to those ratios.

5-24.   Mr. Gow needs to build a wheelchair access ramp for the school's auditorium. The ramp must rise a total of 3 feet to get from the ground to the entrance of the building. In order to follow the state building code, the angle formed by the ramp and the ground cannot exceed 4.76°.

Mr. Gow has plans from the planning department that call for the ramp to start 25 feet away from the building. Will this ramp meet the state building code?

a.   Draw an appropriate diagram. Add all the measurements you can. What does Mr. Gow need to find?

b.   To find an angle from a trigonometric ratio you need to "undo" it, just like you can undo addition with subtraction, multiplication with division, or squaring by finding the square root. These examples are all pairs of **inverse** operations.

When you use a calculator to do this, you use inverse trigonometric functions which are usually labeled "**sin⁻¹**", "**cos⁻¹**", and "**tan⁻¹**". These are pronounced, "inverse sine," "inverse cosine," and "inverse tangent." On many calculators, you must press the "inv" or "2nd" key first, then the "sin", "cos", or "tan" key.

Verify that your calculator can find an inverse trig value using the triangle at right from Lesson 5.1.2. When you find $\cos^{-1}\frac{8}{16}$, do you get 60°?

c.   Return to your diagram from part (a). According to the plan, what angle will the ramp make with the ground? Will the ramp be to code?

d.   At least how far from the building must the ramp start in order to meet the building code? If Mr. Gow builds the ramp exactly to code, how long will the ramp be? Show all work.

Core Connections Geometry

5-25. For the triangle at right, find the measures of $\angle A$ and $\angle B$. Once you have found the measure of the first acute angle (either $\angle A$ or $\angle B$), what knowledge about the angles in triangles could help you find the second acute angle?

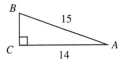

5-26. Examine the triangles below. Note: The diagrams are not drawn to scale.

  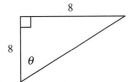

$$\cos \theta = \frac{\text{adj}}{\text{hyp}} \qquad \sin \theta = \frac{\text{opp}}{\text{hyp}} \qquad \tan \theta = \frac{\text{opp}}{\text{adj}}$$

With your study team:

- Look through all the triangles first and see if any look familiar or are ones that you know how to answer right away without using a trigonometric tool.

- Then, for all the other triangles, identify which tool to use based on where the reference angle (θ) is located and which side lengths are involved.

- Write and solve an equation to find the missing side length or angle.

a.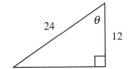
b.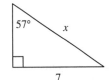
c.

5-27. Peter cannot figure out what he did wrong. He wrote the equation below to find the missing angle of a triangle. However, his calculator gives him an error message each time he tries to calculate the angle.

Peter's work: $\cos \theta = \frac{8}{2.736}$

Jeri, his teammate, looked at his work and exclaimed, "*Of course your calculator gives you an error! Your cosine ratio is impossible!*" What is Jeri talking about? And how could she tell without seeing the triangle or checking on her calculator?

5-28.   **LEARNING LOG**

Write a Learning Log entry describing what you know
about inverse trig functions. Be sure to include an example
and a description of how to solve it. Title this entry,
"Inverse Trig Functions" and label it with today's date.

─────── Review & Preview ───────

5-29.   Solve the following equations for the given variable, if possible. Remember to
check your answers.

a. $6x^2 = 150$ b. $4m + 3 - m = 3(m+1)$

c. $\sqrt{5x-1} = 3$ d. $(k-4)^2 = -3$

5-30.   Use two different trig ratios to find the measure of $\angle A$.
Did you get the same answer both ways?

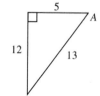

5-31.   Mervin and Leela are in bumper cars. They are at opposite ends of a 100-meter
track heading toward each other. If Mervin moves at a rate of 5.5 meters per
second and Leela moves at a rate of 3.2 meters per second, how long does it take
for them to collide?

5-32.   Assume that two standard dice are being rolled. Let event A = {the sum is a
multiple of 3} and event B = {the sum is a multiple of 4}. The $P(A) = \frac{12}{36}$ and
the $P(B) = \frac{9}{36}$.

a.   How many outcomes are in the intersection of events A and B?

b.   What is P(A or B)?

Core Connections Geometry

5-33.   Find the area and the perimeter of the figure at right. Be sure to organize your work so you can explain your method later.

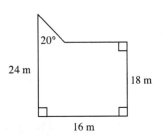

5-34.   Jerry was trying to use a flowchart to describe how his friend Marcy feels about Whizzbangs candy. Examine his flowchart below.

a.   How do you know Jerry's flowchart is incorrect?

b.   Make a flowchart on your paper with the same three ovals, but with arrows drawn in so the flowchart makes sense. Explain why your flowchart makes more sense than the one at right.

5-35.   While playing a board game, Mimi noticed that she could roll the dice 8 times in 30 seconds. How many minutes should it take her to roll the dice 150 times?

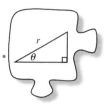

5.1.4 How can I use trig ratios?

Trigonometric Applications

Throughout this chapter, you have developed new tools to help you determine the length of any side or the measurement of any angle of a right triangle. Trigonometric ratios, coupled with the Pythagorean Theorem, give you the powerful ability to solve problems involving right triangles. Today you will apply this knowledge to solve some real world problem situations.

As you are working with your team on the problems below, be sure to draw and label a diagram and determine which trigonometric ratio to use before you start solving.

5-36.   CLIMBING IN YOSEMITE

David and Emily are climbing El
Capitan, a big cliff wall in Yosemite
National Park. David is on the ground
holding the rope attached to a
carabiner (a rope "pulley" that is on
the wall) above Emily as she climbs.
When Emily stops to rest, David
wonders how high she has climbed.
The rope is attached to his waist,
about 3 feet off of the ground, and he
has let out 48 feet of rope which goes
up to the carabiner and then back
down the wall to Emily's harness.
The rope at David's waist makes a 55°
angle with the ground and he is
standing 20 feet away from the base of
the wall.

a.   Assuming that the rope is taut (i.e., pulled tight), approximately how long is the rope between David and the carabiner above Emily?

b.   How high up the wall has Emily climbed? Describe your method.

Core Connections Geometry

5-37.   The Bungling Brothers Circus is in town and you are part of the crew that is setting up its enormous tent. The center pole that holds up the tent is 70 feet tall. To keep it upright, a support cable needs to be attached to the top of the pole so that the cable forms a 60° angle with the ground.

  a.   How long is the cable?

  b.   How far from the pole should the cable be attached to the ground?

5-38.   Nathan is standing in a meadow, exactly 185 feet from the base of El Capitan. At 11:00 a.m., he observes Emily climbing up the wall, and determines that his angle of sight up to Emily is about 10°.

  a.   If Nathan's eyes are about 6 feet above the ground, about how high is Emily at 11:00 a.m.?

  b.   At 11:30 a.m., Emily has climbed some more, and Nathan's angle of sight to her is now 25°. How far has Emily climbed in the past 30 minutes?

  c.   If Emily climbs 32 feet higher in ten more minutes, at what angle will Nathan have to look in order to see Emily?

5-39.   Forest needs to repaint the right side of his house because sunlight and rain have caused the paint to peel. Each can of paint states that it will cover 150 sq. feet. Help Forest decide how many cans of paint he should buy.

  a.   Copy the shaded diagram below onto your paper. Work with your team to find the area that will be painted.

  b.   Assuming that Forest can only buy whole cans of paint, how many cans of paint should he buy? (Note: 1 square meter ≈ 10.764 square feet)

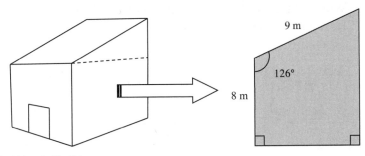

5-40.   TEAM CHALLENGE

It is 11:55 a.m., and Emily has climbed even higher. The rope now makes an angle of 6° with the cliff wall. If David is 18 feet away from the base of El Capitan, at what angle should Nathan (who is 185 feet from the base) look up to see Emily?

Ⓜ ETHODS AND MEANINGS

Inverse Trigonometry

Just as subtraction "undoes" addition and multiplication "undoes" division, the inverse trigonometric functions "undo" the trigonometric functions tangent, sine, and cosine. Specifically, **inverse trigonometric functions** are used to find the measure of an acute angle in a right triangle when a ratio of two sides is known. This is the **inverse**, or opposite, of finding the trigonometric ratio from a known angle.

The inverse trigonometric functions that will be used in this course are **sin⁻¹**, **cos⁻¹**, and **tan⁻¹** (pronounced "inverse sine," "inverse cosine," and "inverse tangent"). Below is an example that shows how $\cos^{-1}$ may be used to find a missing angle, θ.

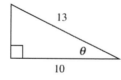

$$\cos \theta = \frac{10}{13}$$
$$\theta = \cos^{-1}\left(\frac{10}{13}\right)$$
$$\theta \approx 39.7°$$

To evaluate $\cos^{-1}\left(\frac{10}{13}\right)$ on a scientific calculator, most calculators require the "2nd" or "INV" button to be pressed before the "cos" button.

Review & Preview

5-41.   Which of the triangles below are similar to $\triangle LMN$ at right? How do you know? Explain.

a.

b.

c.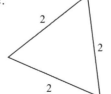

d.

Core Connections Geometry

5-42. Find the equation of the line that has a 33.7° slope angle and a y-intercept at $(0, 7)$. Assume the line has a positive slope.

5-43. Write an equation for each sequence.

a. $108, 120, 132, \ldots$

b. $\frac{2}{5}, \frac{4}{5}, \frac{8}{5}, \ldots$

c. $3741, 3702, 3663, \ldots$

d. $117, 23.4, 4.68, \ldots$

5-44. For each triangle below, write a trigonometric equation relating a, b, and θ.

a.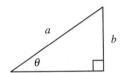

b.

c.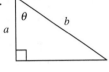

5-45. In a standard deck of 52 playing cards, 13 cards are clubs, and 3 of the clubs are "face" cards (K, Q, J). What is the probability of drawing one card that is:

a. A club or a face card? Is this a union or an intersection?

b. A club and a face card? Is this a union or an intersection?

c. Not a club and not a face card?

5-46. Estelle is trying to find x in the triangle at right. She lost her scientific calculator, but luckily her teacher told her that $\sin 23° \approx 0.391$, $\cos 23° \approx 0.921$, and $\tan 23° \approx 0.424$.

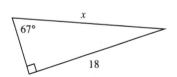

a. Write an equation that Estelle could use to solve for x.

b. Without a calculator, how could Estelle find $\sin 67°$? Explain.

5.2.1 Is there a shortcut?

Special Right Triangles

You know when triangles are similar and how to find missing side lengths in similar triangles. Today you will be using both of those ideas to investigate patterns within two types of special right triangles. These patterns will allow you to use a shortcut whenever you need to find side lengths in these particular types of right triangles.

5-47. Darren wants to find the side lengths of the triangle at right. The only problem is that he left his calculator at home and he does not remember the value of cos 60°.

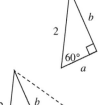

a. *"That's okay,"* says his teammate, Jan. *"I think I see a shortcut."* Using tracing paper, she created the diagram at right by reflecting the triangle across the side with length b. What is the resulting shape? How do you know?

b. What if Jan had reflected across a different side? Would the result still be an equilateral triangle? Why or why not?

c. Use Jan's diagram to find the value of a without using a trigonometric ratio.

d. Now find the length of b without a calculator. Leave your answer in exact form. In other words, do not approximate the height with a decimal.

5-48. Darren's triangle is an example of a half-equilateral triangle, also known as a 30°- 60°- 90° triangle because of its angle measures. Darren is starting to understand Jan's shortcut, but he still has some questions. Help Darren by answering his questions below.

a. *"Will this approach work on all triangles?"* In other words, can you always form an equilateral triangle by reflecting a right triangle? Explain your reasoning.

b. *"What if the triangle is a different size?"* Use tracing paper to show how Darren can reflect the triangle at right to form an equilateral triangle. Then find the lengths of *x* and *y* without a calculator.

c. *"Is the longer leg of a 30°- 60°- 90° triangle always going to be the length of the shorter leg multiplied by $\sqrt{3}$?"* Explain why or why not.

d. *"What if I only know the length of the shorter leg?"* Consider the triangle at right. Visualize the equilateral triangle. Then find the values of *n* and *m* without using a calculator.

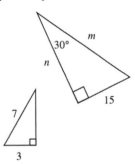

e. Darren drew the triangle at right and is wondering if it also is a 30°- 60°- 90° triangle. What do you think? How do you know?

5-49. Darren wonders if he can find a similar pattern in another special triangle he knows, shown at right.

a. Use what you know about this triangle to help Darren find the lengths of *a* and *b* without a trig tool or a calculator. Leave your answer in exact form.

b. What should Darren name this triangle?

c. Use the fact that all 45°- 45°- 90° triangles are similar to find the missing side lengths in the right triangles below. Leave your answers in exact, radical form.

5-50.   Use your new 30°- 60°- 90° and 45°- 45°- 90° triangle patterns to quickly find
the lengths of the missing sides in each of the triangles below. Do not use a
calculator. Leave answers in exact form. Note: The triangles are not
necessarily drawn to scale.

a.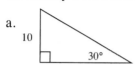

b.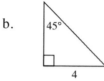

c.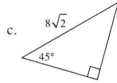

d.

e.

f.

5-51.   LEARNING LOG

In your Learning Log, explain what you know about
30°- 60°- 90° and 45°- 45°- 90° triangles. Include diagrams
of each. Label this entry "Special Right Triangles" and
label it with today's date.

METHODS AND **M**EANINGS

Rationalizing a Denominator

In Lesson 5.2.1, you developed some shortcuts to help find the lengths of the sides of a 30°- 60°- 90° and 45°- 45°- 90° triangle. This will enable you to solve similar problems in the future without a calculator or your Trig Table Toolkit.

However, sometimes using the shortcuts leads to some strange looking answers. For example, when finding the length of a in the triangle at right, you will get the expression $\frac{6}{\sqrt{2}}$.

A number with a radical in the denominator is difficult to estimate. Therefore, it is sometimes beneficial to **rationalize the denominator** so that no radical remains in the denominator. Study the example below.

Example: Simplify $\frac{6}{\sqrt{2}}$.

First, multiply the numerator and denominator by the radical in the denominator. Since $\frac{\sqrt{2}}{\sqrt{2}} = 1$, this does not change the value of the expression.

Example

$$\frac{6}{\sqrt{2}} \cdot \frac{\sqrt{2}}{\sqrt{2}} = \frac{6\sqrt{2}}{2}$$
$$= 3\sqrt{2}$$

After multiplying, notice that the denominator no longer has a radical, since $\sqrt{2} \cdot \sqrt{2} = 2$.

Often, the product can be further simplified. Since 2 divides evenly into 6, the expression $\frac{6\sqrt{2}}{2}$ can be rewritten as $3\sqrt{2}$.

5-52.   For each triangle below, use your triangle shortcuts from this lesson to find the missing side lengths. Then find the area and perimeter of the triangle.

a.

b.

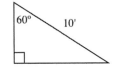

5-53. Use the relationships found in each of the diagrams below to solve for x and y. Assume the diagrams are not drawn to scale. State which geometric relationships you used.

a.

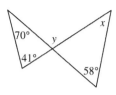

b.

c.

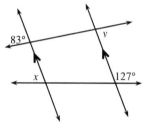

d.

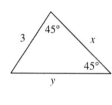

5-54. On graph paper, graph $\overline{AB}$ if $A(1, 6)$ and $B(5, 2)$.

a. Find AB (the length of $\overline{AB}$). Leave your answer in exact form. That is, do not approximate with a decimal. Explain your method.

b. Reflect $\overline{AB}$ across the y-axis to create $\overline{A'B'}$. What type of shape is $ABB'A'$ if the points are connected in order? Then find the area of $ABB'A'$.

5-55. In a random sample of 10,000 college students, a research company found that 35.7% were involved in a club and 27.8% studied 4 or more hours per day. When they reported their findings, the research company indicated that 53.4% of college students were either involved in a club or they studied 4 or more hours per day. Given this information, what is the probability that a college student is involved in a club and studies 4 or more hours per day?

5-56.   Fill in the blank ovals below so that each flowchart is correct.

a.

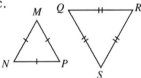

b.

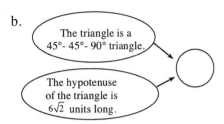

5-57.   Write an explicit equation for the following sequences.

a. $500, 2000, 3500, \ldots$

b. $30, 150, 750, 3750, \ldots$

5-58.   Decide if each pair of triangles below are similar. If they are similar, give a sequence of transformations that justifies your conclusion. If they are not similar, explain how you know.

a.

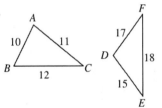

b.

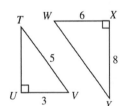

c.

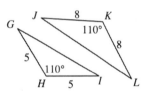

d.

5.2.2 How can I use similar triangles?

Pythagorean Triples

In Lesson 5.2.1, you developed shortcuts that will help you quickly find the lengths of the sides of certain right triangles. What other shortcuts can be helpful? As you work today with your study team, look for patterns and connections between triangles.

5-59.   Use the tools you have developed thus far to find the lengths of the missing sides of the triangles below. If you know of a shortcut, share it with your team. Be ready to share your strategies with the class.

a.
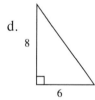

b.
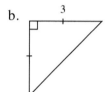

c.

d.
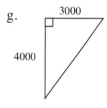

e.
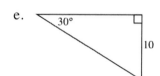

f.
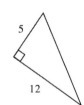

g.
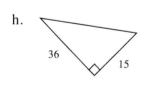

h.
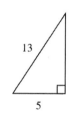

i.

5-60.   Karl noticed some patterns as he was finding lengths of the missing sides of the triangles in problem 5-59. He recognized that the side lengths of the triangles in parts (c), (d), (f), (g), (h), and (i) were integers. He also noticed that knowing the side lengths of the triangle in part (c) could help find the length of the hypotenuse in parts (d) and (g).

   a.   Groups of numbers like 3, 4, 5 and 5, 12, 13 are called **Pythagorean Triples**. Why do you think they are called Pythagorean Triples?

   b.   What other sets of numbers are also Pythagorean Triples? How many different sets can you find?

5-61.   With your team, find the missing side lengths for each triangle below. Try to use your new shortcuts whenever possible.

   a.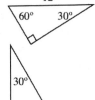

   b.

   c.

   d.

   e.

   f.

5-62.   Diana looked at the next problems and thought she could not do them. Erik pointed out that they are the same as the previous triangles, but instead of numbers, each side length is given in terms of a variable. Use Erik's idea to help you find the missing side lengths of the triangles below:

   a.

   b.

   c.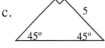

   d.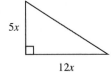

   e.

5-63.   Use your shortcuts to find the area and perimeter of each shape below:

a. 6″ 60°

b. 6√2 cm 45°

c.  8′ 5′ 3′

ⓂETHODS AND MEANINGS

Expected Value

MATH NOTES

The amount you would expect to win (or lose) per game after playing a game of chance many times is called the **expected value**. This value does not need to be a possible outcome of a single game, but instead reflects an average amount that will be won or lost per game.

For example, the "$9" portion of the spinner at right makes up $\frac{30°}{360°} = \frac{1}{12}$ of the spinner, while the "$4" portion is the rest, or $\frac{11}{12}$, of the spinner. If the spinner was spun 12 times, probability predicts that it would land on "$9" once and "$4" eleven times. Therefore, someone spinning 12 times would expect to receive $1(\$9) + 11(\$4) = \$53$. On average, each spin would earn an expected value of $\frac{\$53}{12 \text{ spins}} \approx \$4.42$ per spin . You could use this value to predict the result for any number of spins. For example, if you play 30 times, you would expect to win 30($4.42) = $132.50.

Another way to calculate expected value involves the probability of each possible outcome. Since "$9" is expected $\frac{1}{12}$ of the time, and "$4" is expected $\frac{11}{12}$ of the time, then the expected value can be calculated with the expression $(\$9)(\frac{1}{12}) + (\$4)(\frac{11}{12}) = \frac{\$53}{12} \approx \$4.42$.

A **fair game** is one in which the expected value is zero. Neither player expects to win or lose if the game is played numerous times.

5-64. The sides of each of the triangles below can be found using one of the shortcuts from Section 5.2. Try to find the missing lengths using your patterns. Do not use a calculator.

a.
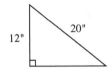

b.

c.
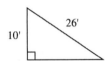

d.

5-65. Copy the diagram at right onto your paper.

a. Find the measures of all the angles in the diagram.

b. Make a flowchart showing that the triangles are similar.

c. Cheri and Roberta noticed their similarity statements for part (b) were not the same. Cheri had stated $\triangle ABC \sim \triangle DEC$, while Roberta maintained that $\triangle ABC \sim \triangle EDC$. Who is correct? Or are they both correct? Explain your reasoning.

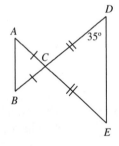

5-66. Using the triangle at right, write an expression representing $\cos 52°$. Then write an expression for $\tan 52°$ and $\cos 38°$. What other ratio is equivalent to $\cos 38°$?

5-67.   Hadrosaurs, a family of duck-billed, plant-eating dinosaurs, were large creatures with thick, strong tails. It has recently been determined that hadrosaurs probably originated in North America.

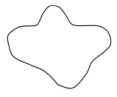

Example of a hadrosaur footprint.

Scientists in Alaska recently found a hadrosaur footprint like the one at right that measured 14 inches across. It is believed that the footprint was created by a young dinosaur that was approximately 27 feet long. Adult hadrosaurs have been known to be 40 feet long. How wide would you expect a footprint of an adult hadrosaur to be? Show your reasoning.

5-68.   A sequence starts $-3, 1, 5, 9...$

  a.   If you wanted to find the 50th term of the sequence, would an explicit equation or a recursive equation be more useful?

  b.   Write an equation that represents the sequence.

  c.   What is the 50th term of the sequence?

  d.   Write an explicit equation for the sequence $3, 2\frac{2}{3}, 2\frac{1}{3}, 2, 1\frac{2}{3}, ...$

5-69.   The probability of winning \$3 on the spinner at right is equal to the chance of winning \$5. Find the expected value for one spin. Is this game fair?

5-70.   Jeynysha has a Shape Bucket with a trapezoid, right triangle, scalene triangle, parallelogram, square, rhombus, pentagon, and kite. If she reaches in the bucket and randomly selects a shape, find:

  a.   P(at least one pair of parallel sides)   b.   P(hexagon)

  c.   P(not a triangle)   d.   P(has at least 3 sides)

5.3.1 What triangle tools do I still need?

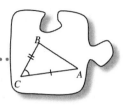

Finding Missing Parts of Triangles

When do you have enough information to find all of the angle measures and side lengths of a triangle? For example, can you find all of the side lengths if you are only informed about the three angles? Does it matter if the triangle has a right angle or not? Today you will organize your triangle knowledge so that you know what tools you have and for which triangles you can accurately find all of the angle measures and side lengths.

5-71.   How many ways can three pieces of information about
         a triangle be given? For example, the three given
         measurements could be one angle and two side
         lengths, as shown in the triangle at right. List as many
         other combinations of three pieces of information
         about a triangle as you can.

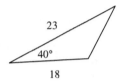

5-72.   HOW MUCH INFORMATION DO YOU NEED?

         So far in this course you have developed several tools to find missing parts of
         triangles. But how complete is your Triangle Toolkit? Are there more tools
         that you need to develop?

         Your Task: With your team, find the missing angles and sides of the triangles
         below. (Also printed on the Lesson 5.3.1 Resource Page). Notice that each
         triangle has three given pieces of information about its angles and sides. If
         there is not enough information or if you do not yet have the tools to find the
         missing information, explain why.

Discussion Points

- Are there any triangles that look familiar or that you already have a
  strategy for?

- What tools do you have to solve for parts of triangles? For what types of
  triangles do these tools work?

- Would it be helpful to subdivide any of the triangles into right triangles?

Problem continues on next page →

5-72.   *Problem continued from previous page.*

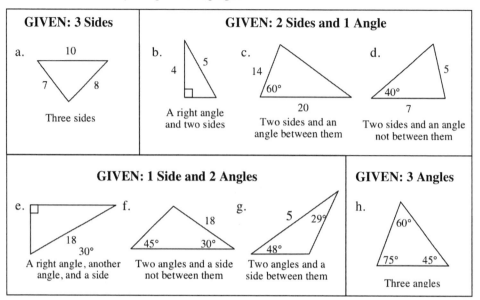

GIVEN: 3 Sides	GIVEN: 2 Sides and 1 Angle
a. 10 / 7 / 8 — Three sides	b. 4, 5 — A right angle and two sides c. 14, 60°, 20 — Two sides and an angle between them d. 5, 40°, 7 — Two sides and an angle not between them

GIVEN: 1 Side and 2 Angles	GIVEN: 3 Angles
e. 18, 30° — A right angle, another angle, and a side f. 18, 45°, 30° — Two angles and a side not between them g. 5, 29°, 48° — Two angles and a side between them	h. 60°, 75°, 45° — Three angles

Further Guidance

5-73.   While looking for different strategies to use, advice from a teammate can often help.

   a.   Angelo thinks that the Pythagorean Theorem is a useful tool. For which types of triangles is the Pythagorean Theorem useful? Look for these types of triangles in problem 5-72 and use the theorem to solve for any missing sides.

   b.   Tomas remembers using trigonometric ratios to find the missing sides and angles of a triangle. Which triangles from problem 5-72 can be analyzed using this strategy?

   c.   Ngoc thinks that more than one triangle exists with the angles at right. Is she correct? If so, how are these triangles related?

60° / 75° / 45° — Three angles

   d.   Does it matter if the triangle is a right triangle? For example, both of these triangles (from parts (b) and (d)) give an angle and two sides. Can you use the same tool for both? Why or why not?

4, 5 — A right angle and two sides   5, 40°, 7 — Two sides and an angle not between them

———   *Further Guidance*   ———
            section ends here.

Core Connections Geometry

5-74.   WHAT IF IT DOES NOT HAVE A RIGHT ANGLE?

If your team needs help on parts (c) and (f) of
problem 5-72, Leila has an idea. She knows
that she has some tools to use with right
triangles but noticed that some of the
triangles in problem 5-72 are *not* right
triangles. Therefore, she thinks it is a good
idea to split a triangle into two right triangles.

a.   Discuss with your team how to change the diagram
      at right so that the triangle is divided into two right
      triangles. Then use your right triangle tools to solve
      for the missing sides and angles.

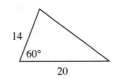

b.   Leila wonders if her method would work for other
      triangles too. Test her method on the triangle from
      part (f) of problem 5-72 (also shown at right). Does
      her method work?

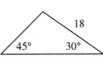

5-75.   Ryan liked Leila's idea so much that he looked for a way
         to create a right triangle in the triangle from part (g) of
         problem 5-72. He decided to draw a height *outside* the
         triangle, forming a large right triangle. Use the right
         triangle to help you find the missing side lengths of the
         original triangle.

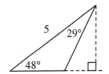

5-76.   LEARNING LOG

Return to problem 5-72 and examine all of the ways that
three pieces of information can be given about a triangle.
For which triangle(s) were you able to find missing side
lengths and angles? For which triangle(s) do you not have enough information
given? For which triangle(s) do you need a new strategy? Reflect on the
strategies you have developed so far. Title this entry "Strategies to find Sides
and Angles of a Triangle" and label it with today's date.

METHODS AND MEANINGS

Special Right Triangles

So far in this chapter, you have learned about several special right triangles. Being able to recognize these triangles will enable you to quickly find the lengths of the sides and will save you time and effort in the future.

The half-equilateral triangle is also known as the **30°- 60°- 90° triangle**. The sides of this triangle are always in the ratio $1:\sqrt{3}:2$, as shown at right.

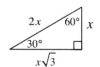

Another special triangle is the **45°- 45°- 90° triangle**. This triangle is also commonly known as an isosceles right triangle. The ratio of the sides of this triangle is always $1:1:\sqrt{2}$.

You also discovered several **Pythagorean Triples**. A Pythagorean Triple is any set of 3 positive integers a, b, and c for which $a^2 + b^2 + = c^2$. Two of the common Pythagorean Triples that you will see throughout this course are shown at right.

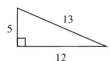

5-77.   To paint a house, Travis leans a ladder against the wall. If the ladder is 16 feet long and it makes contact with the house 14 feet above ground, what angle does the ladder make with the ground? Draw a diagram of this situation and show all work.

5-78.   WACKY DIAGRAMS

After drawing some diagrams on his paper, Jason thinks there is
something wrong. Examine each diagram below and decide
whether or not the triangle could exist. If it cannot exist, explain
why not.

a.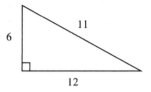

b.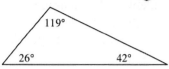

5-79.   William thinks that the hypotenuse must be the longest side of a right triangle,
but Chad does not agree. Who is correct? Support your answer with an
explanation and a counterexample, if possible.

5-80.   Plot $\triangle ABC$ on graph paper with points $A(3, 3)$, $B(1, 1)$, and $C(6, 1)$.

a.   Multiply all of the y-coordinates of $\triangle ABC$ by -1. Then use the function
$(x, y) \rightarrow (x - 6, y - 3)$ to translate the triangle. Name the coordinates of the
result.

b.   Rotate $\triangle ABC$ 90° counterclockwise (↺) about the origin. Then reflect the
result across the y-axis. Name the coordinates of the result.

5-81.   Solve the equations below, if possible. If there is no solution, explain why.

a. $\frac{8-x}{x} = \frac{3}{2}$

b. $-2(5x - 1) - 3 = -10x$

c. $x^2 + 8x - 33 = 0$

d. $\frac{2}{3}x - 12 = 180$

5-82.   **Multiple Choice:** Based on the relationships provided in
the diagram, which of the equations below is correct?
Justify your solution.

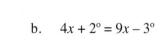

a. $4x + 2° + 9x - 3° = 90°$

b. $4x + 2° = 9x - 3°$

c. $4x + 2° + 9x - 3° = 180°$

d. $(4x + 2°)(9x - 3°) = 90°$

5.3.2 Is there a faster way?

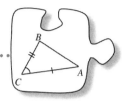

Law of Sines

In problem 5-74, you used a complicated strategy to find the lengths of sides and measures of angles for a non-right triangle. Is there a tool you can use to find angles and side lengths of non-right triangles directly, using fewer steps? Today you will explore the relationships that exist among the sides and angles of triangles and will develop a new tool called the Law of Sines.

5-83.   Is there a relationship between a triangle's side and the angle opposite to it? For example, assume that the diagram for $\triangle ABC$, shown at right, is not drawn to scale. Based on the angle measures provided in the diagram, which side must be longest? Which side must be shortest? How do you know?

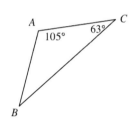

5-84.   When Madelyn examined the triangle at right, she said, "*I don't think this diagram is drawn to scale because I think the side labeled x has to be longer than 4 cm.*"

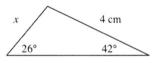

   a.   Do you agree with Madelyn? Why or why not?

   b.   Leila thinks that x can be found by using right triangles. Review what you learned in Lesson 5.3.1 by finding the value of x.

   c.   Find the area of the triangle.

5-85.   Thui and Ivan came up with two different ways to find the height of the triangle below.

   - Using the right triangle on the left, Thui wrote: $\sin 58° = \frac{h}{12}$.

   - Ivan also used the sine function, but his equation looked like this: $\sin 24° = \frac{h}{25}$.

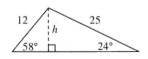

   a.   Which triangle did Ivan use?

   b.   Calculate h using Thui's equation and again using Ivan's equation. How do their answers compare?

Core Connections Geometry

5-86.   LAW OF SINES

Edwin wonders if Thui's and Ivan's methods can
be used to find a way to relate the sides and angles
of a non-right triangle. To find the height, Ivan
and Thui drew a perpendicular line from point C
to side $\overline{AB}$. Then each used the sine ratio with an
acute angle and the hypotenuse of a right triangle.

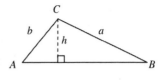

a.   Use the triangle above to find two expressions for h using the individual
right triangles like you did in problem 5-85.

b.   Use your expressions from part (a) to show that $\frac{\sin(m\angle B)}{b} = \frac{\sin(m\angle A)}{a}$.

c.   Describe where $\angle B$ is located in relation to the side labeled b. How is $\angle A$
related to the side labeled a?

d.   The relationship $\frac{\sin(m\angle B)}{b} = \frac{\sin(m\angle A)}{a}$ is called the **Law
of Sines**. Read the Math Notes box for this lesson to
learn more about this relationship. Then use this
relationship to solve for x in the triangle at right.

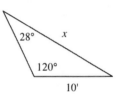

5-87.   The sine ratio can also help to find the area of
a triangle when any two side lengths and the
measure of the included angle is given.
Explore this fact below.

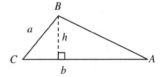

a.   Assume for the triangle above that you know the lengths of a and b and the
measure of the angle at C. Also assume that h is the height of the triangle
found by dropping a perpendicular from B to its opposite side. Write an
equation for the area of this triangle using its base and height.

b.   What if the height is unknown? Since $m\angle C$ is known, write an equation
for $\sin C$ using one of the right triangles. Solve for h.

c.   Use your equation for h in part (b) to rewrite the area equation you wrote
for part (a). You now have a relationship that you can use to find the area
of any triangle when you know two sides lengths and the measure of the
angle between them.

d.   Use your relationship from part (c) to find the area of the triangle in
part (d) of problem 5-86. Remember that you will need the measure of the
angle between the two side lengths.

5-88.   LEARNING LOG

Reflect on what you have learned during this lesson about
the sides and angles of a triangle. What is the Law of Sines
and when can it be used? Include an example. Title this
entry "Law of Sines" and label it with today's date.

MᴇTHODS AND Mᴇᴀɴɪɴɢs

MATH NOTES

Law of Sines

For any $\triangle ABC$, the ratio of the sine of an
angle to the length of the side opposite
the angle is constant. This means that:

$$\frac{\sin(m\angle A)}{a} = \frac{\sin(m\angle B)}{b},$$

$$\frac{\sin(m\angle B)}{b} = \frac{\sin(m\angle C)}{c}, \text{ and}$$

$$\frac{\sin(m\angle A)}{a} = \frac{\sin(m\angle C)}{c}.$$

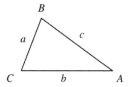

This property is called the **Law of Sines**. This is a powerful tool because
you can use the sine ratio to solve for measures of angles and lengths of sides
of *any* triangle, not just right triangles. The law works for angle measures
between 0° and 180°.

Review & Preview

5-89.   Lizzie noticed that two angles in $\triangle DEF$, shown at
right, have the same measure. Based on this
information, what statement can you make about the
relationship between $\overline{ED}$ and $\overline{EF}$?

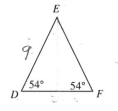

5-90.   Find the length of $\overline{DF}$ in the diagram from problem 5-89 if $DE = 9$ mm.

5-91. Find the area of the triangle at right. Show all work.

5-92. In the diagram at right, $\triangle ABC$ and $\triangle ADE$ are similar. If $AB = 5$, $BD = 4$, and $BC = 7$, then what is DE?

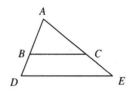

5-93. Stephen does not like yogurt very much, but he loves apples. Since both make a good snack, Stephen's mom makes a deal with Stephen. She will keep the refrigerator stocked with 5 yogurts, 2 green apples, and 3 red apples every day. Each day, Stephen will randomly pick a snack. What is the probability Stephen will *not* get three yogurts on three consecutive days? Use a tree diagram or area model to show all the possible outcomes in the sample space.

5-94. Solve each equation below for x. Check your solution if possible.

a. $\frac{4}{5}x - 2 = 7$

b. $3x^2 = 300$

c. $\frac{4x-1}{2} = \frac{x+5}{3}$

d. $x^2 - 4x + 6 = 0$

5-95. Solve the system of equations below. Write your solution as a point in (x, y) form. Check your solution.

$$y = -3x - 2$$
$$2x + 5y = 16$$

5.3.3 How can I complete my triangle toolkit?

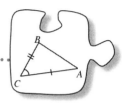

Law of Cosines

So far, you have three tools that will help you solve for missing sides and lengths of a triangle. In fact, one of those tools, the Law of Sines, even helps when the triangle is not a right triangle. There are still two triangles from our exploration in Lesson 5.3.1 that you cannot solve directly with any of your existing tools. Today you will develop a tool to help find missing side lengths and angle measures for triangles such as those shown at right.

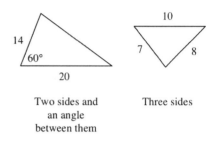

Two sides and an angle between them

Three sides

By the end of this lesson, you will have a complete set of tools to help solve for the side lengths and angle measures of *any* triangle, as long as enough information is given.

5-96.   LAW OF COSINES

Leila remembers that in problem 5-74, she solved for the side lengths and missing angles of the triangle at right by dividing the triangle into two right triangles. She thinks that using two right triangles may help find a tool that works for any triangle with two given sides and a given angle between them. Help Leila generalize this process by answering the questions below.

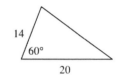

a.   Examine △ABC at right. Assume that you know the lengths of sides a and b and the measure of ∠C. Notice how the side opposite ∠A is labeled a and the side opposite ∠B is labeled b, and so on. Line segment $\overline{BD}$ is drawn so that △ABC is divided into two right triangles. If $CD = x$, then what is DA?

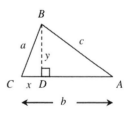

b.   Write an equation relating a, x, and y. Likewise, write an equation relating the side lengths of △BDA.

Problem continues on next page →

Core Connections Geometry

5-96.   *Problem continued from previous page.*

    c.   Leila noticed that both expressions from part (b) have a y^2-term. *"Can we combine these equations so that we have one equation that links sides a, b, and c?"* she asked. With your team, use algebra to combine these two equations so that y^2 is eliminated. Then simplify the resulting equation as much as possible.

    d.   The equation from part (c) still has an x-term. Using only a and $m\angle C$, find an expression for x using the left-hand triangle. Solve your equation for x, then substitute this expression into your equation from part (c) for x.

    e.   Solve your equation from part (d) for c^2. You have now found an equation that links the lengths of two sides and the measure of the angle between them to find the length of the side opposite the angle. This relationship is called the **Law of Cosines**. Read the Math Notes box for this lesson to learn more about the Law of Cosines.

    f.   Use the Law of Cosines to solve for x in the triangle at right.

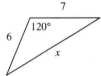

5-97.   You now have several tools to solve for missing side lengths and angle measures. Decide which tool to use for each of the triangles below and solve for x. Decide if your answer is reasonable based on the diagram.

    a.   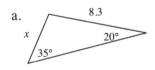   b.   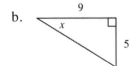   c.   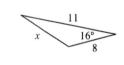

5-98.   EXTENSION

Not only can the Law of Cosines be used to solve for side lengths, but it can also be used to solve for angles. Consider the triangle from Lesson 5.3.1, shown at right.

    a.   Write an equation that relates the three sides and the angle α. Then solve the equation for α.

    b.   Now solve for the other two angles using any method. Be sure to name which tool(s) you used!

5-99. You have now completed your Triangle Toolkit and can find the missing side lengths and angle measures for *any* triangle, provided that enough information is given. Add the Law of Sines and Law of Cosines to your Triangle Toolkit for reference later in this course.

METHODS AND MEANINGS

Law of Cosines

Just like the Law of Sines, the **Law of Cosines** represents a relationship between the sides and angles of a triangle.

Specifically, when given the lengths of any two sides, such as a and b, and the angle between them, $\angle C$, the length of the third side, in this case c, can be found using this relationship:

$$c^2 = a^2 + b^2 - 2ab\cos C$$

Similar equations can be used to solve for a and b.

5-100. Eugene wants to use the cosine ratio to find y on this triangle.

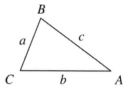

a. Which angle should he use to write an equation and solve for y using the cosine ratio? Why?

b. Set up an equation, and solve for y using cosine.

5-101. Copy the graph at right onto graph paper.

a. If the shape *ABCDE* were rotated about the origin 180°, where would point A' be?

b. If the shape *ABCDE* were reflected across the x-axis, where would point C' be?

c. If the shape *ABCDE* were translated so that each point (x, y) corresponds to $(x - 1, y + 3)$, where would point B' be?

Core Connections Geometry

5-102. On graph paper, graph the line $y = \frac{3}{4}x + 6$. Then find the slope angle (the acute angle the line makes with the *x*-axis).

5-103. An 8 foot ladder leaning against a house touches 7 feet above the ground. Draw a diagram and determine the measure of the angle created by the ladder and the ground.

5-104. This problem is a checkpoint for multiplying polynomials and solving quadratic equations. It will be referred to as Checkpoint 5A.

In parts (a) and (b) rewrite the expression without parentheses. In parts (c) and (d) solve each equation.

a. $2x(x+3)$

b. $(3x+2)(x-3)$

c. $x^2 - 8x + 7 = 0$

d. $y^2 - 2y = 15$

Check your answers by referring to the Checkpoint 5A materials located at the back of your book.

Ideally, at this point you are comfortable working with these types of problems and can solve them correctly. If you feel that you need more confidence when solving these types of problems, then review the Checkpoint 5A materials and try the practice problems provided. From this point on, you will be expected to do problems like these correctly and with confidence.

5-105. The spinners at right are spun and the results are added.

a. Find P(sum is 4).

b. Find P(sum is 8).

Spinner #1　　　**Spinner #2**

5.3.4 Is there more than one possible triangle?

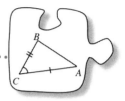

Ambiguous Triangles

Now that you have completed your Triangle Toolkit, you can solve for the missing angles or sides of any triangle, provided that enough information is given. But how do you know if you have enough information? What if there is more than one possible triangle? Today you will explore situations where your tools may not be adequate to solve for the missing side lengths and angle measures of a triangle.

5-106.   Examine the triangle at right from part (d) of problem 5-72. Notice that two side lengths and an angle measure not between the labeled sides are given. (This situation is sometimes referred to as SSA.)

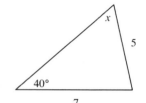

a.   Assuming that the triangle is not drawn to scale, what do you know about x? Is it more than 40° or less than 40°? Justify your conclusion.

b.   Solve for x. Was your conclusion from part (a) correct?

c.   "*Hold on!*" proclaims your teammate, Missy. "*That's not what I got. I found out that x ≈ 115.9°.*" She then drew the triangle at right. Do you agree with Missy? Use the Law of Sines to test her answer. That is, find out if the ratios of $\frac{\sin(angle)}{\text{opposite side}}$ are equal for each angle and its opposite side.

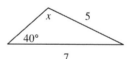

d.   What happened? How can there be two possible answers for x? Examine the diagram at right for clues.

e.   What is the relationship between the two solution angles? Do you think this relationship always exists? Examine the diagram above, which shows the two angle solutions, and use it to explain how the solutions are related.

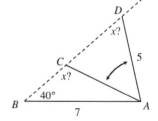

5-107.   In problem 5-106, you determined that it was possible to create two different triangles because you were given only two side lengths and an angle not between them. When this happens, it is called **triangle ambiguity** since you cannot tell which triangle was the one you were supposed to find. Will there always be two possible triangles? Can there ever be more than two possible triangles? Think about this as you answer the questions below.

a.   Obtain the Lesson 5.3.4 Resource Page and some linguini (or other flat manipulative) from your teacher. Prepare pieces of linguini that are 1 inch, 1.5 inches, 2 inches, 2.5 inches, and 3 inches long.

b.   For each length of linguini, place one end at point A in the diagram on the resource page. Determine if you can form a triangle by connecting the linguini with the dashed side to close the triangle. If you can make a triangle, label the third vertex C and label $\overline{AC}$ with its length. Can you form more than one triangle with the same side length? Is a triangle always possible? Record any conjectures you make.

c.   If the technology is available, test your conjectures from part (b) with a technology tool. Try to learn everything you can about SSA triangles. Use the questions below to guide your investigation.

   • Can you find a way to create three possible triangles with one set of SSA information?

   • Is it ever impossible to form a triangle?

   • Is it possible to choose SSA information that will create only one triangle? How?

5-108.   Now that Alex knows that SSA (two
          sides and an angle not between them)
          can result in more than one possible
          triangle, he wants to know if other types
          of given information can also create
          ambiguous results. For example, when
          given three side lengths, is more than
          one triangle possible?

          Examine each of the diagrams below
          (from problem 5-72) and determine if
          any other types of triangles are also
          ambiguous. You may want to imagine
          building the shapes with linguini. Remember that the given information cannot
          change – thus, if a side length is given, it cannot be lengthened or shortened.

a.

   Three sides (SSS)

b.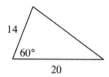

   Two sides and an angle
   between them (SAS)

c.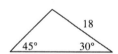

   Two angles and a side not
   between them (AAS)

d.

   Three angles (AAA)

5-109.   You now have several tools to use when solving for missing sides lengths and
          angle measures. Decide which tool to use for each of the triangles below and
          solve for x. If there is more than one solution, find both. Name the tool you
          use.

a.

b.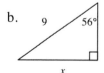

c.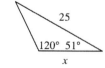

5-110.   EXTENSION

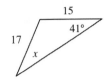

While examining the triangle at right, Alex stated, *"Well, I know that there can be at most one solution."*

a.   Examine the information given in the triangle. What do you know about *x*? Is it more than 41° or less? How can you tell?

b.   Alex remembered that if there were two solutions, then they had to be supplementary. Explain why this triangle cannot have two different values for *x*.

5-111.   Farmer Jill has a problem. She lives on a triangular plot of land that is surrounded on all three sides by a fence. Yesterday, one side of the fence was torn down in a storm. She wants to determine the length of the side that needs to be rebuilt so she can purchase enough lumber. Since the weather is still too poor for her to go outside and measure the distance, she decides to use the lengths of the two sides that are still standing (116 feet and 224 feet) and the angle between them (58°).

a.   Draw a diagram of this situation. Label all of the sides and angles that Farmer Jill has measurements for.

b.   Find the length of the fence that needs to be replaced. Show all work. Which tool did you use?

5-112.   Mr. Miller has informed you that two shapes are similar.

a.   What does this tell you about the angles in the shapes?

b.   What does this tell you about the lengths of the sides of the shapes?

5-113.   Find the equation of the line that has a slope angle of 25° and a *y*-intercept of (0, 4). Sketch a graph of this line. Assume the slope of the line is positive.

5-114.   Two sides of a triangle have lengths 9 and 14 units. Describe what you know about the length of the third side.

5-115.   How many terms are in the arithmetic sequence shown below?

$$15, 7, -1, -9, ..., -225$$

5-116.   Mr. Kyi has placed 3 red, 7 blue, and 2 yellow beads in a hat. If a person selects a red bead, he or she wins $3. If that person selects a blue bead, he or she loses $1. If the person selects a yellow bead, he or she wins $10. What is the expected value for one draw? Is this game fair?

5-117.   Tehachapi High School has 839 students and is increasing by 34 students per year. Meanwhile, Fresno High School has 1644 students and is decreasing by 81 students per year. In how many years will the two high schools have the same number of students? Be sure to show all work.

5.3.5 Which tool should I use?

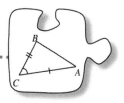

Choosing a Tool

During this section, you have developed new tools such as the Law of Sines and the Law of Cosines to find the lengths of sides and the measures of angles of a triangle. These strategies are very useful because they work with all triangles, not just right triangles. But when is each strategy the best one to use? Today you will focus on which strategy is most effective to use in different situations. You will also apply your strategies to triangles in different contexts.

As you work on these problems, keep in mind that good communication and a joint brainstorming of ideas will greatly enhance your team's ability to choose a strategy and to solve these problems.

5-118.   LAKE TOFTEE, Part One

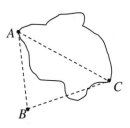

A bridge is being designed to connect two towns along the shores of Lake Toftee in Minnesota (one at point *A* and the other at point *C*). Lavanne has been given the responsibility of determining the length of the bridge.

Since he could not accurately measure across the lake (*AC*), he measured the only distance he could by foot (*AB*). He drove a stake into the ground at point *B* and found that $AB = 684$ feet. He also used a protractor to determine that $m\angle B = 79°$ and $m\angle C = 53°$. How long will the bridge need to be?

5-119.   LAKE TOFTEE, Part Two

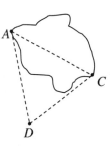

Lavanne was not convinced that his measurements from problem 5-118 were correct. He decided to measure the distance between towns *A* and *C* again using a different method to verify his results.

This time, he decided to drive a stake in the ground at point *D*, which is 800 feet from town *A* and 694 feet from town *C*. He also determined that $m\angle D = 68°$. Using these measurements, how wide is the lake between points *A* and *C*? Does this confirm the results from problem 5-118?

5-120.   The lid of a grand piano is propped open by
a supporting arm, as shown in the diagram
at right. Carson knows that the supporting
arm is 2 feet long and makes a 60° angle
with the piano. He also knows that the
piano lid makes a 23° angle with the piano.
How wide is the piano?

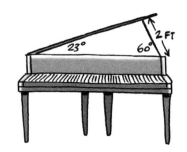

5-121.   PENNANT RACE

Your basketball team has made it to the
semi-finals and now needs to win only two
more games to go to the finals. Your plan
is to leave Philadelphia, travel 138 miles
to the town of Euclid to play the team
there. Then you will leave Euclid, travel
to Pythagoras, and play that team. Finally,
you will travel 97 miles to return home.

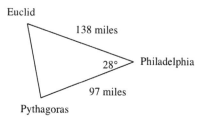

Your team bus can travel only 300 miles on one tank of gas. Assuming that all
of the roads connecting the three towns are straight and that the two roads that
connect in Philadelphia form a 28° angle, will one tank of gas be enough for the
trip? Justify your solution.

5-122.   Shonte is buying pipes to install sprinklers for her
front lawn. She needs to fit the pipes into the bed
of her pickup truck to get them home from the
store. She knows that the longest dimension in
her truckbed is from the top of one corner to the
bottom of the bed at the opposite corner. After
measuring the truckbed, she drew the diagram at
right. What is the longest pipe she can buy?

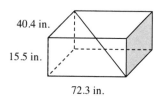

5-123.   You have previously used your intuition to state that if a
triangle has two angles that are equal, then the triangle has
two sides that are the same length. Now use your triangle
tools to show that your intuition was correct. For example,
for $\triangle PQR$, show that if $m\angle Q = m\angle R$, then $PQ = PR$.

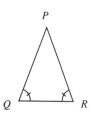

5-124.   As Freda gazes at the edge of the Grand Canyon, she decides to try to determine the height of the wall opposite her. Using her trusty clinometer, she determines that the top of the wall is at a 38° angle above her, while the bottom is at a 46° angle below her, as shown in the diagram at right. If the base of the wall is 253 feet from the point on the ground directly below Freda, determine the height of the wall opposite her.

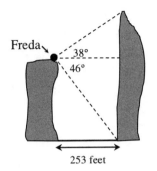

5-125.   While facing north, Lisa and Aaron decide to hike to their campsite. Lisa plans to hike 5 miles due north to Lake Toftee before she goes to the campsite. Aaron plans to turn 38° east and hike 7.4 miles directly to the campsite. How far will Lisa have to hike from the lake to meet Aaron at the campsite? Start by drawing a diagram of the situation, then calculate the distance.

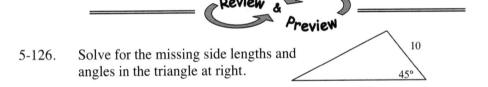
Review & Preview

5-126.   Solve for the missing side lengths and angles in the triangle at right.

5-127.   Examine the triangle shown at right. Solve for *x twice*, using two different methods. Show your work for each method clearly.

5-128.   In Chapter 1 you learned that all rectangles are parallelograms because they all have two pairs of opposite parallel sides. Does that mean that all parallelograms are rectangles? Why or why not? Support your statements with reasons.

5-129.   Find the area and perimeter of each shape below. Show all work.

a.
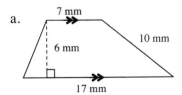

b.
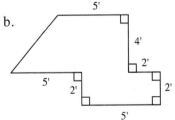

5-130. $\triangle ABC$ was reflected across the *x*-axis, and then that result was rotated 90° clockwise about the origin to result in $\triangle A'B'C'$, shown at right. Find the coordinates of points A, B, and C of the original triangle.

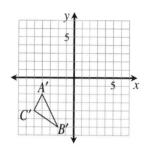

5-131.   Marina needs to win 10 tickets to get a giant stuffed panda bear. To win tickets, she throws a dart at the dartboard at right and wins the number of tickets listed in the region where her dart lands. Unfortunately, she only has enough money to play the game three times. If she throws the dart randomly, do you expect that she will be able to win enough tickets? Assume that each dart will land on the dartboard.

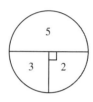

5-132.   Find the equation of a line parallel to the line $y = \frac{3}{4}x - 5$ that passes through the point $(-4, 1)$. Show how you found your answer.

5-133.   Examine trapezoid *ABCD* at right.

   a.   Find the measures of all the angles in the diagram.

   b.   What is the sum of the angles that make up the trapezoid *ABCD*? That is, what is $m\angle A + m\angle ABC + m\angle BCD + m\angle D$?

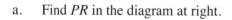

5-134.   Use your triangle tools to solve the problems below.

   a.   Find *PR* in the diagram at right.

   b.   Find the perimeter of quadrilateral *PQRS*.

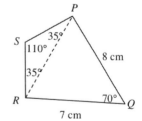

5-135.   Find the area and perimeter of $\triangle ABC$ at right. Give approximate (decimal) answers, not exact answers.

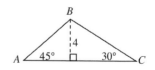

5-136.   This problem is a checkpoint for writing equations for arithmetic and geometric sequences. It will be referred to as Checkpoint 5B.

a.   Write an explicit and recursive rule for $t(n) = 1, 4, 7, 10, ...$

b.   Write an explicit and recursive rule for $t(n) = 3, \frac{3}{2}, \frac{3}{4}, \frac{3}{8}, ...$

In parts (c) and (d), write an explicit rule for the sequence given in the $n \to t(n)$ tables.

c.   An arithmetic sequence

n	$t(n)$
1	17
2	
3	3
4	

d.   A geometric sequence

n	$t(n)$
1	
2	7.2
3	8.64
4	

e.   If an arithmetic sequence has $t(7) = 1056$ and $t(12) = 116$, what is $t(4)$?

Check your answers by referring to the Checkpoint 5B materials located at the back of your book.

Ideally, at this point you are comfortable working with these types of problems and can solve them correctly. If you feel that you need more confidence when solving these types of problems, then review the Checkpoint 5B materials and try the practice problems provided. From this point on, you will be expected to do problems like these correctly and with confidence.

5-137.   Bob is hanging a swing from a pole high off the ground so that it can swing a total angle of 120°. Since there is a bush 5 feet in front of the swing and a shed 5 feet behind the swing, Bob wants to ensure that no one will get hurt when they are swinging. What is the maximum length of chain that Bob can use for the swing?

a.   Draw a diagram of this situation.

b.   What is the maximum length of chain that Bob can use? State what tools you used to solve this problem.

5-138.   On graph paper, draw $\triangle ABC$ if $A(3, 2)$, $B(-1, 4)$, and $C(0, -2)$.

a.   Find the perimeter of $\triangle ABC$.

b.   Dilate $\triangle ABC$ from the origin by a factor of 2 to create $\triangle A'B'C'$. What is the perimeter of $\triangle A'B'C'$?

c.   If $\triangle ABC$ is rotated 90° clockwise ($\circlearrowright$) about the origin to form $\triangle A''B''C''$, name the coordinates of C''.

Chapter 5 Closure What have I learned?

Reflection and Synthesis

The activities below offer you a chance to
reflect about what you have learned during this
chapter. As you work, look for concepts that
you feel very comfortable with, ideas that you
would like to learn more about, and topics you
need more help with. Look for connections
between ideas as well as connections with
material you learned previously.

①   TEAM BRAINSTORM

What have you studied in this chapter? What ideas were important in what you
learned? With your team, brainstorm a list. Be as detailed as you can. To help
get you started, lists of Learning Log entries, Toolkit Entries, and Math Notes
boxes are below.

What topics, ideas, and words that you learned *before* this chapter are connected
to the new ideas in this chapter? Again, be as detailed as you can.

How long can you make your list? Challenge yourselves. Be prepared to share
your team's ideas with the class.

Learning Log Entries
- Lesson 5.1.2 – Choosing a Trig Tool
- Lesson 5.1.3 – Inverse Trig Functions
- Lesson 5.2.1 – Special Right Triangles
- Lesson 5.3.1 – Strategies to find Sides and Angles of a Triangle
- Lesson 5.3.2 – Law of Sines

Toolkit Entries
- Triangle Toolkit (Lesson 5.1.1 and Lesson 5.3.1 Resource
  Pages, and problems 5-6 and 5-99)

Math Notes
- Lesson 5.1.2 – Trigonometric Ratios
- Lesson 5.1.4 – Inverse Trigonometry
- Lesson 5.2.1 – Rationalizing a Denominator
- Lesson 5.2.2 – Expected Value
- Lesson 5.3.1 – Special Right Triangles
- Lesson 5.3.2 – Law of Sines
- Lesson 5.3.3 – Law of Cosines

② MAKING CONNECTIONS

Below is a list of the vocabulary used in this chapter. Make sure that you are familiar with all of these words and know what they mean. Refer to the glossary or index for any words that you do not yet understand.

30°- 60°- 90° triangle	45°- 45°- 90° triangle	adjacent side
ambiguous triangle	angle	cosine ratio
counterexample	equilateral	hypotenuse
inverse sine	inverse cosine	inverse tangent
isosceles	Law of Cosines	Law of Sines
leg	opposite side	Pythagorean Triple
reference angle	right triangle	sine ratio
slope angle	tangent ratio	theta (θ)
trigonometric ratio		

Make a concept map showing all of the connections you can find among the key words and ideas listed above. To show a connection between two words, draw a line between them and explain the connection, as shown in the model below. A word can be connected to any other word as long as you can justify the connection. For each key word or idea, provide an example or sketch that shows the idea.

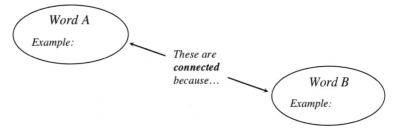

Your teacher may provide you with vocabulary cards to help you get started. If you use the cards to plan your concept map, be sure either to re-draw your concept map on your paper or to glue the vocabulary cards to a poster with all of the connections explained for others to see and understand.

While you are making your map, your team may think of related words or ideas that are not listed here. Be sure to include these ideas on your concept map.

PORTFOLIO: EVIDENCE OF MATHEMATICAL PROFICIENCY

This closure activity will focus on choosing a
strategy or tool. Think about the problems you
have worked on in this chapter. When did you
need to think about what method you would use to
solve a problem? What helped you decide how to
approach a problem? Were there times when more
than one strategy seemed most useful? You may
want to flip through the chapter to refresh your
memory about the problems that you have worked on.

Once your discussion is complete, think about the way you think as you answer
the questions below.

a.   List all the triangle tools that you have learned so far in this course. For
     each tool, find or create a problem that can be solved with this strategy.

b.   Sometimes, the key to being able to choose a strategy or tool is to
     recognize that different tools can be used on the same problem, but that
     sometimes some tools are more efficient than others.

     Solve for x in each diagram below *twice*. Each time, use a different
     strategy or tool. Then decide which method was easiest for that problem
     or state that both methods were of equal value.

(1) 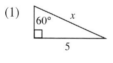   (2)   (3)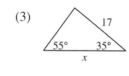

c.   While you have focused most of this chapter on developing strategies for
     measuring triangles, you have developed strategies for several other topics
     so far in this course. Consider your strategy options as you answer the
     questions below.

     (1)   Examine the diagram at right.
           Assume you know the measure of
           $\angle b$. How could you find $m\angle h$?
           Describe two different strategies.

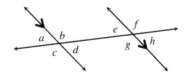

Activity continues on next page →

Activity continued from previous page.

(2) Now consider the trapezoid below. Find the area of the shape twice, using two different strategies.

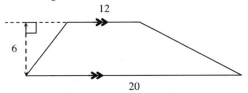

(3) While shopping at the Two Tired Bike Shop, Barry notices that he may choose from many bicycles. Of the bikes at the store, $\frac{1}{4}$ were mountain bikes, while the rest were racing bikes. Also, $\frac{1}{2}$ of the bikes were blue, $\frac{1}{3}$ of the bikes were red, and $\frac{1}{6}$ of the bikes were purple. Barry decides that he will randomly choose a bicycle from the store. The color of the bike is independent of its type.

Choose a probability model to represent this situation. Then find the probability that he chooses a purple racing bike.

d. What about multiple strategies that you have learned in an earlier class? For example, you have multiple ways to approach a problem involving a system of equations. Consider the system below. Solve the system *twice*: once by graphing and again algebraically. Which strategy seemed most efficient? Why?

$$y = -x + 8$$
$$y = \tfrac{1}{2}x - 7$$

Your teacher may give you the Chapter 5 Closure Resource Page: Choosing a Strategy/Tool Graphic Organizer to work on (or you can download it from www.cpm.org). A Graphic Organizer is a tool you can use to organize your thoughts, showcase your knowledge, and communicate your ideas clearly.

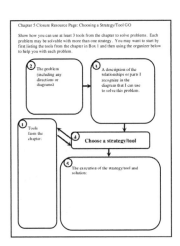

WHAT HAVE I LEARNED?

Most of the problems in this section represent typical problems found in this chapter. They serve as a gauge for you. You can use them to determine which types of problems you can do well and which types of problems require further study and practice. Even if your teacher does not assign this section, it is a good idea to try these problems and find out for yourself what you know and what you still need to work on.

Solve each problem as completely as you can. The table at the end of the closure section has answers to these problems. It also tells you where you can find additional help and practice with problems like these.

CL 5-139. For each diagram, write an equation and solve to find the value for each variable.

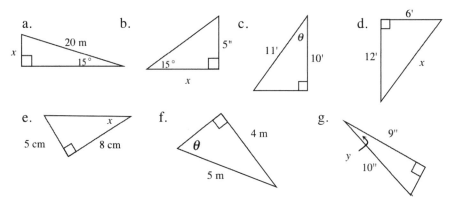

a.

b.

c.

d.

e.

f.

g.

CL 5-140. Copy the diagram at right onto your paper.

a. Are the triangles similar? If so, show your reasoning with a flowchart.

b. If $m\angle B = 80°$, $m\angle ACB = 29°$, $AB = 14$, and $DE = 12$, find CE.

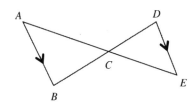

CL 5-141.   STEP RIGHT UP!

At a fair, Cyrus was given the following opportunity.
He could roll the die formed by the net at right one
time. If the die landed so that a shaded die faced up,
then Cyrus would win $10. Otherwise, he would lose
$5. Is this game fair? Explain how you know.

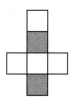

CL 5-142.   Use your knowledge of special right triangles to find the missing side
lengths and angle measures exactly. No calculators are needed.

a.   b.   c.

$4^2 + b^2 = c^2$ $B^2 = 48$
$16 + b^2 = 64$
$-16 \quad -16$

CL 5-143.   While working on homework, Zachary was finding the
value of each variable in the diagrams below. His first step
for each problem is shown under the diagram. If his first
step is correct, continue solving the problem to find the
solution. If his first step is incorrect, explain his mistake
and solve the problem correctly.

a.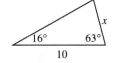

$$\sin 16° = \frac{x}{10}$$

b.

$$x^2 = 10^2 + 70^2 - 2(10)(70)\cos 50°$$

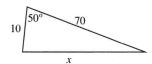

CL 5-144.   In parts (a) and (b), use what you know about Pythagorean Triples to find the third side quickly. In parts (c) and (d), give all possible lengths for the third side of the triangle.

a.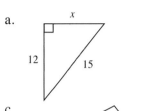

b.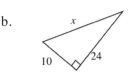

c.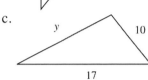

d.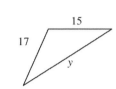

CL 5-145.   Kayla brought snacks for her and her partner on the volleyball team. She packed flavored water (2 berry and 4 citrus), fruit (5 apricots, 2 apples, and 3 bunches of grapes), and small packages of crackers (2 regular and 2 whole wheat). Kayla will randomly choose one flavored water, one fruit, and one package of crackers.

a.   Show all the possible combinations of three snacks that Kayla could choose.

b.   What is the probability that Kayla will choose a high-fiber snack (any combination that includes both an apple and whole-wheat crackers).

CL 5-146.   Examine the triangle at right. Solve for *x* *twice* using two different methods.

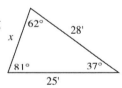

CL 5-147.   Graph the points $(3, -4)$ and $(7, 2)$ on graph paper and draw the line segment and a slope triangle that connects the points. Find:

a.   The length of the segment.

b.   The slope of the line segment.

c.   The area of the slope triangle that connects the points.

d.   The measure of the slope angle.

CL 5-148.   Trace the figure at right onto your paper and then perform all of
the transformations listed below on the same diagram. Then
find the perimeter of the final shape.

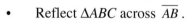

•   Reflect △ABC across $\overline{AB}$.

•   Rotate △ABC 180° around the midpoint of $\overline{BC}$.

•   Reflect △ABC across $\overline{AC}$.

CL 5-149.   A snack cracker company surveyed 1000 people, in different age groups, to
determine their favorite cracker.

Age of Participants (years)

	Under 20	20 to 39	40 to 59	60 and over
# people	250	250	250	250

Favorite Cracker

	Cracker A	Cracker B	Cracker C
# people	371	308	321

a.   What is the probability (represented as a percent) that a randomly
selected participant was 20 years old or older?

b.   152 of the participants under 20 years old chose cracker A as their
favorite. Calculate the probability that a participant chose cracker A *or*
was under 20 years old.

c.   What is the probability that a participant did not choose cracker A *and*
was 20 or over years old? Show how you used a complement to answer
this problem.

CL 5-150.   Check your answers using the table at the end of this section. Which
problems do you feel confident about? Which problems were hard? Have
you worked on problems like these in math classes you have taken before?
Use the table to make a list of topics you need help on and a list of topics
you need to practice more.

Answers and Support for Closure Activity #4
What Have I Learned?

Note: MN = Math Notes, LL = Learning Logs

Problem	Solutions	Need Help?	More Practice
CL 5-139.	a. $\sin 15° = \frac{x}{20}$; $x \approx 5.176$ m	Lessons 2.3.2, 4.1.4, and Section 5.1	Problems 5-17, 5-18, 5-30, 5-44, 5-46, 5-77, 5-100, 5-103, and 5-137
	b. $\tan 15° = \frac{5}{x}$; $x \approx 18.66$ in	MN: 2.3.2, 4.1.4, 5.1.2, and 5.1.4	
	c. $\cos \theta = \frac{10}{11}$; $\theta \approx 24.62°$		
	d. $6^2 + 12^2 = x^2$; $x \approx 13.416$ ft		
	e. $\tan^{-1} \frac{5}{8} \approx 32.0°$	LL: 4.1.4, 5.1.2, 5.1.3, and 5.3.1	
	f. $\sin^{-1} \frac{4}{5} \approx 53.1°$		
	g. $\cos^{-1} \frac{9}{10} \approx 25.8°$	Triangle Toolkit	
CL 5-140.	a.	Section 3.2 MN: 3.2.1, 3.2.4, 3.2.5, and 5.3.2	Problems CL 3-121, CL 4-123, 5-23, 5-34, and 5-65
	b. $CE \approx 24.38$	LL: 3.2.2, 3.2.4, and 5.3.2	
CL 5-141.	Yes, the game is fair because the expected value is $\frac{2}{6}(10) + \frac{4}{6}(-5) = 0$.	Lesson 4.2.5 MN: 5.2.2	Problems 5-20, 5-69, 5-116, and 5-131
CL 5-142.	a. 2 cm, $2\sqrt{2}$ cm, 90°	Lesson 5.2.1 MN: 5.3.1 LL: 5.2.1	Problems 5-52, 5-53 (d), 5-64 (b), 5-127, and 5-135
	b. $30°, 60°, 4\sqrt{3}$ units		
	c. $30°, 3$ m, $3\sqrt{3}$ m		
CL 5-143.	a. Cannot use sine in this manner in a non-right triangle. Use the Law of Sines instead: $\frac{x}{\sin(16°)} = \frac{10}{\sin(101°)}$; $x \approx 2.807$	Lessons 5.3.1, 5.3.2, and 5.3.3 MN: 5.3.2 and 5.3.3 LL: 5.3.1 and 5.3.2	Problems 5-90, 5-97, and 5-134
	b. $x \approx 64.03$ units		

Problem	Solutions	Need Help?	More Practice
CL 5-144.	a. 9 b. 26 c. $7 < y < 27$ d. $2 < y < 32$	Lesson 2.3.1 MN: 5.3.1 LL: 2.3.1	Problems CL 3-117, 4-85, 5-64, 5-78, 5-79, 5-89, 5-113, 5-129, and 5-138
CL 5-145.	a. See tree diagram below. An area model is not practical. b. See tree diagram above. $\frac{8}{240} + \frac{16}{240} = \frac{24}{240} = 10\%$	Lessons 4.2.1, 4.2.2, and 4.2.3 MN: 4.2.3 LL: 4.2.2 and 4.2.3 $\frac{2}{6} \cdot \frac{2}{10} \cdot \frac{2}{4} = \frac{8}{240}$	Problems CL 4-127, 5-20, and 5-93
CL 5-146.	Both the Law of Sines and the Law of Cosines will work, as does dividing the triangle into two right triangles; $x \approx 17.06$ ft.	Section 5.3 MN: 5.3.2 and 5.3.3 LL: 5.3.1 and 5.3.2	Problems 5-90, 5-126, and 5-134

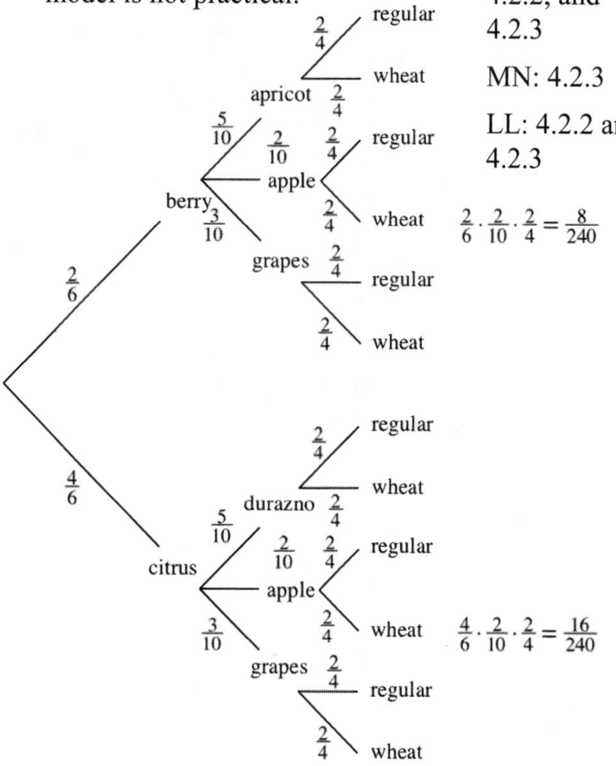

Problem	Solutions		Need Help?	More Practice
CL 5-147.	a. $\sqrt{52} \approx 7.21$ units	b. $\frac{3}{2}$	Lessons 2.3.2 and 4.1.2	Problems CL 2-121, CL 3-116, 5-42, 5-102, and 5-113
	c. 12 sq. units	d. 56.31°	Checkpoint 3	
			MN: 1.2.6, 2.3.2, 4.1.1, and 4.1.2	
			LL: 2.3.2 and 4.1.3	
CL 5-148.	The final shape is shown below: Perimeter: 24 feet 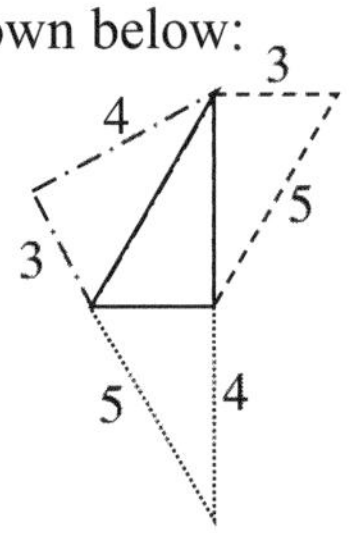		Lessons 1.2.2 and 1.2.4 MN: 1.1.3, 1.2.2, and 1.2.4	Problems CL 4-126, 5-80, 5-101, 5-130, and 5-138
CL 5-149.	a. The complement of being under 20 years old is $1 - \frac{250}{1000} = \frac{750}{1000} = 75\%$, or, the probability is $\frac{250+250+250}{1000} = \frac{750}{1000} = 75\%$		Lesson 4.2.4 MN: 4.2.4	Problems 5-10, 5-32, 5-45, 5-55, and 5-93
	b. $\frac{371}{1000} + \frac{250}{1000} - \frac{152}{1000} = \frac{469}{1000} = 46.9\%$			
	c. $1 - \frac{469}{1000} = \frac{531}{1000} = 53.1\%$			

CHAPTER 6 Congruent Triangles

In Chapter 5, you completed your work with the measurement of triangles, so you can now find the missing side lengths and angles of a triangle when sufficient information is given. Earlier, you developed ways to determine if two triangles are similar, and can use the ratios of similarity to learn more about the sides and angles of similar figures. But what if two triangles are congruent? What information can congruent triangles provide? In this chapter, you will find ways to determine whether two triangles are congruent.

In addition, Section 6.2 offers several projects and activities that will help you synthesize your understanding and make connections between different concepts you have learned so far. You will consolidate what you know, apply it in new ways, and identify what you still need to learn.

Guiding Question

Mathematically proficient students construct viable arguments and critique the reasoning of others.

As you work through this chapter, ask yourself:

How can I use information to construct arguments, justify my conclusions and respond to the arguments presented by others?

In this chapter, you will learn:

➢ The information that is needed in order to conclude that two triangles are congruent.

➢ The converse of a conditional statement and how to recognize whether or not the converse is true.

➢ How to organize a flowchart that concludes two triangles are congruent.

Chapter Outline

Section 6.1   This section turns the focus to congruent triangles. You will develop strategies to directly conclude that two triangles are congruent without first concluding that they are similar.

Section 6.2   This section includes several big problems and activities to help you learn how different threads of geometry are connected and to help you assess what you know and what you still need to learn.

6.1.1 Are the triangles congruent?

Congruent Triangles

In Chapter 3, you learned how to identify similar triangles and used them to solve problems. But what can be learned when triangles are congruent? In today's lesson, you will practice identifying congruent triangles using what you know about similarity. As you search for congruent triangles in today's problems, focus on these questions:

What do I know about these triangles?

How can I show similarity?

What is the common ratio?

6-1.   Examine the triangles at right.

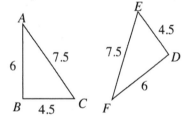

a.   Make a flowchart showing that these triangles are similar.

b.   Are these triangles also congruent? Explain how you know.

c.   While the symbol for similar figures is "~", the symbol for congruent figures is "≅". How is the congruence symbol related to the similarity symbol? Why do you think mathematicians chose this symbol for congruence?

d.   Luis wanted to write a statement to convey that these two triangles are congruent. He started with "Δ*CAB* ...", but then got stuck because he did not know the symbol for congruence. Now that you know the symbol for congruence, complete Luis's statement for him.

6-2.   The diagrams below are not drawn to scale. For each pair of triangles:

- Determine if the two triangles are congruent.

- If you find congruent triangles, write a congruence statement (such as $\triangle PQR \cong \triangle XYZ$).

- If the triangles are not congruent or if there is not enough information to determine congruence, then write "cannot be determined."

a. $\overline{AC}$ is a straight segment:

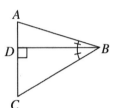

b.

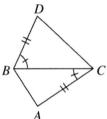

c.

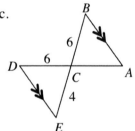

d.

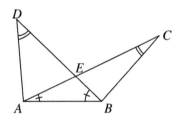

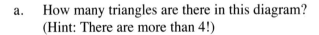

6-3.   Consider square *MNPQ* with diagonals intersecting at *R*, as shown at right.

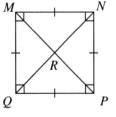

a.   How many triangles are there in this diagram?
     (Hint: There are more than 4!)

b.   How many lines of symmetry does *MNPQ* have? On your paper, trace *MNPQ* and indicate the location of each line of symmetry with a dashed line.

c.   Write as many triangle congruence statements as you can that involve triangles in this diagram. Be prepared to justify each congruence statement you write.

d.   Write a similarity statement for two triangles in the diagram that are not congruent. Justify your similarity statement with a flowchart.

METHODS AND MEANINGS

Congruent Shapes

MATH NOTES

The information below is from Chapter 3 and is reprinted here for your convenience.

If two figures have the same shape and are the same size, they are **congruent**. Since the figures must have the same shape, they must be similar.

Two figures are congruent if there is a sequence of rigid transformations that carry one onto the other. Two figures are also congruent if they meet both the following conditions:

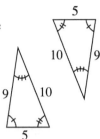

- The two figures are similar, and

- Their side lengths have a common ratio of 1.

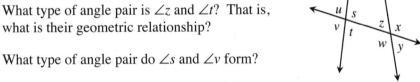

6-4. Use the diagram at right to answer the following questions.

a. What type of angle pair is ∠z and ∠t? That is, what is their geometric relationship?

b. What type of angle pair do ∠s and ∠v form?

c. Name all pairs of corresponding angles in the diagram. Hint: There are four different pairs.

6-5. Examine the triangles at right.

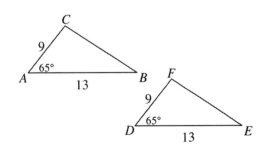

a. Are these triangles similar? If so, use a flowchart to show how you know. If they are not similar, explain how you know.

b. Are the triangles congruent? Explain your reasoning.

6-6.   Using the diagram at right, write an equation
         and find x. Check your answer.

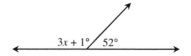

6-7.   For each of the triangles below, find x.

a. 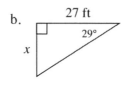   b. 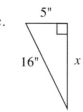   c.

8 cm

27 ft
29°

5"
16"

6-8.   Joey is in charge of selling cupcakes at the basketball games. The game is
         today at 5:00 p.m. At 3:00 p.m., Joey put some cupcakes into the oven and
         started working on his homework. He fell asleep and did not wake up until
         3:55 p.m. What do you think happened?

         Joey knows that the following four statements are facts:

         i.   If the cupcakes are burned, then the fans that attend the varsity
               basketball games will not buy them.

         ii.   If cupcakes are in the oven for more than 50 minutes, they will burn.

         iii. If the fans do not buy the cupcakes, then the team will not have enough
               money for new uniforms next year.

         iv.   The cupcakes are in the oven from 3:00 p.m. to 3:55 p.m.

         Copy the flowchart at right and decide how to
         organize the facts into the ovals. You will need
         to fill in one of the ovals with your own logical
         conclusion. Be sure that your ovals are in the correct
         order and that the arrows really show connections
         between the ovals. What conclusion should your
         flowchart make?

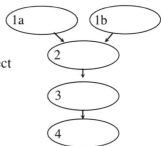

6-9.   Assume that 25% of the student body at your school is male and that 40% of the students walk to school. If a student from this school is selected at random, find the following probabilities.

   a.   P(student is female)

   b.   P(student is male and does not walk to school)

   c.   P(student walks to school or does not walk to school)

   d.   Identify the sample space in parts (b) and (c) above as a "union" or a "intersection."

6-10.   **Multiple Choice:** $\triangle ABC$ is defined by points $A(3, 2)$, $B(4, 9)$, and $C(6, 7)$. Which triangle below is the image of $\triangle ABC$ when it is rotated 90° counter-clockwise (↺) about the origin?

   a. $A'(-2, 3)$, $B'(-9, 4)$, $C'(-7, 6)$ b. $A'(-3, 2)$, $B'(-4, 9)$, $C'(-6, 7)$

   c. $A'(-2, 3)$, $B'(-7, 6)$, $C'(-9, 4)$ d. $A'(2, -3)$, $B'(9, -4)$, $C'(7, -6)$

   e.   None of these

6.1.2 What information do I need?

Conditions for Triangle Congruence

In Lesson 6.1.1, you identified congruent triangles by looking for similarity and a common side length ratio of 1. Must you go through this two-step process every time you want to argue that triangles are congruent? Are there shortcuts for establishing triangle congruence? Today you will investigate multiple triangle congruence conditions in order to quickly determine if two triangles are congruent.

6-11. Review your work from problem 6-5, which required you to determine if two triangles are congruent. Then work with your team to answer the questions below.

    a. Derek wants to find general conditions that can help determine if triangles are congruent. To help, he draws the diagram at right to show the relationships between the triangles in problem 6-5.

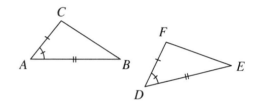

       If two triangles have the relationships shown in the diagram, do they have to be congruent? How do you know?

    b. Write a theorem in the form of a conditional statement or arrow diagram based on this relationship. If you write a conditional statement, it should look like, "If two triangles …, then the triangles are congruent." What would be a good name (abbreviation) for this theorem?

6-12. TRIANGLE CONGRUENCE THEOREMS

Derek wonders, *"What other types of information can determine that two triangles are congruent?"*

Your Task: Examine the pairs of triangles below to decide what other types of information force triangles to be congruent. Notice that since no measurements are given in the diagrams, you are considering the general case of each type of pairing. For each pair of triangles below that you can prove must be congruent, enter the appropriate triangle congruence theorem on your Lesson 6.1.2 Resource Page with an explanation defending your decision. An entry for SAS $\cong$ (the theorem you looked at problem 6-11) is already created on the resource page as an example. Be prepared to share your results with the class.

Problem continues on next page →

6-12.   *Problem continued from previous page.*

Discussion Points

- For those triangles that must be congruent, how can you prove it?

- Which of the conditions below assure congruence?

- Which of the conditions below DO NOT assure congruence?

a.

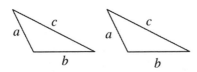

Side-Side-Side: SSS

b.

Hypotenuse-Leg: HL

c.

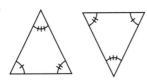

Angle-Angle-Angle: AA

d.

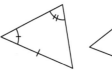

Angle-Angle-Side: AAS

e.

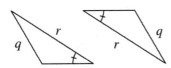

Side-Side-Angle: SSA

f.

Angle-Side-Angle: ASA

6-13.   Use your triangle congruence theorems to determine if the following pairs of triangles must be congruent. Note: The diagrams are not necessarily drawn to scale.

a.

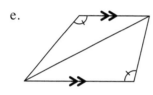

b.

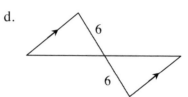

c.

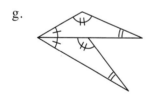

d.

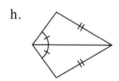

e.

f.

g.

h.

━━━━━━━━ Review & Preview ━━━━━━━━

6-14.   Examine the relationships that exist in the diagram at right. Find the measures of angles a, b, c, and d. Remember that you can find the angles in any order, depending on the angle relationships you use.

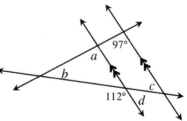

Core Connections Geometry

6-15.   Examine the triangles below. For each one, solve for x and name which tool you used. Show all work.

a.

b.

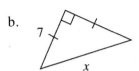

7

x

c.

15   32°   18

x

6-16.   The two shapes at right are similar.

a.   Find the value of x. Show all work.

b.   Find the area of each shape.

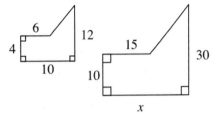

6
12
4
10
15
30
10
x

6-17.   On graph paper, graph $\triangle ABC$ if its vertices are $A(-2, 7)$, $B(-5, 8)$, and $C(-3, 1)$.

a.   Reflect $\triangle ABC$ across the x-axis to form $\triangle A'B'C'$. Name the coordinates of each new vertex.

b.   Now rotate $\triangle A'B'C'$ from part (a) 180° about the origin $(0, 0)$ to form $\triangle A''B''C''$. Name the coordinates of each new vertex.

c.   Describe a single transformation that would change $\triangle ABC$ to $\triangle A''B''C''$.

6-18.   Earl hates to take out the garbage and to wash the dishes, so he decided to make a deal with his parents: He will flip a coin once for each chore and will perform the chore if the coin lands on heads. What he doesn't know is that his parents are going to use a weighted coin that lands on heads 80% of the time!

a.   What is the probability that Earl will have to do both chores?

b.   What is the probability that Earl will have to take out the garbage, but will not need to wash the dishes?

6-19.   **Multiple Choice:** Which list of side lengths below could form a triangle?

a.   2, 6, 7   b.   3, 8, 13   c.   9, 4, 2   d.   10, 20, 30

6.1.3 How can I prove it?

· ·

Congruence of Triangles Through Rigid Transformations

In Lesson 6.1.2, you identified five conditions that guarantee triangle congruence. They are true because they require the triangles to be similar and because you know the ratio of the side lengths equals 1. However, the definition of congruence uses rigid transformations. So it is reasonable to assume these conditions can be proved without similarity. In this lesson, you will revisit each condition and develop new logic for why each one is true.

6-20.   PROVING SAS TRIANGLE CONGRUENCE

A team is working together to try to prove SAS≅. Given the triangles shown at right, they want to prove that $\triangle ABC \cong \triangle DEF$.

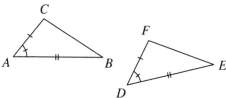

Jurgen said, *"We know that congruent means that the two triangles have the same size and shape, so we have to be able to move $\triangle ABC$ right on top of $\triangle DEF$ using rigid motions, since they preserve lengths and angles. Does anyone see how we can do this?"*

Carlos suggested, *"Well, we can certainly move point A on top of point D with a translation to get $\triangle A'B'C'$ with points $A' = D$, but nothing else matches."*

Then Mary Sue added, *"Oh, then we can rotate $\triangle A'B'C'$ about point D to get $\triangle A''B''C''$ with $\overline{A''B''}$ pointing in the same direction as , and since point $A'' = D$, the two rays are the same. But does point B'' lie on top of point E then?"*

After a moment Emmy said, *"Sure. We know that rigid motions like translation and rotations preserve angles and lengths. So $AB = A'B' = A''B''$, right? And since we are assuming that $AB = DE$, then $A''B'' = DE$. Since point A'' is on point D, then point B'' must be at point E."*

Jurgen added, *"And look, since $\triangle A''B''C''$ lies on top of $\triangle DEF$, they are congruent."*

a.   Use the SAS ~ tech tool and repeat their strategy to move $\triangle ABC$ onto $\triangle DEF$ to prove these triangles are congruent.

Problem continues on next page →

6-20.   *Problem continued from previous page.*

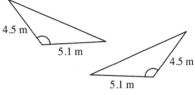

b.   Emmy asks, *"What about these triangles? How can we make them coincide?"* Discuss how their previous strategy needs to be changed to show that these triangles are congruent using rigid transformations. Explain why this proves that all pairs of triangles with SAS ≅ must be congruent.

6-21.   PROVING ASA TRIANGLE CONGRUENCE

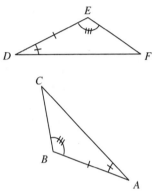

In problem 6-20 you proved SAS ≅ by finding a sequence of rigid transformations that would move one triangle onto another. A similar strategy can be used to prove the ASA ≅ condition. Suppose that $\triangle ABC$ and $\triangle DEF$ are triangles with $\overline{AB} \cong \overline{DE}$, $\angle A \cong \angle D$, and $\angle B \cong \angle E$ as shown in the diagram at right. Look at the work of a second team below as they work to prove that $\triangle ABC \cong \triangle DEF$ using rigid transformations.

a.   Janet said, *"Like last time, we can translate and then rotate the triangle so that A″ lies on D and B″ lies on E. Except this time, we have to show that even though these points are on top of each other, the others (C and F) are also."*

She thinks for a bit and adds, *"I think $\angle E \cong \angle B''$."* How can she be sure that $\angle E \cong \angle B''$?

b.   Patrick points out, *"This means that $\overrightarrow{B''C''}$ is identical to $\overrightarrow{EF}$. Using the same reasoning, I know that $\overrightarrow{A''C''}$ is identical to $\overrightarrow{DF}$."* Is Patrick correct? Explain why or why not.

c.   Aleesha then exclaimed, *"That's it! They must be congruent because this means that point C″ is the same as point F."* Help her justify this conclusion.

d.   Eddie asks, *"What if we need a reflection to have the triangles lie on top of each other?"* Does this affect the result? Explain why or why not.

6-22.   PROVING SSS, ASA, AND HL TRIANGLE CONGRUENCE

Interestingly, each of the other triangle congruence conditions can be shown to be true by either ASA ≅ or SAS ≅. Finish proving these three remaining conditions by answering the questions below.

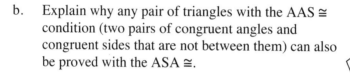

a.   For the SSS ≅ condition, start with two triangles that have three pairs of congruent sides and explain why the triangles must be congruent. (Hint: Think about why the Law of Cosines guarantees that at least one of the pairs of angles has the same measure. To help, consider how you would calculate $m\angle A$ and $m\angle D$ at right.)

b.   Explain why any pair of triangles with the AAS ≅ condition (two pairs of congruent angles and congruent sides that are not between them) can also be proved with the ASA ≅.

c.   Finally, consider what you know about the side lengths of right triangles. How can you use SAS ≅ to prove the HL ≅ condition, that is, that right triangles with a pair of congruent legs and a pair of congruent hypotenuses must be congruent?

Review & Preview

6-23.   For each pair of triangles below, decide if the pair is similar, congruent or neither. Justify your conclusion with a flowchart or the reasons why the triangles cannot be similar or congruent. Assume that the diagrams are not drawn to scale.

a.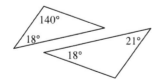

b.

Core Connections Geometry

6-24.   Use what you know about the slopes of parallel and perpendicular lines to find the equation of each line described below.

    a.   Find the equation of the line that goes through the point $(2, -3)$ and is perpendicular to the line $y = -\frac{2}{5}x + 6$.

    b.   Find the equation of the line that is parallel to the line $-3x + 2y = 10$ and goes through the point $(4, 7)$.

6-25.   In the diagram at right, $\triangle ABC \sim \triangle ADE$.

    a.   Draw each triangle separately on your paper. Be sure to include all measurements in your diagrams.

    b.   Find the length of $\overline{DE}$.

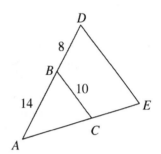

6-26.   Examine the two triangles at right.

    a.   Are the triangles congruent? Justify your conclusion. If they are congruent, complete the congruence statement $\triangle DEF$ _____ .

    b.   What series of transformation(s) are needed to change $\triangle DEF$ to $\triangle LJK$?

    c.   If $DE = 4$ units, find KL.

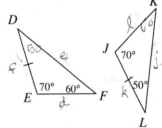

6-27.   If $b + 2a = c$ and $2a + b = 10$, then what is c? Explain how you know.

6-28.   There are 212 students enrolled in geometry at West Valley High School. 64 are freshman, and 112 are sophomores.

    a.   If a random geometry student is chosen, what is the chance (in percent) the student is a freshman or sophomore? Show how you can use the Addition Rule to answer this question. What was unusual about using the Addition Rule to answer this question?

    b.   114 of the geometry students perform in band and 56 perform in chorus. There is a 75% chance that a geometry student performs in either band or chorus. What is the probability a geometry student performs both in band and in chorus?

6.1.4 How can I organize my reasoning?

Flowcharts for Congruence

Now that you have shortcuts for establishing triangle congruence, how can you organize information in a flowchart to show that triangles are congruent? Consider this question as you work today with your team.

6-29. In problem 6-1, you determined that the triangles at right are congruent.

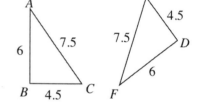

a. Which triangle congruence theorem shows that these triangles are congruent?

b. Make a flowchart showing your argument that these triangles are congruent.

c. How is a flowchart showing congruence different from a flowchart showing similarity? List every difference you can find.

6-30. In Don's congruence flowchart for problem 6-29, one of the ovals said "$\frac{AB}{FD} = 1$". In Phil's flowchart, one of the ovals said, "$AB = FD$". Discuss with your team whether these ovals say the same thing. Can equality statements like Phil's always be used in congruence flowcharts?

6-31. Make a flowchart showing that the triangles below are congruent.

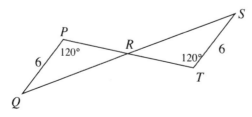

6-32.   In each diagram below, determine whether the triangles are congruent, similar but not congruent, or not similar. If you claim the triangles are similar or congruent, make a flowchart justifying your answer.

a.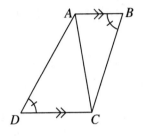

b.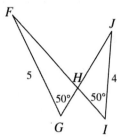

c.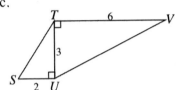

d.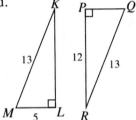

6-33.   Suppose you are working on a problem involving the two triangles $\triangle UVW$ and $\triangle XYZ$ and you know that $\triangle UVW \cong \triangle XYZ$. What can you conclude about the sides and angles of $\triangle UVW$ and $\triangle XYZ$? Write down every equation involving side lengths or angle measures that must be true.

Ⓜ ETHODS AND MEANINGS

Triangle Congruence Conditions

To show that triangles are congruent, you can show that the triangles are similar and that the common ratio between side lengths is 1 or you can use rigid motions (transformations). However, you can also use certain combinations of congruent, corresponding parts as shortcuts to determine if triangles are congruent. These combinations, called **triangle congruence conditions**, are:

SSS ≅ (Pronounced "side–side–side")
If all three pairs of corresponding sides have equal lengths, then the triangles are congruent.

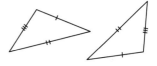

SAS ≅ (Pronounced "side–angle–side")
If two pairs of corresponding sides have equal lengths *and* the angles between them (the included angle) are equal, then the triangles are congruent.

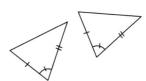

ASA ≅ (Pronounced "angle–side–angle") If two angles and the side between them in a triangle are congruent to the corresponding angles and side in another triangle, then the triangles are congruent.

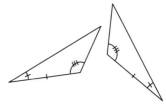

AAS ≅ (Pronounced "angle–angle–side")
If two pairs of corresponding angles *and* a pair of corresponding sides that are not between them have equal measures, then the triangles are congruent.

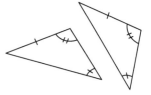

HL ≅ (Pronounced "hypotenuse–leg")
If the hypotenuse and a leg of one right triangle have the same lengths as the hypotenuse and a leg of another right triangle, the triangles are congruent.

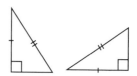

6-34.   Use your theorems about parallel lines and the angles formed with a third line to find the measures of the labeled angles below. Show each step you use and be sure to justify each one with an angle theorem from your Angle Relationships Toolkit. Be sure to write down your reasoning in the order that you find the angles.

a.

b.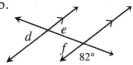

c.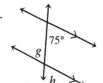

6-35.   For each pair of triangles below, decide if the pair is similar, congruent or neither. Justify your conclusion using a flowchart. Assume that the diagrams are not drawn to scale.

a.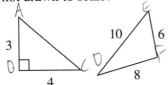

b.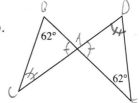

6-36.   Solve the systems of equations below using any method, if possible. Show all work and check your solution. If there is no solution, explain why not.

a. $y = 2x + 8$

    $3x + 2y = -12$

b. $2x - 5y = 4$

    $5y - 2x = 10$

6-37.   Examine the triangles at right. Solve for x.

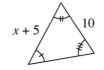

6-38.   Solve the problem below using any method. Show all work.

Angle A of $\triangle ABC$ measures 5° more than 3 times the measure of angle B. Angle C measures 20° less than angle B. Find the measure of angles A, B, and C.

6-39.   Kendra has programmed her cell phone to randomly show one of six photos
        when she turns it on. Two of the photos are of her parents, one is of her niece,
        and three are of her boyfriend, Bruce. Today she will need to turn her phone on
        twice: once before school and again after school.

        a.   Choose a model (such as a tree diagram or generic area model) to
              represent this situation.

        b.   What is the probability that both photos will be of her boyfriend?

        c.   What is the probability that neither photo will be of her niece?

6-40.   **Multiple Choice:** Given the diagram at right, which
        of the statements below is not necessarily true?

        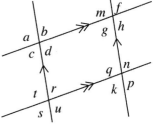

        a. $a = d$ b. $d + r = 180°$

        c. $u = n$ d. $t = m$

        e.   These all must be true.

6.1.5 What is the relationship?

Converses

So far in this chapter, you have completed several problems in which you were given certain information and had to determine whether triangles were congruent. But what if you already know triangles are congruent? What information can you conclude then? Thinking this way requires you to reverse your triangle congruence theorems. Today you will look more generally at what happens when you reverse a theorem.

6-41. Jorge is working with the diagram at right, and concludes that $\overleftrightarrow{AB} \parallel \overleftrightarrow{CD}$. He writes the following conditional statement to justify his reasoning:

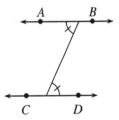

If alternate interior angles are equal, then lines are parallel.

a. Margaret is working with a different diagram, shown at right. She concludes that $x = y$. Write a conditional statement or arrow diagram that justifies her reasoning.

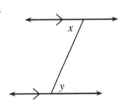

b. How are Jorge's and Margaret's statements related? How are they different?

c. Conditional statements that have this relationship are called **converses**. Write the converse of the conditional statement below.

If lines are parallel, then corresponding angles are equal.

6-42. In problem 6-41, you learned that each conditional statement has a converse. Do you think that all converses of true statements are also true? Consider the arrow diagram of a familiar theorem below.

Triangles congruent → *corresponding sides are congruent.*

a. Is this arrow diagram true?

b. Write the converse of this arrow diagram as an arrow diagram or as a conditional statement. Is this converse true? Justify your answer.

Problem continues on next page →

6-42.   *Problem continued from previous page.*

    c.   Now consider another true congruence conjecture below. Write its converse and decide if it is true. If it is true, prove it. If it is not always true, explain why not.

        Triangles congruent ➔ *corresponding angles are congruent.*

    d.   Write the converse of the arrow diagram below. Is this converse true? Justify your answer.

        A shape is a rectangle ➔ *the area of the shape is b · h.*

6-43.   CRAZY CONVERSES

For each of these problems below, make up a conditional statement or arrow diagram that meets the stated conditions. You must use a different example each time, and none of your examples can be about math!

    a.   A true statement whose converse is true.

    b.   A true statement whose converse is false.

    c.   A false statement whose converse is true.

    d.   A false statement whose converse is false.

6-44.   INFORMATION OVERLOAD

Raj is solving a problem about three triangles. He is trying to find the measure of $\angle H$ and the length of $\overline{HI}$. Raj summarizes the relationships he has found so far in the diagrams below:

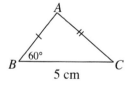
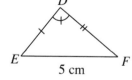
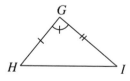

    a.   Help Raj out! Assuming everything marked in the diagram is true, find $m\angle H$ and the length of $\overline{HI}$. Make sure to justify all your claims – do not make assumptions based on how the diagram looks!

    b.   Raj is still confused. Write a careful explanation of the reasoning you used to find the values in part (a). Whenever possible, use arrow diagrams or conditional statements in explaining your reasoning.

6-45. LEARNING LOG

Write an entry in your Learning Log about the converse relationship. Explain what a converse is, and give an example of a conditional statement and its converse. Also discuss the relationship between the truth of a statement and its converse. Title this entry "Converses" and label it with today's date.

METHODS AND MEANINGS

MATH NOTES

Converses

When conditional statements (also called "If …, then …" statements) are written backwards so that the condition (the "if" part) is switched with the conclusion (the "then" part), the new statement is called a **converse**. For example, examine the theorem and its converse below:

Theorem: If two parallel lines are cut by a transversal, then pairs of corresponding angles are equal.

Converse: If two corresponding angles formed when two lines are cut by a transversal are equal, then the lines cut by the transversal are parallel.

Since the second statement is a reversal of the first, it is called its converse. Note that just because a theorem is true does not mean that its converse must be true. For example, if the conditional statement, "If the dog has a meaty bone, then the dog is happy," is true, then its converse, "If the dog is happy, then the dog has a meaty bone," is not necessarily true. The dog could be happy for other reasons, such as going for a walk.

6-46. Copy the diagram at right onto your paper. If $a = 53°$ and $g = 125°$, find the measures of each labeled angle. Explain how you find each angle, citing definitions and theorems from your toolkit that support your steps. Remember that you can find the angles in any order, depending on the angle relationships you use.

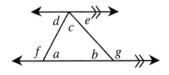

6-47.   As Samone looked at the triangles at right, she
         said, *"I think these triangles are congruent."* Her
         teammate, Darla, said, *"But they don't look the
         same. How can you tell?"* Samone smiled and
         said, *"Never trust the picture! Look at the angles
         and the sides. The measures are all the same."*

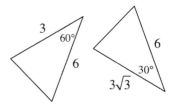

     a.   Solve for the missing side of each triangle.
            How do they compare?

     b.   Are you convinced that Samone is correct? Explain.

6-48.   Write a converse for each conditional statement below. Then, assuming the
         original statement is true, decide if the converse must be true or not.

     a.   If it rains, then the ground is wet.

     b.   If a polygon is a square, then it is a rectangle.

     c.   If a polygon is a rectangle, then it has four 90° angles.

     d.   If the shape has three angles, it is a triangle.

     e.   If two lines intersect, then vertical angles are congruent.

6-49.   On graph paper, graph the line $y = -\frac{3}{2}x + 6$. Name the x- and y-intercepts.

6-50. This problem is a checkpoint for solving proportional equations and similar figures. It will be referred to as Checkpoint 6.

a. $\frac{7-y}{5} = \frac{3}{4}$

b. $\frac{3}{y} = \frac{6}{y-2}$

c. Sam grew $1\frac{3}{4}$ inches in $4\frac{1}{2}$ months. If he continued at the same rate, how much would he grow in one year?

d. Use the figure at right to solve for x.

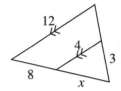

Check your answers by referring to the Checkpoint 6 materials located at the back of your book.

Ideally, at this point you are comfortable working with these types of problems and can solve them correctly. If you feel that you need more confidence when solving these types of problems, then review the Checkpoint 6 materials and try the practice problems provided. From this point on, you will be expected to do problems like these correctly and with confidence.

6-51. Donnell has a bar graph which shows the probability of a colored section coming up on a spinner, but part of the graph has been ripped off.

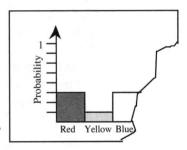

a. What is the probability of spinning red?

b. What is the probability of spinning yellow?

c. What is the probability of spinning blue?

d. If there is only one color missing from the graph, namely green, what is the probability of spinning green? Why?

6-52.

One measurement used in judging kite-flying competitions is the size of the angle formed by the kite string and the ground. This angle can be used to find the height of the kite. Suppose the length of the string is 600 feet and the angle at which the kite is flying measures 40°. Calculate the height, h, of the kite.

6.2.1 How can I use it? What is the connection?

• •

Angles on a Pool Table

The activities in this section review several big topics you have studied so far. Work with your team to decide which combination of tools you will need for each problem. As you work together, think about which skills and tools you are comfortable using and which ones you need more practice with.

As you work on this activity, keep in mind the following questions:

What mathematical concepts did you use to solve this problem?

What do you still want to know more about?

What connections did you find?

6-53.   TAKE IT TO THE BANK

Ricky just watched his favorite pool player, Montana Mike, make a double bank shot in a trick-shot competition. Montana bounced a ball off two rails (sides) of the table and sank it in the corner pocket. *"That doesn't look too hard,"* Ricky says, *"I just need to know where to put the ball and in which direction to hit it."*

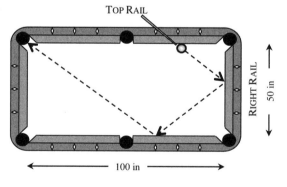

A diagram of Montana's shot is shown at right. The playing area of a tournament pool table is 50 inches by 100 inches. Along its rails, a pool table is marked with a diamond every 12.5 inches. Montana started the shot with the ball against the top rail and the ball hit the bottom rail three diamonds from the right rail.

Your Task: Figure out where on the top rail Ricky needs to place his ball and where he needs to aim to repeat Montana Mike's bank shot. Write instructions that tell Ricky how to use the diamonds on the table to place his ball correctly, and at what angle from the rail to hit the ball.

6-54.   EXTENSIONS

The algebraic and geometric tools you have developed so far will enable you to answer many questions about the path of a ball on a pool table. Work with your team to analyze the situations below.

a.   Ricky decided he wants to alter Montana's shot so that it hits the right rail exactly at its midpoint. Where would Ricky need to place the ball along the top rail so that his shot bounces off the right rail, then the bottom rail, and enters the upper left pocket? At what angle with the top rail would he need to hit the ball?

b.   During another shot, Ricky noticed that Montana hit the ball as shown in the diagram at right. He estimated that the ball traveled 18 inches before it entered the pocket. Before the shot, the announcers noted that the distance of the ball to the top rail was 2 inches more than the distance along the top rail, as shown in the diagram. Where was the ball located before Montana hit it?

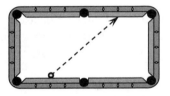

c.   Ricky wants to predict how Montana's next shot will end. The ball is placed at the second diamond from the left along the bottom rail, as shown at right. Montana is aiming to hit the ball toward the second diamond from the right along the top rail. Assuming he hits the ball very hard so that the ball continues traveling indefinitely, will the ball ever reach a pocket? If so, show the path of the ball. If not, explain how you know.

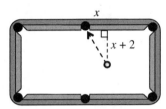

d.   After analyzing the path in part (c), Montana decided to start his ball from the third diamond from the left along the bottom rail, as shown at right. He is planning to aim at the same diamond as he did in part (c). If he hits the ball sufficiently hard, will the ball eventually reach a pocket? If so, show the path of the ball. If not, explain how you know.

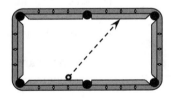

6-55.   Use your triangle tools to solve for x in the triangles below.

a.

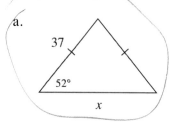

b.

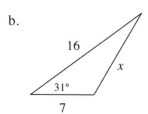

c.

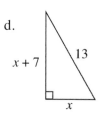

d.

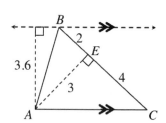

6-56.   Penelope measured several sides and heights of $\triangle ABC$, as shown in the diagram at right. Find the area of $\triangle ABC$ *twice*, using two different methods.

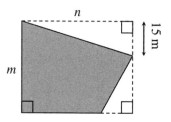

6-57.   The shaded figures at right are similar.

a.   Solve for m and n.

b.   Find the area and perimeter of each figure.

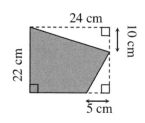

6-58. Decide if each triangle below is congruent to △*ABC* at right, similar but not congruent to △*ABC*, or neither. Justify each answer. If you decide that they are congruent, organize your reasoning into a flowchart.

a.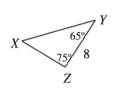

b.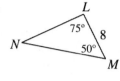

c.

6-59. On graph paper, graph the line $y = 3x + 1$.

    a. What is the slope angle of the line? That is, what is the acute angle the line makes with the *x*-axis?

    b. Find the equation of a new line that has a slope angle of 45° and passes through the point (0, 3). Assume that the slope is positive.

    c. Find the intersection of these two lines using any method. Write your solution as a point in the form (x, y).

6-60. **Multiple Choice:** Listed below are the measures of several different angles. Which angle is obtuse?

    a. 0°   b. 52°   c. 210°   d. 91°

6.2.2 How can I use it? What is the connection?

Investigating a Triangle

The activities in this section review several big topics you have studied so far. Work with your team to decide which combination of tools you will need for each problem. As you work together, think about which skills and tools you are comfortable using and which ones you need more practice with.

As you work on this activity, keep in mind the following questions:

What mathematical concepts did you use to solve this problem?

What do you still want to know more about?

What connections did you find?

6-61. GETTING TO KNOW YOUR TRIANGLE

a. If you were asked to give every possible measurement of a triangle, what measurements could you include?

b. Consider a triangle on a coordinate grid with the following vertices:

$A(2, 3), B(32, 15), C(12, 27)$

Your Task: On graph paper, graph $\triangle ABC$ and find all of its measurements. Be sure to find every measurement you listed in part (a) of this problem and show all of your calculations. With your team, be prepared to present your method for finding the area.

6-62. Examine the diagram at right. Based on the information below, what statement can you make about the relationships between the lines? Be sure to justify each conclusion. Remember: each part below is a separate problem.

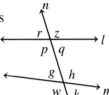

a. $p = h$

b. $w = k$

c. $r = q$

d. $z + k = 160°$

6-63. Determine if each pair of triangles below are congruent, similar but not congruent, or if they are neither. If they are congruent, organize your reasoning into a flowchart. Remember that the triangles below may not be drawn to scale.

a.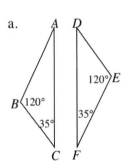

b.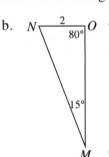

c.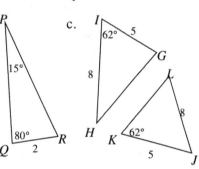

6-64. Write a converse for each conditional statement below. Then, assuming the original statement is true, decide if the converse must be true or not.

a. If the cat knocks over the lamp, then it will run away frightened.

b. If a 6-sided die is rolled, then the chances of getting a 3 are $\frac{1}{6}$.

c. If a triangle has a 90° angle, then it is a right triangle.

6-65. For the spinner at right, find the expected value of one spin.

6-66.   **Multiple Choice:** Which equation below correctly represents the relationship of the sides given in the diagram at right?

$3x - 2$ $2x + 17$

a. $3x - 2 + 2x + 17 = 360°$

b. $3x - 2 + 2x + 17 = 180°$

c. $3x - 2 + 2x + 17 = 90°$

d. $3x - 2 = 2x + 17$

6-67.   On graph paper, plot and connect the points to form quadrilateral *WXYZ* if its vertices are $W(3, 7)$, $X(3, 4)$, $Y(9, 1)$, and $Z(5, 6)$.

a.   What is the shape of quadrilateral *WXYZ*? Justify your conclusion.

b.   Find the perimeter of quadrilateral *WXYZ*.

c.   If quadrilateral *WXYZ* is reflected using the transformation function $(x \rightarrow -x, y \rightarrow y)$ to form quadrilateral *W′X′Y′Z′*, then where is *Y′*?

d.   Rotate quadrilateral *WXYZ* about the origin 90° clockwise (↻) to form quadrilateral *W″X″Y″Z″*. What is the slope of $\overline{W''Z''}$?

6.2.3 How can I use it? What is the connection?

Creating a Mathematical Model

The activities in this section review several big topics you have studied so far. Work with your team to decide which combination of tools you will need for each problem. As you work together, think about which skills and tools you are comfortable using and which ones you need more practice with.

As you work on this activity, keep in mind the following questions:

What mathematical concepts did you use to solve this problem?

What do you still want to know more about?

What connections did you find?

6-68. **AT YOUR SERVICE**

Carina, a tennis player, wants to make her serve a truly powerful part of her game. She wants to hit the ball so hard that it appears to travel in a straight path. Unfortunately, the ball always lands beyond the service box. After a few practice serves, she realizes that the height at which you hit the ball determines where the ball lands. Before she gets tired from serving, she sits down to figure out how high the ball must be when she hits it so that her serve is legal.

In the game of tennis, every point begins with one player serving the ball. For a serve to be legal, the player must stand outside the court and hit the ball so that it crosses over the net and lands within the service box (shown shaded below). It can be difficult to make the ball land in the service box because the ball is often hit too low and touches the net or is hit too high and lands beyond the service box.

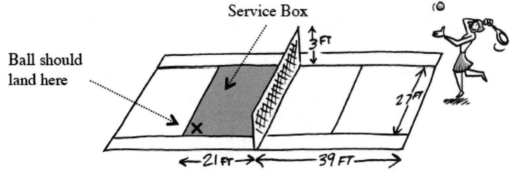

A tennis court is 78 feet long with the net stretched across the center. The distance from the net to the back of the service box is 21 feet, and the net is 3 feet tall.

Problem continues on next page →

6-68.   *Problem continues from previous page.*

Your Task: Assuming Carina can hit the ball so hard that its path is linear, from what height must she hit the ball to have the serve just clear the net and land in the service box? Decide whether or not it is reasonable for Carina to reach this height if she is 5'7" tall. Also, at what angle does the ball hit the ground?

Your solution should include:

- A labeled diagram that shows a birds' eye view of the path of the ball.

- A labeled diagram that shows the side view of Carina, the ideal height of the tennis racket, the ideal path of the tennis ball, and the measurements that are needed from the birds' eye view diagram.

Discussion Points

What would you see if you were a bird looking down
on the court as Carina served?

Which distances do you know and which do you need to find?

Further Guidance

6-69.   To help solve this problem, copy the diagram at right, which shows the tennis court from above (called a "birds-eye" view). On your diagram, locate the position of Carina and the spot where the ball should land. Be sure to include the path of the ball.

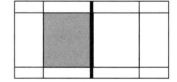

a.   Label all distances you already know. Do you see any triangles?

b.   What distance(s) can you find? What geometric tool(s) can you use?

6-70.   Next visualize the situation from the side and draw the path of the ball.

a.   As you draw this diagram, be sure to include Carina, the net, and the spot where the ball should land.

b.   Are there any similar triangles? Be careful to include any measurements that might help you determine the height of the serve.

c.   What triangle tool can you use to find the angle of the path of the ball? Find the acute angle the path of the ball makes with the ground.

6-71. How high must the ball be hit so that it just clears the net and lands in the service box? If Carina is 5'7" tall, is it possible for her to accomplish this serve? Assume that a tennis racquet is 2 feet long.

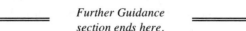

Further Guidance
section ends here.

6-72. You've been hired as a consultant for the National Tennis Association. They are considering raising the net to make the serve even more challenging. They want players to have to jump to make a successful serve (assuming that the powerful serves will be hit so hard that the ball will travel in a straight line). Determine how high the net should be so that the players must strike the ball from at least 10 feet.

6-73. Examine the triangles in the diagram at right.

a. Are the triangles similar? If you decide that they are, then justify your conclusion using a flowchart.

b. Solve for x. Show all work.

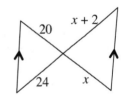

6-74. For each diagram below, use geometric relationships to solve for the given variable(s). Check your answer.

a.

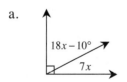

b.

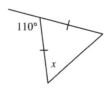

c.

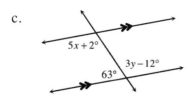

d.

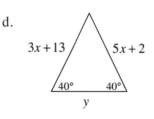

6-75.	Refrigerators that are produced on an assembly line sometimes contain defects. The probability a refrigerator has a paint blemish is 4%. The probability that it has a dent is $\frac{1}{2}$%. The probability it has both a paint blemish and a dent is also $\frac{1}{2}$%. What is the probability a refrigerator has a paint blemish or a dent? What can you conclude about defects on these refrigerators?

6-76.	Find the area and perimeter of the trapezoid at right.

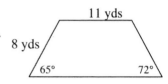

6-77.	A map of an island is shown at right. Each unit of length on the grid represents 32 feet.

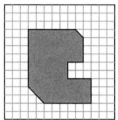

a.	Find the actual dimensions of the island (the overall width and length).

b.	Find the area of the shape at right and the actual area of the island.

6-78.	**Multiple Choice:** The length of a rectangle is three units shorter than twice its width. Which expression below could represent the area of the rectangle?

a.	$2x^2 - 3$	b.	$2x^2 - 6x$	c.	$2x^2 - 3x$	d.	$(2x - 3)^2$

6.2.4 How can I use it? What's the connection?

Analyzing a Game

The activities in this section review several big topics you have studied so far. Work with your team to decide which combination of tools you will need for each problem. As you work together, think about which skills and tools you are comfortable using and which ones you need more practice with.

As you work on this activity, keep in mind the following questions:

What mathematical concepts did you use to solve this problem?

What do you still want to know more about?

What connections did you find?

6-79. THE MONTY HALL PROBLEM

Wow! Your best friend, Lee, has been selected as a contestant in the popular "Pick-A-Door" game show. The game show host, Monty, has shown Lee three doors and, because he knows what is behind each door, has assured her that behind one of the doors lies a new car! However, behind each of the other two doors is a goat.

Lee's original choice

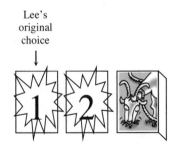

"Which door do you pick?" Monty asks.

"I pick Door #1," Lee replies confidently.

"Okay. Now, before I show you what is behind Door #1, let me show you what is behind Door #3. It is a goat! Now, would you like to change your mind and choose Door #2 instead?" Monty asks.

What should Lee do? Should she stay with Door #1 or should she switch to Door #2? Does she have a better chance of winning if she switches, or does it not matter? Discuss this situation with the class and make sure you provide reasons for your statements.

6-80.   Now test your prediction from problem 6-79 by simulating this game with a partner using either a computer or a programmable calculator. If no technology is available, collect data by playing the game with a partner as described below.

Choose one person to be the contestant and one person to be the game show host. As you play, carefully record information about whether the contestant switches doors and whether the contestant wins. Play as many times as you can in the time allotted, but be sure to record at least 10 results from switching and 10 results from not switching. Be ready to report your findings with the class.

If playing this game without technology, the host should:

- Secretly choose the winning door. Make sure that the contestant has no way of knowing which door has been selected.

- Ask the contestant to choose a door.

- "Open" one of the remaining two doors that does not have the winning prize.

- Ask the contestant if he or she wants to change his or her door.

- Show if the contestant has won the car and record the results.

6-81.   Examine the data the class collected in problem 6-80.

a.   What does this data tell you? What should Lee do in problem 6-79 to maximize her chance of winning?

b.   Your teammate, Kaye, is confused. *"Why does it matter? At the end, there are only two doors left. Isn't there a 50-50 chance that I will select the winning door?"* Explain to Kaye why switching is better.

c.   Gerald asks, *"What if there are 4 doors? If Monty now reveals two doors with a goat, is it still better to switch?"* What do you think? Analyze this problem and answer Gerald's question.

6-82.   LEARNING LOG

One of the topics you studied during Chapters 1 through 6 was probability. You investigated what made a game fair and how to predict if you would win or lose. Reflect on today's activity and write a Learning Log entry about the mathematics you used today to analyze the "Monty Hall" game. Title this entry "Game Analysis" and label it with today's date.

6-83. Determine whether or not the triangles in each pair below are congruent. Justify your conclusion with a triangle congruency condition. Then choose one pair of congruent triangles and show your reasoning with a flowchart.

a.

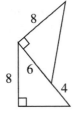

b.

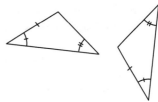

c.

d.

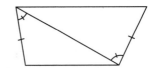

6-84. Examine the geometric relationships in each of the diagrams below. For each one, write and solve an equation to find the value of the variable. Name all geometric relationships or theorems that you use.

a.

b.

c.

d.

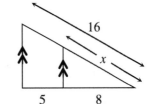

6-85.　In the diagram at right, $\overrightarrow{BD}$ **bisects** $\angle ABC$. This means that $\overrightarrow{BD}$ divides the angle into two equal parts. If $m\angle ABD = 3x + 24°$ and if $m\angle CBD = 5x + 2°$, solve for x. Then find $m\angle ABC$.

6-86.　Write a converse for each conditional statement below. Then, assuming the original statement is true, decide if the converse must be true or not.

　　a.　If the base angles of a triangle are congruent, then it is isosceles.

　　b.　If a figure is a triangle, then the sum of the angles in the figure is $180°$.

　　c.　If I clean my room, then my mom will be happy.

6-87.　A particular spinner only has two regions: green and purple. If the spinner is randomly spun twice, the probability of it landing on green twice is 16%. What is the probability of the spinner landing on purple twice?

6-88.　**Multiple Choice:** The measure of $\angle ABD$ at right is:

　　a.　$27°$　　　　b.　$161°$

　　c.　$118°$　　　　d.　$153°$

　　e.　None of these

6.2.5 How can I use it? What is the connection?

Using Transformations and Symmetry to Design Snowflakes

The activities in this section review several big topics you have studied so far. Work with your team to decide which combination of tools you will need for each problem. As you work together, think about which skills and tools you are comfortable using and which ones you need more practice with. As you work on this activity, keep in mind the following questions:

What mathematical concepts did you use to solve this problem?

What do you still want to know more about?

What connections did you find?

6-89.   THE PAPER SNOWFLAKE

You have volunteered to help the decorating committee make paper snowflakes for the upcoming winter school dance. A paper snowflake is made by folding and cutting a square piece of paper in such a way that when the paper is unfolded, the result is a beautiful design with symmetric patterns similar to those of a real snowflake.

Looking through your drawer of craft projects, you find the directions for how to fold the paper snowflake (see below). However you cannot find any directions for how to cut the folded paper to make specific designs in the final snowflake.

> DESIGNING A PAPER SNOWFLAKE: Cut out a 20 unit by 20 unit square from a piece of graph paper. Making sure that the gridlines are visible on the outside of the shape, fold the square three times as shown in the diagram below. Your final shape should be a 45°- 45°- 90° triangle that has folds along the hypotenuse.
>
>
>
> Once you have folded your paper, correctly label the sides of your folded triangle "hypotenuse," "folded leg," and "open leg" (the leg comprised of the edges of your original square). Orient your triangle as shown in the diagram at right.
>
>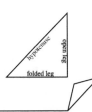

Problem continues on next page →

6-89. *Problem continued from previous page.*

Your Task: You want to be fully prepared to help the decorating committee for the school dance. Explore and be ready to explain the relationships between the shapes that are cut out and the design that appears after unfolding the paper. For each possible location of a cutout, use what you know about symmetry and transformations to describe the shapes that result when you unfold the paper.

Discussion Points

What are your goals for this task?

What tools would be useful to complete this task?

Visualize the result when a shape is cut along the hypotenuse.
What qualities will the result have?

Further Guidance

6-90. Since there are so many cuts that are possible, it is helpful to begin by considering a simple cutout along one side of the triangle.

a. Sketch triangles onto your folded paper according to these directions, making sure that none of the shapes share a side or overlap:

- A 45°-45°-90° triangle with its hypotenuse along the paper triangle's hypotenuse. Each leg should be 3 units long.

- A 45°-45°-90° triangle with a 3-unit leg along the paper triangle's folded leg.

- A 45°-45°-90° triangle with a 3-unit leg along the paper triangle's open leg.

b. Cut out the shapes you sketched from part (a). Then unfold the paper to view your snowflake. Identify the three different kinds of shapes that resulted from the triangles you cut. Describe them with as much specific vocabulary as you can.

c. Find each pair of shapes shown below on your own snowflake. For each pair, describe *two different ways* to transform one shape into the other.

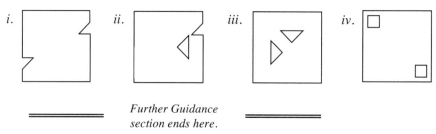

*Further Guidance
section ends here.*

6-91.   Some possible folded triangles with cutouts are shown below. What would each of these snowflakes look like when unfolded? Draw the resulting designs on the squares provided on the Lesson 6.2.5 Resource Page (or draw the result on your paper.)

a.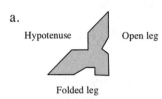

b.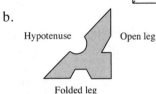

6-92.   What shape must you cut out along your folded triangle hypotenuse to get the following shapes on your snowflake when your paper is unfolded? Sketch and label diagrams to show that you can accomplish each result.

a.   Rectangle with a length that is twice its width

b.   Kite

c.   Rhombus

d.   Pentagon

6-93.   EXTENSION

Get a final piece of grid paper from your teacher. Make one more snowflake that includes at least four of the following shapes. Make sure you sketch all of your planned cuts before cutting the paper with scissors. After you cut out your shapes and unfold your snowflake, answer questions (a) through (d) below.

*   Draw a shape at the vertex where the hypotenuse and folded leg intersect that results in a shape with 8 lines of symmetry. Note that you will actually have to cut the vertex off to do this.

*   Many letters, such as E, H, and I have reflection symmetry. Pick a letter (maybe one of your initials) and draw a shape along the folded triangle's hypotenuse or folded leg that results in a box letter when cut out and the snowflake is unfolded.

*   Draw a shape along the folded triangle's hypotenuse or folded leg that results in a regular hexagon when cut out and the snowflake is unfolded.

Problem continues on next page →

6-93.   *Problem continued from previous page.*

  •   Draw a shape along the folded triangle's hypotenuse or folded leg
       that results in a star when cut out and the snowflake is unfolded.

  •   Draw curved shapes along the open leg so that there is at least one
       line of symmetry that is perpendicular to the open leg.

  a.   What has to be true about the shape you cut out in order for your unfolded
        shape to have 8 lines of symmetry?

  b.   There are two different shapes you could have drawn that would result in a
        regular hexagon. Sketch both shapes. Why do both shapes work?

  c.   Some shapes are impossible to create by cutting along the hypotenuse of
        the folded paper triangle. Sketch several different examples of these
        shapes. What is the common characteristic of these impossible shapes?

  d.   How is cutting along the open leg different from cutting along the folded
        leg or hypotenuse? Try to describe the difference in terms of symmetry.
        Use a diagram to help make your description clear.

6-94.   Examine the angles formed by parallel lines at right.

  a.   If $r = 5x + 3°$ and $k = 4x + 9°$, solve for x.
        Justify your answer.

  b.   If $c = 114°$, what is q? Justify your answer.

  c.   If $g = 88°$, then what is q? Justify your answer.

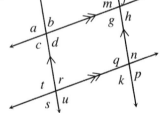

6-95.   Write the equation of each line described below in slope-intercept form
         ($y = mx + b$).

  a. $m = \frac{6}{5}$ and $b = -3$ b. $m = -\frac{1}{4}$ and $b = 4.5$

  c. $m = \frac{1}{3}$ and the line passes   d. $m = 0$ and $b = 2$
        through the origin $(0, 0)$

6-96.   For each part below, decide if the triangles are similar. If they are similar, use their similarity to solve for x. If they are not similar, explain why not.

a.
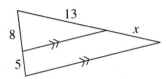

b.
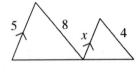

c.
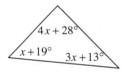

6-97.   For each shape below, use the geometric relationships to solve for the given variable(s). Show all work. Name the geometric relationships you used.

a.
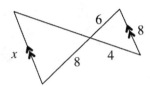

b.
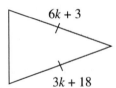

c.
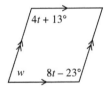

d.
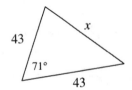

6-98.   Jinning is going to flip a coin. If the result is "heads," he wins $4. If the result is "tails," he loses $7.

a.   What is his expected value per flip?

b.   If he flips the coin 8 times, how much should he win or lose?

6-99.   **Multiple Choice:** What is the distance between the points $(-2, -5)$ and $(6, 3)$?

a.   8   b. $8\sqrt{2}$ c.   16   d.   64

Chapter 6 Closure   What have I learned?

Reflection and Synthesis

The activities below offer you a chance to
reflect about what you have learned during this
chapter. As you work, look for concepts that
you feel very comfortable with, ideas that you
would like to learn more about, and topics you
need more help with. Look for connections
between ideas as well as connections with
material you learned previously.

①   TEAM BRAINSTORM

What have you studied in this chapter? What ideas were important in what you
learned? With your team, brainstorm a list. Be as detailed as you can. To help
get you started, lists of Learning Log entries and Math Notes boxes are below.

What topics, ideas, and words that you learned *before* this chapter are connected
to the new ideas in this chapter? Again, be as detailed as you can.

How long can you make your list? Challenge yourselves. Be prepared to share
your team's ideas with the class.

Learning Log Entries
- Lesson 6.1.5 – Converses
- Lesson 6.2.4 – Game Analysis

Math Notes
- Lesson 6.1.1 – Congruent Shapes
- Lesson 6.1.4 – Triangle Congruence Conditions
- Lesson 6.1.5 – Converses

②   MAKING CONNECTIONS

Below is a list of the vocabulary used in this chapter. Make sure that you are familiar with all of these words and know what they mean. Refer to the glossary or index for any words that you do not yet understand.

AAS $\cong$	arrow diagrams	ASA $\cong$
bisect	conditional statement	congruent
conjecture	converse	corresponding parts
flowchart	HL $\cong$	SAS $\cong$
similar	SSS $\cong$	

triangle congruence conditions

Make a concept map showing all of the connections you can find among the key words and ideas listed above. To show a connection between two words, draw a line between them and explain the connection, as shown in the model below. A word can be connected to any other word as long as you can justify the connection. For each key word or idea, provide an example or sketch that shows the idea.

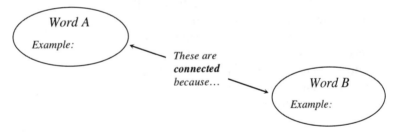

Your teacher may provide you with vocabulary cards to help you get started. If you use the cards to plan your concept map, be sure either to re-draw your concept map on your paper or to glue the vocabulary cards to a poster with all of the connections explained for others to see and understand.

While you are making your map, your team may think of related words or ideas that are not listed here. Be sure to include these ideas on your concept map.

③   PORTFOLIO: EVIDENCE OF MATHEMATICAL PROFICIENCY

This portfolio entry gives you the opportunity to showcase your understanding of the geometric concepts studied so far in the course.

Your teacher will indicate which of the problems from Lessons 6.2.1 through 6.2.5 you are to use as your portfolio entry. Revise your initial work if you need to so that you are showing off the very best work you know how to do. Record your work neatly and justify each step as evidence of the mathematics you are now able to do. Include as much detail as you can.

④   WHAT HAVE I LEARNED?

Most of the problems in this section represent typical problems found in this chapter. They serve as a gauge for you. You can use them to determine which types of problems you can do well and which types of problems require further study and practice. Even if your teacher does not assign this section, it is a good idea to try these problems and find out for yourself what you know and what you still need to work on.

Solve each problem as completely as you can. The table at the end of the closure section has answers to these problems. It also tells you where you can find additional help and practice with problems like these.

CL 6-100.   Write the converse of each statement and then determine whether or not the converse is true.

       a.   If two lines are parallel, then pairs of corresponding angles are equal.

       b.   In $\triangle ABC$, if the sum of $m\angle A$ and $m\angle B$ is $110°$, then $m\angle C = 70°$.

       c.   If alternate interior angles k and s are not equal, then the two lines cut by the transversal are not parallel.

       d.   If Johan throws coins in the fountain, then he loses his money.

CL 6-101. Determine whether or not the two triangles in each part below are congruent. If they are congruent, show your reasoning in a flowchart. If the triangles are not congruent or you cannot determine that they are, justify your conclusion.

a.

b.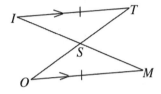

c.

d.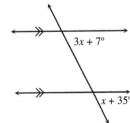

CL 6-102. For each part, determine which lines, if any, are parallel. Be sure to justify your decisions.

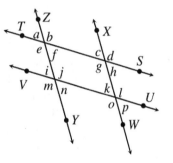

a. $\angle e \cong \angle m$

b. $\angle c \cong \angle o$

c. $\angle d \cong \angle o$

d. $\angle a \cong \angle m \cong \angle o$

e. $\angle a \cong \angle k$

f. $\angle k \cong \angle c \cong \angle f$

CL 6-103. For each diagram, solve for the variable. Be sure to include the names of any relationships you used to get your solution.

a.

b.

c.

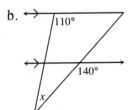

CL 6-104.   Cynthia is planning a party. For entertainment, she has designed a game
            that involves spinning two spinners. If the sum of the numbers on the
            spinners is 10 or greater, the guests can choose a prize from a basket of
            candy bars. If the sum is less than 10, then the guest will be thrown in the
            pool. She has two possible pairs of spinners, shown below. For each pair of
            spinners, determine the probability of getting tossed in the pool. Assume
            that Spinners B, C, and D are equally subdivided.

a. 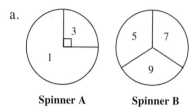   b.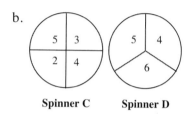

      Spinner A   Spinner B   Spinner C   Spinner D

CL 6-105.   Yee Ping thought about swimming
            across Redleaf Lake. She knows that
            she can swim about 1000 meters. She
            decided that she would feel more
            confident if she knew how far she
            would have to swim. To determine
            the length of the lake, she put posts at
            both ends of the lake (points A and B)
            and a third post on one side of the lake
            (point C). The distances between the
            posts are shown in the diagram at
            right. She measured the angle
            between the two posts and found that it was 150°. Use this information to
            determine the length of the lake. Do you think that Yee Ping will be able to
            swim between points A and B?

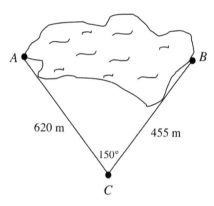

CL 6-106.   Your teacher has constructed a spinner like the one at
            right. He has informed you that the class gets one spin.
            If the spinner lands on the shaded region, you will have a
            quiz tomorrow. What is the probability that you will
            have a quiz tomorrow? Explain how you know.

CL 6-107.   For each spinner below, find the expected value of one spin.

a. 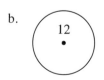   b.

CL 6-108.   Margarite has 9 pieces of copper pipe with which she plans to make 3 triangular frames. She has organized them into groups of three based on their coloring. The lengths of the pipes in each group are listed below.

      i. $23, 21, 4$ *ii.* $2, 11, 10$ *iii.* $31, 34, 3$

    a.   Which groups, if any, will she actually be able to use to make a triangular frame if she is unable to cut any of the pipes? How do you know?

    b.   If possible, arrange the 9 pieces she has so that she can make 3 triangular frames. If so, how? If not, why not?

CL 6-109.   At a story-telling class, Barbara took notes on the following story. However, all the parts of the story got mixed up. Help her make sense of the story by organizing the following details in a flowchart.

    a.   Maggie was happy she could play on the same team as Julie and Cheryl.

    b.   Julie was hoping to make the A team again this year as she grabbed her basketball and got on a bus in Bellingham.

    c.   Cheryl, having been named most valuable player in Port Townsend, started the drive to the statewide basketball camp.

    d.   Because of her skill in the first game, Maggie moved up to the A team.

    e.   At camp, Julie and Cheryl were placed on the A team.

    f.   Julie, Maggie and Cheryl met at a statewide basketball camp. Shortly after they met, they were placed on teams.

    g.   This year was Maggie's first year at camp, and was placed on the B team.

    h.   On the train to camp, Maggie thought about how surprising it was that her basketball coach chose her to attend camp.

CL 6-110.   Check your answers using the table at the end of this section. Which problems do you feel confident about? Which problems were hard? Have you worked on problems like these in math classes you have taken before? Use the table to make a list of topics you need help on and a list of topics you need to practice more.

Answers and Support for Closure Activity #4
What Have I Learned?

MN = Math Notes, LL = Learning Log

Problem	Solutions	Need Help?	More Practice
CL 6-100.	a. True; If a pair of corresponding angles formed by two lines and a transversal are equal, then the two lines are parallel.	Lesson 6.1.5 MN: 6.1.5 LL: 6.1.5	Problems 6-48, 6-64, and 6-86
	b. True; In $\triangle ABC$, if angle C is 70°, then the sum of angles A and B is 110°.		
	c. True; If lines cut by a transversal that form alternate interior angles are not parallel, then those angles are not equal.		
	d. False; If Johan loses money, then he has thrown coins in the fountain.		
CL 6-101.	a. Congruent 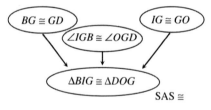	Lessons 6.1.1, 6.1.2, 6.1.3, and 6.1.4 MN: 3.2.2, 3.2.4, 3.2.5, 6.1.1, and 6.1.4 LL: 3.2.2	Problems 6-26, 6-47, 6-58, 6-63, and 6-83
	b. Congruent 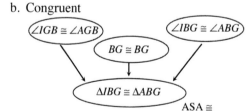		
	c. Not enough information.		
	d. Congruent 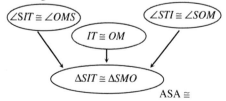		

Problem	Solutions	Need Help?	More Practice
CL 6-102.	a. $\overline{ST} \parallel \overline{UV}$; corres. angles are equal. b. Not enough information. c. $\overline{ST} \parallel \overline{UV}$; alt. interior angles are equal. d. $\overline{ZY} \parallel \overline{XW}$; corres. angles are equal. e. Not enough information. f. $\overline{ZY} \parallel \overline{XW}$; $\overline{ST} \parallel \overline{UV}$; corres. angles and alternate interior angles are equal.	Section 2.1 MN: 2.1.1, 2.1.4, and 2.2.1 LL: 2.1.1 Angle Relationship Toolkit	Problems CL 2-122, CL 4-125, 6-14, 6-34, 6-40, 6-46, 6-62, and 6-94
CL 6-103.	Reasons may vary. One possible set of reasons is listed for each: a. $x = 100°$ Triangle Angle Sum Theorem and supplementary angles b. $x = 30°$ Triangle Angle Sum Theorem, corresponding and supplementary angles c. $x = 14°$ corresponding angles	Section 2.1 MN: 2.1.1, 2.1.4, and 2.2.1 LL: 2.1.1 Angle Relationship Toolkit	Problems CL 2-122, CL 4-125, 6-14, 6-34, 6-40, 6-46, 6-62, 6-88, and 6-94
CL 6-104.	a. $\frac{3}{12} + \frac{3}{12} + \frac{1}{12} = \frac{7}{12}$ b. $\frac{9}{12}$	Section 4.2 MN: 1.2.1, 4.1.5, 4.2.3, and 4.2.4 LL: 4.2.3	Problems CL 4-127, CL 5-145, 6-18, 6-28, 6-39, 6-75, and 6-87
CL 6-105.	The lake is about 1039 meters wide. This means Yee might have a problem.	Lesson 5.3.3 MN: 5.3.3	Problems CL 5-146, and 6-15(c)
CL 6-106.	$360° - 40° = 320°$, so $\frac{320}{360} = \frac{8}{9} \approx 89\%$	Section 4.2 MN: 1.2.1, 4.1.5, 4.2.3, and 4.2.4 LL: 4.2.3	Problems CL 4-127 and 6-51
CL 6-107.	a. $\frac{53}{12}$, or ≈ 4.42 b. 12	Lesson 4.2.5 MN: 5.2.2	Problems CL 5-141, 6-65, and 6-98

Problem	Solutions	Need Help?	More Practice

CL 6-108.	a. Sets *i* and *ii* work.
	
	b. It is possible.
	   i. 4, 31, 34
	   ii. 3, 21, 23
	   iii. 2, 10, 11
		Lesson 2.3.1
		
		LL: 2.3.1
			Problems CL 3-117, CL 5-144, and 6-19

CL 6-109.	One possible solution: 	Lesson 3.2.2 MN: 3.2.4 LL: 3.2.2	Problems CL 3-121, 4-72, 5-34, 5-56, and 6-8

CHAPTER 7   Proof and Quadrilaterals

This chapter opens with a set of explorations designed to introduce you to new geometric topics that you will explore further in Chapters 8 through 12. You will learn about the special properties of a circle, explore three-dimensional shapes, and use a hinged mirror to learn more about a rhombus.

Section 7.2 then builds on your work from Chapters 3 through 6. Using congruent triangles, you will explore the relationships of the sides and diagonals of a parallelogram, kite, trapezoid, rectangle, and rhombus. As you explore new geometric properties, you will formalize your understanding of proof.

Guiding Question

Mathematically proficient students will construct viable arguments and critique the reasoning of others.

As you work through this chapter, ask yourself:

How can I use the given information to construct arguments, how can I justify my conclusions and how can I respond to the arguments of others.

This chapter ends with an exploration of coordinate geometry.

In this chapter, you will learn:

➢ The relationships of the sides, angles, and diagonals of special quadrilaterals, such as parallelograms, rectangles, kites, and rhombi (plural of rhombus).

➢ How to write a convincing proof in a variety of formats, such as a flowchart or two-column proof.

➢ How to find the midpoint of a line segment.

➢ How to use algebraic tools to explore quadrilaterals on coordinate axes.

Chapter Outline

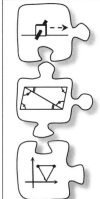

Section 7.1 This section contains four large investigations introducing you to geometry topics that will be explored further in Chapters 8 through 12.

Section 7.2 While investigating what congruent triangles can inform you about the sides, angles, and diagonals of a quadrilateral, you will develop an understanding of proof.

Section 7.3 This section begins a focus on coordinate geometry, that is, the study of geometry on coordinate axes. During this section, you will use familiar algebraic tools (such as slope) to make and justify conclusions about shapes.

7.1.1 Does it roll smoothly?

Properties of a Circle

In Chapters 1 through 6, you studied many different types of two-dimensional shapes, explored how they could be related, and developed tools to measure their lengths and areas. In Chapters 7 through 12, you will examine ways to extend these ideas to new shapes (such as polygons and circles) and will thoroughly investigate what you can learn about three-dimensional shapes.

Section 7.1 contains four key investigations that will touch upon the big ideas of the following chapters. As you explore these lessons, take note of what mathematical tools from Chapters 1 through 6 you are using and think about what new directions this course will take. Generate "What if…" questions that can be answered later once new tools are developed.

Since much of the focus of Chapters 7 through 12 is on the study of circles, this lesson will first explore the properties of a circle. What makes a circle special? Today you are going to answer that question and, at the same time, explore other shapes with surprisingly similar qualities.

7-1. THE INVENTION OF THE WHEEL

One of the most important human inventions was the wheel. Many archeologists estimate that the wheel was probably first invented about 10,000 years ago in Asia. It was an important tool that enabled humans to transport very heavy objects long distances. Most people agree that impressive structures, such as the Egyptian pyramids, could not have been built without the help of wheels.

a. One of the earliest types of "wheels" used were actually logs. Ancient civilizations laid multiple logs on the ground, parallel to each other, under a heavy item that needed to be moved. As long as the logs had the same diameter and the road was even, the heavy object had a smooth ride. What is special about a circle that allows it to be used in this way? In other words, why do circles enable this heavy object to roll smoothly?

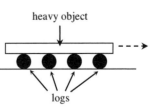

Problem continues on next page →

7-1. *Problem continued from previous page.*

b. What happens to a point on a wheel as it turns? For example, as the wheel at right rolls along the line, what is the path of point P? Imagine a piece of gum stuck to a tire as it rolls. On your paper, draw the motion of point P. If you need help, find a coin or other round object and test this situation.

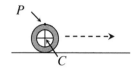

c. Now turn your attention to the center of the wheel (labeled C in the diagram above). As the wheel rolls along the line, what is the path of point C? Describe its motion. Why does that happen?

7-2. DO CIRCLES MAKE THE BEST WHEELS?

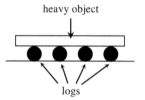

As you read in problem 7-1, ancient civilizations used circular logs to roll heavy objects. However, is a circle the only shape they could have chosen? Are there any other shapes that could rotate between a flat road and a heavy object in a similar fashion?

Examine the shapes below. Would logs of any of these shapes be able to roll heavy objects in a similar fashion? Be prepared to defend your conclusion!

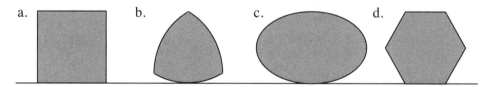

7-3.   Stan says that he has a tricycle with square wheels and
        claims that it can ride as smoothly as a tricycle with
        circular wheels! Rosita does not believe him. Analyze
        this possibility with your team as you answer the
        questions below.

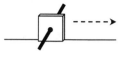

a.   Is Stan's claim possible? Describe what it would be like to ride a tricycle
      with square tires. What type of motion would the rider experience? Why
      does this happen?

b.   When Rosita challenged him, Stan confessed that he needed a special road
      so that the square wheels would be able to rotate smoothly and would keep
      Stan at a constant height. What would his road need to look like? Draw
      an example on your paper.

c.   How would Stanley need to change his road to be able to ride a tricycle
      with rectangular (but non-square) wheels? Draw an example on your
      paper.

d.   As the picture at right[1] shows,
      square wheels are possible if
      the road is specially curved to
      accommodate the change in
      the length of the radius of the
      wheel as it rotates. An
      example is shown below.

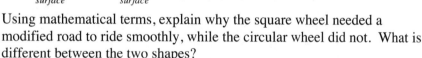

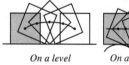

On a level   *On a curved*
surface   *surface*

Using mathematical terms, explain why the square wheel needed a
modified road to ride smoothly, while the circular wheel did not. What is
different between the two shapes?

_____

[1] The picture above shows Stan Wagon riding his special square-wheeled tricycle. This tricycle is on display at
Macalester College in St. Paul, Minnesota. *Reprinted with permission.*

7-4.   REULEAUX CURVES

Reuleaux (pronounced "roo LOW") curves are special
because they have a constant diameter. That means that as a
Reuleaux curve rotates, its height remains constant. Although
the diagram at right is an example of a Reuleaux curve based
on an equilateral triangle, these special curves can be based
on any regular polygon with an odd number of sides.

a.   What happens to the center (point C)
as the Reuleaux wheel at right rolls?

b.   Since logs with a Reuleaux curve shape can also smoothly roll heavy
objects, why are these shapes not used for bicycle wheels? In other words,
what is the difference between a circle and a Reuleaux curve?

7-5.   LEARNING LOG

A big focus of Chapters 7 through 12 is on circles. What
did you learn about circles today? Did you learn anything
about other shapes that was new or that surprised you?
Write a Learning Log entry explaining what you learned about the shapes of
wheels. Title this entry "Shapes of Wheels" and label it with today's date.

7-6.   Examine $\triangle ABC$ and $\triangle DEF$ at right.

a.   Assume the triangles at right are not drawn
to scale. Complete a flowchart to justify
the relationship between the two triangles.

b.   Find AC and DF.

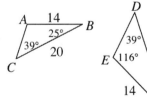

7-7.   Use the relationships in the diagram at right to find the
values of each variable. Name which geometric
relationships you used.

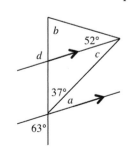

Core Connections Geometry

7-8.   A rectangle has one side of length 11 mm and a diagonal of 61 mm. Draw a diagram of this rectangle and find its width and area.

7-9.   Troy is thinking of a shape. He says that it has four sides and that no sides have equal length. He also says that no sides are parallel. What is the best name for his shape?

7-10.   Without using your calculator, find the exact values of x and y in each diagram below.

a.
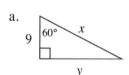

b.
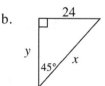

c.

7-11.   Solve each system of equations below, if possible. If it is not possible, explain what the lack of an algebraic solution tells you about the graphs of the equations. Write each solution in the form (x, y). Show all work.

a. $y = -2x - 1$
     $y = \frac{1}{2}x - 16$

b. $y = x^2 + 1$
     $y = -x^2$

7.1.2 What can I build with a circle?

Building a Tetrahedron

In later chapters, you will learn more about polygons, circles, and three-dimensional shapes. Later investigations will require that you remember key concepts you have already learned about triangles, parallel lines, and other angle relationships. Today you will have the opportunity to review some of the geometry you have learned while also beginning to think about what you will be studying in the future.

As you work with your team, consider the following focus questions:

Is there more than one way?

How can you be sure that is true?

What else can we try?

7-12.   IS THERE MORE TO THIS CIRCLE?

Circles can be folded to create many different shapes. Today, you will work with a circle and use properties of other shapes to develop a three-dimensional shape. Be sure to have reasons for each conclusion you make as you work. Each person in your team should start by obtaining a copy of a circle from your teacher and cutting it out.

a.   Fold the circle in half to create a crease that lies on a line of symmetry of the circle. Unfold the circle and then fold it in half again to create a new crease that is perpendicular to the first crease. Unfold your paper back to the full circle. How could you convince someone else that your creases are perpendicular? What is another name for the line segment represented by each crease?

b.   On the circle, label the endpoints of one diameter A and B. Fold the circle so that point A touches the center of the circle and create a new crease. Then label the endpoints of this crease C and D. What appears to be the relationship between $\overline{AB}$ and $\overline{CD}$? Discuss and justify with your team. Be ready to share your reasons with the class.

c.   Now fold the circle twice to form creases $\overline{BC}$ and $\overline{BD}$ and use scissors to cut out $\triangle BCD$. What type of triangle is $\triangle BCD$? How can you be sure? Be ready to convince the class.

7-13.   ADDING DEPTH

Your equilateral triangle should now be flat (also called two-dimensional).
Two-dimensional shapes have length and width, but not depth (or "thickness").

a.   If you cut the labels off when creating your equilateral triangle, label the
vertices of $\triangle BCD$ again. Then, with the unmarked side of the triangle
facedown, fold and crease the triangle so that B touches the midpoint of
$\overline{CD}$. Keep it in the folded position.

What does the resulting shape appear to be? What smaller shapes do you
see inside the larger shape? Justify that your ideas are correct. For
example, if you think that lines are parallel, you must provide evidence.

b.   Open your shape again so that you have the large equilateral triangle in
front of you. How does the length of a side of the large triangle compare
to the length of the side of the small triangle formed by the crease? How
many of the small triangles would fit inside the large triangle? In what
ways are the small and large triangles related?

c.   Repeat the fold in part (a) so that C touches the midpoint of $\overline{BD}$. Unfold
the triangle and fold again so that D touches the midpoint of $\overline{BC}$. Create a
three-dimensional shape by bringing points B, C, and D together. A **three-
dimensional** shape has length, width, and depth. Use tape to hold your
shape together.

d.   Three-dimensional shapes formed with polygons have **faces** and **edges**, as
well as **vertices** (plural of vertex). Faces are the flat surfaces of the shape,
while edges are the line segments formed when two faces meet. Vertices
are the points where edges intersect. Discuss with your team how to use
these words to describe your new shape. Then write a complete
description. If you think you know the name of this shape, include it in
your description.

7-14. Your team should now have 4 three-dimensional shapes (called tetrahedra). If you are working in a smaller team, you should quickly fold more shapes so that you have a total of four.

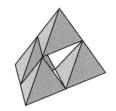

a. Put four tetrahedra together to make an enlarged tetrahedron like the one pictured at right. Is the larger tetrahedron similar to the small tetrahedron? How can you tell?

b. To determine the edges and faces of the new shape, pretend that it is solid. How many edges does a tetrahedron have? Are all of the edges the same length? How does the length of an edge of the team shape compare with the length of an edge of one of the small shapes?

c. How many faces of the small tetrahedral would it take to cover the face of the large tetrahedron? Remember to count gaps as part of a face. Does the area of the tetrahedron change in the same way as the length?

Enlarged tetrahedron   Original

METHODS AND MEANINGS

Parts of a Circle

A **circle** is the set of all points on a flat surface that are the same distance from a fixed central point, C, referred to as its **center**. This text will use the notation $\odot C$ to name a circle with center at point C.

circle

The **radius** is a line segment from the center to a point on the circle. Its length is usually denoted r. However, a line segment drawn through the center of the circle with both endpoints on the circle is called a **diameter** and its length is usually denoted d.

Notice that a diameter of a circle is always twice as long as the radius.

7-15. What is the relationship between $\triangle ABC$ and $\triangle GHJ$ at right? Create a flowchart to justify your conclusion.

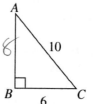

7-16. The area of the trapezoid at right is 56 cm². What is h? Show all work.

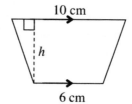

7-17. Line L is perpendicular to the line $6x - y = 7$ and passes through the point $(0, 6)$. Line M is parallel to the line $y = \frac{2}{3}x - 4$ and passes through the point $(-3, -1)$. Where do these lines intersect? Explain how you found your solution.

7-18. Examine the geometric relationships in each of the diagrams below. For each one, write and solve an equation to find the value of the variable. Name any geometric property or conjecture that you used.

a.

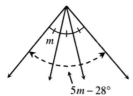

b.

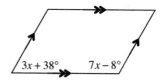

c. $\triangle ABC$ is equilateral.

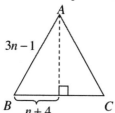

d. Point C is the center of the circle.
$AB = 11x - 1$ and $CD = 3x + 12$

7-19.   In the Shape Factory, you created many shapes by
         rotating triangles about the midpoint of its sides.
         (Remember that the **midpoint** is the point exactly
         halfway between the endpoints of the line segment.)
         However, what if you rotate a trapezoid instead?

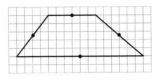

         Carefully draw the trapezoid above on graph paper, along with the given
         midpoints. Then rotate the trapezoid 180° about one of the midpoints and
         examine the resulting shape formed by both trapezoids (the original and its
         image). Continue this process with each of the other midpoints, until you
         discover all the shapes that can be formed by a trapezoid and its image when
         rotated 180° about the midpoint of one of its sides.

7-20.   On graph paper, plot the points $A(-5, 7)$ and $B(3, 1)$.

         a.   Find AB (the length of $\overline{AB}$).

         b.   Locate the midpoint of $\overline{AB}$ and label it C. What are the coordinates of C?

         c.   Find AC. Can you do this without using the Pythagorean Theorem?

Core Connections Geometry

7.1.3 What is the shortest distance?

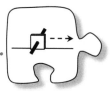

Shortest Distance Problems

Questions such as, "What length will result in the largest area?" or "When was the car traveling the slowest?" concern *optimization*. To optimize a quantity is to find the "best" possibility. Calculus is often used to solve optimization problems, but geometric tools can sometimes offer surprisingly simple and elegant solutions.

7-21.   INTERIOR DESIGN

Laura needs your help. She needs to order expensive wire to connect her sound system to her built-in speakers and would like your help to save her money.

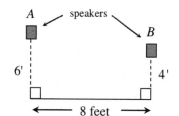

She plans to place her sound system somewhere on a cabinet that is 8 feet wide. Speaker A is located 6 feet above one end of the cabinet, while speaker B is located 4 feet above the other end. She will need wire to connect the sound system to speaker A, and additional wire to connect it to speaker B.

Where should she place her sound system that she needs the least amount of wire?

Your Task: Before you discuss this with your team, make your own guess. What does your intuition tell you? Then, using the Lesson 7.1.3 Resource Page, work with your team to determine where on the cabinet the sound system should be placed. How can you be sure that you found the best answer? In other words, how do you know that the amount of wire you found is the least amount possible?

Discussion Points

What is this problem about? What are you supposed to find?

What is a reasonable estimate of the total length of speaker wire?

What mathematical tools could be helpful to solve this problem?

Further Guidance

7-22.   To help solve problem 7-21, first collect some data.

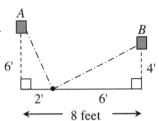

a.   Calculate the total length of wire needed if the sound system is placed 2 feet from the left edge of the cabinet (the edge below Speaker A), as shown in the diagram at right.

b.   Now calculate the total length of wire needed if the sound system is placed 3 feet from the same edge. Does this placement require more or less wire than that from part (a)?

c.   Continue testing placements for the sound system and create a table with your results. Where should the sound system be placed to minimize the amount of wire?

Further Guidance section ends here.

7-23.   This problem reminds Bradley of problem 3-105, *You Are Getting Sleepy…*, in which you and a partner created two triangles by standing and gazing into a mirror. He remembered that the only way two people could see each other's eyes in the mirror was when the triangles were similar. Examine your solution to problem 7-21. Are the two triangles created by the speaker wires similar? Justify your conclusion.

7-24.   Bradley enjoyed solving problem 7-21 so much that he decided to create other "shortest distance" problems. For each situation below, first predict where the shortest path would be using visualization and intuition. Then find a way to determine whether the path you chose is, in fact, the shortest.

a.   In this first puzzle, Bradley decided to test what would happen on the side of a cylinder, such as a soup can. On a can provided by your teacher, find points *A* and *B* labeled on the outside of the can. With your team, determine the shortest path from point *A* to point *B* along the surface of the can. (In other words, no part of your path can go inside the can.) Describe how you found your solution.

b.   What if the shape is a cube? Using a cube provided by your teacher, predict which path would be the shortest path from opposite corners of the cube (labeled points *C* and *D* in the diagram at right). Then test your prediction. Describe how you found the shortest path.

7-25.   MAKING CONNECTIONS

As Bradley looked over his answer from
problem 7-21, he couldn't help but wonder if
there is a way to change this problem into a
straight-line problem like those in problem 7-24.

a.   On the Lesson 7.1.3 Resource Page, reflect
one of the speakers so that when the two
speakers are connected with a straight line,
the line passes through the horizontal cabinet.

b.   When the speakers from part (a) are
connected with a straight line, two triangles
are formed. How are the two triangles
related? Justify your conclusion.

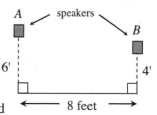

c.   Use the fact that the triangles are similar to find
where the sound system should be placed. Did
your answer match that from problem 7-21?

7-26.   TAKE THE SHOT

While playing a game of pool,
Montana Mike needed to hit the
last remaining ball into pocket A,
as shown in the diagram below.
However, to show off, he decided
to make the ball first hit at least
one of the rails of the table.

Your Task: On the Lesson 7.1.3
Resource Page provided by your
teacher, determine where Mike
could bounce the ball off a rail so
that it will land in pocket A.
Work with your team to find as
many possible locations as you
can. Can you find a way he
could hit the ball so that it would
rebound twice before entering
pocket A?

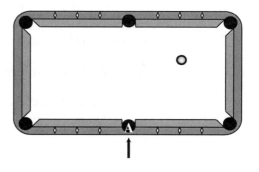

Be ready to share your solutions with the class.

7-27. LEARNING LOG

Look over your work from this lesson. What mathematical
ideas did you use? What connections, if any, did you find?
Can any other problems you have seen so far be solved
using a straight line? Describe the mathematical ideas you developed during
this lesson in your Learning Log. Title this entry "Shortest Distance" and label
it with today's date.

Mᴇᴛʜᴏᴅꜱ ᴀɴᴅ Mᴇᴀɴɪɴɢꜱ

Congruent Triangles → Congruent Corresponding Parts

MATH NOTES

As you learned in Chapter 3, if two shapes are congruent, then
they have exactly the same shape and the same size. This means that if
you know two triangles are congruent, you can state that corresponding
parts are congruent. This can be also stated with the arrow diagram:

$$\cong \Delta s \to \,\cong \text{parts}$$

For example, if $\triangle ABC \cong \triangle PQR$, then it follows that $\angle A \cong \angle P$,
$\angle B \cong \angle Q$, and $\angle C \cong \angle R$. Also, $\overline{AB} \cong \overline{PQ}$, $\overline{AC} \cong \overline{PR}$, and $\overline{BC} \cong \overline{QR}$.

Review & Preview

7-28. $\triangle XYZ$ is reflected across $\overline{XZ}$, as shown at right.

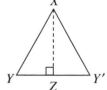

a. How can you justify that the points Y, Z, and Y'
all lie on a straight line?

b. What is the relationship between $\triangle XYZ$ and $\triangle X'Y'Z'$? Why?

c. Read the Math Notes box for this lesson. Then make all the statements
you can about the corresponding parts of these two triangles.

7-29.   Remember that a midpoint of a line segment is the point that divides the segment into two segments of equal length. On graph paper, plot the points $P(0, 3)$ and $Q(0, 11)$. Where is the midpoint M if $PM = MQ$? Explain how you found your answer.

7-30.   Examine the diagram at right. Find two equivalent expressions that represent the area of the *inner* square.

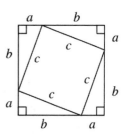

7-31.   For each pair of triangles below, decide whether the triangles are similar and/or congruent. Justify each conclusion.

a.

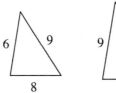

b.

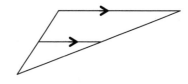

c.

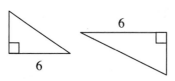

d.

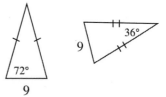

7-32.   On graph paper, plot and connect the points $A(1, 1)$, $B(2, 3)$, $C(5, 3)$, and $D(4, 1)$ to form quadrilateral $ABCD$.

    a.   What is the best name for quadrilateral $ABCD$? Justify your answer.

    b.   Find and compare $m\angle DAB$ and $m\angle BCD$. What is their relationship?

    c.   Find the equations of diagonals $\overline{AC}$ and $\overline{BD}$. Are the diagonals perpendicular?

    d.   Find the point where diagonals $\overline{AC}$ and $\overline{BD}$ intersect.

7-33.   Solve each system of equations below, if possible. If it is not possible, explain what having "no solution" tells you about the graphs of the equations. Write each solution in the form (x, y). Show all work.

a. $y = -\frac{1}{3}x + 7$

$y = -\frac{1}{3}x - 2$

b. $y = 2x + 3$

$y = x^2 - 2x + 3$

7-34.   How long is the longest line segment that will fit inside a square of area 50 square units? Show all work.

7-35.   Graph and connect the points $G(-2, 2)$, $H(3, 2)$, $I(6, 6)$, and $J(1, 6)$ to form $GHIJ$.

a.   What specific type of shape is quadrilateral $GHIJ$? Justify your conclusion.

b.   Find the equations of the diagonals $\overline{GI}$ and $\overline{HJ}$.

c.   Compare the slopes of the diagonals. How do the diagonals of a rhombus appear to be related?

d.   Find J' if quadrilateral $GHIJ$ is rotated 90° clockwise (↻) about the origin.

e.   Find the area of quadrilateral $GHIJ$.

7-36.   The four triangles at right are placed in a bag. If you reach into the bag without looking and pull out one triangle at random, what is the probability that:

a.   The triangle is scalene?

b.   The triangle is isosceles?

c.   at least one side of the triangle is 6 cm?

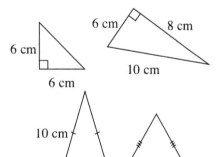

7-37.   Examine the relationships in the diagrams below. For each one, write an equation and solve for the given variable(s). Show all work.

a.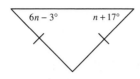

b.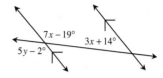

c.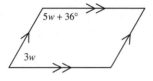

d.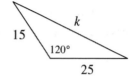

7-38.   Copy the table below on your paper and complete it for the equation $y = x^2 + 2x - 3$. Then graph and connect the points on graph paper. Name the roots (x-intercepts).

x	−4	−3	−2	−1	0	1	2
y							

7-39.   Find the perimeter of the shape at right. Show all work.

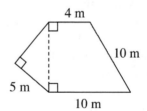

7.1.4 How can I create it?

Using Symmetry to Study Polygons

In Chapter 1, you used a hinged mirror to study the special angles associated with regular polygons. In particular, you investigated what happens as the angle formed by the sides of the mirror is changed. Toda y, you will use a hinged mirror to determine if there is more than one way to build each regular polygon using the principles of symmetry. And what about other types of polygons? What can a hinged mirror help you understand about them?

As your work with your study team, keep these focus questions in mind:

Is there another way?

What types of symmetry can I find?

What does symmetry tell me about the polygon?

7-40.   THE HINGED MIRROR TEAM CHALLENGE

Obtain a hinged mirror, a piece of unlined colored paper, and a protractor from your teacher.

With your team, spend five minutes reviewing how to use the mirror to create regular polygons. Remember that a **regular polygon** has equal sides and angles. Once everyone remembers how the hinged mirror works, select a team member to read the directions of the task below.

Your Task: Below are four challenges for your team. Each requires you to find a creative way to position the mirror in relation to the colored paper. You can tackle the challenges in any order, but you must work together as a team on each of them. Whenever you successfully create a shape, do not forget to measure the angle formed by the mirror, as well as draw a diagram on your paper of the core region in front of the mirror. If your team decides that a shape is impossible to create with the hinged mirror, explain why.

- Create a regular hexagon.

- Create an equilateral triangle at least *two* different ways.

- Create a rhombus that is *not* a square.

- Create a circle.

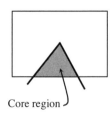

Core region

414   *Core Connections Geometry*

7-41.   ANALYSIS

How can symmetry help you to learn more about shapes? Discuss each question below with the class.

a.   One way to create a regular hexagon with a hinged mirror is with six triangles, as shown in the diagram at right. Note: The gray lines represent reflections of the bottom edges of the mirrors and the edge of the paper, while the core region is shaded.

What is special about each of the triangles in the diagram? What is the relationship between the triangles? Support your conclusions. Would it be possible to create a regular hexagon with 12 triangles? Explain.

b.   If you have not done so already, create an equilateral triangle so that the core region in front of the mirror is a right triangle. Draw a diagram of the result that shows the different reflected triangles like the one above. What special type of right triangle is the core region? Can all regular polygons be created with a right triangle in a similar fashion?

c.   In problem 7-40, your team formed a rhombus that is not a square. On your paper, draw a diagram like the one above that shows how you did it. How can you be sure your resulting shape is a rhombus? Using what you know about the angle of the mirror, explain what must be true about the diagonals of a rhombus.

7-42.   Use what you learned today to answer the questions below.

a.   Examine the regular octagon at right. What is the measure of angle θ? Explain how you know.

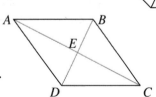

b.   Quadrilateral *ABCD* at right is a rhombus. If *BD* = 10 units and *AC* = 18 units, then what is the perimeter of *ABCD*? Show all work.

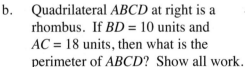

METHODS AND MEANINGS

Regular Polygons

MATH NOTES

A polygon is **regular** if all its sides are congruent and its angles have equal measure. An equilateral triangle and a square are each regular polygons since they are both *equilateral* and *equiangular*. See the diagrams of common regular polygons below.

Equilateral
Triangle

Square

Regular
Hexagon

Regular
Octagon

Regular
Decagon

7-43. Felipe set his hinged mirror so that its angle was 36° and the core region was isosceles, as shown at right.

a. How many sides did his resulting polygon have? Show how you know.

b. What is another name for this polygon?

7-44. In problem 7-41 you learned that the diagonals of a rhombus are perpendicular bisectors. If *ABCD* is a rhombus with side length 15 mm and if *BD* = 24 mm, then find the length of the other diagonal, $\overline{AC}$. Draw a diagram and show all work.

7-45. Joanne claims that $(2, 4)$ is the midpoint of the segment connecting the points $(-3, 5)$ and $(7, 3)$. Is she correct? Explain how you know.

7-46. For each pair of triangles below, determine whether or not the triangles are similar. If they are similar, show your reasoning in a flowchart. If they are not similar, explain how you know.

a.   b.   c.

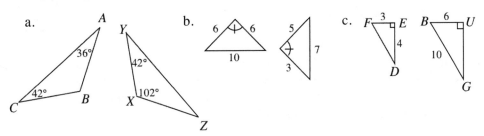

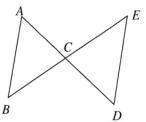

7-47. If $\triangle ABC \cong \triangle DEC$, which of the statements below must be true? Justify your conclusion. Note: More than one statement may be true.

a. $\overline{AC} \cong \overline{DC}$ b. $m\angle B = m\angle D$

c. $\overline{AB} \parallel \overline{DE}$ d. $AD = BE$

e. None of these are true.

7-48. On graph paper, graph the points $A(2, 9)$, $B(4, 3)$, and $C(9, 6)$. Which point (A or C) is closer to point B? Justify your conclusion.

7.2.1 What can congruent triangles tell me?

Special Quadrilaterals and Proof

In earlier chapters you studied the relationships between the sides and angles of a triangle, and solved problems involving congruent and similar triangles. Now you are going to expand your study of shapes to quadrilaterals. What can triangles tell you about parallelograms and other special quadrilaterals?

By the end of this lesson, you should be able to answer these questions:

> What are the relationships between the sides, angles, and diagonals
> of a parallelogram?

> How are congruent triangles useful?

7-49.   Carla is thinking about parallelograms and wondering if there are as many special properties for parallelograms as there are for triangles. She remembers that it is possible to create a shape that looks like a parallelogram by rotating a triangle about the midpoint of one of its sides.

a.   Carefully trace the triangle at right onto tracing paper. Be sure to copy the angle markings as well. Then rotate the triangle about a midpoint of a side to make a shape that looks like a parallelogram.

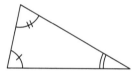

b.   Is Carla's shape truly a parallelogram? Use the angles to convince your teammates that the opposites sides must be parallel. Then write a convincing argument.

c.   What else can the congruent triangles tell you about a parallelogram? Look for any relationships you can find between the angles and sides of a parallelogram.

d.   Does this work for all parallelograms? That is, does the diagonal of a parallelogram always split the shape into two congruent triangles? Draw the parallelogram at right on your paper. Knowing only that the opposite sides of a parallelogram are parallel, create a flowchart to show that the triangles are congruent.

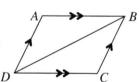

7-50.   CHANGING A FLOWCHART INTO A PROOF

The flowchart you created for part (d) of problem 7-49 shows how you can conclude that if a quadrilateral is a parallelogram, then its each of its diagonals splits the quadrilateral into two congruent triangles.

However, to be convincing, the facts that you listed in your flowchart need to have justifications. This shows the reader how you know the facts are true and helps to prove your conclusion.

Therefore, with the class or your team, decide how to add reasons to each statement (bubble) in your flowchart. You may need to add more bubbles to your flowchart to add justification and to make your proof more convincing.

7-51.   Kip is confused. He put his two triangles from problem 7-49 together as shown at right, but he did not get a parallelogram.

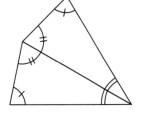

a.   What shape did he make? Justify your conclusion.

b.   What transformation(s) did Kip use to form his shape?

c.   What do the congruent triangles tell you about the angles of this shape?

7-52.   KITES

Kip shared his findings about his kite with his teammate,
Carla, who wants to learn more about the diagonals of a kite.
Carla quickly sketched the kite at right onto her paper with a
diagonal showing the two congruent triangles.

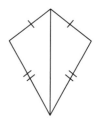

a.   **EXPLORE:** Trace this diagram onto tracing paper and
carefully add the other diagonal. Then, with your team,
consider how the diagonals may be related. Use tracing
paper to help you explore the relationships between the
diagonals. If you make an observation you think is true,
move on to part (b) and write a conjecture.

b.   **CONJECTURE:** If you have not already done so, write a conjecture
based on your observations in part (a).

c.   **PROVE:** When she drew the second diagonal, Carla noticed that four new
triangles appeared. *"If any of these triangles are congruent, then they may
be able to help us prove our conjecture from part (b),"* she said. Examine
△*ABC* below. Are △*ACD* and △*BCD* congruent? Create a flowchart proof
like the one from problem 7-50 to justify your conclusion.

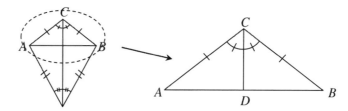

d.   Now extend your proof from part (c) to prove your conjecture from
part (b).

7-53.   Reflect on all of the interesting facts about parallelograms
and kites you have proven during this lesson. Obtain a
Theorem Toolkit (Lesson 7.2.1A Resource Page) from your
teacher. On it, record each **theorem** (proven conjecture) that
you have proven about the sides, angles, and diagonals of a
parallelogram in this lesson. Do the same for a kite. Be sure
your diagrams contain appropriate markings to represent
equal parts.

METHODS AND MEANINGS

Reflexive Property of Equality

In this lesson, you used the fact that two triangles formed by the diagonal of a parallelogram share a side of the same length to help show that the triangles were congruent.

The **Reflexive Property of Equality** states that the measure of any side or angle is equal to itself. For example, in the parallelogram at right, $\overline{BD} \cong \overline{DB}$ because of the Reflexive Property.

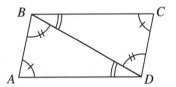

Review & Preview

7-54.   Use the information given for each diagram below to solve for x. Show all work.

a. $\overrightarrow{BD}$ bisects $\angle ABC$. (Remember that this means it divides the angle into two equal parts.) If $m\angle ABD = 5x - 10°$ and $m\angle ABC = 65°$, solve for x.

b.   Point M is a midpoint of $\overline{EF}$. If $EM = 4x - 2$ and $MF = 3x + 9$, solve for x.

c. $WXYZ$ at right is a parallelogram. If $m\angle W = 9x - 3°$ and $m\angle Z = 3x + 15°$, solve for x.

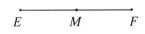

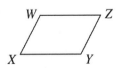

7-55.   Jamal used a hinged mirror to create a regular polygon like you did in Lesson 7.1.4.

$360 / 72 = 5$

a.   If his hinged mirror formed a 72° angle and the core region in front of the mirror was isosceles, how many sides did his polygon have?

b.   Now Jamal has decided to create a regular polygon with 9 sides, called a nonagon. If his core region is again isosceles, what angle is formed by his mirror?

$360 / 4 = x$

7-56.   Sandra wants to park her car so that she optimizes the distance she has to walk to the art museum and the library. That is, she wants to park so that her total distance directly to each building is the shortest. Find where she should park.

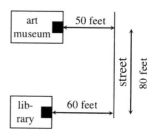

7-57.   Write an equation for each of the following sequences.

a. $40, 60, 80, ...$

b. $3, \frac{3}{2}, \frac{3}{4}, ...$

7-58.   Earl (from Chapter 6) still hates to wash the dishes and take out the garbage. He found his own weighted coin, one that would randomly land on heads 30% of the time. He will flip a coin once for each chore and will perform the chore if the coin lands on heads.

a.   What is the probability that Earl will get out of doing both chores?

b.   What is the probability that Earl will have to take out the garbage, but will not need to wash the dishes?

7-59.   Which pairs of triangles below are congruent and/or similar? For each part, explain how you know using an appropriate triangle congruence or similarity condition. Note: The diagrams are not necessarily drawn to scale.

a.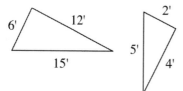

b.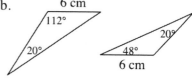

c.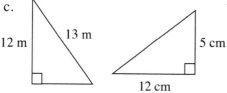

d.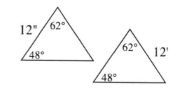

7-60.   For part (b) of problem 7-59, explain how the triangles are congruent using a sequence of rigid transformations.

7.2.2 What is special about a rhombus?

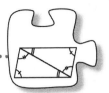

Properties of Rhombi

In Lesson 7.2.1, you learned that congruent triangles can be a useful tool to discover new information about parallelograms and kites. But what about other quadrilaterals? Today you will use congruent triangles to investigate and prove special properties of rhombi (the plural of rhombus). At the same time, you will continue to develop your ability to make conjectures and prove them convincingly.

7-61.   Audrey has a favorite quadrilateral – the rhombus. Even though a rhombus is defined as having four congruent sides, she suspects that the sides of a rhombus have other special properties.

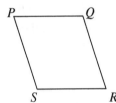

a.   **EXPLORE:** Draw a rhombus like the one at right on your paper. Mark the side lengths equal.

b.   **CONJECTURE:** What else might be special about the sides of a rhombus? Write a conjecture.

c.   **PROVE:** Audrey knows congruent triangles can help prove other properties about quadrilaterals. She starts by adding a diagonal $\overline{PR}$ to her diagram so that two triangles are formed. Add this diagonal to your diagram and prove that the created triangles are congruent. Then use a flowchart with reasons to show your logic. Be prepared to share your flowchart with the class.

d.   How can the triangles from part (c) help you prove your conjecture from part (b) above? Discuss with the class how to extend your flowchart to convince others. Be sure to justify any new statements with reasons.

7-62.   Now that you know the opposite sides of a rhombus are parallel, what else can you prove about a rhombus? Consider this as you answer the questions below.

a.   **EXPLORE:** Remember that in Lesson 7.1.4, you explored the shapes that could be formed with a hinged mirror. During this activity, you used symmetry to form a rhombus. Think about what you know about the reflected triangles in the diagram. What do you think is true about the diagonals $\overline{SQ}$ and $\overline{PR}$? What is special about $\overline{ST}$ and $\overline{QT}$? What about $\overline{PT}$ and $\overline{RT}$?

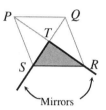

b.   **CONJECTURE:** Use your observations from part (a) to write a conjecture on the relationship of the diagonals of a rhombus.

c.   **PROVE:** Write a flowchart proof that proves your conjecture from part (b). Remember that to be convincing, you need to justify each statement with a reason. To help guide your discussion, consider the questions below. Which triangles should you use? Find two triangles that involve the segments $\overline{ST}$, $\overline{QT}$, $\overline{PT}$, and $\overline{RT}$.

- How can you prove these triangles are congruent? Create a flowchart proof with reasons to prove these triangles must be congruent.

- How can you use the congruent triangles to prove your conjecture from part (b)? Extend your flowchart proof to include this reasoning and prove your conjecture.

7-63.   There are often many ways to prove a conjecture. You have rotated triangles to create parallelograms and used congruent parts of congruent triangles to justify that opposite sides are parallel. But is there another way?

Ansel wants to prove the conjecture "*If a quadrilateral is a parallelogram, then opposite angles are congruent.*" He started by drawing parallelogram *TUVW* at right. Copy and complete his flowchart. Make sure that each statement has a reason.

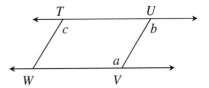

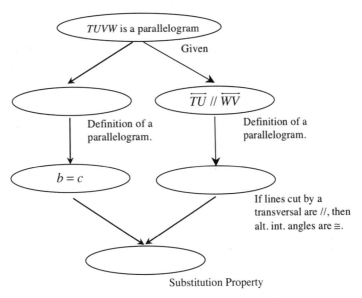

Substitution Property

7-64.   Think about the new facts you have proven about rhombi during this lesson. On your Theorem Toolkit (Lesson 7.2.1A Resource Page), record each new theorem you have proven about the angles and diagonals of a rhombus. Include clearly labeled diagrams to illustrate your findings.

METHODS AND MEANINGS

MATH NOTES

Exponential Functions

An **exponential function** has the general form $y = a \cdot b^x$, where a is the **initial value** (the y-intercept) and b is the **multiplier** (the growth). Be careful: The independent variable x has to be in the exponent. For example, $y = x^2$ is *not* an exponential equation, even though it has an exponent.

For example, in the multiple representations below, the y-intercept is $(0, 4)$ and the growth factor is 3 because the y-value is increasing by multiplying by 3.

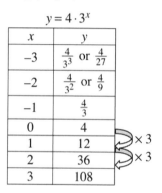

$y = 4 \cdot 3^x$

x	y
-3	$\frac{4}{3^3}$ or $\frac{4}{27}$
-2	$\frac{4}{3^2}$ or $\frac{4}{9}$
-1	$\frac{4}{3}$
0	4
1	12
2	36
3	108

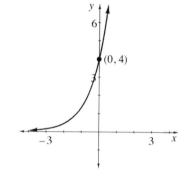

To increase or decrease a quantity by a percentage, use the multiplier for that percentage. For example, the multiplier for an increase of 7% is $100\% + 7\% = 1.07$. The multiplier for a decrease of 7% is $100\% - 7\% = 0.93$.

Review & Preview

7-65. Point M is the midpoint of $\overline{AB}$ and B is the midpoint of $\overline{AC}$. What are the values of x and y? Show all work and reasoning.

$$\underset{A}{\bullet} \overset{4x-1}{\underset{M}{\bullet}} \overset{x+8}{\underset{B}{\bullet}} \overset{5y+2}{\underset{C}{\bullet}}$$

7-66. Read the Math Notes box in this lesson and then answer the following questions.

The cost of large flat-screen televisions is decreasing 20% per year.

a. What is the multiplier?

b. If a 50-inch flat-screen now costs $1200, what will it cost in three years?

c. At the same rate, what did it cost two years ago?

7-67. A light directed from point E is pointed at a hinged mirror with right angle as shown at right.

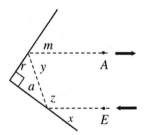

a. If $\angle x$ measures $36°$, find the measures of $\angle a, \angle r, \angle m, \angle y$, and $\angle z$.

b. Why must the arrows at points A and E be parallel?

7-68. On graph paper, graph quadrilateral $MNPQ$ if $M(-3, 6), N(2, 8), P(1, 5)$, and $Q(-4, 3)$.

a. What shape is $MNPQ$? Show how you know.

b. Use the function $x \rightarrow x, y \rightarrow -y$ to reflect $MNPQ$ across the x-axis and create $M'N'P'Q'$. What are the coordinates of P'?

7-69. Jester started to prove that the triangles at right are congruent. He was only told that point E is the midpoint of segments $\overline{AC}$ and $\overline{BD}$.

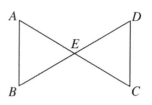

Copy and complete his flowchart below. Be sure that a reason is provided for every statement.

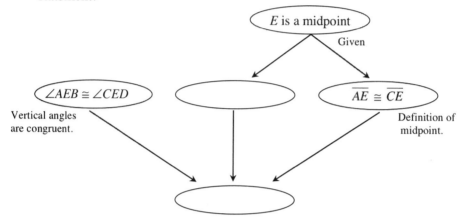

E is a midpoint

Given

$\angle AEB \cong \angle CED$

Vertical angles are congruent.

$\overline{AE} \cong \overline{CE}$

Definition of midpoint.

7-70. For a school fair, Donny is going to design a spinner with red, white, and blue regions. Since he has a certain proportion of three types of prizes, he wants the P(red) = 40% and P(white) = 10%.

a. If the spinner only has red, white, and blue regions, then what is P(blue)? Explain how you know.

b. Find the central angles of this spinner if it has only three sections. Then draw a sketch of the spinner. Be sure to label the regions accurately.

c. Is there a different spinner that has the same probabilities? If so, sketch another spinner that has the same probabilities. If not, explain why there is no other spinner with the same probabilities.

7-71. On graph paper, graph and shade the solutions for the inequality below.

$$y < -\tfrac{2}{3}x + 5$$

7.2.3 What else can be proved?

More Proofs with Congruent Triangles

In Lessons 7.2.1 and 7.2.2, you used congruent triangles to learn more about parallelograms, kites, and rhombi. You now possess the tools to do the work of a geometer (someone who studies geometry): to discover and prove new properties about the sides and angles of shapes.

As you investigate these shapes, focus on proving your ideas. Remember to ask yourself and your teammates questions such as, "*Why does that work?*" and "*Is it always true?*" Decide whether your argument is convincing and work with your team to provide all of the necessary justification.

7-72. Carla decided to turn her attention to rectangles. Knowing that a rectangle is defined as a quadrilateral with four right angles, she drew the diagram at right.

After some exploration, she conjectured that all rectangles are also parallelograms. Help her prove that her rectangle *ABCD* must be a parallelogram. That is, prove that the opposite sides must be parallel. Then add this theorem to your Theorem Toolkit (Lesson 7.2.1A Resource Page).

7-73.   For each diagram below, find the value of x, if possible. If the triangles are congruent, state which triangle congruence condition was used. If the triangles are not congruent or if there is not enough information, state, "Cannot be determined."

a. ABC below is a triangle.

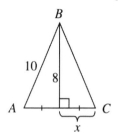

b.

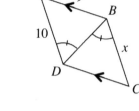

c.

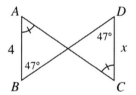

d. $\overline{AC}$ and $\overline{BD}$ are straight line segments.

7-74.   With the class or your team, create a flowchart to prove your answer to part (b) of problem 7-73. That is, prove that $\overline{AD} \cong \overline{CB}$. Be sure to include a diagram for your proof and reasons for every statement. Make sure your argument is convincing and has no "holes."

Core Connections Geometry

ETHODS AND MEANINGS

Definitions of Quadrilaterals

When proving properties of shapes, it is necessary to know exactly how a shape is defined. Below are the definitions of several quadrilaterals that you developed in Lesson 1.3.2 and that you will need to refer to in this chapter and the chapters that follow.

Quadrilateral: A closed four-sided polygon.

Kite: A quadrilateral with two distinct pairs of consecutive congruent sides.

Trapezoid: A quadrilateral with at least one pair of parallel sides.

Parallelogram: A quadrilateral with two pairs of parallel sides.

Rhombus: A quadrilateral with four sides of equal length.

Rectangle: A quadrilateral with four right angles.

Square: A quadrilateral with four sides of equal length and four right angles.

7-75. Identify if each pair of triangles below is congruent or not. Remember that the diagram may not be drawn to scale. Justify your conclusion.

a.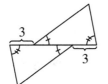

b.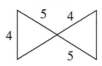

c.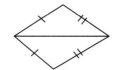

d.

7-76. For either part (a), (c) or (d) of problem 7-75, create a flowchart to prove your conclusion. Remember to start with the given information and include a reason or justification for each "bubble" in your flowchart.

7-77. In the diagram at right, ∠DCA is referred to as an **exterior angle** of ΔABC because it lies outside the triangle and is formed by extending a side of the triangle.

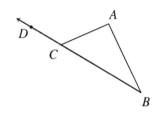

a. If $m\angle CAB = 46°$ and $m\angle ABC = 37°$, what is $m\angle DCA$? Show all work.

b. If $m\angle DCA = 135°$ and $m\angle ABC = 43°$, then what is $m\angle CAB$?

7-78. Tromika wants to find the area of the isosceles triangle at right.

a. She decided to start by drawing a height from vertex A to side $\overline{BC}$ as shown below. Will the two smaller triangles be congruent? In other words, is $\triangle ABC \cong \triangle ABD$? Why or why not?

b. What is $m\angle DAB$? BD?

c. Find AD. Show how you got your answer.

d. Find the area of $\triangle ABC$.

7-79. On graph paper, graph quadrilateral $ABCD$ if $A(0,0)$, $B(6,0)$, $C(8,6)$, and $D(2,6)$.

a. What is the best name for $ABCD$? Justify your answer.

b. Find the equation of the lines containing each diagonal. That is, find the equations of lines $\overleftrightarrow{AC}$ and $\overleftrightarrow{BD}$.

7-80. It is often useful to estimate the value of a square root to determine if your answer is reasonable.

a. What would be a reasonable estimate of $\sqrt{68}$? Explain your thinking. After you have made an estimate, check your estimation with a calculator.

b. Repeat this process to estimate the values below.

    (1) $\sqrt{5}$ (2) $\sqrt{85}$ (3) $\sqrt{50}$ (4) $\sqrt{22}$

7-81.   For each diagram below, solve for x. Show all work.

a.

b.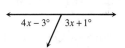

c.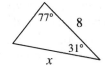

d.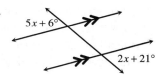

7.2.4 What else can I prove?

More Properties of Quadrilaterals

Today you will work with your team to apply what you have learned to other shapes. Remember to ask yourself and your teammates questions such as, *"Why does that work?"* and *"Is it always true?"* Decide whether your argument is convincing and work with your team to provide all of the necessary justification. By the end of this lesson, you should have a well-crafted mathematical argument proving something new about a familiar quadrilateral.

7-82. **WHAT ELSE CAN CONGRUENT TRIANGLES TELL US?**

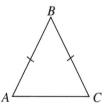

Your Task: For each situation below, determine how congruent triangles can tell you more information about the shape. Then prove your conjecture using a flowchart. Be sure to provide a reason for each statement. For example, stating *"m∠A = m∠B"* is not enough. You must give a convincing reason, such as *"Because vertical angles are equal"* or *"Because it is given in the diagram."* Use your triangle congruence conditions to help prove that the triangles are congruent.

Later, your teacher will select one of these flowcharts for you to place on a poster. On your poster, include a diagram and all of your statements and reasons. Clearly state what you are proving and help the people who look at your poster understand your logic and reasoning.

a. In Chapter 1, you used the symmetry of an isosceles triangle to show that the base angles must be congruent. How can you prove this result using congruent triangles?

Assume that $\overline{AB} \cong \overline{CB}$ for the triangle at right. With your team, decide how to split $\triangle ABC$ into two triangles that you can show are congruent to show that $\angle BAC \cong \angle BCA$.

Problem continues on next page →

7-82.   *Problem continued from previous page.*

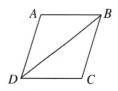

b.   What can congruent triangles tell us about the
     diagonals and angles of a rhombus? Examine
     the diagram of the rhombus at right. With
     your team, decide how to prove that the
     diagonals of a rhombus bisect the angles.
     That is, prove that $\angle ABD \cong \angle CBD$.

c.   What can congruent triangles tell us about the
     diagonals of a rectangle? Examine the
     rectangle at right. Using the fact that the
     opposite sides of a rectangle are parallel
     (which you proved in problem 7-72), prove
     that the diagonals of the rectangle are
     congruent. That is, prove that $AC = BD$.

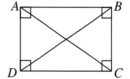

ⓂETHODS AND MEANINGS

Diagonals of a Rhombus

A **rhombus** is defined as a quadrilateral
with four sides of equal length. In addition, you
proved in problem 7-62 that the diagonals of a
rhombus are perpendicular bisectors of each
other.

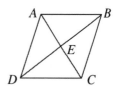

For example, in the rhombus at right, E is a
midpoint of both $\overline{AC}$ and $\overline{DB}$. Therefore, $AE = CE$ and $DE = BE$. Also,
$m\angle AEB = m\angle BEC = m\angle CED = m\angle DEA = 90°$.

In addition, you proved in problem 7-82 that the diagonals bisect the
angles of the rhombus. For example, in the diagram above,
$m\angle DAE = m\angle BAE$.

7-83.   Use Tromika's method from problem 7-78 to find the area of an equilateral
         triangle with side length 12 units. Show all work.

7-84.   The guidelines set forth by the National
         Kitchen & Bath Association recommends that
         the perimeter of the triangle connecting the
         refrigerator (F), stove, and sink of a kitchen be
         26 feet or less. Lashayia is planning to
         renovate her kitchen and has chosen the
         design at right. Does her design conform to
         the National Kitchen and Bath Association's
         guidelines? Show how you got your answer.

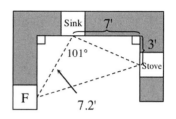

7-85.   Examine the triangles below. For each, solve for x and name which tool you
         use. Show all work.

a.
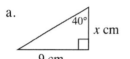

b.
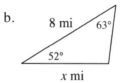

c.
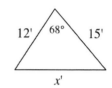

7-86.   For each figure below, determine if the two smaller triangles in each figure are
         congruent. If so, create a flowchart to explain why. Then, solve for x. If the
         triangles are not congruent, explain why not.

a.
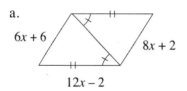

b.
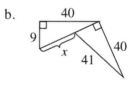

7-87.   The diagonals of a rhombus are 6 units and 8 units long. What is the area of the
         rhombus? Draw a diagram and show all reasoning.

7-88.   Kendrick is frantic. He remembers
that several years ago he buried his
Amazing Electron Ring in his little
sister's sandbox, but he cannot
remember where. A few minutes
ago he heard that someone is
willing to pay $1000 for it. He has
his shovel and is ready to dig.

a.   The sandbox is rectangular, measuring 4 feet by
5 feet, as shown at right. If Kendrick only has
time to search in the 2 foot-square shaded
region, what is the probability that he will find
the ring?

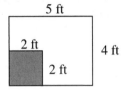

b.   What is the probability that he will not find the ring?
Explain how you found your answer.

c.   Kendrick decides instead to dig in the square
region shaded at right. Does this improve his
chances for finding the ring? Why or why not?

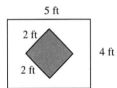

7-89.   What is the 50th term in this sequence?

$$17, 14, 11, 8, \ldots$$

7.2.5 How else can I write it?

Two-Column Proofs

Today you will continue to work with constructing a convincing argument, otherwise known as writing a proof. In this lesson, you will use what you know about flowchart proofs to write a convincing argument using another format, called a two-column proof.

7-90.   The following pairs of triangles are not necessarily congruent even though they appear to be. Use the information provided in the diagram to show why. Justify your statements.

a.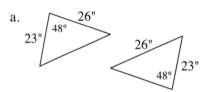

b.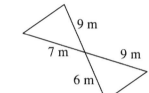

7-91.   Write a flowchart to prove that if point P on line l (not on $\overline{AB}$) is a point on the perpendicular bisector of $\overline{AB}$, then $\overline{PA} \cong \overline{PB}$. That is, point P is the same distance from points A and B *(called "equidistant" in mathematics)*. Assume the intersection of $\overline{AB}$ and line l is point M as shown in the diagram.

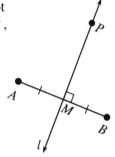

7-92.   Another way to organize a proof is called a **two-column proof**. Instead of using arrows to indicate the order of logical reasoning, this style of proof lists statements and reasons in a linear order, first to last, in columns.

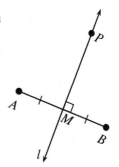

The proof from problem 7-91 has been converted to a two-column proof below. Copy and complete the proof on your paper using your statements and reasons from problem 7-91.

If: M is on $\overline{AB}$ and $\overrightarrow{PM}$ is the perpendicular bisector of $\overline{AB}$

Prove: $\overline{PA} \cong \overline{PB}$

Statements	Reasons (This statement is true because…)
Point M is on $\overline{AB}$ and $\overrightarrow{PM}$ is the perpendicular bisector of $\overline{AB}$.	Given
$m\angle PMA = m\angle PMB = 90°$	Definition of perpendicular and angles with the same measure are congruent.
	Definition of a bisector.
$\overline{PM} \cong \overline{PM}$	

7-93.   Examine the posters of flowchart proofs from problem 7-82. Convert each flowchart proof to a two-column proof. Remember that one column must contain the ordered statements of fact while the other must provide the reason (or justification) explaining why that fact must be true.

7-94.   So far in Section 7.2, you have proven many special properties of quadrilaterals and other shapes. Remember that when a conjecture is proven, it is called a theorem. For example, once you proved the relationship between the lengths of the sides of a right triangle, you were able to refer to that relationship as the Pythagorean Theorem. Find your Theorem Toolkit (Lesson 7.2.1A Resource Page) and make sure it contains all of the theorems you and your classmates have proven so far about various quadrilaterals. Be sure that your records include diagrams for each statement.

7-95.   **LEARNING LOG**

Reflect on the new proof format you learned today.
Compare it to the flowchart proof format that you have used
earlier. What are the strengths and weaknesses of each
style of proof? Which format is easier for you to use? Which is
easier to read? Title this entry "Two-Column Proofs" and label
it with today's date.

7-96.   Suppose you know that $\triangle TAP \cong \triangle DOG$ where $TA = 14$, $AP = 18$, $TP = 21$, and
$DG = 2y + 7$.

a.   On your paper, draw a reasonable sketch of $\triangle TAP$ and $\triangle DOG$.

b.   Find y. Show all work.

7-97.   Graph the equation $y = -\frac{3}{2}x + 6$ on graph paper. Label the points where the line
intersects the x- and y-axes.

7-98. $\angle a$, $\angle b$, and $\angle c$ are exterior angles of the triangle at right.
Find $m\angle a$, $m\angle b$, and $m\angle c$. Then find
$m\angle a + m\angle b + m\angle c$.

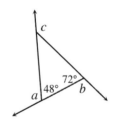

7-99.   The principal's new car cost \$35,000 but in three years it will only be worth
\$21,494. What is the annual percent of decrease?

7-100. What else can you prove about parallelograms? Prove that if a pair of opposite sides of a quadrilateral are congruent and parallel, then the quadrilateral must be a parallelogram. For example, for the quadrilateral *ABCD* at right, given that $\overline{AB} \parallel \overline{CD}$ and $\overline{AB} \cong \overline{CD}$, show that $\overline{BC} \parallel \overline{AD}$. Organize your reasoning in a flowchart. Then record your theorem in your Theorem Toolkit (Lesson 7.2.1A Resource Page).

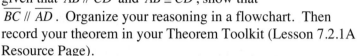

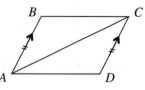

7-101. As Ms. Dorman looked from the window of her third-story classroom, she noticed Pam in the courtyard. Ms. Dorman's eyes were 52 feet above ground and Pam was 38 feet from the building. Draw a diagram of this situation. What is the angle at which Ms. Dorman had to look down, that is, what is the angle of depression? (Assume that Ms. Dorman was looking at the spot on the ground below Pam.)

7-102. For each pair of triangles below, determine if the triangles are congruent. If the triangles are congruent,

- complete the correspondence statement,
- state the congruence property,
- and record any other ideas you use that make your conclusion true.

Otherwise, explain why you cannot conclude that the triangles are congruent. Note that the figures are not necessarily drawn to scale.

a. $\triangle ABC \cong \triangle$ _____   b. $\triangle SQP \cong \triangle$ _____   c. $\triangle PLM \cong \triangle$ _____

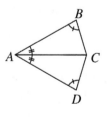

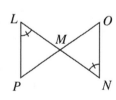

d. $\triangle WXY \cong \triangle$ _____   e. $\triangle EDG \cong \triangle$ _____   f. $\triangle ABC \cong \triangle$ _____

midpoint of $\overline{WT}$ and $\overline{XZ}$

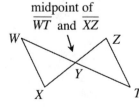

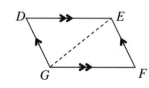

7.2.6 What can I prove?

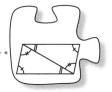

Explore-Conjecture-Prove

So far, congruent triangles have helped you to discover and prove many new facts about triangles and quadrilaterals. But what else can you discover and prove? Today your work will mirror the real work of professional mathematicians. You will investigate relationships, write a conjecture based on your observations, and then prove your conjecture.

7-103. TRIANGLE MIDSEGMENT THEOREM

As Sergio was drawing shapes on his paper, he drew a line segment that connected the midpoints of two sides of a triangle. This is called the **midsegment** of a triangle. "*I wonder what we can find out about this midsegment,*" he said to his team. Examine his drawing at right.

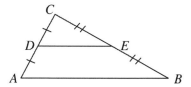

a. **EXPLORE:** Examine the diagram of $\triangle ABC$, drawn to scale above. How do you think $\overline{DE}$ is related to $\overline{AB}$? How do their lengths seem to be related?

b. **CONJECTURE:** Write a conjecture about the relationship between segments $\overline{DE}$ and $\overline{AB}$.

c. **PROVE:** Sergio wants to prove that $AB = 2DE$. However, he does not see any congruent triangles in the diagram. How are the triangles in this diagram related? How do you know? Prove your conclusion with a flowchart.

d. What is the common ratio between side lengths in the similar triangles? Use this to write a statement relating lengths DE and AB.

e. Now Sergio wants to prove that $\overline{DE} \parallel \overline{AB}$. Use the similar triangles to find all the pairs of equal angles you can in the diagram. Then use your knowledge of angle relationships to make a statement about parallel segments.

Core Connections Geometry

7-104.   The work you did in problem 7-103 mirrors the work of many professional
mathematicians. In the problem, Sergio examined a geometric shape and
thought there might be something new to learn. You then helped him by finding
possible relationships and writing a conjecture. Then, to find out if the
conjecture was true for all triangles, you wrote a convincing argument (or
proof). This process is summarized in the diagram below.

Explore		Conjecture		Prove
Use any tools that are available to explore a shape and discover any possible relationships.	⟹	Write a conditional statement or arrow diagram based on your observations from the investigation.	⟹	Convince yourself (and others) that your conjecture is always true with a convincing argument.

Discuss this process with the class and describe when you have used this
process before (either in this class or outside of class). Why do mathematicians
rely on this process?

7-105.   RIGHT TRAPEZOIDS

Consecutive angles of a polygon occur at opposite ends of a side of the
polygon. What can you learn about a quadrilateral with two consecutive right
angles?

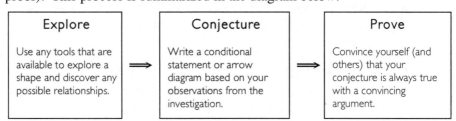

a.   EXPLORE: Examine the quadrilateral at right
with two consecutive right angles. What do
you think is true about $\overline{AB}$ and $\overline{DC}$?

b.   CONJECTURE: Write a conjecture about what type of quadrilateral has
two consecutive right angles. Write your conjecture in conditional ("If…,
then…") form.

c.   PROVE: Prove that your conjecture from part (b) is true for all
quadrilaterals with two consecutive right angles. Write your proof using
the two-column format introduced in Lesson 7.2.4. Hint: Look for angle
relationships.

d.   The quadrilateral you worked with in this problem is called a **right
trapezoid**. Are all quadrilaterals with two right angles a right trapezoid?

7-106.   ISOSCELES TRAPEZOIDS

An **isosceles trapezoid** is a trapezoid with a pair
of congruent base angles. What can you learn
about the sides of an isosceles trapezoid?

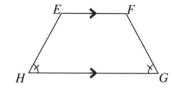

a.   **EXPLORE:** Examine trapezoid *EFGH* at
right. How do the non-parallel side lengths
appear to be related?

b.   **CONJECTURE:** Write a conjecture about side
lengths in an isosceles trapezoid. Write your
conjecture in conditional ("If…, then…") form.

c.   **PROVE:** Now prove that your conjecture
from part (b) is true for all isosceles
trapezoids. Write your proof using the two-
column format introduced in Lesson 7.2.5.
To help you get started, the isosceles
trapezoid is shown at right with its sides
extended to form a triangle.

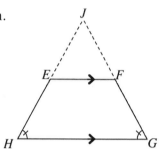

7-107.   Add the theorems you have proved in this lesson to your
Theorem Toolkit (Lesson 7.2.1A Resource Page). Be sure
to include diagrams for each statement.

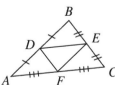

MATH NOTES

METHODS AND MEANINGS

Triangle Midsegment Theorem

A **midsegment** of a triangle is a segment
that connects the midpoints of any two
sides of a triangle. Every triangle has
three midsegments, as shown at right.

A midsegment between two sides of a triangle is
half the length of and parallel to the third side of the
triangle. For example, in $\triangle ABC$ at right, $\overline{DE}$ is a
midsegment, $\overline{DE} \parallel \overline{AC}$, and $DE = \frac{1}{2} AC$.

7-108.   What else can you prove about parallelograms?
Prove that the diagonals of a parallelogram
bisect each other. For example, assuming that
quadrilateral *WXYZ* at right is a parallelogram,
prove that $\overline{WM} \cong \overline{YM}$ and $\overline{ZM} \cong \overline{XM}$.
Organize your reasoning in a
flowchart. Then record your theorem
in your Theorem Toolkit (Lesson
7.2.1A Resource Page).

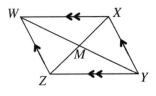

7-109.   One way a shape can be special is to have two congruent sides. For example,
an isosceles triangle is special because it has a pair of sides that are the same
length. Think about all the shapes you know and list the other special
properties shapes can have. List as many as you can. Be ready to share your
list with the class at the beginning of Lesson 7.3.1.

7-110.   Carefully examine each diagram below and explain why the
geometric figure cannot exist. Support your statements with
reasons. If a line looks straight, assume that it is.

a.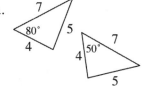

b.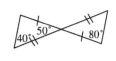

c.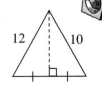

d.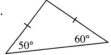

e.

f.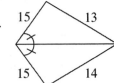

7-111.   Remember that if a triangle has two equal sides, it is called isosceles. Decide whether each triangle formed by the points below is isosceles. Explain how you decided.

a. $(6, 0), (0, 6), (6, 6)$

b. $(-3, 7), (-5, 2), (-1, 2)$

c. $(4, 1), (2, 3), (9, 2)$

d. $(1, 1), (5, -3), (1, -7)$

7-112.   For each pair of numbers, find the number that is exactly halfway between them.

a.   9 and 15

b.   3 and 27

c.   10 and 21

7-113.   Penn started the proof below to show that if $\overline{AD} \parallel \overline{EH}$ and $\overline{BF} \parallel \overline{CG}$, then $a = d$. Unfortunately, he did not provide reasons for his proof. Copy his proof and provide a justification for each statement.

Statements	Reasons
1. $\overline{AD} \parallel \overline{EH}$ and $\overline{BF} \parallel \overline{CG}$	
2. $a = b$	
3. $b = c$	
4. $a = c$	
5. $c = d$	
6. $a = d$	

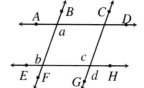

7-114.   After finding out that her kitchen does not conform to industry standards, Lashayia is back to the drawing board (see problem 7-84). Where can she locate her sink along her top counter so that its distance from the stove and refrigerator is as small as possible? And will this location keep her perimeter below 26 feet? Show all work.

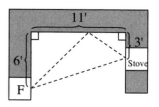

7.3.1 What makes a quadrilateral special?

Studying Quadrilaterals on a Coordinate Grid

In Section 7.2 you investigated special types of quadrilaterals, such as parallelograms, kites, and rhombi. Each of these quadrilaterals has special properties you have proved: parallel sides, sides of equal length, equal opposite angles, bisected diagonals, etc.

But not all quadrilaterals have a special name. How can you tell if a quadrilateral belongs to one of these types? And if a quadrilateral does not have a special name, can it still have special properties? In Section 7.3 you will use both algebra and geometry to investigate quadrilaterals defined on coordinate grids.

7-115.   PROPERTIES OF SHAPES

Think about the special quadrilaterals you have studied in this chapter. Each shape has some properties that make it special. For example, a rhombus has two diagonals that are perpendicular. With the class, brainstorm the other types of properties that a shape can have. You may want to refer to your work from problem 7-109. Be ready to share your list with the class.

7-116.   Review some of the algebra tools you already have. Consider two line segments $\overline{AB}$ and $\overline{CD}$, given $A(0, 8)$, $B(9, 2)$, $C(1, 3)$, and $D(9, 15)$.

   a.   Draw these two segments on a coordinate grid. Find the length of each segment.

   b.   Find the equation of $\overleftrightarrow{AB}$ and the equation of $\overleftrightarrow{CD}$. Write both equations in $y = mx + b$ form.

   c.   Is $\overline{AB} \, // \, \overline{CD}$? Is $\overline{AB} \perp \overline{CD}$? Justify your answer.

   d.   Use algebra to find the coordinates of the point where $\overline{AB}$ and $\overline{CD}$ intersect.

7-117.   AM I SPECIAL?

Shayla just drew quadrilateral *SHAY*, shown at
right. The coordinates of its vertices are:

   $S(0, 0)$ $H(0, 5)$ $A(4, 8)$ $Y(7, 4)$

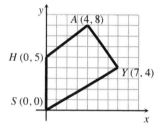

a.   Shayla thinks her quadrilateral is a trapezoid.
      Is she correct? Be prepared to justify your
      answer to the class.

b.   Does Shayla's quadrilateral look like it is one of the other kinds of special
      quadrilaterals you have studied? If so, which one?

c.   Even if Shayla's quadrilateral does not have a special name, it may still
      have some special properties like the ones you listed in problem 7-115.
      Use algebra and geometry tools to investigate Shayla's quadrilateral and
      see if it has any special properties. If you find any special properties, be
      ready to justify your claim that this property is present.

7-118.   MUST BE, COULD BE

Mr. Quincey likes to play a game with his class. He
says, "*My quadrilateral has four right angles.*" His
students say, "*Then it MUST BE a rectangle*" and "*It
COULD BE a square.*" For each description of a
quadrilateral below, say what special type the
quadrilateral *must be* and/or what special type the
quadrilateral *could be*. Look out, some descriptions
may have no *must be* statements and some
descriptions may have many *could be* statements!

a.   My quadrilateral has four equal sides.

b.   My quadrilateral has two pairs of opposite parallel sides.

c.   My quadrilateral has two consecutive right angles.

d.   My quadrilateral has two pairs of equal sides.

7-119.   The diagram at right shows three bold
segments. Find the coordinates of the midpoint
of each segment.

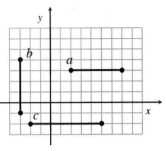

7-120.   Examine the diagram at right.

a.   Are the triangles in this diagram similar? Justify
your answer using similarity transformations.

b.   What is the relationship between the lengths of *HR* and
AK? Between the lengths of *SH* and *SA*? Between the
lengths of *SH* and *HA*?

c.   If *SK* = 20 units and *RH* = 8 units, what is *HA*?

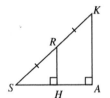

7-121.   Examine the spinner at right. Assume that the probability of
spinning a –8 is equal to that of spinning a 0.

a.   Find the spinner's expected value if the value of
region *A* is 8.

b.   Find the spinner's expected value if the value of region *A* is – 4.

c.   What does the value of region *A* need to be so that the expected value of
the spinner is 0?

7-122. For each pair of triangles below, determine if the triangles are congruent. If the triangles are congruent, state the triangle congruence condition that justifies your conclusion. If you cannot conclude that the triangles are congruent, explain why not.

a. $\triangle CAB \cong \triangle$ _____

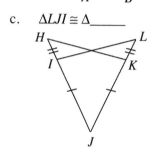

b. $\triangle CBD \cong \triangle$ _____

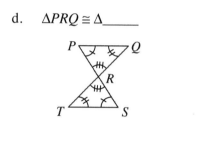

c. $\triangle LJI \cong \triangle$ _____

d. $\triangle PRQ \cong \triangle$ _____

7-123. For one of parts (a), (b) or (c) of problem 7-122, create a flowchart or a two-column proof for your conclusion. Remember to start with the given facts and to provide a justification for each step.

7-124. Carolina compared her proof to Penn's work in problem 7-113. Like him, she wanted to prove that if $\overline{AD} \parallel \overline{EH}$ and $\overline{BF} \parallel \overline{CG}$, then $a = d$. Unfortunately, her statements were in a different order. Examine her proof below and help her decide if her statements are in a logical order in order to prove that $a = d$.

Statements	Reasons
1. $\overline{AD} \parallel \overline{EH}$ and $\overline{BF} \parallel \overline{CG}$	Given
2. $a = b$	If lines are parallel, alternate interior angles are equal.
3. $a = c$	Substitution
4. $b = c$	If lines are parallel, corresponding angles are equal.
5. $c = d$	Vertical angles are equal.
6. $a = d$	Substitution

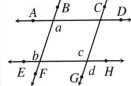

7-125. Describe the minimum information you would need to know about the shapes below in order to identify it correctly. For example, to know that a shape is a square, you must know that it has four sides of equal length and at least one right angle. Be as thorough as possible.

a. rhombus

b. trapezoid

7.3.2 How can I find the midpoint?

Coordinate Geometry and Midpoints

In Lesson 7.3.1, you applied your existing algebraic tools to analyze geometric shapes on a coordinate grid. What other algebraic processes can help us analyze shapes? And what else can be learned about geometric shapes?

7-126. Cassie wants to confirm her theorem on triangle midsegments (from Lesson 7.2.6) using a coordinate grid. She started with $\triangle ABC$ with $A(0,0)$, $B(2,6)$, and $C(7,0)$.

a. Graph $\triangle ABC$ on graph paper.

b. With your team, find the coordinates of P, the midpoint of $\overline{AB}$. Likewise, find the coordinates of Q, the midpoint of $\overline{BC}$.

c. Prove that the length of the midsegment, $\overline{PQ}$, is half the length of $\overline{AC}$. Also verify that $\overline{PQ}$ is parallel to $\overline{AC}$.

7-127. As Cassie worked on problem 7-126, her teammate, Esther, had difficulty finding the midpoint of $\overline{BC}$. The study team decided to try to find another way to find the midpoint of a line segment.

a. To help Cassie, draw $\overline{AM}$ with $A(3,4)$ and $M(8,11)$ on graph paper. Then extend the line segment to find a point B so that M is the midpoint of $\overline{AB}$. Justify your location of point B by drawing and writing numbers on the graph.

b. Esther thinks she understands how to find the midpoint on a graph. *"I always look for the middle of the line segment. But what if the coordinates are not easy to graph?"* she asks. With your team, find the midpoint of $\overline{KL}$ if $K(2,125)$ and $L(98,15)$. Be ready to share your method with the class.

c. Test your team's method by verifying that the midpoint between $(-5,7)$ and $(9,4)$ is $(2,5.5)$.

7-128.   Randy has decided to study the triangle graphed at right.

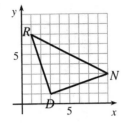

a.   Consider all the special properties this triangle can have. Without using any algebra tools, predict the best name for this triangle.

b.   For your answer to part (a) to be correct, what is the minimum amount of information that must be true about $\triangle RND$?

c.   Use your algebra tools to verify each of the properties you listed in part (b). If you need, you may change your prediction of the shape of $\triangle RND$.

d.   Randy wonders if there is anything special about the midpoint of $\overline{RN}$. Find the midpoint M, and then find the lengths of $\overline{RM}$, $\overline{DM}$, and $\overline{MN}$. What do you notice?

7-129.   On a map, Cary drew a set of coordinate axes. He noticed that the town of Coyner is located at the point $(3, 1)$ and Woottonville is located at $(15, 7)$, where 1 grid unit represents 1 mile.

a.   If the towns want to place a school at the midpoint between the towns, where should it be located? How far would it be from each town?

b.   Woottonville argues that since it will have twice as many students attending the school, it should be closer to Woottonville. Where should the school be if it is:

   i. $\frac{1}{3}$ of the way from Woottonville to Coyner?

   ii. $\frac{1}{4}$ of the way from Woottonville to Coyner?

   iii. $\frac{2}{3}$ of the way from Coyner to Woottonville?

c.   Cary's brother is confused and needs help. Describe how he can find a point a certain fraction of the distance from one point to another?

7-130.   LEARNING LOG

In your Learning Log, explain what a midpoint is and the method you prefer for finding midpoints of a line segment when given the coordinates of its endpoints. Include any diagram or example that helps explain why this method works. Title this entry "Finding a Midpoint" and label it with today's date.

METHODS AND MEANINGS

Coordinate Geometry

Coordinate geometry is the study of geometry on a coordinate grid. Using common algebraic and geometric tools, you can learn more about a shape, such as, *"Does it have a right angle?"* or *"Are there two sides with the same length?"*

One useful tool is the Pythagorean Theorem. For example, the Pythagorean Theorem could be used to determine the length of side $\overline{AB}$ of $ABCD$ at right. By drawing the slope triangle between points A and B, the length of $\overline{AB}$ can be found to be $\sqrt{2^2 + 5^2} = \sqrt{29}$ units.

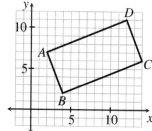

Similarly, slope can help analyze the relationships between the sides of a shape. If the slopes of two sides of a shape are equal, then those sides are **parallel**. For example, since the slope of $\overline{BC} = \frac{2}{5}$ and the slope of $\overline{AD} = \frac{2}{5}$, then $\overline{BC} \parallel \overline{AD}$.

Also, if the slopes of two sides of a shape are opposite reciprocals, then the sides are **perpendicular** (meaning they form a 90° angle). For example, since the slope of $\overline{BC} = \frac{2}{5}$ and the slope of $\overline{AB} = -\frac{5}{2}$, then $\overline{BC} \perp \overline{AB}$.

By using multiple algebraic and geometric tools, you can identify shapes. For example, further analysis of the sides and angles of $ABCD$ above shows that $AB = DC$ and $BC = AD$. Furthermore, all four angles measure 90°. These facts together indicate that $ABCD$ must be a rectangle.

7-131. Tomika remembers that the diagonals of a rhombus are perpendicular to each other.

a. Graph $ABCD$ if $A(1, 4)$, $B(6, 6)$, $C(4, 1)$, and $D(-1, -1)$. Is $ABCD$ a rhombus? Show how you know.

b. Find the equation of the lines on which the diagonals lie. That is, find the equations of $\overleftrightarrow{AC}$ and $\overleftrightarrow{BD}$.

c. Compare the slopes of $\overleftrightarrow{AC}$ and $\overleftrightarrow{BD}$. What do you notice?

7-132. Find another valid, logical order for the statements for Penn's proof from problem 7-113. Explain how you know that changing the order the way you did does not affect the logic.

7-133. Each of these number lines shows a segment in bold. Find the midpoint of the segment in bold. Note that the diagrams are *not* drawn to scale.

a. ↤——•——————•——→ 3   9

b. ↤——•——————•——→ -1   7

c. ↤——•——————•——→ -15   2

7-134. Examine the diagram at right.

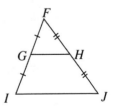

a. Are the triangles in this diagram similar? If they are, use a flowchart with justifications or a two-column proof to prove similarity. If they are not similar, explain why not. Explain.

b. Name all the pairs of congruent angles in this diagram you can.

c. Are $\overline{GH}$ and $\overline{IJ}$ parallel? Explain how you know.

d. If $GH = 4x - 3$ and $IJ = 3x + 14$, find x. Then find the length of $\overline{GH}$.

7-135. Consider $\triangle ABC$ with vertices $A(2, 3)$, $B(6, 6)$, and $C(8, -5)$.

    a. Draw $\triangle ABC$ on graph paper. What kind of triangle is $\triangle ABC$? Prove your result.

    b. Reflect $\triangle ABC$ across $\overline{AC}$. Find the location of B'. What name best describes the resulting figure? Prove your claim.

7-136. This problem is a checkpoint for solving with trigonometric ratios and the Pythagorean Theorem. It will be referred to as Checkpoint 7.

    a. Compute the perimeter.   b. Solve for x.

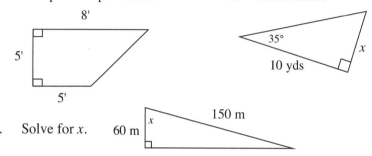

    c. Solve for x.

    d. Juanito is flying a kite at the park and realizes that all 500 feet of string are out. Margie measures the angle of the string with the ground using her clinometer and finds it to be 42°. How high is Juanito's kite above the ground? Draw a diagram and use the appropriate trigonometric ratio.

Check your answers by referring to the Checkpoint 7 materials located at the back of your book.

Ideally, at this point you are comfortable working with these types of problems and can solve them correctly. If you feel that you need more confidence when solving these types of problems, then review the Checkpoint 7 materials and try the practice problems provided. From this point on, you will be expected to do problems like these correctly and with confidence.

7-137. MUST BE, COULD BE

    Here are some more challenges from Mr. Quincey. For each description of a quadrilateral below, say what special type the quadrilateral *must be* and/or what special type the quadrilateral *could be*. Look out: Some descriptions may have no *must be* statements, and some descriptions may have many *could be* statements!

    a. My quadrilateral has a pair of equal sides and a pair of parallel sides.

    b. The diagonals of my quadrilateral bisect each other.

                                                                        Core Connections Geometry

7.3.3 What kind of quadrilateral is it?

Identifying Quadrilaterals on a Coordinate Grid

Today you will use algebra tools to investigate the properties of a quadrilateral and then will use those properties to identify the type of quadrilateral it is.

7-138.   MUST BE, COULD BE

Mr. Quincey has some new challenges for you! For each description below, decide what special type the quadrilateral *must be* and/or what special type the quadrilateral *could be*. Look out: Some descriptions may have no *must be* statements, and some descriptions may have many *could be* statements!

a.   My quadrilateral has three right angles.

b.   My quadrilateral has a pair of parallel sides.

c.   My quadrilateral has two consecutive equal angles.

7-139.   THE SHAPE FACTORY

You just got a job in the Quadrilaterals Division of your uncle's Shape Factory. In the old days, customers called up your uncle and described the quadrilaterals they wanted over the phone: *"I'd like a parallelogram with…"*.

"But nowadays," your uncle says, *"customers using computers have been emailing orders in lots of different ways."* Your uncle needs your team to help analyze his most recent orders listed below to identify the quadrilaterals and help the shape-makers know what to produce.

Your Task: For each of the quadrilateral orders listed below,

*   Create a diagram of the quadrilateral on graph paper.

*   Decide if the quadrilateral ordered has a special name. To help the shape-makers, your name must be as specific as possible. (For example, do not just call a shape a rectangle when it is also a square!)

*   Record and be ready to present a proof that the quadrilateral ordered must be the kind you say it is. It is not enough to say that a quadrilateral *looks* like it is of a certain type or *looks* like it has a certain property. Customers will want to be sure they get the type of quadrilateral they ordered!

Problem continues on next page →

Discussion Points

What special properties might a quadrilateral have?

What algebra tools could be useful?

What types of quadrilaterals might be ordered?

The orders:

a.   A quadrilateral formed by the intersection of these lines:

$$y = -\tfrac{3}{2}x + 3 \qquad y = \tfrac{3}{2}x - 3 \qquad y = -\tfrac{3}{2}x + 9 \qquad y = \tfrac{3}{2}x + 3$$

b.   A quadrilateral with vertices at these points:

$A(0, 2)$ $\qquad\qquad$ $B(1, 0)$ $\qquad\qquad$ $C(7, 3)$ $\qquad\qquad$ $D(4, 4)$

c.   A quadrilateral with vertices at these points:

$W(0, 5)$ $\qquad\qquad$ $X(2, 7)$ $\qquad\qquad$ $Y(5, 7)$ $\qquad\qquad$ $Z(5, 1)$

METHODS AND MEANINGS

MATH NOTES

Finding a Midpoint

A **midpoint** is a point that divides a line segment into two parts of equal length. For example, M is the midpoint of $\overline{AB}$ at right.

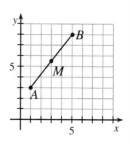

There are several ways to find the midpoint of a line segment if the coordinates of the endpoints are known. One way is to add half the change in x ($\tfrac{1}{2}\Delta x$) and half of the change in y ($\tfrac{1}{2}\Delta y$) to the x- and y-coordinates of the starting point, respectively.

Thus, if $A(1, 3)$ and $B(5, 8)$, then $\Delta x = 5 - 1 = 4$ and $\Delta y = 8 - 3 = 5$. Then the x-coordinate of M is $1 + \tfrac{1}{2}(4) = 3$ and the y-coordinate is $3 + \tfrac{1}{2}(5) = 5.5$. So point M is at $(3, 5.5)$.

This strategy can be used to find other points between A and B that are a proportion of the way from a starting point. For example, if you wanted to find a point $\tfrac{4}{5}$ of the way from point A to point B, then this could be found by adding $\tfrac{4}{5}$ of Δx to the x-coordinate of point A and adding $\tfrac{4}{5}$ of Δy to the y-coordinate of point A. This would be the point $((1 + \tfrac{4}{5}(4), 3 + \tfrac{4}{5}(5))$ which is $(4.2, 7)$. Generally, a point a ratio r from $A(x_0, y_0)$ to $B(x_1, y_1)$ is at $(x_0 + r(x_1 - x_0), y_0 + r(y_1 - y_0))$.

7-140. Each problem below gives the endpoints of a segment. Find the coordinates of the midpoint of the segment. If you need help, consult the Math Notes box for this lesson.

a. (5, 2) and (11, 14)

b. (3, 8) and (10, 4)

7-141. Below are the coordinates of three points and the equations of two lines. For each line, determine which of the points, if any, lie on that line. (There may be more than one!)

$$X(0, 15) \quad Y(3, 16) \quad Z(7, 0)$$

a. $y = \frac{1}{3}x + 15$

b. $y - 16 = -4(x - 3)$

7-142. MUST BE, COULD BE

Here are some more challenges from Mr. Quincey. For each description of a quadrilateral below, say what special type the quadrilateral *must be* and/or what special type the quadrilateral *could be*. Look out: Some descriptions may have no *must be* statements, and some descriptions may have many *"could be"* statements!

a. My quadrilateral has two right angles.

b. The diagonals of my quadrilateral are perpendicular.

7-143. Examine the arrow diagram below.

Polygon is a parallelogram → *area of the polygon equals base times height.*

a. Write this conjecture as a conditional ("If, then") statement.

b. Write the converse of this conditional statement. Is the converse statement a true statement?

c. Write a similar conjecture about triangles. Write it once as a conditional statement and once as an arrow diagram.

d. Write the converse of your triangle conjecture from part (c). Is the converse statement true?

7-144. The angle created by a hinged mirror when forming a
regular polygon is called a **central angle**. For example,
∠*ABC* in the diagram at right is the central angle of the
regular hexagon.

a. If the central angle of a regular polygon measures 18°,
how many sides does the polygon have?

b. Can a central angle measure 90°? 180°? 13°? For each angle measure,
explain how you know.

7-145. Jamika designed a game that allows some people to win
money and others to lose money, but overall Jamika will
neither win nor lose money. Each player will spin the spinner
at right and will win the amount of money shown in the
result. How much should each player pay to spin the spinner?
Explain your reasoning.

7-146. Suppose *ADBC* is a quadrilateral and the diagonal $\overline{AB}$ lies on $y = -\frac{4}{3}x + 5$ and
diagonal $\overline{CD}$ lies on $y = \frac{3}{4}x - 1$. Assume the diagonals intersect at point *E*.

a. Without graphing, what is the relationship between the diagonals? How do
you know?

b. Graph the lines on graph paper. If *E* is a midpoint of $\overline{CD}$, what type of
quadrilateral could *ADBC* be? Is there more than one possible type?
Explain how you know.

Core Connections Geometry

Chapter 7 Closure What have I learned?

Reflection and Synthesis

The activities below offer you a chance to reflect about what you have learned during this chapter. As you work, look for concepts that you feel very comfortable with, ideas that you would like to learn more about, and topics you need more help with. Look for connections between ideas as well as connections with material you learned previously.

①   TEAM BRAINSTORM

What have you studied in this chapter? What ideas were important in what you learned? With your team, brainstorm a list. Be as detailed as you can. To help get you started, a list of Learning Log entries, Toolkit Entries, and Math Notes boxes are below.

What topics, ideas, and words that you learned *before* this chapter are connected to the new ideas in this chapter? Again, be as detailed as you can.

Next consider the Standards for Mathematical Practice that follow Activity ③: Portfolio. What Mathematical Practices did you use in this chapter? When did you use them? Give specific examples.

How long can you make your lists? Challenge yourselves. Be prepared to share your team's ideas with the class.

Learning Log Entries
- Lesson 7.1.1 – Shapes of Wheels
- Lesson 7.1.3 – Shortest Distance
- Lesson 7.2.5 – Two-Column Proofs
- Lesson 7.3.2 – Finding a Midpoint

Toolkit Entries
- Theorem Toolkit (Lesson 7.2.1A Resource Page and problems 7-53, 7-64, 7-72, 7-94, 7-100, 7-107, and 7-108.)

Math Notes
- Lesson 7.1.2 – Parts of a Circle
- Lesson 7.1.3 – Congruent Triangles → Congruent Corresponding Parts
- Lesson 7.1.4 – Regular Polygons
- Lesson 7.2.1 – Reflexive Property of Equality
- Lesson 7.2.2 – Exponential Functions
- Lesson 7.2.3 – Definitions of Quadrilaterals
- Lesson 7.2.4 – Diagonals of a Rhombus
- Lesson 7.2.6 – Triangle Midsegment Theorem
- Lesson 7.3.2 – Coordinate Geometry
- Lesson 7.3.3 – Finding a Midpoint

②   MAKING CONNECTIONS

Below is a list of the vocabulary used in this chapter. Make sure that you are familiar with all of these words and know what they mean. Refer to the glossary or index for any words that you do not yet understand.

bisect	center	central angle
circle	congruent	conjecture
consecutive angles	coordinate geometry	diagonal
diameter	edge	exterior angle
face	flowchart	isosceles trapezoid
kite	midpoint	midsegment
opposite	parallel	parallelogram
perpendicular	proof	quadrilateral
radius	rectangle	Reflexive Property
regular polygon	rhombus	right trapezoid
square	tetrahedron	theorem
three-dimensional	trapezoid	two-column proof
two-dimensional	vertex	

Make a concept map showing all of the connections you can find among the key words and ideas listed above. To show a connection between two words, draw a line between them and explain the connection, as shown in the model below. A word can be connected to any other word as long as you can justify the connection. For each key word or idea, provide an example or sketch that shows the idea.

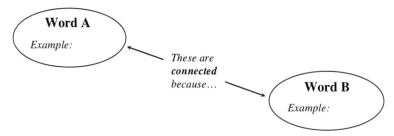

Your teacher may provide you with vocabulary cards to help you get started. If you use the cards to plan your concept map, be sure either to re-draw your concept map on your paper or to glue the vocabulary cards to a poster with all of the connections explained for others to see and understand.

While you are making your map, your team may think of related words or ideas that are not listed here. Be sure to include these ideas on your concept map.

Re-create your proof from problem 7-100 to showcase your current understanding of formal proof. Make sure your flowchart includes given information, bubbles that contain statements, and justifications for the statements. Do *not* use quadrilateral theorems from your Theorem Toolkit or elsewhere in this chapter as part of your flowchart. In other words, start with the given information and make statements based on angle relationships, shape definitions, triangle properties, and triangle similarity, as needed, but do not use quadrilateral theorems (such as "diagonals of a parallelogram bisect each other").

Then rewrite your proof, showcasing your ability to write a two-column proof.

Your teacher may give you the Chapter 7 Closure Resource Page: Quadrilaterals Graphic Organizer to record your work. A Graphic Organizer is a tool you can use to organize your thoughts, showcase your knowledge, and communicate your ideas clearly.

Next, consider the Standards for Mathematical Practice that follow. What Mathematical Practices did you use in this chapter? When did you use them? Give specific examples.

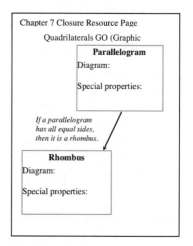

BECOMING MATHEMATICALLY PROFICIENT
The Common Core State Standards for Mathematical Practice

This book focuses on helping you use some very specific Mathematical Practices. The Mathematical Practices describe ways in which mathematically proficient students engage with mathematics everyday.

Make sense of problems and persevere in solving them:

Making sense of problems and persevering in solving them means that you can solve problems that are full of different kinds of mathematics. These types of problems are not routine, simple, or typical. Instead, they combine lots of math ideas and everyday situations. You have to stick with challenging problems, try different strategies, use multiple representations, and use a different method to check your results.

Reason abstractly and quantitatively:

Throughout this course, everyday situations are used to introduce you to new math ideas. Seeing mathematical ideas within a context helps you make sense of the ideas. Once you learn about a math idea in a practical way, you can "**reason abstractly**" by thinking about the concept more generally, representing it with symbols, and manipulating the symbols. **Reasoning quantitatively** is using numbers and symbols to represent an everyday situation, taking into account the units involved, and considering the meaning of the quantities as you compute them.

Construct viable arguments and critique the reasoning of others:

To **construct a viable argument** is to present your solution steps in a logical sequence and to justify your steps with conclusions, relying on number sense, facts and definitions, and previously established results. You communicate clearly, consider the real-life context, and provide clarification when others ask. In this course, you regularly share information, opinions, and expertise with your study team. You **critique the reasoning of others** when you analyze the approach of others, build on each other's ideas, compare the effectiveness of two strategies, and decide what makes sense and under what conditions.

Model with mathematics:

When you **model with mathematics**, you take a complex situation and use mathematics to represent it, often by making assumptions and approximations to simplify the situation. Modeling allows you to analyze and describe the situation and to make predictions. For example, to find the density of your body, you might model your body with a more familiar shape, say, a cylinder of the same diameter and height. Although a model may not be perfect, it can still be very useful for describing data and making predictions. When you interpret the results, you may need to go back and improve your model by revising your assumptions and approximations.

Core Connections Geometry

Use appropriate tools strategically:

To **use appropriate tools strategically** means that you analyze the task and decide which tools may help you model the situation or find a solution. Some of the tools available to you include diagrams, graph paper, calculators, computer software, databases, and websites. You understand the limitations of various tools. A result can be check or estimated by strategically choosing a different tool.

Attend to precision:

To **attend to precision** means that when solving problems, you need to pay close attention to the details. For example, you need to be aware of the units, or how many digits your answer requires, or how to choose a scale and label your graph. You may need to convert the units to be consistent. At times, you need to go back and check whether a numerical solution makes sense in the context of the problem.

You need to **attend to precision** when you communicate your ideas to others. Using the appropriate vocabulary and mathematical language can help make your ideas and reasoning more understandable to others.

Look for and make use of structure:

Looking for and making use of structure is a guiding principle of this course. When you are involved in analyzing the structure and in the actual development of mathematical concepts, you gain a deeper, more conceptual understanding than when you are simply told what the structure is and how to do problems. You often use this practice to bring closure to an investigation.

There are many concepts that you learn by looking at the underlying structure of a mathematical idea and thinking about how it connects to other ideas you have already learned. For example, geometry theorems are developed from the structure of translations.

Look for and express regularity in repeated reasoning:

To **look for and express regularity in repeated reasoning** means that when you are investigating a new mathematical concept, you notice if calculations are repeated in a pattern. Then you look for a way to generalize the method for use in other situations, or you look for shortcuts. For example, the investigations with simple shapes can be applied to more complex shapes using repeated reasoning.

④   WHAT HAVE I LEARNED?

Most of the problems in this section
represent typical problems found in
this chapter. They serve as a gauge
for you. You can use them to
determine which types of problems
you can do well and which types of
problems require further study and
practice. Even if your teacher does
not assign this section, it is a good
idea to try these problems and find
out for yourself what you know and what you still need to work on.

Solve each problem as completely as you can. The table at the end of the
closure section has answers to these problems. It also tells you where you
can find additional help and practice with problems like these.

CL 7-147.   Julius set his hinged mirror so that its angle was 72° and the
core region was isosceles, as shown at right.

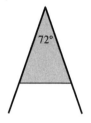

a.   How many sides did his resulting polygon have?
Show how you know.

b.   What is another name for this polygon?

CL 7-148.   Kelly started the proof below to show that if $\overline{TC} \cong \overline{TM}$
and $\overline{AT}$ bisects $\angle CTM$, then $\overline{CA} \cong \overline{MA}$. Copy and
complete her proof.

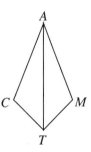

Statements	Reasons
1. $\overline{TC} \cong \overline{TM}$ and $\overline{AT}$ bisects $\angle CTM$	
2.	Definition of bisect
3. $\overline{AT} \cong \overline{AT}$	
4.	
5.	$\cong \triangle s \rightarrow \cong$ parts

CL 7-149.   Examine the spinner at right.

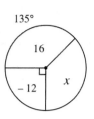

a.   Find the expected value of the spinner if $x = 4$.

b.   Find the expected value of the spinner if $x = -8$.

c.   Find x so that the expected value of the spinner is 6.

CL 7-150.   *ABCD* is a parallelogram. If $A(3, -4), B(6, 2), C(4, 6)$, then what are the possible locations of point *D*? Draw a graph and justify your answer.

CL 7-151.   Each problem below gives the endpoints of a segment. Find the coordinates of the midpoint of the segment.

a. $(-3, 11)$ and $(5, 6)$ b. $(-4, -1)$ and $(8, 9)$

CL 7-152.   For each diagram below, solve for the variable.

a.   b.   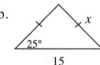   c.

CL 7-153.   On graph paper, draw quadrilateral *MNPQ* if $M(1, 7), N(-2, 2), P(3, -1)$, and $Q(6, 4)$.

a.   Find the slopes of $\overline{MN}$ and $\overline{NP}$. What can you conclude about $\angle MNP$?

b.   What is the best name for *MNPQ*? Justify your answer.

c.   Which diagonal is longer? Explain how you know your answer is correct.

d.   Find the midpoint of $\overline{MN}$.

CL 7-154.   Examine the geometric relationships in each of the diagrams below. For each one, write and solve an equation to find the value of the variable. Name any geometric property or conjecture that you used.

a.

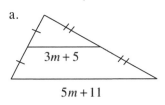

$3m + 5$

$5m + 11$

b.   *PQRS* is a rhombus with perimeter = 28 units and *PR* = 8 units, find *b* (*QT*)

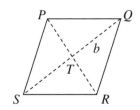

c.

$3x + 17°$

$x - 5°$

d.

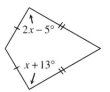

$2x - 5°$

$x + 13°$

CL 7-155.   Given the information in the diagram at right, use a flowchart to prove that $\triangle WXY \cong \triangle YZW$.

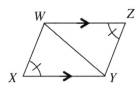

CL 7-156.   MUST BE, COULD BE

Here are some more challenges from Mr. Quincey. For each description of a quadrilateral below, say what special type the quadrilateral *must be* and/or what special type the quadrilateral *could be*. Remember: Some descriptions may have no *must be* statements, and some descriptions may have many "*could be* statements!

a.   The diagonals of my quadrilateral are equal.

b.   My quadrilateral has one right angle.

c.   My quadrilateral has one pair of equal adjacent sides.

CL 7-157.   Check your answers using the table at the end of the closure section. Which problems do you feel confident about? Which problems were hard? Use the table to make a list of topics you need help on and a list of topics you need to practice more.

Answers and Support for Closure Activity #4
What Have I Learned?

Note: MN = Math Note, LL = Learning Log

Problem	Solution	Need Help?	More Practice
CL 7-147.	a. $360° \div 72° = 5$ sides b. regular pentagon	Lesson 7.1.4 MN: 7.1.4	Problems 7-43, 7-55, and 7-144
CL 7-148.	<table><tr><th>Statements</th><th>Reasons</th></tr><tr><td>1. $\overline{TC} \cong \overline{TM}$ and $\overline{AT}$ bisects $\angle CTM$</td><td>Given</td></tr><tr><td>2. $\angle CTA \cong \angle MTA$</td><td>Definition of bisect</td></tr><tr><td>3. $\overline{AT} \cong \overline{AT}$</td><td>Reflexive Property</td></tr><tr><td>4. $\triangle CAT \cong \triangle MAT$</td><td>SAS $\cong$</td></tr><tr><td>5. $\overline{CA} \cong \overline{MA}$</td><td>$\cong \triangle s \rightarrow \cong$ parts</td></tr></table>	Lesson 7.2.5 MN: 7.1.3 and 7.2.1 LL: 7.2.5 Theorem Toolkit	Problems 7-102, 7-113, 7-122, and 7-124
CL 7-149.	a. 4.5 b. 0 c. $x = 8$	Lesson 4.2.5 MN: 5.2.2	Problems CL 5-141, CL 6-107, 7-121, and 7-145
CL 7-150.	Point D is at $(1, 0), (5, -8)$, or $(7, 12)$.	Lessons 7.3.1 and 7.3.3 MN: 7.2.3 and 7.3.2	Problems 7-32, 7-35, 7-68, and 7-79
CL 7-151.	a. $(1, 8.5)$ b. $(2, 4)$	Lesson 7.3.2 MN: 7.3.3 LL: 7.3.2	Problems 7-20, 7-29, 7-45, 7-119, and 7-140
CL 7-152.	a. $x \approx 7.43$ b. $x \approx 8.28$ c. $\theta \approx 33.7°$	Lesson 2.3.2, Sections 4.1 and 5.1 MN: 2.3.2, 4.1.2, 4.1.4, 5.1.2, and 5.1.4 LL: 2.3.2, 4.1.3, 4.1.4, 5.1.2, 5.1.3, and 5.3.1 Triangle Toolkit	Problems CL 3-119(a), CL 4-122, CL 5-139, 7-10, 7-85, and 7-136

Problem	Solution	Need Help?	More Practice
CL 7-153.	a. Slope of $\overline{MN} = \frac{5}{3}$ and $\overline{NP} = -\frac{3}{5}$, $\angle MNP$ is a right angle. b. It is a square because all sides are equal and all angles are right angles. c. The diagonals have equal length. Each is $\sqrt{68}$ units long. d. $(-\frac{1}{2}, \frac{9}{2})$	Section 7.3 MN: 7.2.3, 7.3.2, and 7.3.3 LL: 7.3.3	Problems 7-20, 7-32, 7-35, 7-48, 7-79, and 7-131
CL 7-154.	a. $2(3m+5) = 5m+11$, $m = 1$ b. $b^2 + 4^2 = 7^2$, so $b = \sqrt{33} \approx 5.74$ units c. $3x + 17° + x - 5° = 180°$, so $x = 42°$ d. $2x - 5° = x + 13°$, so $x = 18°$	Section 2.1, Lessons 2.3.2 and 7.2.6 MN: 2.1.1, 2.1.4, 2.3.2, 7.2.4, and 7.2.6 LL: 2.1.1, 2.3.2 Angle Relationships Toolkit Theorem Toolkit	Problems 7-7, 7-18, 7-37, and 7-81
CL 7-155.		Section 3.2 and Lessons 6.1.1 through 6.1.4 MN: 3.2.2, 3.2.4, 6.1.4, and 7.2.1 LL: 3.2.2	Problems CL 3-121, CL 4-123, CL 5-140, CL 6-101, 7-6, 7-15, 7-46, 7-69, 7-76, 7-86, 7-100, 7-108, 7-123, and 7-134(a)
CL 7-156.	a. Must be: none; Could be: rectangle, square, isosceles trapezoid b. Must be: none; Could be: any quadrilateral c. Must be: none; Could be: kite, rhombus, square	Lessons 7.3.1 and 7.3.3 MN: 7.2.3	Problems 7-9, 7-125, 7-137, and 7-142

CHAPTER 8   Polygons and Circles

In previous chapters, you have extensively studied triangles and quadrilaterals to learn more about their sides and angles. In this chapter, you will broaden your focus to include polygons with 5, 8, 10, and even 100 sides. You will develop a way to find the area and perimeter of a regular polygon and will study how the area and perimeter changes as the number of sides increases.

In Section 8.2, you will re-examine similar shapes to study what happens to the area and perimeter of a shape when the shape is enlarged or reduced.

Finally, in Section 8.3, you will connect your understanding of polygons with your knowledge of the area ratios of similar figures to find the area and circumference of circles of all sizes.

Guiding Question

Mathematically proficient students express regularity in repeated reasoning.

As you work through this chapter, ask yourself:

Can I find the shortcuts and generalize the rules for finding perimeters and areas of polygons?

In this chapter, you will learn:

➢ About special types of polygons, such as regular and non-convex polygons.

➢ How the measures of the interior and exterior angles of a regular polygon are related to the number of sides of the polygon.

➢ How the areas of similar figures are related.

➢ How to find the area and circumference of a circle and parts of circles and use this ability to solve problems in various contexts.

Chapter Outline

Section 8.1   This section begins with an investigation of the interior and exterior angles of a polygon and ends with a focus on the areas and perimeters of regular polygons.

Section 8.2   In this section, similar figures are revisited in order to investigate the ratio of the areas of similar figures.

Section 8.3   While answering the question, *"What if the polygon has an infinite number of sides?"*, a process will be developed to find the area and circumference of a circle.

8.1.1 How can I build it?

Pinwheels and Polygons

In previous chapters, you have studied triangles and quadrilaterals. In Chapter 8, you will broaden your focus to include all polygons and will study what triangles can tell us about shapes with 5, 8, or even 100 sides.

By the end of this lesson, you should be able to answer these questions:

How can you use the number of sides of a regular polygon to find the measure of the central angle?

What type of triangle is needed to form a regular polygon?

8-1.   PINWHEELS AND POLYGONS

Inez loves pinwheels. One day in class, she noticed that if she put three congruent triangles together so that one set of corresponding angles are adjacent, she could make a shape that looks like a pinwheel.

a.   Can you determine any of the angles of her triangles? Explain how you found your answer.

b.   The overall shape (outline) of Inez's pinwheel is shown at right. How many sides does it have? What is another name for this shape?

c.   Inez's shape is an example of a **polygon** because it is a <u>closed</u>, two-dimensional figure made of <u>non-intersecting straight line segments connected end-to-end</u>. As you study polygons in this course, it is useful to use the names below because they identify how many sides a particular polygon has. Some of these words may be familiar, while others may be new. On your paper, draw an example of a *heptagon*.

Name of Polygon	Number of Sides	Name of Polygon	Number of Sides
Triangle	3	Octagon	8
Quadrilateral	4	Nonagon	9
Pentagon	5	Decagon	10
Hexagon	6	11-gon	11
Heptagon	7	*n*-gon	*n*

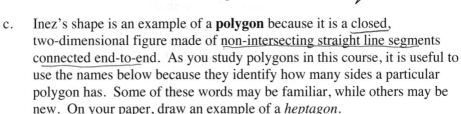

8-2.   Inez is very excited. She wants to know if you can build a pinwheel using *any* angle of her triangle. Obtain a Lesson 8.1.1 Resource Page from your teacher and cut out Inez's triangles. Then work with your team to build pinwheels and polygons by placing different corresponding angles together at the center. You will need to use the triangles from all four team members together to build one shape. Be ready to share your results with the class.

8-3.   Jorge likes Inez's pinwheels but wonders, *"Will all triangles build a pinwheel or a polygon?"*

a. If you have not already done so, cut out the remaining triangles on the Lesson 8.1.1 Resource Page. Work together to determine which congruent triangles can build a pinwheel (or polygon) when corresponding angles are placed together at the center. For each successful pinwheel, answer the questions below.

   • How many triangles did it take to build the pinwheel?

   • Calculate the measure of a central angle of the pinwheel. (Remember that a central angle is an angle of a triangle with a vertex at the center of the pinwheel.)

   • Is the shape familiar? Does it have a name? If so, what is it?

b. Explain why one triangle may be able to create a pinwheel or polygon while another triangle cannot.

c. Jorge has a triangle with angle measures 32°, 40°, and 108°. Will this triangle be able to form a pinwheel? Explain.

8-4.   Jasmine wants to create a pinwheel with equilateral triangles.

    a.   How many equilateral triangles will she need? Explain how you know.

    b.   What is the name for the polygon she created?

    c.   Jasmine's shape is an example of a **convex polygon**, while Inez's shape, shown at right, is **non-convex**. Study the examples of convex and non-convex polygons below and then write a definition of a convex polygon on your paper.

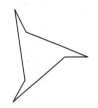

Examples of Non-Convex Polygons	Examples of Convex Polygons
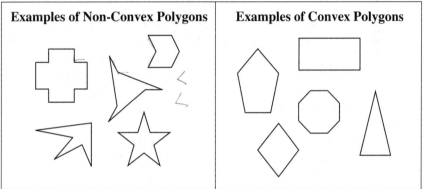	

8-5.   When corresponding angles are placed together, why do some triangles form convex polygons while others result in non-convex polygons? Consider this as you answer the following questions.

    a.   Carlisle wants to build a convex polygon using congruent triangles. He wants to select one of the triangles below to use. Which triangle(s) will build a convex polygon if multiple congruent triangles are placed together so that they share a common vertex and do not overlap? Explain how you know.

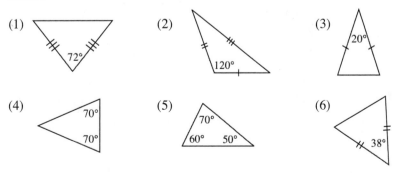

    b.   For each triangle from part (a) that creates a convex polygon, how many sides would the polygon have? What name is most appropriate for the polygon?

METHODS AND MEANINGS

Convex and Non-Convex Polygons

A **polygon** is defined as a two-dimensional closed figure made up of straight line segments connected end-to-end. These segments may not cross (intersect) at any other points.

A polygon is referred to as a **regular polygon** if it is equilateral (all sides have the same length) and equiangular (all interior angles have equal measure). For example, the hexagon shown at right is a regular hexagon because all sides have the same length and each interior angle has the same measure.

A polygon is called **convex** if each pair of interior points can be connected by a segment without leaving the interior of the polygon. See the example of convex and non-convex shapes in problem 8-4.

Review & Preview

8-6.   Solve for x in each diagram below.

a.
75°
35°
$x = 110$
$160 - 75$
$105 - 35$
70

b.
x
140° 40
$40 + 2x = 180$
-40 $2x = 140$ $x = 70$
2 2

c.
148°
x 100°

d.

x
36°
$180 - 72$
$x = 108$

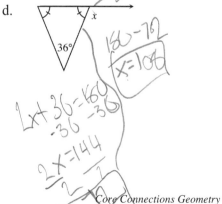
$2x + 36 = 180$
-36 -36
$2x = 144$
2 2
$x = 72$

Core Connections Geometry

8-7.   Using the definition of polygon from the Math Notes box in this lesson determine whether each of the following figures is or is not a polygon. Justify your decisions for each figure.

a.   b. 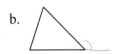   c.   d.

e.   f. ☆   g. ◺   h. ⌐⌐

8-8.   After solving for *x* in each of the diagrams in problem 8-6, Jerome thinks he sees a pattern. He notices that the measure of an exterior angle of a triangle is related to two of the angles of a triangle.

    a.   Do you see a pattern? To help find a pattern, study the results of problem 8-6.

    b.   In the example at right, angles *a* and *b* are called **remote interior angles** of the given exterior angle because they are not adjacent to the exterior angle. Write a conjecture about the relationships between the remote interior and exterior angles of a triangle.

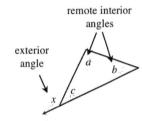

    c.   Prove that the conjecture you wrote for part (b) is true for all triangles. Your proof can be written in any form, as long as it is convincing and provides reasons for all statements.

8-9.   Examine the geometric relationships in the diagram at right. Show all of the steps in your solutions for *x* and *y*.

8-10.   Steven has 100 congruent triangles that each has an angle measuring 15°. How many triangles would he need to use to make a pinwheel? Explain how you found your answer.

8-11.   Find the value of *x* in each diagram below, if possible. If the triangles are congruent, state which triangle congruence property was used. If the triangles are not congruent or if there is not enough information, state, "Cannot be determined."

a.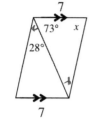

b.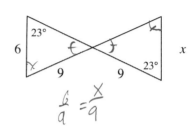

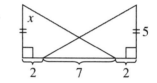

c.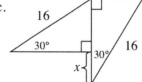

d.

8-12.   Decide if the following statements are true or false. If a statement is false, provide a diagram of a counterexample.

a.   All squares are rectangles.

b.   All quadrilaterals are parallelograms.

c.   All rhombi are parallelograms.

d.   All squares are rhombi.

e.   The diagonals of a parallelogram bisect the angles.

8.1.2 What is its measure?

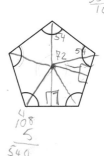

Interior Angles of Polygons

In an earlier chapter you discovered that the sum of the interior angles of a triangle is always 180°. What about other polygons, such as hexagons or decagons? What about the sum of their interior angles? Do you think it matters if the polygon is convex or not? Consider these questions today as you investigate the angles of a polygon.

8-13. Copy the diagram of the regular pentagon at right onto your paper. Then, with your team, find the *sum* of the measures of its interior angles *as many ways as you can*. You may want to use the fact that the sum of the angles of a triangle is 180°. Be prepared to share your team's methods with the class.

8-14. SUM OF THE INTERIOR ANGLES OF A POLYGON

In problem 8-13, you found the sum of the angles of a regular pentagon. But what about other polygons?

a. Obtain a Lesson 8.1.2 Resource Page from your teacher. Then use one of the methods from problem 8-13 to find the sum of the interior angles of other polygons. Complete the table (also shown below) on the resource page.

Number of Sides of the Polygon	3	4	5	6	7	8	9	10	12
Sum of the Interior Angles of the Polygon	180°	360	540	720	900	1080			

b. Does the interior angle sum depend on whether the polygon is convex? Test this idea by drawing a few non-convex polygons (like the one at right) on your paper and determine if it matters whether the polygon is convex. Explain your findings.

c. Find the sum of the interior angles of a 100-gon. Explain your reasoning.

d. LEARNING LOG

In your Learning Log, write an expression that represents the sum of the interior angles of an *n*-gon. Title this entry "Sum of Interior Angles of a Polygon" and include today's date.

8-15. The pentagon at right has been dissected (broken up) into three triangles with the angles labeled as shown. Use the three triangles to prove that the sum of the interior angles of *any* pentagon is always 540°. If you need help doing this, answer the questions below.

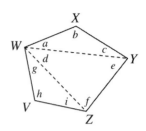

a. What is the sum of the angles of a triangle? Use this fact to write three equations based on the triangles in the diagram.

b. Add the three equations to create one long equation that represents the sum of all nine angles.

c. Substitute the three-letter name for each angle of the pentagon for the lower case letters at each vertex of the pentagon. For example, $m\angle XYZ = c + e$.

8-16. Use the angle relationships in each of the diagrams below to solve for the given variables. Show all work.

a.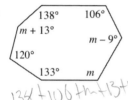

138° 106°
$m + 13°$
          $m - 9°$
120°
    133° m

$138 + 106 + m + 13 + m - 9 + 120 + 133th \vdots$

b.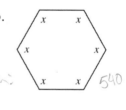

x x
x x
x x 540

c.

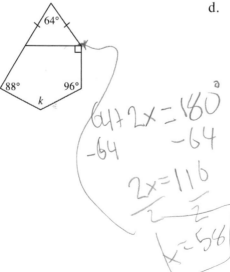

64°
88°   96°
    k

$64 + 2x = 180$
-64 -64
$2x = 116$
$\frac{2x}{2} = \frac{116}{2}$
$x = 58$

d.

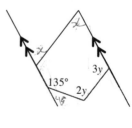

x
x
135° $3y$
   $2y$
48°

METHODS AND **M**EANINGS

MATH NOTES

Special Quadrilateral Properties

In Chapter 7, you examined several special quadrilaterals and proved conjectures regarding many of their special properties. Review what you learned below.

Parallelogram: Opposite sides of a parallelogram are congruent and parallel. Opposite angles are congruent. Also, since the diagonals create two pair of congruent triangles, the diagonals bisect each other.

Parallelogram

Rhombus: Since a rhombus is a parallelogram, it has all of the properties of a parallelogram. In addition, its diagonals are perpendicular bisectors that bisect the angles of the rhombus; the diagonals also create four congruent triangles.

Rhombus

Rectangle: Since a rectangle is a parallelogram, it has all of the properties of a parallelogram. In addition, its diagonals must be congruent.

Rectangle

Isosceles Trapezoid: The base angles (angles joined by a base) of an isosceles trapezoid are congruent.

Isosceles Trapezoid

Review & Preview

8-17.   On graph paper, graph $\triangle ABC$ if $A(3, 0)$, $B(2, 7)$, and $C(6, 4)$.

   a.   What is the most specific name for this triangle? Prove your answer is correct using both slope and side length.

   b.   Find $m\angle A$. Explain how you found your answer.

8-18.   The exterior angles of a quadrilateral are labeled a, b, c, and d in the diagram at right. Find the measures of a, b, c, and d and then find the sum of the exterior angles.

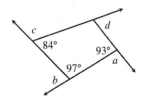

8-19.   Find the area and perimeter of the shape at right. Show all work.

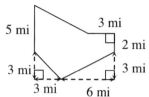

8-20.   Crystal is amazed! She graphed $\triangle ABC$ using the points $A(5,-1)$, $B(3,-7)$, and $C(6,-2)$. Then she rotated $\triangle ABC$ 90° counterclockwise ($\circlearrowleft$) about the origin to find $\triangle A'B'C'$. Meanwhile, her teammate took a different triangle ($\triangle TUV$) and rotated it 90° clockwise ($\circlearrowright$) about the origin to find $\triangle T'U'V'$. Amazingly, $\triangle A'B'C'$ and $\triangle T'U'V'$ ended up using exactly the same points! Name the coordinates of the vertices of $\triangle TUV$.

8-21.   Write an equation for each of the following sequences.

a. $-30,-15,0,...$ b. $9,3,1,...$

8-22.   Suzette started to set up a proof to show that if $\overline{BC} \parallel \overline{EF}$, $\overline{AB} \parallel \overline{DE}$, and $AF = DC$, then $\overline{BC} \cong \overline{EF}$. Examine her work below. Then complete her missing statements and reasons.

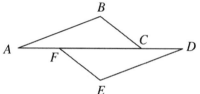

Statements	Reasons
1. $\overline{BC} \parallel \overline{EF}$, $\overline{AB} \parallel \overline{DE}$, and $AF = DC$	1.
2. $m\angle BCF = m\angle EFC$ and $m\angle EDF = m\angle CAB$	2.
3.	3. Reflexive Property
4. $AF + FC = FC + DC$	4. Additive Property of Equality (adding the same amount to both sides of an equation keeps the equation true)
5. $AC = DF$	5. Segment addition
6. $\triangle ABC \cong \triangle DEF$	6.
7.	7. $\cong \triangle s \rightarrow \cong$ parts

8-23.   **Multiple Choice:** Which equation below is *not* a correct statement based on the information in the diagram?

a. $3x + y = 180°$ b. $2x - 1° = 4° - x$

c. $2x - 1° = 5y - 10°$ d. $2x - 1° + 3x = 180°$

e.   All of these are correct

8.1.3 What if it is a regular polygon?

. . . .

Angles of Regular Polygons

In Lesson 8.1.2 you discovered how to determine the sum of the interior angles of a polygon with any number of sides. What more can you learn about a polygon? Today you will focus on the interior and exterior angles of regular polygons.

As you work today, keep the following focus questions in mind:

Does it matter if the polygon is regular?

Is there another way to find the answer?

What's the connection?

8-24. Diamonds, a very valuable naturally-occurring gem, have been popular for centuries because of their beauty, durability, and ability to reflect a spectrum of light. In 1919, a diamond cutter from Belgium, Marcel Tolkowsky, used his knowledge of geometry to design a new shape for a diamond, called the "round brilliant cut" (top view shown at right). He discovered that when diamonds are carefully cut with flat surfaces (called facets or faces) in this design, the angles maximize the brilliance and reflective quality of the gem.

Notice that at the center of this design is a regular octagon with equal sides and equal interior angles. For a diamond cut in this design to achieve its maximum value, the octagon must be cut carefully and accurately. One miscalculation, and the value of the diamond can be cut in half!

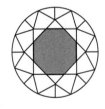

a. Determine the measure of each interior angle of a regular octagon. Explain how you found your answer.

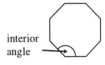

interior angle

b. What about the interior angles of other regular polygons? Find the interior angles of a regular nonagon and a regular 100-gon.

c. Will the process you used for part (a) work for any regular polygon? Write an expression that will calculate the interior angle of an n-gon.

8-25.   Fern states, *"If a triangle is equilateral, then all angles have equal measure and it must be a regular polygon."* Does this reasoning work for polygons with more than three sides? Investigate this idea below.

   a.   If all of the sides of a polygon, such as a quadrilateral, are equal, does that mean that the angles must be equal? If you can, draw a counterexample.

   b.   What if all of the angles are equal? Does that force a polygon to be equilateral? Explain your thinking. Draw a counterexample on your paper, if possible.

8-26.   Jeremy asks, *"What about exterior angles? What can we learn about them?"*

   a.   Examine the regular hexagon shown at right. Angle *a* is an example of an **exterior angle** because it is formed on the outside of the hexagon by extending one of its sides. Are all of the exterior angles of a regular polygon equal? Explain how you know.

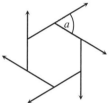

   b.   Find *a*. Be prepared to share how you found your answer.

   c.   This regular hexagon has six exterior angles, as shown in the diagram above. What is the sum of the exterior angles of a regular hexagon?

   d.   What can you determine about the exterior angles of other regular polygons? Explore this with your team. Have each team member choose a different shape from the list below to analyze. For each shape:

   •   Find the measure of one exterior angle of that shape, and

   •   Find the sum of the exterior angles.

   (1)   equilateral triangle   (2)   regular octagon

   (3)   regular decagon   (4)   regular dodecagon (12-gon)

   e.   Compare your results from part (d). As a team, write a conjecture about the sum of the exterior angles of polygons based on your observations. Be ready to share your conjecture with the rest of the class.

   f.   Is your conjecture from part (e) true for all polygons or for only regular polygons? Does it matter if the polygon is not convex? Explore these questions using a technology tool or obtain the Lesson 8.1.3 Resource Page and tracing paper from your teacher. Write a statement explaining your findings.

8-27.   Use your understanding of polygons to answer the questions below, if possible. If there is no solution, explain why not.

   a.   Gerardo drew a regular polygon that had exterior angles measuring 40°. How many sides did his polygon have? What is the name for this polygon?

   b.   A polygon has an interior angle sum of 2520°. How many sides does it have?

   c.   A quadrilateral has four sides. What is the measure of each of its interior angles?

   d.   What is the measure of an interior angle of a regular 360-gon? Is there more than one way to find this answer?

8-28.   LEARNING LOG

How can you find the interior angle of a regular polygon? What is the sum of the exterior angles of a polygon? Write a Learning Log entry about what you learned during this lesson. Title this entry "Interior Angles and Sum of Exterior Angles of a Polygon" and include today's date.

8-29.   Find the area and perimeter of each shape below. Show all work.

   a. 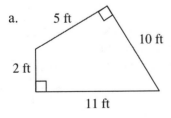   b.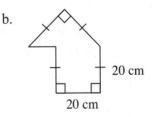

8-30.   In the figure at right, if $PQ = RS$ and $PR = SQ$, prove that $\angle P \cong \angle S$. Write your proof either in a flowchart or in two-column proof form.

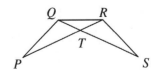

8-31.   Joey used 10 congruent triangles to create a regular decagon.

   a.   What kind of triangles is he using?

   b.   Find the three angle measures of one of the triangles. Explain how you know.

   c.   If the area of each triangle is 14.5 square inches, then what is the area of the regular decagon? Show all work.

8-32.   On graph paper, plot $A(2, 2)$ and $B(14, 10)$.

   a.   If C is the midpoint of $\overline{AB}$, D is the midpoint of $\overline{AC}$, and E is the midpoint of $\overline{CD}$, find the coordinates of E.

   b.   What fraction of the distance from A to B is E?

   c.   Use the ratio from part (b) to find the coordinates of point E.

8-33.   Use the geometric relationships in the diagrams below to solve for x.

   a.
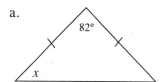

   b.
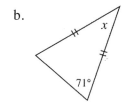

8-34.   The arc at right is called a quarter circle because it is one-fourth of a circle.

   a.   Copy Region A at right onto your paper. If this region is formed using 4 quarter circles, can you find another shape that must have the same area as Region A? Justify your conclusion.

   b.   Find the area of Region A. Show all work.

8-35.   **Multiple Choice:** Which property below can be used to prove that the triangles at right are similar?

   a.   AA ~   b.   SAS ~

   c.   SSS ~   d.   HL ~   e.   None of these

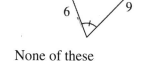

8.1.4 Is there another way?

Regular Polygon Angle Connections

During Lessons 8.1.1 through 8.1.3, you have discovered several ways the number of sides of a regular polygon is related to the measures of the interior and exterior angles of the polygon. These relationships can be represented in the diagram at right.

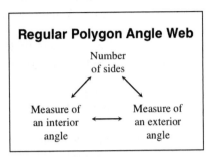

How can these relationships be useful? What is the most efficient way to go from one measurement to another? This lesson will explore these questions so that you will have a complete set of tools to analyze the angles of a regular polygon.

8-36. Which connections in the Regular Polygon Angle Web do you already have? Which do you still need? Explore this as you answer the questions below.

   a. If you know the number of sides of a regular polygon, how can you find the measure of an interior angle directly? Find the measurements of an interior angle of a 15-gon.

   b. If you know the number of sides of a regular polygon, how can you find the measure of an exterior angle directly? Find the measurements of an exterior angle of a 10-gon.

   c. What if you know that the measure of an interior angle of a regular polygon is 162°? How many sides must the polygon have? Show all work.

   d. If the measure of an exterior angle of a regular polygon is 15°, how many sides does it have? What is the measure of an interior angle? Show how you know.

8-37. Suppose a regular polygon has an interior angle measuring 120°. Find the number of sides using *two* different strategies. Show all work. Which strategy was most efficient?

8-38.   Use your knowledge of polygons to answer the questions below, if possible.

   a.   How many sides does a polygon have if the sum of the measures of the interior angles is 1980°? 900°?

   b.   If the exterior angle of a regular polygon is 90°, how many sides does it have? What is another name for this shape?

   c.   Each interior angle of a regular pentagon has measure $2x+4°$. What is x? Explain how you found your answer.

   d.   The measures of four of the exterior angles of a pentagon are 57°, 74°, 56°, and 66°. What is the measure of the remaining angle?

   e.   Find the sum of the interior angles of an 11-gon. Does it matter if it is regular or not?

8-39.   LEARNING LOG

In a Learning Log entry, copy the Regular Polygon Angle Web that your class created. Explain what it represents and give an example of at least two of the connections. Title this entry "Regular Polygon Angle Web" and include today's date.

8-40.   Esteban used a hinged mirror to create an equilateral triangle, as shown in the diagram at right. If the area of the shaded region is 11.42 square inches, what is the area of the entire equilateral triangle? Justify your solution.

8-41.   A house purchased for $135,000 has an annual appreciation of 4%.

   a.   What is the multiplier?

   b.   Write a function of the form $f(t)=ab^t$ that represents the situation, where t is the time in years after the house was purchased.

   c.   At the current rate, what will be the value of the house in 10 years?

8-42.   Copy each shape below on your paper and state if the shape is convex or non-convex. You may want to compare each figure with the examples provided in problem 8-4.

a.   b.   c.   d.

8-43.   Find the area of each figure below. Show all work.

a. 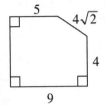   b.   c.

8-44.   Find the number of sides in a regular polygon if each interior angle has the following measures.

a.   60°   b.   156°   c.   90°   d.   140°

8-45.   Determine if the figures below (not drawn to scale) are similar. Justify your decision.

8-46.   At right is a scale drawing of the floor plan for Nzinga's dollhouse. The actual dimensions of the dollhouse are 5 times the measurements provided in the floor plan at right.

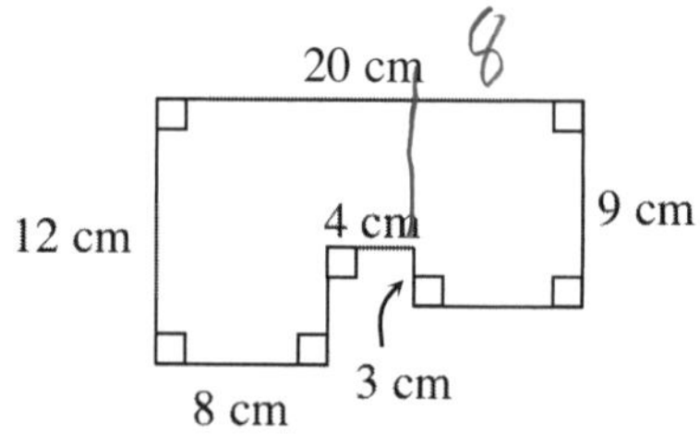

20 cm

12 cm

4 cm

9 cm

8 cm   3 cm

a.   Use the measurements provided in the diagram to find the area and perimeter of her floor plan.

b.   Draw a similar figure on your paper. Label the sides with the actual measurements of Nzinga's dollhouse. What is the perimeter and area of the floor of her actual dollhouse? Show all work.

c.   Find the ratio of the perimeters of the two figures. What do you notice?

d.   Find the ratio of the areas of the two figures. How does the ratio of the areas seem to be related to the zoom factor?

8.1.5 What is the area?

Finding Areas of Regular Polygons

In Lesson 8.1.4, you developed a method to find the measures of the interior and exterior angles of a regular polygon. How can this be useful? Today you will use what you know about the angles of a regular polygon to explore how to find the area of any regular polygon with *n* sides.

8-47.   USING MULTIPLE STRATEGIES

With your team, find the area of each shape below *twice*, each time using a distinctly different method or strategy. Make sure that your results from using different strategies are the same. Be sure that each member of your team understands each method.

a.   square

b.   regular hexagon

8-48.   Create a presentation that shows the two different methods that your team used to find the area of the regular hexagon in part (b) of problem 8-47.

Then, as you listen to other teams present, look for strategies that are different than yours. For each one, consider the questions below.

- *Which geometric tools does this method use?*

- *Would this method help find the area of other regular polygons (like a pentagon or 100-gon)?*

8-49. Which method presented by teams in problem 8-48 seemed able to help find the area of other regular polygons? Discuss this with your team. Then find the area of the two regular polygons below. If your method does not work, switch to a different method. Assume *C* is the center of each polygon.

a.

C

11

b.

C

5

8-50. LEARNING LOG

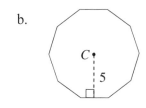

So far, you have found the area of a regular hexagon, nonagon, and decagon. How can you calculate the area of *any* regular polygon? Write a Learning Log entry describing a general process for finding the area of a polygon with *n* sides. Title this entry "Area of a Regular Polygon" and label it with today's date.

8-51. Beth needs to fertilize her flowerbed, which is in the shape of a regular pentagon. A bag of fertilizer states that it can fertilize up to 150 square feet, but Beth is not sure how many bags of fertilizer she should buy.

Beth does know that each side of the pentagon is 15 feet long. Copy the diagram of the regular pentagon below onto your paper. Find the area of the flowerbed and tell Beth how many bags of fertilizer to buy. Explain how you found your answer.

15 ft

8-52.   **GO, ROWDY RODENTS!**

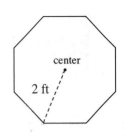

Recently, your school ordered a stained-glass window with the design of the school's mascot, the rodent. Your student body has decided that the shape of the window will be a regular octagon, shown at right. To fit in the space, the window must have a radius of 2 feet. The **radius of a regular polygon** is the distance from the center to each vertex.

a.   A major part of the cost of the window is the amount of glass used to make it. The more glass used, the more expensive the window. Your principal has turned to your class to determine how much glass the window will need. Copy the diagram onto your paper and find its area. Explain how you found your answer.

b.   The edge of the window will have a polished brass trim. Each foot of trim will cost $48.99. How much will the trim cost? Show all work.

Ⓜ️ETHODS AND MEANINGS

Interior and Exterior Angles of a Polygon

The properties of interior and exterior angles in polygons (which includes regular and non-regular polygons), where n represents the number of sides in the polygon (n-gon), can be summarized as follows:

- The sum of the measures of the interior angles of an n-gon is $180°(n - 2)$.

- The sum of the measures of the exterior angles of an n-gon is always $360°$.

- The measure of any interior angle plus its corresponding exterior angle is $180°$.

In addition, for *regular* polygons:

- The measure of each interior angle in a regular n-gon is $\frac{180°(n-2)}{n}$.

- The measure of each exterior angle in a regular n-gon is $\frac{360°}{n}$.

Review & Preview

8-53.   The exterior angle of a regular polygon is $20°$.

    a.   What is the measure of an interior angle of this polygon? Show how you know.

    b.   How many sides does this polygon have? Show all work.

8-54.   Examine the triangle and line of reflection at right.

    a.   On your paper, trace the triangle and the line of reflection. Then draw the image of the triangle after it is reflected across the line. Verify your reflection is correct by folding your paper along the line of reflection.

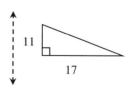

    b.   Find the perimeter of the image. How does it compare with the perimeter of the original figure?

    c.   Find the measure of both acute angles in the original triangle.

8-55.   Find the coordinates of the point at which the diagonals of parallelogram *ABCD* intersect if $B(-3, -17)$ and $D(15, 59)$. Explain how you found your answer.

8-56.   Find the area of an equilateral triangle with side length 20 mm. Draw a diagram and show all work.

8-57.   A hotel in Las Vegas is famous for its large-scale model of the Eiffel Tower. The model, built to scale, is 128 meters tall and 41 meters wide at its base. If the real tower is 324 meters tall, how wide is the base of the real Eiffel Tower?

8-58.   For each equation below, solve for *w*, if possible. Show all work.

   a. $5w^2 = 17$ b. $5w^2 - 3w - 17 = 0$ c. $2w^2 = -3$

8-59.   **Multiple Choice:** The triangles at right are congruent because of:

   a.   SSA $\cong$ b.   HL $\cong$ c.   SAS $\cong$

   d.   SSS $\cong$ e.   None of these

8-60.   Solve for *x* in each diagram below.

   a.

   b.
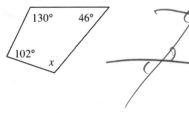

   c.
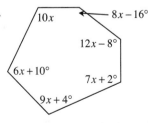

   d.
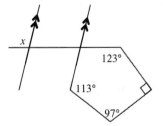

8-61.   What is another (more descriptive) name for each polygon described below?

a.   A regular polygon with an exterior angle measuring 120°.

b.   A quadrilateral with four equal angles.

c.   A polygon with an interior angle sum of 1260°.

d.   A quadrilateral with diagonals that are perpendicular bisectors of each other.

8-62.   If $\triangle ABC$ is equilateral and if $A(0,0)$ and $B(12,0)$, then what do you know about the coordinates of vertex C? Prove your answer is true.

8-63.   In the figure at right, $\overline{AB} \cong \overline{DC}$ and $\angle ABC \cong \angle DCB$.

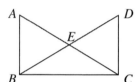

a.   Is $\overline{AC} \cong \overline{DB}$? Prove your answer using a flowchart or two-column proof.

b.   Do the measures of $\angle ABC$ and $\angle DCB$ make any difference in your solution to part (a)? Explain why or why not.

8-64.   On graph paper, graph the parabola $y = 2x^2 - x - 15$.

a.   What are the roots (x-intercepts) of the parabola? Write your points in (x, y) form.

b.   How would the graph of $y = -(2x^2 - x - 15)$ be the same or different? Can you tell without graphing?

8-65.   **Multiple Choice:** To decide if his class would take a quiz today, Mr. Chiu will flip a coin three times. If all three results are heads or all three results are tails, he will give the quiz. Otherwise, his students will not be tested. What is the probability that his class will take the quiz?

a. $\frac{1}{8}$ b. $\frac{1}{4}$ c. $\frac{1}{2}$ d.   1

8-66.   **Multiple Choice:** Approximate the length of $\overline{AB}$.

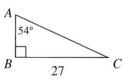

a.   15.87   b.   21.84   c.   37.16

d.   19.62   e.   None of these

8.2.1 How does the area change?

Area Ratios of Similar Figures

Much of this course has focused on similarity. In Chapter 3, you investigated how to enlarge and reduce a shape to create a similar figure. You also have studied how to use proportional relationships to find the measures of sides of similar figures. Today you will study how the areas of similar figures are related. That is, as a shape is enlarged or reduced in size, how does the area change?

8-67.　MIGHTY MASCOT

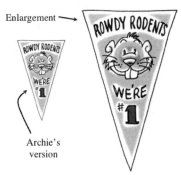

Enlargement →

Archie's version

To celebrate the victory of your school's championship girls' ice hockey team, the student body has decided to hang a giant flag with your school's mascot on the gym wall.

To help design the flag, your friend Archie has created a scale version of the flag measuring 1 foot wide and 1.5 feet tall.

a.　The student body thinks the final flag should be 3 feet tall. How wide would this enlarged flag be? Justify your solution.

b.　If Archie used $2 worth of cloth to create his scale model, then how much will the cloth cost for the full-sized flag? Discuss this with your team. Explain your reasoning.

c.　Obtain the Lesson 8.2.1A Resource Page and scissors from your teacher. Carefully cut enough copies of Archie's scale version to fit into the large flag. How many did it take? Does this confirm your answer to part (b)? If not, what will the cloth cost for the flag?

d.

The student body is reconsidering the size of the flag. It is now considering enlarging the flag so that it is 3 or 4 times the width of Archie's model. How much would the cloth for a similar flag that is 3 times as wide as Archie's model cost? What if the flag is 4 times as wide?

To answer this question, first *estimate* how many of Archie's drawings would fit into each enlarged flag. Then obtain one copy of the Lesson 8.2.1B Resource Page for your team and confirm each answer by fitting Archie's scale version into the enlarged flags.

8-68.   Write down any observations or patterns you found while working on problem 8-67. For example, if the area of one shape is 100 times larger than the area of a similar shape, then what is the ratio of the corresponding sides (also called the **linear scale factor**)? And if the linear scale factor is r, then how many times larger is the area of the new shape?

8-69.   Use your pattern from problem 8-68 to answer the following questions.

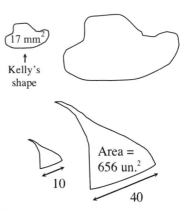

Kelly's shape

a.   Kelly's shape at right has an area of 17 mm^2. If she enlarges the shape with a linear scale (zoom) factor of 5, what will be the area of the enlargement? Show how you got your answer.

b.   Examine the two similar shapes at right. What is the linear scale factor? What is the area of the smaller figure?

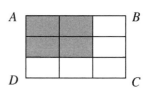

Area = 656 un.^{2}

c.   Rectangle *ABCD* at right is divided into nine smaller congruent rectangles. Is the shaded rectangle similar to *ABCD*? If so, what is the linear scale factor? And what is the ratio of the areas? If the shaded rectangle is not similar to *ABCD*, explain how you know.

d.   While ordering carpet for his rectangular office, Trinh was told by the salesperson that a 16' by 24' piece of carpet costs $800. Trinh then realized that he read his measurements wrong and that his office is actually 8' by 12'. *"Oh, that's no problem,"* said the salesperson. *"That is half the size and will cost $400 instead."* Is that fair? Decide what the price should be.

8-70.   If the side length of a hexagon triples, how does the area increase? First make a prediction using your pattern from problem 8-68. Then confirm your prediction by calculating and comparing the areas of the two hexagons shown at right.

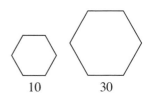

METHODS AND MEANINGS

Ratios of Similarity

Since Chapter 3, you have used the term **zoom factor** to refer to the ratio of corresponding dimensions of two similar figures. However, now that you will be using other ratios of similar figures (such as the ratio of the areas), this ratio needs a more descriptive name. From now on, this text will refer to the ratio of corresponding sides as the **linear scale factor**. The word "linear" is a reference to the fact that the ratio of the lengths of line segments is a comparison of a single dimension of the shapes. Often, this value is represented with the letter r, for ratio.

For example, notice that the two triangles at right are similar because of AA ~. Since the corresponding sides of the new and original shape are 9 and 6, it can be stated that $r = \frac{9}{6} = \frac{3}{2}$.

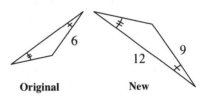

Original   New

8-71.   Examine the shape at right.

a.   Find the area and perimeter of the shape.

b.   On graph paper, enlarge the figure so that the linear scale factor is 3. Find the area and perimeter of the new shape.

c.   What is the ratio of the perimeters of both shapes? What is the ratio of the areas?

8-72.   Sandip noticed that when he looked into a mirror that was lying on the ground 8 feet from him, he could see a clock on the wall. If Sandip's eyes are 64 inches off the ground, and if the mirror is 10 feet from the wall, how high above the floor is the clock? Include a diagram in your solution.

8-73.   Mr. Singer has a dining table in the shape of a regular
         hexagon. While he loves this design, he has trouble finding
         tablecloths to cover it. He has decided to make his own
         tablecloth!

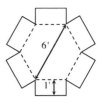

         In order for his tablecloth to drape over each edge, he will
         add a rectangular piece along each side of the regular hexagon
         as shown in the diagram at right. Using the dimensions given in
         the diagram, find the total area of the cloth Mr. Singer will need.

8-74.   What is the probability that $x^2 + 7x + k$ is factorable if $0 \le k \le 20$ and k is an
         integer?

8-75.   Your teacher has offered your class extra credit.
         She has created two spinners, shown at right.
         Your class gets to spin only one of the spinners.
         The number that the spinner lands on is the
         number of extra credit points each member of
         the class will get. Study both spinners carefully.

         a.   Assuming that each spinner is divided into equal portions, which spinner
               do you think the class should choose to spin and why?

         b.   What if the spot labeled "20" were changed to "100"? Would that make
               any difference?

8-76.   If the rectangles below have the same area, find x. Is there more than one
         answer? Show all work.

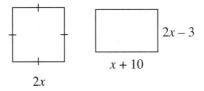

8-77.   **Multiple Choice:** A cable 100 feet long is attached 70 feet up the side of a
         building. If it is pulled taut (i.e., there is no slack) and staked to the ground as
         far away from the building as possible, approximately what angle does the cable
         make with the ground?

         a.   39.99°   b.   44.43°   c.   45.57°   d.   12.22°

8.2.2 How does the area change?

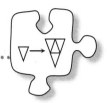

Ratios of Similarity

Today you will continue investigating the ratios between similar figures. As you solve today's problems, look for connections between the ratios of similar figures and what you already know about area and perimeter.

8-78.   TEAM PHOTO

Alice has a 4-inch by 5-inch photo of your school's championship girls' ice hockey team. To celebrate their recent victory, your principal wants Alice to enlarge her photo for a display case near the main office.

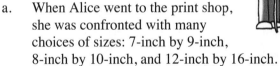

a.   When Alice went to the print shop, she was confronted with many choices of sizes: 7-inch by 9-inch, 8-inch by 10-inch, and 12-inch by 16-inch.

She's afraid that if she picks the wrong size, part of the photo will be cut off. Which size should Alice pick and why?

b.   The cost of the photo paper to print Alice's 4-inch-by-5-inch picture is $0.45. Assuming that the cost per square inch of photo paper remains constant, how much should it cost to print the enlarged photo? Explain how you found your answer.

c.   Unbeknownst to her, the vice-principal also went out and ordered an enlargement of Alice's photo. However, the photo paper for his enlargement cost $7.20! What are the dimensions of his photo?

8-79.   So far, you have discovered and used the relationship between the areas of similar figures. How are the perimeters of similar figures related? Confirm your intuition by analyzing the pairs of similar shapes below. For each pair, calculate the areas and perimeters and complete a table like the one shown below. To help see patterns, reduce fractions to lowest terms or find the corresponding decimal values.

	Ratio of Sides	Perimeter	Ratio of Perimeters	Area	Ratio of Areas
small figure					
large figure					

a.
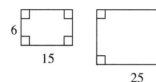

b.
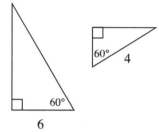

c.
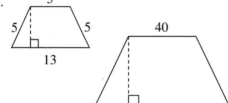

8-80.   While Jessie examines the two figures at right, she wonders if they are similar. Decide with your team if there is enough information to determine if the shapes are similar. Justify your conclusion.

8-81.   Your teacher enlarged the figure at right so that the area of the similar shape is 900 square cm. What is the perimeter of the enlarged figure? Be prepared to explain your method to the class.

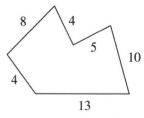

Area = 100 cm²

8-82.   LEARNING LOG

Reflect on what you have learned in Lessons 8.2.1 and
8.2.2. Write a Learning Log entry that explains what you
know about the areas and perimeters of similar figures.
What connections can you make with other geometric concepts? Be sure to
include an example. Title this entry "Areas and Perimeters of Similar Figures"
and include today's date.

8-83.   Assume Figure A and Figure B, at right, are similar.

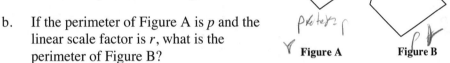

a.   If the ratio of similarity is $\frac{3}{4}$, then what is the
ratio of the perimeters of Figures A and B?

b.   If the perimeter of Figure A is p and the
linear scale factor is r, what is the
perimeter of Figure B?

c.   If the area of Figure A is a and the linear scale factor is r, what is the area
of Figure B?

8-84.   Always a romantic, Marris decided to bake his girlfriend a cookie in the shape of
a regular dodecagon (12-gon) for Valentine's Day.

a.   If the edge of the dodecagon is 6 cm, what is the area of the top of the
cookie?

b.   His girlfriend decides to divide the cookie into 12 congruent pieces. After
9 of the pieces have been eaten, what area of the cookie is left?

8-85.   As her team was building triangles with linguini, Karen asked for help building
a triangle with sides 5, 6, and 1. *"I don't think that's possible,"* said her
teammate, Kelly.

a.   Why is this triangle not possible?

b.   Change the lengths of one of the sides so that the triangle is possible.

8-86.   What is the 150th term in this sequence?

$$17, 16\tfrac{1}{2}, 16, 15\tfrac{1}{2}, \ldots$$

8-87.   Callie started to prove that given the information in the
         diagram at right, then $AB \cong CD$. Copy her flowchart below
         on your paper and help her by justifying each statement.

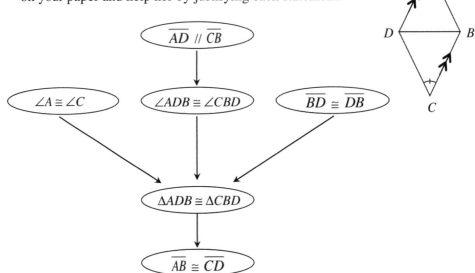

8-88.   For each pair of triangles below, decide if the triangles are congruent. If the
         triangles are congruent:

   • State which triangle congruence property proves that the triangles are
     congruent.

   • Write a congruence statement (such as $\triangle ABC \cong \triangle$ _____).

a. 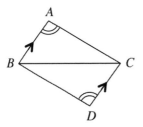   b.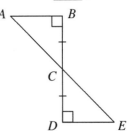

8-89.   **Multiple Choice:** What is the solution to the $y = \frac{1}{2}x - 4$
         system of equations at right? $x - 4y = 12$

   a. $(2, 0)$ b. $(16, 4)$

   c. $(-2, -5)$ d. $(4, -2)$

   e.   None of these

8.3.1 What if it has infinitely many sides?

A Special Ratio

In Section 8.1, you developed a method to find the area and perimeter of a regular polygon with *n* sides. You carefully calculated the area of regular polygons with 5, 6, 8, and even 10 sides. But what if the regular polygon has an infinite number of sides? How can you predict its area?

As you investigate this question today, keep the following focus questions in mind:

What is the connection?

Do I see any patterns?

How are the shapes related?

8-90.   POLYGONS WITH INFINITELY MANY SIDES

In order to predict the area and perimeter of a polygon with infinitely many sides, your team is going to work with other teams to generate data in order to find a pattern.

Your teacher will assign your team three of the regular polygons below. For each polygon, find the area and perimeter if the radius is 1 (as shown in the diagram of the regular pentagon at right). Leave your answer accurate to the nearest 0.01. Place your results into a class chart to help predict the area and perimeter of a polygon with infinitely many sides.

a.   equilateral triangle   b.   regular octagon   c.   regular 30-gon

d.   square   e.   regular nonagon   f.   regular 60-gon

g.   regular pentagon   h.   regular decagon   i.   regular 90-gon

j.   regular hexagon   k.   regular 15-gon   l.   regular 180-gon

8-91.   ANALYSIS OF DATA

With your team, analyze the chart created by the class.

a.   What do you predict the area will be for a regular polygon with infinitely many sides? What do you predict its perimeter will be?

b.   What is another name for a regular polygon with infinitely many sides?

c.   Does the number 3.14… look familiar? If so, share what you know with your team. Be ready to share your idea with the class.

8-92.   LEARNING LOG

Record the area and circumference of a circle with radius 1 in your Learning Log. Then, include a brief description of how you "discovered" π. Title this entry "Pi" and include today's date.

![M]ETHODS AND MEANINGS

Area of a Regular Polygon

If a polygon is regular with n sides, it can be subdivided into n congruent isosceles triangles. One way to calculate the area of a regular polygon is to multiply the area of one isosceles triangle by n.

n-gon

To find the area of the isosceles triangle, it is helpful to first find the measure of the polygon's central angle by dividing 360° by n. The height of the isosceles triangle divides the top vertex angle in half.

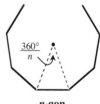

For example, suppose you want to find the area of a regular decagon with side length 8 units. The central angle is $\frac{360°}{10} = 36°$. Then the top angle of the shaded right triangle at right would be $36° \div 2 = 18°$.

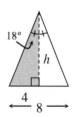

Use right triangle trigonometry to find the measurements of the right triangle, then calculate its area. For the shaded triangle above, $\tan 18° = \frac{4}{h}$ and $h \approx 12.311$. Use the height and the base to find the area of the isosceles triangle: $\frac{1}{2}(8)(12.311) \approx 49.242$ sq. units. Then the area of the regular decagon is approximately $10 \cdot 49.242 \approx 492.42$ sq. units.

Core Connections Geometry

8-93.   Find the area of the shaded region for the regular
         pentagon at right if the length of each side of the
         pentagon is 10 units. Assume that point C is the
         center of the pentagon.

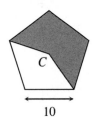

8-94.   For each triangle below, find the value of x, if possible. Name the triangle tool
         that you used. If the triangle cannot exist, explain why.

a.   b.   c.   d.

    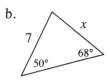

                                                                   Area of the
                                                                   shaded region is
                                                                   96 square units.

8-95.   Find the measure of each interior angle of a regular 30-gon using two different
         methods.

8-96.   Examine the diagram at right. Assume that $\overline{AD}$ and
         $\overline{BE}$ are line segments, and that $\overline{BC} \cong \overline{DC}$ and
         $\angle A \cong \angle E$. Prove that $\overline{AB} \cong \overline{ED}$. Use the form of
         proof that you prefer (such as the flowchart or
         two-column proof format). Be sure to copy the
         diagram onto your paper and add any appropriate
         markings.

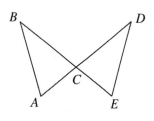

8-97.   For each diagram below, write and solve an equation to find x.

a.   b.

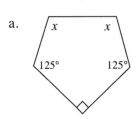   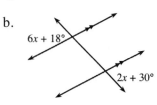

8-98.   On graph paper, plot the points $A(-3, -1)$ and $B(6, 11)$.

   a.   Find the midpoint M of $\overline{AB}$.

   b.   Find the point P, on $\overline{AB}$, that is $\frac{2}{3}$ of the way from A to B.

   c.   Find the equation of the line that passes through points A and B.

   d.   Find the distance between points M and P.

8-99.   **Multiple Choice:** What fraction of the circle at right is shaded?

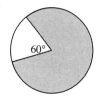

   a. $\frac{60}{360}$ b. $\frac{300}{360}$ c. $\frac{60}{180}$

   d. $\frac{120}{180}$ e.   None of these

8.3.2 What is the relationship?

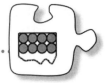

Area and Circumference of a Circle

In Lesson 8.3.1, your class discovered that the area of a circle with radius 1 unit is π units^2 and that the circumference is 2π units. But what if the radius of the circle is 5 units or 13.6 units? Today you will develop a method to find the area and circumference of circles when the radius is not 1. You will also explore parts of circles (called sectors and arcs) and learn about their measurements.

As you and your team work together, remember to ask each other questions such as:

Is there another way to solve it?

What is the relationship?

What is area? What is circumference?

8-100. AREA AND CIRCUMFERENCE OF A CIRCLE

Now that you know the area and circumference (perimeter) of a circle with radius 1, how can you find the area and circumference of a circle with any radius?

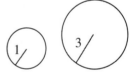

a. First examine how the circles at right are related. Since circles always have the same shape, what is the relationship between any two circles?

b. What is the ratio of the circumferences (perimeters)? What is the ratio of the areas? Explain.

c. If the area of a circle with radius of 1 is π square units, what is the area of a circle with radius 3 units? With radius 10 units? With radius r units?

d. Likewise, if the circumference (perimeter) of a circle is 2π units, what is the circumference of a circle with radius 3? With radius 7? With radius r?

8-101.   Read the definitions of radius and diameter in the Math Notes box for this lesson. Then answer the questions below.

a.   Find the area of a circle with radius 10 units.

b.   Find the circumference of a circle with diameter 7 units.

c.   If the area of a circle is 121π square units, what is its diameter?

d.   If the circumference of a circle is 20π units, what is its area?

8-102.   The giant sequoia trees in California are famous for their immense size and old age. Some of the trees are more than 2500 years old and tourists and naturalists often visit to admire their size and beauty. In some cases, you can even drive a car through the base of a tree!

One of these trees, the General Sherman tree in Sequoia National Park, is the largest living thing on the earth. The tree is so gigantic, in fact, that the base has a circumference of 102.6 feet! Assuming that the base of the tree is circular, how wide is the base of the tree? That is, what is its diameter? How does that diameter compare with the length and width of your classroom?

8-103. To celebrate their victory, the girls'
ice-hockey team went out for pizza.

a. The goalie ate half of a pizza that
had a diameter of 20 inches! What
was the area of pizza that she ate?
What was the length of crust that she
ate? Leave your answers in exact
form. That is, do not convert your
answer to decimal form.

b. Sonya chose a slice from another pizza that had a diameter of 16 inches.
If her slice had a central angle of 45°, what is the area of this slice? What
is the length of its crust? Show how you got your answers.

c. As the evening drew to a close, Sonya noticed that
there was only one slice of the goalie's pizza
remaining. She measured the central angle and found
out that it was 72°. What is the area of the remaining
slice? What is the length of its crust? Show how you
got your answer.

d. A portion of a circle (like the crust of a slice of pizza) is
called an **arc**. This is a set of connected points a fixed
distance from a central point. The length of an arc is a part
of the circle's circumference. If a circle has a radius of
6 cm, find the length of an arc with a central angle of 30°.

arc

e. A region that resembles a slice of pizza is called a **sector**. It
is formed by two radii of a central angle and the arc between
their endpoints on the circle. If a circle has radius 10 feet,
find the area of a sector with a central angle of 20°.

sector

8-104. LEARNING LOG

Reflect on what you have learned today. How did you use
similarity to find the areas and circumferences of circles?
How are the radius and diameter of a circle related? Write
a Learning Log entry about what you learned today. Title this entry
"Area and Circumference of a Circle" and include today's date.

MᴇᴛHODS AND MᴇᴀNINGS

MATH NOTES

Circle Facts

The area of a circle with radius $r = 1$ unit is π units^2. (Remember that $\pi \approx 3.1415926...$)

Since all circles are similar, their areas increase by a square of the linear scale (zoom) factor. That is, a circle with radius 6 has an area that is 36 times the area of a circle with radius 1. Thus, a circle with radius 6 has an area of 36π units^2, and a circle with radius r has **area** $A = \pi r^2$ units^2.

Area $= \pi r^2$
Circumference $= 2\pi r = \pi d$

The **circumference** of a circle is its perimeter. It is the distance around a circle. The circumference of a circle with radius $r = 1$ unit is 2π units. Since the perimeter ratio is equal to the ratio of similarity, a circle with radius r has circumference $C = 2\pi r$ units. Since the diameter of a circle is twice its radius, another way to calculate the circumference is $C = \pi d$ units.

A part of a circle is called an **arc**. This is a set of points a fixed distance from a center and is defined by a central angle. Since a circle does not include its interior region, an arc is like the edge of a crust of a slice of pizza.

arc

A region that resembles a slice of pizza is called a **sector**. It is formed by two radii of a central angle and the arc between their endpoints on the circle.

sector

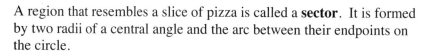

8-105. A regular hexagon with side length 4 has the same area as a square. What is the length of the side of the square? Explain how you know.

8-106. Use what you know about similar figures to complete the following tasks.

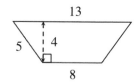

a. Find the area and perimeter of the trapezoid at right.

b. Find the area and perimeter of the trapezoid that is similar to this one, but has been reduced by a linear scale factor of $\frac{1}{3}$.

Core Connections Geometry

8-107.   An exterior angle of a regular polygon measures 18°.

    a.   How many sides does the polygon have?

    b.   If the length of a side of the polygon is 2 units, what is the area of the polygon?

8-108.   Find the missing angle(s) in each problem below using the geometric relationships shown in the diagram at right. Be sure to write down the conjecture that justifies each calculation. Remember that each part is a separate problem.

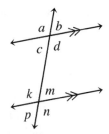

    a.   If $d = 110°$ and $k = 5x - 20°$, write an equation and solve for x.

    b.   If $b = 4x - 11°$ and $n = x + 26°$, write an equation and solve for x. Then find the measure of $\angle n$.

8-109.   Reynaldo has a stack of blocks on his desk, as shown below at right.

    a.   If his stack is 2 blocks wide, 2 blocks long, and 2 blocks tall, how many blocks are in his stack?

    b.   What if his stack instead is 3 blocks wide, 3 blocks long, and 2 blocks tall? How many blocks are in this stack?

    c.   What if his stack contains 99 blocks, is 3 blocks tall, x blocks long, and y blocks wide? What could x and y be?

8-110.   Krista is trying to solve for x in the triangle at right.

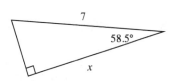

    a.   What equation would Krista write?

    b.   Krista does not have a calculator, but she remembered something funny her friend Juanisha told her. Juanisha's favorite sine ratio is $\sin 35° \approx 0.522$ because 5/22 is Juanisha's birthday! Without a calculator, use Juanisha's favorite ratio to solve your equation from part (a).

8-111.   **Multiple Choice:** Which type of quadrilateral below does not necessarily have diagonals that bisect each other?

    a.   square   b.   rectangle   c.   rhombus   d.   trapezoid

8.3.3 How can I use it?

Circles in Context

In Lesson 8.3.2, you developed methods to find the area and circumference of a circle with radius r. During this lesson, you will work with your team to solve problems from different contexts involving circles and polygons.

8-112.   While the earth's orbit (path) about the sun is slightly elliptical, it can be approximated by a circle with a radius of 93,000,000 miles.

a.   How far does the earth travel in one orbit about the sun? That is, what is the approximate circumference of the earth's path?

b.   Approximately how fast is the earth traveling in its orbit in space? Calculate your answer in miles per hour.

8-113.   A certain car's windshield wiper clears a portion of a sector as shown shaded at right. If the angle the wiper pivots during each swing is 120°, find the area of the windshield that is wiped during each swing.

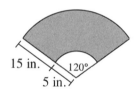

8-114.   THE GRAZING GOAT

Zoe the goat is tied by a rope to one corner of a 15 meter-by-25 meter rectangular barn in the middle of a large, grassy field. Over what area of the field can Zoe graze if the rope is:

a.   10 meters long?

b.   20 meters long?

c.   30 meters long?

d.   Zoe is happiest when she has at least 400 m² to graze. What possible lengths of rope could be used?

8-115.   THE COOKIE CUTTER

A cookie baker has an automatic mixer that
turns out a sheet of dough in the shape of a
square 12 inches wide. His cookie cutter cuts
3-inch diameter circular cookies as shown at
right. The supervisor complained that too much
dough was being wasted and ordered the baker
to find out what size cookie would have the
least amount of waste.

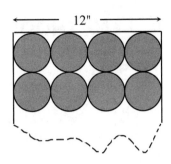

Your Task:

- Analyze this situation and determine how
  much cookie dough is "wasted" when
  3-inch cookies are cut. Then have each
  team member find the amount of dough
  wasted when a cookie of a different
  diameter is used. Compare your results.

- Write a note to the supervisor explaining
  your results. Justify your conclusion.

METHODS AND MEANINGS

Arc Length and Area of a Sector

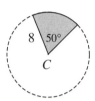

The ratio of the area of a sector to the area of a circle with the same radius equals the ratio of its central angle to 360°. For example, for the sector in circle C at right, the area of the entire circle is $\pi(8)^2 = 64\pi$ square units. Since the central angle is 50°, then the area of the sector can be found with the proportional equation:

$$\frac{50°}{360°} = \frac{\text{area of sector}}{64\pi}$$

Thus, the area of the sector is $\frac{50°}{360°}(64\pi) = \frac{80\pi}{9} \approx 27.93$ sq. units.

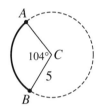

The length of an arc can be found using a similar process. The ratio of the length of an arc to the circumference of a circle with the same radius equals the ratio of its central angle to 360°. To find the length of $\overset{\frown}{AB}$ at right, first find the circumference of the entire circle, which is $2\pi(5) = 10\pi$ units. Then:

$$\frac{104°}{360°} = \frac{\text{arc length}}{10\pi}$$

Multiplying both sides of the equation by 10π, the arc length is $\frac{104°}{360°}(10\pi) = \frac{26\pi}{9} \approx 9.08$ units.

You may be surprised to learn that there are other units of measure (besides degrees) to measure an angle. A very special angle measure is called a **radian** and is defined as the measure of a central angle when the length of the arc equals the length of the radius. 1 radian = $\frac{360°}{2\pi} \approx 57.296°$.

8-116.   Use what you know about the area and circumference of circles to answer the questions below. Show all work. Leave answers in terms of π.

    a.   If the radius of a circle is 14 units, what is its circumference? What is its area?

    b.   If a circle has diameter 10 units, what is its circumference? What is its area?

    c.   If a circle has circumference 100π units, what is its area?

    d.   If a circle has circumference C, what is its area in terms of C?

8-117.   In 2000 a share of Jiffy Stock was worth $20 and in 2010 it was worth $50. What was the annual multiplier and the annual percent of increase?

8-118.   Larry started to set up a proof to show that if $\overline{AB} \perp \overline{DE}$ and $\overline{DE}$ is a diameter of $\odot C$, then $\overline{AF} \cong \overline{FB}$. Examine his work below. Then complete his missing statements and reasons.

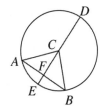

Statements	Reasons
1. $\overline{AB} \perp \overline{DE}$ and $\overline{DE}$ is a diameter of $\odot C$.	1.
2. $\angle AFC$ and $\angle BFC$ are right angles.	2.
3. $FC = FC$	3.
4. $AC = BC$	4. Definition of a Circle (radii must be equal)
5.	5. HL $\cong$
6. $\overline{AF} \cong \overline{FB}$	6.

8-119.   Match each regular polygon named on the left with a statement about its qualities listed on the right.

a.   regular hexagon   (1)   Central angle of 36°

b.   regular decagon   (2)   Exterior angle measure of 90°

c.   equilateral triangle   (3)   Interior angle measure of 120°

d.   square   (4)   Exterior angle measure of 120°

8-120.   Examine the graph of $f(x)$ at right. Use the graph to find the following values.

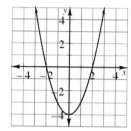

a. $f(1)$ b. $f(0)$

c. x if $f(x) = 4$ d. x if $f(x) = 0$

8-121.   Examine the relationships that exist in the diagram at right. Find the measures of angles $a, b, c,$ and d. Remember that you can find the angles in any order, depending on the angle relationships you use.

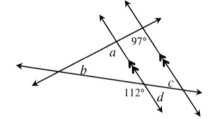

8-122.   **Multiple Choice:** How many cubes with edge length 1 unit would fit in a cube with edge length 3 units?

a.   3   b.   9

c.   10   d.   27

e.   None of these

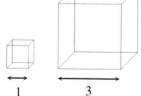

8-123. The city of Denver wants you to help build a dog park. The design of the park is a rectangle with two semicircular ends. (Note: A semicircle is half of a circle.)

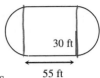

a. The entire park needs to be covered with grass. If grass is sold by the square foot, how much grass should you order?

b. The park also needs a fence for its perimeter. A sturdy chain-linked fence costs about $8 per foot. How much will a fence for the entire park cost?

c. The local design board has rejected the plan because it was too small. "*Big dogs need lots of room to run,*" the president of the board said. Therefore, you need to increase the size of the park with a linear scale factor of 2. What is the area of the new design? What is the perimeter?

8-124. This problem is a checkpoint for angle relationships in geometric figures. It will be referred to as Checkpoint 8.

For each diagram, solve for the variable and name the relationship used.

a. $4x - 3°$ $3x + 1°$

b.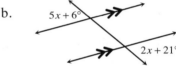

c.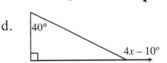

d. $40°$ $4x - 10°$

Check your answers by referring to the Checkpoint 8 materials located at the back of your book.

Ideally, at this point you are comfortable working with these types of problems and can solve them correctly. If you feel that you need more confidence when solving these types of problems, then review the Checkpoint 8 materials and try the practice problems provided. From this point on, you will be expected to do problems like these correctly and with confidence.

8-125. $\overline{BE}$ is the midsegment of $\triangle ACD$, shown at right.

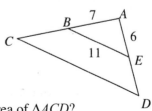

a. Find the perimeter of $\triangle ACD$.

b. If the area of $\triangle ABE$ is 19 cm^2, what is the area of $\triangle ACD$?

8-126. Christie has tied a string that is 24 cm long into a closed loop, like the one at right.

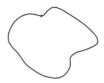

    a.   She decided to form an equilateral triangle with her string. What is the area of the triangle?

    b.   She then forms a square with the same loop of string. What is the area of the square? Is it more or less than the equilateral triangle she created in part (a)?

    c.   If she forms a regular hexagon with her string, what would be its area? Compare this area with the areas of the square and equilateral triangle from parts (a) and (b).

    d.   What shape do you think that Christie conjectures will enclose the greatest area?

8-127. Three spinners are shown at right. If each spinner is randomly spun and if spinners #2 and #3 are each equally divided, find the following probabilities.

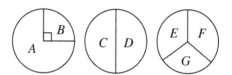

    a.   P(spinning A, C, and E)

    b.   P(spinning at least one vowel)

8-128. The **Isoperimetric Theorem** states that of all closed figures on a flat surface with the same perimeter, the circle has the greatest area. Use this fact to answer the questions below.

    a.   What is the greatest area that can be enclosed by a loop of string that is 24 cm long?

    b.   What is the greatest area that can be enclosed by a loop of string that is 18π cm long?

8-129. **Multiple Choice:** The diagram at right is not drawn to scale. If $\triangle ABC \sim \triangle KLM$, find KM.

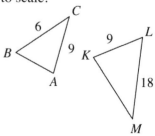

    a.   6   b.   12

    c.   15   d.   21

    e.   None of these

Chapter 8 Closure   What have I learned?

Reflection and Synthesis

The activities below offer you a chance to
reflect about what you have learned during this
chapter. As you work, look for concepts that
you feel very comfortable with, ideas that you
would like to learn more about, and topics you
need more help with. Look for connections
between ideas as well as connections with
material you learned previously.

①   TEAM BRAINSTORM

What have you studied in this chapter? What ideas were important in what you
learned? With your team, brainstorm a list. Be as detailed as you can. To help
get you started, lists of Learning Log entries and Math Notes boxes are below.

What topics, ideas, and words that you learned *before* this chapter are connected
to the new ideas in this chapter? Again, be as detailed as you can.

How long can you make your list? Challenge yourselves. Be prepared to share
your team's ideas with the class.

Learning Log Entries
- Lesson 8.1.2 – Sum of Interior Angles of a Polygon
- Lesson 8.1.3 – Interior Angles and Sum of Exterior
  Angles of a Polygon
- Lesson 8.1.4 – Regular Polygon Angle Web
- Lesson 8.1.5 – Area of a Regular Polygon
- Lesson 8.2.2 – Areas and Perimeters of Similar Figures
- Lesson 8.3.1 – Pi
- Lesson 8.3.2 – Area and Circumference of a Circle

Math Notes
- Lesson 8.1.1 – Convex and Non-Convex Polygons
- Lesson 8.1.2 – Special Quadrilateral Properties
- Lesson 8.1.5 – Interior and Exterior Angles of a Polygon
- Lesson 8.2.1 – Ratios of Similarity
- Lesson 8.3.1 – Area of a Regular Polygon
- Lesson 8.3.2 – Circle Facts
- Lesson 8.3.3 – Arc Length and Area of a Sector

②　　MAKING CONNECTIONS

Below is a list of the vocabulary used in this chapter. Make sure that you are familiar with all of these words and know what they mean. Refer to the glossary or index for any words that you do not yet understand.

arc	area	central angle
circumference	convex (polygon)	diameter
exterior angle	interior angle	linear scale factor
non-convex (polygon)	perimeter	pi (π)
polygon	radius	radius of a regular polygon
regular polygon	remote interior angle	sector
similar	zoom factor	

Make a concept map showing all of the connections you can find among the key words and ideas listed above. To show a connection between two words, draw a line between them and explain the connection. A word can be connected to any other word as long as you can justify the connection. For each key word or idea, provide an example or sketch that shows the idea.

While you are making your map, your team may think of related words or ideas that are not listed here. Be sure to include these ideas on your concept map.

③　　PORTFOLIO: EVIDENCE OF MATHEMATICAL PROFICIENCY

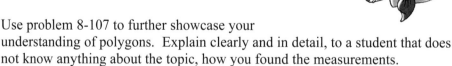

Write down all the ways that you can find the interior and exterior angles of a regular polygon. Make a sketch of a seven-sided regular polygon and any other regular polygon you choose. Showcase your understanding of regular polygons by finding all the interior and exterior angles of these two polygons.

Use problem 8-107 to further showcase your understanding of polygons. Explain clearly and in detail, to a student that does not know anything about the topic, how you found the measurements.

Choose one or two problems from Lesson 8.3.3 that you feel best exhibits your understanding of circles and carefully copy your work, modifying and expanding it if needed. Again, make sure your explanation is clear and detailed. Remember you are not only exhibiting your understanding of the mathematics, but you are also exhibiting your ability to communicate your justifications.

④ WHAT HAVE I LEARNED?

Most of the problems in this section represent typical problems found in this chapter. They serve as a gauge for you. You can use them to determine which types of problems you can do well and which types of problems require further study and practice. Even if your teacher does not assign this section, it is a good idea to try these problems and find

out for yourself what you know and what you still need to work on.

Solve each problem as completely as you can. The table at the end of the closure section has answers to these problems. It also tells you where you can find additional help and practice with problems like these.

CL 8-130. Mrs. Frank loves the clock in her classroom because it has the school colors, green and purple. The shape of the clock is a regular dodecagon with a radius of 14 centimeters. Centered on the clock's face is a green circle of radius 9 cm. If the region outside the circle is purple, which color has more area? (See problem 8-52 in Lesson 8.1.5 for the definition of the radius of a polygon.)

CL 8-131. Graph the quadrilateral $ABCD$ if $A(-2, 6)$, $B(2, 3)$, $C(2, -2)$, and $D(-2, 1)$.

    a. What is the most descriptive name for this quadrilateral? Justify your conclusion.

    b. Find the area of $ABCD$.

    c. Find the slope of the diagonals, $\overline{AC}$ and $\overline{BD}$. How are the slopes related?

    d. Find the point of intersection of the diagonals. What is the relationship between this point and diagonal $\overline{AC}$?

CL 8-132.   Examine the triangle pairs below, which are not necessarily drawn to scale. For each pair, determine:

- If they must be congruent. If they are congruent, write a correct congruence statement (such as $\triangle PQR \cong \triangle STU$) and state the congruence property (such as SAS $\cong$).

- If there is not enough information, explain why you cannot assure congruence.

- If they cannot be congruent, and explain why.

a.   b.   c.

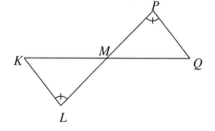

CL 8-133.   Complete the following statements.

a.   If $\triangle YSR \cong \triangle NVD$, then $\overline{DV} \cong$ ___?___ and $m\angle RYS =$ ___?___ .

b.   If $\overrightarrow{AB}$ bisects $\angle DAC$, then ___?___ $\cong$ ___?___ .

c.   In $\triangle WQY$, if $\angle WQY \cong \angle QWY$, then ___?___ $\cong$ ___?___ .

d.   If $ABCD$ is a parallelogram, and $m\angle B = 148°$, then $m\angle C =$ ___?___ .

CL 8-134.   Examine the diagram at right. If M is the midpoint of $\overline{KQ}$ and if $\angle P \cong \angle L$, prove that $\overline{KL} \cong \overline{QP}$. Use a flowchart or a two-column proof format.

CL 8-135.   A running track design is composed of two half circles connected by two straight-line segments. Garrett is jogging on the inner lane (with radius r) while Devin is jogging on the outer (with radius R). If $r = 30$ meters and $R = 33$ meters, how much longer does Devin have to run to complete one lap?

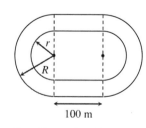

CL 8-136.   Use the relationships in the diagrams below to solve for the given variable.
             Justify your solution with a definition or theorem.

a.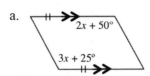

b.   The perimeter of the quadrilateral
      below is 202 units.

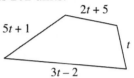

c.   *CARD* is a rhombus.

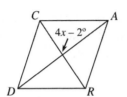

d.

CL 8-137.   Use the relationships in the diagrams below to find the values of the
             variables, if possible. The diagrams are not drawn to scale.

a.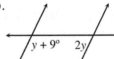

b.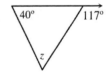

c.

CL 8-138.   Answer the following questions about polygons. If there is not enough
             information or the problem is impossible, explain why.

a.   Find the sum of the interior angles of a dodecagon.

b.   Find the number of sides of a regular polygon if its central angle
      measures 35°.

c.   If the sum of the interior angles of a regular polygon is 900°, how
      many sides does the polygon have?

d.   If the exterior angle of a regular polygon is 15°, find its central angle.

e.   Find the exterior angle of a polygon with 10 sides.

CL 8-139.   Examine the diagram at right.

a.   Find the measures of each of
      the angles below, if possible.
      If it is not possible, explain
      why it is not possible. If it is
      possible, state your reasoning.

      (1) $m\angle b$ (2) $m\angle f$

      (3) $m\angle m$ (4) $m\angle g$

      (5) $m\angle h$ (6) $m\angle i$

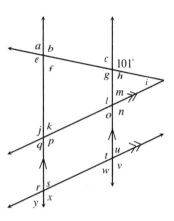

b.   If $m\angle p = 130°$, can you now find the measures of any of the angles
      from part (a) that you couldn't before? Find the measures for all that
      you can. Be sure to justify your reasoning.

CL 8-140.   Check your answers using the table at the end of the closure section. Which
             problems do you feel confident about? Which problems were hard? Use the
             table to make a list of topics you need help on and a list of topics you need
             to practice more.

Answers and Support for Closure Activity #4
What Have I Learned?

MN: Math Notes, LL: Learning Log

Problem	Solution	Need Help?	More Practice
CL 8-130.	Area of green $= 81\pi \approx 254.5$ cm^2; area of purple $= 588 - 81\pi \approx 333.5$ cm^2, so the area of purple is greater.	Lessons 8.1.5 and 8.3.2 MN: 8.1.5, 8.3.1, and 8.3.2 LL: 8.1.4, 8.1.5, and 8.3.2	Problems 8-67, 8-84, 8-93, 8-107(b), and 8-126
CL 8-131.	a. Rhombus. It is a quadrilateral with four equal sides. b. 20 square units c. The slopes are -2 and $\frac{1}{2}$. They are opposite reciprocals. d. The point of intersection is $(0, 2)$. It is the midpoint of the diagonal.	Section 7.3 MN: 7.2.3, 7.3.2, 7.3.3, and 8.1.2 LL: 7.3.3	Problems CL 7-153, 8-17, 8-32, 8-55, and 8-98

Problem	Solution	Need Help?	More Practice
CL 8-132.	a. Congruent (SAS $\cong$), $\triangle ABD \cong \triangle CBD$ b. Not enough information (the triangles are similar (AA $\sim$), but no side lengths are given to know if they are the same size.) c. Congruent (ASA $\cong$ or AAS $\cong$), $\triangle ABC \cong \triangle DEF$	Section 3.2 and Lessons 6.1.1 through 6.1.4 MN: 3.2.2 and 6.1.4	Problems CL 3-121, CL 4-123, CL 5-140, CL 6-101, CL 7-155, 8-11, and 8-88
CL 8-133.	a. $\overline{DV} \cong \overline{RS}$, $m\angle RYS = m\angle DNV$ b. $\angle DAB \cong \angle CAB$ c. $\overline{WY} \cong \overline{QY}$ d. $m\angle C = 32°$	MN: 7.1.3	Problems 7-24, 7-38, 7-48, 7-75, 8-22, 8-30, and 8-88
CL 8-134.		Section 3.2 and Lessons 6.1.1 through 6.1.4 MN: 3.2.2, 3.2.4, 6.1.4, and 7.1.3 LL: 3.2.2	Problems CL 3-121, CL 4-123, CL 5-140, CL 6-101, CL 7-155, 8-22, 8-30, 8-63, 8-87, 8-96, and 8-118
CL 8-135.	Devin must run 6π meters farther than Garrett on each lap.	Lesson 8.3.2 MN: 8.3.2 LL: 8.3.2	Problems 8-116 and 8-123(b)

Problem	Solution	Need Help?	More Practice
CL 8-136.	a. $x = 25°$ (Opposite angles in a parallelogram are equal.) b. $t = 18$ (Perimeter equals the sum of the sides.) c. $x = 23°$ (Diagonals of a rhombus are perpendicular.) d. $m = 4$ (Nonparallel sides of an isosceles trapezoid are congruent.)	Section 2.1, Lessons 2.3.2 and 7.2.6 MN: 2.1.1, 2.1.4, 2.3.2, 7.2.4, 7.2.6, and 8.1.2 LL: 2.1.1, 2.3.2 Angle Relationships Toolkit	Problems CL 7-154, 8-6, 8-60, 8-97, 8-108, 8-121, and 8-124
CL 8-137.	a. $x = 4°$ b. Cannot determine because the lines are not marked parallel. c. $z = 77°$	Section 2.1 MN: 2.1.1 and 2.1.4 LL: 2.1.1	Problems 8-6, 8-23, 8-33, 8-60, 8-97, 8-108, 8-121, and 8-124
CL 8-138.	a. $1800°$ b. Impossible. In a regular polygon, the central angle must be a factor of $360°$. c. 7 sides d. $15°$ e. $36°$	Lessons 8.1.2, 8.1.3, and 8.1.4 MN: 7.1.4 and 8.1.5 LL: 8.1.2, 8.1.3, and 8.1.4	Problems 8-8, 8-18, 8-44, 8-53, 8-95, 8-107(a), and 8-119
CL 8-139.	a. (1) $b = 101°$, corresponding angles are equal (2) $f = 79°$, supplementary angles (3) not enough information (4) $g = 101°$, vertical angles are equal (5) $h = 79°$, supplementary angles (6) not enough information b. $m = 50°$, supplementary angles $i = 51°$, Triangle Angle Sum Theorem	Section 2.1 MN: 2.1.1, 2.1.4, and 2.2.1 LL: 2.1.1	Problems 8-6, 8-23, 8-33, 8-60, 8-97, 8-108, 8-121, and 8-124

SOLIDS AND CONSTRUCTIONS

9

CHAPTER 9   Solids and Constructions

In your study of geometry so far, you have focused your attention on two-dimensional shapes. You have investigated the special properties of triangles, parallelograms, regular polygons and circles, and have developed tools to help you describe and analyze those shapes. For example, you have tools to find an interior angle of a regular hexagon, to calculate the length of the hypotenuse of a right triangle, and to measure the perimeter of a triangle or the area of a circle.

In Section 9.1, you will turn your focus to three-dimensional shapes (called **solids**), such as cubes and cylinders. You will learn several ways to represent three-dimensional solids and develop methods to measure their volumes and surface areas.

Then, in Section 9.2, you will learn how to use special tools to construct accurate diagrams of two-dimensional shapes and geometric relationships. During this investigation, you will revisit many of the geometric conjectures and theorems that you have developed so far.

In this chapter, you will learn how to:

> ➢ Find the surface area and volume of three-dimensional solids, such as prisms and cylinders.

> ➢ Represent a three-dimensional solid with a mat plan, a net, and side and top views.

> ➢ Determine the changes to volume when a three-dimensional solid is enlarged proportionally.

> ➢ Construct familiar geometric shapes (such as a rhombus or a regular hexagon) using construction tools such as tracing paper, a compass and straightedge, or a technology tool.

Guiding Question

Mathematically proficient students use appropriate tools strategically.

As you work through this chapter, ask yourself:

How can I represent it, what tools can I use, and how can I construct it?

Chapter Outline

Section 9.1   This section is devoted to the study of three-dimensional solids and their measurement. You will also learn to use a variety of methods to represent the shapes of solids.

Section 9.2   This section will introduce you to the study of constructing geometric shapes and relationships. For example, you will learn how to construct a perpendicular bisector using only a compass and a straightedge.

9.1.1 How can I build it?

Three-Dimensional Solids

With your knowledge of polygons and circles, you are able to create and explore new, interesting shapes and make elaborate designs such as the one shown in the stained glass window at right. However, in the physical world, the objects you encounter every day are three-dimensional. In other words, physical objects cannot exist entirely on a flat surface, such as a tabletop.

To understand the shapes that you encounter daily, you will need to learn more about how three-dimensional shapes, called **solids**, can be created, described, and measured.

Reprinted with permission by Rob Mielke, Blue Feather Stained Glass Designs.

As you work with your team today, be especially careful to explain to your teammates how you "see" each solid. Remember that spatial visualization takes time and effort, so be patient with your teammates and help everyone understand how each solid is built.

9-1.   Using blocks provided by your teacher, work with your team to build the three-dimensional solid at right. Assume that blocks cannot hover in midair. That is, if a block is on the second level, assume that it has a block below it to prop it up.

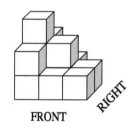

a.   Is there more than one arrangement of blocks that could look like the solid drawn at right? Why or why not?

b.   To avoid confusion, a **mat plan** can be used to show how the blocks are arranged in the solid. The number in each square represents the number of the blocks stacked in that location if you are looking from above. For example, in the right-hand corner, the solid is only 1 block tall, so there is a "1" in the corresponding corner of its mat plan.

2	1	0
3	2	1
2	1	1

FRONT
Mat Plan

Verify that the solid your team built matches the solid represented in the mat plan above.

c.   What is the **volume** of the solid? That is, if each block represents a cubic unit, how many blocks (cubic units) make up this solid?

9-2.   Another way to represent a
three-dimensional solid is by
its **side** and **top views**.

For example, the solid from
problem 9-1 can also be
represented by a top, front, and
right-hand view, as shown at right.
Each view shows *all* of the blocks
that are visible when looking
directly at the solid from that
direction.

Examine the diagram of blocks at
right. On graph paper, draw the
front, right, and top views of this
solid. Assume that there are no
hidden blocks.

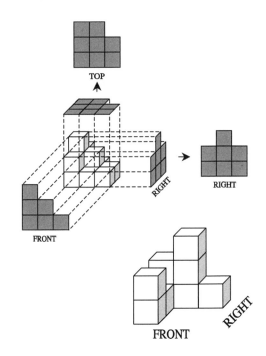

9-3.   For each of the mat plans below:

  •   Build the three-dimensional solid with the blocks provided by your
      teacher.

  •   Find the volume of the solid in cubic units.

  •   Draw the front, right, and top views of the solid on a piece of graph paper.

a.
0	3	0
2	3	1
0	2	0

RIGHT
FRONT

b.
0	2	1
0	3	0
3	2	1

RIGHT
FRONT

c.
1	1	3
2	1	2
0	0	1

RIGHT
FRONT

9-4.   Meagan built a shape with blocks and then drew
the views shown at right.

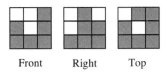

Front   Right   Top

a.   Build Meagan's shape using blocks
     provided by your teacher. Use as few
     blocks as possible.

b.   What is the volume of Meagan's shape?

c.   Draw a mat plan for her shape.

Core Connections Geometry

9-5.   Draw a mat plan for each of the following solids. There may be more than one
        possible answer! Then find the possible volumes of each one.

a.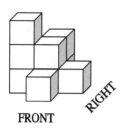

FRONT   RIGHT

b.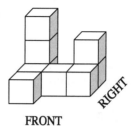

FRONT   RIGHT

9-6.   LEARNING LOG

        During this lesson, you have found the volume of several
        three-dimensional solids. However, what *is* volume? What
        does it measure? Write a Learning Log entry describing
        volume. Add at least one example. Title this entry
        "Volume of a Three-Dimensional Shape" and include today's date.

Review & Preview

9-7.   Examine the solid at right.

        a. On your paper, draw a possible mat
            plan for this solid.

        b. Find the volume of this solid.

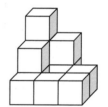

9-8.   Assume that two figures on a flat surface, A and B, are similar.

        a. If the linear scale factor is $\frac{2}{5}$, then what is the ratio of the areas of A and B?

        b. If the ratio of the perimeters of A and B is 14:1, what is the ratio of the
            areas?

        c. If the area of A is 81 times that of B, what is the ratio of the perimeters?

9-9.   Find the area of a regular decagon with perimeter 100 units. Show all work.

9-10.   The diagram at right shows a circle inscribed in a square. Find the area of the shaded region if the side length of the square is 6 meters.

9-11.   Solve each system of equations below. Write your solution in the form (x, y). Check your solution.

a. $3x - y = 14$
        $x = 2y + 8$

b. $x = 2y + 2$
        $x = -y - 10$

c. $16x - y = -4$
        $2x + y = 13$

9-12.   Gino looked around at the twelve students in his lunchtime computer science club and wrote down the following descriptions of their sex, clothing, and shoes:

male, long pants, tennis shoes   male, shorts, tennis shoes

female, shorts, tennis shoes   male, shorts, other shoes

female, dress or skirt, other shoes   female, dress or skirt, tennis shoes

female, long pants, tennis shoes   male, long pants, other shoes

male, long pants, other shoes   female, shorts, other shoes

female, long pants, other shoes   male, long pants, tennis shoes

a.   Make an area model or tree diagram of all the possible outfits in the sample space. Organize the combinations of sex, clothing, and shoes.

b.   In your model or diagram from part (a), indicate the probabilities for each option. What is the probability that a randomly selected student is wearing long pants?

c.   Which outcomes are in the event which is the union of {long pants} and {tennis shoes}? Which outcomes are in the intersection of {long pants} and {tennis shoes}?

9-13.   **Multiple Choice:** What information would you need to know about the diagram at right in order to prove that $\triangle ABD \cong \triangle CBD$ by SAS $\cong$?

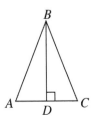

a. $\overline{AD} \cong \overline{CD}$

b. $\overline{AB} \cong \overline{CB}$

c. $\angle A \cong \angle C$

d. $\angle ABD \cong \angle CBD$

e.   None of these

9.1.2 How can I measure it?

Volumes and Surface Areas of Prisms

Today you will continue to study three-dimensional solids and will practice representing a solid using a mat plan and its side and top views. You will also learn a new way to represent a three-dimensional object, called a net. As you work today, you will learn about a special set of solids called prisms and will study how to find the surface area and volume of a prism.

9-14. The front, top, and right-hand views of Heidi's solid are shown at right.

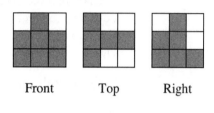

Front　　　Top　　　Right

a. Build Heidi's solid using blocks provided by your teacher. Use the smallest number of blocks possible. What is the volume of her solid?

b. Draw a mat plan for Heidi's solid. Be sure to indicate where the front and right sides are located.

c. Oh no! Heidi accidentally dropped her entire solid into a bucket of paint! What is the **surface area** of her solid? That is, what is the area that is now covered in paint?

9-15. So far, you have studied three ways to represent a solid: a three-dimensional drawing, a mat plan, and its side and top views.

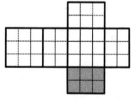

Another way to represent a three-dimensional solid is with a **net**, such as the one shown at right. When folded, a net will form the three-dimensional solid it represents.

a. With your team, predict what the three-dimensional solid formed by this net will look like. Assume the shaded squares make up the base (or bottom) of the solid.

b. Obtain a Lesson 9.1.2 Resource Page and scissors from your teacher and cut out the net. Fold along the solid lines to create the three-dimensional solid. Did the result confirm your prediction from part (a)?

c. Now build the shape with blocks and complete the mat plan at right for this solid.

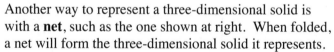

d. What is the volume of this solid? How did you get your answer?

e. What is the surface area of the solid? How did you find your answer? Be prepared to share any shortcuts with the class.

9-16.   Paul built a tower by stacking six identical
         layers of the shape at right on top of each
         other.

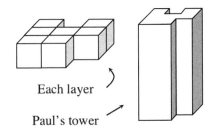

Each layer

Paul's tower

a.   What is the volume of his tower?
      How can you tell without building
      the shape?

b.   What is the surface area of his tower?

c.   Paul's tower is an example of a **prism** because it is a solid and two of its
      faces (called **bases**) are congruent and parallel. A prism must also have
      sides that connect the bases (called **lateral faces**). Each lateral face must
      be a parallelogram (and thus may also be a rectangle, rhombus or a
      square).

      For each of the prisms below, find the volume and surface area.

(1) 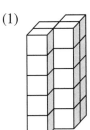   (2) 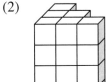   (3)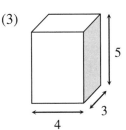

5

4

3

9-17.   Heidi created several more solids, represented below. Find the volume of each
         one.

a.

0	3	5
22	10	25
18	15	8
16	12	0

RIGHT

FRONT

b. 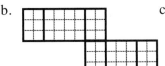   c.

9-18.   Pilar built a tower by stacking identical layers on top of each other. If her tower
         used a total of 312 blocks and if the bottom layer has 13 blocks, how tall is her
         tower? Explain how you know.

9-19.   LEARNING LOG

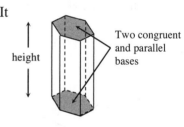

What is the relationship between the area of the base of a
prism, its height, and its volume? In a Learning Log
entry, summarize how to find the volume of a solid. Be
sure to include an example. Title this entry "Finding Volume"
and include today's date.

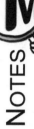

Review & Preview

9-20.   Mr. Wallis is designing a home. He found
the plan for his dream house on the Internet
and printed it out on paper.

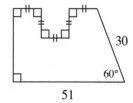

30

60°

51

a.   The design of the home is shown at right.
If all measurements are in millimeters,
find the area of the diagram.

b.   Mr. Wallis took his home design to the copier and enlarged it 400%.
What is the area of the diagram now? Show how you know.

9-21.   At right is the solid from problem 9-7.

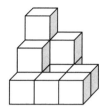

    a.   On graph paper, draw the front, right, and top views.

    b.   Find the total surface area of the solid.

9-22.   Review what you know about the angles of polygons below.

    a.   If the exterior angle of a polygon is 29°, what is the interior angle?

    b.   If the interior angle of a polygon is 170°, can it be a regular polygon? Why or why not?

    c.   Find the sum of the interior angles of a regular 29-gon.

9-23.   For each geometric relationship represented below, write and solve an equation for x. Show all work.

    a.

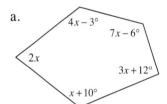

    b.

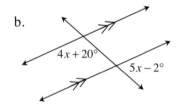

9-24.   At the band's peak of popularity, a personally signed Black Diamond poster sold for $500. Three years later the band was almost forgotten and the poster was worth only $10. What were the annual multiplier and annual percent of decrease?

9-25.	On graph paper, graph $\triangle ABC$ if $A(-3,-4)$, $B(-1,-6)$, and $C(-5,-8)$.

    a.	What is AB (the length of $\overline{AB}$)?

    b.	Reflect $\triangle ABC$ across the x-axis to form $\triangle A'B'C'$. What are the coordinates of B'? Describe the function that would change the coordinates of $\triangle ABC$ to $\triangle A'B'C'$.

    c.	Rotate $\triangle A'B'C'$ 90° clockwise ($\circlearrowright$) about the origin to form $\triangle A''B''C''$. What are the coordinates of C''?

    d.	Translate $\triangle ABC$ so that $(x,y) \rightarrow (x+5, y+1)$. What are the new coordinates of point A?

9-26.	Compute the volume of the figure at right.

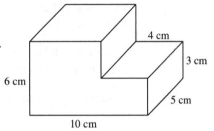

9-27.	**Multiple Choice:** Find the perimeter of the sector at right.

    a.	12π ft b.	3π ft c.	$6 + 3\pi$ ft

    d.	$12 + \pi$ ft e.	None of these

9.1.3 What if the bases are not rectangles?

Prisms and Cylinders

In Lessons 9.1.1 and 9.1.2, you investigated volume, surface area, and special three-dimensional solids called prisms. Today you will explore different ways to find the volume and surface area of a prism and a related solid called a cylinder. You will also consider what happens to the volume of a prism or cylinder if it slants to one side or if it is enlarged proportionally.

9-28. Examine the three-dimensional solid at right.

   a. On graph paper, draw a net that, when folded, will create this solid.

   b. Compare your net with those of your teammates. Is there more than one possible net? Why or why not?

   c. Find the surface area and volume of this solid.

9-29. SPECIAL PRISMS

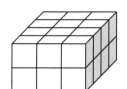

The prism in problem 9-28 is an example of a **rectangular prism**, because its bases are rectangular. Similarly, the prism at right is called a **triangular prism** because the two congruent bases are triangular.

   a. Carefully draw the prism at right onto your paper. One way to do this is to draw the two triangular bases first and then to connect the corresponding vertices of the bases. Notice that hidden edges are represented with dashed lines.

   b. Find the surface area of the triangular prism. Remember that the surface area includes the areas of *all* surfaces – the sides and the bases. Carefully organize your work and verify your solution with your teammates.

   c. Find the volume of the triangular prism. Be prepared to share your team's method with the class.

   d. Does your method for finding surface area and volume work on other prisms? For example, what if the bases are hexagonal, like the one shown at right? Work with your team to find the surface area and volume of this hexagonal prism. Assume that the bases are regular hexagons with side length 4 inches.

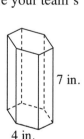

9-30.   CYLINDERS

Carter wonders, *"What if the bases are circular?"* Copy the
cylinder at right onto your paper. Discuss with your team
how to find its surface area and volume if the radius of the
base is 5 units and the height of the cylinder is 8 units.

9-31.   CAVALIERI'S PRINCIPLE

Bonaventura Cavalieri (1598-1647) was a mathematician who helped to
develop calculus, but is best remembered today for a principle named for
him. Cavalieri's Principle can be thought of as a way of finding volumes in a
relatively easy way.

a.   Suppose you have a stack of 25 pennies piled one on top of the other. You
decide to slant the stack by sliding some of the pennies over. Does the
volume of the 25 pennies change even though they are no longer stacked
one on top of another?

b.   Would the same thing be true of a stack of 15 books that you slide to the
side or twist some of them? What about a stack of 1000 sheets of paper?

c.   The idea of viewing solids as slices that can be moved
around without affecting the volume is called **Cavalieri's
Principle**. Use this principle to find the volume of the
cylinder at right. Note that when the lateral faces of a
prism or cylinder are not perpendicular to its base, the
solid is referred to as an **oblique** cylinder or prism. How is the
volume of this prism related to the one in problem 9-30?

9-32.   Hernando needs to replace the hot water tank at his
house. He estimates that his family needs a tank
that can hold at least 75 gallons of water. His local
water tank supplier has a cylindrical model that has
a diameter of 2 feet and a height of 3 feet. If
1 gallon of water is approximately 0.1337 cubic
feet, determine if the supplier's tank will provide
enough water.

MᴇᴛHODS AND Mᴇᴀɴɪɴɢs

Volume and Total Surface Area of a Solid

Volume measures the size of a three-dimensional space enclosed within an object. It is expressed as the number of $1 \times 1 \times 1$ cubes (or parts of cubes) that fit inside a solid.

For example, the solid shown above right has a volume of 6 cubic units.

Since volume reflects the number of cubes that fit within a solid, it is measured in **cubic units**. For example, if the dimensions of a solid are measured in feet, then the volume would be measured in cubic feet (a cube with dimensions $1' \times 1' \times 1'$).

On the other hand, the total **surface area** of a solid is the area of all of the external faces of the solid. For example, the total surface area of the solid above is 24 square units.

Cavalieri's Principle states that when the corresponding slices of two solids (with equal heights) have equal area, then the solids have equal volume. One way to think about Cavalieri's Principle is to think about how the volume of a stack of identical books would not change when you slide or twist some of them in the stack.

9-33.   In the diagram at right, $\overline{DE}$ is a midsegment of $\triangle ABC$. If the area of $\triangle ABC$ is 96 square units, what is the area of $\triangle ADE$? Explain how you know.

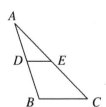

9-34.   A regular hexagonal prism has a volume of 2546.13 cm³ and the base has an edge length of 14 cm. Find the height and surface area of the prism.

9-35.   Are $\triangle EHF$ and $\triangle FGE$ congruent? If so, explain how you know. If not, explain why not.

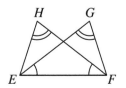

9-36.   A sandwich shop delivers lunches by bicycle to nearby office buildings. Unfortunately, sometimes the delivery is made later than promised. A delay can occur either because food preparation took too long, or because the bicycle rider got lost. Last month the food preparation took too long or the rider got lost, 7% of the time. During the same month, the food preparation took longer than expected 11 times and the bicycle rider got lost 4 times. There were 200 deliveries made during the month. For a randomly selected delivery last month, find the probability that both the food preparation took too long and the rider got lost.

9-37.   Remember that the absolute value of a number is its positive value. For example, $|-5| = 5$ and $|5| = 5$. Use this understanding to solve the equations below, if possible. If there is no solution, explain how you know.

   a. $|x| = 6$ b. $|x| = -2$ c. $|x+7| = 10$

9-38.   Cindy's cylindrical paint bucket has a diameter of 12 inches and a height of 14.5 inches. If 1 gallon $\approx$ 231 in.^{3}, how many gallons does her paint bucket hold?

9-39.   Write the equation of an exponential function that passes through the points (0, 32) and (3, 4).

9-40.   A cork in the shape of a cylinder has a radius of 2 cm, a height of 5 cm, and weighs 2.5 grams.

   a.   What is the volume of the cork?

   b.   What is the cork's density in grams per cubic centimeter? That is, how many grams of cork are there per cubic centimeter?

9.1.4 How does the volume change?

Volumes of Similar Solids

As you continue your study of three-dimensional solids, today you will explore how the volume of a solid changes as the solid is enlarged proportionally.

9-41.   HOW DOES THE VOLUME CHANGE?

In Lesson 9.1.3, you began a study of the surface area and volume of solids. Today, you will continue that investigation in order to generalize about the ratios of similar solids.

a.   Describe the solid formed by the net at right. What are its dimensions (length, width, and height)?

b.   Have each team member select a different enlargement ratio from the list below. On graph paper, carefully draw the net of a similar solid using your enlargement ratio. Then cut out your net and build the solid (so that the gridlines end up on the outside the solid) using scissors and tape.

   (1) 1   (2) 2   (3) 3   (4) 4

c.   Find the volume of your solid and compare it to the volume of the original solid. What is the ratio of these volumes? Share the results with your teammates so that each person can complete a table like the one below.

Linear Scale Factor	Original Volume	New Volume	Ratio of Volumes
1			
2			
3			
4			
r			

d.   How does the volume change when a three-dimensional solid is enlarged or reduced to create a similar solid? For example, if a solid's length, width, and depth are enlarged by a linear scale factor of 10, then how many times bigger does the volume get? What if the solid is enlarged by a linear scale factor of r? Explain.

9-42.   Examine the $1 \times 1 \times 3$ solid at right.

a.   Build this solid with blocks provided by your teacher.

b.   If this shape is enlarged by a linear scale factor of 2, how wide will the new shape be? How tall? How deep?

c.   How many of the $1 \times 1 \times 3$ solids would you need to build the enlargement described in part (b) above? Use blocks to prove your answer.

d.   What if the $1 \times 1 \times 3$ solid is enlarged with a linear scale factor of 3? How many times larger would the volume of the new solid be? Explain how you found your answer.

9-43.      At the movies, Maurice counted the number of kernels of popcorn that filled his tub and found that it had 320 kernels. He decided that next time, he will get an enlarged tub that is similar, but has a linear scale factor of 1.5. How many kernels of popcorn should the enlarged tub hold?

9-44.   LEARNING LOG

In your Learning Log, explain how the volume changes when a solid is enlarged proportionally. That is, if a three-dimensional object is enlarged by a linear scale factor of 2, by what factor does the volume increase? Title this entry "Volumes of Similar Solids" and include today's date.

9-45.   Koy is inflating a spherical balloon for her brother's birthday party. She has used three full breaths so far and her balloon is only half the width she needs. Assuming that she puts the same amount of air into the balloon with each breath, how many more breaths does she need to finish the task? Explain how you know.

9-46.   Draw a cylinder on your paper. Assume the radius of the cylinder is 6 inches and the height is 9 inches.

   a.   What is the surface area of the cylinder? What is the volume?

   b.   If the cylinder is enlarged with a linear scale factor of 3, what is the volume of the enlarged cylinder? How do you know?

9-47.   While Katarina was practicing her figure skating, she wondered how far she had traveled. She was skating a "figure 8," which means she starts between two circles and then travels on the boundary of each circle, completing the shape of a sideways 8. If both circles have a radius of 5 feet, how far does she travel when skating one "figure 8"?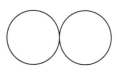

9-48.   For each triangle below, solve for x, if possible. If no solution is possible, explain why.

   a.   b.   c.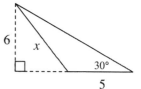

9-49.   The mat plan for a three-dimensional solid is shown at right.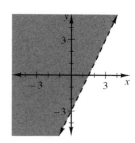

   a.   On your paper, draw the front, right, and top views of this solid.

   b.   Find the volume and surface area of the solid.

9-50.   The graph of the inequality $y > 2x - 3$ is shown at right. On graph paper, graph the inequality $y \leq 2x - 3$. Explain what you changed about the graph.

9-51. An international charity builds homes for disaster victims. Often the materials are donated. The charity recently built 45 homes. 20% used granite for the kitchen countertops, while the rest used porcelain tile. 15 of the homes used red oak for the wooden kitchen floor, 20 used white oak, and 10 used maple. If a disaster victim is randomly assigned to a home, what is the probability (in percent) of getting an oak floor with granite countertops?

9-52. **Multiple Choice:** The point $A(-2, 5)$ is rotated 90° counter-clockwise (↺) about the origin. What are the new coordinates of point A?

a. $(2, 5)$ b. $(5, -2)$ c. $(2, -5)$ d. $(-5, -2)$

9.1.5 How does the volume change?

Ratios of Similarity

Today, work with your team to analyze the following problems. As you work, think about whether the problem involves volume or area. Also think carefully about how similar solids are related to each other.

9-53.   A statue to honor Benjamin Franklin will be placed outside the entrance to the Liberty Bell exhibit hall in Philadelphia. The designers decide that a smaller, similar version will be placed on a table inside the building. The dimensions of the life-sized statue will be four times those of the smaller statue. Planners expect to need 1.5 pints of paint to coat the small statue. They also know that the small statue will weigh 14 pounds.

   a.   How much paint will be needed to paint the life-sized statue?

   b.   If the small statue is made of the same material as the enlarged statue, then its weight will change just as the volume changes as the statue is enlarged. How much will the life-size statue weigh?

9-54.   The Blackbird Oil Company is considering the purchase of 20 new jumbo oil storage tanks. The standard model holds 12,000 gallons. Its dimensions are $\frac{4}{5}$ the size of the similarly shaped jumbo model, that is, the ratio of the dimensions is 4:5.

   a.   How much more storage capacity would the twenty jumbo models give Blackbird Oil?

   b.   If jumbo tanks cost 50% more than standard tanks, which tank is a better buy?

Core Connections Geometry

9-55. In problem 7-14 your class constructed a large tetrahedron like the one at right. Assume the dimensions of the shaded tetrahedron at right are half of the dimensions of the similar enlarged tetrahedron.

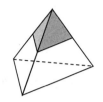

a. If the volume of the large tetrahedron is 138 in.³, find the volume of the small shaded tetrahedron.

b. Each face of a tetrahedron is an equilateral triangle. If the small shaded tetrahedron has an edge length of 16 cm, find the total surface area for each of the tetrahedra.

c. Your class tried to construct a tetrahedron using four smaller congruent tetrahedra. However, the result left a gap in the center, as shown in the diagram at right. If the volume of each small shaded tetrahedron is 50 in.³, what is the volume of the gap? Explain how you know.

METHODS AND MEANINGS

The $r : r^2 : r^3$ Ratios of Similarity

MATH NOTES

When a two-dimensional figure is enlarged proportionally, its perimeter and area also grow. If the linear scale factor is r, then the perimeter of the figure is enlarged by a factor of r while the area of the figure is enlarged by a factor of r^2. Examine what happens when the square at right is enlarged by a linear scale factor of 3.

$P = 4$ units $P = 4 \cdot 3 = 12$ units
$A = 1$ units² $A = 1 \cdot 3^2 = 9$ units²

When a solid is enlarged proportionally, its surface area and volume also grow. If it is enlarged by a linear scale factor of r, then the surface area grows by a factor of r^2 and the volume grows by a factor of r^3. The example at right shows what happens to a solid when it is enlarged by a linear scale factor of 2.

Original solid   Width, height,   **Result:**
SA = 14   and depth are   SA = 56
units²   doubled   units²
V = 3 units³   V = 24 units³

Thus, if a solid is enlarged proportionally by a linear scale factor of r, then:

New edge length = $r \cdot$ (corresponding edge length of original solid)

New surface area = $r^2 \cdot$ (original surface area)

New volume = $r^3 \cdot$ (original volume)

9-56.   Consider the two similar solids at right.

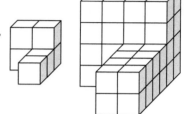

a.   Create a mat plan and draw the front, right, and top views for the solid on the left.

b.   What is the linear scale factor between the two solids?

c.   Find the surface area of each solid. What is the ratio of the surface areas? How is this ratio related to the linear scale factor?

d.   Now find the volumes of each solid. How are the volumes related? Compare this to the linear scale factor and record your observations.

9-57.   Elliot has a modern fish tank that is in the shape of an oblique prism, shown at right.

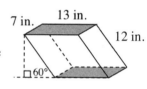

a.   If the slant of the prism makes a 60° angle with the flat surface on which the prism is placed, find the volume of water the tank can hold. Assume that each base is a rectangle.

b.   If Elliot has 25 fish, how crowded are the fish? That is, what is the density of fish, measured in number of fish per cubic inch?

c.   What is the density of fish in Elliot's tank in fish per cubic *foot*?

9-58.   Decide if the following statements are true or false. If they are true, explain how you know. If they are false, provide a counterexample.

a.   If a quadrilateral has two sides that are parallel and two sides that are congruent, then the quadrilateral must be a parallelogram.

b.   If the interior angles of a polygon add up to 360°, then the polygon must be a quadrilateral.

c.   If a quadrilateral has 3 right angles, then the quadrilateral must be a rectangle.

d.   If the diagonals of a quadrilateral bisect each other, then the quadrilateral must be a rhombus.

9-59.   Write and solve an equation based on the geometric
         relationship shown at right.

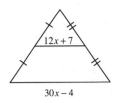

9-60.   Solve each equation below. Check your solution.

         a. $20 - 6(5 + 2x) = 10 - 2x$ b. $2x^2 - 9x - 5 = 0$

         c. $\frac{3}{5x-1} = \frac{1}{x+1}$ d. $|2x - 1| = 5$

9-61.   A new car purchased for \$27,000 loses 15% of its value each year.

         a.   What is the multiplier?

         b.   Write a function of the form $f(t) = ab^t$ that represents the situation.

         c.   At the current rate, what will be the value of the car in 5 years?

9-62.   Examine the information provided in each diagram below.
         Decide if each figure is possible or not. If the figure is not
         possible, explain why.

         a.   b.   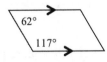   c.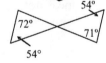

9-63.   **Multiple Choice:** For $\angle ABE \cong \angle BEF$ in the diagram below, what must be true?

         a. $\angle ABE \cong \angle BED$

         b. $\angle ABE \cong \angle GBC$

         c. $\overline{AC} \parallel \overline{GH}$

         d. $\overline{AC} \parallel \overline{DF}$

         e.   None of these.

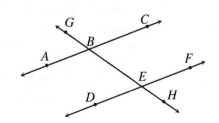

9.2.1 How can I construct it?

Introduction to Constructions

So far in this course, you have used tools such as rulers, tracing paper, protractors, and even computers to draw geometric relationships and shapes. But how did ancient mathematicians accurately construct shapes such as squares or equilateral triangles without these types of tools?

Today you will start by exploring how to construct several geometric relationships and figures with tracing paper. You will then investigate how to construct geometric shapes with tools called a compass and a straightedge, much like the ancient Greeks did more than 2000 years ago. As you study these forms of **construction**, you will not only learn about new geometric tools, but also gain a deeper understanding of some of the special geometric relationships and shapes you have studied so far in this course.

9-64.   CONSTRUCTING WITH TRACING PAPER

To start this focus on construction, you will begin with a familiar tool: tracing paper. Obtain several sheets of tracing paper and a straightedge from your teacher. Note: A straightedge is *not* a ruler. It does not have any markings or measurements on it. For example, a 3" × 5" index card makes a good straightedge.

a.   Starting with a smooth, square piece of tracing paper, find a way to create parallel lines (or creases). Make sure the lines are *exactly* parallel. Be ready to share with the class how you accomplished this.

b.   With a new piece of tracing paper, trace line segment $\overline{AB}$ at right. Use your straightedge for accuracy. Can you fold the tracing paper so that the resulting crease not only finds the midpoint of $\overline{AB}$ but also is perpendicular to $\overline{AB}$? Remember that this is the **perpendicular bisector** of $\overline{AB}$. Prove that your crease is the perpendicular bisector.

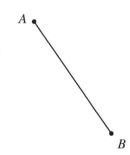

Problem continues on next page →

9-64.   *Problem continued from previous page.*

   c.   On the perpendicular bisector from part (b) above, choose a point *C* and
        then connect $\overline{AC}$ and $\overline{BC}$ to form $\triangle ABC$. What type of triangle did you
        construct? Use your geometry knowledge to justify your answer.

   d.   In part (b), you determined how to use tracing paper and a straightedge to
        construct a line that bisects another line. How can you construct an angle
        bisector?

        On a piece of tracing paper, trace
        ∠*BAC* at right. Construct the
        angle bisector. That is, find $\overrightarrow{AD}$
        such that ∠*BAD* ≅ ∠*CAD*.

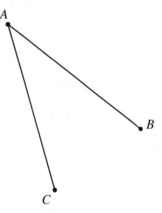

   e.   Did you know that the angle bisectors of a
        triangle intersect at a single point? On
        your tracing paper, connect $\overline{BC}$ to form
        $\triangle ABC$. Then fold to find the angle
        bisectors of the other two angles, ∠*ABC*
        and ∠*BCA*. Mark this special "center" of
        the triangle, which is sometimes referred
        to as the **incenter** of the triangle, with a
        point. Put this tracing paper aside but
        keep it for problem 9-66.

9-65.   CONSTRUCTING WITH A COMPASS AND A STRAIGHTEDGE

Other tools that are often used to construct
geometric figures are a compass and a
straightedge. Obtain a Lesson 9.2.1 Resource
Page from your teacher and explore what types of
shapes you can construct using these tools.

a.   Find point *C* on the resource page. Use your compass to construct two
      circles with different radii that have a center at point *C*. Circles that have
      the same center are called **concentric** circles.

b.   With tracing paper, copying a line segment means just putting the tracing
      paper over the line and tracing it. But how can you copy a line segment
      using only a compass and a straightedge?

      On the resource page, find $\overline{AB}$. Next to $\overline{AB}$, use your straightedge to draw
      a new line segment. With your team, decide how to use the compass to
      mark off two points (*C* and *D*) so that $\overline{AB} \cong \overline{CD}$. Be ready to share your
      method with the class.

c.   Now construct a new line segment, labeled $\overline{EF}$, that is twice as long as
      $\overline{AB}$. How can you be sure that $\overline{EF}$ is twice as long as $\overline{AB}$?

d.   How can you use these tools to copy an angle? On
      your resource page, find $\angle X$. With your team,
      discuss how you can use your compass to construct a
      new angle ($\angle Y$) on your resource page that is
      congruent to $\angle X$. Start by drawing a ray with
      endpoint *Y*.

9-66.   The incenter of a triangle is special because it is also the center of a circle that
         lies inside the triangle and intersects each side of the triangle exactly once. This
         circle is called an **inscribed circle**. To construct this circle, you will need to
         use both your tracing paper from part (d) and (e) of problem 9-64 and your
         compass.

a.   As Shui thought about constructing a circle that fits inside the triangle, she
      observed, "*I think △ABC is an isosceles triangle.*" Do you agree? How
      can you test her conjecture with your tracing paper?

b.   Shui thinks that the inscribed circle must pass through the midpoint of
      $\overline{BC}$. Is this correct? Explain why or why not.

c.   With your compass, construct the inscribed circle of △*ABC* with the center
      at the incenter.

9-67.   **REGULAR HEXAGON**

As Shui was completing her homework, she noticed that a
regular hexagon has a special quality: when dissected into
congruent triangles, the hexagon contains triangles that are
all equilateral! *"I bet I can use this fact to help me
construct a regular hexagon,"* she told her team.

a.   On the Lesson 9.2.1 Resource Page, construct a circle with radius *r* and
       center *H*.

b.   Mark one point on the circle to be a starting vertex. Since each side of the
       hexagon has length *r*, the radius of the circle, carefully use the compass to
       mark off the other vertices of the hexagon on the circle. Then connect the
       vertices to create the regular hexagon.

c.   When all vertices of a polygon lie on the same circle, the polygon is
       inscribed in the circle. For example, the hexagon you constructed in part
       (b) is inscribed in ⊙*H* . After consulting with your teammates, construct
       an equilateral triangle that is also inscribed in ⊙*H* . You may want to use
       colored markers or pencils to help distinguish between the hexagon and
       the triangle.

9-68.   Examine the diagram of *ABCD* at right.

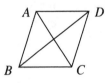

a.   If opposite sides of the quadrilateral are parallel
       and all sides are congruent, what type of
       quadrilateral is *ABCD*?

b.   List what you know about the diagonals of *ABCD*.

c.   Find the area of *ABCD* if *BC* = 8 and *m∠ABC* = 60°.

9-69. A butterfly house at a local zoo is a rectangular prism with dimensions $20' \times 15' \times 10'$ and contains 625 butterflies.

   a. Sketch the prism on your paper.

   b. What is the volume of the butterfly house? Show your work.

   c. How many cubic feet of air is there for each butterfly?

   d. **Density** is the quantity of something per unit measure, especially length, area, or volume. For example you might talk about the density of birds on a power wire (maybe a flock lands with 7 birds/meter), population density (the density of Singapore is 7301 people per square kilometer), or the mass density of an element (iron has density of $7.874 \frac{g}{cm^3}$).

   Assuming the butterflies are equally distributed inside the butterfly house, what is the density of butterflies? Explain.

9-70. Use the relationships given in the diagram at right to write and solve an equation for x. Show all work.

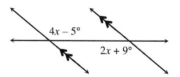

9-71. For each pair of triangles below, determine if the triangles are congruent. If they are congruent, state the congruence property that assures their congruence and write a congruence statement (such as $\triangle ABC \cong \triangle$_____).

   a.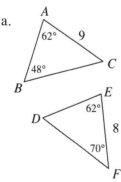

   b.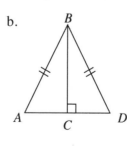

   c.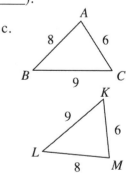

9-72. Write the equation represented by the table below.

IN (x)	−4	−3	−2	−1	0	1	2	3	4
OUT (y)	−26	−20	−14	−8	−2	4	10	16	22

9-73. This problem is a checkpoint for finding probabilities. It will be referred to as Checkpoint 9A.

Because students complained that there were not enough choices in the cafeteria, the student council decided to collect data about the sandwich choices that were available. The cafeteria supervisor indicated that she makes 36 sandwiches each day. Each sandwich consists of bread, a protein, and a condiment. Twelve of the sandwiches were made with white bread, and 24 with whole-grain bread. Half of the sandwiches were made with salami, and the other half were evenly split between turkey and ham. Two-thirds of the sandwiches were made with mayonnaise, and the rest were left plain with no condiment.

a. Organize the possible sandwich combinations of bread, protein, and condiment by making an area model or tree diagram, if possible.

b. Wade likes any sandwich that has salami or mayonnaise on it. Which outcomes are sandwiches that Wade likes? If Wade randomly picks a sandwich, what is the probability he will get a sandwich that he likes? (Hint: You can use W and G to abbreviate the breads. Then use S, T, and H to abbreviate the proteins, and M and P to abbreviate the condiments.)

c. Madison does not like salami or mayonnaise. Which outcomes are sandwiches that Madison likes? If Madison randomly picks a sandwich, what is the probability she will get a sandwich that she likes?

d. If you have not already done so in part (c), show how to use a complement to find the probability Madison gets a sandwich that she likes.

e. Which outcomes are in the event for the intersection of {salami} and {mayonnaise}?

Check your answers by referring to the Checkpoint 9A materials located at the back of your book.

Ideally, at this point you are comfortable working with these types of problems and can solve them correctly. If you feel that you need more confidence when solving these types of problems, then review the Checkpoint 9A materials and try the practice problems provided. From this point on, you will be expected to do problems like these correctly and with confidence.

9-74. **Multiple Choice:** Which net below will not produce a closed cube?

a. 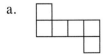   b. 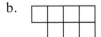   c.   d.

9.2.2 How can I construct it?

· ·

Constructing Bisectors

During Lesson 9.2.1, you studied how to construct geometric relationships such as congruent line segments using tools that include a compass and tracing paper. But what other geometric relationships and shapes can you construct using these tools? Today, as you investigate new ways to construct familiar geometric figures, look for connections to previous course material.

9-75.   INTERSECTING CIRCLES

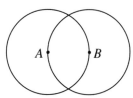

As Ventura was doodling with his compass, he drew the diagram at right. Assume that each circle passes through the center of the other circle.

a.   Explain why ⊙*A* and ⊙*B* must have the same radius.

b.   On the Lesson 9.2.2 Resource Page provided by your teacher, construct two intersecting circles so that each passes through the other's center. Label the centers *A* and *B*.

c.   On your construction, locate the two points where the circles intersect each other. Label these points *C* and *D*. Then construct quadrilateral *ACBD*. What type of quadrilateral is *ACBD*? Justify your answer.

d.   Use what you know about the diagonals of *ACBD* to describe the relationship of $\overline{AB}$ and $\overline{CD}$. Make as many statements as you can.

e.   What else can this diagram help you construct when given a line segment such as $\overline{AB}$? Share your ideas with the class.

9-76.   In problem 9-75, you constructed a rhombus
and a perpendicular bisector.

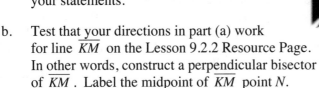

a.   In your own words, describe how this process
works. That is, given any line segment, how
can you find its midpoint? How can you find
a line perpendicular to it? Be sure to justify
your statements.

b.   Test that your directions in part (a) work
for line $\overline{KM}$ on the Lesson 9.2.2 Resource Page.
In other words, construct a perpendicular bisector
of $\overline{KM}$. Label the midpoint of $\overline{KM}$ point N.

c.   Return to your work from part (b) and use it to construct a 45°- 45°- 90°
triangle. Prove that your triangle must be isosceles.

9-77.   In problem 9-75, you used the fact that the diagonals of a rhombus are
perpendicular bisectors of each other to develop a construction. In fact, most
constructions are rooted in the properties of many of the geometric shapes you
have studied so far. A rhombus can help you with another important
construction.

a.   Examine the rhombus ABCD at right. What is the
relationship between ∠ABC and $\overline{BD}$?

b.   Since the diagonals of a rhombus bisect the angles,
use this relationship to construct an angle bisector of
∠R on the resource page. That is, construct a
rhombus so that R is one of its vertices. Use only a
compass, a straightedge, and a pencil.

9-78.   CONSTRUCTION CHALLENGE

On the Lesson 9.2.2 Resource Page, locate $\overline{PQ}$, $\overline{ST}$, and ∠V. In the space
provided, use the construction strategies you have developed so far to construct
a triangle with legs congruent to $\overline{PQ}$ and $\overline{ST}$, with an angle congruent to ∠V in
between. Be sure you know how to do this two ways: with a compass and a
straightedge and with tracing paper.

METHODS AND MEANINGS

Rhombus Facts

Review what you have previously learned about a rhombus below.

A **rhombus** is a quadrilateral with four equal sides. All rhombi (the plural of rhombus) are parallelograms.

Starting with the definition of a rhombus above, there are several facts about rhombi that can be proved. For example, the diagonals of a rhombus are perpendicular bisectors of each other. That is, they intersect each other at their midpoints and form right angles at that point. Also, all four small triangles are congruent (as well as the larger triangles formed by any two of the smaller triangles). In addition, the diagonals of a rhombus bisect the opposite angles.

9-79.   Unlike a straightedge, a ruler has measurement markings. With a ruler, it is fairly simple to construct a line segment of length 6 cm or a line segment with length 3 inches. But how can you construct a line segment of $\sqrt{2} \approx 1.414213562...$ centimeters? Consider this as you answer the questions below.

   a.   With a ruler, construct a line segment of 1 cm.

   b.   What about 1.4 cm? Adjust your line segment from part (a) so that its length is 1.4 cm. Did your line get longer or shorter?

   c.   Now change the line segment so that its length is 1.41 cm. How did it change?

   d.   Karen wants to draw a line segment is exactly $\sqrt{2} \approx 1.414213562...$ centimeters long. Is this possible? Why or why not?

9-80.   Describe a sequence of steps to construct an equilateral triangle.

9-81.   The floor plan of Marina's local drug store is shown at right. While shopping one day, Marina tied her dog, Mutt, to the building at point F. If Mutt's leash is 4 meters long, what is the area that Mutt can roam? Draw a diagram and show all work.

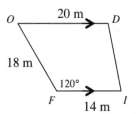

9-82.    Find the area of the Marina's drugstore (*FIDO*) in problem 9-81 Show all work.

9-83.   Compute the volume of the figure at right.

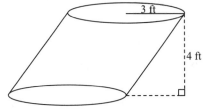

9-84.   Which has greater measure: an exterior angle of an equilateral triangle or an interior angle of a regular heptagon (7-gon)? Show all work.

9-85.   On graph paper, graph the line $y = -\frac{3}{2}x + 6$. State the x- and y-intercepts.

9-86.   **Multiple Choice:** A solid with a volume of 26 in.^{3} was enlarged to create a similar solid with a volume of 702 in.^{3}. What is the linear scale factor between the two solids?

   a.   1   b.   2   c.   3   d.   4

9.2.3 How do I construct it?

More Explorations with Constructions

So far, several geometric relationships and properties have helped you develop constructions using a compass and a straightedge. For example, constructing a rhombus helped you construct an angle bisector. Constructing intersecting circles helped you construct a perpendicular bisector. What other relationships can help you develop constructions?

Today you will investigate how to use parallel line theorems to construct a line parallel to a given line through a point not on the line. You will also use the different construction techniques you have learned to construct a square, and will justify that the shape you created meets the definition of a square.

9-87. CONSTRUCTING PARALLEL LINES

In this chapter you have used geometric concepts such as triangle congruence and the special properties of a rhombus to create constructions. How can angle relationships formed by parallel lines help with construction? Consider this question as you answer the questions below.

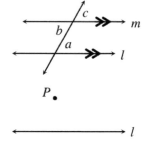

a. Examine the diagram at right. If $l \mathbin{/\mkern-4mu/} m$, what do you know about $\angle a$ and $\angle b$? What about $\angle a$ and $\angle c$? Justify your answer.

b. Neelam thinks that angle relationships can help her construct a line parallel to another line through a given point not on the line. On the Lesson 9.2.3 Resource Page, find line l and point P. Help Neelam construct a line parallel to l through point P by first constructing a transversal through point P that intersects line l.

c. If you have not already done so, complete Neelam's construction by copying an angle formed by the transversal and line l. Explain how you used alternate interior angles or corresponding angles.

Core Connections Geometry

9-88.   CONSTRUCTING A SQUARE

So far, you have developed techniques for constructing congruent angles, congruent line segments, perpendicular and parallel lines, and bisectors of angles and segments. You have constructed a rhombus, a regular hexagon, and an equilateral triangle using just a compass and straightedge. Now you will use what you know to construct a square.

a.   What makes a square a square? In other words, what are its unique characteristics? What shapes is it related to?

b.   Based on the characteristics you identified in part (a), work with your team to develop a strategy for constructing a square. Keep track of the steps you take on the Lesson 9.2.3 Resource Page, so that you can share them with the class.

c.   In order for the shape you constructed in part (c) to be a square, it must have four right angles and four congruent sides. Prove that your shape is a square using the steps of your construction and your geometry knowledge. Be ready to share your justification.

9-89.   Consider what you know about all 30°- 60°- 90° triangles.

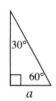

a.   Using the information in the triangle at right, how long is the hypotenuse? Explain how you know.

b.   Negin (pronounced "Nay-GEEN") wants to use this relationship to construct a 30°- 60°- 90° triangle. On the Lesson 9.2.3 Resource Page, locate her work so far. She has constructed perpendicular lines and has constructed one side ($\overline{MN}$). Complete her construction so that her triangle has angles 30°, 60°, and 90°.

9-90.   CONSTRUCTING OTHER GEOMETRIC SHAPES

What about constructing a kite? On the Lesson 9.2.3 Resource Page, use a compass and a straightedge to construct a kite. Remember that a kite is defined as a quadrilateral with two pairs of adjacent, congruent sides. Be prepared to explain to the class how you constructed your kite.

METHODS AND MEANINGS

MATH NOTES

Constructing a Perpendicular Bisector

A perpendicular bisector of a given segment can be constructed using tracing paper or using a compass and a straightedge.

With tracing paper: To construct a perpendicular bisector with tracing paper, first copy the line segment onto the tracing paper. Then fold the tracing paper so that the endpoints coincide (so that they lie on top of each other). When the paper is unfolded, the resulting crease is the perpendicular bisector of the line segment.

With a compass and a straightedge: One way to construct a perpendicular bisector with a compass and a straightedge is to construct a circle at each endpoint of the line segment with a radius equal to the length of the line segment. Then use the straightedge to draw a line through the two points where the circles intersect. This line will be the perpendicular bisector of the line segment.

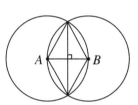

Review & Preview

9-91. Examine the mat plan of a three-dimensional solid at right.

6	0	0
3	0	1
2	6	6

FRONT

Mat Plan

RIGHT

a. On your paper, draw the front, right, and top views of this solid.

b. Find the volume of the solid.

c. If the length of each edge of the solid is divided by 2, what will the new volume be? Show how you got your answer.

9-92. Examine the diagram at right. Given that $\triangle ABC \cong \triangle EDF$, prove that $\triangle DBG$ is isosceles. Use any format of proof that you prefer.

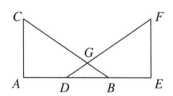

9-93. The Portland Zoo is building a new children's petting zoo pen that will contain 6 goats. One of the designs being considered is shown at right (the shaded portion). Assume the measurements are in meters.

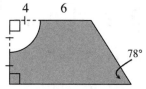

a. What is the area of the petting zoo?

b. How many meters of fence are needed to enclose the petting zoo area.

c. What will be the density of goats in the pen? Show how you got your answer.

9-94. Sylvia has 14 coins, all nickels and quarters. If the value of the coins is $2.90, how many of each type of coin does she have? Explain your method.

9-95. West High School has a math building in the shape of a regular polygon. When Mrs. Woods measured an interior angle of the polygon (which was inside her classroom), she got 135°.

a. How many sides does the math building have? Show how you got your answer.

b. If Mrs. Wood's ceiling is 10 feet high and the length of one side of the building is 25 feet, find the volume of West High School's math building.

9-96. Given the information in the diagram at right, prove that $\angle C \cong \angle D$. Write your proof using any format studied so far.

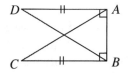

9-97. Write the equation of an exponential function that passes through the points (2, 48) and (5, 750).

9-98. **Multiple Choice:** Jamila has started to construct a line parallel to line m through point Q at right. Which of the possible strategies below make the most sense to help her find the line parallel to m through point Q?

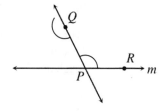

a. Measure $\angle QPR$ with a protractor.

b. Use the compass to measure the arc centered at P, then place the point of the compass where the arc centered at Q meets $\overline{QP}$, and mark that measure off on the arc.

c. Construct $\overline{QR}$.

d. Measure PR with a ruler.

9.2.4 What more can I construct?

Other Constructions

So far in this section, you have developed a basic library of constructions that can help create many of the geometric shapes and relationships you have studied in Chapters 1 through 8. For example, you can construct a rhombus, an isosceles triangle, a right triangle, a regular hexagon, and an equilateral triangle.

As you continue your investigation of geometric constructions today, keep in mind the following focus questions:

What geometric principles or properties can I use?

Why does it work?

Is there another way?

9-99.   TEAM CHALLENGE

Albert has a neat trick. Given any triangle, he can place it on the tip of his pencil and it balances on his first try! The whole class wonders, *"How does he do it?"*

Your Task: Construct a triangle and find its point of balance. This point, called a **centroid**, is special not only because it is the center of balance, but also because it is where the **medians** of the triangle meet. Read more about medians of a triangle in the Math Notes box for this lesson and then follow the directions below.

a.   After reading about medians and centroids in the Math Notes box for this lesson, draw a large triangle on a piece of unlined paper provided by your teacher. (Note: Your team will work together on one triangle.)

b.   Working together, carefully construct the three medians and locate the centroid of the triangle.

c.   Once your team is convinced that your centroid is accurate, glue the paper to a piece of cardstock or cardboard provided by your teacher. Carefully cut out the triangle and demonstrate that your centroid is, in fact, the center of balance of your triangle! Good luck!

9-100.   In problem 9-99, you constructed a centroid of a triangle, which is special
          because it is a center of balance in a triangle. However, there are other
          important points in a triangle. For example, visualize a point inside of △ABC
          below that is the same distance from each vertex.

    a.   Find △ABC on the Lesson 9.2.4 Resource Page
          provided by your teacher. Using a compass and a
          straightedge, find a line that represents all the
          points that are equidistant (the same distance)
          from point A and point B. Justify your answer.

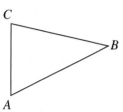

    b.   Joanna asks, "*How can we find one point that is the same distance from C,
          too?*" Talk about this with your team and test out your ideas until you find
          one point that is equidistant from A, B, and C.

    c.   Joanna points out that the intersection of the perpendicular bisectors of the
          sides of the triangle is equidistant from the vertices. "*That means there is
          a circle that passes through all three vertices!*" she noted. Use your
          compass to draw this circle. Where is its center?

9-101.   As the Math Notes box for this lesson states, the point at which the medians of a
          triangle meet is called the **centroid**. However, how can you be certain that the
          medians of a triangle will always meet at a single point? In this problem, you
          will provide some of the reasoning for a proof that the medians will always
          meet at a single point.

    a.   △ABC has midpoints E and F on sides
          $\overline{AC}$ and $\overline{AB}$ as shown in the diagram at
          right. $\overline{BE}$ and $\overline{CF}$ intersect at P. Why
          are $\overline{BE}$ and $\overline{CF}$ medians?

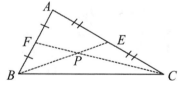

    b.   Draw segment $\overline{FE}$ and explain how you know that $\overline{FE}$ is parallel to $\overline{BC}$
          and half its length.

    c.   Prove that △FPE ~△CPB.

    d.   Use the relationship of the triangles to identify the ratios $\frac{EP}{PB}$ and $\frac{FE}{BC}$.
          How does this help explain that $\frac{BP}{BE} = \frac{2}{3}$?

    e.   What if you had started with a different pair of medians for this triangle?
          Let point D be the midpoint of $\overline{BC}$. Can the same logic be used to show
          that $\overline{AD}$ and $\overline{BE}$ will intersect at a point with the same ratio of lengths as
          in part (d)? Explain.

    f.   Explain how this proves that the medians will intersect at a single point.

9-102. What other specific triangles can you construct? Choose at least three of the different triangles below and, if possible, construct them using compass and straightedge or tracing paper and the techniques you have developed so far. Be prepared to share your strategies, and to justify your steps for creating each shape or to justify why the shape could not be constructed.

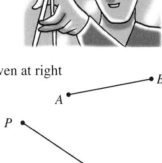

- An isosceles triangle with side length $\overline{AB}$ given at right

- A triangle with side lengths 3, 4, and 5 units

- A 30°-60°-90° triangle

- A triangle with side lengths 2, 3 and 6 units

- An isosceles right triangle with leg length $\overline{PQ}$

- A scalene triangle

METHODS AND **M**EANINGS

Centroid and Medians of a Triangle

MATH NOTES

A line segment connecting a vertex of a triangle to the midpoint of the side opposite the vertex is called a **median**.

Since a triangle has three vertices, it has three medians. An example of a triangle with its three medians is provided at right.

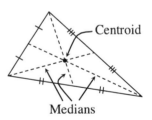

The point at which the three medians intersect is called a **centroid**. The centroid is also the center of balance of a triangle.

Since the three medians intersect at a single point, this point is called a **point of concurrency**. You will learn about other points of concurrency in a later chapter.

568

9-103.   Find the volumes of the solids below.

a.   cylinder with a hole

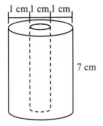

b.   regular octagonal prism

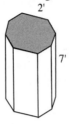

9-104.   Jillian is trying to construct a square. She has started by constructing two perpendicular lines, as shown at right. If she wants each side of the square to have length k, as shown at right, describe how she should finish her construction.

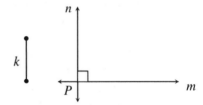

9-105.   Without using a calculator, find the sum of the interior angles of a 1002-gon. Show all work.

9-106.   York County, Maine, is roughly triangular in shape. To help calculate its area, Sergio has decided to use a triangle to model the region, as shown at right. According to his map, the border with New Hampshire is 165 miles long, while the coastline along the Atlantic Ocean is approximately 100 miles long. If the angle at the tip of Maine is 43°, as shown in the diagram, what is the approximate area of York County?

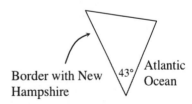

9-107. This problem is a checkpoint for exponential function problems. It will be referred to as Checkpoint 9B.

a. Graph $y = 2(0.75)^x$.

b. Write the equation for the exponential function based on the table at right.

x	$f(x)$
1	23
2	52.9
3	121.67
4	

c. The population of Flood River City is now 42,000. Experts predict the population will decrease 25% each year for the next five years. What will be the population in five years?

d. A share of Orange stock that was worth $25 in 2000 was worth $60 in 2010. What is the annual multiplier and percent increase?

Check your answers by referring to the Checkpoint 9B materials located at the back of your book.

Ideally, at this point you are comfortable working with these types of problems and can solve them correctly. If you feel that you need more confidence when solving these types of problems, then review the Checkpoint 9B materials and try the practice problems provided. From this point on, you will be expected to do problems like these correctly and with confidence.

9-108. Copy the following words and their lines of reflection onto your paper. Then use your visualization skills to help draw the reflected images.

a. **REFLECT**
        ←-------------→

b. **PRISM** ⁞

9-109. **Multiple Choice:** Solve this problem without a calculator: Examine the triangle at right. Find the approximate value of x. Use the values in the trigonometric table below as needed.

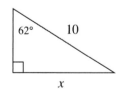

a. 4.69   b. 5.32

c. 8.83   d. 18.81

e. None of these

θ	$\cos\theta$	$\sin\theta$	$\tan\theta$
28°	0.883	0.469	0.532
62°	0.469	0.883	1.881

Chapter 9 Closure   What have I learned?

Reflection and Synthesis

The activities below offer you a chance to reflect
about what you have learned during this chapter. As
you work, look for concepts that you feel very
comfortable with, ideas that you would like to learn
more about, and topics you need more help with.
Look for connections between ideas as well as
connections with material you learned previously.

①   TEAM BRAINSTORM

What have you studied in this chapter? What ideas were important in what you
learned? With your team, brainstorm a list. Be as detailed as you can. To help
get you started, lists of Learning Log entries, Toolkit entries, and Math Notes
boxes are given below.

What topics, ideas, and words that you learned *before* this chapter are connected
to the new ideas in this chapter? Again, be as detailed as you can.

How long can you make your list? Challenge yourselves. Be prepared to share
your team's ideas with the class.

Learning Log Entries
- Lesson 9.1.1 – Volume of a Three-Dimensional Shape
- Lesson 9.1.2 – Finding Volume
- Lesson 9.1.4 – Volumes of Similar Solids

Toolkit Entries
- Construction Toolkit (Lesson 9.2,1. 9.2.2, and 9.2.3
  Resource Pages)

Math Notes
- Lesson 9.1.2 – Polyhedra and Prisms
- Lesson 9.1.3 – Volume and Total Surface Area of a Solid
- Lesson 9.1.5 – The $r : r^2 : r^3$ Ratios of Similarity
- Lesson 9.2.2 – Rhombus Facts
- Lesson 9.2.3 – Constructing a Perpendicular Bisector
- Lesson 9.2.4 – Centroid and Medians of a Triangle

Below is a list of the vocabulary used in this chapter. Make sure that you are familiar with all of these words and know what they mean. Refer to the glossary or index for any words that you do not yet understand.

base	bisect	centroid
circle	compass	concentric circles
construction	cylinder	density
incenter	inscribed	lateral face
line segment	linear scale factor	mat plan
median	net	oblique
perimeter	perpendicular bisector	polygon
polyhedron	point of concurrency	prism
ratio	rhombus	similar
solid	straightedge	surface area
three-dimensional	volume	

Make a concept map showing all of the connections you can find among the key words and ideas listed above. To show a connection between two words, draw a line between them and explain the connection. A word can be connected to any other word as long as you can justify the connection. For each key word or idea, provide an example or sketch that shows the idea.

While you are making your map, your team may think of related words or ideas that are not listed here. Be sure to include these ideas on your concept map.

PORTFOLIO: EVIDENCE OF MATHEMATICAL PROFICIENCY

Showcase your understanding of the different representations of a three-dimensional solid by describing the advantages and disadvantages of each representation, including how each representation makes it easier or more difficult to find the surface area and volume of the solid.

Showcase your constructions ability by using only a compass and straightedge to construct a line segment that is $\sqrt{5}$ units long. Assume the segment below is one unit long and use it to make your line segment. Show your construction marks, and explain each step clearly and in detail to a student that does not know how to complete this construction.

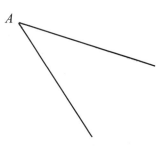

Copy the angle at right. Explain each step clearly and in detail in constructing its angle bisector.

Your teacher may give you the Chapter 9 Closure Resource Page: Representations of a Solid Graphics Organizer, and/or the Chapter 9 Closure Resource Page: Constructions Graphics Organizer to work on (or you can download these pages from www.cpm.org). A Graphic Organizer is a tool you can use to organize your thoughts, showcase your knowledge, and communicate your ideas clearly.

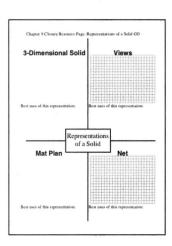

④ WHAT HAVE I LEARNED?

Most of the problems in this section represent typical problems found in this chapter. They serve as a gauge for you. You can use them to determine which types of problems you can do well and which types of problems require further study and practice. Even if your teacher does not assign this section, it is a good idea to try these problems and find out for yourself what you know and what you still need to work on.

Solve each problem as completely as you can. The table at the end of the closure section has answers to these problems. It also tells you where you can find additional help and practice with problems like these.

CL 9-110. On her paper, Kaye has a line with points A and B on it. Explain how she can use a compass to find a point C so that B is a midpoint of $\overline{AC}$. If you have access to a compass, try this yourself.

CL 9-111. Assume that the solid at right has no hidden cubes.

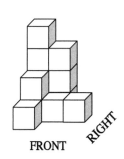

a. On graph paper, draw the front, right, and top views of this solid.

b. Find the volume and surface area of the cube.

c. Which net(s) below would have the same volume as the solid at right when it is folded to create a box?

FRONT   RIGHT

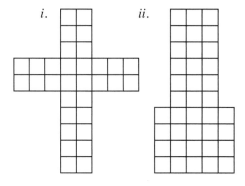

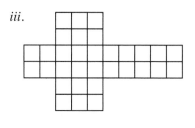

CL 9-112.   The solid from problem CL 9-111 is redrawn at right.

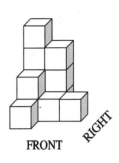

FRONT   RIGHT

a.   If this solid were enlarged by a linear scale factor of 4, what would the volume and surface area of the new solid be?

b.   Enrique enlarged the solid at right so that its volume was 1500 cubic units. What was his linear scale factor? Justify your answer.

CL 9-113.   After constructing a $\triangle ABC$, Pricilla decided to try a little experiment. She chose a point V outside of $\triangle ABC$ and then constructed rays $\overrightarrow{VA}$, $\overrightarrow{VB}$, and $\overrightarrow{VC}$. Her result is shown at right. Copy this diagram onto your paper.

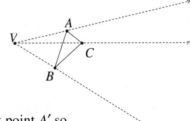

a.   Pricilla then used a compass to mark point A' so that $VA = AA'$. She also constructed points B' and C' using the same method. For the diagram on your paper, locate A', B', and C'.

b.   Now connect the new points to form $\triangle A'B'C'$. What is the relationship between $\triangle ABC$ and $\triangle A'B'C'$? Explain what happened.

c.   If the area of $\triangle ABC$ is 19 cm² and its perimeter is 15 cm, find the area and perimeter of $\triangle A'B'C'$.

CL 9-114.   A restaurant has a giant fish tank, shown at right, in the shape of an octagonal prism.

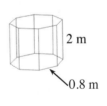

2 m

0.8 m

a.   Find the volume and surface area of the fish tank if the base is a regular octagon with side length 0.8 m and the height of the prism is 2 m.

b.   What is the density of fish if there are 208 fish in the tank?

CL 9-115.   Answer the questions about the angles of polygons below, if possible. If it is not possible, explain how you know it is not possible.

a.   Find the sum of the interior angles of a 28-gon.

b.   If the exterior angle of a regular polygon is 42°, how many sides does the polygon have?

c.   Find the measure of each interior angle of a pentagon.

d.   Find the measure of each interior angle of a regular decagon.

CL 9-116.   Fill in the blanks in each statement below with one of the quadrilaterals listed at right so that the statement is *true*. Use each quadrilateral name only once.

List:

Kite

Rectangle

Rhombus

Trapezoid

a.   If a shape is a square, then it must also be a _____.

b.   The diagonals of a _____ must be perpendicular to each other.

c.   If the quadrilateral has only one line of symmetry, then it could be a _____.

d.   If a quadrilateral has only two sides that are congruent, then the shape could be a _____.

CL 9-117.   Copy quadrilateral *DART*, shown at right, onto your paper. If $\overline{DR}$ bisects $\angle ADT$ and if $\angle A \cong \angle T$, prove that $\overline{DA} \cong \overline{DT}$.

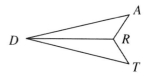

CL 9-118.   After Myong's cylindrical birthday cake was sliced, she received the slice at right. If her birthday cake originally had a diameter of 14 inches and a height of 6 inches, find the volume of her slice of cake.

CL 9-119.   Check your answers using the table at the end of the closure section. Which problems do you feel confident about? Which problems were hard? Use the table to make a list of topics you need help on and a list of topics you need to practice more.

Answers and Support for Closure Activity #4
What Have I Learned?

Note: MN = Math Note, LL = Learning Log

Problem	Solution	Need Help?	More Practice
CL 9-110.	She should match the length of $\overline{AB}$ with her compass. Then, with the point of the compass at point B, she should mark a point on the line on the side of point B opposite point A. Then she should label that point C.	Lesson 9.2.1 Construction Toolkit	Problems 9-79, 9-80, 9-98, and 9-104
CL 9-111.	a. Front Right Top b. $V = 12$ un^3, SA = 42 units^2 c. All three nets will form a box with volume 12 units^3.	Lessons 9.1.1 and 9.1.2 MN: 9.1.3 LL: 9.1.1	Problems 9-7, 9-21, 9-49, 9-56, 9-74, and 9-91
CL 9-112.	a. $V = 12(4)^3 = 768$ units^3, $SA = 42(4)^2 = 672$ units^2 b. Linear scale factor = 5	Lessons 9.1.4 and 9.1.5 MN: 9.1.5	Problems 9-45, 9-46, 9-56, 9-86, and 9-91
CL 9-113.	a. b. $\triangle ABC$ was enlarged (or dilated) to create a similar triangle with a linear scale factor of 2. c. $A = 19(2)^2 = 76$ units^2; $P = 15(2) = 30$ units	Lessons 8.2.1, 8.2.2, and 9.2.1 MN: 3.1.1, 8.2.1, and 9.1.5 Construction Toolkit	Problems 8-71, 8-83, 9-8, 9-20, and 9-33

Problem	Solution	Need Help?	More Practice
CL 9-114.	a. Area of base ≈ 3.09 m^2 Volume ≈ 6.18 m^3 Surface Area ≈ 18.98 m^2 b. density ≈ 33.66 fish/m^3	Lessons 9.1.2 and 9.1.3 MN: 8.3.1 and 9.1.3 LL: 8.1.5 and 9.1.2	Problems 9-26, 9-34, 9-38, 9-40, 9-46, 9-57, 9-69, 9-83, 9-95, and 9-103
CL 9-115.	a. 4680° b. Not possible because 42° does not divide evenly into 360°. c. Not possible because it is not stated that the pentagon is regular. d. 144°	Lessons 8.1.2, 8.1.3, and 8.1.4 MN: 7.1.4 and 8.1.5 LL: 8.1.2, 8.1.3, and 8.1.4	Problems CL 8-138, 9-22, 9-84, 9-95, and 9-105
CL 9-116.	a. Rectangle b. Rhombus c. Kite d. Trapezoid	Lessons 7.3.1 and 7.3.3 MN: 7.2.3, 8.1.2, and 9.2.2	Problems CL 7-156, 8-12, 8-61, and 9-58
CL 9-117.		Section 3.2 and Lessons 6.1.1 through 6.1.4 MN: 3.2.2, 3.2.4, 6.1.4, 7.1.3, and 7.2.1 LL: 3.2.2	Problems CL 3-123, CL 4-123, CL 5-140, CL 6-101, CL 7-155, CL 8-134, 9-35, 9-92, and 9-96
CL 9-118.	$V \approx 97.49$ cubic inches	Lesson 9.1.3 MN: 8.3.2, 8.3.3, and 9.1.3 LL: 9.1.2	Problems 9-38, 9-40, 9-46, and 9-103

CIRCLES 10
and
Conditional
Probability

Build a FARM

Blue   Red

CHAPTER 10

Circles and
Conditional Probability

In Chapter 8, you developed a method for finding the area and circumference of a circle, and in Chapter 9 you constructed many shapes using circles as a starting point. In Section 10.1, you will explore the relationships between angles, arcs, and chords in a circle.

The focus of your work turns to probability in Section 10.2. As you analyze probabilities, you will develop an understanding of conditional probability and more formal mathematical definitions of independence. With that you can determine if two categorical variables are associated with each other. To calculate and display probabilities, you will add the additional tool of two-way tables to your existing tools of area models and tree diagrams.

Guiding Question

Mathematically proficient students use appropriate tools strategically.

As you work through this chapter, ask yourself:

What tools do I have available to help me solve this problem?

Chapter Outline

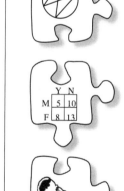

Section 10.1 The relationships between angles, arcs, and line segments in a circle will be investigated to develop "circle tools" that can help solve problems involving circles.

Section 10.2 Area models and two-way tables provide the basis for calculating conditional probabilities and determining whether events are independent.

Section 10.3 Some sample spaces are so large that models cannot easily represent them. Based on the Fundamental Principal of Counting, other formulas for permutations and combinations are developed that can be used to solve more complex problems.

10.1.1 What is the length of the diameter?

....

Introduction to Chords

In Chapter 8, you learned that the diameter of a circle is the distance across the center of the circle. This length can be easily determined if the entire circle is in front of you and the center is marked, or if you know the length of the radius of the circle. However, what if you only have part of a circle, called an **arc**? Or what if the circle is so large that it is not practical to measure its diameter using standard measurement tools, such as finding the diameter of the Earth's equator?

Today you will consider a situation that demonstrates the need to learn more about the parts of a circle and the relationships between them.

10-1.   THE WORLD'S WIDEST TREE

The baobab tree is a species of tree found in Africa and Australia. It is often referred to as the world's widest tree because it has been known to be up to 45 feet in diameter!

While digging at an archeological site, Rafi found a fragment of a fossilized baobab tree that appears to be wider than any tree on record! However, since he does not have the remains of the entire tree, he cannot simply measure across the tree to find its diameter. He needs your help to determine the length of the radius of this ancient tree. Assume that the shape of the tree's cross-section is a circle.

Tree fragment

a.   Obtain the Lesson 10.1.1 Resource Page from your teacher. On it, locate $\overset{\frown}{AB}$, which represents the curvature of the tree fragment. Trace this arc as neatly as possible on tracing paper. Then decide with your team how to fold the tracing paper to find the center of the tree. (Hint: This will take more than one fold.) Be ready to share with the class how you found the center.

b.   In part (a), you located the center of a circle. Use a ruler to measure the radius of that circle. If 1 cm represents 10 feet of tree, find the approximate length of the radius and diameter of the tree. Does the tree appear to be larger than 45 feet in diameter?

10-2.   PARTS OF A CIRCLE, Part One

A line segment that connects the endpoints of an arc is called a **chord**. Thus, $\overline{AB}$ in the diagram below is an example of a chord.

a.   One way to find the center of a circle when given an arc is to fold it so that the two parts of the arc coincide (lie on top of each other).

If you fold $\overset{\frown}{AB}$ so that A lies on B, what is the relationship between the resulting crease and the chord $\overline{AB}$? Explain how you know.

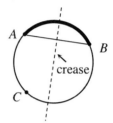

b.   The tree fragment in problem 10-1 was an arc between points A and B. However, the missing part of the tree formed another larger arc of the tree. With your team, find the larger arc formed by the circle and points A and B above. Then propose a way to use the points to name the larger arc to distinguish it from $\overset{\frown}{AB}$.

c.   In problem 10-1, the tree fragment formed the shorter arc between two endpoints. The shorter arc between points A and B is called the **minor arc** and is written $\overset{\frown}{AB}$. The larger arc is called a **major arc** and is usually written using three points, such as $\overset{\frown}{ACB}$. What do you know about $\overline{AB}$ if the minor and major arcs are the same length? Explain how you know.

10-3.   In problem 10-1, folding the arc several times resulted in a point that seemed to be the center of the circle. But how can you prove that the line bisecting an arc (or chord) will pass through the center? To consider this, first assume that the perpendicular bisector does *not* pass through the center. This is an example of a proof by contradiction.

a.   According to our assumption, if the perpendicular bisector does not pass through the center, then the center, C, will be off the line in the circle, as shown at right. Copy this diagram onto your paper.

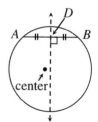

b.   Now consider $\triangle ACD$ and $\triangle BCD$. Are these two triangles congruent? Why or why not?

c.   Explain why your result from part (b) contradicts the original assumption. That is, explain why the center must lie on the perpendicular bisector of $\overline{AB}$.

Core Connections Geometry

10-4.   What if you are given two non-parallel chords in a circle and nothing else? How can you use the chords to find the center of the circle?

    a.   On the Lesson 10.1.1 Resource Page, locate the chords provided for ⊙P and ⊙Q. Work with your team to determine how to find the center of each circle. Then use a compass to draw the circles that contain the given chords. Tracing paper may be helpful.

    b.   Describe how to find the center of a circle without tracing paper. That is, how would you find the center of ⊙P with only a compass and a straightedge? Be prepared to share your description with the rest of the class.

10-5.   Examine the chord $\overline{WX}$ in ⊙Z at right. If $WX = 8$ units and the length of the radius of ⊙Z is 5 units, how far from the center is the chord? Draw the diagram on your paper and show all work.

ETHODS AND **MEANINGS**

Circle Vocabulary

MATH NOTES

An **arc** is a part of a circle. Remember that a circle does not contain its interior. A bicycle tire is an example of a circle. The spokes and the space in between them are not part of the circle. The piece of tire between any two spokes of the bicycle wheel is an example of an arc.

Any two points on a circle create two arcs. When these arcs are not the same length, the larger arc is referred to as the **major arc**, while the smaller arc is referred to as the **minor arc**.

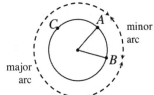

To name an arc, an arc symbol is drawn over the endpoints, such as $\overparen{AB}$. To refer to a major arc, a third point on the arc should be used to identify the arc clearly, such as $\overparen{ACB}$.

A **chord** is a line segment that has both endpoints on a circle. $\overline{AB}$ in the diagram at right is an example of a chord. When a chord passes through the center of the circle, it is called a **diameter**.

10-6. A rectangular prism has a cylindrical hole removed, as shown at right.

    a.   If the length of the radius of the cylindrical hole is 0.5 cm, find the volume of the solid.

    b.   What could this geometric figure represent? That is, if it were a model for something that exists in the world, what might it be? Also, how might you change it to make it a better model?

10-7. In the diagram below, $\overline{AD}$ is a diameter of $\odot B$.

    a.   If $m\angle A = 35°$, what is $m\angle CBD$?

    b.   If $m\angle CBD = 100°$, what is $m\angle A$?

    c.   If $m\angle A = x$, what is $m\angle CBD$?

10-8. Lavinia started a construction at right. Explain what she is constructing. Then copy her diagram and finish her construction.

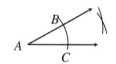

10-9. A sector is attached to the side of a parallelogram, as shown in the diagram at right. Find the area and perimeter of the figure.

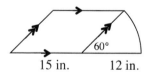

10-10. For each recursively defined sequence, list the first five terms and identify the sequence as arithmetic, geometric, or neither.

    a. $a_1 = 17$, $a_{n+1} = -a_n$

    b. $a_1 = 32$, $a_{n+1} = -5 + \frac{1}{2}a_n$

    c. $a_1 = 81$, $a_{n+1} = a_n$

10-11.　On the same set of axes, graph both equations listed below. Then name all points of intersection in the form (x, y). How many times do the graphs intersect?

$$y = 4x - 7$$
$$y = x^2 - 2x + 2$$

10-12.　**Multiple Choice:** A penny, nickel, and dime are all flipped once. What is the probability that at least one coin comes up heads?

　a.　$\frac{1}{3}$　　　　b.　$\frac{3}{8}$　　　　c.　1　　　　d.　$\frac{7}{8}$

10.1.2 What is the relationship?

• •

Angles and Arcs

In order to learn more about circles, you need to investigate different types of angles and chords that are found in circles. In Lesson 10.1.1, you studied an application with a tree to learn about the chords of a circle. Today you will study a different application that will demonstrate the importance of knowing how to measure the angles and arcs within a circle.

10-13.

ERATOSTHENES' REMARKABLE DISCOVERY

Eratosthenes, who lived in the 3rd century B.C., was able to determine the circumference of the Earth at a time when most people thought the world was flat! Since he was convinced that the Earth was round, he realized that he could use a shadow to help calculate the length of the Earth's radius.

Eratosthenes knew that Alexandria was located about 500 miles north of a town that was closer to the equator, called Syene. When the sun was directly overhead at Syene, a meter stick had no shadow. However, at the same time in Alexandria, a meter stick had a shadow due to the curvature of the Earth. Since the sun is so far away from the Earth, Eratosthenes assumed that the sun's rays were essentially parallel once they entered the Earth's atmosphere and realized that he could therefore use the stick's shadow to help calculate the length of the Earth's radius.

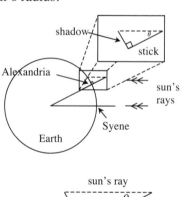

a. Unfortunately, the precise data used by Eratosthenes was lost long ago. However, if Eratosthenes used a meter stick for his experiment today, then the stick's shadow in Alexandria would be 127 mm long. Determine the angle θ that the sunrays made with the meter stick. Remember that a meter stick is 1000 millimeters long.

b. Assuming that the sun's rays are essentially parallel, determine the central angle of the circle if the angle passes through Alexandria and Syene. How did you find your answer?

Problem continues on next page →

10-13.   *Problem continued from previous page.*

c.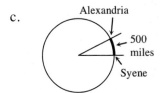

Since the distance along the Earth's surface from Alexandria to Syene is about 500 miles, that is the length of the arc between Alexandria and Syene. Use this information to approximate the circumference of the Earth.

d.   Use your result from part (c) to approximate the length of the radius of the Earth.

10-14.   PARTS OF A CIRCLE, Part Two

In order to find the circumference of the Earth, Eratosthenes used an angle that had its vertex at the center of the circle. Like the angles in polygons that you studied in Chapter 8, this angle is called a **central angle**.

a.   An **arc** is a part of a circle. Every central angle has a corresponding arc. For example, in $\odot T$ at right, $\angle STU$ is a central angle and corresponds to $\overset{\frown}{SU}$. Since the measure of an angle helps us know its part of the whole 360° of a circle, an arc can also be measured in degrees, representing its fraction of an entire circle. Thus, the **measure of an arc** is defined to be equal to the measure of its corresponding central angle.

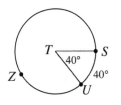

Examine the circle above. What is the measure of $\overset{\frown}{SU}$ (written $m\overset{\frown}{SU}$)? What is $m\overset{\frown}{SZU}$? Show how you got your answer.

b.   When Eratosthenes measured the distance from Syene to Alexandria, he measured the length of an arc. This distance is called **arc length** and is measured with units like centimeters or feet. One way to find arc length is to wrap a string about a part of a circle and then to straighten it out and measure its length. Calculate the arc length of $\overset{\frown}{SU}$ above if the length of the radius of $\odot T$ is 12 inches.

10-15.   INSCRIBED ANGLES

In the diagram at right, ∠BDC is an example of
an **inscribed angle**, because it lies within ⊙A and
its vertex lies on the circle. It corresponds to
central angle ∠BAC because they both intercept
the same arc, $\overset{\frown}{BC}$. (An **intercepted arc** is an arc
with endpoints on each side of the angle.)

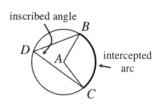

Investigate the measure of inscribed angles as you
answer the questions below.

a.   In the circle at right, ∠F, ∠G, and ∠H are
      examples of inscribed angles. Notice that all
      three angles intercept the same arc ($\overset{\frown}{JK}$). Use
      tracing paper to compare their measures. What
      do you notice?

b.   Now compare the measurements of the central
      angle (such as ∠WZY in ⊙Z at right) and an
      inscribed angle (such as ∠WXY). What is the
      relationship of an inscribed angle and its
      corresponding central angle? Use tracing
      paper to test your idea.

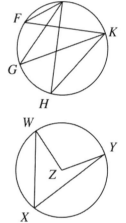

10-16.   In problem 10-15, you found that the measure of an inscribed angle was half of
the measure of its corresponding central angle in the cases you tested. Later
you will prove that this is always true and since the measure of the central angle
always equals the measure of its intercepted arc, then the measure of the
inscribed angle must be half of the measure of its intercepted arc.

Examine the diagrams below. Find the measures of the indicated angles. If a
point is labeled C, assume it is the center of the circle.

a.

118°

b.

41°

c.

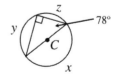

78°

d.

56°

e.

114°

f.

28°

10-17.   LEARNING LOG

Reflect on what you have learned during this lesson.
Write a Learning Log entry describing the relationships
between inscribed angles and their intercepted arcs. Be
sure to include an example. Title this entry "Inscribed
Angles" and include today's date.

METHODS AND MEANINGS

More Circle Vocabulary

The vertex of a **central angle** is at the center of a circle. An
inscribed angle has its vertex on the circle with each side
intersecting the circle at a different point.

One way to discuss an arc is to consider it as a fraction of 360°, that is, as
a part of a full circle. When speaking about an arc using degrees, this is
called the **arc measure**. The arc between the endpoints of the sides of a
central angle has the same measure (in degrees) as its corresponding
central angle.

When you want to know how *far* it is from one point to another as you
travel along an arc, you call this the **arc length** and measure it in feet,
miles, etc.

For example, point O is the center of $\odot O$ at right,
and $\angle AOB$ is a central angle. The sides of the angle
intersect the circle at points A and B, so $\angle AOB$
intercepts $\overset{\frown}{AB}$. In this case, the measure of $\overset{\frown}{AB}$ is 60°,
while the measure of the major arc, $m\overset{\frown}{ACB}$, is 300°
because the sum of the major and minor arcs is 360°.
The length of $\overset{\frown}{AB}$ is $\frac{60}{360} = \frac{1}{6}$ of the circumference.

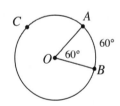

10-18.   In $\odot A$ at right, $\overline{CF}$ is a diameter and $m\angle C = 64°$. Find:

a. $m\angle D$ b. $m\overset{\frown}{BF}$

c. $m\angle E$ d. $m\overset{\frown}{CBF}$

e. $m\angle BAF$ f. $m\angle BAC$

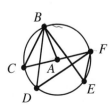

10-19.   Find the area of a regular polygon with 100 sides and with a perimeter of 100 units.

10-20.   For each of the geometric relationships represented below, write and solve an equation for the given variable. For parts (a) and (b), assume that *C* is the center of the circle. Show all work.

a.
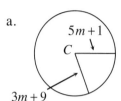

b.
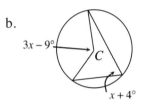

c.
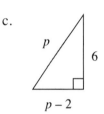

d.
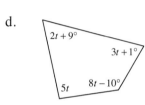

10-21.   On graph paper, plot $\triangle ABC$ if $A(-1,-1)$, $B(1,9)$, and $C(7,5)$.

a.   Find the midpoint of $\overline{AB}$ and label it *D*. Also find the midpoint of $\overline{BC}$ and label it *E*.

b.   Find the length of the midsegment, $\overline{DE}$. Use it to predict the length of $\overline{AC}$.

c.   Now find the length of $\overline{AC}$ and compare it to your prediction from part (b).

10-22.   *ABCDE* is a regular pentagon inscribed in $\odot O$, meaning that each of its five vertices just touches the circle.

a.   Draw a diagram of *ABCDE* and $\odot O$ on your paper.

b.   Find $m\angle EDC$. How did you find your answer?

c.   Find $m\angle BOC$. What relationship did you use?

d.   Find $m\widehat{EBC}$. Is there more than one way to do this?

10-23. Create mat plans from the following isometric views and find the volume of each.

a.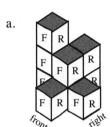

b.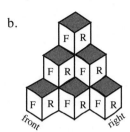

c. Did you have to make any assumptions about hidden cubes when you drew the mat plans? If so, what assumptions did you make in each case and why?

d. What other view would you need to see to be sure how many cubes there are? Explain.

10-24. **Multiple Choice:** Jill's car tires are spinning at a rate of 120 revolutions per minute. If her car tires' radii are each 14 inches, how far does she travel in 5 minutes?

a. 140π in.　　b. 8400π in.　　c. 3360π in.　　d. 16800π in.

10.1.3 What more can I learn about circles?

Chords and Angles

As you investigate more about the parts of a circle, look for connections that you can make to other shapes and relationships you have studied so far in this course.

10-25.   WHAT IF IT'S A SEMICIRCLE?

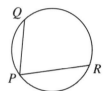

What is the measure of an angle when it is inscribed in a **semicircle** (an arc with measure 180°)? Consider this as you answer the questions below.

a.   Assume that the diagram at right is not drawn to scale. If $m\widehat{QR} = 180°$, then what is $m\angle P$? Why?

b.   Since you have several tools to use with right triangles, the special relationship you found in part (a) can be useful. For example, $\overline{UV}$ is a diameter of the circle at right. If $TU = 6$ units and $TV = 8$ units, what is the length of the radius of the circle? What is its area?

10-26.   In Lesson 10.1.1, you learned that a chord is a line segment that has its endpoints on a circle. What geometric tools do you have that can help find the length of a chord?

a.   Examine the diagram of chord $\overline{LM}$ in $\odot P$ at right. If the length of the radius of $\odot P$ is 6 units and if $m\widehat{LM} = 150°$, find LM. Be ready to share your method with the class.

b.   What if you know the length of a chord? How can you use it to reverse the process? Draw a diagram of a circle with radius with length 5 units and chord $\overline{AB}$ with length 6 units. Find $m\widehat{AB}$.

Core Connections Geometry

10-27. Timothy asks, *"What if two chords intersect inside a circle? Can triangles help me learn something about these chords?"* Copy his diagram at right in which chords $\overline{AB}$ and $\overline{CD}$ intersect at point E.

a. Timothy decided to create two triangles ($\triangle BED$ and $\triangle AEC$). Add line segments $\overline{BD}$ and $\overline{AC}$ to your diagram.

b. Compare $\angle B$ and $\angle C$. Which is bigger? How can you tell? Likewise, compare $\angle D$ and $\angle A$. Write down your observations.

c. How are $\triangle BED$ and $\triangle AEC$ related? Justify your answer.

d. If $DE = 8$, $AE = 4$, and $EB = 6$, then what is EC? Show your work.

10-28. A polygon is said to be **inscribed** in a circle when each of its vertices touch the circle. How are the angles of a quadrilateral inscribed in a circle related? Consider this as you answer the questions below.

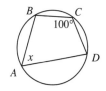

a. For *ABCD* inscribed in the circle at right, solve for x. Explain how you found your answer.

b. Alejandra noticed something. *"I think that the opposite angles of a quadrilateral inscribed in a circle are always supplementary."* Is she correct? Prove your conclusion.

10-29. Use the relationships in the diagrams to solve for *x*.
Justify your solutions.

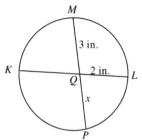

a. $\overline{KL}$ and $\overline{MP}$ intersect at *Q* and *KL* = 8 inches

b. $\overline{RT}$ is a diameter

c.

10-30. **LEARNING LOG**

Look over your work from today. Consider all the
geometric tools you applied to learn more about angles and
chords of circles. In a Learning Log entry, describe which
connections you made today. Title this entry "Connections with
Circles" and include today's date.

METHODS AND MEANINGS

Inscribed Angle Theorem

The measure of any inscribed angle is half of the measure of its intercepted arc. Likewise, any intercepted arc is twice the measure of any inscribed angles whose sides pass through the endpoints of the arc.

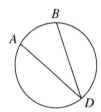

For example, in the diagram at right:

$$m\angle ADB = \tfrac{1}{2} m\widehat{AB} \text{ and } m\widehat{AB} = 2m\angle ADB$$

Proof:

To prove this relationship, consider the relationship between an inscribed angle and its corresponding central angle. In problem 10-7, you used the isosceles triangle $\triangle ABC$ to demonstrate that if one of the sides of the inscribed angle is a diameter of the circle, then the inscribed angle must be half of the measure of the corresponding central angle. Therefore, in the diagram at right, $m\angle DAC = \tfrac{1}{2} m\widehat{DC}$.

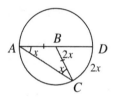

But what if the center of the circle instead lies in the interior of an inscribed angle, such as $\angle EAC$ shown at right? By extending $\overline{AB}$ to construct the diameter $\overline{AD}$, the work above shows that if $m\angle EAD = k$ then $m\widehat{ED} = 2k$ and if $m\angle DAC = p$, then $m\widehat{DC} = 2p$. Since $m\angle EAC = k + p$, then $m\widehat{EC} = 2k + 2p = 2(k + p) = 2m\angle EAC$.

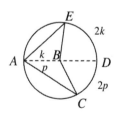

The last possible case to consider is when the center lies outside of the inscribed angle, as shown at right. Again, constructing a diameter $\overline{AD}$ helps show that if $m\angle CAD = k$ then $m\widehat{CD} = 2k$ and if $m\angle EAD = p$, then $m\widehat{ED} = 2p$. Since $m\angle EAC = p - k$, then $m\widehat{EC} = 2p - 2k = 2(p - k) = 2m\angle EAC$.

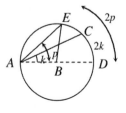

Therefore, an arc is always twice the measure of any inscribed angle that intercepts it.

10-31. Assume point B is the center of the circle below. Match each item in the left column with the best description for it in the right column.

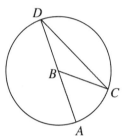

a. $\overline{AB}$ 1. inscribed angle

b. $\overline{CD}$ 2. semicircle

c. $\overarc{AD}$ 3. radius

d. $\angle CDA$ 4. minor arc

e. $\overarc{AC}$ 5. central angle

f. $\angle ABC$ 6. chord

10-32. The figure at right shows two concentric circles.

a. What is the relationship between $\overarc{AB}$ and $\overarc{CD}$? How do you know?

b. Which has greater measure, $\overarc{AB}$ or $\overarc{CD}$? Which has greater length? Explain.

c. If $m\angle P = 60°$ and $PD = 14$, find the length of $\overarc{CD}$. Show all work.

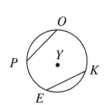

10-33. In $\odot Y$ at right, assume that $m\overarc{PO} = m\overarc{EK}$. Prove that $\overline{PO} \cong \overline{EK}$. Use the format of your choice.

Core Connections Geometry

10-34.   While working on the quadrilateral hotline, Jo
Beth got this call: "*I need help identifying the
shape of the quadrilateral flowerbed in front of
my apartment. Because a shrub covers one side,
I can only see three sides of the flowerbed.
However, of the three sides I can see, two are
parallel and all three are congruent. What are
the possible shapes of my flowerbed?*" Help Jo
Beth answer the caller's question.

10-35.   Compute the volume of the solid shown at right.

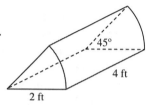

10-36.   For each pair of triangles below, decide if the triangles are similar or not and
explain how you know. If the triangles are similar, complete the similarity
statement $\triangle ABC \sim \triangle$ _____.

a. 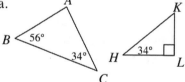   b.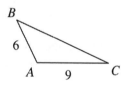

c.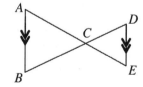

10-37.   **Multiple Choice:** Which equation below is perpendicular to $y = \frac{-2}{5}x - 7$ and
passes through the point $(4, -1)$?

a. $2x - 5y = 13$ b. $2x + 5y = 3$ c. $5x - 2y = 22$

d. $5x + 2y = 18$ e.   None of these

10.1.4 What is the relationship?

Tangents and Secants

So far, you have studied the relationships that exist between angles and chords (line segments) in a circle. Today you will extend these ideas to include the study of lines and circles.

10-38. Consider all the ways a circle and a line can intersect. Can you visualize a line and a circle that intersect at exactly one point? What about a line that intersects a circle twice? On your paper, draw a diagram for each of the situations below, if possible. If it is not possible, explain why.

a. Draw a line and a circle that do not intersect.

b. Draw a line and a circle that intersect at exactly one point. When this happens, the line is called a **tangent**.

c. Draw a line and a circle that intersect at exactly two points. A line that intersects a circle twice is called a **secant**.

d. Draw a line and a circle that intersect three times.

10-39. A line that intersects a circle exactly once is called a **tangent**. What is the relationship of a tangent to a circle?

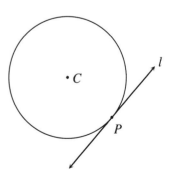

To investigate this question, carefully copy the diagram showing line *l* tangent to ⊙*C* at right onto tracing paper. Fold the tracing paper so that the crease is perpendicular to line *l* through point *P*. Your crease should pass through point *C*. What does this tell you about the tangent line?

10-40.   Ventura began to think about perpendicularity in a circle. He wondered, *"If a radius is perpendicular to a line at a point on the circle, how do we know if the line is a secant or a tangent?"* His team decided to tackle his question.

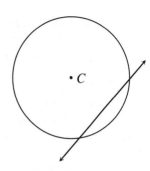

a.   Ho says, *"Let's assume the line perpendicular to the radius is a secant."* On your paper, draw a diagram, like the one at right, with $\odot C$ and a secant. Label the points where the secant intersects the circle A and B. Since Ventura's question assumes that the line is perpendicular to a radius, assume that $\overleftrightarrow{AB}$ is perpendicular to $\overline{CA}$ at A.

b.   Ventura adds *"I think △CAB is isosceles."* Do you agree? Explain how you know.

c.   Sandra chimes in with, *"Then ∠CBA must be a right angle too."* Ventura quickly adds, *"But that's impossible!"* What do you think? Discuss this with your team and give reasons to support your conclusions.

d.   Explain to Ventura what this contradiction reveals about the line perpendicular to the radius of a circle at a point on the circle.

10-41.   Use the relationships in the diagrams below to answer the following questions. Be sure to name what relationship(s) you used.

a. $\overrightarrow{PQ}$ is tangent to $\odot C$ at P. If $PQ = 5$ and $CQ = 6$, find CP and $m\angle C$.

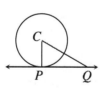

b.   In $\odot H$, $m\overset{\frown}{DR} = 40°$ and $m\overset{\frown}{GOR} = 210°$. Find $m\overset{\frown}{GD}$, $m\overset{\frown}{OR}$, and $m\angle RGO$.

c. $\overline{AC}$ is a diameter of $\odot E$ and $\overline{BC} \parallel \overline{ED}$. Find the measure of $\overset{\frown}{CD}$.

d. $\overline{HJ}$ and $\overline{IK}$ intersect at G. If $HG = 9$, $GJ = 8$, and $GK = 6$, find IG.

e. $\overline{AC}$ is a diameter of $\odot E$, the area of the circle is 289π units^2, and $AB = 16$ units. Find BC and $m\overset{\frown}{BC}$.

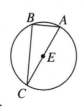

f.   △ABC is inscribed in the circle at right. Using the measurements provided in the diagram, find $m\overset{\frown}{AB}$.

10-42. In Chapter 9, it was stated that the intersection of the angle bisectors of a triangle is the center of a circle inscribed in the triangle. You now have enough information to prove this relationship.

   a.   Assume that in $\triangle ABC$, $\overrightarrow{AG}$ and $\overrightarrow{BH}$ are angle bisectors of $\angle CAB$ and $\angle CBA$, respectively. Draw this diagram on your paper. Label the intersection of the angle bisectors P.

   b.   You need to show that P is the same distance from sides $\overline{AB}$ and $\overline{AC}$. Draw a perpendicular from P to $\overline{AB}$ and label its intersection D. Similarly, draw a perpendicular from P to $\overline{AC}$ and label its intersection E. How can you prove that $\triangle ADP \cong \triangle AEP$?

   c.   Explain why $PE = PD$.

   d.   Use similar reasoning to show that P must also be the same distance from $\overline{BC}$. For example, if the perpendicular from P to $\overline{BC}$ intersects $\overline{BC}$ at F, why is $PF = PD$?

   e.   Explain why there must be a circle through points D, E, and F with center P and that each side of $\triangle ABC$ must be tangent to this circle, making the circle inscribed in the triangle.

MᴇᴛʜᴏᴅS AND Mᴇᴀɴɪɴɢs

Intersecting Chords

MATH NOTES

When two chords in a circle intersect, an interesting relationship between the lengths of the resulting segments occurs. If the ends of the chords are connected as shown in the diagram, similar triangles are formed (see problem 10-27). Then, since corresponding sides of similar triangles have a common ratio, $\frac{a}{d} = \frac{c}{b}$, and so

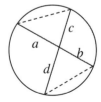

$$ab = cd.$$

10-43. If $\overline{QS}$ is a diameter and $\overline{PO}$ is a chord of the circle at right, find the measure of the geometric parts listed below.

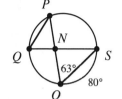

a. $m\angle QSO$

b. $m\angle QPO$

c. $m\angle ONS$

d. $m\overset{\frown}{PS}$

e. $m\overset{\frown}{PQ}$

f. $m\angle PQN$

10-44. For each triangle below, solve for the given variables.

a.
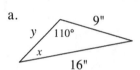

b.
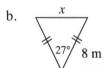

c.
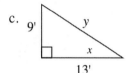

10-45. The spinner at right is designed so that if you randomly spin the spinner and land in the shaded sector, you win $1,000,000. Unfortunately, if you land in the unshaded sector, you win nothing. Assume point C is the center of the spinner.

a. If $m\angle ACB = 90°$, how many times would you have to spin to reasonably expect to land in the shaded sector at least once? How did you get your answer?

b. What if $m\angle ACB = 1°$? How many times would you have to spin to reasonably expect to land in the shaded sector at least once?

c. Suppose $P(\text{winning } \$1,000,000) = \frac{1}{5}$ for each spin. What must $m\angle ACB$ equal? Show how you got your answer.

10-46. Calculate the total surface area and volume of the prism at right. Assume that the base is a regular pentagon.

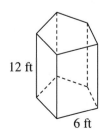

10-47. Quadrilateral *ABCD* is graphed so that $A(3, 2), B(1, 6), C(5, 8)$, and $D(7, 4)$.

    a.   Graph *ABCD* on graph paper. What shape is *ABCD*? Justify your answer.

    b.   *ABCD* is rotated 180° about the origin to create *A'B'C'D'*. Then *A'B'C'D'* is reflected across the *x*-axis to form *A"B"C"D"*. Name the coordinates of *C'* and *D"*.

10-48. Polly has a pentagon with angle measures $3x - 26°$, $2x + 70°$, $5x - 10°$, $3x$, and $2x + 56°$. Find the probability that if one vertex is selected at random, then the measure of its angle is more than or equal to 90°.

10-49. **Multiple Choice:** Which graph below represents $y > -\frac{1}{2}x + 1$?

a. 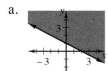   b. 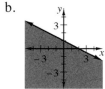   c. 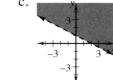   d.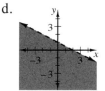

10.1.5 How can I solve it?

Problem Solving with Circles

Your work today is focused on consolidating your understanding of the relationships between angles, arcs, chords, and tangents in circles. As you work today, ask yourself the following focus questions:

Is there another way?

What is the relationship?

10-50. On a map, the coordinates of towns A, B, and C are $A(-3, 3)$, $B(5, 7)$, and $C(6, 0)$. City planners have decided to connect the towns with a circular freeway.

    a. Graph a map of the towns on graph paper. Once the freeway is built, $\overline{AB}$, $\overline{BC}$, and $\overline{AC}$ will be chords of the circle. Use this information to find the center of the circle.

    b. Draw triangle ABC and use a compass to draw the circle connecting all three towns on your graph paper. Then, find the length of the radius of the circular freeway.

        The circle that you drew **circumscribes** triangle $\triangle ABC$, because $\triangle ABC$ is inscribed in the circle. The center of the circle is called the **circumcenter** of the triangle, because it is the center of the circle that circumscribes the triangle.

    c. The city planners also intend to locate a new restaurant at the point that is an equal distance from all three towns. Where on the map should that restaurant be located? Justify your conclusion.

10-51. An 8-inch dinner knife is sitting on a circular plate so that its ends are on the edge of the plate. If the minor arc that is intercepted by the knife measures 120°, find the length of the diameter of the plate. Show all work.

10-52. A cylindrical block of cheese has a 6-inch diameter and is 2 inches thick. After a party, only a sector remains that has a central angle of 45°. Find the volume of the cheese that remains. Show all work.

10-53. Dennis plans to place a circular hot tub in the corner of his backyard so that it is tangent to a fence on two sides, as shown in the diagram at right.

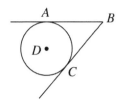

a. Prove that $\overline{AB} \cong \overline{CB}$.

b. The switch to turn on the air jets is located at point B. If the length of the diameter of the hot tub is 6 feet and $AB = 4$ feet, how long does his arm need to be for him to reach the switch from the edge of the tub? (Assume that Dennis will be in the tub when he turns the air jets on and that the switch is level with the top edge of the hot tub.)

Ⓜ️ETHODS AND MEANINGS

MATH NOTES

Points of Concurrency

You learned that the **centroid** of a triangle is the point at which the three medians of a triangle intersect, as shown at right. When three lines intersect at a single point, that point is called a **point of concurrency**. Refer to the Math Notes box in Lesson 9.2.4.

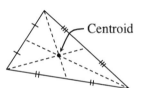

A circle that **circumscribes** a triangle touches all three vertices of the triangle. The center of this circle is called the **circumcenter**. The circumcenter is another point of concurrency because it is located where the perpendicular bisectors of each side of a triangle meet. See the example at right.

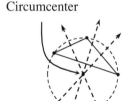

A circle that **inscribes** a triangle touches all three sides of the triangle just once. The center of this circle is called the **incenter**. The incenter is yet another point of concurrency because it is located where the three angle bisectors of a triangle meet.

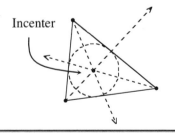

10-54. In the diagram at right, $\odot M$ has radius length of 14 feet and $\odot A$ has radius length of 8 feet. $\overleftrightarrow{ER}$ is tangent to both $\odot M$ and $\odot A$. If $NC = 17$ ft feet, find ER.

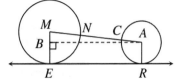

10-55. Use the sectors in circles D and E to answer the following questions.

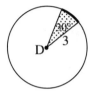

a. What is the ratio of the arc length to the radius of circle D? Leave your answer in terms of π.

b. What is the ratio of the arc length to the radius of circle E?

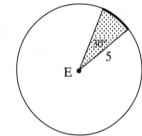

c. The ratio of the arc length to the radius of a circle is called a **radian**. Why will all sectors with a central angle of 30° have the same radian measure?

10-56. In the figure at right, find the interior height (h) of the obtuse triangle. Show all work.

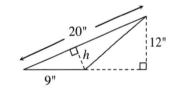

10-57. A cylinder with volume 500π cm³ is similar to a smaller cylinder. If the scale factor is $\frac{1}{5}$, what is the volume of the smaller cylinder? Explain your reasoning.

10-58. A six-year old house, now worth $175,000, has had an annual appreciation of 5%.

a. What is the multiplier?

b. What did it cost when new?

c. Write a function of the form $f(t) = ab^t$, where t is the time in years, that represents the value of the house since it was new.

10-59.   In the figure at right, $\overline{EX}$ is tangent to $\odot O$ at point X.
$OE = 20$ cm and $XE = 15$ cm.

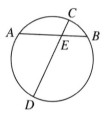

a.   What is the area of the circle?

b.   What is the area of the sector bounded by
$\overline{OX}$ and $\overline{ON}$?

c.   Find the area of the region bounded by $\overline{XE}$, $\overline{NE}$, and $\overparen{NX}$.

10-60.   **Multiple Choice:** In the circle at right, $\overline{CD}$ is a
diameter. If $AE = 10$, $CE = 4$, and $AB = 16$, what is
the length of the radius of the circle?

a.   15   b.   16

c.   18   d.   19

e.   None of these

10.2.1 What does independence tell me?

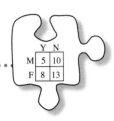

Conditional Probability and Independence

When two events can occur, either simultaneously or one after the other, how can you calculate the probability of one of them when you know the other has already happened? You will investigate this question today. Then you will see how finding **conditional probabilities** will help you determine if two events are independent of each other.

10-61. EIGHT THE HARD WAY

Maribelle is playing the board game Eight The Hard Way with her friends. Each player rolls two dice on their turn, and moves according to the sum on the dice. However, if a player rolls two fours (called "eight the hard way"), they instantly win the round of play and a new round is started.

Shayna stepped into the kitchen to get snacks when she heard Maribelle shout *"Woo Hoo! I got an eight!"*

Shayna knows Maribelle got an eight. With your team, help Shayna investigate the probability that Maribelle rolled two fours and won the round of play. In other words calculate the **conditional probability** that Maribelle rolled two fours, given that you know she already rolled a sum of eight.

a. Use an area model to represent all of the possible sums of numbers when rolling two dice.

b. However, since you know that Maribelle rolled a sum of eight, the sample space is changed. Now the sample space is only all the ways a sum of eight can be rolled. On your area model, shade all of the ways a sum of eight can be rolled. How many different ways can a sum of eight be rolled, that is, how many outcomes are in the new sample space?

c. You are interested in the event {eight the hard way}. How many different ways can two fours be rolled?

d. What is the probability of the event {eight the hard way} given that you know Maribelle already rolled a sum of eight?

e. Becca rolls "high" (meaning that she rolled a sum of nine or more). What is the conditional probability that she rolled an odd number, given that you know she rolled high?

10-62.   At Einstein Technical University (ETU), data on
engineering majors was collected:

	Engineering majors	Other majors
Live Off Campus	30	170
Live On Campus	6	34

a.   What is the probability of a student living on
campus at ETU?

b.   Copy the table and shade the cells with engineering majors. What is the
conditional probability of a student living on campus, given that you know
a student is an engineering major?

c.   Two events, A and B, are **independent** if knowing that B occurred does
not change the probability of event A occurring. That is, two events, A
and B, are independent if P(A given B) = P(A). Are the events
{live on campus} and {engineering} independent?

d.   Two events are **mutually exclusive** (or **disjoint**) if they cannot both occur
at the same time. That is, two events are mutually exclusive if
P(A and B) = 0. Are the events {on campus} and {engineering} mutually
exclusive?

10-63. The following data was collected about students in Mr. Rexinger's high school statistics class.

	Wearing jeans	Not wearing jeans
Male	7	7
Female	5	13

a. Mr. Rexinger is playing a game with his students. He randomly chooses a student from his class roster. If a player guesses the gender of the student correctly, the player gets an early-lunch pass. Madeline is the next player. Which gender should she guess to have the greatest chances of winning the lunch pass? Explain.

b. Mr. Rexinger tells Madeline that the student is wearing jeans. Should Madeline change her guess? Explain.

c. In a previous course, you may have studied the **association** of two *numerical* variables by analyzing scatterplots and least squares regression lines. Associations between *categorical* variables are determined by independence – if two variables are independent then they are not associated.

Are the events {female} and {wearing jeans} associated for the students in Mr. Rexinger's class today? Explain using the independence relationship from part (c) of problem 10-62.

d. Are the events {female} and {wearing jeans} mutually exclusive? Explain.

10-64. At Digital Technical Institute, the following data was collected:

	Engineering majors	Other majors
Live Off Campus	30	170
Live On Campus	0	40

a. Are the events {live on campus} and {engineering majors} associated at this institute?

b. Are the events {live on campus} and {engineering} mutually exclusive at this institute? What outcomes are in the intersection of {live on campus} and {engineering}?

10-65.   LEARNING LOG

Explain in your Learning Log what it means for two
numerical variables to be associated, and give an example.
What does it mean for two *categorical* variables to be
associated? Give an example. Think of a new situation in which two events are
associated mathematically, and explain the difference between mutually
exclusive and independent events in your own words. Title this entry,
"Independent or Mutually Exclusive?" and include today's date.

METHODS AND MEANINGS

Mutually Exclusive

MATH NOTES

Mutually exclusive events, also called **disjoint** events, can never
both happen at the same time. When one of the events occurs, it
means the other cannot possibly occur. If event B occurs, then you
know that event A cannot occur: $P(A \text{ and } B) = 0$ and the intersection
of {A} and {B} contains no outcomes.

If events A and B are mutually exclusive, the occurrence of B tells
you precisely about the probability of A occurring (A cannot occur). The
probabilities of mutually exclusive events depend on each other. Mutually
exclusive events are never independent (and thus always associated).

For example, suppose natural blondes occur in about 10% of the students at your
school. Being naturally blonde and having naturally black hair are mutually
exclusive – if one occurs, the other cannot possibly occur. If your friend tells
you that a randomly selected person has naturally black hair, the probability they
have naturally blonde hair is 0%. The probability of blonde has changed,
knowing that the person has black hair. The events {blonde hair} and {black
hair} are not independent.

10-66.   Natalie has a bag that contains eight marbles. She
          draws out a marble, records its color, and puts it back.

    a.   If Natalie repeats this eight times and does not
          record any red marbles, can she conclude that
          there are not any red marbles in the bag? Explain.

    b.   If she repeats this 100 times and does not record any red marbles, can she
          conclude that there are not any red marbles in the bag? Explain.

    c.   How many times would she have to draw marbles (putting them back each
          time) to be absolutely certain that there are no red marbles in the bag?

10-67.   When the net at right is folded, it creates a die with values as
          shown.

    a.   If the die is rolled randomly, what is P(even)? P(1)?

    b.   If the die is rolled randomly 60 times, how many times would you expect
          an odd number to land side-up? Explain how you know.

    c.   Now create your own net so that the resulting die has P(even) = $\frac{1}{3}$,
          P(3) = 0, and P(a number less than 5) = 1.

10-68.   In the diagram at right, $\overline{AB}$ is a diameter of $\odot L$. If
          $BC = 5$ and $AC = 12$, use the relationships shown in the
          diagram to solve for the quantities listed below.

          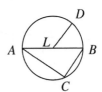

    a. AB b.   length of the radius of $\odot L$

    c. $m\angle ABC$ d. $m\overset{\frown}{AC}$

10-69.   When Erica and Ken explored a cave, they each found a gold nugget. Erica's nugget is similar to Ken's nugget. They measured the length of two matching parts of the nuggets and found that Erica's nugget is five times as long as Ken's. When they took their nuggets to the metallurgist to be analyzed, they learned that it would cost $30 to have the surface area and weight of the smaller nugget calculated, and $150 to have the same analysis done on the larger nugget.

"I won't have that kind of money until I sell my nugget, and then I won't need it analyzed!" Erica says.

"Wait, Erica. Don't worry. I'm pretty sure we can get all the information we need for only $30."

a.   Explain how they can get all the information they need for $30.

b.   If Ken's nugget has a surface area of 20 cm², what is the surface area of Erica's nugget?

c.   If Ken's nugget weighs 5.6 g (about 0.2 oz), what is the weight of Erica's nugget?

10-70.   Find x if the angles in a quadrilateral are $2x$, $3x$, $4x$, and $5x$.

10-71.   A graph of an inequality is shown at right. Decide if each of the points (x, y) listed below would make the inequality true or not. For each point, explain how you know.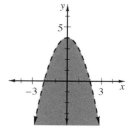

a. $(1, 1)$ b. $(-3, 2)$

c. $(-2, 0)$ d. $(0, -2)$

10-72.   **Multiple Choice:** Which expression below represents the length of the hypotenuse of the triangle at right?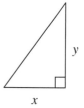

a. $\frac{y}{x}$ b. $\sqrt{x^2 + y^2}$ c. $x + y$

d. $\sqrt{y^2 - x^2}$ e.   None of these

10.2.2 Is there another way to organize data?

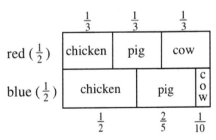

Two-Way Tables

In the previous lesson, you were given the counts (or the frequency) of the number of people or objects in a given situation, and then, from this, you computed conditional probabilities. In this lesson, you will extend your understanding of conditional probabilities by starting from probabilities rather than counts. You will see how data or probabilities are often organized into **two-way tables**, and you will continue to investigate the association of two categorical variables.

10-73.   BUILD-A-FARM

In the children's game, Build-a-Farm, each player first spins a spinner. Half of the time the spinner comes up red and half of the time the spinner comes up blue. If the spinner is red, the player reaches into the red box. If the spinner is blue, the player reaches into the blue box. The red box has 10 chicken counters, 10 pig counters, and 10 cow counters, while the blue box has 5 chicken counters, 4 pig counters, and 1 cow counter.

a.   Draw a tree diagram, including probabilities, to represent the sample space for this game.

b.   What is the probability of getting a cow counter in one turn?

c.   Even though the events {spin} and {animal counter} are not independent, a modified area model, as shown at right, is possible for this situation.

	$\frac{1}{3}$	$\frac{1}{3}$	$\frac{1}{3}$
red ($\frac{1}{2}$)	chicken	pig	cow
blue ($\frac{1}{2}$)	chicken	pig	cow
	$\frac{1}{2}$	$\frac{2}{5}$	$\frac{1}{10}$

Copy the area model and shade the parts of the diagram that correspond to getting a cow counter. Using the diagram, verify that P(cow) is the same as the one that you found in part (b).

Problem continues on next page →

10-73.   *Problem continued from previous page.*

    d.   Let's investigate the conditional probability that a child's spin was red, given that you know the child got a cow counter.

        Since you know that the child got a cow counter, the new sample space is limited to only the outcomes that contain cow – which is the area that you shaded in part (c). Considering only the outcomes that contain cow, what is the conditional probability that a child spun red, knowing that the child got a cow counter?

    e.   Using the method in part (d), find the conditional probability that if you got a pig counter, your spin was blue.

10-74.   FLIP TO SPIN OR ROLL

On the midway at the county fair, there are many popular games to play. One of them is Flip to Spin or Roll. First, the player flips a coin. If a head comes up, the player gets to spin the big wheel, which has ten equal sections: three red, three blue, and four yellow. If the coin shows a tail, the player gets to roll a cube with three red sides, two yellow sides, and one blue side. If the wheel spin lands on blue, or if the blue side of the cube comes up, the player wins a stuffed animal.

    a.   Draw a modified area model to represent the sample space for Flip to Spin or Roll. Note that the rectangles for heads will have different areas than the rectangles for tails.

    b.   Suppose that you know that Tyler won a stuffed animal. Discus this with your team and then shade the appropriate parts of the modified area model to help you figure out the probability that he started off by getting a head. Be prepared to share your ideas with the class.

10-75.   Raul is conducting a survey for the school news blog. He surveyed 200 senior-class students and found that 78 students had access to a car on weekends, 54 students had regular chores assigned at home, and 80 students neither had access to a car, nor had regular chores to do. Raul said he couldn't figure out how to put the data into a table like the one at right.

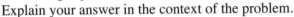

	car	no car
chores		
no chores		

a.   Copy and complete Raul's table to figure out the number of students in each cell.

b.   This type of table is called a **two-way table** and is often used to organize information and calculate probabilities. Two-way tables often include row and column totals also. If you have not already done so, add row and column totals to your two-way table. Is there an association between car privileges and having regular chores for this group? Explain your answer in the context of the problem.

10-76.   There are 30 students in Mr. Cooper's class; 18 boys and 12 girls. Mr. Cooper chooses a student at random to take the attendance folder to the office. Four of the boys have previously taken the folder to the office, and 3 of the girls have previously taken it.

a.   Create a two-way table to display this data.

b.   If Mr. Cooper randomly selects a student, what is the probability he selects a boy who previously took the folder? Make a new two-table table, and fill in that probability. Then fill in the remaining cells with their respective probabilities. Include row and column totals.

c.   If a student is chosen at random, what is the probability that the student is a girl or is a student that has taken the folder previously? Use the probabilities from the table that you made in part (b).

d.   Shade the cells in your table from part (b) where a student has previously taken the folder. If a student previously took the folder, what is the probability that the student is a girl?

10-77.   If Letitia studies for her math test tonight, she has an
         80% chance of getting an A. If she does not study,
         she only has a 10% chance. Whether she can study or
         not depends on whether she has to work at her
         parents' store. Earlier in the day, her father said there
         is a 50% chance that Letitia would be able to study.

   a.   Draw a modified area model for the situation.

   b.   Find the probability that Letitia gets an A on the
        math test.

   c.   What are the chances that Letitia studied, given that she got an A? Show
        how you shaded the diagram.

   d.   Create a two-way table that shows the probabilities for this situation.
        Include row and column totals. Verify using your table that if she studies,
        Letitia has an 80% chance of getting an A as described in the beginning of
        this problem.

Review & Preview

10-78.   For each diagram below, write an equation to represent the relationship between
         x and y.

   a.   b.   c.   d.

     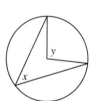   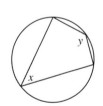

10-79.   For each triangle below, use the information in the diagram to decide if it is a
         right triangle. Justify each conclusion. Assume the diagrams are not drawn to
         scale.

   a.   b.

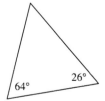   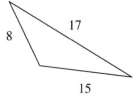

Core Connections Geometry

10-80.   A cement block is the shape of a prism with length 1.5 ft, width 1 ft and height 1 ft. Centered on the top of the block and passing all the way through the block are two 0.25 ft by 0.2 ft rectangular holes.

   a.   Draw a diagram of the block.

   b.   What is the volume of the block?

10-81.   A spinner is divided into two regions. One region, red, has a central angle of 60°. The other region is blue.

   a.   On your paper, sketch a picture of this spinner.

   b.   If the spinner is spun twice, what is the probability that both spins land on blue?

   c.   If the radius of the spinner is 7 cm, what is the area of the blue region?

   d.   A different spinner has three regions: purple, mauve, and green. If the probability of landing on purple is $\frac{1}{4}$ and the probability of landing on mauve is $\frac{2}{3}$, what is the central angle of the green region?

10-82.   After doing well on a test, Althea's teacher placed a gold star on her paper. When Althea examined the star closely, she realized that it was really a regular pentagon surrounded by 5 isosceles triangles, as shown in the diagram at right. If the star has the angle measurements shown in the diagram, find the sum of the angles inside the shaded pentagon. Show all work.

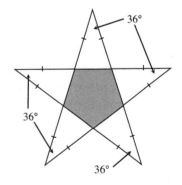

10-83.   Remember that the radian measure of a central angle of a circle is the ratio of the arc length to the radius (see problem 10-55).

   a.   What is the radian measure for a 45-degree central angle on a circle with radius 5 cm? What is the radian measure for a 45-degree central angle on a circle with radius 1 cm? Answer in terms of π.

   b.   The central angle of a circle has a radian measure of $\frac{\pi}{3}$. What is the measure of the central angle of the sector in degrees?

10-84.   **Multiple Choice:** $\triangle ABC$ is a right triangle and is graphed on coordinate axes. If $m\angle B = 90°$ and the slope of $\overline{AB}$ is $-\frac{4}{5}$, what is the slope of BC?

a. $\frac{4}{5}$ b. $\frac{5}{4}$ c. $-\frac{5}{4}$ d. $-\frac{4}{5}$

e. Cannot be determined

10-85.   At the University of the Great Plains the following data about engineering majors was collected:

	Engineering major	Other major	
Live Off Campus	800	7200	8000
Live On Campus	120	11,880	12,000
	920	19,080	20,000

a.   What is the conditional probability of living on campus, given that you know a student is an engineering major?

b.   Compare your answer to part (a) to the probability of living on campus.

c.   Are the two events, {living on campus} and {engineering major} associated? Use the probabilities to explain why or why not.

10-86.   The spinner at right has three regions: A, B, and C. If it is spun 80 times, how many times would you expect each region to result? Show your work.

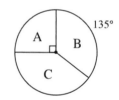

10-87.   Review what you know about the angles and arcs of circles below.

a.   A circle is divided into nine congruent sectors. What is the measure of each central angle?

b.   In the diagram at right, find $m\overarc{AD}$ and $m\angle C$ if $m\angle B = 97°$.

c.   In $\odot C$ at right, $m\angle ACB = 125°$ and $r = 8$ inches. Find $m\overarc{AB}$ and the length of $\overarc{AB}$. Then find the area of the smaller sector.

10-88.   Examine the diagram at right. Use the given geometric relationships to solve for x, y, and z. Be sure to justify your work by stating the geometric relationship and applicable theorem.

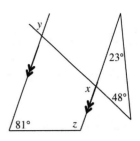

10-89.   Solve each equation below for x. Check your work.

a. $\frac{x}{2} = 17$ b. $\frac{x}{4} = \frac{1}{3}$ c. $\frac{x+6}{2} + 2 = \frac{5}{2}$ d. $\frac{4}{x} = \frac{5}{8}$

10-90.   Mrs. Cassidy solved the problem $(w-3)(w+5) = 9$ and got $w = 3$ and $w = -5$. Is she correct? If so, show how you know. If not, show how you know and find the correct solution.

10-91.   **Multiple Choice:** Which expression represents the area of the trapezoid at right?

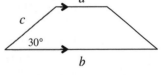

a. $\frac{c(a+b)}{4}$ b. $\frac{c(a+b)}{2}$

c. $\frac{bc}{2}$ d. $\frac{a+b+c}{2}$

e.   None of these

10.2.3 How can I pull it all together?

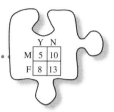

Applications of Probability

Probability has uses far beyond its origins in games of chance. Often, probabilities are based on survey data or data taken from a sample population. Today you will learn two new probability rules, and at the end of the lesson you will be given an opportunity to summarize the probability rules that you know.

10-92.   In a recent survey of college freshman, 35% of students checked the box next to "Exercise regularly," 33% checked the box next to "Eat five servings of fruits and vegetables a day," and 57% checked the box next to "Neither."

a.   Create a two-way table to represent this situation. Include row and column totals.

b.   What is the probability that a freshman in this study exercises regularly *and* eats 5 servings of fruits and vegetables each day?

c.   What is the probability that a freshman in this study exercises regularly *or* eats 5 servings of fruits and vegetables each day?

d.   Do you think that freshmen who eat 5 servings of fruit and vegetables per day are more likely to exercise? In other words, are exercising and eating associated?

e.   Compare and contrast a two-way table with an area model.

10-93. DOUBLE SPIN

Remember Double Spin, the game at the fair from Chapter 4?
The player gets to spin a spinner twice, but only wins if the
same amount comes up both times. The $100 sector is $\frac{1}{8}$ of the
circle. Nick is currently playing the game.

a.   Make an area model to show the sample space of every possible outcome
     for two spins. What is the probability that Nick wins?

b.   When Nick came home from the fair, he told Zack that he had won some
     money in the Double Spin game. Knowing that Nick won some money,
     what are the chances that he won $100?

c.   Make a two-way table that shows the probabilities for the Double Spin
     game. How does your table compare to the area model from part (a)?
     Explain.

d.   A mathematical way to express the conditional probability relationship is:

$$P(A \text{ given } B) = \frac{P(A \text{ and } B)}{P(B)} .$$

     This relationship is called the **Multiplication Rule**. (You will learn why it
     is called that in the next problem.) Verify your answer to part (b) using
     the Multiplication Rule. Be sure to define events A and B.

10-94. ANOTHER DEFINITION FOR INDEPENDENCE

a.   To learn how the Multiplication Rule got its name, rewrite the
     Multiplication Rule starting with "P(A and B) = ".

b.   Write the relationship between event A and event B for when they are
     independent using symbols.

c.   Substitute the independence relationship from part (b) into the
     Multiplication Rule that you wrote for part (a) to get another definition for
     independence.

10-95. The Laundry Shop sells washers and dryers. The owner of the store, Mr. McGee, thinks that a customer who purchases a washer is more likely to purchase a dryer than a customer that did not purchase a washer. He analyzes the sales from the last month and finds that a total of 240 customers made purchases. He counts 180 washers that were purchased and 96 dryers that were purchased.

Mr. McGee then counts the number of sales that included both a washer and a dryer and finds 72 customers purchased both.

Is there an association between the purchase of washers and dryers? Explain and show your reasoning using the relationships that you have learned in this lesson.

10-96. SHIFTY SHAUNA

Shauna has a bad relationship with the truth – she doesn't usually tell it! In fact, whenever Shauna is asked a question, she rolls a die. If it comes up 6, she tells the truth. Otherwise, she lies.

a. If Shauna flips a fair coin and you ask her how it came out, what is the probability that she says "heads" *and* is telling the truth? Choose a method to solve this problem and carefully record your work. Be ready to share your solution method with the class.

b. Suppose Shauna flips a fair coin and you ask her whether it came up heads or tails. What is the probability that she says "heads"? (Hint: The answer is not $\frac{1}{12}$!)

c. Suppose Shauna tells you that the coin says heads. What is the probability that she really did flip heads?

d. Is whether Shauna lies or tells the truth independent of whether the coin lands on heads or tails?

10-97.   It is generally assumed that there is no relationship between height and IQ (a measure of intelligence). Thus, the heights for 175 randomly selected people are independent of their IQs.

Using this assumption, complete the two-way table below.

	Below average height	Above average height	
Below average IQ			70
Above average IQ			105
	50	125	175

10-98.   A spinner has just two colors, red and blue. The probability the spinner will land on blue is x.

a.   What is the probability it will land on red?

b.   Sketch an area model for spinning this spinner twice.

c.   When the spinner is spun twice, what is the probability that it will land on the same color both times?

d.   Given that the spinner lands on the same color twice, what is the probability that it landed on blue both times?

10-99.   On another spinner, blue occurs a fraction x of the time, while the red and green portions have equal area. There are no other colors on the spinner.

a.   Find the probability that the spinner will land on green.

b.   Sketch an area diagram for spinning the spinner twice.

c.   Shade the region on your area diagram corresponding to getting the same color on the spinner twice.

d.   What is the probability that both spins give the same color?

e.   If you know that you got the same color twice, what is the probability that the color was blue?

10-100.   LEARNING LOG

First, consider the Build-a-Farm game described in
problem 10-73. What are three different models you can
use to find probabilities? Title this Learning Log entry,
"Probability Rules" and include today's date.

Then summarize the probability rules you know as follows:

- State the Addition Rule. Also state the rule as a union or intersection,
  whichever is appropriate.

- State both versions of the Multiplication Rule (the multiplication and the
  division versions).

- State two different rules that define independence.

- For each rule, create examples from the Build-a-Farm game.

ETHODS AND MEANINGS

Conditional Probability and Independence

MATH NOTES

When you are calculating a probability, but have been given
additional information about an event that has already occurred,
you are calculating a **conditional probability**. For the conditional
probability P(A given B), you know that event B has occurred, so
event B becomes the sample space of all possible outcomes.
P(A given B) is the fraction of event B's outcomes that also include
event A, which is formally stated as the **Multiplication Rule**:

$$P(A \text{ given } B) = \frac{P(A \text{ and } B)}{P(B)}$$

Two events are **independent** when the outcome of one does not influence the
outcome of the other. Two independent events could both occur, but knowing event
B has occurred does not change the probability of event A occurring, thus
P(A given B) = P(A). When events are not independent, you say that they are
associated. That is, one event influences the other.

If you substitute the definition for independence, P(A given B) = P(A), into the
Multiplication Rule and rearrange the result, you get an alternate definition for
independence: If events A and B are independent, then P(A and B) = P(A) · P(B).
The converse of this statement is also true: If P(A and B) = P(A) · P(B), then A and
B are independent.

10-101. A technology group wants to determine if bringing a laptop on a trip that involves flying is related to people being on business trips. Data for 1000 random passengers at an airport was collected and summarized in the table below.

	Laptop	No laptop
Traveling for business	236	274
Not traveling for business	93	397

a. What is the probability of traveling with a laptop if someone is traveling for business?

b. Does it appear that there is an association between bringing a laptop on a trip that involves flying and traveling for business?

10-102. In a certain small town, 65% of the households subscribe to the daily paper, 37% subscribe to the weekly local paper, and 25% subscribe to both papers.

a. Make a two-way table to represent this data.

b. If a household is selected at random, what is the probability that it subscribes to at least one of the two papers? Shade these areas in your table.

c. Charlie's neighbor subscribes to a paper. What is the probability that he receives the daily paper?

10-103. The Sunshine Orange Juice Company wants its product in a one-quart container (1 quart equals 107.75 cubic inches). The manufacturer for their containers makes cylindrical cans that have a base that is 5 inches in diameter. What will be the height of the one-quart container?

10-104. The radian measure of a central angle of 90° is $\frac{\pi}{2}$. What must the radian measure of a central angle of 180° be? How can you tell without actually computing the radian measure?

10-105. The mat plan for a three-dimensional solid is shown at right.

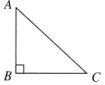

a. On graph paper, draw *all* of views of this solid. (There are six views.) Compare the views. Are any the same?

b. Find the volume and surface area of the solid. Explain your method.

c. Do the views you drew in part (a) help calculate volume or surface area? Explain.

10-106. For the triangle at right, find each trigonometric ratio below. The first one is done for you.

a. $\tan C = \frac{AB}{BC}$

b. $\sin C$

c. $\tan A$

d. $\cos C$

e. $\cos A$

f. $\sin A$

10-107. Review circle relationships as you answer the questions below.

a. On your paper, draw a diagram of $\odot B$ with $\overset{\frown}{AC}$. If $m\overset{\frown}{AC} = 80°$ and the length of the radius of $\odot B$ is 10, find the length of chord $\overline{AC}$.

b. Now draw a diagram of a circle with two chords, $\overline{EF}$ and $\overline{GH}$, that intersect at point K. If $EF = 15$, $EK = 6$, and $HK = 3$, what is GK?

10.3.1 What if the sample space is very large?

•••

The Fundamental Principle of Counting

Phone numbers in the U.S. are composed of a three-digit area code followed by seven digits. License plates in some states are made up of three letters followed by a three-digit number. Postal ZIP codes are made up of five digits, and another four digits are often added. To win the lottery in one state you need to select the correct five numbers from all the possible choices of five numbers out of 56. Consider these questions:

- How likely is it that you could win the lottery?

- Are there enough phone numbers for the dramatic increase in cell phones, tablets, and e-readers for books, many of which use unseen phone numbers to download information?

- Jay wants to know the probability of randomly getting JAY on his license plates so he can avoid paying the extra amount for a personalized license plate.

The sample spaces for these questions are very large. Imagine trying to draw a tree diagram! Tree diagrams with three or four branches, branching two or three times, are messy enough. You need a way to count possibilities without having to draw a complete diagram. In this and the next two lessons, you and your team will develop some strategies that will allow you to account for all possibilities without having to make a complete list or draw a complete tree diagram. As you work on the problems in this lesson, discuss the following questions with your team:

What decisions am I making when I make a systematic list?

How many decisions do I need to make?

How many ways are there to make each decision?

How can I use the patterns in a tree diagram to find the total number of branches?

10-108. Nick came across the following problem: If a 4-digit number is randomly selected from all of the 4-digit numbers that use the digits $1, 2, 3, 4, 5, 6,$ and 7, with repeated digits allowed, what is the probability that the selected number is 2763? Nick knew that he had to figure out how many numbers were possible, in order to know the size of his sample space.

a. Nick started to make a systematic list of the possibilities, but after the first few he gave up. What is the difficulty in trying to create a list?

b. Next he started a tree diagram. What problem did he encounter with the tree?

c. Nick decided he needed a shortcut strategy for organizing this problem; otherwise he was going to be up all night. He started by asking himself, *"How many decisions (about the digits) do I need to make?"* With your team discuss his first question and then consider his next question, *"How many choices do I have for each decision (each digit)?"*

d. Audrey was at her house working on the same problem. She was thinking of a tree diagram, when she asked herself, *"How many branch points will this tree have?"* and *"How many branches at each point?"* What are the answers to her questions? How are these questions related to the one that Nick was pondering?

e. At the same moment, they text messaged each other that they were stuck. When they talked, they realized they were on the same track. The problem asks for four-digit numbers, so there are four decisions. Simultaneously they said, *"We need a **decision chart**."* They wrote the following on their papers:

$$\overline{} \quad \overline{} \quad \overline{} \quad \overline{}$$
1st digit   *2nd digit*   *3rd digit*   *4th digit*

How many choices are there for each decision? How many four digit numbers are there?

f. What is the probability that the randomly selected number will be 2763?

10-109. How many four-digit numbers could you make with the digits $1, 2, 3, 4, 5, 6,$ and 7 if you could not use any digit more than once in the four-digit number? Make a decision chart and explain the similarities and differences between this situation and the one described in problem 10-108.

10-110. The basis for a decision chart is the **Fundamental Principle of Counting**.
Read the Math Notes box at the end of this lesson to help you understand the
Fundamental Principle of Counting. Then use a decision chart to answer each
question below.

    a.   A game contains nine discs, each with one of the numbers 1, 2, 3, 4, 5, 6,
7, 8, or 9 on it. How many different three-digit numbers can be formed by
choosing any three discs, without replacing the discs?

    b.   A new lotto game called Quick Spin has three wheels, each with the
numbers 1, 2, 3, 4, 5, 6, 7, 8, and 9 equally spaced around the rim. Each
wheel is spun once, and the numbers the arrows point to are recorded in
order. How many three-digit numbers are possible?

    c.   Explain the similarities and differences between part (a) and part (b).

10-111. Marcos is selecting classes for next year. He
plans to take English, physics, government, pre-
calculus, Spanish, and journalism. His school
has a six-period day, so he will have one of these
classes each period.

    a.   How many different schedules are
possible?

    b.   How many schedules are possible with
first-period pre-calculus?

    c.   What is the probability that Marcos will get first-period pre-calculus?

    d.   What is the probability that Marcos will get both first-period pre-calculus
and second-period physics?

10-112. CAN MY CALCULATOR FIND IT FASTER?

a. How many possible ways can the letters in the word MATH be arranged?

b. On your calculator, find the **factorial** function, $n!$ or !. On many scientific calculators, it can be found by pressing the PRB key. On many graphing calculators, it is a function in the math menu and probability submenu.

Find the value of 7 factorial (written 7!), then 6!, then 5!, 4!, ... , 1!

c. How do you think your calculator computes 5!

d. Explain why 4! gives the correct solution to the possible number of ways to arrange the letters M A T H.

e. What happens when you try to find 70! with your calculator? Why?

10-113. Remembering what $n!$ means can help you do some messy calculations quickly, as well as help you do problems that might be too large for your calculator's memory.

For instance, if you wanted to calculate $\frac{9!}{6!}$, you could use the $n!$ button on your calculator and find that 9! = 362,880 and 6! = 720, so $\frac{9!}{6!} = \frac{362880}{720} = 504$.

You could also use a simplification technique. Since
$9! = 9 \bullet 8 \bullet 7 \bullet 6 \bullet 5 \bullet 4 \bullet 3 \bullet 2 \bullet 1$ and $6! = 6 \bullet 5 \bullet 4 \bullet 3 \bullet 2 \bullet 1$, you can rewrite $\frac{9!}{6!} = \frac{9 \cdot 8 \cdot 7 \cdot 6 \cdot 5 \cdot 4 \cdot 3 \cdot 2 \cdot 1}{6 \cdot 5 \cdot 4 \cdot 3 \cdot 2 \cdot 1} = 9 \cdot 8 \cdot 7 = 504$.

Use this simplification technique to simplify each of the following problems before computing the result.

a. $\frac{10!}{8!}$
b. $\frac{70!}{68!}$
c. $\frac{7!}{4!3!}$
d. $\frac{20!}{18!2!}$

METHODS AND MEANINGS

MATH NOTES

Fundamental Principle of Counting

The **Fundamental Principle of Counting** is a method for counting the number of outcomes (the size of the sample space) of a probabilistic situation, often where the order of the outcomes matters. If event {A} has *m* outcomes, and event {B} has *n* outcomes after event {A} has occurred, then the event {A} followed by event {B} has *m* • *n* outcomes.

For a sequence of events, a tree diagram could be used to count the number of outcomes, but if the number of outcomes is large a **decision chart** is more useful.

For example, how many three-letter arrangements could be made by lining up any three blocks, chosen from a set of 26 alphabet blocks, if the first letter must be a vowel? There are three decisions (three blocks to be chosen), with 5 choices for the first letter (a vowel), 25 for the second, and 24 for the third. According to the Fundamental Principle of Counting, the total number of possibilities is:

$$\underset{\text{1st decision}}{\underline{5}} \cdot \underset{\text{2nd decision}}{\underline{25}} \cdot \underset{\text{3rd decision}}{\underline{24}} = 3000 \ .$$

This decision chart is a way to represent a tree with 5 branches for the first alphabet block, followed by 25 branches for each of those branches; each of those 125 branches would then have 24 branches representing the possibilities for the third alphabet block.

10-114. A Scrabble® player has four tiles with the letters A, N, P, and S.

a. How many arrangements of these letters are possible?

b. Draw a tree diagram that shows how to get the arrangements and explain how a decision chart represents the tree.

c. What is the probability of a two-year-old randomly making a word using the four letters?

10-115. Five students are running for Junior class president. They must give speeches before the election committee. They draw straws to see who will go first, second, etc. In how many different orders could they give their speeches?

10-116. Parents keep telling their teens to "turn down the music" or "turn off the computer" when studying. But teens insist that these "distractions" actually help them study better! In order to put this argument to rest, a psychologist studied whether subjects were able to memorize 20 index cards while listening to loud music or studying in silence. The sixty subjects had these results:

	Able to memorize	Not able to memorize
Loud music	9	36
Silence	3	12

a. What is the probability that a randomly chosen subject is able to memorize the index cards?

b. What is the probability that a music listener memorizes the index cards?

c. According to the data from this study, is the ability to memorize independent of listening to loud music?

10-117. Marty and Gerri played Pick a Tile, in which the player reaches into two bags. One bag contains square tiles and the other circular tiles. The bag with squares contains three yellow, one blue, and two red squares. The bag with circles has one yellow and two red circles. In order to win the game (and a large stuffed animal), a player must choose one blue square and one red circle.

a. Complete the two-way table below.

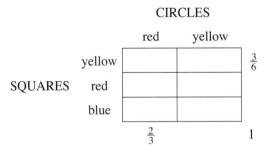

b. What is the probability of a player choosing the winning blue-red combination?

c. When Marty pulled her hand out of the bag, Gerri squealed with delight because she thought she saw something blue. If it was something blue, what is the probability that Marty won a stuffed animal?

10-118. The *sum* of the lengths of the edges of a cube is 1200 cm. Find the surface area and the volume of the cube.

10-119. The circle at right is inscribed in a regular hexagon. Find the area of the shaded region.

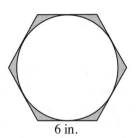

6 in.

10-120. **Multiple Choice:** Examine ⊙*L* at right. Which of the mathematical statements below is not necessarily true?

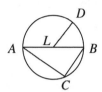

a. $LD = AL$

b. $m\angle DLB = m\widehat{DB}$

c. $\overline{LD} \parallel \overline{CB}$

d. $m\widehat{BC} = 2m\angle BAC$

e. $2AL = AB$

10.3.2 How can I count arrangements?

Permutations

There are many kinds of counting problems. In this lesson you will learn to recognize problems that involve arrangements. In some cases outcomes will be repeated, but in others they will not. A list of **permutations** includes different arrangements of distinct objects chosen from a set of objects. In other words, permutations are arrangements of elements without using any element more than once, and without repetition. As you work on the problems in this lesson discuss the following questions with your team:

> When I make a decision chart, how many choices do I have after I make the
> first choice? The second? The third? …

> Can I use the same choice again?

> Can this situation be represented as a permutation?

> What patterns can I find in these problems?

10-121.   Jasper finally managed to save enough money to open a savings account at the credit union. When he went in to open the account, the accounts manager told him that he needed to select a four-digit PIN (personal identification number). She also said that he could not repeat a digit, but that he could use any of the digits 0, 1, 2, …, 9 for any place in his four-digit PIN.

   a.   How many different PIN's are possible?

   b.   Notice that the decision chart for this problem looks like the beginning of 10!, but it does not go all the way down to 1. Factorials can be used to represent this problem, but you must compensate for the factors that you do not use, so you can write $\frac{10!}{6!}$. Discuss with your team how this method gives the same result as your decision chart.

10-122.   With your team, discuss how you could use factorials to represent each of the following situations. Then find the solutions. Four of the five problems involve permutations, and one does not. As you work, discuss with your team which problems fit the definition for permutations and why or why not. Write your answers both as factorials and as whole numbers.

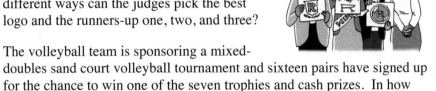

a.   Fifty-two contestants entered a contest for a new school logo design. In how many different ways can the judges pick the best logo and the runners-up one, two, and three?

b.   The volleyball team is sponsoring a mixed-doubles sand court volleyball tournament and sixteen pairs have signed up for the chance to win one of the seven trophies and cash prizes. In how many different ways can the teams finish in the top seven slots?

c.   Carmen is getting a new locker at school, and the first thing she must do is decide on a new locker combination. The three-number locker combination can be picked from the numbers 0 through 35. How many different locker combinations could she create if none of the numbers can be repeated?

d.   How many three-number locker combinations could Carmen make up if zero could only be the second or third number and none of the numbers can be repeated?

e.   How many locker combinations can Carmen have if she can use any of the numbers 0 through 35 and she can repeat numbers? Is this still a permutation? Explain why you think that it is or is not.

10-123. Problems about the order of teams or winners, and questions about how many numbers you could make without repeating any digits, are called **permutations**.

a. Below is a list of all of the license plate letter triples that can be made with the letters A, B, and C.

AAA	BBB	CCC	AAB	ABA
BAA	AAC	ACA	CAA	ABB
BAB	BBA	ACC	CAC	CCA
ABC	ACB	CAB	BAC	CBA
BCA	BCC	CBC	CCB	CBB
BCB	BBC			

How is this list different from all the arrangements a child can make on a line on the refrigerator door with three magnetic letters A, B, and C? Make the list of arrangements the child can make with the refrigerator magnets. Why are the lists different? Which one is a permutation?

b. Imagine a group of 8 candidates: one will become president, one vice president, and one secretary of the school senate. Now imagine a different group of 8 applicants, three of whom will be selected to be on the spirit committee. How will the lists of three possible people selected from the 8 people differ? Which list would be longer? Which is a permutation?

c. Consider these two situations. Decide if they are permutations. Why or why not?

• The possible 4-digit numbers you could write if you could choose any digit from the numbers 2, 3, 4, 5, 6, 7, 8, and you could use digits several times.

• All the 4-digit numbers you could make using seven square tiles numbered 2, 3, 4, 5, 6, 7, and 8.

d. What are the important characteristics that a counting problem has to have in order to classify it as a permutation problem? Discuss this with your team and then write a *general* method for counting the number of arrangements in any problem that could be identified as a permutations problem.

10-124. **WHAT IS THE FORMULA?**

a. In part (a) of problem 10-122 you calculated how many ways judges could pick the logo contest winner and three runners up from 52 contestants. The answer can be written using factorials as $\frac{52!}{48!}$. Explain where these numbers came from.

b. The logo contest situation can be thought of as finding the number of possible arrangements of 52 elements arranged 4 at a time. Reexamine your answers to parts (b) and (c) of problem 10-122 and use your answers to write a general formula to calculate the number of possible arrangements of n objects arranged r at a time. Begin your formula with $_nP_r = .$

c. Use your formula from part (b) above to calculate:

   i. $_7P_4$ *ii.* $_{52}P_4$ *iii.* $_{16}P_7$

10-125. **ANAGRAMS**

a. How many distinct ways can the letters in the word MASH be arranged?

b. How many distinct ways can the letters in the word SASH be arranged? Use a tree diagram if it helps.

c. How many distinct ways can the letters in the word SASS be arranged?

d. Express your answers to parts (b) and (c) using fractions with factorials. The numerators should both be 4!.

e. How can you use fractions with factorials to account for repeated letters when counting the number of arrangements?

10-126. Sasha wonders how many distinct ways she can arrange the letters in her name. She thinks the answer is $\frac{5!}{4!} = 5$. What is her mistake? What is the correct answer, written using factorials?

METHODS AND MEANINGS

MATH NOTES

n! and Permutations

A **factorial** is shorthand for the product of a list of consecutive, descending whole numbers from the largest down to 1:

$$n! = n(n-1)(n-2) \ldots (3)(2)(1)$$

For example, 4 factorial or $4! = 4 \cdot 3 \cdot 2 \cdot 1 = 24$ and
$6! = 6 \cdot 5 \cdot 4 \cdot 3 \cdot 2 \cdot 1 = 720$.

A **permutation** is an arrangement of items in which the order of selection matters and items cannot be selected more than once. The number of permutations that can be made by selecting r items from a set of n items can be represented with tree diagrams or decision charts, or calculated
$_nP_r = \frac{n!}{(n-r)!} = n(n-1)(n-2)\ldots(n-r+1)$.

For example, eight people are running a race. In how many different ways can they come in first, second, and third? The result can be represented $_8P_3$, which means the number of ways to choose *and* arrange three different (not repeated) things from a set of eight.

$$_8P_3 = \frac{8!}{(8-3)!} = \frac{8!}{5!} = \frac{8 \cdot 7 \cdot 6 \cdot 5 \cdot 4 \cdot 3 \cdot 2 \cdot 1}{5 \cdot 4 \cdot 3 \cdot 2 \cdot 1} = 8 \cdot 7 \cdot 6 = 336$$

Review & Preview

10-127. For the homecoming football game the cheerleaders at High Tech High printed each letter of the name of the school's mascot, WIZARDS, on a large card. Each card has one letter on it, and each cheerleader is supposed to hold up one card. At the end of the first quarter, they realize that someone has mixed up the cards.

    a. How many ways are there to arrange the cards?

    b. If they had not noticed the mix up, what would be the probability that the cards would have correctly spelled out the mascot?

10-128.   Twelve horses raced in the CPM Derby.

    a.   How many ways could the horses finish in the top three places?

    b.   If you have not already done so, write your answer to part (a) as a fraction with factorials.

10-129.   An engineer is designing the operator panel for a water treatment plant. The operator will be able to see four LED lights in a row that indicate the condition of the water treatment system. LEDs can be red, yellow, green, or off. How many different conditions can be signaled with the LEDs?

10-130.   An insurance company wants to charge a higher premium to drivers of red cars because they believe that they get more speeding tickets. A research company collected the following data to investigate their claim. Use the data below to decide if the insurance company should be charging a higher premium to drivers of red cars.

Total: 20,000 cars with 507 speeding tickets

Red Cars: 348 red cars with 9 speeding tickets.

10-131.   A survey of local car dealers revealed that 64% of all cars sold last month had a Green Fang system, 28% had alarm systems, and 22% had both Green Fang and alarm systems.

    a.   What is the probability one of these cars selected at random had neither Green Fang nor an alarm system?

    b.   What is the probability that a car had Green Fang and was not protected by an alarm system?

    c.   Are having Green Fang and an alarm system disjoint (mutually exclusive) events?

    d.   Use the alternative definition of independence (see the Math Notes box in Lesson 10.2.3) to determine if having Green Fang is associated with having an alarm.

10-132. In the past, many states had license plates composed of three letters followed by three digits (0 to 9). Recently, many states have responded to the increased number of cars by adding one digit (1 to 9) ahead of the three letters. How many more license plates of the second type are possible? What is the probability of being randomly assigned a license plate containing ALG 2?

10-133. Describe the solid represented by each net below.

a.

b.

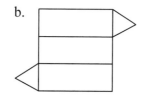

c.

10.3.3 How many groups are possible?

··

Combinations

In the previous lesson you learned a method for counting arrangements, including permutations. In this lesson you will consider questions such as how many five-card poker hands are possible, how many spirit committees can be selected from the Junior class, or your chances of winning the lottery.

In a five-card poker hand, the *arrangement* of the cards does *not* matter. Since all the spirit committee members have equal status, the *order* in which they are selected does *not* matter. If you have a winning lottery ticket, you will not care about the order in which the numbers are drawn. In these situations, you need to count the **combinations**. As you work with your team on the problems in this lesson, use the following questions to help focus your discussion:

Does the particular arrangement matter?

What are the relationships among these situations?

10-134. Five members of the Spirit Club have volunteered for the club governing board. These members are Al, Barbara, Carl, Dale, and Ernie. The club members will select three of the five as board members for the next year. One way to do this would be to elect a governing committee of three in which all members would have the same title. A second way would be to select a president, vice-president, and secretary.

a. How many different lineups of officers are possible? This means a president, vice-president, and a secretary are chosen. Thus, Al as president, Barbara as vice-president, and Carl as secretary would be a different possibility from Al as president, Barbara as secretary, and Carl as vice-president.

b. How many different three-member committees are possible? In this case, it is a good idea to make a list of all the possibilities, which are called **combinations**.

c. Felicia decides that she wants to volunteer as well.

   i. How many different possibilities for officers are possible now?

   ii. How many different governing committees are possible now? Again, make the list of all of the possibilities, or combinations.

Problem continues on next page →

10-134.   *Problem continued from previous page.*

> d.   Since there are more volunteers, the spirit club has decided to appoint another committee member.
>
> > i.   If they add a treasurer to the list of officers, how many different ways are there to select the four officers are possible?
> >
> > ii. If they choose a governing committee of four, how many possibilities are there?

10-135.   Compare the results you got for each set of numbers in problem 10-134 when the roles were determined (permutations) and when there were no specific roles (combinations).

> a.   How do the number of combinations and permutations compare in each situation?
>
> b.   Work with your team to develop a conjecture about the mathematical relationship between permutations and combinations chosen from the same sized groups. Be prepared to share your thinking with the class.
>
> c.   Test your conjecture by calculating the number of permutations and combinations of 2 items chosen from 6. Does it work?
>
> d.   How can you generalize your conjecture so that it can be applied to permutations and combinations of r items chosen from n? Write a formula relating permutations (written $_nP_r$) and combinations (written $_nC_r$).

10-136.   Now you will use your calculator to test the formula you wrote in problem 10-135.

> a.   Try 4 items chosen from 20. Does your formula work?
>
> b.   With your team, find a way to justify the logic of your formula. How can you convince someone that it has to be correct for all numbers?

10-137.   In one state lottery, there are 56 numbers from which a player can choose six.

> a.   Does the order in which the numbers are chosen matter?
>
> b.   Find the number of possible combinations for a set of 6 winning lottery numbers.
>
> c.   What is the probability of selecting the six winning numbers?

10-138.   In the game of poker called Five-Card Draw, each player is dealt five cards from a standard deck of 52 cards. While players tend to arrange the cards in their hands, the order in which they get them does not matter. How many five-card poker hands are possible? Use the methods you developed in today's investigation to answer this question.

MᴇᴛHODS AND Mᴇᴀɴɪɴɢs

MATH NOTES

Combinations

When selecting committees, it matters who is selected but not the **order** of selection or any **arrangement** of the groups. Selections of committees, or of lists of groups without regard to the order within the group, are called **combinations**. Note that combinations do not include repeated elements.

For example: Eight people are eligible to receive $500 scholarships, but only three will be selected. How many different ways are there to select a group of three?

This is a problem of counting combinations. $_8C_3$ represents the number of ways to choose three from a set of eight. This is sometimes read as "eight *choose* three."

To compute the number of combinations, first calculate the number of permutations and then divide by the number of ways to arrange each permutation.

$$_8C_3 = \frac{_8P_3}{3!} = \frac{8!}{5!3!} = 56$$

In general: Number of ways to choose = $\frac{\text{\# of ways to choose and arrange}}{\text{\# of ways to arrange}}$

$$_nC_r = \frac{_nP_r}{r!} = \frac{n!}{(n-r)!r!}$$

10-139.   How many different batting orders can be made from the nine starting players on a baseball team? Write the answer using factorials and as a number.

10-140.   What do you think 0! is equal to?

   a.   Try it on your calculator to see what you get.

   b.   What does $_8P_8$ mean? What *should* $_8P_8$ be equal to? Write $_8P_8$ using the factorial formula. Why is it necessary for 0! to equal 1?

   c.   Do you remember how to show that $2^0 = 1$? You can use a sequence of powers of two like this: $\frac{2^4}{2} = 2^3$, $\frac{2^3}{2} = 2^2$, $\frac{2^2}{2} = 2^1$, so $\frac{2^1}{2} = 2^0$. Since $\frac{2^1}{2} = 1$ you also know that $2^0 = 1$.

         You can construct a similar pattern for 0!, starting with $\frac{5!}{5} = 4!$ and then $\frac{4!}{4} = 3!$. Continue the pattern and make an argument to justify that 0! = 1.

10-141.   For each of the following expressions, write a factorial expression and then compute the value. Use the $_nC_r$ and $_nP_r$ functions on your calculator to make the computation.

   a. $_{10}P_8$ b. $_{10}C_8$ c. $_6C_1$

10-142.   Of the 63 drinks at Joe's Java and Juice Hut, 42 contain coffee and 21 contain dairy products. If Alexei randomly chooses a drink, what is the probability of getting a drink with both coffee and a dairy product? What is the probability of getting neither coffee nor a dairy product? Assume that choosing a coffee drink is independent of choosing a dairy-product drink. See if you can answer these questions without making a two-way table first.

10-143.   Akio coaches the girls volleyball team. He needs to select players for the six different starting positions from his roster of 16 players. On Akio's teams, each position has its own special responsibility: setter, front left-side and middle hitters, back right- and left-side passers, and libero.

   a.   If he chooses randomly, how many ways can Akio form his starting lineup?

   b.   How many of those teams have Sidney playing in the libero position?

   c.   If Akio chooses starting teams randomly, what is the probability (in percent) that Sidney gets chosen as the starting libero?

   d.   If Akio just randomly chooses six players to start, without regard to who plays which position, what is the probability that Sidney gets chosen?

10-144. If $f(n)=n!$, evaluate each of the following ratios.

   a. $\dfrac{f(5)}{f(3)}$ b. $\dfrac{f(6)}{f(4)}$ c. $\dfrac{f(9)}{f(7)f(2)}$

10-145. Consider the following anagrams.

   a. How many distinct ways can the letters in the word ITEMS be arranged?

   b. How many distinct ways can the letters in the word STEMS be arranged?

   c. How many distinct ways can the letters in the word SEEMS be arranged?

   d. What makes these counts different?

10.3.4 What kind of counting problem is this?

Categorizing Counting Problems

One of the biggest challenges in solving problems that involve counting techniques is deciding which method of counting to use. Selecting a counting method depends on whether different arrangements of elements will be considered to be different outcomes and on whether elements can be repeated in an outcome. As you work with your team on the Ice Cream Shop problem, starting a list of possibilities will be a useful strategy. The list may be too long to complete, but starting it might help you decide which counting technique to use.

10-146. THE ICE-CREAM SHOP

Friday was the seventh day of the heat wave with temperatures over 95° F, and DJ's Gourmet Ice-Cream Shop had only five flavors left: chocolate fudge, French vanilla, maple nut, lemon custard, and blueberry delight. Some customers ordered their ice cream in cones and some in a dish, but everyone ordered three scoops, the maximum DJ was allowing to ensure that the inventory would last.

On Saturday the temperature hit 100° F. DJ still had five flavors and both cones and dishes, but he decided to allow no more than one scoop of a particular flavor per customer in order to keep a balanced variety on hand. On Friday, the customers had more choices than on Saturday because they could order a cone (which most people eat from the top down) or a dish (where scoops can be eaten in any order) and they could have three different flavors or more than one scoop of their favorite.

DJ's Gourmet Ice-Cream Shop advertises that it has ***Over 100 Choices!*** When DJ's customers complained that he did not have 100 flavors, he responded, "*But I still offer more than 100 choices!*" Was that true on both Friday and Saturday?

Your Task: There are four counting problems here, two for Friday and two for Saturday. Describe each situation and show how to calculate the number of choices customers have once they decide on a cone or a dish.

Discussion Points

What are some possible outcomes for this situation? Can I start a list?

Does the arrangement or order of the scoops matter?

Can the choices be repeated?

Does the description of the outcomes for this situation fit any of the counting formulas I know?

Could this situation involve several different counting situations?

Further Guidance

10-147.   It is useful to organize the information in a large 2×2 chart with columns for Friday and Saturday and rows for dishes and cones. With your team, set up a 2×2 chart or obtain the Lesson 10.3.4 Resource Page from your teacher and use it to organize the different possibilities. Describe each problem in relation to whether it involves arrangements or repeats elements, and make a prediction about which situation has the greatest number of choices and which has the least.

10-148.   Use what you have learned about the Fundamental Principal of Counting, permutations, and combinations to solve three of the four problems.

10-149.   The fourth problem is more cumbersome because the order of the scoops does not matter and all of the scoops could be different, two could be the same and one different, or all could be the same. This problem has a number of subproblems, and for at least one of them you may need to make a list. Work with your team to identify and solve each subproblem.

Further Guidance section ends here.

10-150. Charlie and his nephew, Jake, who is a
bottomless hunger pit, went to the state fair.
Charlie had promised he would buy Jake three
snacks. He can have one when they arrive, one
mid-afternoon, and one when they were about to
leave or, as Jake prefers, he can have all of the
snacks all at once. At the food stand the menu
included seven items:

Corn Dogs	Popcorn
Root Beer	Orange Soda
Sno Cones	Cotton Candy
Candied Apples	

Jake likes everything on the menu so much that he would not mind having any
three items, or even any two or three of the same thing. Uncle Charlie thinks
variety is good, so he wants Jake to choose three different things.

Your Task: With your team, categorize the alternatives for Jake and Charlie in
terms of arrangements and repetition. Then describe and justify the solution
method you would use to count the number of possibilities for each situation.
Finally, figure out how many possible ways there are for Jake to choose his
snacks for each situation.

10-151. When Jake and Charlie disagree, Jake has a two-thirds chance of getting his
way. Draw an area model or tree diagram and calculate the probability that
Charlie prevails and Jake has to order three different items and have his snacks
spread out.

10-152. LEARNING LOG

Summarize the differences between combinations and
permutations, anagrams, and other counting problems
that involve the Fundamental Principle of Counting.
Make your explanation clear and thorough enough that a
student who is just transferring into your class could
understand counting techniques. Include information about whether
arrangements are important and whether elements can be repeated and give
examples that illustrate the different possibilities. Title this entry, "Counting
Problems and Strategies" and label it with today's date.

10-153.   From a batch of 500 light bulbs, how many ways can three be tested to see if they are defective?

10-154.   Mr. K wants to bring a variety of language textbooks to the classroom in which he teaches French. From his library at home, he found some that would be appropriate for the classroom: 4 Russian texts, 7 German texts, 1 Japanese text, 2 Italian texts, and 3 Danish texts. If he decides to bring one book of each language to the classroom, and put them in alphabetical order by language on his bookshelf (Danish, German, Italian, and so forth), how many different ways can Mr. K arrange the new language books?

10-155.   Joaquin is getting a new locker at school and the first thing he must do is decide on a new combination. The three number locker combination can be selected from the numbers 0 through 21.

   a.   How many different locker combinations can Joaquin choose if none of the numbers can be repeated?

   b.   With your understanding of permutations, combinations, and factorials, decide if the name "combination lock" is appropriate.

   c.   How many mathematical combinations are possible?

   d.   How many choices would there be if you could repeat a number, but not use the same number twice in a row?

10-156.   This problem is a checkpoint for finding angles in and areas of regular polygons. It will be referred to as Checkpoint 10.

   a.   What is the measure of each interior angle of a regular 20-gon?

   b.   Each angle of a regular polygon measures 157.5°. How many sides does this polygon have?

   c.   Find the area of a regular octagon with sides 5 cm.

   Check your answers by referring to the Checkpoint 10 materials located at the back of your book.

   Ideally, at this point you are comfortable working with these types of problems and can solve them correctly. If you feel that you need more confidence when solving these types of problems, then review the Checkpoint 10 materials and try the practice problems provided. From this point on, you will be expected to do problems like these correctly and with confidence.

10-157.   The first four factors of 7! are 7, 6, 5, and 4 or 7, $(7-1)$, $(7-2)$, and $(7-3)$.

      a.   Show the first four factors of 12! in the same way the factors of 7! are shown above.

      b.   What are the first six factors of $n!$?

      c.   What is $_nP_6$?

10-158.   Here is another way to think about the question: *"What is 0! ?"*

      a.   How many ways are there to choose all five items from a group of five items? What happens when you substitute into the factorial formula to compute $_5C_5$? Since you know (logically) what the result has to be, use this to explain what 0! must be equal to.

      b.   On the other hand, how many ways are there to choose *nothing* from a group of five items? And what happens when you try to use the factorial formula to compute $_5C_0$?

10-159.   A European high-speed passenger train is made up of two first-class passenger cars, five second-class cars, and a restaurant car. How many ways can the train be made up?

10.3.5 What are my chances of winning?

Some Challenging Probability Problems

In this lesson, you will have the opportunity to apply what you have learned about probability and counting principles to solve some interesting (and very challenging) problems. As you work with your team on one of the following problems, you may get stuck at some point along the way. Below are discussion questions that can help you to get started again.

What subproblems do I need to solve?

What simpler problem would help us to understand this problem?

How would I start a tree or a list?

Does order matter? Are the outcomes combinations, permutations, or something else?

Are these separate groups of outcomes? Are the probabilities independent?
Should I add or do I need to multiply?

Would it be easier to consider what is *not* an outcome?

10-160. THE CANDY DISH

A bowl contains three candies: two red and one green. Work with a partner and decide who is player A and who is player B. Then take turns choosing a candy from the bowl without looking. Player A takes one and holds on to it, then player B takes one. If the colors match, player A gets a point; if they differ, player B gets a point. Is this a fair game?

a. First try the game experimentally. Then show your analysis of the probabilities.

b. Now put four candies in the bowl, three of one color and one of another. Will this game be fair? Again, check experimentally then give your analysis using probabilities.

c. Are there other ways to put different numbers of two colors of candy in the bowl that would lead to a fair game while keeping the rest of the rules the same as in the previous two problems? Try a number of different possibilities (up to at least a total of 20 candies). Analyze each one using probability, make some hypotheses, and report any patterns you see in the results, conclusions, or generalizations that you can justify mathematically.

Problem continues on next page →

10-160.   *Problem continued from previous page.*

Your Task: Prepare a report or poster that shows:

- The number and variety of cases you investigated and analyzed.

- Your organization of the data, your analyses, and your general conclusions.

- The extent to which you can mathematically generalize your observations and justify your generalizations.

10-161.   CASINO DICE GAME

To play this game, you roll two dice. If your total on the first roll is 7 or 11 points, you win. If your total is 2, 3, or 12 points, you lose. If you get any other number (4, 5, 6, 8, 9, or 10), that number becomes your point. You then continue to roll until your point comes up again or until a 7 comes up. If your point comes up before you roll a 7, you win. If 7 comes up first, you lose. You ignore any outcomes that are not your point or 7.

a.   In pairs, play the game ten times. Record how many wins and losses your team has. Combine your information with other teams working on the problem. Are the results fairly even or were there many more wins or losses?

b.   The game you have been playing is the basic dice game played in casinos worldwide. What is the probability of winning?

Your Task: To calculate the probability of winning, you will need to identify and solve several subproblems. Prepare a report that shows each of the subproblems clearly, as well as how you solved each one. Your report should also show the exact probability of winning as a fraction as well as a decimal approximation.

10-162.   **An extra challenge:** Most casinos allow bettors to bet against the dice roller. In this case, the bettor wins whenever the roller would lose *except when the roller gets a 12 on the first roll.* When 12 comes up, the bettor does not win or lose and he or she just waits for the next roll. What is the probability of winning a bet against the roller? Which is the better bet, for or against? By how much?

10-163. Start with a list of the ways to get each sum 2, 3, ..., 12. For the remaining parts of this work, it will help to keep answers in fraction form.

    a. Find the probability of winning on the first roll.

    b. Find the probability of losing on the first roll.

    c. Find the probability of the game ending on the first roll.

10-164. Now consider the other ways to win by rolling the point before rolling a 7.

    a. Find the probability of rolling a 4.

    b. Find the probability of rolling a 4 before a 7. (Note that you are only interested in 4's and 7's for this problem.)

    c. Find the probability of rolling a 4 and then rolling another 4 before a 7. In other words, what is the probability of getting the outcome in part (a) and then the outcome in part (b)?

    d. Find the probability of rolling a 5.

    e. Find the probability of rolling a 5 before a 7. (You only care about 5's and 7's here.)

    f. Find the probability of rolling a 5 and another 5 before a 7.

    g. Find the probabilities for winning when your first roll is 6, 8, 9, or 10. Look for symmetry as you do this.

10-165. Make a list of all the ways to win.

    a. What is the probability of winning?

    b. If you won the game, what is the probability that you won by throwing 7 or 11 on the first throw?

    c. What is the probability of losing this game?

    d. Is it a fair game? Is it close to fair? Explain why casinos can allow betting on this game without expecting to lose money.

━━━━━━━ *Further Guidance* ━━━━━━━
section ends here.

10-166. TRIANGLES BY CHANCE

Obtain three dice from your teacher. You may also want some string, linguini, a compass, or some other building material.

a. Roll the three dice and use the numbers on the dice to represent the lengths of sides of a triangle. Build (or draw) the triangle. Record the three numbers in a table according to the type of triangle formed (scalene, isosceles, equilateral, or no triangle). For example, if 3, 3, and 5 came up on the dice, you would record 3, 3, 5 under the heading isosceles since a triangle with sides of length 3, 3, and 5 is isosceles.

b. Repeat this ten times, and then combine your information with the other teams working on this problem. Examine the data and discuss the results.

c. Based on your discussion, make an estimate for the probability of each outcome. Then calculate the theoretical probabilities.

Your Task: Complete a team report or poster that includes:

*   Initial estimates of probabilities with your team justification for each one.

*   The subproblems you solved, including how you counted the possible outcomes.

*   The theoretical probability for each case.

Further Guidance

10-167. First you will need to calculate the size of the sample space for rolling three dice.

a. How many ways come up so that the result is an equilateral triangle?

b. How many ways can the dice come up so that the result is an isosceles triangle?

c. How many ways can the dice come up so that the result is a scalene triangle?

d. How many outcomes lead to no triangle?

e. Use your results from parts (a) through (d) to compute the probabilities for each outcome.

———————— *Further Guidance* ————————
section ends here.

Core Connections Geometry

10-168.   POKER

In the basic game of five-card-draw poker, five cards are dealt to each player from a standard deck of 52 cards. Players place bets based on their estimate of their chances of winning. They then draw any number of cards (up to five) to see if they can improve their hands, and they make another round of placing bets.

The winning poker hands (assuming no wild cards) are described below, in order from best to worst. Poker is a game that has been played for many centuries. Players had established the order of winning hands centuries before mathematicians developed the counting techniques, which verified that the order was mostly correct based on the probability of getting the hand.

(Note: In the list below, J stands for Jack, Q stands for Queen, K stands for King, A stands for Ace, and X stands for any card.)

1.   Royal flush: 10-J-Q-K-A, all the same suit.

2.   Straight flush: such as, 7-8-9-10-J, any five in a row, all the same suit (A can be used before 2 or after K).

3.   Four of a kind: 2-2-2-2-X, four of a number or face card, and any other card.

4.   Full house: 7-7-7-A-A-, three of one kind and two of another.

5.   Flush: any five cards of the same suit, not all consecutive.

6.   Straight: 3-4-5-6-7, any five in a row, a mixture of 2 or more suits.

7.   Three of a kind: 8-8-8-J-A, three of a number or face card, the other two different.

8.   Two pair: 9-9-5-5-2, pairs of two different numbers or face cards, with one other number or face card.

9.   Two of a kind: A-A-7-8-J, any pair with three random others that do not match.

10.   Bust: no matches, no runs of five in a row, different suits.

Your Task: Calculate the number of five-card hands that can be selected from a deck of 52 cards, and then, for the first six of the above hands, calculate the number of ways the hand can be dealt, and the probability that a player will be dealt that hand. Prepare a team report or poster that describes your work on both the counting problems and the probabilities.

10-169. The most difficult Poker hand to get is a royal flush. To calculate the probability of getting a royal flush, you first need to determine the size of the sample space. How many five-card hands are possible if there are 52 cards to choose from? Then decide how many ways there are to make a royal flush.

    a.   What is the probability of getting a royal flush?

    b.   How many straight flushes are there that are all spades? Making a list will help you decide. Then how many straight flushes are there altogether?

    c.   What is the probability of getting a straight flush that is not a royal flush?

10-170. Flushes are five cards of one suit.

    a.   How many flushes are possible?

    b.   What is the probability of getting a flush?

10-171. Straights are five cards in a row, such as 4-5-6-7-8 of any suit.

    a.   How many straights are possible that include 2 or more suits? In other words, how many straights are possible that are not also straight flushes or royal flushes?

    b.   What is the probability of getting a straight?

10-172. How many ways are there to draw four cards that are the same number? Making a list will help. And how many ways are there to get the fifth card? What do you need to do to get the total number of five-card hands that contain four of a kind?

a. What is the probability of getting four of a kind?

b. Now consider a full house. First, think of listing the number of ways to get exactly three cards that are the same number. Once you know the three cards, how many ways are there to get the other two cards in your hand the same? What should you do with these two results to get the number of full houses possible?

c. What is the probability of getting a full house?

d. Recall your result for the number of ways to get three of a kind and figure out how many ways there are to get two cards that are different from the rest of the deck. Use this information to calculate the number of five-card hands with three matching numbers.

e. What is the probability of getting three of a kind?

f. Use a similar method for calculating the probability of getting two of a kind.

g. Think about how you calculated the number of full houses and about how you calculated the number of hands with four of a kind. Then calculate the number of hands with two pairs. What is the probability of getting two pairs?

h. What is the probability of drawing a hand that is a "bust?" How can you use the probabilities you have already calculated?

————— *Further Guidance* —————
section ends here.

MᴇTHODS AND Mᴇᴀɴɪɴɢꜱ

Definition of 0!

The use of the combinations formula when $r = n$ (when the number to be chosen is the same as the total number in the group) leads to a dilemma, as illustrated in the following example.

Suppose the Spirit Club has a total of three faithful members. Only one three-member governance committee is possible. If you apply the formula for combinations, you get $_3C_3 = \frac{_3P_3}{3!} = \frac{3!}{(3-3)!3!} = \frac{3!}{0!3!} = 1$. Does this make sense?

To resolve this question and make the formulas useful for all cases, mathematicians decided on this definition: $0! = 1$.

Review & Preview

10-173.   From a new shipment of 100 video games, how many ways can three games be tested to see if they are defective?

10-174.   Which is greater: $(5 - 2)!$ or $(5 - 3)!$? Justify your answer.

10-175.   Write an equivalent expression for each of the following situations that does not include the factorial (!) symbol.

a.   The first five factors of $(n - 3)!$

b.   The first five factors of $(n + 2)!$

c. $\frac{n!}{(n-3)!}$

d. $\frac{(n+2)!}{(n-2)!}$

Core Connections Geometry

10-176.   Of the students who choose to live on campus at Coastal College, 10% are
          seniors. The most desirable dorm rooms are in the newly constructed
          OceanView dorm, and 60% of the seniors live there, while 20% of the rest of
          the students live there.

          a.   Represent these probabilities in a two-way table.

          b.   What is the probability that a randomly selected resident of the OceanView
               dorm is a senior?

          c.   Use the alternative definition of independence (see the Math Notes box in
               Lesson 10.2.3) to determine if being a senior is associated with living in
               the Ocean View dorm.

10-177.   At 10:00 a.m. a radioactive material weighed 2 grams but at 6:00 p.m. it only
          weighed 0.45 grams. What were the approximate hourly multiplier and the
          hourly percent of decrease?

10-178.   A triangular prism has a volume of 600 cubic cm. The base is a right triangle
          with a hypotenuse of length 17 cm and one leg with length 15 cm.

          a.   Draw the figure.

          b.   Find the height of the prism.

          c.   Find the surface area of the prism.

          d.   Find all three angles of the triangle in the base of the prism.

10-179.   A pizza parlor has 12 toppings other than cheese.
          How many different pizzas can they create with five
          or fewer toppings? List all subproblems and
          calculate the solution.

10-180. Mike was asked to make his popular ten-layer dip for the tailgate party at the big football game. The ten layers are: three layers of mashed avocado, two layers of cheddar cheese, and one layer each of refried beans, sour cream, sliced olives, chopped tomatoes, and green onions. How many ways can Mike make the ten layers in a glass serving pan?

10-181. Write an equation and use it to solve this problem.

Jill has a 9-inch tall cylinder that she is using to catch water leaking from a pipe. The water level in the cylinder is currently 2 inches deep and is increasing at a rate of $\frac{1}{4}$-inch per hour. How long will it be before the water overflows?

10-182. Determine whether or not the two triangles in each pair below are similar. If so, write a flowchart to show your reasoning. If not, explain why not.

a.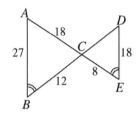

b.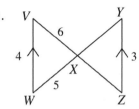

10-183. For each mat plan, create an isometric view of the solid.

a.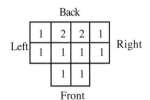

b.

10-184. Calculate the total surface area and volume of the prism at right. The bases are equilateral triangles.

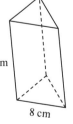

Chapter 10 Closure   What have I learned?

Reflection and Synthesis

The activities below offer you a chance to reflect
about what you have learned during this chapter. As
you work, look for concepts that you feel very
comfortable with, ideas that you would like to learn
more about, and topics you need more help with.
Look for connections between ideas as well as
connections with material you learned previously.

①   TEAM BRAINSTORM

What have you studied in this chapter? What ideas were important in what you
learned? With your team, brainstorm a list. Be as detailed as you can. To help
get you started, lists of Learning Log entries and Math Notes boxes are below.

What topics, ideas, and words that you learned *before* this chapter are connected
to the new ideas in this chapter? Again, be as detailed as you can.

How long can you make your list? Challenge yourselves. Be prepared to share
your team's ideas with the class.

Learning Log Entries
  - Lesson 10.1.2 – Inscribed Angles
  - Lesson 10.1.3 – Connections with Circles
  - Lesson 10.2.1 – Independent or Mutually Exclusive?
  - Lesson 10.2.3 – Probability Rules
  - Lesson 10.3.4 – Counting Problems and Strategies

Math Notes
  - Lesson 10.1.1 – Circle Vocabulary
  - Lesson 10.1.2 – More Circle Vocabulary
  - Lesson 10.1.3 – Inscribed Angle Theorem
  - Lesson 10.1.4 – Intersecting Chords
  - Lesson 10.1.5 – Points of Concurrency
  - Lesson 10.2.1 – Mutually Exclusive
  - Lesson 10.2.3 – Conditional Probability and Independence
  - Lesson 10.3.1 – Fundamental Principle of Counting
  - Lesson 10.3.2 – $n!$ and Permutations
  - Lesson 10.3.3 – Combinations
  - Lesson 10.3.5 – Definition of 0!

②   MAKING CONNECTIONS

Below is a list of the vocabulary used in this chapter. Make sure that you are familiar with all of these words and know what they mean. Refer to the glossary or index for any words that you do not yet understand.

arc length	arc measure	association
center	center-radius form	central angle
chord	circle	circumcenter
circumference	circumscribed	combination
conditional probability	decision chart	diameter
factorial	Fundamental Principle of Counting	
independent events	inscribed	Inscribed Angle Theorem
intercepted arc	major arc	minor arc
Multiplication Rule	mutually exclusive	permutation
perpendicular	probability	radius
sample space	secant	semicircle
similar	tangent	two-way table
$x^2 + y^2 = r^2$	zero factorial	

Make a concept map showing all of the connections you can find among the key words and ideas listed above. To show a connection between two words, draw a line between them and explain the connection. A word can be connected to any other word as long as you can justify the connection.

While you are making your map, your team may think of related words or ideas that are not listed here. Be sure to include these ideas on your concept map.

③   PORTFOLIO: EVIDENCE OF MATHEMATICAL PROFICIENCY

Showcase your new knowledge of circles by describing all the new circle tools you have developed (such as lengths of two intersecting chords are related, and what is special about an angle inscribed in a semicircle). Be sure to include diagrams.

Choose one or two problems from Lesson 10.1.5 that you feel best showcases your understanding of circles and carefully copy your work, modifying and expanding it if needed. Make sure your explanation is clear and in detail. Remember you are not only showcasing your understanding of the mathematics, but you are also showcasing your ability to communicate your justifications.

Showcase your understanding of counting methods by copying one of the solutions from Lesson 10.3.5, modifying and expanding it as needed. Again, make sure your explanation is clear and detailed.

           Core Connections Geometry

④   WHAT HAVE I LEARNED?

Most of the problems in this section represent typical problems found in this chapter. They serve as a gauge for you. You can use them to determine which types of problems you can do well and which types of problems require further study and practice. Even if your teacher does not assign this section, it is a good idea to try these problems and find out for yourself what you know and what you still need to work on.

Solve each problem as completely as you can. The table at the end of the closure section has answers to these problems. It also tells you where you can find additional help and practice with problems like these.

CL 10-185.   Copy the diagram at right onto your paper. Assume $\overline{AD}$ is tangent to $\odot C$ at D. Assume each part is a separate problem.

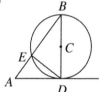

     a.   If $AD = 9$ cm and $AB = 15$ cm, what is the area of $\odot C$?

     b.   If the length of the radius of $\odot C$ is 10 cm and the $m\overarc{ED} = 30°$, what are $m\overarc{EB}$ and AD?

     c.   If $m\overarc{EB} = 86°$ and $BC = 7$ cm, find EB.

CL 10-186.   A circle has two intersecting chords as shown in the diagram at right. Find the value of x.

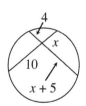

CL 10-187. Eight friends go to the movies to celebrate their win in academic facts competition. They want to sit together in a row with a student on each aisle. (Assume the row is 8 seats wide including 2 aisle seats.)

a. If Kristen wants to sit in an aisle seat, how many ways can they all sit in the row?

b. If they sit down randomly, what is the probability they end up with five boys on the left and three girls on the right?

c. They decide to arrange themselves randomly by using the first letter of their last names. But two of the students' last names begin with K, and three begin with S. How many ways can they arrange themselves by using the first letter of their last name?

CL 10-188. At East College, 7776 students are in the freshman class, 6750 are sophomores, 6750 are juniors, and the rest are seniors. About 18% of students in each class are in the performing arts.

a. If there are 27,000 undergraduates at the school, what is the probability of being a senior in the performing arts?

b. Is being in a performing art independent of your class standing?

c. If a student is in the performing arts, what is the probability that he or she is a senior?

CL 10-189. Beethoven wrote nine symphonies and Mozart wrote 27 piano concertos.

a. If the local radio station KALG wants to play two pieces, a Beethoven symphony and then a Mozart concerto, in how many ways can this be done?

b. The station manager has decided that on each successive night (seven days a week), a Beethoven symphony will be played, followed by a Mozart concerto, followed by a Schubert string quartet (there are 15 of those). How long could this policy be continued before exactly the same program would have to be repeated?

CL 10-190. Antonio and Giancarlo are playing a board game that uses three spinners, which are shown in the diagrams at right. On each turn the player has to spin the first spinner. The first spinner determines which of the other two spinners the player also has to spin. The second spin determines how far the player gets to move his marker.

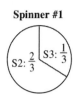

Spinner #1

a. What is the probability that Giancarlo will get to move his marker 4 or 6 spaces? Use a two-way table as needed.

Spinner #2

b. What is the probability he will have to stay put?

c. What is the probability that he will get to move?

Spinner #3

d. Antonio moved his marker 2 spaces. What is the probability that he spun S2 on the first spinner?

e. Explain your method for finding the probability in part (d) so that a student who was absent for today's work would understand conditional probability.

CL 10-191. Consider the solid represented by the mat plan at right.

a. Draw the front, right, and top view of this solid on graph paper.

3	1	0
0	1	1
0	2	3

Right

Front

b. Find the volume and surface area of this solid.

c. If this solid is enlarged by a linear scale factor of 3.5, what will be its new volume and surface area?

CL 10-192. Consider the descriptions of the different shapes below. Which shapes *must* be a parallelogram? If a shape does not have to be a parallelogram, what other shapes could it be?

a. A quadrilateral with two pairs of parallel sides.

b. A quadrilateral with two pairs of congruent sides.

c. A quadrilateral with one pair of sides that is both congruent and parallel.

d. A quadrilateral with two diagonals that are perpendicular.

e. A quadrilateral with four congruent sides.

CL 10-193. In $\odot C$ at right, $\overline{AB} \cong \overline{DE}$.
Prove that $\angle ACB \cong \angle DCE$.

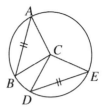

CL 10-194. Find the measure of x in each diagram below. Assume each polygon is regular.

a.
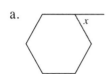

b.
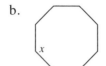

c.

CL 10-195. Check your answers using the table at the end of the closure section. Which problems do you feel confident about? Which problems were hard? Use the table to make a list of topics you need help on and a list of topics you need to practice more.

Answers and Support for Closure Activity #4
What Have I Learned?

Note: MN = Math Note, LL = Learning Log

Problem	Solution	Need Help?	More Practice
CL 10-185.	a. 36π cm^2 b. $m\overset{\frown}{EB} = 150°$, $AD = 20\tan 15° \approx 5.36$ cm c. $14\sin 43° \approx 9.55$ cm	Lesson 8.3.2 and Section 10.1 MN: 5.1.2, 8.3.2, 10.1.1, 10.1.2, and 10.1.3 LL: 5.1.2, 8.3.2, 10.1.2, and 10.1.3	Problems 10-7, 10-18, 10-43, 10-54, 10-59, 10-68, 10-87, and 10-119
CL 10-186.	$4(x+5) = 10x$ $x = \frac{20}{6} \approx 3.33$	Lesson 10.1.3 MN: 10.1.4 LL: 10.1.3	Problems 10-60, 10-78(c), and 10-107
CL 10-187.	a. $2 \cdot 7! = 10080$ b. $\frac{_5P_5 \cdot _3P_3}{_8P_8} = \frac{720}{40320} \approx 1.8\%$ c. This is an anagram. $\frac{8!}{2!3!} = 3360$	Section 10.3 MN: 10.3.1 and 10.3.2 LL: 10.2.3 and 10.3.4	Problems 10-114, 10-115, 10-127, 10-128, 10-132, 10-139, 10-145, and 10-154

Problem	Solution	Need Help?	More Practice
CL 10-188.	a. About 18% of the 5724 seniors are in the performing arts, so P(senior and performing arts) = $\frac{(0.18)(5724)}{27,000} \approx \frac{1030}{27,000} \approx 3.8\%$. b. They are independent. The probability of being in a performing art is always 18%; it does not change knowing the class standing of a student. Or, make a two-way table and check if P(A given B) = P(A), for example, P(art given soph) = $\frac{1215}{6750}$ which equals P(art) = $\frac{1400+1215+1215+1030}{27,000}$. c. Since they are independent, P(senior given performing arts) = P(senior) = $\frac{5724}{27000} = 21.2\%$.	Section 10.2 MN: 10.2.1 and 10.2.3 LL: 10.2.1 and 10.2.3	Problems 10-85, 10-101, 10-116, and 10-130
CL 10-189.	a. 243 b. 3645 ways, 9.98 years	Section 10.3 MN: 10.3.1 and 10.3.2 LL: 10.2.3 and 10.3.4	Problems 10-114, 10-115, 10-127, 10-128, 10-132, 10-139, 10-145, and 10-154
CL 10-190.	a. Since the spinners are independent of each other, we can find entries in a two-way table by using P(A and B) = P(A) · P(B). See table below. $\frac{2}{12}+\frac{2}{12}+\frac{2}{15}+\frac{1}{12} \approx 63.3\%$	Section 10.2 MN: 10.2.3 LL: 10.2.1 and 10.2.3	Problems 10-102, 10-117, 10-131, 10-142, and 10-176

	0 spaces	2 spaces	4 spaces	6 spaces	
Spinner 2	$\frac{1}{4} \cdot \frac{2}{3} = \frac{2}{12}$	$\frac{2}{12}$	$\frac{2}{12}$	$\frac{2}{12}$	$\frac{2}{3}$
Spinner 3	0	$\frac{7}{20} \cdot \frac{1}{3} = \frac{7}{60}$	$\frac{2}{15}$	$\frac{1}{12}$	$\frac{1}{3}$

$\frac{2}{12}+0=\frac{2}{12}$

b. P(0 spaces) = $\frac{2}{12} \approx 16.7\%$

c. $1-\frac{2}{12} \approx 83.3\%$

d. P(Spinner 2 given 2 spaces) = $\frac{\frac{2}{12}}{\frac{2}{12}+\frac{7}{60}} \approx 58.8\%$

e. Answers will vary.

Problem	Solution	Need Help?	More Practice
CL 10-191.	a. Front Right Top b. $V = 11$ units^3, $SA = 42$ units^2 c. $V = 11(3.5)^3 = 471.625$ units^3, $42(3.5)^2 = 514.5$ units^2	Lessons 9.1.1 and 9.1.2 MN: 9.1.3 LL: 9.1.1	Problems CL 9-111, 10-23, 10-105, and 10-183
CL 10-192.	Must be a parallelogram: (a), (c), and (e) (b) could be a kite (d) could be a kite	Lessons 7.3.1 and 7.3.3 MN: 7.2.3 and 8.1.2	Problems CL 7-156, CL 9-116, and 10-34
CL 10-193.		Section 3.2 and Lessons 6.1.1 through 6.1.4 MN: 3.2.2, 3.2.4, 6.1.4, and 7.1.3 LL: 3.2.2	Problems CL 3-123, CL 4-123, CL 5-140, CL 6-101, CL 7-155, CL 8-134, CL 9-117, 10-30, 10-36, and 10-47
CL 10-194.	a. 60° b. 135° c. 36°	Lessons 8.1.2, 8.1.3, and 8.1.4 Checkpoint 10 MN: 7.1.4 and 8.1.5 LL: 8.1.2, 8.1.3, and 8.1.4	Problems CL 8-138, CL 9-115, 10-22, 10-82, and 10-156

11

SOLIDS AND CIRCLES

CHAPTER 11

Solids and Circles

In Chapter 9, you looked at how to find the volume and surface area of three-dimensional solids formed with blocks. You extended these concepts to include prisms and cylinders. In this chapter, you will complete your study of three-dimensional solids to include pyramids, cones, and spheres. You will learn how to identify the cross-sections of a solid and will investigate a special group of solids known as Platonic Solids.

As the word *geometry* literally means the "measurement of the Earth," it is only fitting that Section 11.2 focuses on developing the geometric tools that are used to learn more about the Earth. For example, by studying the height at which satellites orbit the Earth, you will get a chance to develop tools to work with the angle and arc measures that occur when two lines that are tangent to the same circle intersect each other.

Guiding Question

Mathematically proficient students will make sense of problems and persevere in solving them.

As you work through this chapter ask yourself:

What information do I need, what do I already know, and how can I use this information to solve the problem?

In this chapter, you will learn:

➢ How to find the volume and surface area of a pyramid, a cone, and a sphere.

➢ About the properties of special polyhedra (Platonic Solids).

➢ How to find the cross-section of a solid.

➢ How to find the measure of angles and arcs that are formed by tangents and secants.

➢ About the relationships between the lengths of segments created when tangents or secants intersect outside a circle.

Chapter Outline

Section 11.1   In this section, you will learn how regular polygons can be used to form three-dimensional solids called "polyhedra." You will extend your knowledge of finding volume and surface area to include other solids, such as pyramids, cones, and spheres.

Section 11.2   By studying the coordinate system of latitude and longitude lines that help refer to locations on the Earth, you will learn about great circles and how to find the distance between two points on a sphere. You will also investigate the geometric relationships created when tangents and secants intersect a circle.

11.1.1 How can I build it?

Platonic Solids

In Chapter 9, you explored three-dimensional solids such as prisms and cylinders. You developed methods to measure their sizes using volume and surface area and learned to represent three-dimensional solids using mat plans and two-dimensional (front, right, and top) views.

But what other types of three-dimensional solids can you learn about? During Section 11.1, you and your team will examine new types of solids made from regular polygons in order to expand your understanding of three-dimensional shapes.

11-1. EXAMINING A CUBE

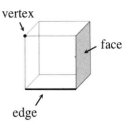

In Chapter 9, you studied the volume and surface area of three-dimensional solids, such as prisms and cylinders. A **cube** is a special type of rectangular prism because each face is a square.

a. What are some examples of cubes you remember seeing?

b. Find the volume and surface area of a cube with an edge length of 10 units.

c. Remember that a "flat side" of a prism is called a **face**, as shown in the diagram above. Notice that the line segment where two faces meet is called an **edge**, while the point where the edges meet is called a **vertex**. How many faces does a cube have? How many edges? How many vertices? (Vertices is plural for vertex.)

d. Confirm with your team that a cube has three square faces that meet at each vertex. Is it possible to have a solid where only two square faces and no other faces meet at a vertex? Could a solid have four or more square faces at a vertex? Explain.

11-2.   OTHER REGULAR POLYHEDRA

A three-dimensional solid made up of
flat, polygonal faces is called a
polyhedron (*poly* is the Greek root for
"many," while *hedron* is the Greek root
for "faces"). A cube, like the one you
studied in problem 11-1, is an example
of a **regular polyhedron** because all of
the faces are congruent, regular polygons
and the same number of faces meet at
each vertex. In fact, you found that a
cube is the *only* regular polyhedron with
square faces.

But what if the faces are equilateral triangles? Or what if the faces are other
regular polygons such as pentagons or hexagons?

Your Task: With your team, determine what other regular polyhedra are
possible. First, obtain building materials from your teacher. Then work
together to build regular polyhedra by testing how the different types of regular
polygons can meet at a vertex. For example, what type of solid is formed when
three equilateral triangle faces meet at each vertex? Four? Five? Six? Do
similar tests for regular pentagons and hexagons. For each regular polyhedron,
describe its shape and count its faces. Be ready to discuss your results with the
class.

Discussion Points

• What is this task asking you to do?

• How should you start?

• How can your team organize the task among the members
  to complete the task efficiently?

11-3.   For help in testing the various ways that congruent, regular polygons can build regular polyhedra, follow the directions below.

a.   Start by focusing on equilateral triangles. Attach three equilateral triangles so that they are adjacent and share a common vertex, as shown at right. Then fold and attach the three triangles so that they completely surround the common vertex. Complete the solid with as many equilateral triangles as needed so that each vertex is the intersection of three triangles. How would you describe this shape?

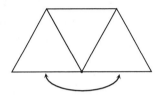

Fold so that these edges meet.

b.   Now repeat your test to determine what solids are possible when 4, 5, or more equilateral triangles meet at each vertex. If a regular polyhedron is possible, describe it and state the number of faces it has. If a regular polyhedron is not possible, explain why not.

c.   What if the faces are regular pentagons? Try building a regular polyhedron so that each vertex is the intersection of three regular pentagons. What if four regular pentagons meet at a vertex? Explain what happens in each case.

d.   End your investigation by considering regular hexagons. Place three or more regular hexagons at a common vertex and explain what solids are formed. If no solid is possible, explain why.

11-4.   POLYHEDRA VOCABULARY

The regular polyhedra you discovered in
problem 11-2 (along with the cube from
problem 11-1) are sometimes referred to as
Plato's Solids (or **Platonic Solids**) because
the knowledge about them spread about
2300 years ago during the time of Plato, a
Greek philosopher and mathematician.

In addition, polyhedra are classified by the
number of faces they have. For example, a
cube is a solid with six faces, so it can be
called a regular hexahedron (because *hexa*
is the Greek root meaning "six" and *hedron*
is the Greek root for "face").

Plato (490 – 430 B.C.)

Examine the table of names below. Then return to your results from problem
11-2 and determine the name for each regular polyhedron you discovered.

4 faces	Tetrahedron	**9 faces**	Nonahedron
5 faces	Pentahedron	**10 faces**	Decahedron
6 faces	Hexahedron	**11 faces**	Undecahedron
7 faces	Heptahedron	**12 faces**	Dodecahedron
8 faces	Octahedron	**20 faces**	Icosahedron

11-5.   Find the surface area of each of Plato's Solids you built in problem 11-2 (the
regular tetrahedron, octahedron, dodecahedron, and icosahedron) if the length
of each edge is 2 inches. Show all work and be prepared to share your method
with the class.

11-6.   DUAL POLYHEDRA

Ivan wonders, *"What happens when the centers of adjacent faces of a regular polyhedron are connected?"* These connections form the edges of a solid, which can be called a **dual polyhedron**.

To investigate dual polyhedra, first predict the results for each regular polyhedron with your team using spatial visualization. Then use a technology tool to test your prediction of what solid is formed when the centers of adjacent faces of a Platonic Solid are connected. Be sure to test all five Platonic Solids (tetrahedron, cube, octahedron, dodecahedron, and icosahedron) and record the results.

11-7.   Reflect on what you learned about Plato's Solids during this lesson. What connections did you make to previous material? Write an entry in your Learning Log explaining what is special about this group of solids. Name and describe each Platonic Solid. Title this entry "Plato's Solids" and include today's date.

11-8.   Draw a hexagon on your paper.

a.   Do all hexagons have an interior angle sum of 720°?

b.   Does every hexagon have an interior angle measuring 120°? Explain your reasoning.

c.   Does every hexagon have 6 sides? Explain your reasoning.

11-9.   The mascot for Sacramento High School is the DRAGONS.

a.   How many ways can the cheerleaders rearrange the letters in the school mascot?

b.   How many ways can the letters be rearranged if the first and last letters are correctly placed?

11-10. The **lateral surface** of a cylinder is the surface connecting the bases. For example, the label from a soup can would represent the lateral surface of a cylindrical can. If the radius of a cylinder is 4 cm and the height is 15 cm, find the lateral surface area of the cylinder. Note: It may help you to think of "unrolling" a soup can label and finding the area of the label.

11-11. For each of the relationships represented in the diagrams below, write and solve an equation for x and/or y. Justify your method. In part (a), assume that C is the center of the circle.

a.

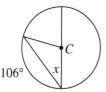

b.

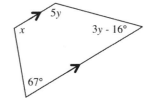

c.

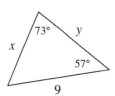

d.

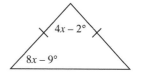

11-12. Garland is having trouble with the copy machine. He is trying to copy a triangle with an area of 36 square units and a perimeter of 42 units.

a. After he pressed the button to copy, Garland noticed the copier's zoom factor (the linear scale factor) was set to 200%. What is the area and perimeter of the resulting triangle?

b. Now Garland takes the result from part (a) and accidentally shrinks it by a linear scale factor of $\frac{1}{3}$! What is the area and perimeter of the resulting triangle?

11-13.   Three flags are shown below on flagpoles. For each flag, determine what shape appears if the flag is spun very quickly about its pole. If you do not know the name of the shape, describe it.

a.

← pole

b.
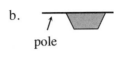
pole

c.
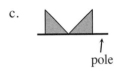
pole

11-14.   **Multiple Choice:** $\triangle ABC$ has a right angle at B. If $m\angle A = 42°$ and $BC = 7$ mm, what is the approximate length of AC?

a.   9.4 mm   b.   10.5 mm   c.   7.8 mm   d.   4.7 mm

11-15.   Draw a tetrahedron on your paper.

a.   How many faces does the tetrahedron have?

b.   How many edges does it have?

c.   How many vertices does it have?

11-16.   If $n > 3$, write a shorter, equivalent expression for $n \cdot (n-1) \cdot (n-2) \cdot (n-3)$.

11-17.   Mia found the volume of a rectangular prism to be 840 mm³. As she was telling her father about it, she remembered that the base had a length of 10 mm and a width of 12 mm, but she could not remember the height. *"Maybe there's a way you can find it by going backwards,"* her father suggested. Can you help Mia find the height of her prism? Explain your solution.

11-18.   For each geometric relationship below, determine whether a or b is larger, or if they are equal. Assume that the diagrams are not drawn to scale. If there is not enough information, explain what information is missing.

a.

b.

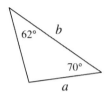

c.

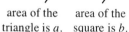

area of the triangle is a.   area of the square is b.

11-19.   Examine the diagram of the triangle at right.

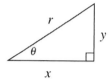

a.   Write an equation representing the relationship between x, y, and r.

b.   Write an expression for $\sin\theta$. What is $\sin\theta$ if $r = 1$?

c.   Write an expression for $\cos\theta$. What is $\cos\theta$ if $r = 1$?

11-20.   In a circle, chord $\overline{AB}$ has length 10 units, while $m\overset{\frown}{AB} = 60°$. What is the area of the circle? Draw a diagram and show all work.

11-21.   **Multiple Choice:** Assume that the coordinates of $\triangle ABC$ are $A(5, 1)$, $B(3, 7)$, and $C(2, 2)$. If $\triangle ABC$ is rotated 90° clockwise (↻) about the origin, the coordinates of the image of B would be:

a. $(-3, 7)$ b. $(-7, 3)$ c. $(7, -3)$ d. $(7, 3)$

11.1.2 How can I measure it?

Pyramids

In Lesson 11.1.1, you explored Plato's five special solids: the tetrahedron, the octahedron, the cube (also known as the hexahedron), the dodecahedron, and the icosahedron. You discovered why these are the only regular polyhedra and developed a method to find their surface area.

Today you will examine the tetrahedron from a new perspective: as a member of the **pyramid** family. As you work today with your team, you will discover ways to classify pyramids by their shape and will develop new tools of measurement.

11-22. A **pyramid** is a polyhedron with a polygonal base formed by connecting each point of the base to a single given point (the **apex**) that is above or below the flat surface containing the base. Each triangular lateral face of a pyramid is formed by the segments from the apex to the endpoints of a side of the base and the side itself. A tetrahedron is a special pyramid because any face can act as its base.

Obtain the four Lesson 11.1.2 Resource Pages, a pair of scissors, and either tape or glue from your teacher. Have each member of your team build one of the solids. When assembling each solid, be sure to have the printed side of the net on the exterior of the pyramid for reference later. Then answer the questions below.

a. Sketch each pyramid onto your paper. What is the same about each pyramid? What is different? With your team, list as many qualities as you can.

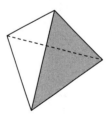

b. A tetrahedron can also be called a **triangular-based pyramid**, because its base is always a triangle. Choose similar, appropriate names for the other pyramids that your team constructed.

c. Find the surface area of pyramids B and D. Use a ruler to find the dimensions of the edges in centimeters.

d. Compare pyramids B and C. Which do you think has more volume? Justify your reasoning.

11-23.   THE TRANSAMERICA BUILDING

The TransAmerica building in San Francisco is built of
concrete and is shaped like a square-based pyramid. The
building is periodically power-washed using one gallon
of cleaning solution for every 250 square meters of
surface. As the new building manager, you need to order
the cleaning supplies for this large task. The problem is
that you do not know the height of each triangular face of
the building; you only know the vertical height of the
building from the base to the top vertex.

Your Task: Determine the amount of cleaning solution needed to wash the
TransAmerica building if an edge of the square base is 96 meters and the height
of the building is 220 meters. Include a sketch in your solution.

11-24.   Read the Math Notes box for this lesson, which introduces new vocabulary
terms such as **slant height** and **lateral surface area**. Explain the difference
between the slant height and the height of a pyramid. How can you use one to
find the other?

METHODS AND **M**EANINGS

Pyramid Vocabulary

If a face of a pyramid (defined in problem 11-22) or prism is not
a base, it is called a **lateral face**.

The **lateral surface area** of a pyramid or prism is the sum of the
areas of all faces of the pyramid or prism, not including the base(s).
The area of the exterior of the TransAmerica building that needs
cleaning (from problem 11-23) is an example of lateral surface area,
since the exterior of the base of the pyramid cannot be cleaned.

The **total surface area** of a pyramid or prism is the sum of the areas of
all faces, including the bases.

Sometimes saying the word "height" for a
pyramid can be confusing, since it could refer to
the height of one of the triangular faces or it
could refer to the overall height of the pyramid.
Therefore, the height of each lateral face is called
a **slant height** to distinguish it from the **height** of
the pyramid itself. See the diagram at right.

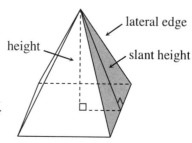

11-25.   A pyramid has a volume of 108 cubic inches and a base area of 27 square inches. Find its height.

11-26.   Connie and Nora went into Ready Scoop to get ice cream cones, but Nora cannot make up her mind. They have 23 flavors and she wants 3 scoops.

a.   If Nora is very particular about the order of the scoops, how many choices does she have if all of the scoops are different?

b.   Nora changes her mind. She wants a dish, not a cone, but she still wants three different flavors. How many ways can she order?

c.   Connie says, *"I still want a cone with dark chocolate on the bottom and then any other two scoops."* How many cones are possible with dark chocolate on the bottom?

d.   Vlad came in as they were leaving and saw Connie's cone. He said, *"Oh, that's what I want, a cone with chocolate on the bottom, and then two other flavors that are not chocolate."* The clerk, said, *"Okay, but we have four kinds of chocolate."* Vlad replied, *"Any kind of chocolate will do."* How many different cones could fill Vlad's order?

11-27.   Examine $\triangle ABC$, $\triangle ABD$, and $\triangle ABE$ in the diagram at right. If $\overline{CE} \parallel \overline{AB}$, explain what you know about the areas of the three triangles. Justify your statements.

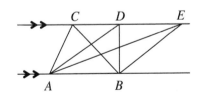

11-28.   Solve each equation below, if possible. Show all work.

a. $\frac{3}{5} = \frac{2x}{3} - 8$

b. $\frac{9x}{5000} + \frac{2}{1000} = \frac{28}{5000}$

c. $\frac{2x}{3} + \frac{x}{2} = \frac{2x}{3}$

d. $\frac{3}{2}(2x - 5) = \frac{1}{6}$

11-29.   Prove that when two lines that are tangent to the same circle intersect, the lengths between the point of intersection and the points of tangency are equal. That is, in the diagram at right, if $\overline{AB}$ is tangent to ⊙P at B, and $\overrightarrow{AC}$ is tangent to ⊙P at C, prove that $AB = AC$. Use either a flowchart or a two-column proof.

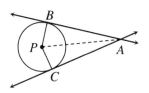

11-30.   On graph paper, plot the points $A(4, 1)$ and $B(10, 9)$.

a.   Find the distance between points A and B. That is, find AB.

b.   If point C is at $(10, 1)$, find $m\angle CAB$. Show all work.

11-31.   Find the missing terms in this geometric sequence.

$$2, \_\_\_, \_\_\_, \_\_\_, 162$$

11-32.   **Multiple Choice:** Which net below *cannot* create a regular octahedron when folded, like the one at right?

a.

b.

c.

d.

e.   None of these

11.1.3 What is the volume?

Volume of a Pyramid

Today, as you continue your focus on pyramids, look for and utilize connections to other geometry concepts. The models of pyramids that you constructed in Lesson 11.1.2 will be useful as you develop a method for finding the volume of a pyramid.

11-33.   GOING CAMPING

As Soraya shopped for a tent, she came across two models that she liked best, shown at right. However, she does not know which one to pick! They are both made by the same company and appear to have the same quality. She has come to you for help in making her decision.

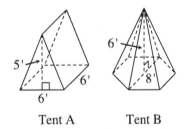

Tent A   Tent B

While she says that her drawings are not to scale, below are her notes about the tents:

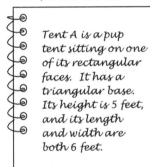

Tent A is a pup tent sitting on one of its rectangular faces. It has a triangular base. Its height is 5 feet, and its length and width are both 6 feet.

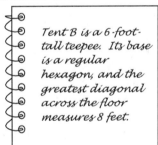

Tent B is a 6-foot-tall teepee. Its base is a regular hexagon, and the greatest diagonal across the floor measures 8 feet.

JAKE'S SPORTING GOODS

With your team, discuss the following questions in any order.
Be prepared to share your discussion with the class.

- What are the shapes of the two tents?

- Without doing any calculations, which tent do you think Soraya should buy and why?

- What types of measurement might be useful to determine which tent is better?

- What do you still need to know to answer her question?

11-34.   COMPARING SOLIDS

To analyze Tent B from problem 11-33, you need to know how to find the volume of a pyramid. But how can you find that volume?

To start, consider a simpler pyramid with a square base, such as pyramid B that your team built in Lesson 11.1.2. To develop a method to find the volume of a pyramid, first consider what solids(s) you could compare it to. For example, when finding the area of a triangle, you compared it to the area of a rectangle and figured out that the area of a triangle is always half the area of a rectangle with the same base and height. To what solids(s) can you compare the volume of pyramid B? Discuss this with your team and be prepared to share your thinking with the class.

11-35.   VOLUME OF A PYRAMID

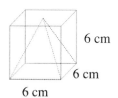

Soraya thinks that pyramid B could be compared to a cube, like the one shown at right, since the base edges and heights of both are 6 cm.

6 cm

6 cm

6 cm

a.   First estimate. What proportion of the cube is pyramid B? Discuss this with your team.

b.   Soraya remembers comparing pyramids B and C in Lesson 11.1.2. She decided to compare the volumes by thinking of it as a stack of slices. When thinking of it this way, what is the shape of each layer? Note: The name for the shape of a layer of a three-dimensional solid is called a **cross-section**.

c.   Soraya then slid all of the layers of the pyramid so that the top vertex was directly above one of the corners of the base, like Pyramid C from problem 11-22.

When the top vertex of a pyramid is directly above (or below) the center of the base, the pyramid is called a **right pyramid**, while all other pyramids are referred to as **oblique pyramids**.

When Soraya slid the layers to create an oblique pyramid, she did not add or take away any foam layers. How does the volume of her oblique pyramid compare with the right pyramid in part (b) above?

d.   Test your estimate from part (a) by using as many copies of pyramid C as you need to assemble a cube. Was your estimate accurate? Now explain how to find the volume of a pyramid.

11-36.   In problem 11-35, you may have noticed that the special square-based pyramid had one-third the volume of the cube. It turns out that this relationship between a pyramid and a prism with the same base area and height works for all other pyramids as well.

   a.   Write an expression for the volume of a pyramid with base area B and height h.

   b.   Use your expression from part (a) to find the volume of a pyramid with base area of 34 square units and height of 9 units.

11-37.   Now return to problem 11-33 and help Soraya decide which tent to buy for her backpacking trip. To make this decision, compare the volumes, base areas, and surface areas of both tents. Be ready to share your decision with the class.

Tent A   Tent B

11-38.   THREE-DIMENSIONAL SOLIDS TOOLKIT

   Obtain the Lesson 11.1.3A Resource Pages ("Three-Dimensional Solids Toolkit") from your teacher. On the Resource Page, write everything you know about finding the volume and surface area of all of the solids that you have studied so far. In later lessons, you will continue to add information to this toolkit, so be sure to keep this resource page in a safe place. At this point, your Toolkit should include:

   Prisms   Cylinders   Pyramids

METHODS AND MEANINGS

Cross-Sections of Three-Dimensional Solids

The intersection of a three-dimensional solid and a plane is called a **cross-section** of the solid. The result is a two-dimensional diagram that represents the flat surface of a slice of the solid.

One way to visualize a cross-section is to imagine the solid sliced into thin slices like a ream of paper. Since a solid can be sliced in any direction and at any angle, you need to know the direction of the slice to find the correct cross-section.

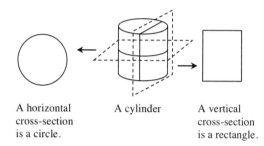

A horizontal cross-section is a circle.

A cylinder

A vertical cross-section is a rectangle.

For example, the cylinder at right has several different cross-sections depending on the direction of the slice. When this cylinder is sliced vertically, the resulting cross-section is a rectangle, while the cross-section is a circle when the cylinder is sliced horizontally.

Review & Preview

11-39. Review the information about cross-sections in the Math Notes box for this lesson. Then answer the questions below.

    a. Draw a cube on your paper. Is it possible to slice a cube and get a cross-section that is not a quadrilateral? Explain how.

    b. Barbara has a solid on her desk. If she slices it horizontally at any level, the cross-section is a triangle. If she slices it vertically in any direction, the cross-section is a triangle. What could her shape be? Draw a possible shape.

11-40. Find the volume and surface area of a square-based right pyramid if the base edge has length 6 units and the height of the pyramid is 4 units. Assume the diagram at right is not to scale.

11-41.   Twelve students will be chosen at random from the 900 students at Rolling Meadows High School to serve as the Judicial Board for minor student infractions.

a.   How many different Judicial Boards are possible?

b.   Mariko hopes to be on the board. How many possible boards include her?

c.   What is the probability (in percent) that Mariko is chosen for the board?

11-42.   The solid at right is a regular octahedron.

a.   Trace the shape on your paper. How many faces does it have? How many edges? Vertices?

b.   If an octahedron is sliced horizontally, what shape is the resulting cross-section?

11-43.   Assume that the prisms at right are similar.

a.   Solve for x and y.

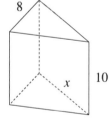

b.   What is the ratio of the corresponding sides of Solid B to Solid A?

c.   If the base area of Solid A is 27 square units, find the base area of Solid B.

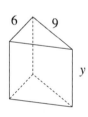

Solid A   Solid B

11-44.   Find the area and circumference of $\odot C$ at right. Show all work.

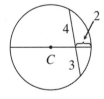

11-45.   **Multiple Choice:** The volume of the square-based pyramid with base edge 9 units and height 48 units is:

a.   324 units^3 b.   1296 units^3

c.   3888 units^3 d.   not enough information

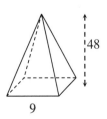

11-46.   Examine the Venn diagram at right. In which region should the figure below be placed? Show all work to justify your conclusion.

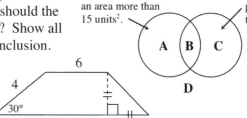

These shapes have an area more than 15 units².

These shapes have perimeter more than 20 units.

11-47.   While volunteering for a food sale, Aimee studied a cylindrical can of soup. She noticed that it had a diameter of 3 inches and a height of 4.5 inches.

a.   Find the volume of the soup can.

b.   If Aimee needs to fill a cylindrical pot that has a diameter of 14 inches and a height of 10 inches, how many cans of soup will she need?

c.   What is the area of the soup can label?

11-48.   In the diagram at right, assume that $m\angle ECB = m\angle EAD$ and point E is the midpoint of $\overline{AC}$. Prove that $\overline{AD} \cong \overline{CB}$.

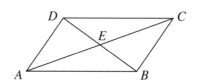

11-49.   Next June, Joanna is taking a vacation to do some sightseeing and visit relatives. She will make four stops while she is gone. They might include Baltimore, Pittsburgh, Washington D.C., Philadelphia, New York City, and the New Jersey shore. Joanna is not sure in what order to visit these places.

a.   In how many ways can she organize her drive from place to place?

b.   How many of these trips will include the New Jersey Shore?

11-50.   A snack cracker company conducted a taste test for the three different types of crackers it makes. It surveyed 250 people in each age group in the table below. Participants chose their favorite type of cracker. Use the results to answer the questions.

Age	Cracker A	Cracker B	Cracker C
Under 20	152	54	44
20 to 39	107	85	58
40 to 59	78	101	71
60 and over	34	68	148

a.   Calculate the probability that a participant chose cracker A or was under 20 years old. Show how you used the Addition Rule.

b.   What is the probability that a participant did not choose cracker A and was over 20 years old? Show how you used a complement to answer this problem.

c.   What is the probability that a participant was 20 years old or older. Show how you used a complement to answer this problem.

d.   A randomly-selected participant says he is 15 years old. What is the probability that he chose cracker A?

11-51.   Write and solve an equation from the geometric relationships provided in the diagrams below.

a.
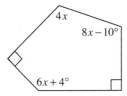

b.
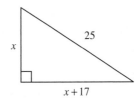

c.

d.
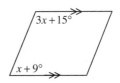

11-52.   **Multiple Choice:** Calculate the volume of the rectangle-based pyramid at right.

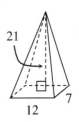

a.   84 units^3 b.   648 units^3 c.   882 units^3

d.   1764 units^3 e.   None of these

11.1.4 What if it is a cone?

• •

Surface Area and Volume of a Cone

Today you will continue to use what you know about the volume and surface area of prisms and pyramids and will extend your understanding to include a new three-dimensional shape: a cone. As you work with your team, look for connections to previous course material.

11-53.   Review what you learned in Lesson 11.1.3 by finding the volume of each pyramid below. Assume that the pyramid in part (a) corresponds to a rectangular-based prism and that the base of the pyramid and prism in part (b) is a regular hexagon.

a.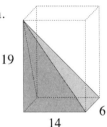

b.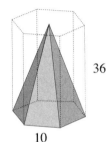

c.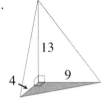

11-54.   While finding the volumes of the pyramids in problem 11-53, Jamal asked, *"But what if it is a cone? How would you find its volume?"* Note that a **cone** is somewhat like a pyramid, but it has a circular base. Every point on the perimeter of the circular base connects to a point above the base called the apex.

a.   Discuss Jamal's question with your team. How might you use what you learned about the volume of pyramids to reason about the volume of a cone?

b.   Lekili said, *"Remember when we found the area of a circle by finding what happens to the area of a regular polygon and the number of sides increase? I think we can use that approach here."* What do you think Lekili means? Explain how this can help find a method to compute the volume of a cone.

c.   Use your ideas from part (b) to write an expression for the volume of a cone with radius of length r and height h.

d.   Use your expression from part (c) to find the volume of a cone at right. Show all work.

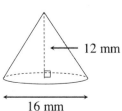

11-55.   HAPPY BIRTHDAY!

Your class has decided to throw your principal a surprise
birthday party tomorrow. The whole class is working together
to create party decorations, and your team has been assigned the
job of producing party hats. Each party hat will be created out
of special decorative paper and will be in the shape of a cone.

Your Task: Use the sample party hat provided by your teacher to determine the
size and shape of the paper that forms the hat. Then determine the amount of
paper (in square inches) needed to produce one party hat and figure out the total
amount of paper you will need for each person in your class to have a party hat.

11-56.   The Math Club has decided to sell giant waffle ice-
cream cones at the Spring Fair. Lekili bought a cone,
but then he got distracted. When he returned to the
cone, the ice cream had melted, filling the cone to the
very top!

If the diameter of the base of the cone is 4 inches and
the slant height is 6 inches, find the volume of the ice
cream and the area of the waffle that made the cone.

11-57.   THREE-DIMENSIONAL SOLIDS TOOLKIT

Add details to your Lesson 11.1.3A Resource Pages
("Three-Dimensional Solids Toolkit") for finding the
volume and surface area of cones.

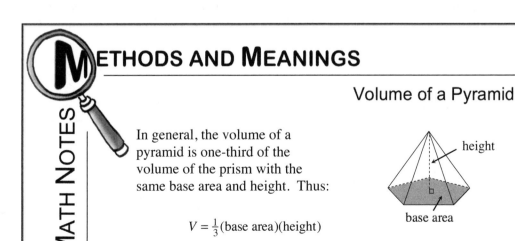

METHODS AND MEANINGS

MATH NOTES

Volume of a Pyramid

In general, the volume of a
pyramid is one-third of the
volume of the prism with the
same base area and height. Thus:

$$V = \tfrac{1}{3}(\text{base area})(\text{height})$$

height

base area

11-58.   Find the volume and total surface area of each solid below. Show all work.

a.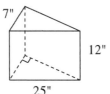

b.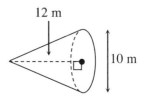

11-59.   Each of the *petit fours* (tiny bite-sized layered cakes) at Pauline's Pastries are
          made with three layers of filling. The pastry chef made one *petit four* for each
          possible choice of three different fillings of the eight that were available. The
          assistant iced them all with chocolate icing before marking which petit four
          contained which fillings. Since they are eaten in one bite, the order of the
          fillings does not matter.

          a.   How many *petit fours* did the chef make?

          b.   How many have raspberry, custard, and one
                other filling?

          c.   What is the probability (in percent) of getting a *petit four* that has apricot
                filling?

11-60.   You roll three different-colored dice and use the numbers on the dice to
          determine the lengths of the sides of a triangle. For example, 3-3-5 would be an
          isosceles triangle with base 5. What is the probability of building a right
          triangle?

11-61.   Examine the diagram of the cone at right.

          a.   How could you slice the cone so that the cross-section
                is a triangle?

          b.   What cross-section do you get if you slice the cone
                horizontally?

          c.   Lois is thinking of a shape. She says that no matter how you slice it, the
                cross-section will always be a circle. What shape is she thinking of?
                Draw and describe this shape on your paper.

11-62. For each triangle below, decide if it is similar to the triangle at right. If it is similar, justify your conclusion and complete the similarity statement $\triangle ABC \sim \triangle$_____. If the triangle is not similar, explain how you know. Assume that the diagrams are not drawn to scale.

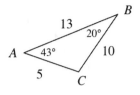

a.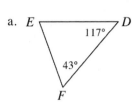

b.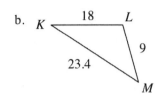

c.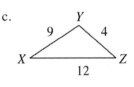

11-63. On graph paper, graph the following system of inequalities. Be sure that your shaded region represents all of the points that make both inequalities true.

$$y < \tfrac{2}{3}x - 2$$
$$y \geq -5x - 2$$

11-64. Examine the diagram at right. State the relationship between each pair of angles listed below (such as vertical angles) and state whether the angles are congruent, supplementary, or neither.

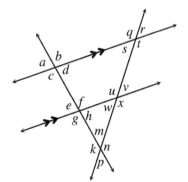

a. $\angle e$ and $\angle a$

b. $\angle t$ and $\angle u$

c. $\angle v$ and $\angle x$

d. $\angle g$ and $\angle v$

11-65. **Multiple Choice:** In the diagram at right, the value of y is:

a. $\sin \theta$ b. $\cos \theta$ c. $\tan \theta$

d. x e.   None of these

11.1.5 What is the relationship?

Surface Area and Volume of a Sphere

This lesson will complete your Three-Dimensional Solids Toolkit. You will learn about a new shape that you encounter often in your daily life: a sphere. You will also make connections between a cylinder, cone, and sphere of the same radius and height.

As you work with your team, keep the following focus questions in mind:

> What's the relationship?
>
> What other tools or information do I need?

11-66.   Alonzo was blowing bubbles to amuse his little sister. He wondered, *"Why are bubbles always perfectly round?"*

   a.   Discuss Alonzo's question with the class. Why are free-floating bubbles always shaped like a perfectly round ball?

   b.   The shape of a bubble is called a **sphere**. What other objects can you remember seeing that are shaped like a sphere?

   c.   What shapes are related to spheres? How are they related?

11-67.   GEOGRAPHY LESSON, Part One

Alonzo learned in his geography class that about 70% of the Earth's surface is covered in water. *"That's amazing!"* he thought. This information only made him think of new questions, such as *"What is the area of land covered in water?"*, *"What percent of the Earth's surface is the United States?"*, and *"What is the volume of the entire Earth?"*

Discuss Alonzo's questions with your team. Decide:

   •   What facts about the Earth would be helpful to know?

   •   What do you still need to learn to answer Alonzo's questions?

Core Connections Geometry

11-68.   In order to answer his questions, Alonzo decided to get out his set of plastic geometry models. He has a sphere, cone, and cylinder that each has the same radius and height.

   a.   Draw an example diagram of each shape.

   b.   If the radius of the sphere is r, what is the height of the cylinder? How do you know?

   c.   Alonzo's models are hollow and are designed to hold water. Alonzo was pouring water between the shapes, comparing their volumes. He discovered that when he poured the water in the cone and the sphere into the cylinder, the water filled up the cylinder without going over! Determine what the volume of the sphere must be if the radius of the sphere is r units. Show all work.

11-69.   Now that Alonzo knows that spheres, cylinders, and cones with the same height and radius are related, he decides to examine the surface area of each one. As he paints the exterior of each shape, he notices that the lateral surface area of the cylinder and the surface area of the sphere take exactly the same amount of paint! If the radius of the sphere and cylinder is r, what is the surface area of the sphere?

11-70.   GEOGRAPHY LESSON, Part Two

   Now that you have strategies for finding the volume and surface area of a sphere, return to problem 11-67 and help Alonzo answer his questions. That is, determine:

   • The area of the Earth's surface that is covered in water.

   • The percent of the Earth's surface that lies in the United States.

   • The volume of the entire Earth.

   Remember that in Chapter 10, you determined that the radius of the Earth is about 4,000 miles. Alonzo did some research and discovered that the land area of the United States is approximately 3,537,438 square miles.

11-71.   THREE-DIMENSIONAL SOLIDS TOOLKIT

Retrieve the Three-Dimensional Solids Toolkit. Complete
the entry for a sphere. That is, write everything you know
about finding the volume and surface area of spheres. Be
sure you include the relationships between the volumes of a
cone, cylinder, and sphere with the same radius and height.

$\mathbf{M}$ETHODS AND $\mathbf{M}$EANINGS

MATH NOTES

Volume and Lateral Surface of a Cone

The general formula for the volume of a
cone (defined in problem 11-54) is the same as
the formula for the volume of a pyramid:

$$\text{Volume} = \tfrac{1}{3}(\text{Base Area})(\text{Height})$$

In the case of the cone, the Base Area $= \pi r^2$ where r
is the length of the radius of the circular base. So if
h is the height of the cone then the volume is:

$$V = \tfrac{1}{3}(\text{Base Area})(\text{Height}) = \tfrac{1}{3}\pi r^2 h .$$

To find the lateral surface area of a cone, imagine
unrolling the lateral surface of the cone to create a
sector. The radius of the sector would be the slant
height, l, of the cone, and the arc length would be
the circumference of the base of the cone, $2\pi r$.

Therefore, the area of the sector (the lateral surface area of the cone) is:

$$LA = \tfrac{2\pi r}{2\pi l}\, \pi l^2 = \pi r l$$

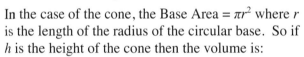

11-72.   As Shannon peeled her orange for lunch, she realized that it was very close to
being a sphere. If her orange has a diameter of 8 centimeters, what is its
approximate surface area (the area of the orange peel)? What is the approximate
volume of the orange? Show all work.

11-73. How many committees of three juniors and three seniors can be formed from the student government class of eight juniors and 10 seniors?

11-74. Pauline's Pastries is making special *petit fours* (as in problem 11-59). The chef is making *petit fours* with three or four fillings. For Valentine's Day they have twelve fillings available and they make one *petit four* for each of the possible three or four different fillings.

a. How many *petit fours* did they make?

b. What is the probability of getting a *petit four* that has both raspberry and custard?

11-75.  Martha was playing with a hollow plastic cone that had a diameter of 12 inches and a height of 5 inches. Her brother Matt snatched the cone, cut two inches off the top, and placed the cut piece upside down in the lower portion of the cone as shown at right. How many cubic inches of water would fit inside the space of her redesigned cone?

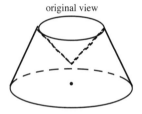

original view

original view upside-down

11-76. Review what you know about polyhedra as you answer the questions below. Refer to the table in problem 11-4 if you need help.

a. Find the total surface area of a regular icosahedron if the area of each face is 45 mm². Explain your method.

b. The total surface area of a regular dodecahedron is 108 cm². What is the area of each face?

c. A regular tetrahedron has an edge length of 6 inches. What is its total surface area? Show all work.

11-77.   Hokiri's ladder has two legs that are each 8 feet
          long. When the ladder is opened safely and locked
          for use, the legs are 4 feet apart on the ground.
          What is the angle that is formed at the top of the
          ladder where the legs meet?

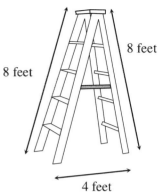

8 feet

8 feet

4 feet

11-78.   Find the area of the region that represents the
          solution of the inequality $x^2 + y^2 \le 72$.

11-79.   Solve each system of equations below. Write the solution
          in the form (x, y). Show all work.

    a. $y + 3x = 14$ b. $y = 6 - 3x$
          $y - 3x = 6$ $2x + y = 7$

11.2.1 Where is this location?

Coordinates on a Sphere

As you learned in Chapter 1, the word *geometry* literally means "measurement of the Earth." In fact, so far in this course, you have used your geometric tools to learn more about Earth. For example, in Lesson 11.1.5, you learned that the United States only makes up 1.8% of the Earth's surface. Also, in Lesson 10.1.1, you learned how Eratosthenes used shadows to estimate the Earth's radius.

Today, you will examine other earthly questions that can be answered using geometry. Since you can approximate the shape of the earth as a sphere, you will be able to use many of the tools you have used previously. As you work with your team, consider the following focus questions:

What strategy or tool can I use?

Is there another way?

Does this strategy always work?

11-80.   YOU ARE HERE

The reference lines connecting the north and south poles of the earth are called lines of **longitude**, as shown in the diagram at right. These lines have been used for hundreds of years to help navigators determine how many degrees east or west they have traveled. While these reference markings are referred to as "lines," they are technically circles that wrap around the Earth.

Lines of Longitude

Lines of longitude extend north and south, while lines of **latitude** circle east and west, as shown in the diagrams below. These lines help to mark off arc measures on the planet's surface. In the diagrams at right, the lines of latitude are marked every 15° while the lines of longitude are marked every 30°. The most famous line of latitude is the **equator**, which separates the Earth into two **hemispheres** (half a sphere).

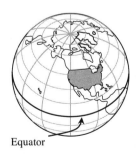

Equator

Problem continues on next page →

11-80.   *Problem continued from previous page.*

Another name for these lines of longitude is **meridians**, which is Latin from *medius* (which means "middle") and *diem* (which means "day"). The word meridian also used to refer to noon, since it was the time the sun was directly overhead. In the morning, it was "ante meridian" or before noon. This is where the abbreviation **a.m.** comes from. Likewise, **p.m.** is short for "post meridian," which means after noon.

a. The equator is an example of a **great circle**, which means that it is a circle that lies on the sphere and has the same diameter as the sphere. Compare the equator with the other lines of latitude. What do you notice?

Lines of Latitude

Lines of Longitude

b. Is it possible for two great circles on the same sphere to intersect? If so, draw an example on your paper. If not, explain why not.

North Pole

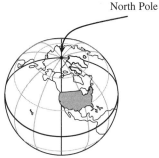

c. On the sphere provided by your teacher, carefully draw circles to represent the lines of latitude (every 30°) and longitude (every 30°) on the Earth. Highlight the equator by making it darker or a different color than the other lines of latitude. Also choose one line of longitude to represent 0° (called the **prime meridian**, which passes through Greenwich, England, on the eastern edge of London) and highlight it as well.

d. Norman is exactly 1 mile north of Sula. If they both travel due west, will their paths cross? Why or why not? Assume that people can travel over water and all types of terrain.

e. Erin is exactly 1 mile east of Wilber. If they both travel due south at the same rate, will their paths cross? Why or why not?

11-81.   DEAR PEN PAL

Brianna, who lives in New Orleans, has been writing
to her pen pal in Jacksonville, Florida. *"Gosh,"* she
wonders, *"How far away is my friend?"*

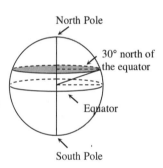

a.   On your spherical model of the globe from
problem 11-80, locate Brianna's home. (New
Orleans, LA, is approximately 90° west of the prime meridian and 30°
north of the equator.) Mark it with a pushpin.

b.   Now, with a second pushpin, mark the location of Brianna's friend, if
Jacksonville is 82° west of the prime meridian and 30° north of the
equator. Use a rubber band to locate the circle with the smallest radius
that passes through these two locations.

c.   What is the measure of the arc connecting these two cities? Show how
you know.

d.   Brianna thinks that if she knew the
circumference of the circle marked with the
rubber band, then she could use the arc
measure to approximate the distance between
the two cities. The shaded circle in the
diagram at right represents the cross-section of
the earth 30° above the equator. If the radius
of the earth is approximately 4000 miles, find
the circumference of the shaded circle.

e.   Use what you found in part (d) to find the
distance between New Orleans and Jacksonville.

11-82.   Obtain a Lesson 11.2.1 Resource Page from your teacher. On it, mark and label
the following locations:

a.   London, England, which is on the prime meridian and is approximately
51° north of the equator.

b.   Narsarssuaq, Greenland, which is approximately 45° west of the prime
meridian and 61° north of the equator.

c.   Quito, Ecuador, which is on the equator and is approximately 79° west of
the prime meridian.

d.   Cairo, Egypt, which is approximately 31° east of the prime meridian and
30° north of the equator.

e.   Buenos Aires, Argentina, which is approximately 58° west of the prime
meridian and 35° south of the equator.

11-83.   EXTENSION

a.   If a polar bear travels 1 mile south
      from the North Pole, travels one mile
      east, and then travels one mile north,
      where does it end up? Explain what
      happens and why.

b.   Is there another location the polar bear could have started from so that it
      still ends up where it started after following the same directions? Explain.

11-84.   The moon is an average distance of 238,900 miles away from the Earth. While
          that seems very far, how far is it?

a.   Compare that distance with the circumference of the Earth's equator.
      Assume that the Earth's radius is 4000 miles. How many times greater
      than the Earth's circumference is the distance to the moon?

b.   One way to estimate the distance
      between the Earth and the sun is
      to consider the triangle formed
      by the sun, Earth, and moon
      when the moon appears to be
      half-full. (See the diagram at
      right.) When the moon appears
      from earth to be half-full, it can
      be assumed that the moon forms
      a 90° angle with the sun and the Earth.

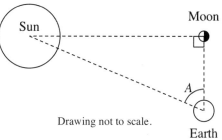

Drawing not to scale.

      Using special equipment, Ray found the measure of angle A to be 89.85°.
      If the moon is 238,900 miles away from the Earth, then how far is the sun
      from the Earth?

11-85.   The length of chord $\overline{AB}$ in $\odot D$ is 9 mm. If the $m\overset{\frown}{AB} = 32°$, find the length of
          $\overset{\frown}{AB}$. Draw a diagram.

11-86.   On your paper, draw a diagram of a square-based pyramid if the side length of
          the base is 9 cm and the height of the pyramid is 12 cm.

a.   Find the volume of the pyramid.

b.   If a smaller pyramid is similar to the pyramid in part (a), but has a linear
      scale factor of $\frac{1}{3}$, find its volume.

Core Connections Geometry

11-87.   In the card game called "Twenty-One," two cards are dealt from a randomly shuffled deck of playing cards. The player's goal is to get the sum of his or her cards to be as close (or equal) to 21 as possible, without going over 21. To establish the sample space for this problem, you need to think of choosing two from a set of 52.

    a.   How many ways are there to be dealt two cards?

    b.   The tens, jacks, queens, and kings all have a value of 10 points. There are four of each in a standard deck. What is the probability of being dealt two ten-valued cards?

    c.   If you did not already do so, write your solution to part (b) in the form $\frac{{}_aC_b}{{}_dC_e}$.

    d.   What is the probability (as a percent) of being dealt two face cards? (Face cards are Kings, Queens, and Jacks, that is, the cards that have faces.) Also write your answer as $\frac{{}_aC_b}{{}_dC_e}$.

    e.   In "Twenty-One" an Ace can count as 1 point or 11 points. The deal is called "soft" when the Ace is counted as 11 points. What is the probability of being dealt a "soft 21," that is, a card worth ten points and an Ace?

11-88.   Mr. McGee, the owner of The Laundry Shop (from problem 10-95) has a different question that he wants to answer with data and probability. He wants to estimate the probability that a customer who comes into his store will buy a washer or dryer. He collected the following data during one week: 177 customers came to his store, 88 purchased washers, 64 purchased dryers, and 69 did not make a purchase.

    a.   Using this data, what is the probability that the next customer who comes to his store will purchase a washer or a dryer?

    b.   Mr. McGee promises his salespeople a bonus if they can increase the probability that the customers who buy washers also buy dryers. For the week's data above, what is the probability that if a customer bought a washer, he or she also bought a dryer?

11-89.   In the picture of a globe at right, the lines of latitude are concentric circles. Where else might you encounter concentric circles?

11-90.   **Multiple Choice:** The volume of a solid is V. If the solid is enlarged proportionally so that its side lengths increase by a factor of 9, what is the volume of the enlarged solid?

    a. $9V$ b. $\frac{81}{4}V$ c. $81V$ d. $729V$

11.2.2 What is the relationship?

Tangents and Arcs

Today, you will develop new geometric tools as you continue to study the Earth and its measure.

11-91.   EYE IN THE SKY

Did you know that as of 2012, there were approximately 3000 operating satellites orbiting the Earth performing various functions such as taking photographs of the planet? One way that scientists learn more about the Earth is to carefully examine photographs that are taken by an orbiting satellite. Everyday citizens also use imagery from these satellites in applications such as maps on cell phones.

Satellite

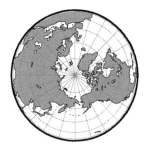

However, how much of the Earth can a satellite see? What does this depend upon? In other words, what information would you need to know in order to figure out how much of the planet is in view of a satellite in space? Discuss this with your team and be ready to share your ideas with the rest of the class.

11-92.   Locate Satellites A, B, and C on the Lesson 11.2.2 Resource Page (or on a computer if you are using the technology tool).

a.   Draw an angle from Satellite A that shows the portion of the Earth's equator that is visible from the satellite. What is the relationship of the sides of the angle and the circle that represents the equator of the Earth?

b.   Draw quadrilateral *ADEF* that connects Satellite A, the points of tangency, and the center of the Earth (point *E*). If the measure of the angle at Satellite A is 90°, what is the measure of the equator's arc that is in view? Explain how you know.

c.   What is the relationship of *AD* and *AF*? Prove the relationship using congruent triangles.

d.   If $m\angle A = 90°$ and the radius of the Earth is 4000 miles, how far above the surface of the planet is Satellite A?

Core Connections Geometry

11-93.   What if the satellite is placed higher in orbit? Consider this as you answer the
          questions below.

    a.   Using a different colored line, draw the viewing angle from Satellite B.
          Label the points of tangency *G* and *H*. Will Satellite B see more or less of
          the Earth's equator than Satellite A?

    b.   If $m\angle B = 60°$, find the length of the equator in view of Satellite B.
          Assume that the radius of the Earth is 4000 miles.

    c.   Use a third color to draw the viewing angle from Satellite C. Label the
          points of tangency *J* and *K*. If $m\angle C = 45°$, find the $m\widehat{JK}$ and $m\widehat{JZK}$.

    d.   Is it possible for a satellite to see 50% of the Earth's equator? Why or why
          not?

11-94.   CONSTRUCTING A TANGENT TO A CIRCLE THROUGH A POINT

          In problems 11-92 and 11-93, you drew tangents to a circle through a given
          point. You may have done this by "eye-balling" a point on the circle.
          However, how can the point of tangency be found using geometric
          construction? Do the following to find the answer to this question.

    a.   On a blank piece of paper, use a compass to construct a circle *E*. Then
          mark and label a point outside the circle *A*.

    b.   Tyler remembers that a line tangent to a circle at a point must be
          perpendicular to the radius of the circle at that same point. *"How can we
          find a point that makes a right triangle with the center of the circle and the
          location of Satellite A?"*

          Shana said "Maybe a different circle will
          help. If $\overline{EA}$ *is a diameter of a circle, then*
          any other points on that circle must form a
          right triangle with points E and A." She
          drew the diagram at right. Is Shana correct?
          Discuss Shana's idea with your team.

    c.   With your compass and straightedge, construct $\overline{EA}$ and mark its midpoint,
          M. Then construct the circle through *A* with center *M*. Label one of the
          points where ⊙*M* intersects ⊙*E* point *B*.

    d.   Construct $\overleftrightarrow{AB}$. Prove that $\overleftrightarrow{AB}$ is tangent to ⊙*E* at *B*.

11-95.   HOW ARE THEY RELATED?

In problems 11-92 and 11-93, you found the
measures of angles and arcs formed by two
tangents to a circle that intersect each other.

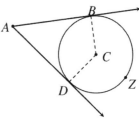

a.   Copy the diagram at right onto your paper.
Using intuition, describe how the measure
of the angle formed by the tangents ($m\angle A$) seems to be related to the
measures of the major and minor arcs formed by the points of tangency
($\overset{\frown}{BD}$ and $\overset{\frown}{BZD}$).

b.   If $m\angle A = x$, find $m\overset{\frown}{BD}$ and $m\overset{\frown}{BZD}$ in terms of x. Compare the measure of
the angle with the measure of the major and minor arcs. What do you
notice?

c.   LEARNING LOG

Write an entry in your Learning Log describing the
relationship between the angles and arcs formed by
two intersecting tangents to a circle. Also record
what you found out about the lengths of the tangents
from the point of tangency to their point of intersection. Title this entry
"Tangents and Arcs" and include today's date.

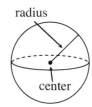

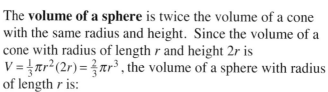

METHODS AND **M**EANINGS

Volume and Surface Area of a Sphere

A **sphere** is a three-dimensional solid formed
by points that are equidistant from its center.

radius

The **volume of a sphere** is twice the volume of a cone
with the same radius and height. Since the volume of a
cone with radius of length r and height $2r$ is
$V = \frac{1}{3}\pi r^2 (2r) = \frac{2}{3}\pi r^3$, the volume of a sphere with radius
of length r is:

center

$$V = \tfrac{4}{3}\pi r^3$$

The **surface area of a sphere** is four times the area of a circle with
the same radius. Thus, the surface area of a sphere with radius of
length r is:

$$SA = 4\pi r^2$$

11-96. While making his lunch, Alexander sliced off a portion of his grapefruit. If the area of the cross-section of the slice (shaded at right) was 3 in.^{2}, and if the diameter of the grapefruit was 5 inches long, find the distance between the center of the grapefruit and the slice. Assume the grapefruit is a sphere.

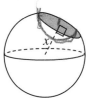

11-97. The approximate surface areas of the seven Earth continents are shown in the table at right. If the radius of the Earth's moon is approximately 1080 miles, how would its surface area compare with the size of the continents?

Continent	Area (sq. miles)
Asia	17,212,048.1
Africa	11,608,161.4
North America	9,365,294.0
South America	6,879,954.4
Antarctica	5,100,023.4
Europe	3,837,083.3
Australia/Oceania	2,967,967.3

11-98. A bag contains four red pens, six green pens, and two blue pens. If three pens are chosen at random, what is the probability that one of each color is picked?

11-99. Find the area of a regular decagon if the length of each side is 20 units.

11-100. The solid at right is an example of a **truncated pyramid**. It is formed by slicing and removing the top of a pyramid so that the slice is parallel to the base of the pyramid. If the original height of the square-based pyramid at right was 12 cm, find the volume of this truncated pyramid. (Hint: You may find your results from problem 11-86 useful.)

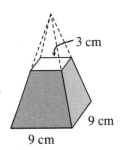

11-101. Examine the triangles at right. Are they similar? Are they congruent? Explain how you know. Then write an appropriate similarity or congruence statement.

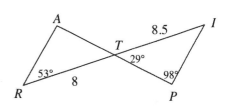

11-102. This problem is a checkpoint for computing volumes and surface areas of prisms and cylinders. It will be referred to as Checkpoint 11.

Compute the volume and surface area of each solid.

a.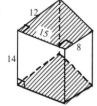

b.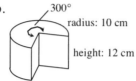
radius: 10 cm

height: 12 cm

c.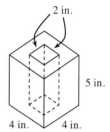

Check your answers by referring to the Checkpoint 11 materials located at the back of your book.

Ideally, at this point you are comfortable working with these types of problems and can solve them correctly. If you feel that you need more confidence when solving these types of problems, then review the Checkpoint 11 materials and try the practice problems provided. From this point on, you will be expected to do problems like these correctly and with confidence.

11-103. **Multiple Choice:** Which shape below has the *least* area?

a.   A circle with radius 5 units.

b.   A square with side length 9 units.

c.   A trapezoid with bases of length 8 and 10 units and height of 9 units.

d.   A rhombus with side length 9 units and height of 8 units.

11.2.3 What is the measure?

Secant and Tangent Relationships

In Lesson 11.2.2, you studied the angles and arcs formed by tangents when a satellite orbits the Earth, as shown in the diagram at right. Today, you will consider a related question: What if the sides of the angle intersect the circle more than once? What are the relationships between the angles and arcs formed when this happens? And what can you learn about the lengths of the segments created by the points of intersection?

Satellite

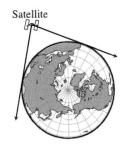

As you work with your team, carefully record your team's conjectures. And while you work, keep the following questions in mind:

What patterns do I see?

Is this relationship always true?

11-104. Review what you learned in Lesson 11.2.2 by solving for the given variables in the diagrams below. Show all work.

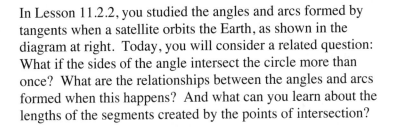

a. 68° x y   b. x 152° y   c. x 8

11-105. While a tangent is a line that intersects a circle (such as $\odot C$ in the diagram at right) at exactly one point, a **secant** is a line that intersects a circle twice. $\overleftrightarrow{PR}$ is an example of a secant, while $\overleftrightarrow{QS}$ is an example of a tangent.

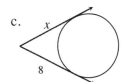

a. What happens to the measure of the angles and arcs when a secant intersects the circle at the point of tangency? Namely, how are the angles located at point P in the diagram above related to $m\overarc{PR}$ and $m\overarc{PTR}$? First make an educated guess. Then test your ideas out using a technology tool. Write a conjecture and be ready to share it with the class.

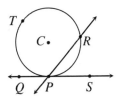

Problem continues on next page →

11-105. *Problem continued from previous page.*

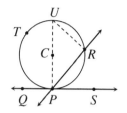

b. Uri wants to prove his conjecture from part (a) for a non-special secant (meaning that $\overline{PR}$ is not a diameter). He decided to extend a diameter from point P and to create an inscribed angle that intercepts $\overset{\frown}{PR}$. With your team, examine Uri's diagram carefully and consider all the relationships you can identify that could be useful. To get you started, use the list below.

   i.   What is $m\angle URP$?

   ii. How is $m\angle RUP$ related to $m\overset{\frown}{PR}$?

   iii. What is the sum of the angles in $\triangle PRU$?

   iv. How are $\angle UPR$ and $\angle RPS$ related?

c. Using the relationships you explored in part (b), prove that if $m\angle RPS = x$ in the diagram from part (b), then $m\overset{\frown}{PR} = 2x$. Remember to justify each step.

11-106. Uri now has this challenge for you: *What happens when secants and tangents intersect outside a circle?* To consider this, you need to examine two separate cases: One is when a secant and tangent intersect outside a circle (case *i* below). The other is when two secants intersect outside a circle (case *ii* below). As with your earlier investigations,

- First make a prediction about the relationship between the measures of x, a, and b for each case.

- Then use your technology tool to test your conjectures.

- For each case, write an algebraic statement (equation) that relates x, a, and b. Be ready to share each equation with the rest of the class.

i.

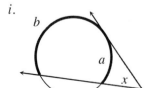

ii.

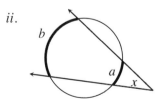

11-107. Now prove your conjectures from problem 11-106. For each diagram, add a line segment that will help to create an inscribed angle. Then use angle relationships (such as the sum of the angles of a triangle must be 180°) to then find the measures of all the angles in terms of x, a, and b. Be sure to show that in each case, $x = \frac{b-a}{2}$. Remember to justify each statement.

i.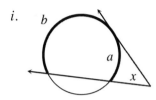

ii.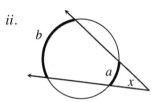

11-108. Camille is interested in the lengths of segments that are created by the points of intersection. She remembers proving in Lesson 11.2.2 that the lengths of the tangents between their intersection and the points of tangency are equal, as shown in the diagram at right. She figures that there must be some relationships in the lengths created by the intersections of secants, too.

a. The first case she wants to consider is when a tangent and secant intersect outside a circle, as shown in the figure at right. Copy this diagram onto your paper.

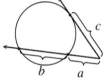

b. *"To find a relationship, I think we need to add some line segments to create some inscribed angles and triangles,"* Camille tells her team. She decides to add the line segments shown at right. Show why the angles marked x and y must be congruent.

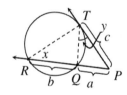

c. *"If some of these triangles are similar, I can use that to find a relationship between these side lengths,"* Camille explains. Help her prove that $\triangle PQT \sim \triangle PTR$.

d. Use the fact that $\triangle PQT \sim \triangle PTR$ to write a proportion using a, b, and c. Simplify this equation as much as possible to find an equation that helps you understand the relationship between a, b, and c.

e. Use the same process to find the relationship between the lengths created when two secants intersect outside a circle. Two extra segments have been added to the diagram to help create similar triangles. Be ready to justify your relationship.

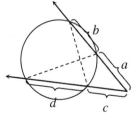

11-109. Use all your circle relationships to solve for the variables in each of the diagrams below.

a.

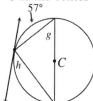

31° x y 168°

b.

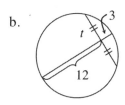

t 3   12

c.

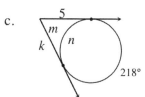

5   m n k 218°

d. C is the center

57°

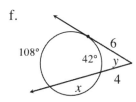

g h C

e.

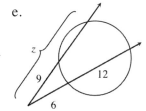

z 9   6   12

f.

108°   42°   6 y x 4

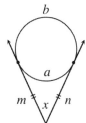

11-110. Solve for the variables in each of the diagrams below. Assume point C is the center of the circle in part (b).

a.

b.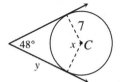

c.

11-111. In part (c) of problem 11-110, you used the relationship between the segment lengths formed by intersecting chords to find a missing length. But how are the arc measures of two random intersecting chords related? Examine the diagram at right.

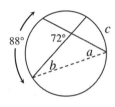

a. Solve for a, b, and c using what you know about inscribed angles and the sum of the angles of a triangle.

b. Compare the result for c with 88° and 72°. Is there a relationship?

11-112. Dr. G, the principal at Westside High School Academy, is worried that the students who win academic awards might also be the ones more likely to win awards in the Fine Arts. He would like to spread out the awards more. Does Dr. G have anything to worry about? Out of the 768 students, 128 won academic awards of some sort, and 48 won Fine Arts awards. 8 won both kinds of awards.

11-113. On your paper, draw a diagram of a square-based right pyramid. If the base has side length 6 units and the height of the pyramid is 10 units, find the total surface area. Show all your work.

11-114. Perhaps you think the Earth is big? Consider the sun!

a. Assume that the radius of the Earth is 4000 miles. The sun is approximately 109 times as wide. Find the sun's radius.

b. The distance between the Earth and the moon is 238,900 miles. Compare this distance with the radius of the sun you found in part (a).

c. If the sun were hollow, how many Earths would fill the inside of it?

11-115. A cube has an edge length of 16 units. Draw a diagram of the cube and find its volume and surface area.

11-116. **Multiple Choice:** Which of the following cannot be the measure of an exterior angle of a regular polygon?

a. 18°   b. 24°   c. 28°   d. 40°

11-117. Solve for the variables in each of the diagrams below. Assume that point C is the center of the circle in part (b).

a.
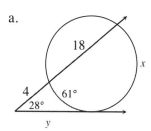

b.
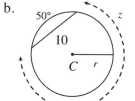

c.
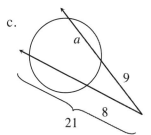

11-118. Which has greater volume: a cylinder with radius 38 units and height 71 units or a rectangular prism with dimensions 34, 84, and 99 units? Show all work and support your reasoning.

11-119. Jean Luc's favorite Asian restaurant has six dishes on its lunch menu. He wants to get their three-item combo for lunch. The server reminds Jean Luc that he can choose two or three servings of the same dish if he wants. How many different ways could he order lunch?

11-120. Copy the diagram at right onto your paper. Use the process from problem 11-111 to find the measure of x. Show all work.

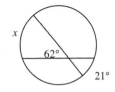

11-121. Find the equation of an exponential function that passes through the points $(1, 6)$ and $(5, 30.375)$.

11-122. A solar eclipse occurs when the moon passes between the Earth and the sun and is perfectly aligned so that it blocks the Earth's view of the sun.

Note: This diagram is not to scale.

How do scientists figure out what areas of the Earth will see an eclipse? To find out, copy the diagram above onto your paper. Then use tangents representing the sun's rays to visually show the portion of the Earth's equator that will see the total eclipse. You do not need to calculate this area, just show it on the diagram.

11-123. **Multiple Choice:** The Mona Lisa, by Leonardo da Vinci, is arguably the most famous painting in existence. The rectangular artwork, which hangs in the Musée du Louvre, measures 77 cm by 53 cm. When the museum created a billboard with an enlarged version of the portrait for advertisement, they used a linear scale factor of 20. What was the area of the billboard?

a. 4081 cm²   b. 32,638,000 cm²

c. 81,620 cm²   d. 1,632,400 cm²

e. None of these

Chapter 11 Closure   What have I learned?

Reflection and Synthesis

The activities below offer you a chance to reflect
about what you have learned during this chapter. As
you work, look for concepts that you feel very
comfortable with, ideas that you would like to learn
more about, and topics you need more help with.
Look for connections between ideas as well as
connections with material you learned previously.

①   TEAM BRAINSTORM

What have you studied in this chapter? What ideas were important in what you
learned? With your team, brainstorm a list. Be as detailed as you can. To help
get you started, lists of Learning Log entries, Toolkit Entries, and Math Notes
boxes are below.

What topics, ideas, and words that you learned *before* this chapter are connected
to the new ideas in this chapter? Again, be as detailed as you can.

Next consider the Standards for Mathematical Practice that follow Activity ③:
Portfolio. What Mathematical Practices did you use in this chapter? When did
you use them? Give specific examples.

How long can you make your lists? Challenge yourselves. Be prepared to
share your team's ideas with the class.

Learning Log Entries
- Lesson 11.1.1 – Plato's Solids
- Lesson 11.2.2 – Tangents and Arcs

Toolkit Entries
- Three-Dimensional Solids Toolkit (Lesson 11.1.3A
  Resource Pages, problems 11-38, 11-57, and 11-71)

Math Notes
- Lesson 11.1.2 – Pyramid Vocabulary
- Lesson 11.1.3 – Cross-Sections of Three-Dimensional Solids
- Lesson 11.1.4 – Volume of a Pyramid
- Lesson 11.1.5 – Volume and Lateral Surface of a Cone
- Lesson 11.2.2 – Volume and Surface Area of a Sphere
- Lesson 11.2.3 – Intersecting Tangents

MAKING CONNECTIONS

Below is a list of the vocabulary used in this chapter. Make sure that you are familiar with all of these words and know what they mean. Refer to the glossary or index for any words that you do not yet understand.

apex	arc	base
circle	cone	cross-section
cube	cylinder	diameter
edge	equator	face
great circle	height	hemisphere
lateral face	latitude	longitude
meridian	oblique	octahedron
platonic solid	polyhedron	pyramid
radius	secant	slant height
sphere	surface area	tangent
tetrahedron	volume	

Make a concept map showing all of the connections you can find among the key words and ideas listed above. To show a connection between two words, draw a line between them and explain the connection. A word can be connected to any other word as long as you can justify the connection. For each key word or idea, provide an example or sketch that shows the idea.

While you are making your map, your team may think of related words or ideas that are not listed here. Be sure to include these ideas on your concept map.

③ PORTFOLIO: EVIDENCE OF MATHEMATICAL PROFICIENCY

Showcase your ability to work with solids by solving the following problem. Make sure your explanation is clear and in detail. Remember you are not only showcasing your understanding of the mathematics, but you are also showcasing your ability to communicate your justifications.

The Germany Historical Society has just acquired a castle on the Rhine River and wishes to turn it into a museum. But for it to be inviting to guests, they must heat the castle and place a new layer of plaster around the outside. If one commercial heater can heat about 16,000 cubic feet, how many heaters will the Society need to purchase? How many square feet of plaster will they need (ignoring the windows)? The Society has modeled the castle with the following diagram:

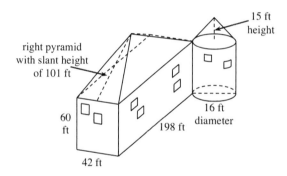

Next, consider the Standards for Mathematical Practice that follow. What Mathematical Practices did you use in this chapter? When did you use them? Give specific examples.

BECOMING MATHEMATICALLY PROFICIENT
The Common Core State Standards for Mathematical Practice

This book focuses on helping you use some very specific Mathematical Practices. The Mathematical Practices describe ways in which mathematically proficient students engage with mathematics everyday.

Make sense of problems and persevere in solving them:

Making sense of problems and persevering in solving them means that you can solve problems that are full of different kinds of mathematics. These types of problems are not routine, simple, or typical. Instead, they combine lots of math ideas and everyday situations. You have to stick with challenging problems, try different strategies, use multiple representations, and use a different method to check your results.

Reason abstractly and quantitatively:

Throughout this course, everyday situations are used to introduce you to new math ideas. Seeing mathematical ideas within a context helps you make sense of the ideas. Once you learn about a math idea in a practical way, you can **reason abstractly** by thinking about the concept more generally, representing it with symbols, and manipulating the symbols. **Reasoning quantitatively** is using numbers and symbols to represent an everyday situation, taking into account the units involved, and considering the meaning of the quantities as you compute them.

Construct viable arguments and critique the reasoning of others:

To **construct a viable argument** is to present your solution steps in a logical sequence and to justify your steps with conclusions, relying on number sense, facts and definitions, and previously established results. You communicate clearly, consider the real-life context, and provide clarification when others ask. In this course, you regularly share information, opinions, and expertise with your study team. You **critique the reasoning of others** when you analyze the approach of others, build on each other's ideas, compare the effectiveness of two strategies, and decide what makes sense and under what conditions.

Model with mathematics:

When you **model with mathematics**, you take a complex situation and use mathematics to represent it, often by making assumptions and approximations to simplify the situation. Modeling allows you to analyze and describe the situation and to make predictions. For example, to find the density of your body, you might model your body with a more familiar shape, say, a cylinder of the same diameter and height. Although a model may not be perfect, it can still be very useful for describing data and making predictions. When you interpret the results, you may need to go back and improve your model by revising your assumptions and approximations.

Use appropriate tools strategically:

To **use appropriate tools strategically** means that you analyze the task and decide which tools may help you model the situation or find a solution. Some of the tools available to you include diagrams, graph paper, calculators, computer software, databases, and websites. You understand the limitations of various tools. A result can be checked or estimated by strategically choosing a different tool.

Attend to precision:

To **attend to precision** means that when solving problems, you need to pay close attention to the details. For example, you need to be aware of the units, or how many digits your answer requires, or how to choose a scale and label your graph. You may need to convert the units to be consistent. At times, you need to go back and check whether a numerical solution makes sense in the context of the problem.

You need to **attend to precision** when you communicate your ideas to others. Using the appropriate vocabulary and mathematical language can help make your ideas and reasoning more understandable to others.

Look for and make use of structure:

Looking for and making use of structure is a guiding principle of this course. When you are involved in analyzing the structure and in the actual development of mathematical concepts, you gain a deeper, more conceptual understanding than when you are simply told what the structure is and how to do problems. You often use this practice to bring closure to an investigation.

There are many concepts that you learn by looking at the underlying structure of a mathematical idea and thinking about how it connects to other ideas you have already learned. For example, geometry theorems are developed from the structure of translations.

Look for and express regularity in repeated reasoning:

To **look for and express regularity in repeated reasoning** means that when you are investigating a new mathematical concept, you notice if calculations are repeated in a pattern. Then you look for a way to generalize the method for use in other situations, or you look for shortcuts. For example, the investigations with simple shapes can be applied to more complex shapes using repeated reasoning.

④   WHAT HAVE I LEARNED?

Most of the problems in this section
represent typical problems found in
this chapter. They serve as a gauge
for you. You can use them to
determine which types of problems
you can do well and which types of
problems require further study and
practice. Even if your teacher does
not assign this section, it is a good
idea to try these problems and find out
for yourself what you know and what
you still need to work on.

Solve each problem as completely as you can. The table at the end of the
closure section has answers to these problems. It also tells you where you
can find additional help and practice with problems like these.

CL 11-124. Use all your circle relationships to solve for the variables in each of the
diagrams below.

a.

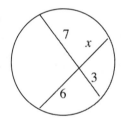

b.

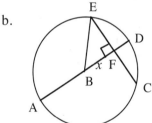

EC = 8 and AB = 5

c. $\overline{MN} \cong \overline{PQ}$, MN = $7x+13$,
and PQ = $10x-8$.

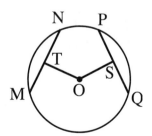

CL 11-125. On graph paper, draw $\triangle ABC$ if $A(2,4)$, $B(9,5)$, and $C(4,10)$.

    a.   Verify that $D(3,7)$ is a midpoint of $\overline{AC}$.

    b.   Find the equation of the line through points D and B.

    c.   Is $\overline{BD}$ a height of $\triangle ABC$? Use slope to show that $\overline{BD}$ is perpendicular to $\overline{AC}$.

CL 11-126. Four brown dogs and two white dogs are in a large doghouse. Someone tells you that exactly two dogs are asleep.

    a.   What is the probability that the two dogs are brown?

    b.   What is the probability that the two dogs are both white?

    c.   What is the probability that one dog is white and the other is brown?

    d.   If someone also told you the two sleeping dogs were the same color, what is the probability they are brown?

CL 11-127. In the game Tic Tac Toe, players can choose to put their marker in any square that is not already occupied. The rows can be labeled **T**op, **M**iddle, **B**ottom, and the columns **L**eft, **I**nner, **R**ight, as shown in the diagram below. For example, the first three moves might be MI, BR, then TL.

	Left	Inner	Right
Top	✓		
Middle		✓	
Bottom			✓

    a.   How many different ways are there to make the first three moves in Tic Tac Toe? In this case, you are not concerned with which player made the move, just what the first three moves were.

    b.   If you have not done so already, write your answer to part (a) as a fraction with factorials.

CL 11-128. Find the volume and surface area of a right pyramid if its height is 7 mm and its base is a regular pentagon with perimeter 20 mm.

CL 11-129. According to a survey, in 2010 pet ownership in the U.S. was distributed as shown in the table below (out of every 1000 households).

Household income	Number with primarily dogs	Number with primarily cats	Number with primarily birds	Number with primarily horses	Number with no pets
under $20,000	64	63	9	3	70
$20,000 to $34,999	66	59	7	3	41
$35,000 to $54,999	77	66	8	4	38
$55,000 to $84,999	82	68	7	4	31
$85,000 and over	97	77	9	5	42

    a.   What is the probability of having no pets?

    b.   What is the probability of having a pet?

    c.   If a person is selected at random, what is the probability the person earns under $35,000 *and* owns a dog?

    d.   What is the probability the person earns under $35,000 *or* owns a dog?

    e.   Use another method for determining the probability of earning under $35,000 *or* owning a dog to verify your result for part (d).

    f.   What is the probability that a randomly-selected person who earns under $35,000 owns a dog?

CL 11-130. Examine the triangles below. Based on the markings and measurements provided in the diagrams, which are similar to $\triangle ABC$ at right? Which are congruent? Are there any that you cannot determine? Justify your conclusion and, if appropriate, write a similarity or congruence statement. Note: The diagrams are not drawn to scale.

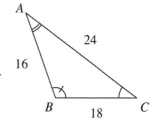

    a.

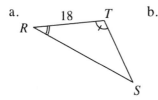

    b.   c.

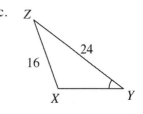

CL 11-131. Talila is planning on giving her geometry teacher a gift. She has two containers to choose from:

- A cylinder tube with diameter 6 inches and height 10 inches.

- A rectangular box with dimensions 5 inches by 6 inches by 9 inches.

a. Assuming that her gift can fit in either box, which will require the least amount of wrapping paper?

b. She plans to tie three loops of ribbon about the package as shown at right. Which package will require the least amount of ribbon? Ignore any ties or bows.

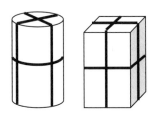

CL 11-132. A big warehouse carrying tents has a miniature model that is similar to the full-sized tent. The tent is a triangular-based prism and the miniature model has dimensions shown in the diagram at right.

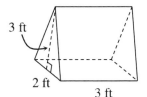

a. How much fabric does the small tent use? That is, what is its surface area?

b. What is the volume of the small model?

c. If the volume of the full-sized model is 72 ft^3, how tall is the full-sized tent?

d. How much fabric does the full-sized tent use?

CL 11-133. Check your answers using the table at the end of the closure section. Which problems do you feel confident about? Which problems were hard? Use the table to make a list of topics you need help on and a list of topics you need to practice more.

Answers and Support for Closure Activity #4
What Have I Learned?

Note: MN = Math Note, LL = Learning Log

Problem	Solution	Need Help?	More Practice
CL 11-124.	a. $x = 3.5$ b. $x = 3$ c. $x = 7$	Section 10.1 MN: 10.1.2, 10.1.3, and 10.1.4 LL: 10.1.2 and 10.1.3	Problems CL 10-185, CL 10-186, 11-44, 11-110, 11-111, 11-117, and 11-120
CL 11-125.	a. Typical response: The distance between A and D ($\sqrt{10}$) equals the distance between B and D (also $\sqrt{10}$). b. $y = -\frac{1}{3}x + 8$ c. Yes, the slope of $\overline{BD}$ is $-\frac{1}{3}$ while the slope of $\overline{AC}$ is 3. Since the slopes are opposite reciprocals, $\overline{BD}$ is perpendicular to $\overline{AC}$.	Lessons 2.3.2 and 7.3.2 Checkpoint 3 MN: 1.2.6, 2.3.2, and 7.3.3 LL: 2.3.2 and 7.3.2	Problems CL 2-121, CL 3-116, CL 5-147, CL 7-151, and CL 7-153
CL 11-126.	a. $\frac{_4C_2}{_6C_2} = \frac{6}{15} = 40\%$, or $\frac{_4P_2}{_6P_2} = \frac{4\cdot3}{6\cdot5} = 40\%$ b. $\frac{_2C_2}{_6C_2} = \frac{1}{15} \approx 6.7\%$ or $\frac{_2P_2}{_6P_2} = \frac{2}{30} \approx 6.7\%$ c. $1 - (\frac{6}{15} + \frac{1}{15}) = \frac{8}{15} \approx 53.3\%$ d. P(brown given same color) = $\frac{\frac{6}{15}}{\frac{6}{15} + \frac{1}{15}} = \frac{6}{7}$	Lesson 10.3.3 MN: 10.3.3 LL: 10.3.4	Problems 10-153, 10-155, 10-173, 11-26, 11-41, 11-59, and 11-87
CL 11-127.	a. $_9P_3 = 504$ b. $_9P_3 = \frac{9!}{(9-3)!} = \frac{9!}{6!}$	Lesson 10.3.2 MN: 10.3.2 LL: 10.3.4	Problems 10-128, 10-143, 10-155, 11-9, 11-26, 11-49, 11-60

Problem	Solution	Need Help?	More Practice
CL 11-128.	$V \approx 64.23$ mm.^{3}, SA $= 102.75$ mm^2	Lessons 8.1.5, 11.1.2, and 11.1.3 MN: 8.3.1, 11.1.2, and 11.1.4 LL: 8.1.4 and 8.1.5 Three-Dimensional Solids Toolkit	Problems CL 9-114, 10-46, 11-25, 11-40, 11-52, 11-86, 11-100, and 11-113
CL 11-129.	a. $\frac{222}{1000} = 22.2\%$ b. $1 - \frac{222}{1000} = \frac{778}{1000} = 77.8\%$ c. $\frac{130}{1000} = 13\%$ d. See solution to part (e) below. e. Either sum the appropriate cells: $\frac{64+63+9+3+70+66+59+7+3+41+77+82+97}{1000} = 64.1\%$ or use the Addition Rule: $\frac{385}{1000} + \frac{386}{1000} - \frac{130}{1000} = \frac{641}{1000} = 64.1\%$ f. P(dog given < \$35,000) = $\frac{64+66}{64+63+9+3+70+66+59+7+3+41} = 33.7\%$	Section 10.2 MN: 10.2.1 and 10.2.3 LL: 10.2.1 and 10.2.3	Problems CL 10-188, 11-50, and 11-88
CL 11-130.	a. $\triangle ABC \sim \triangle RTS$ (AA~) b. $\triangle ABC \sim \triangle MPK$ (AAS $\cong$) c. Cannot be determined because there are two possible triangles when SSA is given.	Section 3.2 MN: 3.1.4, 3.2.1, and 3.2.5 LL: 3.1.2 and 3.2.4	Problems CL 3-122, CL 4-123, CL 5-140, 11-62, and 11-101
CL 11-131.	a. The cylinder needs less paper (SA $= 78\pi$ in.^{2}). b. The prism requires less ribbon (80 in.).	Lessons 9.1.2 and 9.1.3 Checkpoint 11 MN: 9.1.2 and 9.1.3 Three-Dimensional Solids Toolkit	Problems 11-10, 11-47, 11-58, and 11-102

Problem	Solution	Need Help?	More Practice
CL 11-132.	a. SA ≈ 31.0 ft^2 b. V ≈ 9 ft^3 c. linear scale factor = 2, height = 6 ft d. SA ≈ 124 ft^2	Lessons 9.1.4 and 9.1.5 MN: 9.1.3 and 9.1.5 LL: 9.1.1, 9.1.2, and 9.1.4 Three-Dimensional Solids Toolkit	Problems CL 9-112, CL 10-191, 11-12, 11-43, 11-86, 11-90, and 11-123

CHAPTER 12   Conics and Closure

As this course draws to a close, it is appropriate to reflect on what you have learned so far as you continue to see connections between topics in both algebra and geometry.

For example, in Section 12.1, you will extend your geometric understanding of circles to write algebraic equations for circles. Then you will look at the cross-sections of a cone, called conic sections and learn about the geometric properties of parabolas.

Then in Section 12.2, four activities offer a chance for you to apply your geometric tools in new ways. You will find new connections between familiar geometric ideas and learn more special properties of familiar shapes.

Guiding Question

Mathematically proficient students look for and make use of structure.

As you work through this chapter, ask yourself:

How can I connect these ideas to previous topics, and can I make it simpler or make a generalization?

Chapter Outline

Section 12.1   You will start with what you know geometrically about a circle, and extend it to write an algebraic equation for a circle. By studying the different cross-sections of a cone (the conic sections), and a parabola in particular, you will further discover how geometry and algebra can each define a shape.

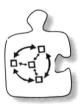

Section 12.2   As you complete the course closure activities in this section, you will apply the mathematics you have learned throughout this course. For example, you will discover a special ratio that seems to occur in nature and art, find new relationships that exist in basic polyhedra, learn about a shape created when the midpoints of the sides of a quadrilateral are connected, and determine where a goat should be tethered to a barn so that it has the lowest probability of eating a poisoned weed.

12.1.1 What is the equation?

The Equation of a Circle

During Chapters 7 through 10, you studied circles *geometrically*, that is, based on the geometric shape of a circle. For example, the relationship between circles and polygons helped you develop a method to find the area and circumference of a circle, while geometric relationships of intersecting circles helped you develop constructions of shapes such as a rhombus and a kite.

However, how can circles be represented *algebraically* or *graphically*? And how can you use these representations to learn more about circles? Today your team will develop the equation of a circle.

12-1. **EQUATION OF A CIRCLE**

You know equations for lines and parabolas, but what type of equation could represent a circle? On a piece of graph paper, draw a set of *xy*-axes. Then use a compass to construct a circle with radius of length 10 units centered at the origin $(0, 0)$.

a. What do all of the points on this circle have in common? That is, what is true about each point on the circle?

b. Find all of the points on the circle where $x = 6$. For each point, what is the *y*-value? Use a right triangle (like the one shown at right) to justify your answer.

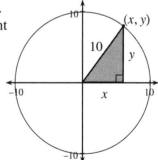

c. What if $x = 3$? For each point on the circle where $x = 3$, find the corresponding *y*-value. Use a right triangle to justify your answer.

d. Mia picked a random point on the circle and labeled it (x, y). Unfortunately, she does not know the value of *x* or *y*! Help her write an equation that relates *x*, *y*, and 10 based on her diagram above.

e. Does your equation from part (d) work for the points $(10, 0)$ and $(0, 10)$? What about $(-8, -6)$? Explain.

12-2.   In problem 12-1, you wrote an equation of a circle with radius of length 10 units and center at $(0, 0)$.

   a.   What if the radius were instead 4 units long? Discuss this with your team and write an equation of this circle.

   b.   Write the equation of a circle centered at $(0, 0)$ with radius r.

   c.   On graph paper, sketch the graph of $x^2 + y^2 = 36$. Can you graph it without a table? Explain your method.

   d.   Describe the graph of the circle $x^2 + y^2 = 0$.

12-3.   What if the center of the circle is not at $(0, 0)$? On graph paper, construct a circle with a center $A(3, 1)$ and radius of length 5 units.

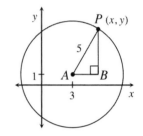

   a.   On the diagram at right, point P represents a point on the circle with no special characteristics. Add a point P to your diagram and then draw a right triangle like $\triangle ABP$ in the circle at right.

   b.   What is the length of $\overline{PB}$? Write an expression to represent this length. Likewise, what is the length of $\overline{AB}$?

   c.   Use your expressions for AB and BP, along with the fact that the length of the radius of the circle is 5 units, to write an equation for this circle. (Note: You do not need to worry about multiplying any binomials.)

   d.   Find the equation of each circle represented below.

      (1) The circle with center $(2, 7)$ (2)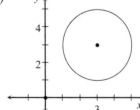
           and radius of length 1 unit.

      (3) The circle for which $(6, 0)$ and
           $(-6, 0)$ are the endpoints of a
           diameter.

12-4.   On graph paper, graph and shade the solutions for the inequalities below. Then find the area of each shaded region.

   a. $x^2 + y^2 \le 49$ b. $(x - 3)^2 + (y - 2)^2 \le 4$

Core Connections Geometry

12-5.   LEARNING LOG

In a Learning Log entry, describe what you learned in this
lesson about the equation of a circle. What connections did
you make to other areas of algebra or geometry? Be sure to
include an example of how to find the equation of a circle given
its center and the length of its radius. Title this entry "Equation
of a Circle" and include today's date.

─────────── Review & Preview ───────────

12-6.   Examine the graph of the circle at right.

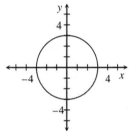

a.   Find the equation of the circle.

b.   On graph paper, sketch the graph of the
        equation $x^2 + y^2 = 49$. What is the radius?

12-7.   Find the volume of each shape below. Assume that all corners in part (b) are
         right angles.

a.   cone

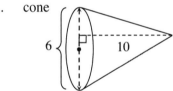

b.

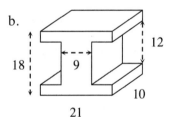

12-8.   Before there were radios and satellite communication systems, ships would
         communicate with each other by using a string of colored flags. With four blue
         flags and two red flags, how many six flag signals are possible?

12-9.   A credit union offers a long-term account that pays 6% interest compounded monthly and your college fund currently contains $8500.

    a.   What is the *monthly* multiplier?

    b.   Write a function of the form $f(t) = ab^t$ that represents the monthly situation.

    c.   At the current rate, what will be the value of the account in 5 years?

12-10.   Examine the diagram at right.

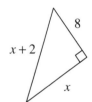

    a.   Write an equation using the geometric relationships in the diagram. Then solve your equation for x.

    b.   Find the measures of the acute angles of the triangle. What tool(s) did you use?

12-11.   Use the diagram of $\odot C$ at right to answer the questions below.

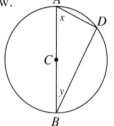

    a.   If $m\angle x = 28°$, what is $m\overset{\frown}{AD}$?

    b.   If $AD = 5$ and $BD = 5\sqrt{3}$, what is the area of $\odot C$?

    c.   If the radius of $\odot C$ is 8 and if $m\overset{\frown}{BD} = 100°$, what is BD?

12-12.   **Multiple Choice:** Based on the markings in the diagrams at right, which statement is true?

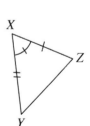
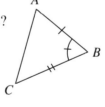

    a. $\triangle ABC \cong \triangle XYZ$

    b. $\triangle ABC \cong \triangle YXZ$

    c. $\triangle ABC \cong \triangle ZXY$

    d. $\triangle ABC \cong \triangle ZYX$

    e.   None of these

12.1.2 How can I graph a circle from its equation?

Completing the Square for Equations of Circles

In this lesson, you will use the technique of completing the square to rewrite the equation of a circle so that it is easier to graph.

12-13. Katelyn is a student assistant in the Musketeers Math Lab. She helps fellow students with their math homework.

Becky and Diego are working on their algebra homework. They have been asked to make a quick sketch of the equation $y = (x-2)^2 - 25$.

a. Becky started by making an $x \to y$ table as shown below. Will her approach work?

x	−10	−8	−6	−4	−2	0	2	4	6	8	10
y	119	75	39	11	−9	−21					

b. Diego started by rewriting the quadratic equation as $y = x^2 - 4x - 21$, then factoring to find $y = (x+3)(x-7)$, because he thought he could find the x-intercepts easier. Will his approach work mathematically?

c. Katelyn complimented Becky and Diego on their mathematical thinking. Then she went on to say that they were both working too hard if their goal was just to make a quick sketch. What did she mean? Be prepared to share your team's thinking with the rest of the class.

12-14. The **standard form** for a quadratic function is $y = ax^2 + bx + c$. But when the equation is rewritten in **graphing form**, $y = a(x-h)^2 + k$, the parabola is easier to graph. In graphing form, the vertex is at the point (h, k), and finding the x-intercept(s) is often easier from the graphing form than from the standard form.

a. Discuss with your team how you would make a quick sketch of $y = x^2 - 6x + 4$. Explain in detail how to find the x- and y-intercept(s) and the vertex. You do not actually have to make the computations or sketch the function.

b. Discuss with your team how you would make a quick sketch of the same equation written in graphing form, $y = (x-3)^2 - 5$. Again, explain in detail how to find the x- and y-intercept(s) and the vertex, but you do not actually have to make the computations or sketch the function.

12-15.   You may have learned the technique of **completing the square** in a previous course. It helps you rewrite a quadratic function that is given in standard form, $y = ax^2 + bx + c$, into graphing form, $y = a(x-h)^2 + k$.

Rewrite $y = x^2 + 8x + 10$ in graphing form and make a quick sketch of the function.

Further Guidance

12-16.   Diego was at the Musketeers Math Lab struggling with his Algebra I homework. He was supposed to **complete the square** to change $y = x^2 + 8x + 10$ to graphing form. Katelyn, the math lab assistant, brought over the algebra tiles. Katelyn explained, "$x^2 + 8x + 10$ *would look like this.*"

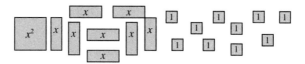

"*Yes,*" said Diego, a little testily. "*We've been using tiles all year, you know.*"

Katelyn patiently continued, "*Now, take the x and x^2 tiles and start making them into a square.*"

"*OK,*" said Diego. He arranged the one x^2-tile and the eight x-tiles as shown below.

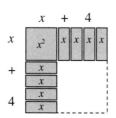

"*So, to make a **complete square**,*" said Katelyn, "*you need 16 small unit tiles to fill in the corner.*"

"*Oh, I get it!*" said Diego. "*The **complete square** is* $(x+4)^2$."

"*Yes, that's right,*" Katelyn continued. "*With the x and x^2 tiles, you can almost make* $(x+4)^2$, *but you are 16 unit tiles short. Therefore, $x^2 + 8x$ is equal to* $(x+4)^2 - 16$."

Diego was excited. "*Wait! Stop! I totally get it! I can change* $y = x^2 + 8x + 10$ *into graphing form now. Look!*" Diego wrote the following on his paper:

$$y = x^2 + 8x \qquad + 10$$
$$y = (x+4)^2 - 16 \ + 10$$
$$y = (x+4)^2 - 6$$

Problem continues on next page →

12-16.   *Problem continued from previous page.*

"Yes, exactly!" said Katelyn.

"Cool. And next time I don't think I even need tiles," said Diego. *"Instead, I can just start with a generic rectangle like this:"*

	x	$+4$
x	x^2	$4x$
$+4$	$4x$	16

Help Diego with a new problem. He needs to complete the square to write $y = x^2 + 4x + 9$ in graphing form. Draw a generic rectangle to help him figure out how to make the x and x^2 part into a square, and then write his equation in graphing form.

12-17.   How could you complete the square to change $f(x) = x^2 + 5x + 2$ into graphing form? How would you split the five x-tiles into two equal parts?

Diego decided to use brute force. He cut one x-tile in half, as shown below.

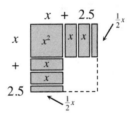

a.   How much is needed to complete the square?

b.   Write the graphing form of the equation.

───────────   *Further Guidance*   ───────────
              section ends here.

12-18.   Rewrite $y = x^2 + 3x + 4$ in graphing form. Then use either equation to find the x-intercepts algebraically. What happens? Why?

12-19. Equations of circles also have two forms.

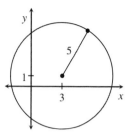

a. Write the equation of the circle graphed at right in **graphing form**, $(x-h)^2 + (y-k)^2 = r^2$, like you did in the previous lesson. What do h, k, and r represent in the graphing form of the equation of a circle?

b. Now, rewrite the equation of the circle from part (a) in **general form**, $ax^2 + ay^2 + bx + cy + d = 0$.

c. How can this process be done backwards? For example, if you are given an equation like $x^2 - 10x + y^2 - 4y = 7$, how can you change it to graphing form? Discuss with your team and be ready to share your strategy with the class.

12-20. Use what you have learned in this lesson to write $x^2 + y^2 - 8x + 6y + 9 = 0$ in a form that allows you to make a quick sketch of the circle.

12-21. A silo (a structure designed to store grain) is designed as a cylinder with a cone on top, as shown in the diagram at right.

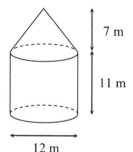

a. If a farmer wants to paint the silo, how much surface area must be painted?

b. What is the volume of the silo? That is, how many cubic meters of grain can the silo hold?

12-22. The figure at right is a **pentagram**. A pentagram is a 5-pointed star that has congruent angles at each of its outer vertices.

a. Use the fact that all pentagrams can be inscribed in a circle to find the measure of angle a at right.

b. Find the measure of angles b, c, and d.

12-23.   In Chapter 7, you discovered that the midsegment of a triangle is not only parallel to the third side, but also half its length. But what about the midsegment of a trapezoid?

The diagram at right shows a midsegment of a trapezoid. That is, $\overline{EF}$ is a midsegment because points E and F are both midpoints of the non-base sides of trapezoid $ABCD$.

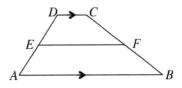

a.   If $A(0,0)$, $B(9,0)$, $C(5,6)$, and $D(2,6)$, find the coordinates of points E and F. Then compare the lengths of the bases ($\overline{AB}$ and $\overline{CD}$) with the length of the midsegment $\overline{EF}$. What seems to be the relationship?

b.   See if the relationship you observed in part (a) holds if $A(-4,0)$, $B(2,0)$, $C(0,2)$, and $D(-2,2)$.

c.   Write a conjecture about the midsegment of a trapezoid.

12-24.   Describe each circle by finding the center and radius. You need to "complete the square" to rewrite the equation in part (b) in graphing form.

a. $(x-2)^2 + (y+3)^2 = 25$ b. $x^2 + 2x + y^2 + 6y - 6 = 0$

12-25.   For each diagram below, solve for x. Show all work.

a.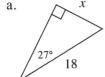

b.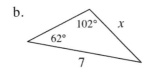

c.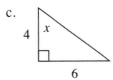

12-26.   For each relationship below, write and solve an equation for x. Justify your method.

a.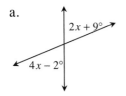

b.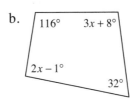

c.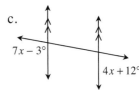

12-27.   **Multiple Choice:** The graph of $x^2 + y^2 = 4$ is:

　　a.　　A parabola with y-intercept $(0, 4)$.

　　b.　　A circle with radius 4 and center $(0, 0)$.

　　c.　　A parabola with x-intercepts $(-2, 0)$ and $(2, 0)$.

　　d.　　A circle with radius 2 and center $(0, 0)$.

　　e.　　None of these.

12-28.   Find the surface area of the solids below. Assume that the solid in part (a) is a prism with a regular octagonal base and the pyramid in part (b) is a square-based pyramid. Show all work.

　　a.

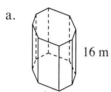

16 m

4 m

　　b.

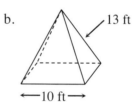

13 ft

←—10 ft—→

12-29.   Solve each equation below for the given variable. Check your solution by verifying that your solution makes the original equation true.

　　a.　　$\frac{2}{3}(15u - 6) = 14u$ 　　　　　b.　　$(5 - x)(3x + 8) = 0$

　　c.　　$2(k - 5)^2 = 32$ 　　　　　　　d.　　$2p^2 + 7p - 9 = 0$

12-30.   Examine the diagram at right.

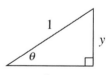

　　a.　　Explain why $y = \sin\theta$ and $x = \cos\theta$.

　　b.　　According to this diagram, what is $(\sin\theta)^2 + (\cos\theta)^2$? Explain how you know.

　　c.　　Does this relationship appear true for all angles? Use your calculator to find $(\sin 23°)^2 + (\cos 23°)^2$ and $(\sin 81°)^2 + (\cos 81°)^2$. Write down your findings.

12-31.   On graph paper, graph a circle with center $(4, 2)$ and radius 3 units.

   a.   Write its equation.

   b.   Find two points on the circle that are on opposite sides of the circle, that is they are 180° from one another. Prove that these two points are exactly one diameter in distance from each other.

12-32.   Solve the following problems:

   a.   How many numbers less than 500 can you make using the digits 0, 2, 4, 6, 8? Digits can be used over. A number cannot start with a zero.

   b.   How many numbers less than 500 are there if the digits 0, 2, 4, 6, 8 cannot be repeated? The lead digit cannot be zero.

12-33.   Use all your circle relationships to solve for the variables in each of the diagrams below.

   a. $\overline{AB}$ and $\overline{CD}$ b.   The area of $\odot C$ is 25π sq. units
         intersect at E.

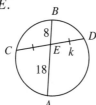   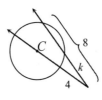

12-34.   **Multiple Choice:** What is the measure of each interior angle of a regular octagon?

   a.   135°   b.   120°   c.   180°   d.   1080°

12.1.3 What is the cross-section?

Introduction to Conic Sections

In Chapter 11 you learned about cross-sections of solids. (Refer to the Math Notes box in Lesson 11.1.3.) In this lesson you and your team will discover the various cross-sections of a cone. As you explore, look for connections with other mathematical concepts that you have studied previously.

12-35.   CONIC SECTIONS

Obtain the Lesson 12.1.3 Resource Page from your teacher and construct a cone. Then, with your team, explore the different cross-sections of a cone, which are called **conic sections**. Imagine slicing a cone as many different ways as you can. Draw and describe the shape of each cross-section on your paper. Do you know the names for any of these shapes?

12-36.   When mathematicians talk about conic sections, they are referring to the cross-sections that can be created from a *double* cone, a shape created with two cones placed in opposite directions with vertices together, as shown at right. The cone continues infinitely in both directions.

a.   Can a single point be a conic section? Explain.

b.   How you can slice the cone so that the cross-section is a line?

c.   What other conic sections are there? You should have seven all together.

12-37.   One of the conic sections that you have discovered
          can be constructed with perpendicular bisectors
          using tracing paper.

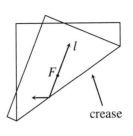

    a.   In your notebook, draw a line *l*, and a point *F* not on
          the line. Imagine (or sketch) all the segments
          connecting *F* with all the points on line *l*. What
          conic section do you think would appear if you drew
          all the perpendicular bisectors of those segments?

    b.   Now try it. On tracing paper, draw a line *l*, and a point *F* not on the line.
          Fold and crease the tracing paper so that line *l* passes through point *F* as
          shown in the figure above. This crease represents the perpendicular
          bisector of one of the segments connecting *F* with a point on line *l*.

          Unfold the tracing paper and fold it again at a different point on line *l* so
          that line *l* still passes through point *F*. Continue this process until you
          have at least 20 creased lines. What conic section appeared?

    c.   Describe where the conic section lies in relationship with the original point
          F and line *l*. Do these relationships seem to hold for the figures
          constructed by your teammates?

12-38.   FOCUS AND DIRECTRIX OF A PARABOLA

          Since the point and line help to determine the parabola, there are special names
          that are used to refer to them. The point is called the **focus** of the parabola,
          while the line is called the **directrix**.

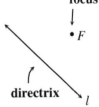

    a.   Together, the focus and the directrix determine the
          parabola. For example, can you visualize the
          parabola formed by the focus and directrix shown at
          right? Trace the point and line on your paper and
          sketch the parabola.

    b.   What is the relationship between the points on the parabola and its focus
          and directrix? Carefully sketch the parabola that formed on your tracing
          paper from problem 12-37. Mark a point on the parabola and label it *P*.
          Notice the segment between *F* and *P*, and compare it to the segment that is
          perpendicular to the directrix *l* and goes to *P*. What do you notice? Does
          this relationship seem to hold for all points on the parabola? Explain.

    c.   How does the distance between the focus (the point) and the
          directrix (the line) affect the shape of the parabola? Explore
          this using a technology tool, if possible. If a technology
          tool is not available, use tracing paper to test several different
          distances between the focus and directrix. Explain the result.

12-39.   LEARNING LOG

Write an entry in your Learning Log describing what you
learned during this lesson. Include information about the
cross-sections of a cone and the geometric relationships in
a parabola. What questions do you have about the other
conic sections? Title this entry "Conic Sections" and include today's date.

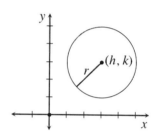

METHODS AND MEANINGS

Equation of a Circle

MATH NOTES

The equation of a circle can be
given in graphing form by the equation
$(x-h)^2 + (y-k)^2 = r^2$, where (h, k) are the
coordinates of the center of the circle, and
r is the radius. Note that the equation of a
circle does not describe a function,
because there are two y-values for most
x-values.

Alternatively, the equation of a circle can be written in general form as
$ax^2 + ay^2 + bx + cy + d = 0$ by multiplying the binomials. To rewrite the
equation of a circle in general form to one in graphing form, the
technique of completing the square can be used.

Review & Preview

12-40.   Cawker City, Kansas, claims to have the
world's largest ball of twine. Started in 1953
by Frank Stoeber, this ball has been created
by wrapping more than 1300 miles of twine.
In fact, this giant ball has a circumference of
40 feet. Assuming the ball of twine is a
sphere, find the surface area and volume of
the ball of twine.

12-41.   The equations below are the types of equations that you will need to be able to solve automatically in a later course. Try to solve these in 10 minutes or less. The solutions are provided after problem 12-46 for you to check your answers.

      a. $2x - 5 = 7$ b. $x^2 = 16$ c. $2(x - 1) = 6$

      d. $\frac{x}{5} = 6$ e. $2x^2 + 5 = x^2 + 14$ f $(x - 3)(x + 5) = 0$

12-42.   Examine the pen or pencil that you are using right now. Imagine slicing it in different directions. On your paper, draw at least three different cross-sections of the pen or pencil.

12-43.   On graph paper, graph $x^2 + y^2 = 9$.

      a.   Consider the inequality $x^2 + y^2 \le 9$. Does the point $(0, 0)$ make this inequality true? What is the graph of $x^2 + y^2 \le 9$? Explain.

      b.   Now consider the inequality $x^2 + y^2 > 9$. Does the point $(0, 0)$ make this inequality true? What region is shaded? Describe the graph of this inequality.

12-44.   Consider the sample space for flipping a coin 10 times in a row. In how many sequences of heads and tails will 5 of the 10 coins show heads?

12-45.   Consider the circle that is centered at the origin and contains the point $(0, 3)$.

      a.   Use geometry and the definition of a circle, but not the algebraic equation for a circle, to prove or disprove that the point $(1, \sqrt{5})$ lies on this circle.

      b.   Find at least one value of x so that the point $(x, \sqrt{5})$ lies on the circle.

      c.   Name 3 other points on this same circle.

12-46.   **Multiple Choice:** In the diagram at right, the value of x is:

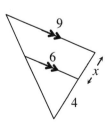

      a.   1   b.   2   c.   3

      d.   4   e.   None of these

Solutions to problem 12-41:

      a: $x = 6$, b: $x = 4$ or -4, c: $x = 4$, d: $x = 30$, e: $x = 3$ or -3, f: $x = 3$ or -5

12.1.4 How can I graph it?

Graphing a Parabola Using The Focus and Directrix

Over the centuries, cones were sliced and the resulting conic sections were described geometrically long before conic sections were described with algebraic equations. For example parabolas were geometrically described as the figure resulting from all the points that are equidistant from the focus and the directrix. A circle is the figure resulting from all the points equidistant from a center point.

You already know how to describe a circle both geometrically and with an algebraic equation, $(x-h)^2 + (x-y)^2 = r^2$. Today you will make an informal connection between the algebraic equation for a parabola, $y = ax^2 + bx + c$, and the geometric description of the focus and directrix of a parabola.

Making a connection between the equation of a cone, and the equations of its parabolas (and other conic sections) is also possible, but that is reserved for a future course.

12-47.   GRAPHING WITH A FOCUS AND DIRECTRIX

In the past, you have graphed conics, such as circles and parabolas, using rectangular graph paper and an equation. However, another way to graph conic sections is to use **focus-directrix graph paper**, that is designed with lines and concentric circles like the example shown in Figure A at right.

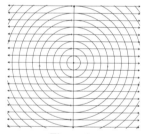

Figure A:
Focus-directrix paper

How can you graph parabolas using this paper? Obtain at least two sheets of focus-directrix paper (Lesson 12.1.4 Resource Page) from your teacher and follow the directions below.

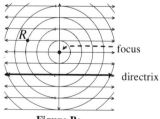

Figure B:
Point R on grid

a.   In problem 12-38, you discovered that each point on a parabola is an equal distance from the focus and the directrix. To graph a parabola, use a colored pen or pencil to mark the center of the concentric circles on your focus-directrix grid. This will be the focus of the parabola. Then draw a colored line that is 2 units away from the focus, as shown in Figure B at right.

Problem continues on next page →

12-47.   *Problem continued from previous page.*

    b.   Examine point R on the focus-directrix grid in Figure B. Notice that the circles help you count the distance between point R and the focus (the center of the circles). Explain how you know that the point R is 3 units from the focus and 3 units from the directrix.

    c.   Use the circles and lines to plot a point that is 1 unit away from the focus and the directrix. Is there another point that is also 1 unit away from both the focus and directrix?

    d.   Likewise, find two points that are 2 units away from both the focus and the directrix. Continue plotting points that are equidistant from the focus and the directrix until the parabola appears. Compare your parabola with those of your teammates to double-check for accuracy.

12-48.   The graphs of points that are equidistant from the focus and directrix *look* like parabolas. However, Tom wants to know how he can know for sure that they *are* parabolas. He wonders, *"If math is about making sense of ideas and not taking someone else's word for it, then there must be a way to figure out if these points really make a parabola."* Tom decided to think about this with his teammates.

    a.   Tom says, *"What if we try to find an equation to represent the points of the graph from problem 12-47 on a coordinate grid? I remember that parabolas have an equation in the form $y = ax^2 + bx + c$. If these points have that type of equation, then the graph is a parabola."*

Joan added, *"Yes, we could let the focus for the graph in problem 12-47 be at (0, 2) on a rectangular coordinate grid, and the directrix be the x-axis."* On graph paper, graph this point and line.

    b.   *"Look, I know that the point (0, 1) will be on my graph because it is equidistant from the line and point. But what about the other points?"* Tom asked. Sofia answered, *"It might make sense to start with a simple case. What if we find the coordinates of the points that are equally distant from the focus and directrix when y = 5?"*

The team thought about this and came up with the equation $x^2 + 3^2 = 5^2$. Where did this equation come from? Discuss this with your team.

Problem continues on next page →

12-48.   *Problem continued from previous page.*

    c.   Sofia added, *"The solutions to that equation are $x = 4$ and $x = -4$."* Joan added, *"So now we know three points on our parabola that has focus at (0, 2) and directrix on the x-axis."* Justify Sofia's statement. What three coordinate points is Joan talking about?

    d.   Tom asked, *"What about all of the other points? This will take us forever if we do them one by one!"* Joan replied, *"What if we just do the same thing except call the y-value 'y' to represent all of the possible y-values?"*

        On your graph, label a point (x,y) and use the same strategy from parts (b) and (c) to generate an equation that relates x and y. Remember the point (x,y) is equally distant from the focus and the directrix.

    e.   Demonstrate that the equation in part (d) is equivalent to $y = \frac{1}{4}x^2 + 1$. What does this show about the set of points graphed in problem 12-47 and in this problem?

12-49.   MORE CROSS-SECTIONS

Find at least three different shapes that can be cross-sections of a cylinder, like the one at right. For each one, draw the resulting cross-section and explain how you sliced the cylinder. Then find as many cross-sections of a sphere as you can. Finally, find as many cross-sections of a cube that you can.

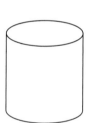

ETHODS AND MEANINGS

Conic Sections

The cross-sections of a cone are also called **conic sections**. The shape of the cross-section depends on the angle of the slice. Three possible cross-sections of a cone (an ellipse, a parabola, and a hyperbola) are shown below. The other four conic sections are special cases of the first three (circle, line, point, and intersecting lines).

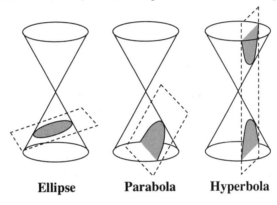

Ellipse   **Parabola**   **Hyperbola**

12-50.   A solid with volume 820 cm³ is reduced proportionally with a linear scale factor of $\frac{1}{2}$. What is the volume of the resulting solid?

12-51.   On graph paper, graph the equations below. For each one, name the center and radius.

a. $x^2 + y^2 = 4.5^2$

b. $x^2 + y^2 = 75$

c. $(x-3)^2 + y^2 = 1$

d. $x^2 - 4x + y^2 - 2y = 14$

12-52.   Use the relationships in each diagram below to solve for the given variables.

a.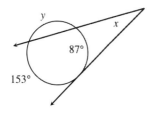

b.   The area of $\odot K$ is 36π sq. units.

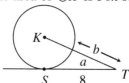

c.   The diameter of $\odot C$ is 13 units. w is the length of $\overline{AB}$.

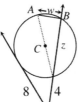

d.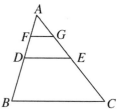

12-53.   In the triangle at right, $\overline{DE}$ is a midsegment of $\triangle ABC$ and $\overline{FG}$ is a midsegment of $\triangle ADE$.

a.   If $DE = 7$ cm, find BC and FG.

b.   If the area of $\triangle AFG$ is 3 cm², what is the area of $DECB$?

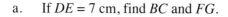

12-54.   Find the volume and lateral surface area of a cone if the circumference of the base is 28π inches and the height is 18 inches.

12-55.   A jar contains five red, four white, and three blue balls. If three balls are randomly selected, find the probability of choosing:

a.   Three white balls.

b.   Two red balls and one white ball.

c.   Three balls of the same color.

12-56.   **Multiple Choice:** Carol was shopping for a spring picnic. She spent $2.00 for each liter of soda and $3.50 for each bag of chips. In all, she bought 18 items for a total of $43.50. Assuming she only bought chips and soda, how many bags of chips did she buy?

a.   9   b.   5   c.   15   d.   3

Core Connections Geometry

12.2.1 What is the shape?

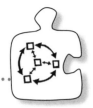

··

Using Coordinate Geometry and Constructions to Explore Shapes

In today's activity, you will learn more about quadrilaterals as you review what you know about coordinate geometry, construction, and proof.

12-57.   Review what you have learned about the
          midsegment of a triangle as you answer the
          questions below. Assume that $\overline{DE}$ is a
          midsegment of $\triangle ABC$.

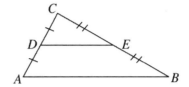

   a.   What is the relationship between $\overline{DE}$
         and AB?

   b.   What is the relationship between $\angle CDE$ and $\angle DAB$? How do you know?

   c.   What is the relationship between $\triangle ABC$ and $\triangle DEC$? Justify your
         conclusion.

   d.   If $DE = 4x + 7$ units and $AB = 34$ units, what is x?

12-58.   QUIRKY QUADRILATERALS

          Quinn decided to experiment with the midpoints
          of the sides of a quadrilateral one afternoon.
          With a compass, he located the midpoint of each
          side of a quadrilateral. He then connected the
          four midpoints together to create a new
          quadrilateral inside his original quadrilateral.

   a.   Without knowing anything about Quinn's original quadrilateral and
         without trying the construction yourself, visualize the result. What can
         you predict about Quinn's resulting quadrilateral? Share your ideas with
         your team.

   b.   Use a compass and straightedge to repeat Quinn's experiment on an unlined
         piece of paper. Make sure each member of your team starts with a
         differently-shaped quadrilateral. Describe your results. Did the results of
         you and your teammates match your prediction from part (a)?

   c.   Does it matter if your starting quadrilateral is convex
         or not? Start with a non-convex quadrilateral, like the
         one shown at right, and repeat Quinn's experiment.
         On your paper, describe your results.

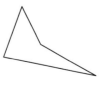

12-59.   Quinn decided to graph his quadrilateral on a set of coordinate axes and prove
          that his inner quadrilateral is, in fact, a parallelogram. His quadrilateral *ABCD*
          uses the points $A(-3, -2)$, $B(-5, 4)$, $C(5, 6)$, and $D(1, -4)$.

          a.   On graph paper, graph the quadrilateral *ABCD*.

          b.   If the midpoint of $\overline{AB}$ is E, the midpoint of $\overline{BC}$ is F, the midpoint of $\overline{CD}$
                is G, and the midpoint of $\overline{DA}$ is H, find and label points E, F, G, and H on
                ABCD.

          c.   Connect the midpoints of the sides you found in part (b). Then find the
                slope of each side of quadrilateral *EFGH* and use these slopes to prove that
                Quinn's inner quadrilateral is a parallelogram.

          d.   Quinn wondered if his parallelogram is also a rhombus. Find *EF* and *FG*,
                and then decide if *EFGH* is a rhombus. Show all work.

12-60.   PROVING THE RESULT FOR ALL QUADRILATERALS

          In problem 12-59, you proved that Quinn's inner
          quadrilateral was a parallelogram when $A(-3, -2)$,
          $B(-5, 4)$, $C(5, 6)$, and $D(1, -4)$. However, what
          about other, random quadrilaterals?

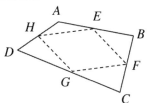

          To prove this works for all quadrilaterals, start with a diagram of a generic
          quadrilateral, like the one above. Assume that the midpoint of $\overline{AB}$ is E, the
          midpoint of $\overline{BC}$ is F, the midpoint of $\overline{CD}$ is G, and the midpoint of $\overline{DA}$ is H.
          Prove that *EFGH* is a parallelogram by proving that its opposite sides are
          parallel. It may help you to draw diagonal $\overline{AC}$ and consider what you know
          about $\triangle ABC$ and $\triangle ACD$. Use any format of proof.

Review & Preview

12-61.   In $\triangle PQR$ at right, what is $m\angle Q$? Explain how you
          found your answer.

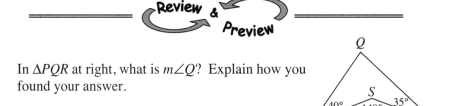

12-62.   The United State Department of Defense is located in a building called the
          Pentagon because it is in the shape of a regular pentagon. Known as "the largest
          office building in the world," its exterior edges measure 921 feet. Find the area
          of land enclosed by the outer walls of the Pentagon building.

12-63.   Examine the triangles below. Decide if each one is a right
triangle. If the triangle is a right triangle, justify your conclusion.
Assume that the diagrams are not drawn to scale.

a.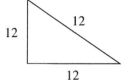

b.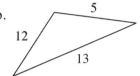

12-64.   On graph paper, graph the equation $x^2 + (y-3)^2 = 25$. State the x- and
y-intercepts.

12-65.   For each equation below, decide if the equation has any real number for the
given variable. For each problem, explain how you know.

a. $4(x-3) = 11$ b. $x^2 = -10$

c. $3x^2 - 18 = 0$ d. $-7 = |x-6|$

12-66.   Using focus-directrix graph paper, create a parabola that has a horizontal
directrix that is six units below the focus. You can get focus-directrix paper on
the Lesson 12.1.4 Resource Page available at www.cpm.org.

12-67.   **Multiple Choice:** Which number below could be the length of the third side of
a triangle with sides of length 29 and 51?

a.   10   b.   18   c.   23   d.   81

12.2.2 What is the pattern?

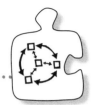

Euler's Formula for Polyhedra

Throughout this course, you have developed your skills of exploring a pattern, forming a conjecture, and then proving your conjecture. Today, with the assistance of materials such as toothpicks and gumdrops, you will review what you know about basic polyhedra (with no holes) as you look for a relationship between the number faces, edges, and vertices each basic polyhedron has. Once you have written a conjecture, your class will discuss how to prove that it must be true.

As you work today, consider the following questions:

Which types of basic polyhedra have I not tested yet?

What relationship can I find between the number of edges, faces, and vertices of a basic polyhedron?

Does this relationship always hold true?

12-68.   POLYHEDRA PATTERNS

Does a basic polyhedron (with no holes) usually have more faces, edges, or vertices? And if you know the number of faces and vertices of a basic polyhedron, can you predict the number of edges? Today you will answer these questions and more as you investigate polyhedra.

Your Task: Obtain the necessary building materials from your teacher, such as toothpicks (for edges) and gumdrops (for vertices). Your team should build *at least* six distinctly different polyhedra and each person in your team is responsible for building *at least* one polyhedron. Be sure to build some regular polyhedra (such as a tetrahedron and an octahedron), basic prisms, pyramids, and unnamed polyhedra.

Create a table like the one at right to hold your data. Once you have recorded the number of vertices, edges, and

Polyhedron	Faces (*F*)	Vertices (*V*)	Edges (*E*)

faces for your team's polyhedra, look for a relationship between the numbers in each row of the table. Try adding, subtracting (or both) the numbers to find a pattern. Write a conjecture (equation) using the variables *F*, *V*, and *E*.

Core Connections Geometry

12-69.   EULER'S FORMULA FOR POLYHEDRA

The relationship you discovered in problem 12-68 between the number of faces, vertices, and edges of a basic polyhedron is referred to as **Euler's Formula for Polyhedra**, after Leonhard Euler (pronounced "oiler"), one of the greatest mathematicians in history. While it is widely believed that Euler independently discovered this relationship, it has been recorded that René Descartes (pronounced "DAY-cart"), the mathematician who invented coordinate geometry, found the relationship over 100 years earlier. This relationship states that if V is the number of vertices, E is the number of edges, and F is the number of faces of a basic polyhedron, then $V - E + F = 2$.

Use Euler's Formula to answer the following questions about basic polyhedra.

a.   If a polyhedron has 5 faces and 6 vertices, how many edges must it have?

b.   What if a polyhedron has 36 edges and 14 faces? How many vertices must it have?

c.   Could a polyhedron have 10 faces, 3 vertices, and 11 edges? Explain why or why not.

12-70.   If V represents the number of vertices, E represents the number of edges, and F represents the number of faces of a basic polyhedron, how can you prove that $V - E + F = 2$? First think about this on your own. Then, as a class, prove Euler's Formula.

12-71. For each situation below, decide if *a* is greater, *b* is greater, if they are the same value, or if not enough information is given.

    a. *a* is the measure of a central angle of an equilateral triangle; *b* is the measure of an interior angle of a regular pentagon.

    b.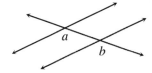
    c.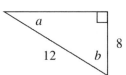

    d. $a = b + 3$
    e.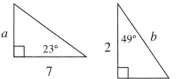

12-72. In the diagram at right, $ABCD \sim DCFE$. Solve for *x* and *y*. Show all work.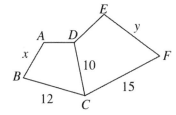

12-73. On graph paper, make a table and graph the function $f(x) = -2(x-1)^2 + 8$.

    a. Label the *x*- and *y*-intercepts and state their coordinates.

    b. Name the vertex.

    c. Find $f(100)$ and $f(-15)$.

12-74. Find the area of the graph of the solution region of $x^2 + y^2 \le 49$.

12-75.   In how many ways can five different French books and three different Spanish books be arranged on a shelf if all of the books of each language must remain together?

12-76.   Find the volume and surface area of the box formed by the shaded net at right.

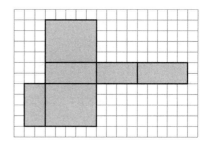

12-77.   **Multiple Choice:** The radius of the front wheel of Gavin's tricycle is 8 inches. If Gavin rode his tricycle for 1 mile in a parade, approximately how many rotations did his front wheel make? (Note: 1 mile = 5280 feet).

    a.   50   b.   1260   c.   660   d.   42,240

12.2.3 What is special about this ratio?

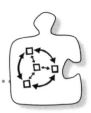

The Golden Ratio

In Chapter 8, you investigated an important irrational number: π. Pi (π) is the ratio of any circle's circumference to its diameter. Today you will discover another special ratio represented by the Greek letter phi (ϕ), pronounced "fee." Phi is also an irrational number. It appears not only in geometry, but also in nature. You will examine several different contexts in which this number appears.

12-78.   While doodling one day, Cyrus drew squares inside of rectangles like the ones below.

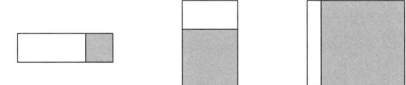

He noticed that if he chose the original rectangle carefully, the rectangle created inside was the same shape as the original rectangle. That is, the two rectangles were similar, as shown below.

Cyrus' teammate, Alex, wondered what the ratio of the sides of the original rectangle had to be to create a similar rectangle inside. So Alex drew and labeled the following rectangle.

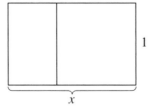

What does x need to be so that the larger rectangle and the smaller rectangle are similar?

12-79.   GOLDEN RECTANGLES

Alex explored his special rectangle further.

a.   What is the scale factor from the smaller rectangle to the larger rectangle?

b.   What is the ratio of the longer side to the shorter side of either of the two rectangles? Express your answer both in exact form and as a decimal approximation.

c.   The ratio you found in part (b) has a special name: the **golden ratio**. It is often represented by the Greek letter lowercase phi, pronounced "fee" and written ϕ or φ. Rectangles whose side lengths are in the proportion ϕ are called **golden rectangles**. Historically many artists and architects have found rectangles whose sides are in the proportion phi to be aesthetically pleasing. Sometimes people see golden rectangles in the shape of the ancient Greek building the Parthenon (447 BC), or in the proportions of the face of the Renaissance painting Mona Lisa (1503 AD), or in the Great Pyramid of Giza (2560 BC).

Surrealist painter Salvador Dali intentionally used the golden rectangle for one of his most famous paintings. The canvas is 267 cm wide. If Dali intended the canvas to be a perfect golden rectangle, what height canvas should he have used?

12-80.   One way to construct golden rectangles is to start from a square and then extend parallel lines as shown at right.

Draw a line from the midpoint of the bottom side of the square to the right upper vertex of the square. Then use this segment as a radius to draw an arc to the bottom line as shown middle right.

Show that the rectangle you can now draw (shown below right) is a golden rectangle.

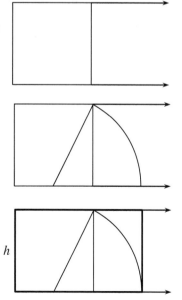

12-81.   GOLDEN SPIRALS

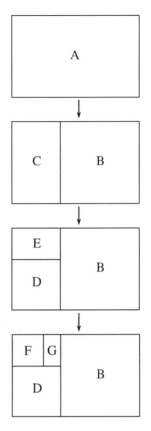

There is no stopping Alex! He continued doodling by
making squares inside of a golden rectangle. First, he
drew golden rectangle A. Then he drew square B
inside the rectangle, creating rectangle C. Then square
D was drawn inside of rectangle C creating square F
and rectangle G, and so on as shown at right.

a.   In problem 12-78, Alex determined the ratios
     needed to draw rectangle A so that it is similar to
     rectangle C. Is rectangle C also a golden
     rectangle?

b.   Is rectangle E a golden rectangle?

c.   The non-square rectangles in Alex's diagrams
     from problem 12-81 are all golden rectangles
     because in each of them the ratio of the longer
     length to the shorter length is ϕ, the golden ratio.
     Alex's process of subdividing each golden
     rectangle into a square and smaller golden
     rectangle can be **iterated** (repeated over and
     over) creating an infinite series of similar golden
     rectangles.

     When connected arcs are placed in each
     of the squares, a spiral forms, like the
     one shown at right.

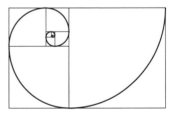

Golden spiral

Use a compass to draw a golden spiral on
the Lesson 12.2.3 Resource Page provided
by your teacher. One place people
sometimes see a golden spiral is the shape
of the human ear, as shown at right.
Where else in nature or art might you have
seen a spiral like this?

12-82.   Alex wonders where else in mathematics the number phi (ϕ) shows up. Look for phi (ϕ) as you analyze the following situations.

a.   Examine the regular decagon at right. If the side length is 1 unit, find the radius of the decagon. What do you notice?

b.   Each central triangle in the regular decagon from part (a) is called a **golden triangle** because the ratio of the congruent sides to the base of each triangle is phi (ϕ). What are the angles of a golden triangle?

c.   Fifteenth century artist and scientist Leonardo da Vinci drew illustrations that he believed showed parts of the human body as golden ratios. Sixteenth century philosopher Heinrich Agrippa illustrated a human on a **star polygon** as shown at right, implying golden ratio proportions in humans. A **star polygon** is created by equally spacing points on the circumference of a circle, and then connecting the points. The star polygon at right is commonly called a **pentagram**. Note that all the corresponding lengths and angles are equal to each other.

With your team investigate the connection between a pentagram and the golden ratio in the diagram that follows. What is the ratio of length *AC* to length *BC*? What is the ratio of length *AB* to length *BD*?

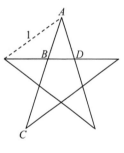

d.   In problem 12-81, you learned about nested golden rectangles (where each golden rectangle is subdivided into a square and a smaller golden rectangle). But what about nested expressions?

Consider either one of the expressions at right. The "…" signifies that the pattern within the expression continues infinitely. With your team, find a way to approximate the value of the expression you chose. Try to find the most accurate approximation that you can. What do you notice?

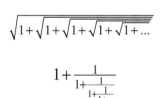

e.   The number ϕ has some interesting properties. What is $\frac{1}{\phi}$? What is ϕ^2? What do you notice? Is this true for other irrational numbers?

f.   Graph $y = x^2 - 1$ and $y = x$ for *x*-values from –3 to 3. Algebraically find the points of intersection. What do you notice?

12-83.   FIBONACCI SPIRALS

You may have seen the Fibonacci sequence in a previous course. Each term in the sequence is created by adding the previous two terms:

$$1, 1, 2, 3, 5, 8, 13, 21, \ldots$$

Fibonacci spirals are created in the same manner that Alex used, but the side-lengths of the starting rectangle are two consecutive Fibonacci numbers. For example, you could start with an 8×13 rectangle.

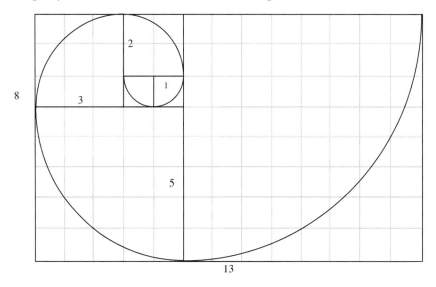

a.   Is a Fibonacci spiral also a golden spiral? How do you know?

b.   Mathematicians say that as a Fibonacci spiral gets larger and larger, it approximates a golden spiral better and better. Why?

12-84.   What if three golden rectangles intersect perpendicularly so that their centers coincide, as shown at right? If each vertex of the golden rectangles is connected with the five closest vertices, what three-dimensional shape appears? First visualize the result. Then, if you have a model available, test your idea with string.

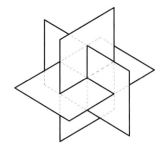

12-85.   If $\triangle ABC$ is equilateral, and if $A(3, 2)$ and $B(7, 2)$, find all possible coordinates of vertex C. Justify your answer.

12-86.   Find the area of the shaded region of the regular pentagon at right. Show all work.

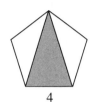

4

12-87.   On graph paper, graph the system of equations at right. Then list all points of intersection in the form (x, y).

$x^2 + y^2 = 25$

$y = x + 1$

12-88.   Jamila solved the quadratic $x^2 + 3x - 10 = 8$ (see her work below). When she checked her solutions, they did not make the equation true. However, Jamila cannot find her mistake. Explain her error and then solve the quadratic correctly.

$$x^2 + 3x - 10 = 8$$
$$(x + 5)(x - 2) = 8$$
$$x + 5 = 8 \quad \text{or} \quad x - 2 = 8$$
$$x = 3 \quad \text{or} \quad x = 10$$

12-89.   If the sum of the interior angles of a regular polygon is $2160°$, how many sides must it have?

12-90.   From the 13 spades in a deck of cards, four are selected. Find the probability that:

a.   Exactly one card is a "face" card (Jack, Queen, or King).

b.   The cards form a consecutive sequence (count both A, 2, 3, 4 and J, Q, K, A as consecutive sequences).

12-91.   **Multiple Choice:** Assume that $A(6, 2)$, $B(3, 4)$, and $C(4, -1)$. If $\triangle ABC$ is rotated $90°$ counterclockwise ($\circlearrowleft$) to form $\triangle A'B'C'$, and then $\triangle A'B'C'$ is reflected across the x-axis to form $\triangle A''B''C''$, then the coordinates of C'' are:

a. $(1, 4)$ b. $(-4, 1)$ c. $(1, -4)$ d. $(4, 1)$

12-92.   Find the area and perimeter of the shape at right.
          Assume that any non-straight portions of the
          shape are part of a circle. Show all work.

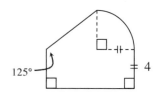

125°

4

12-93.   Examine the diagrams below. For each one, use the geometric relationships to
          solve for the given variable.

    a. $\overleftrightarrow{PR}$ is tangent to $\odot C$ at P and   b.   Radius = 7 cm
          $m\widehat{PMQ} = 314°$. Find QR.

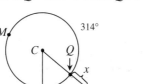

12-94.   Examine the net at right.

    a.   Describe the solid that is formed by this net.
          What are its dimensions?

    b.   Find the surface area and volume of the solid
          formed by this net.

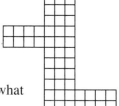

    c.   If all the dimensions of this solid are multiplied by 3, what
          is the SA of the resulting solid? What is the volume?

12-95.   Solve for y in terms of x. That is, rewrite each equation so that it starts "$y =$".

    a. $6x + 5y = 20$ b. $4x - 8y = 16$

12-96.   Using focus-directrix graph paper, create a parabola that has a horizontal
          directrix that is four units above the focus. You can get focus-directrix paper on
          the Lesson 12.1.4 Resource Page available at www.cpm.org.

12-97.   **Multiple Choice:** Dillon starts to randomly select cards out of a normal deck of
          52 playing cards. After selecting a card, he does not return it to the deck. So
          far, he has selected a 3 of clubs, an ace of spades, a 4 of clubs, and a 10 of
          diamonds. Find the probability that his fifth card is an ace.

    a. $\frac{1}{16}$ b. $\frac{3}{52}$ c. $\frac{1}{13}$ d. $\frac{1}{52}$

12.2.4 What is the probability?

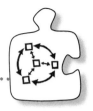

Using Geometry to Find Probabilities

In this final activity, you will connect and apply much of your knowledge from throughout the course to solve a challenging problem.

12-98. ZOE AND THE POISON WEED

Dimitri is getting his prize sheep, Zoe, ready for the county fair. He keeps Zoe in the pasture beside the barn and shed. What he does not know is that there is a single locoweed in this pasture, which will make Zoe too sick to go to the fair if she eats it, and she can eat it in one bite.

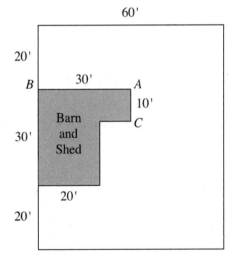

The layout of the field and building is provided at left and on the Lesson 12.2.4 Resource Page provided by your teacher. Assume that the entire field (the unshaded region) has plants growing on it. Also assume that each corner of the barn and field is a right angle.

Dimitri is worried that Zoe will get into trouble unless she is tethered with a rope to the building. He has decided to tether Zoe at point *A* with a 20-foot rope. Zoe is unable to enter the barn or shed while on her tether.

Your Task: Assuming that Zoe will eat all the plants in her tethered region, what is the probability that Zoe will get sick from the poisonous weed?

Discussion Points

What is the problem asking you to find?

What does Zoe's grazing region look like?

What do you need to figure out in order to find the probability?

Further Guidance

12-99. To help find the probability that Zoe will eat the single locoweed, first consider the grazing region if she is tethered to point *A* with a 20-foot rope.

   a. On your Lesson 12.2.4 Resource Page, draw and label the region that Zoe can roam. Then find the area of that region.

   b. What is the probability that the single locoweed is in her region? Find the area of the entire field (the total area region that the locoweed is possibly located) to help you find your answer. Be prepared to explain your answer to the class.

——————— *Further Guidance section ends here.* ———————

12-100. FAMILY DISCUSSION

When Dimitri discussed his idea with his family, he received many suggestions. Analyze each of the ideas given below and then report back to Dimitri about which of them, if any, he should choose. Assume that Zoe needs at least 500 square feet of grazing area between now and the fair. Your analysis should include:

   • A diagram of each proposed region on the Lesson 12.2.4 Resource Page (or use the figure in problem 12-98).

   • All calculations that help you determine the probability that Zoe will eat the poisoned weed for each proposed region.

   a. **Dimitri's Father:** *"Dimitri! Why do you need to waste rope? All you need is to tether your sheep with a 10-foot rope attached at point A. Take it from me: Less area to roam means there is less chance that the sheep will eat the terrible locoweed!"*

   b. **Dimitri's Sister:** *"I don't agree. I think you should consider using a 30-foot rope attached to point B. The longer rope will give Zoe more freedom."*

   c. **Dimitri's Mother:** *"Both of those regions really restrict Zoe to the north-eastern part of the field. That means she won't be able to take advantage of the grass grown in the southern section of the field that is rich in nutrients because of better sunlight. I recommend that you use a 30-foot rope attached to point C. You won't be disappointed!"*

12-101. Find the area of each quadrilateral below. Show all work.

a. Kite

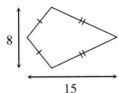

b. Rhombus

12-102. Perry threw a tennis ball up into the air from the edge of a cliff. The height of the ball was $y = -16x^2 + 64x + 80$, where y represents the height in feet of the ball above ground at the bottom of the cliff, and x represents the time in seconds after the ball is thrown.

a. How high was the ball when it was thrown? How do you know?

b. What was the height of the ball 3 seconds after it was thrown? What was its height $\frac{1}{2}$ a second after it was thrown? Show all work.

c. When did the ball hit the ground? Write and solve an equation that represents this situation.

12-103. Examine the triangles below. Which, if any, are similar? Which are congruent? For each pair that must be similar, state how you know. Remember that the diagrams are not drawn to scale.

a.

b.

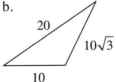

c.

d.

12-104.   Examine the mat plan of a three-dimensional solid at right.

3	1	0
1	2	1
0	2	1

RIGHT

FRONT

mat plan

    a.   On your paper, draw the front, right, and top views of this solid.

    b.   Find the volume of the solid.

    c.   If each edge of the solid is multiplied by 5, what will the new volume be? Show how you got your answer.

12-105.   Describe each circle by finding the center and radius. You need to "complete the square" to rewrite the equation in part (b) in graphing form.

    a. $(x+5)^2 + y^2 = 10$ b. $x^2 - 6x + y^2 - 2y - 5 = 0$

12-106.   Remember that the absolute value function finds the distance on a number line between a number and zero. For example, the absolute value of –6 (written $|-6|$) equals 6, while $|2| = 2$.

On graph paper, copy and complete the table below and graph the function $y = |x| + 2$.

x	-4	-3	-2	-1	0	1	2	3	4
y	6				2				

12-107.   **Multiple Choice:** A square based pyramid has a slant height of 10 units and a base edge of 10 units. What is the height of the pyramid?

    a.   5   b. $5\sqrt{3}$ c.   6   d.   8

Chapter 12 Closure   What have I learned?

Reflection and Synthesis

The activities below offer you a chance to reflect
about what you have learned during this chapter. As
you work, look for concepts that you feel very
comfortable with, ideas that you would like to learn
more about, and topics you need more help with.
Look for connections between ideas as well as
connections with material you learned previously.

①   TEAM BRAINSTORM

What have you studied in this chapter? What ideas were important in what you
learned? With your team, brainstorm a list. Be as detailed as you can. To help
get you started, lists of Learning Log entries and Math Notes boxes are below.

What topics, ideas, and words that you learned *before* this chapter are connected
to the new ideas in this chapter? Again, be as detailed as you can.

How long can you make your list? Challenge yourselves. Be prepared to share
your team's ideas with the class.

Learning Log Entries
- Lesson 12.1.1 – Equation of a Circle
- Lesson 12.1.3 – Conic Sections

Math Notes
- Lesson 12.1.3 – Equation of a Circle
- Lesson 12.1.4 – Conic Sections

②   MAKING CONNECTIONS

Below is a list of the vocabulary used in this chapter. Make sure that you are familiar with all of these words and know what they mean. Refer to the glossary or index for any words that you do not yet understand.

circle	cone	conic section
cross-section	directrix	equidistant
Euler's Formula	focus	focus-directrix graph paper
golden ratio	golden spiral	parabola
phi (ϕ)		

Make a concept map showing all of the connections you can find among the key words and ideas listed above. To show a connection between two words, draw a line between them and explain the connection. A word can be connected to any other word as long as you can justify the connection.

While you are making your map, your team may think of related words or ideas that are not listed here. Be sure to include these ideas on your concept map.

③   PORTFOLIO: EVIDENCE OF MATHEMATICAL PROFICIENCY

Choose one or two of the activities from Lessons 12.2.1 through Lesson 12.2.5 that you feel best exhibits your growth in mathematical understanding this course. Copy your work from that activity, modifying and expanding it if needed. Make sure your explanation is clear and detailed. Remember, you are not only exhibiting your understanding of the mathematics, but you are also exhibiting your ability to communicate your justifications.

WHAT HAVE I LEARNED?

Most of the problems in this section represent typical problems found in this chapter. They serve as a gauge for you. You can use them to determine which types of problems you can do well and which types of problems require further study and practice. Even if your teacher does not assign this section, it is a good idea to try these problems and find out for yourself what you know and what you still need to work on.

Solve each problem as completely as you can. The table at the end of the closure section has answers to these problems. It also tells you where you can find additional help and practice with problems like these.

CL 12-108. A coin is flipped 10 times in a row.

    a.   How many sequences of heads and tails are in the sample space?

    b.   How many ways can 10 heads come up?

    c.   In how many sequences can 0, 1, 2, or 3 heads show, with the rest tails? Hint: You may wish to refer back to problem 12-44.

    d.   Calculate the probability that 0, 1, 2, or 3 heads show up.

    e.   What is the probability that at least 4 heads come up?

CL 12-109. "Complete the square" to rewrite the equation into graphing form. If the equation represents a circle, give the center and radius. If the equation represents a parabola, give the vertex.

    a. $x^2 + 6x + y^2 + 4y = -9$

    b. $x^2 - 4x - y = 1$

    c. $x^2 - 2x + y^2 - 10y = -16$

CL 12-110. Draw a mat plan for each of the following cube stacks and use the mat plan to find the volume of each stack. First find the area of the top of each stack.

a.

b.

c.

d.

CL 12-111. Write an equation for the graph at right.

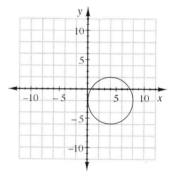

CL 12-112. When considering new plans for a covered baseball stadium, Smallville looked into a design that used a cylinder with a dome in the shape of a hemisphere. The radius of the proposed cylinder is 200 feet and the height is 150 feet. See a diagram of this at right below.

a. One of the concerns for the citizens of Smallville is the cost of heating the space inside the stadium for the fans. What is the volume of this stadium? Show all work.

b. The citizens of Smallville are also interested in having the outside of the new stadium painted in green. What is the surface area of the stadium? Do not include the base of the cylinder.

CL 12-113. An ice-cream cone is filled with ice cream. It also has ice-cream on top that is in the shape of a cylinder. It turns out that the volume of ice cream inside the cone equals the volume of the scoop on top. If the height of the cone is 6 inches and the radius of the scoop of ice cream is 1.5 inches, find the height of the extra scoop on top. Ignore the thickness of the cone.

CL 12-114. Use the diagram at right to prove the
following statement. Use the proof format,
two-column or flowchart, that you prefer.

If $\overline{AB} \cong \overline{AD}$ and $\overline{BC} \cong \overline{DC}$, then $\overline{AC} \perp \overline{BD}$.

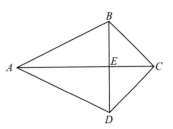

CL 12-115. Examine the diagrams below. For each one, use geometric relationships to
solve for desired information.

a.

b.
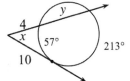

c.
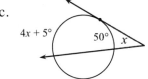

d.

CL 12-116. Using focus-directrix graph paper, create a parabola that has a horizontal
directrix that is five units below the focus. Focus-directrix paper is on the
Lesson 12.1.4 Resource Page, available at www.cpm.org.

CL 12-117. Check your answers using the table at the end of this section. Which
problems do you feel confident about? Which problems were hard? Have
you worked on problems like these in math classes you have taken before?
Use the table to make a list of topics you need help on and a list of topics
you need to practice more.

Answers and Support for Closure Activity #4
What Have I Learned?

Note: MN = Math Note, LL = Learning Log

Problem	Solution	Need Help?	More Practice
CL 12-108.	a. $2^{10} = 1024$ b. 1 c. 0 heads shows up only one way. The others are anagrams of Hs and Ts. $1 + \frac{10!}{9!} + \frac{10!}{8!2!} + \frac{10!}{7!3!} = 176$ d. $\frac{176}{1024} \approx 17.2\%$ e. This is the complement of part (d). $1 - \frac{176}{1024} \approx 82.8\%$	Section 10.2 MN: 10.2.1 and 10.2.3 LL: 10.2.1 and 10.2.3	Problems CL 11-129, 12-44, 12-55, 12-90, and 12-97
CL 12-l09.	a. $(x+3)^2 + (y+2)^2 = 4$; circle; $(-3, -2)$ $r = 2$ b. $y = (x-2)^2 - 5$; parabola; $(2, -5)$ c. $(x-1)^2 + (y-5)^2 = 10$; circle; $(1, 5)$ $r = \sqrt{10}$	Lesson 12.1.2 MN: 12.1.4	Problems 12-6, 12-24, 12-51(d), and 12-105
CL 12-110.	a. $A = 4$ sq. units $V = 8$ cu. units b. $A = 5$ sq. units $V = 15$ cu. units c. $A = 8$ sq. units $V = 16$ cu. units d. $A = 16$ sq. units $V = 48$ cu. units	Lessons 9.1.1 and 9.1.2 MN: 9.1.3 LL: 9.1.1	Problems CL 9-111, CL 10-191, and 12-104

Problem	Solution	Need Help?	More Practice
CL 12-111.	$(x-4)^2+(y+2)^2=16$	Lesson 12.1.1 MN: 12.1.3	Problems 12-6, 12-31, 12-51, 12-64, and 12-87
CL 12-112.	a. Volume of the cylinder is $6,000,000\pi$ cubic feet, volume of the dome is half of $\frac{2}{3}$ of the corresponding cylinder $\frac{1}{2}\cdot\frac{2}{3}\cdot\pi(200)^2\cdot400=\frac{16,000,000}{3}\pi$ cubic feet, so total volume is approximately 35,600,000 cubic feet. b. Lateral area of cylinder is $2\pi(200)(150)=60,000\pi$ sq. feet, surface area of hemisphere is $2\pi(200)^2=80,000\pi$ sq. feet. So total surface to be painted is approximately 440,000 sq. feet.	Lessons 9.1.3 and 11.1.5 MN: 9.1.3 and 11.2.2 Three-Dimensional Solids Toolkit	Problems 11-72, CL 11-132, 12-21, and 12-40
CL 12-113.	Volume of the cone is $\frac{1}{3}\pi(1.5)^2(6)=4.5\pi$ cubic inches. Therefore, $\pi(1.5)^2(x)=4.5\pi$ and $x=2$ inches.	Lessons 11.1.4 and 11.1.5 MN: 11.1.5 Three-Dimensional Solids Toolkit	Problems 11-75, 12-21, and 12-54
CL 12-114.	Condensed proof 1. $\triangle ABC\cong\triangle ADC$; SSS $\cong$ 2. $\angle BCA\cong\angle DCA$; corresponding parts of congruent triangles 3. $\triangle BCE\cong\triangle DCE$; SAS $\cong$ 4. $\angle BEC\cong\angle DEC$; corresponding parts or congruent triangles 5. $m\angle BCA=90°$; $\angle BEC$ and $\angle BEC$ are supplementary and congruent 6. $\overline{AC}\perp\overline{BD}$; definition of perpendicular	Section 7-2. MN: 6.1.4, 7.1.3 LL: 7.2.5	Problems CL 7-148, and CL 9-117

Problem	Solution	Need Help?	More Practice
CL 12-115.	a. $a = 240°$, $b = 60°$, $c = 5\sqrt{3}$ b. $x = 78°$, $y = 21$ c. $x = 22.5$ d. $x = \sqrt{30}$	Section 10.1 and Lessons 11.2.2 and 11.2.3 MN: 10.1.4 LL: 11.2.2	Problems CL 10-186, 11-110, 11-117, CL 11-124, 12-33, 12-52, and 12-93
CL 12-116.		Lesson 12.1.4	Problems 12-66 and 12-96

Core Connections Geometry
Checkpoint Materials

Notes to Students (and their Teachers)

Students master different skills at different speeds. No two students learn exactly the same way at the same time. At some point you will be expected to perform certain skills accurately. Most of the Checkpoint problems incorporate skills that you should have developed in previous courses. If you have not mastered these skills yet it does not mean that you will not be successful in this class. However, you may need to do some work outside of class to get caught up on them.

Starting in Chapter 1 and finishing in Chapter 11, there are 13 problems designed as Checkpoint problems. Each one is marked with an icon like the one above and numbered according to the chapter that it is in. After you do each of the Checkpoint problems, check your answers by referring to this section. If your answers are incorrect, you may need some extra practice to develop that skill. The practice sets are keyed to each of the Checkpoint problems in the textbook. Each has the topic clearly labeled, followed by the answers to the corresponding Checkpoint problem and then some completed examples. Next, the complete solution to the Checkpoint problem from the text is given, and there are more problems for you to practice with answers included.

Remember, looking is not the same as doing! You will never become good at any sport by just watching it, and in the same way, reading through the worked examples and understanding the steps is not the same as being able to do the problems yourself. How many of the extra practice problems do you need to try? That is really up to you. Remember that your goal is to be able to do similar problems on your own confidently and accurately. This is your responsibility. You should not expect your teacher to spend time in class going over the solutions to the Checkpoint problem sets. If you are not confident after reading the examples and trying the problems, you should get help outside of class time or talk to your teacher about working with a tutor.

Another source for help with the Checkpoint problems and other topics in *Core Connections Geometry* is the *Parent Guide with Extra Practice*. This resource is available for download free of charge at www.cpm.org.

Checkpoint Topics

1. Solving Linear Equations
2. Solving Linear Systems of Equations
3. Linear Equations from Multiple Representations
4. Finding Areas and Perimeters of Complex Shapes
5A. Multiplying Polynomials and Solving Quadratics
5B. Writing Equations for Arithmetic and Geometric Sequences
6. Solving Proportional Equations and Similar Figures
7. Solving with Trigonometric Ratios and the Pythagorean Theorem
8. Angle Relationships in Triangles and Lines
9A. Probabilities with Unions, Intersections, and Complements
9B. Exponential Functions
10. Finding Angles in and Areas of Regular Polygons
11. Volumes and Surface Areas of Prisms and Cylinders

Checkpoint 1

Problem 1-127

Solving Linear Equations

Answers to problem 1-127: a. $x = -2$, b. $x = 1\frac{1}{2}$, c. $x = 3$, d. no solution

Equations may be solved in a variety of ways. Commonly, the first steps are to remove parenthesis using the Distributive Property and then simplify by combining like terms. Next isolate the variable on one side and the constant terms on the other. Finally, divide to find the value of the variable. Note: When the process of solving an equation ends with different numbers on each side of the equal sign (for example, $2 = 4$), there is *no solution* to the problem. When the result is the same expression or number on each side of the equation (for example, $x + 3 = x + 3$) it means that *all real numbers* are solutions.

Example 1: Solve $4x + 4x - 3 = 6x + 9$

Solution:

$4x + 4x - 3 = 6x + 9$	problem
$8x - 3 = 6x + 9$	simplify
$2x = 12$	add 3, subtract $6x$ on each side
$x = 6$	divide

Check: $4(6) + 4(6) - 3 = 6(6) + 9$

$24 + 24 - 3 = 36 + 9$

$48 - 3 = 45$

$45 = 45$

Example 2: Solve $-4x + 2 - (-x + 1) = -3 + (-x + 5)$

Solution:

$-4x + 2 - (-x + 1) = -3 + (-x + 5)$	problem
$-4x + 2 + x - 1 = -3 - x + 5$	remove parenthesis (distribute)
$-3x + 1 = -x + 2$	simplify
$-2x = 1$	add x, subtract 1 from each side
$x = -\frac{1}{2}$	divide

Check:

$-4\left(-\frac{1}{2}\right) + 2 - \left(-\left(-\frac{1}{2}\right) + 1\right) = -3 + \left(-\left(-\frac{1}{2}\right) + 5\right)$

$2 + 2 - \left(\frac{1}{2} + 1\right) = -3 + \left(\frac{1}{2} + 5\right)$

$4 - \left(1\frac{1}{2}\right) = -3 + \left(5\frac{1}{2}\right)$

$2\frac{1}{2} = 2\frac{1}{2}$

Now we can go back and solve the original problems.

a. $3x + 7 = -x - 1$
$$4x = -8$$
$$x = -2$$

b. $1 - 2x + 5 = 4x - 3$
$$-2x + 6 = 4x - 3$$
$$9 = 6x$$
$$1\tfrac{1}{2} = x$$

c. $-2x - 6 = 2 - 4x - (x - 1)$
$$-2x - 6 = 2 - 4x - x + 1$$
$$-2x - 6 = -5x + 3$$
$$3x = 9$$
$$x = 3$$

d. $3x - 4 + 1 = -2x - 5 + 5x$
$$3x - 3 = 3x - 5$$
$$-3 = -5$$
$$-3 \neq -5 \Rightarrow \text{no solution}$$

Here are some more to try. Solve each equation.

1. $2x - 3 = -x + 3$

2. $3x + 2 + x = x + 5$

3. $6 - x - 3 = 4(x - 2)$

4. $4x - 2 - 2x = x - 5$

5. $-(x + 3) = 2x - 6$

6. $-x + 2 = x - 5 - 3x$

7. $1 + 3x - x = x - 4 + 2x$

8. $5x - 3 + 2x = x + 7 + 6x$

9. $4y - 8 - 2y = 4$

10. $-x + 3 = 6$

11. $-2 + 3y = y - 2 - 4y$

12. $2(x - 2) + x = 5$

13. $-x - 3 = 2x - 6$

14. $10 = x + 5 + x$

15. $2x - 1 - 1 = x - 3 - (-5 + x)$

16. $3 + 3x - x + 2 = 3x + 4$

17. $-4 + 3x - 1 = 2x + 1 + 2x$

18. $2x - 7 = -x - 1$

19. $7 = 3x - 4 - (x + 2)$

20. $5y + (-y - 2) = 4 + y$

Answers

1. $x = 2$

2. $x = 1$

3. $x = 2\tfrac{1}{5}$

4. $x = -3$

5. $x = 1$

6. $x = -7$

7. $x = 5$

8. no solution

9. $y = 6$

10. $x = -3$

11. $y = 0$

12. $x = 3$

13. $x = 1$

14. $x = 2\tfrac{1}{2}$

15. $x = 2$

16. $x = 1$

17. $x = -6$

18. $x = 2$

19. $x = 6\tfrac{1}{2}$

20. $y = 2$

Checkpoint 2

Problem 2-113

Solving Linear Systems of Equations

Answers to problem 2-113: a. $(-2, 5)$, b. $(1, 5)$, c. $(-12, 14)$, d. $(2, 2)$

When two equations are both in $y = mx + b$ form it is convenient to use the Equal Values Method to solve for the point of intersection. Set the two equations equal to each other to create an equation in one variable and solve for x. Then use the x-value in either equation to solve for y.

If one of the equations has a variable by itself on one side of the equation, then that expression can replace the variable in the second equation. This again creates an equation with only one variable. This is called the Substitution Method. See Example 1 below.

If both equations are in standard form (that is $ax + by = c$), then adding or subtracting the equations may eliminate one of the variables. Sometimes it is necessary to multiply before adding or subtracting so that the coefficients are the same or opposite. This is called the Elimination Method. See Example 2.

Sometimes the equations are not convenient for substitution or elimination. In that case one of both of the equations will need to be rearranged into a form suitable for the previously mentioned methods.

Example 1: Solve the following system. $4x + y = 8$
$$x = 5 - y$$

Solution: Since x is alone in the second equation, substitute $5 - y$ in the first equation, then solve as usual.

$$4(5 - y) + y = 8$$
$$20 - 4y + y = 8$$
$$20 - 3y = 8$$
$$-3y = -12$$
$$y = 4$$

Then substitute $y = 4$ into either original equation to find x. Using the second equation $x = 1$ so the solution is $(1, 4)$.

$$x = 5 - 4$$
$$x = 1$$

Example 2: Solve the following system. $-2x + y = -7$

$\qquad\qquad\qquad\qquad\qquad\qquad\qquad 3x - 4y = 8$

Solution: If we add or subtract the two equations no variable is eliminated. Notice, however, that if everything in the top equation is multiplied by 4, then when the two equations are added together, the y-terms are eliminated.

$$\begin{array}{rcl} -2x + y = -7 \\ 3x - 4y = 8 \end{array} \quad \Rightarrow \quad \begin{array}{c} 4(-2x + y = -7) \\ 3x - 4y = 8 \end{array} \quad \Rightarrow \quad \begin{array}{r} -8x + 4y = -28 \\ 3x - 4y = 8 \\ \hline -5x + 0 = -20 \\ x = 4 \end{array}$$

Substitute $x = 4$ into the first equation: $-2(4) + y = -7 \Rightarrow -8 + y = -7 \Rightarrow y = 1$
The solution is (4, 1).

Now we can go back and solve the original problems.

a. $\quad y = 3x + 11$

$\qquad x + y = 3$

Using substitution:
$$x + (3x + 11) = 3$$
$$4x + 11 = 3$$
$$4x = -8$$
$$x = -2$$
$$y = 3(-2) + 11 = 5$$
The answer is (−2, 5).

b. $\quad y = 2x + 3$

$\qquad x - y = -4$

Using substitution:
$$x - (2x + 3) = -4$$
$$x - 2x - 3 = -4$$
$$-x - 3 = -4$$
$$-x = -1$$
$$x = 1$$
$$y = 2(1) + 3 = 5$$
The answer is (1, 5).

c. $\quad x + 2y = 16$

$\qquad x + y = 2$

Subtracting the second equation from the first eliminates x.

$$\begin{array}{r} x + 2y = 16 \\ -(x + y = 2) \\ \hline y = 14 \end{array}$$
$$x + 14 = 2$$
$$x = -12$$
The answer is (−12, 14).

d. $\quad 2x + 3y = 10$

$\qquad 3x - 4y = -2$

Multiplying the top by 4, the bottom by 3, and adding the equations eliminates y.

$$\begin{array}{r} 8x + 12y = 40 \\ 9x - 12y = -6 \\ \hline 17x \quad\;\; = 34 \\ x = 2 \end{array}$$
$$2(2) + 3y = 10$$
$$3y = 6$$
$$y = 2$$
The answer is (2, 2).

Here are some more to try. Solve each system of equations.

1. $y = -3x$
   $4x + y = 2$

2. $y = 7x - 5$
   $2x + y = 13$

3. $x = -5y - 4$
   $x - 4y = 23$

4. $x + y = -4$
   $-x + 2y = 13$

5. $3x - y = 1$
   $-2x + y = 2$

6. $2x + 5y = 1$
   $2x - y = 19$

7. $x + y = 10$
   $y = x - 4$

8. $y = 5 - x$
   $4x + 2y = 10$

9. $3x + 5y = 23$
   $y = x + 3$

10. $y - x = 4$
    $2y + x = 8$

11. $2x - y = 4$
    $\frac{1}{2}x + y = 1$

12. $-4x + 6y = -20$
    $2x - 3y = 10$

13. $x = \frac{1}{2}y + \frac{1}{2}$
    $2x + y = -1$

14. $a = 2b + 4$
    $b - 2a = 16$

15. $y = 3 - 2x$
    $4x + 2y = 5$

16. $6x - 2y = -16$
    $4x + y = 1$

17. $4x - 4y = 14$
    $2x - 4y = 8$

18. $3x + 2y = 12$
    $5x - 3y = -37$

19. $x + y = 5$
    $2y - x = -2$

20. $2y = 10 - x$
    $3x - 2y = -2$

21. $2x - 3y = 50$
    $7x + 8y = -10$

22. $3x = y - 2$
    $6x + 4 = 2y$

23. $y = -\frac{2}{3}x + 4$
    $y = \frac{1}{3}x - 2$

24. $5x + 2y = 9$
    $2x + 3y = -3$

Answers:

1. $(2, -6)$

2. $(2, 9)$

3. $(11, -3)$

4. $(-7, 3)$

5. $(3, 8)$

6. $(8, -3)$

7. $(7, 3)$

8. $(0, 5)$

9. $(1, 4)$

10. $(0, 4)$

11. $(2, 0)$

12. infinite solutions

13. $(0, -1)$

14. $(-12, -8)$

15. no solution

16. $(-1, 5)$

17. $(3, -\frac{1}{2})$

18. $(-2, 9)$

19. $(4, 1)$

20. $(2, 4)$

21. $(10, -10)$

22. infinite solutions

23. $(6, 0)$

24. $(3, -3)$

Checkpoint 3

Problem 3-111

Linear Equations from Multiple Representations

Answers to problem 3-111: a. $y = -\frac{1}{2}x + 4$, b. $y = 2x - 1$, c. $y = \frac{2}{5}x + \frac{7}{5}$,

d. $C = 15 + 7(t-1) = 8 + 7t$

Linear equations are equations of the form $y = mx + b$. The slope or rate of change is represented by m and the y-intercept or starting value is represented by b. Horizontal lines have a slope of zero and an equation of the form $y = k$. Vertical lines have undefined slope and an equation of the form $x = h$. Parallel lines have the same slope and perpendicular lines have slopes that are opposite reciprocals.

Example 1: Find the equation of the line passing through $(-2, 4)$ and $(4, 7)$. What is the slope of any line perpendicular to this line?

Solution: The slope is $m = \frac{\text{vertical change}}{\text{horizontal change}} = \frac{3}{6} = \frac{1}{2}$ and can be seen in the generic slope triangle at right. Since the line slants upward (when reading from left to right), the slope is positive. The equation of a line is $y = mx + b$ and substituting $\frac{1}{2}$ for b it becomes $y = \frac{1}{2}x + b$. Next choose either given point and substitute for x and y. Choosing $(-2, 4)$, the equation becomes $4 = \frac{1}{2}(-2) + b \Rightarrow b = 5$. The equation of the line is: $y = \frac{1}{2}x + 5$. The slope of any line perpendicular to this line would be $m = -2$.

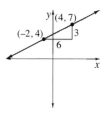

Note: Some people prefer to use formulas that represent the generic slope triangle.

$$\text{slope} = \frac{y_2 - y_1}{x_2 - x_1} = \frac{7 - (4)}{4 - (-2)} = \frac{3}{6} = \frac{1}{2}$$

Notice that $x_2 - x_1$ and $y_2 - y_1$ represent the lengths of the horizontal and vertical legs respectively.

Example 2: The cost to rent a jet ski on Evantown Lake is $30 plus $7.50 per hour. Write an equation that represents the cost for various rental hours. Be sure to define your variables.

Solution: The prices are fixed but the hours and total cost vary. Let C = total cost and h = the hours. A 5-hour rental would cost $30 + $7.50(5), so in general $C = 30 + 7.50h$.

Now we can go back and solve the original problems.

a.   Using the slope triangle formed by the line and the x- and y-axes, $m = -\frac{4}{8} = -\frac{1}{2}$. The y-intercept is the point $(0, 4)$ so $b = 4$. The equation of the line is $y = -\frac{1}{2}x + 4$.

b.   The given line has slope $-\frac{1}{2}$ so the perpendicular line has opposite reciprocal slope of $m = 2$. Using the $y = mx + b$ equation of a line with $m = 2$ and $(x, y) = (-1, -3)$ we have $-3 = 2(-1) + b \Rightarrow b = -1$. The equation of the perpendicular line is $y = 2x - 1$.

c.   Using a generic slope triangle or the formula, $m = \frac{2}{5}$. Choosing $(x, y) = (-1, 1)$ and using $y = mx + b \Rightarrow 1 = \frac{2}{5}(-1) + b \Rightarrow b = \frac{7}{5}$. The equation is $y = \frac{2}{5}x + \frac{7}{5}$.

d.   The parking charges for 6 hours would be $\$15(1) + \$7(6 - 1)$ so in general $C = 15 + 7(t - 1)$ which can also be written as $C = 8 + 7t$.

Here are some more to try. Write an equation for each graphed line.

1.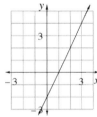

2.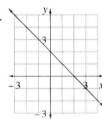

3.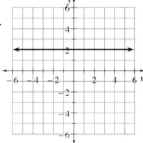

4.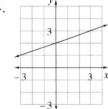

5.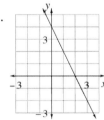

6.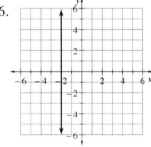

Given each description below, write an equation of the line.

7. Passing through $(1, 1)$ and $(0, 4)$.

8. Passing through $(-2, 3)$ and $(3, 5)$.

9. Perpendicular to the line $y = 2x - 2$ and passing through $(-3, 5)$.

10. Perpendicular to the line $y = x - 2$ and passing through $(-2, 3)$.

11. Passing through $(2, -1)$ and $(3, -3)$.

12. Passing through $(4, 5)$ and $(-2, -4)$.

13. Perpendicular to the line $y = -\frac{3}{2}x + 3$ and passing through $(2, -1)$.

14. Perpendicular to the line $3x - 4y = 12$ and passing through $(4, -2)$.

15. Passing through $(-3, -2)$ and $(5, -2)$.

16. Passing through $(4, 5)$ and $(4, -4)$.

Write a linear equation to represent each situation. Be sure to define your variables.

17. The cost of attending the state fair with a $10 admission fee and cost of $1.50 per ride.

18. The population of Salem that is currently 15,375 but is decreasing by 27 people per year.

19. The weight of Karen who currently weighs 105 pounds but is gaining two pounds per month.

20. The value of Miguel's bank account that currently has $3275 and he is saving $35 per week.

21. Paula's distance from home as her mother drives her home at 50 miles per hour from a camp that is located 250 miles away.

22. The perimeter of a rectangle with length 3 cm more than twice the width.

23. The cost to rent a sailboat that is advertised as $75 for the first 2 hours and $15 for each additional hour.

24. The total ticket receipts for a play with $5 admission for students and $9 admission for adults if there were 40 more student tickets sold than adult tickets.

Answers:

1. $y = 2x - 2$

2. $y = -x + 2$

3. $y = 2$

4. $y = \frac{1}{2}x + 2$

5. $y = -2x + 4$

6. $x = -2$

7. $y = -3x + 4$

8. $y = \frac{2}{5}x + \frac{19}{5}$

9. $y = -\frac{1}{2}x + \frac{7}{2}$

10. $y = -x + 1$

11. $y = -2x + 3$

12. $y = \frac{3}{2}x - 1$

13. $y = \frac{2}{3}x - \frac{7}{3}$

14. $y = -\frac{4}{3}x + \frac{10}{3}$

15. $y = -2$

16. $x = 4$

For answers 17 through 24 different variables are possible but all variables should be defined.

17. $c = 10 + 1.5n$

18. $p = 15375 - 27y$

19. $w = 105 + 2m$

20. $v = 3275 + 35w$

21. $d = 250 - 50h$

22. $p = 2w + 2(2w + 3) = 6w + 6$

23. $c = 75 + 15(h - 2)$

24. $r = 5(a + 40) + 9a$

Checkpoint 4

Problem 4-44

Finding the Areas and Perimeters of Complex Shapes

Answers to problem 4-44: a. 144 cm², 52 cm; b. 696.67 m², 114.67 m; c. 72 cm², 48 cm; d. 130 square units, 58 units

Area is the number of square units in a flat region. The formulas to calculate the area of several kinds of polygons are:

RECTANGLE   PARALLELOGRAM   TRAPEZOID   TRIANGLE

  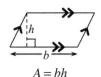   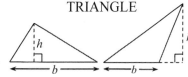

$A = bh$ $A = bh$ $A = \frac{1}{2}\left(b_1 + b_2\right)h$ $A = \frac{1}{2}bh$

Perimeter is the distance around a figure on a flat surface. To calculate the perimeter of a polygon, add together the length of each side.

For complex figures, divide the figure into more recognizable parts. Then find the sum of the area of the parts. When finding the perimeter of a complex region, be sure that the sum only includes the edges on the outside of the region.

Example 1:

Calculate the area and perimeter.

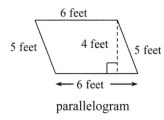

parallelogram

Example 2:

Calculate the area and perimeter.

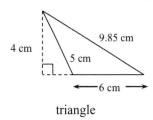

triangle

Solutions:

$A = bh = 6 \cdot 4 = 24$ feet²

$P = 6 + 6 + 5 + 5 = 22$ feet

$A = \frac{1}{2}bh = \frac{1}{2} \cdot 6 \cdot 4 = 12$ cm²

$P = 6 + 5 + 9.85 = 20.85$ cm

Example 3: Calculate the area and perimeter.

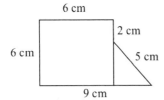

6 cm

6 cm

2 cm

5 cm

9 cm

Solution:

Area of square plus triangle:
$A = s^2 + \frac{1}{2}bh = 6^2 + \frac{1}{2} \cdot 3 \cdot 4 = 42$ cm^2

Add all sides for perimeter:
$6 + 6 + 2 + 5 + 9 = 28$ cm

Now we can go back and solve the original problems.

a. Parallelogram: $A = bh = 16 \cdot 9 = 144$ cm^2; $P = 16 + 16 + 10 + 10 = 52$ cm

b. Trapezoid: $A = \frac{1}{2}(b_1 + b_2)h = \frac{1}{2}(25 + 44.67) \cdot 10 = 696.67$ m^2;
$P = 21 + 25 + 24 + 44.67 = 114.67$ m

c. Rectangle complex: First determine the lengths of the missing sides.
Adding them clockwise
$P = 12 + 2 + 3 + 5 + 3 + 2 + 9 + 7 + 3 + 2 = 48$ cm.
To find the area, imagine two vertical lines that divide the shape into four rectangles–one small rectangle on the left, two small rectangles on the right and a large rectangle in the middle. Each of the small rectangles has a base of 3 cm and a height of 2 cm. The middle rectangle has a base of 6 cm and a height of 9 cm.
Total area = area of 3 small rectangle + area of larger rectangle.
$A = 3bh_{\text{small}} + bh_{\text{big}} = 3(3 \cdot 2) + (6 \cdot 9) = 72$ cm^2.

d. Trapezoid–rectangle: $P = 23 + 10 + 4 + 2 + 3 + 2 + 4 + 10 = 58$ units.
$A = \frac{1}{2}h(b_1 + b_2) - bh = \frac{1}{2} \cdot 8(23 + 11) - 2 \cdot 3 = 130$ units^2

Here are some more to try. Find the area and perimeter of each figure. Note: All angles that look like right angles can be assumed to be right angles.

1.

9 cm
11 cm

2.
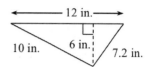
12 in.
10 in.   6 in.
7.2 in.

3. Trapezoid
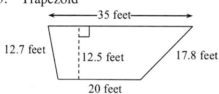
35 feet
12.7 feet   12.5 feet   17.8 feet
20 feet

4. Parallelogram
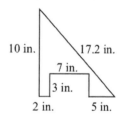
10.8 cm   10 cm   10.8 cm
16 cm

5. Find the area of the shaded region.
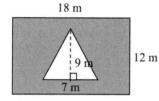
18 m
9 m   12 m
7 m

6.
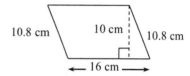
10 in.   17.2 in.
7 in.
3 in.
2 in.   5 in.

7.
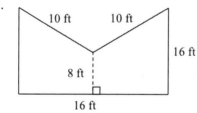
10 ft   10 ft
16 ft
8 ft
16 ft

8. Trapezoid on a rectangle
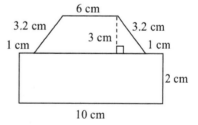
6 cm
3.2 cm   3.2 cm
1 cm   3 cm   1 cm
2 cm
10 cm

9.
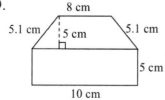
8 cm
5.1 cm   5 cm   5.1 cm
5 cm
10 cm

10.
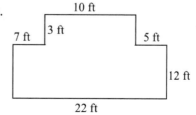
10 ft
7 ft   3 ft   5 ft
12 ft
22 ft

11. Find the area of the shaded region.   12.

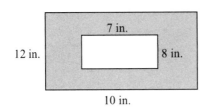

7 in.

12 in.   8 in.

10 in.

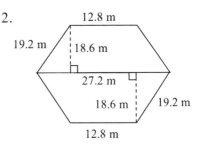

12.8 m

19.2 m   18.6 m

27.2 m

18.6 m   19.2 m

12.8 m

Answers:

1. 99 cm^2, 40 cm

2. 36 in.^{2}, 29.2 in.

3. 343.75 feet^2, 85.5 feet

4. 160 cm^2, 53.6 cm

5. A = 184.5 m^2

6. A = 49 in.^{2}, P = 47.2 in.

7. A = 192 ft^2, P = 68 ft

8. A = 41 cm^2, P = 28.4 cm

9. A = 95 cm^2, P = 38.2 cm

10. A = 294 ft^2, P = 74 ft

11. A = 64 in.^{2}

12. A = 744 m^2, P = 102.4 m

Checkpoint 5A
Problem 5-104
Multiplying Polynomials and Solving Quadratics

Answers to problem 5-104: a. $2x^2 + 6x$, b. $3x^2 - 7x - 6$, c. $x = 7$ or 1, d. $y = 5$ or -3

Polynomials can be multiplied (changed from the area written as a product to the area written as a sum) by using the Distributive Property or generic rectangles.

Example 1: Multiply $-5x(-2x + y)$.

Solution: Using the Distributive Property $\underbrace{-5x(-2x + y)}_{\text{area as a product}} = -5x \cdot -2x + -5x \cdot y = \underbrace{10x^2 - 5xy}_{\text{area as a sum}}$

Example 2: Multiply $(x - 3)(2x + 1)$.

Solution: Although the Distributive Property may be used, for this problem and other more complicated ones, it is beneficial to use a generic rectangle to find all the parts.

$$\Rightarrow (x - 3)(2x + 1) = 2x^2 - 5x - 3$$
$$\underbrace{}_{\text{area as a product}} \quad \underbrace{}_{\text{area as a sum}}$$

Solving quadratics first required factoring the polynomials to change the sum into a product. It is the reverse of multiplying polynomials and using a generic rectangle is helpful. Once the expression is factored, then the factors can be found using the Zero Product Property.

Example 3: Solve $x^2 + 7x + 12 = 0$.

Solution: First, factor the polynomial. Sketch a generic rectangle with 4 sections.

Write the x^2 and the 12 along one diagonal.

Find two terms whose product is $12 \cdot x^2 = 12x^2$ and whose sum is $7x$. That is, $3x$ and $4x$. This is the same as a Diamond Problem.

Write these terms as the other diagonal.

Find the base and height of the rectangle by using the partial areas.

Write the factored equation. $\qquad x^2 + 7x + 12 = (x + 3)(x + 4) = 0$

Then, using the Zero Product Property, we know that either $(x + 3)$ or $(x + 4)$ is equal to zero (since their product is zero). This means that $x = -3$ or $x = -4$.

Example 4: Solve $2x^2 + x = 6$.

Solution: In order to factor and use the Zero Product Property, the equation must be equal to zero. First, rearrange the equation to $2x^2 + x - 6 = 0$. Then factor the expression on the left side.

Sketch a generic rectangle with 4 sections.

Write $2x^2$ and -6 along one diagonal.

Find two terms whose product is $-12x^2$ and whose sum is $1x$. That is, $4x$ and $-3x$.

Write these terms as the other diagonal.

Find the base and height of the rectangle.

Write the factored equation. $\qquad 2x^2 + x - 6 = (2x - 3)(x + 2) = 0$

Then use the Zero Product Property and finish solving.

$$2x - 3 = 0$$
$$2x = 3 \quad \text{and} \quad \begin{aligned} x + 2 &= 0 \\ x &= -2 \end{aligned}$$
$$x = \tfrac{3}{2}$$

Now we can go back and solve the original problems.

a. Using the Distributive Property: $2x(x + 3) = 2x \cdot x + 2x \cdot 3 = 2x^2 + 6x$

b. Using generic rectangles:

$\Rightarrow 3x^2 - 7x - 6$

c. $x^2 - 8x + 7 = 0$

The two terms whose product is $7x^2$ and whose sum is $-8x$ are $-1x$ and $-7x$.

$x^2 - 8x + 7 = (x - 1)(x - 7) = 0$
$x - 1 = 0 \Rightarrow x = 1$
$x - 7 = 0 \Rightarrow x = 7$

d. $y^2 - 2y = 15$

First, rewrite the problem to:
$y^2 - 2y - 15 = 0$.

The two terms whose product is $-15y^2$ and whose sum is $-2y$ are $-5y$ and $3y$.

$y^2 - 2y - 15 = (y - 5)(y + 3) = 0$
$y - 5 = 0 \Rightarrow y = 5$

Here are some more to try. Multiply the expressions in problems 1 through 15 and solve the equations in problems 16 through 30.

1. $2x(x-1)$ 2. $(3x+2)(2x+7)$ 3. $(2x-1)(3x+1)$

4. $2y(x-1)$ 5. $(2y-1)(3y+5)$ 6. $(x+3)(x-3)$

7. $3y(x-y)$ 8. $(2x-5)(x+4)$ 9. $(3x+7)(3x-7)$

10. $(4x+3)^2$ 11. $(x+y)(x+2)$ 12. $(x-1)(x+y+1)$

13. $(2y-3)^2$ 14. $(x+2)(x+y-2)$ 15. $2(x+3)(3x-4)$

16. $x^2+5x+6=0$ 17. $2x^2+5x+3=0$ 18. $3x^2+4x+1=0$

19. $x^2-10x+25=0$ 20. $x^2+15x+44=0$ 21. $x^2-6x=7$

22. $x^2-11x=-24$ 23. $x^2=4x+32$ 24. $4x^2+12x+9=0$

25. $12x^2+11x=5$ 26. $x^2=-x+72$ 27. $3x^2=20x+7$

28. $x^2-11x+28=0$ 29. $3x^2-5=-2x$ 30. $6x^2-2=x$

Answers:

1. $2x^2-2x$ 2. $6x^2+25x+14$ 3. $6x^2-x-1$

4. $2xy-2y$ 5. $6y^2+7y-5$ 6. x^2-9

7. $3xy-3y^2$ 8. $2x^2+3x-20$ 9. $9x^2-49$

10. $16x^2+24x+9$ 11. $x^2+xy+2x+2y$ 12. $x^2+xy-y-1$

13. $4y^2-12y+9$ 14. $x^2+xy+2y-4$ 15. $6x^2+10x-24$

16. $x=-2,-3$ 17. $x=-\frac{3}{2},-1$ 18. $x=-\frac{1}{3},-1$

19. $x=5$ 20. $x=-11,-4$ 21. $x=7,-1$

22. $x=3,8$ 23. $x=8,-4$ 24. $x=-\frac{3}{2}$

25. $x=\frac{1}{3},-\frac{5}{4}$ 26. $x=-9,8$ 27. $x=-\frac{1}{3},7$

28. $x=4,7$ 27. $x=-\frac{5}{3},1$ 30. $x=-\frac{1}{2},\frac{2}{3}$

Checkpoint 5B

Problem 5-136

Writing Equations for Arithmetic and Geometric Sequences

Answers to problem 5-136: a. E $t(n) = -2 + 3n$, R $t(0) = -2$, $t(n+1) = t(n) + 3$;
b. E $t(n) = 6(\frac{1}{2})^n$, R $t(0) = 6$, $t(n+1) = \frac{1}{2}t(n)$; c. $t(n) = 24 - 7n$,
d. $t(n) = 5(1.2)^n$; e. $t(4) = 1620$

An ordered list of numbers such as: $4, 9, 16, 25, 36, \ldots$ creates a sequence. The numbers in the sequence are called terms. One way to identify and label terms is to use function notation. For example, if $t(n)$ is the name of the sequence above, the first term is 4 and the third term is 16. This is written $t(1) = 4$ and $t(3) = 16$. Some books use subscripts instead of function notation. In this case $t_1 = 4$ and $t_3 = 16$.

The initial value is *not* part of the sequence. It is only a reference point and is useful for writing a rule for the sequence. For the sequence above, the initial value, $t(0)$ or t_0, is the value that would come before 4, which is -1. When writing a sequence, start by writing the first term after the initial value, $t(1)$ or t_1. When writing the rule, use the initial value, $t(0)$ or t_0.

Arithmetic sequences have a common difference between the terms. The rule for the values in an arithmetic sequences can be found by $t(n) = a + dn$ where a = the initial value, d = the common difference and n = the number of terms after the initial value.

Geometric sequences have a common ratio between the terms. The rule for the values in a geometric sequence may be found by $t(n) = ar^n$ where a = the initial value, r = the common ratio and n = the number of terms after the initial value.

Example 1: Find a rule for the sequence: $-2, 4, 10, 16, \ldots$

Solution: There is a common difference between the terms $(d = 6)$ so it is an arithmetic sequence. Work backward to find the initial value: $a = -2 - 6 = -8$.
Now use the general rule: $t(n) = a + dn = -8 + 6n$.

Example 2: Find a rule for the sequence: $81, 27, 9, 3, \ldots$

Solution: There is a common ratio between the terms $(r = \frac{1}{3})$ so it is a geometric sequence.
Work backward to find the initial value: $a = 81 \div \frac{1}{3} = 243$.
Now use the general rule: $t(n) = ar^n = 243(\frac{1}{3})^n$.

A rule such as $t(n) = 5 - 7n$ is called an explicit rule because any term can be found by substituting the appropriate value for n into the rule. To find the 10th term after the initial value, $t(10)$, substitute 10 for n. $t(10) = 5 - 7(10) = -65$.

A second way to find the terms in a sequence is by using a recursive formula. A recursive formula tells first term or the initial value and then how to get from one term to the next.

Example 3: Write the first five terms of the sequence determined by $b_1 = 8$, $b_{n+1} = b_n \cdot \frac{1}{2}$ (using subscript notation).

Solution: $b_1 = 8$ tells you the first term and $b_{n+1} = b_n \cdot \frac{1}{2}$ tells you to multiply by $\frac{1}{2}$ to get from one term to the next.

$b_1 = 8$ $\qquad\qquad$ $b_2 = b_1 \cdot \frac{1}{2} = 8 \cdot \frac{1}{2} = 4$ $\qquad\qquad$ $b_3 = b_2 \cdot \frac{1}{2} = 4 \cdot \frac{1}{2} = 2$

$b_4 = b_3 \cdot \frac{1}{2} = 2 \cdot \frac{1}{2} = 1$ $\qquad\qquad$ $b_5 = b_4 \cdot \frac{1}{2} = 1 \cdot \frac{1}{2} = \frac{1}{2}$

The sequence is: $8, 4, 2, 1, \frac{1}{2}, \ldots$

Now we can go back and solve the original problems.

    a.   It is an arithmetic sequence $(d = 3)$. Working backward the initial value is $1 - 3 = -2$. Using the general formula the explicit rule: $t(n) = a + dn = -2 + 3d$.

           A possible recursive rule is $t(0) = -2, t(n+1) = t(n) + 3$.

    b.   It is a geometric sequence $(r = \frac{1}{2})$. Working backward the initial value is $3 \div \frac{1}{2} = 6$. Using the general formula for the explicit rule: $t(n) = ar^n = 6(\frac{1}{2})^n$.

           A possible recursive rule is $t(0) = 6, t(n+1) = \frac{1}{2} t(n)$.

    c. $t(2)$ is halfway between $t(1)$ and $t(3)$ so $t(2) = 10$. This means $d = -7$ and the initial value is 24. Using the general formula the explicit rule: $t(n) = a + dn = 24 - 7d$.

    d.   The common ratio $r = \frac{8.64}{7.2} = 1.2$ so $t(1) = \frac{7.2}{1.2} = 6, t(0) = \frac{6}{1.2} = 5$. Using an initial value of 5 and a common ratio of 1.2 in the general formula for the explicit rule: $t(n) = ar^n = 5(1.2)^n$.

    e.   The common difference is the difference in the values divided by the number of terms. $d = \frac{t(12) - t(7)}{12 - 7} = \frac{116 - 1056}{5} = -188$. Working backward three terms: $t(4) = 1056 - 3(-188) = 1620$.

Here are some more to try.

Write the first 6 terms of each sequence.

1. $t(n) = 5n + 2$

2. $t(n) = 6(-\frac{1}{2})^n$

3. $t(n) = -15 + \frac{1}{2}n$

4. $t_n = -3 \cdot 3^{n-1}$

5. $t(1) = 3,\ t(n+1) = t(n) - 5$

6. $t_1 = \frac{1}{3},\ t_{n+1} = \frac{1}{3}t_n$

For each sequence, write an explicit and recursive rule.

7. $10, 50, 250, 1250, \ldots$

8. $4, 8, 12, 16, \ldots$

9. $-2, 5, 12, 19, \ldots$

10. $16, 4, 1, \frac{1}{4}, \ldots$

11. $-12, 6, -3, \frac{3}{2}, \ldots$

12. $\frac{5}{6}, \frac{2}{3}, \frac{1}{2}, \frac{1}{3}, \ldots$

For each sequence, write an explicit rule.

13. A geometric sequence

n	$t(n)$
0	
1	15
2	45
3	
4	

14. An arithmetic sequence

n	$t(n)$
0	27
1	15
2	
3	
4	

15. An arithmetic sequence

n	$t(n)$
1	
2	$3\frac{1}{3}$
3	
4	
5	$4\frac{1}{3}$

16. A geometric sequence

n	$t(n)$
1	
2	
3	-24
4	48
5	

Solve each problem.

17. An arithmetic sequence has $t(3) = 52$ and $t(10) = 108$. Find a rule for $t(n)$ and find $t(100)$.

18. An arithmetic sequence has $t(1) = -17$, $t(2) = -14$ and $t(n) = 145$. What is the value of n?

19. An arithmetic sequence has $t(61) = 810$ and $t(94) = 1239$. Find a rule for $t(n)$.

20. A geometric sequence has $t(4) = 12$ and $t(7) = 324$. Find the common ratio and a rule for $t(n)$.

Answers:

1. $7, 12, 17, 22, 27, 32$

2. $-3, \frac{3}{2}, -\frac{3}{4}, \frac{3}{8}, -\frac{3}{16}, \frac{3}{32}$

3. $-14\frac{1}{2}, -14, -13\frac{1}{2}, -13, -12\frac{1}{2}, -12$

4. $-3, -9, -27, -81, -243, -729$

5. $3, -2, -7, -12, -17, -22$

6. $\frac{1}{3}, \frac{1}{9}, \frac{1}{27}, \frac{1}{81}, \frac{1}{243}, \frac{1}{729}$

Rules for problems 7 through 20 may vary.

7. $t(n) = 2 \cdot 5^n$; $t(0) = 2, t(n+1) = 5t(n)$

8. $t(n) = 4n$; $t(0) = 0, t(n+1) = t(n) + 4$

9. $t(n) = -9 + 7n$; $t(0) = -9, t(n+1) = t(n) + 7$

10. $t(n) = 64(\frac{1}{4})^n$; $t(0) = 64, t(n+1) = \frac{1}{4}t(n)$

11. $t(n) = 24(-\frac{1}{2})^n$; $t(0) = 24, t(n+1) = -\frac{1}{2}t(n)$

12. $t(n) = 1 - \frac{1}{6}n$; $t(0) = 1, t(n+1) = t(n) - \frac{1}{6}$

13. $t(n) = 5 \cdot 3^n$

14. $t(n) = 27 - 12n$

15. $t(n) = 2\frac{2}{3} + \frac{1}{3}n$

16. $t(n) = 3(-2)^n$

17. $t(n) = 28 + 8n$; $t(100) = 828$

18. $n = 55$

19. $t(n) = 17 + 13n$

20. $r = 3$; $t(n) = \frac{4}{27}(3)^n$

Checkpoint 6
Problem 6-50
Solving Proportional Equations and Similar Figures

Answers to problem 6-50: a. $y = \frac{13}{4}$, b. $y = -2$, c. $4\frac{2}{3}$ inches, d. $x = 4$

A proportion is an equation stating that two ratios are equal. To solve a proportion, begin by eliminating the fractions. Multiply both sides of the proportion by one or both of the denominators. Then solve the resulting equation in the usual way. Setting up the ratios using the unit words consistently helps to proportional situations. To solve problems with similar triangles the corresponding sides must be consistently used in the ratios.

Example 1: Solve: $\frac{x}{x+1} = \frac{3}{5}$

Solution: Multiply by 5 and $(x+1)$ on both sides of the equation.

$5(x+1)\frac{x}{x+1} = \frac{3}{5}(5)(x+1)$

since $\frac{(x+1)}{(x+1)} = 1$ and $\frac{5}{5} = 1$, we have $5x = 3(x+1)$

$5x = 3x + 3 \Rightarrow 2x = 3 \Rightarrow x = \frac{3}{2}$

Example 2: Solve for x in the diagram at right.

Solution: With two sets of congruent angles (alternating interior and vertical), $\triangle ABC \sim \triangle EDC$ and the ratio of corresponding sides is proportional.
$\frac{6}{10} = \frac{x}{6} \Rightarrow 10x = 36 \Rightarrow x = 3.6$

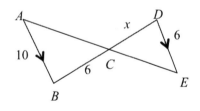

Now we can go back and solve the original problems.

a. $\frac{7-y}{5} = \frac{3}{4}$

$20(\frac{7-y}{5}) = 20(\frac{3}{4})$

$4(7-y) = 15$

$28 - 4y = 15$

$-4y = -13 \Rightarrow y = \frac{13}{4}$

b. $\frac{3}{y} = \frac{6}{y-2}$

$y(y-2)\frac{3}{y} = y(y-2)\frac{6}{y-2}$

$(y-2)3 = (y)6$

$3y - 6 = 6y$

$-6 = 3y \Rightarrow y = -2$

c. $\frac{\text{inches}}{\text{months}} \cdot \frac{1\frac{3}{4}}{4\frac{1}{2}} = \frac{x}{12}$

$4\frac{1}{2}x = 1\frac{3}{4}(12)$

$\frac{9}{2}x = 21$

$x = \frac{2}{9}(21) = \frac{42}{9} = 4\frac{2}{3}$ in

d. Since the triangles are similar, the lengths of corresponding sides are proportional. Separating the figure into two triangles makes it easier to write the ratios.

$\frac{12}{8+x} = \frac{4}{x} \Rightarrow 12x = 4(8+x)$

$12x = 32 + 4x \Rightarrow 8x = 32 \Rightarrow x = 4$

Here are some more to try. Solve for the variable.

1. $\frac{2y-1}{15} = \frac{y}{10}$

2. $\frac{5}{8} = \frac{x}{100}$

3. $\frac{8-x}{x} = \frac{3}{2}$

4. $\frac{4x}{5} = \frac{x-2}{7}$

5. $\frac{9-x}{6} = \frac{24}{2}$

6. $\frac{1}{t} = \frac{5}{t+1}$

7. $\frac{4}{m} = \frac{m}{9}$

8. $\frac{3x}{4} = \frac{x+1}{6}$

Use proportions to solve each problem.

9. A rectangle has length 10 feet and width six feet. It is enlarged to a similar rectangle with length 18 feet. What is the new width?

10. If 300 vitamins cost $5.75, what should 500 vitamins cost?

11. The tax on a $400 statue is $34. What should be the tax on a $700 statue?

12. If a basketball player made 72 of 85 free throws, how many free throws could she expect to make in 200 attempts?

13. A cookie recipe uses $\frac{1}{2}$ teaspoon of vanilla with $\frac{3}{4}$ cups of flour. How much vanilla should be used with five cups of flour?

14. The length of a rectangle is four centimeters more than the width. If the ratio of length to width is seven to five, find the dimensions of the rectangle.

15. Use the similar triangles at right. If, $AB = 14$, $AC = 16$, and $DE = 12$, find CE.

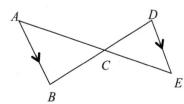

16. In the diagram at right, $\triangle ABC$ and $\triangle ADE$ are similar. If $AB = 6$, $BD = 4$, and $BC = 7$, then what is DE? Start by drawing two separate triangles and labeling the dimensions.

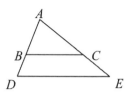

17. The two shapes at right are similar. Find the value of x. Show all work.

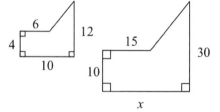

18. Examine the triangles at right. Solve for y.

19. In the diagram at right, $\triangle ABC \sim \triangle ADE$.

   a. Draw each triangle separately on your paper. Be sure to include all measurements in your diagrams.

   b. Find the length of $\overline{DE}$.

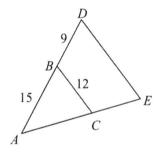

20. Use your knowledge of similar triangles to solve for x.

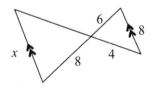

Answers:

1. $y = 2$ 2. $x = 62.5$ 3. $x = 3\frac{1}{5}$ 4. $x = -\frac{10}{23}$

5. $x = -63$ 6. $t = \frac{1}{4}$ 7. $m = \pm 6$ 8. $x = \frac{2}{7}$

9. 10.8 ft 10. \$9.58 11. \$59.50 12. about 169

13. $3\frac{1}{3}$ tsp 14. 10 cm x 14 cm 15. ≈ 13.7 units 16. $11\frac{2}{3}$ units

17. 25 units 18. $12\frac{1}{2}$ units 19. 19.2 units 20. $10\frac{2}{3}$ units

Solving with Trigonometric Ratios and the Pythagorean Theorem

Answers to problem 7-136: a. 23.83 ft, b. $x \approx 7$ yds, c. $x \approx 66.42°$, d. ≈ 334.57 ft

Three trigonometric ratios and the Pythagorean Theorem can used to solve for the missing side lengths and angle measurements in any right triangle.

In the triangle below, when the sides are described relative to the angle θ, the opposite leg is y and the adjacent leg is x. The hypotenuse is h regardless of which acute angle is used.

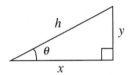

$$\tan \theta = \frac{\text{opposite leg}}{\text{adjacent leg}} = \frac{y}{x}$$

$$\sin \theta = \frac{\text{opposite leg}}{\text{hypotenuse}} = \frac{y}{h}$$

$$\cos \theta = \frac{\text{adjacent leg}}{\text{hypotenuse}} = \frac{x}{h}$$

Also for the triangle above, from the Pythagorean Theorem: $h^2 = x^2 + y^2$.

Example 1: A rectangle has a diagonal of 16 cm and one side of 11 cm. What is the length of the other side?

Solution: The diagonal represents the hypotenuse of a right triangle and the one given side represents one of the legs. Using the Pythagorean Theorem:

$$h^2 = x^2 + y^2 \Rightarrow 16^2 = 11^2 + y^2 \Rightarrow 256 = 121 + y^2$$
$$135 = y^2 \Rightarrow y = \sqrt{135} \approx 11.62 \text{ cm}$$

Example 2: Solve for x in the triangle at right.

Solution: Based on the 40° angle, 11 is the adjacent side and x is the hypotenuse. Use the cosine ratio to solve.

$$\cos 40° = \frac{11}{x}$$
$$x \cos 40° = 11 \Rightarrow x = \frac{11}{\cos 40°} \approx 14.36 \text{ units}$$

Example 3: A ten-foot ladder is leaning against the side of a house. If the top of the ladder touches the house nine feet above the ground, what is the angle made by the ladder and the ground?

Solution: Make a diagram of the situation similar to the one at right. The ladder (10) is the hypotenuse and the house (9) is the opposite leg. Using the sine ratio. To find θ, "undo" the sine function with the inverse sine function ($\sin^{-1} x$) as follows:

$$\sin \theta = \tfrac{9}{10}$$
$$\sin^{-1}(\sin \theta) = \sin^{-1}\left(\tfrac{9}{10}\right)$$
$$\theta = \sin^{-1}\left(\tfrac{9}{10}\right)$$
$$\theta \approx 64.2°$$

Now we can go back and solve the original problems.

a. Separate the trapezoid into a rectangle and a triangle as shown below:

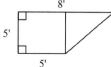

The legs of the triangle are 5 and 3. The hypotenuse or unlabeled side of the trapezoid is found by $h^2 = 5^2 + 3^2 = 34$.
So $h = \sqrt{34} \approx 5.83$.
The perimeter is:
$5 + 5 + 8 + 5.83 = 23.83$ feet

b. $\tan 35° = \tfrac{x}{10}$
$x = 10 \tan 35° \approx 7.0$ yds

c. $\cos x = \tfrac{60}{150}$
$\cos^{-1}(\cos x) = \cos^{-1}(\tfrac{60}{150})$
$x = \cos^{-1}(\tfrac{60}{150})$
$x \approx 66.4°$

d. Using the possible diagram below:
$\sin 42° = \tfrac{x}{500}$
$x = 500 \sin 42° \approx 335$ ft

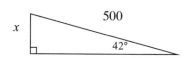

Here are some more to try. Use the right triangle trigonometric ratios or the Pythagorean Theorem to solve for the variable(s).

1.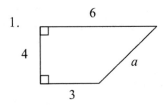

2.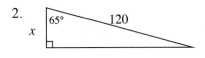

3.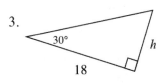

4.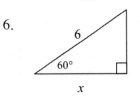

5.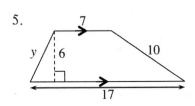

6.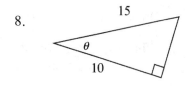

7.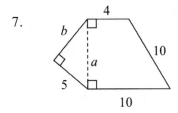

8.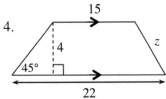

9.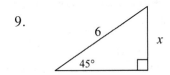

10.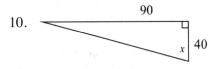

11.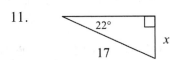

12.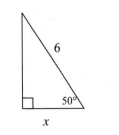

13.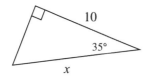

14.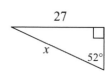

15.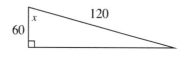

16.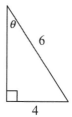

Draw a diagram and solve each of the following problems.

17. The base of a 12-foot ladder is six feet from the wall. How high on the wall does the ladder touch?

18. A garden gate has a six-foot by four-foot rectangular frame that is strengthened by a diagonal brace. How long is the brace?

19. What is the distance between $(-6, -6)$ and $(-3, 2)$?

20. What is the length of the hypotenuse of the right triangle with coordinates: $(-2, -1), (-6, 5),$ and $(4, 3)$?

21. From the takeoff point, the launch crew of a hot air balloon can see the balloon in the sky at an elevation of 13°. The pilot tells the crew that the passenger basket is now 1200 feet above the ground. What is the current ground distance from the crew to the balloon?

22. Federal standards require the angle ramp for wheel chairs to be less than 5°. If the length of a ramp is 20 feet and the vertical rise is 15 inches, does it meet federal standards?

23. If an eight-foot stop sign casts a 10-foot shadow, what is the angle of elevation to the top of the sign?

24. Mayfield High School's flagpole is 15 feet high. Using a clinometer, Tamara measures an angle of 11.3° to the top of the pole. Tamara is 62 inches tall. How far from the flagpole is Tamara standing?

Answers:

1. 5 units

2. ≈ 50.7 units

3. ≈ 10.4 units

4. 5 units

5. $\sqrt{40} \approx 6.32$ units

6. 3 units

7. $a = 8$, $b = \sqrt{39} \approx 6.24$ units

8. $\approx 48.2°$

9. $3\sqrt{2} \approx 4.24$ units

10. $\approx 66.0°$

11. ≈ 6.37 units

12. ≈ 3.86 units

13. ≈ 12.2 units

14. ≈ 34.3 units

15. $60°$

16. $\approx 41.8°$

17. $\sqrt{108} \approx 10.4$ ft

18. $\sqrt{52} \approx 7.2$ ft

19. $\sqrt{73} \approx 8.5$ units

20. $\sqrt{104} \approx 10.2$ units

21. ≈ 5198 ft

22. $3.6°$, yes

23. $\approx 38.7°$

24. ≈ 590.5 in or 49.2 ft

Checkpoint 8

Problem 8-124

Angle Relationships in Triangles and Lines

Answers to problem 8-124: a. supplementary angles sum to 180°; $x = 26°$
b. alternate exterior angles are congruent; $x = 5°$
c. Triangle Angle Sum Theorem; $x = 15°$
d. exterior angle equals sum of remote interior angles; $x = 35°$

Illustrated below are several common relationships between angles in triangles and lines.

Parallel lines

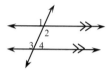

Triangles

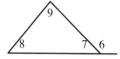

- corresponding angles are equal: $m\angle 1 = m\angle 3$

- alternate interior angles are equal: $m\angle 2 = m\angle 3$

- $m\angle 2 + m\angle 4 = 180°$

- $m\angle 7 + m\angle 8 + m\angle 9 = 180°$

- $m\angle 6 = m\angle 8 + m\angle 9$
  (exterior angle = sum remote interior angles)

Also shown in the above figures:
- vertical angles are equal: $m\angle 1 = m\angle 2$
- linear pairs are supplementary: $m\angle 3 + m\angle 4 = 180°$
  and $m\angle 6 + m\angle 7 = 180°$

In addition, an isosceles triangle, $\triangle ABC$, has $\overline{BA} = \overline{BC}$ and $m\angle A = m\angle C$. An equilateral triangle, $\triangle GFH$, has $\overline{GF} = \overline{FH} = \overline{HG}$ and $m\angle G = m\angle F = m\angle H = 60°$.

Example 1: Solve for x.

Solution: Use the Exterior Angle Theorem:

$6x + 8° = 49° + 67°$

$6x° = 108° \implies x = \frac{108°}{6} \implies x = 18°$

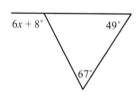

Example 2: Solve for x.

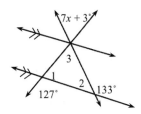

Solution: There are a number of relationships in this diagram. First, $\angle 1$ and the $127°$ angle are supplementary, so we know that $m\angle 1 + 127° = 180°$ so $m\angle 1 = 53°$. Using the same idea, $m\angle 2 = 47°$. Next, $m\angle 3 + 53° + 47° = 180°$, so $m\angle 3 = 80°$. Because angle 3 forms a vertical pair with the angle marked $7x + 3°$, $80° = 7x + 3°$, so $x = 11°$.

Example 3: Find the measure of the acute alternate interior angles.

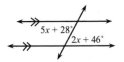

Solution: Parallel lines mean that alternate interior angles are equal, so $5x + 28° = 2x + 46° \Rightarrow 3x = 18° \Rightarrow x = 6°$. Use either algebraic angle measure: $2(6°) + 46° = 58°$ for the measure of the acute angle.

Now we can go back and solve the original problems.

a. Supplementary angles sum to $180°$

$$4x - 3° + 3x + 1° = 180°$$
$$7x - 2° = 180°$$
$$7x = 182°$$
$$x = 26°$$

b. Alt. exterior angles are congruent

$$5x + 6° = 2x + 21°$$
$$3x = 15°$$
$$x = 5°$$

c. Triangle Angle Sum Theorem

$$4x + 28° + x + 19° + 3x + 13° = 180°$$
$$8x + 60° = 180°$$
$$8x = 120°$$
$$x = 15°$$

d. Ext. angle = sum of remote int. angles

$$4x - 10° = 40° + 90°$$
$$4x = 140°$$
$$x = 35°$$

Here are some more to try. For each diagram, name the relationship used and solve for the variable.

1.

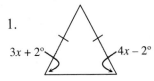

$3x + 2°$ $4x - 2°$

2.

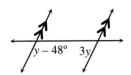

$y - 48°$ $3y$

3.

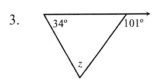

$34°$ $101°$ z

4.

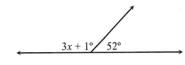

$3x + 1°$ $52°$

5.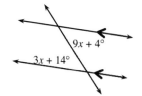

$9x + 4°$

$3x + 14°$

6.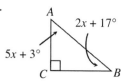

A

$2x + 17°$

$5x + 3°$

C B

7.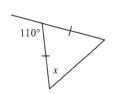

$110°$

x

8.

$3x + 3°$

$x + 7°$

9.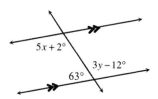

$5x + 2°$

$3y - 12°$

$63°$

10.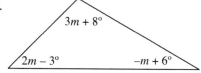

$3m + 8°$

$2m - 3°$ $-m + 6°$

11.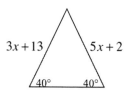

$3x + 13$ $5x + 2$

$40°$ $40°$

12.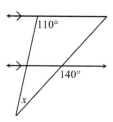

$110°$

$140°$

x

13.

$9k + 3°$

$8k + 9°$

14. $\triangle ABC$ below is equilateral.

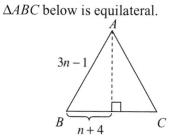

A

$3n - 1$

B C

$n + 4$

15.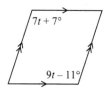

$7t + 7°$

$9t - 11°$

16.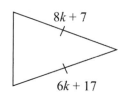

$8k + 7$

$6k + 17$

17.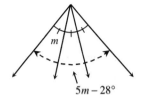

18.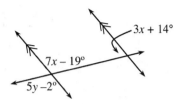

19.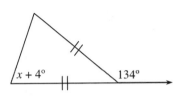

20.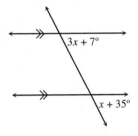

Answers: (explanations may vary)

1. congruent base angles in isosceles triangle; $x = 4°$
2. supplementary same-side interior angles; $y = 57°$
3. exterior angle sum; $z = 67°$
4. supplementary angles; $x = 42\frac{1}{3}°$
5. congruent alternate interior angles; $x = 1\frac{2}{3}°$
6. triangle angle sum; $x = 10°$
7. isosceles triangle and exterior angle sum; $x = 55°$
8. complementary angles; $x = 20°$
9. supplementary angles and congruent alternating interior angles; $y = 43°, x = 23°$
10. triangle angle sum; $m = 42\frac{1}{4}°$
11. isosceles triangle; $x = 5\frac{1}{2}$
12. congruent corresponding angles and exterior angle sum; $x = 30°$
13. congruent vertical angles; $k = 6°$
14. congruent sides on equilateral triangle; $n = 9$
15. two pairs of same-side interior angles; $t = 9°$
16. isosceles triangle; $k = 5$
17. congruent angles and angle sum; $m = 14°$
18. congruent vertical angles, supplementary same-side interior; $x = 18.5°, y = 22.5°$
19. isosceles triangle and exterior angle sum; $x = 63°$
20. congruent corresponding angles; $x = 14°$

Checkpoint 9A

Problem 9-73

Probabilities with Unions, Intersections, and Complements

Answers to problem 9-73:

    a. See tree diagram below.

    b. {WSM, WSP, WTM, WHM, GSM, GSP, GTM, GHM},

        $\frac{2}{18} + \frac{1}{18} + \frac{2}{36} + \frac{2}{36} + \frac{4}{18} + \frac{2}{18} + \frac{4}{36} + \frac{4}{36} = \frac{30}{36} \approx 83.3\%$

    c. {WTP, WHP, GTP, GHP},

        $\frac{2}{36} + \frac{2}{36} + \frac{1}{36} + \frac{1}{36} = \frac{6}{36} \approx 16.7\%$

    d. $100\% - 83.3\% = 16.7\%$

    e. {WSM, GSM}

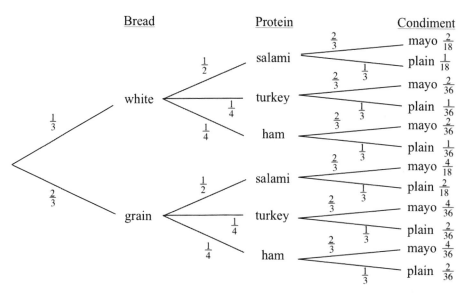

See the Lesson 1.2.1 Math Notes box for definitions of probability terms. There are several models for listing all of the outcomes of a probabilistic situation and showing their probabilities, such as, systematic lists, area models, and tree diagrams. See the Lesson 4.2.3 Math Notes box for an explanation of some of these probability models. An area model is best used when the situation involves exactly two events and the events are independent. See the Lesson 4.1.5 Math Notes box for more information about independent events.

Outcomes from probabilistic situations are called events. Several events can be combined using unions or intersections. See the Lesson 4.2.4 Math Notes box for more information about unions and intersections.

         Core Connections Geometry

Example 1: Howard can never remember what kind of drink he is supposed to get for his wife from the coffee cart on the street. The coffee cart has 5 different hot coffee drinks, 2 different hot tea drinks, and a frozen coffee slush. Harold decides to randomly choose two drinks. When he sees his wife, he learns that she wanted a hot coffee drink. What is the probability (as a percent) that Harold chose at least one hot coffee drink? Make an area model or a tree diagram to justify your solution.

Solution: An area model can be used since there are exactly two events that are independent. The two events are picking the first drink, and picking the second drink. We are only concerned with the events that include a hot coffee drink.

| | | First Drink | | |
		hot coffee $\frac{5}{8}$	hot tea $\frac{2}{8}$	frozen coffee slush $\frac{1}{8}$
	hot coffee $\frac{5}{8}$	$\frac{25}{64}$	$\frac{10}{64}$	$\frac{5}{64}$
Second Drink	hot tea $\frac{2}{8}$	$\frac{10}{64}$		
	frozen coffee slush $\frac{1}{8}$	$\frac{5}{64}$		

A tree diagram could have also been used.

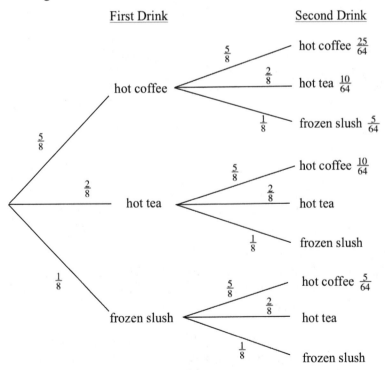

P(at least one hot coffee drink) = $\frac{25}{64} + \frac{10}{64} + \frac{5}{64} + \frac{10}{64} + \frac{5}{64} = \frac{55}{64} \approx 85.9\%$

There is an 85.9% chance that Howard chose at least one hot coffee drink.

Example 2: Denise is also at the coffee cart from Example 1. In addition to one drink, she chooses a bagel. The cart has 8 plain bagels and 5 blueberry bagels. She can top her bagel with cream cheese or butter. If she randomly chooses a drink, a bagel, and a topping, what are all the possible combinations in the sample space? Use the abbreviation C, T or F for the drink, and P or B for the bagel, and Cr or Bu for the topping.

Denise likes hot tea and blueberry bagels. Which outcomes are in the union of the events {hot tea} and {blueberry bagel}? Which outcomes are in the event {hot tea and blueberry bagel}. Are these two events the same? Explain why or why not.

Solution: An area model cannot be used since there are three events (drink, bagel, and topping). The following tree diagram can be used to represent the sample space of all possible outcomes:

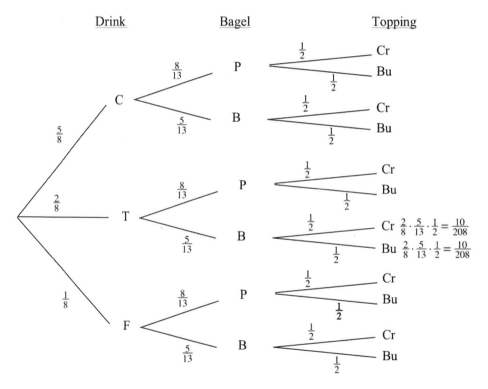

The union of {hot tea} and {blueberry bagel} is any outcome in the sample space above that contains T *or* B or both: {CBCr, CBBu, TPCr, TPBu, TBCr, TBBu, FBCr, FBBu}.

The event {hot tea and blueberry bagel} is different. {hot tea and blueberry bagel} is the *intersection* of {hot tea} and {blueberry bagel} and contains any combination with both T *and* B. Thus, {hot tea and blueberry bagel} = {TBCr, TBBu}.

Core Connections Geometry

Example 3: Denise is randomly handed a drink-bagel-topping combination by the coffee cart owner. Use a complement to find the probability that Denise was not handed a hot tea with a blueberry bagel.

Solution: P(hot tea and blueberry bagel) = $\frac{10}{208} + \frac{10}{208} = \frac{20}{208} \approx 9.6\%$ from the tree diagram in Example 2. The complement is the probability that Denise does not get a hot tea and blueberry bagel: P(not hot tea and blueberry bagel) = $100\% - 9.6\% = 90.4\%$.

There is a 90.4% chance that Denise was not handed a hot tea with a blueberry bagel.

Example 4: Zoey's grandfather has purchased a kit of 75 assorted pieces of sea life for her. The kit contains equal numbers of gastropod seashells, bivalve seashells, sand dollars, sea fans, and starfish. Each type of sea life is divided into equal numbers of large, medium, and small objects. Zoey is creating a piece of display art with the sea life.

To start the artwork, Zoey selects a random piece of sea life. What is the probability that she picks a small seashell?

Solution: There are 5 small gastropod seashells and 5 small bivalve seashells.

$$\text{P(small seashell)} = \frac{\text{number of successful outcomes}}{\text{total number of possible outcomes}} = \frac{10}{75} = \frac{2}{15} \approx 13.3\%$$

Alternatively, an area model, like the one below, could be used.

	gastropod seashells $\frac{1}{5}$	bivalve seashells $\frac{1}{5}$	sand dollar $\frac{1}{5}$	sea fans $\frac{1}{5}$	starfish $\frac{1}{5}$
small $\frac{1}{3}$	$\frac{1}{15}$	$\frac{1}{15}$			
medium $\frac{1}{3}$					
large $\frac{1}{3}$					

P(small seashell) = $\frac{1}{15} + \frac{1}{15} = \frac{2}{15} \approx 13.3\%$

What is the probability that she does *not* pick a small seashell?

Solution: The probability she does *not* pick a small seashell is the complement of the probability that Zoey *does* pick a small seashell.

P(not small seashell) = 1 – P(small seashell)
= $1 - \frac{2}{15} = \frac{13}{15} \approx 86.7\%$ **OR** $100\% - 13.3\% = 86.7\%$

What is the probability she picks a large piece *or* a seashell?

Solution: Use an area model, as shown below, or a tree diagram.

	gastropod seashells $\frac{1}{5}$	bivalve seashells $\frac{1}{5}$	sand dollar $\frac{1}{5}$	sea fans $\frac{1}{5}$	starfish $\frac{1}{5}$
small $\frac{1}{3}$	$\frac{1}{15}$	$\frac{1}{15}$			
medium $\frac{1}{3}$	$\frac{1}{15}$	$\frac{1}{15}$			
large $\frac{1}{3}$	$\frac{1}{15}$	$\frac{1}{15}$	$\frac{1}{15}$	$\frac{1}{15}$	$\frac{1}{15}$

P(large piece or seashell) = $9(\frac{1}{15}) = \frac{9}{15} = 60\%$

Alternatively, the Addition Rule could be used:

P(large piece or seashell) = P(large piece) + P(seashell) − P(large piece and seashell)

P(large piece or seashell) = $\frac{1}{3}$ + $\frac{2}{5}$ − $\frac{2}{15}$

                   = $\frac{9}{15} = 60\%$

Now we can go back and solve the original problems.

a. There are three probabilistic situations, or events, in this situation: choosing a bread (white or grain), choosing a protein (salami, turkey, or ham), and choosing a condiment (mayonnaise or plain). Area models are best used when there are two events, so an area model is not a good choice in this situation. See the answer for part (b) for the tree diagram.

b. The following sandwiches have salami or mayonnaise (or both) on them: {WSM, WSP, WTM, WHM, GSM, GSP, GTM, GHM}.

   To find the probability of any of the sandwiches above, probabilities are added to each branch of the tree diagram, as shown in the part (b) answer above. For example, since 12 of the 36 sandwiches are made with white bread, the probability of randomly selecting a sandwich with white bread is $\frac{12}{36} = \frac{1}{3}$. Once white bread is chosen, the probability of choosing salami is $\frac{1}{2}$. The remaining half of the white-bread sandwiches are split evenly between turkey and ham, so the probability of choosing turkey is $\frac{1}{4}$ and the probability of choosing ham is $\frac{1}{4}$. In this manner, the remainder of the probabilities can be added to the remaining branches. *Note that the sum of the probabilities for any set of branches is always 1.* For example, for white bread, the probabilities of the branches for salami, turkey, and ham add to 1: $\frac{1}{2} + \frac{1}{4} + \frac{1}{4} = 1$.

Solution continues on next page →

Solution continued from previous page.

To find the probability of any one outcome (any one sandwich), multiply the probabilities across all the branches. For example the probability of white-salami-mayonnaise, or WSM, is $\frac{1}{3} \cdot \frac{1}{2} \cdot \frac{2}{3} = \frac{2}{18}$. The probabilities for individual outcomes are indicated in the far right column of the tree diagram.

The probability that Wade randomly picks a sandwich he likes is the sum of the probability of all the outcomes that are successes for Wade:

$$\frac{2}{18} + \frac{1}{18} + \frac{2}{36} + \frac{2}{36} + \frac{4}{18} + \frac{2}{18} + \frac{4}{36} + \frac{4}{36} = \frac{30}{36} \approx 83.3\%$$

c.　Successes for Madison are any sandwich that has neither salami nor mayonnaise. That is, {WTP, WHP, GTP, GHP}. Using the tree diagram from part (b) above, the probability of each of these individual outcomes can be found. For example, P(WTP) $= \frac{1}{3} \cdot \frac{1}{4} \cdot \frac{1}{3} = \frac{1}{36}$.

The probability Madison picks a sandwich she likes is the sum of the probabilities of the sandwiches she considers a success:

$$\frac{2}{36} + \frac{2}{36} + \frac{1}{36} + \frac{1}{36} = \frac{6}{36} \approx 16.7\%$$

d.　The sum of the probabilities of all the outcomes in any probabilistic situation is 1 or 100%. Madison likes any sandwich that Wade does not like. Since the probability of all the outcomes is 100%, and the probability of the outcomes that are success for Wade are about 83.3%, the probability for Madison's success must be 100% − 83.3% = 16.7%.

e.　Intersections are the set of outcomes in which both the first *and* the second event must occur. The outcomes in which both {salami} and {mayonnaise} occur are {WSM, GSM}.

Unions, on the other hand, are the set of outcomes in which either the first *or* the second event must occur. Wade's favorite sandwiches in part (b) were the union of {salami} or {mayonnaise}.

Here are some more to try.

1. As you open the ice chest during your family picnic you find that there are 10 bottles of fruit juice and 10 sandwiches. Unfortunately the bottle labels came off and the sandwiches are not labeled. Your mother says that there are 5 strawberry, 3 grape, and 2 raspberry juices. There are 4 turkey, 3 roast beef, and 3 tuna sandwiches. You are not really picky, but you are hungry and you really do not want grape juice and tuna together.

    a. Draw a diagram to show the sample space for this situation.

    b. What is the probability of picking a grape juice and tuna combination?

    c. What is the probability of picking a lunch with strawberry juice or turkey?

2. A carnival game has a spinner like the one at right. The sections are all the same size.

    R = red   B = blue   G = green

    a. Draw a diagram to show the sample space for spinning twice.

    b. What is the probability of spinning the same color twice?

3. There is a 25% chance that you will have to work tonight and cannot study for the big math test. If you study, then you have an 80% chance of earning a good grade. If you do not study, you only have a 30% chance of earning a good grade.

    a. Draw a diagram to represent this situation.

    b. Calculate the probability of earning a good grade on the math test.

4. For the spinners at right, assume that sections of spinner #1 are all the same size and the R and B sections of spinner #2 are each half the size of section G.

    R = red   B = blue   G = green

    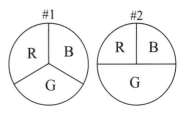

    a. Draw a diagram for the sample space for spinning both spinners.

    b. What is the probability of spinning green on both spinners?

    c. What is the probability of spinning the same color on both spinners?

    d. What is the probability of *not* spinning green on both spinners?

5. Judy's pencil box contains two red, one blue, and three yellow pencils and one yellow and two red erasers. If she randomly picks out one pencil and one eraser, find the following probabilities.

    a. Getting a yellow pencil and red eraser.

    b. Getting a yellow pencil or a red eraser.

    c. Not getting the yellow pencil and red eraser combination.

6. A baseball player gets a hit 40% of the time if the weather is good but only 20% of the time if it is cold or windy. The weather forecast is 70% chance of nice weather, 20% chance of cold weather, and 10% chance of windy. What is the probability of the player getting a hit?

7. The State Fair has the following carnival game.

Pay $5 to spin the wheel at right. Assume that sections B and G are each half the size of section R.

R = red   B = blue   G = green

- If red comes up on the first spin, you win a stuffed animal.
- If blue comes up on the first spin, you spin again. If blue comes up again you win $20. Otherwise you win nothing.
- If green comes up on the first spin, you spin again. If green comes up a second time, you spin again. If green comes up a third time you win $150. Otherwise you win nothing.

    a. Draw a diagram to represent this situation.

    b. What is the probability of winning something in the game?

8. Evan gets up at 4 a.m. each day to deliver newspapers. He does not want to wake up his brother so he gets dressed in the dark and cannot see what clothes he is choosing. In his closet there are three pairs of shoes – one pair of dress shoes and two pairs of tennis shoes. There are also five pairs of pants – three pairs of jeans and two pairs of slacks. In the dresser are eight school shirts – three are blue, two are green and three are Hawaiian. If Evan randomly chooses a pair of shoes, a pair of pants, and a shirt, compute the following probabilities.

    a. Evan wears tennis shoes, jeans, and a Hawaiian shirt.

    b. Evan wears tennis shoes and jeans or tennis shoes and a Hawaiian shirt.

    c. Evan does not wear a dress shoes, slacks, blue shirt combination.

Answers:

1. a.

		Sandwich		
		TY(0.4)	RB(0.3)	TU(0.3)
Drink	S(0.5)	0.20	0.15	0.15
	G(0.3)	0.12	0.09	0.09
	R(0.2)	0.08	0.06	0.06

   b. $0.09 = 9\%$

   c. $0.08 + 0.12 + 0.20 + 0.15 + 0.15 = 0.70 = 70\%$

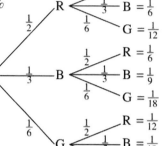

2. a.   See tree diagram at right.

   b. $\{RR\} + \{BB\} + \{GG\} = \frac{1}{4} + \frac{1}{9} + \frac{1}{36} = \frac{7}{18}$

3. a.

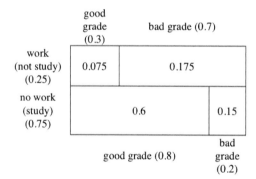

   b. $0.075 + 0.60 = 0.675 = 67.5\%$

4. a.

#1 \ #2	$R\left(\frac{1}{4}\right)$	$B\left(\frac{1}{4}\right)$	$G\left(\frac{1}{2}\right)$
$R\left(\frac{1}{3}\right)$	$\frac{1}{12}$	$\frac{1}{12}$	$\frac{1}{6}$
$B\left(\frac{1}{3}\right)$	$\frac{1}{12}$	$\frac{1}{12}$	$\frac{1}{6}$
$G\left(\frac{1}{3}\right)$	$\frac{1}{12}$	$\frac{1}{12}$	$\frac{1}{6}$

   b. $\frac{1}{6}$ c. $\frac{1}{12} + \frac{1}{12} + \frac{1}{6} = \frac{1}{3}$ d. $1 - \frac{1}{6} = \frac{5}{6}$

5. a. $\frac{1}{2} \cdot \frac{2}{3} = \frac{1}{3}$ b. $\frac{2}{9} + \frac{2}{18} + \frac{1}{6} + \frac{1}{3} = \frac{5}{6}$ c. $1 - \frac{1}{3} = \frac{2}{3}$

Core Connections Geometry

6. $(0.7)(0.4) + (0.2)(0.2) + (0.2)(0.1) = 0.28 + 0.04 + 0.02 = 0.34$

7. a. See tree diagram at right.

   b. $\frac{1}{2} + \frac{1}{16} + \frac{1}{64} = \frac{37}{64} \approx 57.8\%$

8. a. $\frac{3}{20}$

   b. $\frac{2}{3} \cdot \frac{3}{5} + \frac{2}{3} \cdot \frac{3}{8} \cdot \frac{2}{5} = \frac{2}{5} + \frac{2}{20} = \frac{1}{2}$

   c. $1 - \frac{1}{3} \cdot \frac{2}{5} \cdot \frac{3}{8} = \frac{19}{20}$

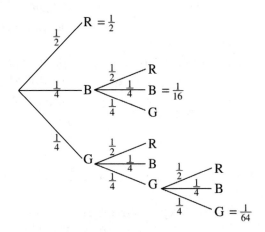

Checkpoint 9B
Problem 9-107
Exponential Functions

Answers to problem 9-107: a. See graph at right.

         b. $f(x) = 10(2.3)^x$

         c. $y = 42,000(0.75)^5 = 9967$

         d. $60 = 25(b)^{10}$, $b = 1.09$, 9% increase

An exponential function is an equation of the form $y = ab^x$ (with $b \geq 0$).

In many cases a represents a starting or initial value, b represents the multiplier or growth/decay factor, and x represents the time. If something is increasing by a percent then the multiplier b is always found by adding the percent increase (as a decimal) to the number 1. If something is decreasing by a percent then the multiplier b is always found by subtracting the percent from the number 1. From a table, the multiplier can be calculated using the ratio of the y-values corresponding to one integer x-value divided by the preceding x-value.

Example 1: Graph $y = 3 \cdot 2^x$.

Solution:
First, make a table of values.

Then, plot the points and connect them to form a smooth curve.

$$y = 3 \cdot 2^x$$

x	-1	0	1	2	3
y	1.5	3	6	12	24

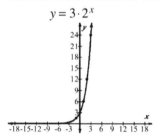

This is called an increasing exponential curve.

Example 2: The ticket prices at African Safari Land have increased annually according to the table at right. Write an equation that represents the cost over various years.

Year	Price
0	$50
1	$55
2	$60.50
3	$66.55

Solution: The initial value is $a = 50$. The multiplier is the ratio of one y-value divided by the previous one:
$b = \frac{55}{50} = \frac{60.50}{55} = \frac{66.55}{60.50} = 1.1$. The prices are increasing by 10% each year. The equation is $y = 50(1.1)^x$.

Example 3: A house that was worth \$200,000 in 2005 was only worth \$150,000 in 2010. Write an equation to represent the value since 2005 and tell the percent of decrease.

Solution: The equation to use is $y = ab^x$. The given initial value is $a = 200{,}000$. The other given value is $y = 150{,}000$ when $x = 5$. Substituting these into the equation and solving for b we get:

$$150{,}000 = 200{,}000b^5$$
$$0.75 = b^5$$
$$b = \sqrt[5]{0.75} \approx 0.944$$

The equation is $y = 200000(0.944)^x$. $1 - 0.944 = 0.056 = 5.6\%$ decrease.

Now we can go back and solve the original problems.

a. Make a table of values. Plot the points and connect them to form a smooth curve. See table below and graph at right.

x	−1	0	1	2	3
y	2.7	2	1.5	1.1	0.8

b. The multiplier $b = \frac{52.9}{23} = 2.3$. The starting value for $x = 0$ can be determined by working backwards from the value of $x = 1$. $a = \frac{23}{2.3} = 10$. The equation represented by the table is: $f(x) = 10(2.3)^x$.

c. $y = ab^x$ $\quad$ $a = 42{,}000$, $b = 1 - 0.25 = 0.75$, $x = 5$
$y = 42{,}000(0.75)^x \Rightarrow 42{,}000(0.75)^5 \approx 9967$

d. $y = ab^x$ $\quad$ $a = 25$, $y = 60$, $x = 10$
$60 = 25b^{10} \Rightarrow \frac{60}{25} = b^{10} \Rightarrow b = \sqrt[10]{\frac{60}{25}} \approx 1.09$ $\quad$ That is a 9% increase.
$y = 25(1.09)^x$

Here are some more to try. Make a table of values and draw a graph of each exponential function.

1. $\quad y = 4(0.5)^x$ $\qquad\qquad$ 2. $\quad y = 2(3)^x$

3. $\quad f(x) = 5(1.2)^x$ $\qquad\qquad$ 4. $\quad f(x) = 10\left(\frac{2}{3}\right)^x$

Write an equation to represent the information in each table.

5.

x	$f(x)$
0	1600
1	2000
2	2500
3	3125

6.

x	y
1	40
2	32
3	25.6

7.

x	$f(x)$
0	1.8
1	5.76
2	18.432

8.

x	y
0	5
1	35
2	245

Write a possible context based on each equation.

9. $y = 32,500(0.85)^x$

10. $f(x) = 2.75(1.025)^x$

Write and use an exponential equation to solve each problem.

11. A powerful computer is purchased for $1500, but on the average loses 20% of its value each year. How much will it be worth 4 years from now?

12. If a gallon of milk costs $3 now and the price is increasing 10% per year, how long before milk costs $10 a gallon? (Note that guess and check will be required to solve the equation after it is written.)

13. Dinner at your grandfather's favorite restaurant now costs $25.25 and has been increasing steadily at 4% per year. How much did it cost 35 *years ago* when he was courting your grandmother?

14. The number of bacteria present in a colony is 280 at 12 noon and the bacteria grows at a rate of 18% per hour. How many will be present at 10 p.m.?

15. A house purchased for $226,000 has lost 4% of its value each year for the past five years. What is it worth now?

16. A 1970 comic book has appreciated 10% per year and originally sold for $0.35. What will it be worth in 2020?

17. A compact car depreciates at 15% per year. Six year ago it was purchased for $21,000. What is it worth now?

18. Inflation is at a rate of 7% per year. Today Janelle's favorite bread costs $4.79. What would it have cost ten years ago?

19.   Ryan's motorcycle is now worth $2500. It has decreased in value 12% each year since it was purchased. If he bought it four years ago, what did it cost new?

20.   The cost of a High Definition television now averages $900, but the cost is decreasing about 12% per year. In how many years will the cost be under $400?

21.   A two-bedroom house in Nashville is worth $110,000. If it appreciates at 2.5% per year, when will it be worth $200,000?

22.   Last year the principal's car was worth $28,000. Next year it will be worth $25,270. What is the annual rate of depreciation? What is the car worth now?

23.   A concert has been sold out for weeks, and as the date of the concert draws closer, the price of the ticket increases. The cost of a pair of tickets was $150 yesterday and is $162 today. Assume that the cost continues to increase at this rate exponentially.

   a.   What is the daily rate of increase? What is the multiplier?

   b.   What will be the ticket cost one week from now, the day before the concert?

   c.   What was the cost two weeks ago?

Answers:

1.

x	−1	0	1	2	3
y	8	4	2	1	0.5

2.

x	−1	0	1	2	3
y	2/3	2	6	18	54

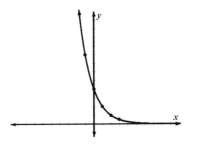

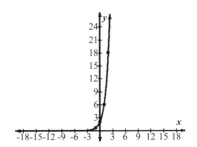

3.

x	−1	0	1	2	3
y	4.17	5	6	7.2	8.64

4.

x	−1	0	1	2	3
y	15	10	6.67	4.44	2.96

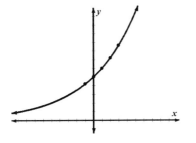

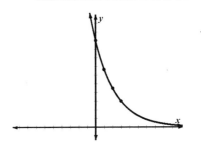

5. $1600(1.25)^x$ 6. $40(0.8)^x$ 7. $1.8(3.2)^x$ 8. $5 \cdot 7^x$

9. Possible answer: If a \$32,500 boat loses 15% of its value each year, what will it be worth x years from now?

10. Possible answer: A soda at the movies now costs \$2.75. If the cost is increasing 2.5% per year, what will it cost x years from now?

11. \$614.40   12. ≈ 12-13 years

13. \$6.40 (Note that answers of \$6.05 used $b = 0.96$ which is incorrect.)

14. ≈ 1465   15. \$184,274   16. \$41.09

17. ≈ \$7920   18. ≈ \$2.43   19. ≈ \$4169

20. ≈ 6-7 years   21. ≈ 24-25 years   22. 5%, ≈ \$26,600

23. a.   8%, 1.08   b.   ≈ \$277.64   c.   ≈ \$55.15

Checkpoint 10
Problem 10-156
Finding Angles in and Areas of Regular Polygons

Answers to problem 10-156: a. $162°$; b. 16 sides; c. $\approx 120.8 \text{ cm}^2$

The sum of the measures of a polygon with n sides is $(n-2)180°$ and therefore each angle in a regular polygon with n sides measures $\frac{(n-2)180°}{n}$.

The sum of the exterior angles of any polygon is $360°$.

To find the area of a regular polygon, use the angles and side length of one of the identical triangles that make up the polygon to find the area of the triangle. Then multiply by the number of identical triangles to determine the area of the polygon.

Example 1: What is the measure of each interior angle of a regular 10-gon?

Solution: Using $n = 10$ in the formula given above $\frac{(n-2)180°}{n} = \frac{8 \cdot 180°}{10} = 144°$

Example 2: If the regular 10-gon in Example 1 has a side length of 6 inches, what is the area of the polygon?

Solution: The regular 10-gon is made is made up of 10 identical isosceles triangles like the one at right. From Example 1, each interior angle is $144°$. The base angle in the triangle is half of the interior angle so $m\angle 1 = 72°$. We can use the tangent ratio to find the height of the triangle:
$\tan 72° = \frac{h}{3} \Rightarrow h = 3\tan 72° \approx 9.23$. The area of the triangle is $\frac{1}{2} \cdot 6 \cdot 9.23 \approx 27.69$.

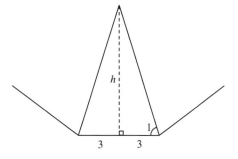

Therefore the area of the 10-gon is $10(27.69) \approx 276.9 \text{ in.}^2$.

Now we can go back and solve the original problems.

a. $\frac{(n-2)180°}{n} = \frac{18 \cdot 180°}{20} = 162°$

b. Method 1 (using the formula): $157.5° = \frac{(n-2)180°}{n} \Rightarrow 157.5° \, n = (n-2)180°$

$\Rightarrow 157.5° \, n = 180° \, n - 360° \Rightarrow -22.5° \, n = -360° \Rightarrow n = 16$

Method 2 (using the exterior angle): If the interior angle is $157.5°$ then the exterior angle is $180°\text{-}157.5° = 22.5°$. Since the sum of the exterior angles of a polygon is $360°$, $360° \div 22.5° = 16$ sides.

c. The octagon is made up of 8 identical triangles. Each interior angle of the polygon measures $\frac{6 \cdot 180°}{8} = 135°$. Using a diagram as in example 2 above, $m\angle 1 = \frac{135°}{2} = 67.5°$. The base of the small triangle is 2.5 cm. To find the height, $\tan 67.5° = \frac{h}{2.5} \Rightarrow h = 2.5 \tan 67.5° \approx 6.04$. The area of the large triangle is $\frac{1}{2} \cdot 5 \cdot 6.04 \approx 15.1$. Eight of these triangles make up the octagon so the area of the octagon is $8 \cdot 15.1 \approx 120.8 \text{ cm}^2$.

Here are some more to try. Find the measure of the angle of each regular polygon.

1. Interior angle, 12 sides
2. Interior angle, 15 sides

3. Interior angle, 7 sides
4. Interior angle, 60 sides

5. Exterior angle, 10 sides
6. Exterior angle, 20 sides

Answer each of the following questions.

7. What is the measure of each interior angle of a regular polygon with 16 sides?

8. What is the measure of each exterior angle of a regular polygon with 16 sides?

9. What is the area of a regular polygon with 16 sides and side length 4 inches?

10. Each interior angle of a regular polygon measures $156°$. How many sides does it have?

11. What is the area of a regular pentagon with side length 10 feet?

12. Each exterior angle of a regular polygon measures $15°$. How many sides does it have?

13. Each interior angle of a regular polygon measures $165.6°$. How many sides does it have?

14. What is the area of a regular octagon with side length 1 meter?

15. Each exterior angle of a regular polygon measures $13\frac{1}{3}°$. How many sides does it have?

16. What is the area of a regular polygon with 15 sides and a side length of 4 inches?

Answers:

1. 150°
2. 156°
3. $128\frac{4}{7}$°

4. 174°
5. 36°
6. 18°

7. 157.5°
8. 22.5°
9. ≈ 321.7 in^2

10. 15 sides
11. ≈ 172.0 ft^2
12. 24 sides

13. 25 sides
14. ≈ 4.83 m^2
15. 27 sides

16. ≈ 282.3 in^2

Checkpoint 11
Problem 11-102
Volumes and Surface Areas of Prisms and Cylinders

Answers to problem 11-102: a. $V = 2100$ units^3, $SA \approx 1007.34$ units^2

b. $V = 1000\pi \approx 3141.59$ cm^3, $SA = \frac{1100\pi}{3} + 240 \approx 1391.92$ cm^2

c. $V = 60$ in.^{3}, $SA = 144$ in.^{2}

The volume (in cubic units) of a prism or cylinder is found by multiplying the area of the base by the height: $V = Bh$.

The surface area (in square units) of either of these solids is found by adding the areas of the bases and the area of the lateral faces (sides).

Example 1: Find the volume and surface area of the cylinder at right.

Solution: To find the volume we need to calculate the area of the base, which in this case is a circle with radius 5 m.

$$B = \pi r^2 = \pi(5)^2 = 25\pi$$
$$V = Bh = (25\pi)(2) = 50\pi \approx 157.08 \text{ m}^3$$

To find the surface area we need to add the area of the two bases and the area of the side. The unrolled side is a rectangle with a base length equal to the circumference of the circle and a height equal to the height of the cylinder.

2(area of the base) + area of the side

$$2(\pi r^2) + \pi 2r(h)$$

$$2\pi \cdot 25 + \pi \cdot 10 \cdot 2 = 70\pi \approx 219.91 \text{ m}^2$$

Example 2: Find the volume and surface area of the prism at right.

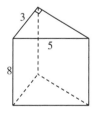

Solution: To find the volume we need to calculate the area of the base, which in this case is a triangle. First use the Pythagorean theorem to find the second leg of the right triangular base. Since $3^2 + \text{leg}^2 = 5^2$, leg = 4.

$$B = \tfrac{1}{2}bh = \tfrac{1}{2}(3)(4) = 6 \qquad V = Bh = (6)(8) = 48 \text{ units}^3$$

To find the surface area we must add together the area of the two bases and the area of the three rectangular sides. The three rectangular sides all have a height of 8 units and the three bases are the lengths of the sides of the triangle.

2(area of the base) + area of side #1 + area of side #2 + area of side #3

$$2(\tfrac{1}{2} \cdot 3 \cdot 4) \;+\; 5 \cdot 8 \;+\; 3 \cdot 8 \;+\; 4 \cdot 8 = 108 \text{ units}^2$$

Now we can go back and solve the original problems.

a. The bases are a trapezoid. $B = \frac{1}{2}h(b_1 + b_2) = \frac{1}{2} \cdot 15(8 + 12) = 150$.

To calculate the volume: $V = Bh = 150 \cdot 14 = 2100$ units^3

To find the surface area we must add together the area of the two bases and the area of the four rectangular sides. The four rectangular sides all have a height of 14 units and the four bases are the lengths of the sides of the trapezoid. To find the missing length of the trapezoid we need to use the Pythagorean Theorem.

Use the triangular part of the trapezoid:
$(12 - 8)^2 + 15^2 = \text{hypotenuse}^2 \Rightarrow 241 = \text{hypotenuse}^2$

The length of the unlabeled side $= \sqrt{241}$.

2(area of the base) + area of side #1 + area of side #2 + area of side #3 + area of side #4
$2(\frac{1}{2} \cdot 15(8 + 12)) + 12 \cdot 14 + 15 \cdot 14 + 8 \cdot 14 + \sqrt{241} \cdot 14 \approx 1007.34$ units^2

b. The base is $\frac{300°}{360°} = \frac{5}{6}$ of a circle. $B = \frac{5}{6}\pi r^2 = \frac{5}{6}\pi \cdot 10^2 = \frac{500\pi}{6}$

To find the volume: $V = Bh = (\frac{500\pi}{6})(12) = 1000\pi \approx 3141.59$ cm^3

To find the surface area we must add together the area of the two bases and the area of the three rectangular sides. The three rectangular sides all have a height of 12 cm and the three bases are two radii and $\frac{5}{6}$ the circumference of the circle.

2(area of the base) + area of side #1 + area of side #2 + area of side #3
$2(\frac{5}{6}\pi \cdot 10^2) + 10 \cdot 12 + 10 \cdot 12 + \frac{5}{6}\pi \cdot 20 \cdot 12 = \frac{1100\pi}{3} + 240 \approx 1391.92$ cm^2

c. The base is a square with a square cut out. $B = 4^2 - 2^2 = 12$

To find the volume: $V = Bh = 12 \cdot 5 = 60$ in.^{3}

To find the surface area we must add together the area of the two bases and the area of the four identical external rectangular sides and the four identical internal rectangular sides.

2(area of the base) + 4(area of external side) + 4(area of internal side)

$2(4^2 - 2^2) + 4(4 \cdot 5) + 4(2 \cdot 5) = 144$ in.^{2}

Here are some more to try. Compute the volume and surface area of each solid.

1.

2.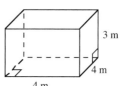

3.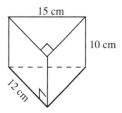

4.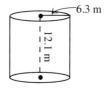

5.

6.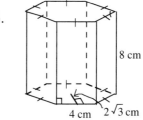

7.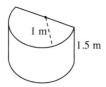

8.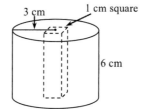

9.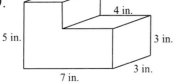

10.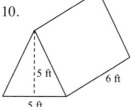

11.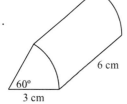

12.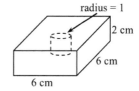

Answers:

1. $V = 200\pi \approx 628.32 \text{ ft}^3$; $SA = 130\pi \approx 408.41 \text{ ft}^2$

2. $V = 48 \text{ m}^3$; $SA = 80 \text{ m}^2$

3. $V = 540 \text{ cm}^3$; $SA = 468 \text{ cm}^2$

4. $V \approx 1508.75 \text{ m}^3$; $SA \approx 728.35 \text{ m}^2$

5. $V = 126 \text{ ft}^3$; $SA \approx 165.19 \text{ ft}^2$

6. $V \approx 332.6 \text{ cm}^3$; $SA \approx 275.14 \text{ cm}^2$

7. $V \approx 2.362 \text{ m}^3$; $SA \approx 10.85 \text{ m}^2$

8. $V \approx 163.65 \text{ cm}^3$; $SA \approx 191.65 \text{ cm}^2$

9. $V = 81 \text{ in.}^3$; $SA = 126 \text{ in.}^2$

10. $V = 75 \text{ ft}^3$; $SA \approx 122.08 \text{ ft}^2$

11. $V \approx 28.27 \text{ cm}^3$; $SA \approx 64.27 \text{ cm}^2$

12. $V \approx 65.72 \text{ cm}^3$; $SA \approx 126.28 \text{ cm}^2$

Glossary

30°-60°-90° triangle A special right triangle with acute angle measures of 30° and 60°. The side lengths are always in the ratio of $1:\sqrt{3}:2$. See the diagram at right. (p. 310)

45°-45°-90° triangle A special right triangle with acute angle measures of 45°. The side lengths are always in the ratio of $1:1:\sqrt{2}$. See the diagram at right. (p. 310)

AA ~ (Triangle Similarity) If two angles of one triangle are congruent to the two corresponding angles of another triangle, then the triangles are similar. For example, given $\triangle ABC$ and $\triangle A'B'C'$ with $\angle A \cong \angle A'$ and $\angle B \cong \angle B'$, then $\triangle ABC \sim \triangle A'B'C'$. You can also show that two triangles are similar by showing that *three* pairs of corresponding angles are congruent (which would be called AAA ~), but two pairs of angles are sufficient to demonstrate similarity. (p. 170)

AAS ≅ (Triangle Congruence) If two angles and a non-included side of one triangle are congruent to the corresponding two angles and non-included side of another triangle, the two triangles are congruent. Note that AAS ≅ is equivalent to ASA ≅. (p. 358)

absolute value The absolute value of a number is the distance of that number from zero. Since absolute value represents a distance, without regard to direction, it is always non-negative. Thus the absolute value of a negative number is its opposite, while the absolute value of a non-negative number is just the number itself. The absolute value of x is usually written $|x|$. For example, $|-5| = 5$ and $|22| = 22$. (p. 768)

acute angle An angle with measure greater than 0° and less than 90°. One example is shown at right. See also *obtuse angle*. (p. 26)

Addition Rule for Probability For any two events {A} and {B}, P(A or B) = P(A) + P(B) – P(A and B). See also *Multiplication Rule for Probability*. (p. 256)

adjacent angles For two angles to be adjacent, they must satisfy these three conditions: (1) The two angles must have a common side; (2) They must have a common vertex; and (3) They can have no interior points in common. This means that the common side must be between the two angles; no overlap between the angles is permitted. In the example at right, $\angle ABC$ and $\angle CBD$ are adjacent angles.

adjacent leg In a right triangle, the leg adjacent to an acute angle is the side of the angle that is not the hypotenuse. For example, in $\triangle ABC$ shown at right, $\overline{AB}$ is the leg adjacent to $\angle A$. (p. 285)

alpha (α) A Greek letter that is often used to represent the measure of an angle. Other Greek letters used to represent the measure of an angle include theta (θ) and beta (β). (p. 214)

alternate interior angles   Angles between a pair of lines that switch sides of a third intersecting line (called a transversal). For example, in the diagram at right the shaded angles are alternate interior angles. If the lines intersected by the transversal are parallel, then the alternate interior angles are congruent. Conversely, if the alternate interior angles are congruent, then the two lines intersected by the transversal are parallel. See also *same-side interior angles* and *corresponding angles*. (p. 100)

altitude   See *height*.

ambiguous   Information is ambiguous when it has more than one interpretation or conclusion.

anagram   A word game in which different arrangements of the letters of a word are created, using all the letters in the original word, one time each. The term anagram is also informally used in this course to refer to permutations in which there are duplicates of some items. For example, finding the number of ways to arrange one red, two blue, and three yellow flags in a row is the same as the number of ways to arrange the "word" RBBYYY. To compute this, find the number of permutations, and divide by the numbers of ways to arrange the repeated items, for example, $\frac{5!}{2!3!}$ for the flags. (p. 637)

angle   In general, an angle is formed by two rays joined at a common endpoint. Angles in geometric figures are usually formed by two segments, with a common endpoint (such as the angle shaded in the figure at right). (p. 26)

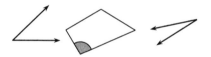

angle bisector   A line segment or ray with an endpoint at the vertex of the angle that divides the angle into two equal pieces. (p. 559)

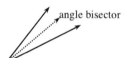

angle measure   See *measurement*.

angle of depression   When an object (B) is below the horizontal line of sight of the observer (A), the angle of depression is the angle formed by the line of sight to the object and the horizontal line of sight.

angle of elevation   When an object (B) is above the horizontal line of sight of the observer (A), the angle of elevation is the angle formed by the line of sight to the object and the horizontal line of sight.

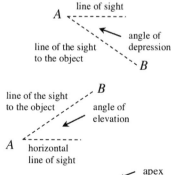

apex   In a cone or pyramid, the apex is the point that is the farthest away from the flat surface (plane) that contains the base. In a pyramid, the apex is also the point at which the lateral faces meet. An apex is also sometimes called the vertex of a pyramid or cone. (p. 679)

apothem   A segment that connects the center of a regular polygon to a point on one of its sides, and is perpendicular to that side.

arc   A connected part of a circle. Because a circle does not contain its interior, an arc is more like a portion of a bicycle tire than a slice of pizza. See also *major arc* and *minor arc* and *sector*. (p. 512)

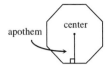

arc length   The length of an arc (in inches, centimeters, feet, etc.) is the distance from one of the arc's endpoints to the arc's other endpoint, measured around the circle. Note that arc length is different from arc measure. Arcs of two different circles may have the same arc measure (like 90°), but have different arc lengths if one circle has a larger radius than the other one. (p. 589)

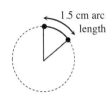

arc measure   The measure in degrees of an arc's central angle. Note that arc measure is measured in degrees and is different from arc length. (p. 589)

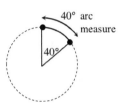

arccosine, arcsine, and arctangent.   Other names for *inverse cosine* ($\cos^{-1} x$), *inverse sine* ($\sin^{-1} x$), and *inverse tangent* ($\tan^{-1} x$). (p. 294)

area   On a flat surface (plane), the number of non-overlapping square units needed to cover the region. See also *surface area*. (p. 16)

area model   A model that uses the area of rectangles to represent the probabilities of possible outcomes when considering two *independent* events. For example, suppose you are going to randomly select a student from a classroom. If the probability of selecting a female student from the room is $\frac{2}{3}$ and the probability of selecting a 9th grader from the room is $\frac{1}{4}$, the area of the shaded rectangle at right represents the probability that a randomly selected student is a female 9th grader ($\frac{2}{3} \cdot \frac{1}{4} = \frac{1}{6}$). A "generic" area model enables you to find the probabilities of outcomes without drawing a diagram to scale. See also *tree diagram*. (p. 249)

	male $\frac{1}{3}$	female $\frac{2}{3}$
9th grader $\frac{1}{4}$	$\frac{1}{12}$	$\frac{1}{6}$
not 9th grader $\frac{3}{4}$	$\frac{1}{4}$	$\frac{1}{2}$

Area model

arithmetic sequence   An ordered sequence of mathematical terms in which a constant number is added to each term to determine the next term in the sequence. The number added to each term to get the next term is called the sequence generator or common difference. The equation for an arithmetic sequence is $t(n) = mn + b$ or $a_n = mn + a_0$, where n is the term number, m is the common difference, and b or a_0 is the zeroth (or initial) term of the sequence. Sequences are usually written starting with the first term, where $n = 1$. For example in the sequence, $4, 7, 10, 13, \ldots$, the common difference is 3, and the equation is $t(n) = 3n + 1$. See also *geometric sequence*. (p. 223)

arrow diagram   A pictorial representation of a conditional statement. The arrow points toward the conclusion of the conditional (the "then" part of the "If… then" statement). For example, the conditional statement *"If two lines cut by a transversal are parallel, then alternate interior angles are congruent"* can be represented by the arrow diagram below. (p. 92)

Lines cut by a transversal are parallel → *alternate interior angles are congruent.*

arrowheads   To indicate a line on a diagram, we draw a segment with arrowheads on its ends. The arrowheads show that our diagram indicates a line, which extends indefinitely, as opposed to a segment, which has endpoints. Marks on pairs of lines or segments such as ">>" and ">>>" indicate that the lines or segments are parallel. Both types of marks are used in the diagrams above.

ASA ≅ (Triangle Congruence)   If two angles and the included side of one triangle are congruent to the corresponding two angles and included side of another triangle, the triangles are congruent. Note that ASA ≅ is equivalent to AAS ≅. (p. 358)

association   A relationship between two (or more) variables. An association between *numerical* variables can be displayed on a scatterplot, and described by its form, direction, strength, and outliers. Possible association between two *categorical* variables can be studied in a two-way table. (p. 609)

auxiliary lines   Segments and lines added to existing figures. Auxiliary lines are usually added to a figure to allow us to prove something about the figure.

axioms   Statements accepted as true without proof. Also known as *postulates*.

base   (a) Triangle: Any side of a triangle to which a height is drawn. There are three possible bases in each triangle; (b) Trapezoid: the two parallel sides; (c) Parallelogram (and rectangle, rhombus, and square): Any side to which a height is drawn (there are four possible bases in each parallelogram); (d) Solid: See *cone, cylinder, prism,* and *pyramid*. (pp. 118, 537)

beta (β)   A Greek letter that is often used to represent the measure of an angle. Other Greek letters used to represent the measure of an angle include alpha (α) and theta (θ). (p. 214)

binomial   An expression that is the sum or difference of exactly two terms, each of which is a monomial. For example, $-2x + 3y^2$ is a binomial.

bisect   To bisect a geometric object is to divide it into two congruent parts. (p. 558)

Cavalieri's Principle Two solids have the same volume if corresponding cross-sectional areas are the same. For example, an oblique solid has the same volume as the corresponding right solid with the same height, as long as all the cross-sections parallel to the base have the same area. See also *oblique prism (or cylinder)* and *oblique pyramid (or cone)*. (p. 542)

center of a circle On a flat surface, the fixed point from which all points on the circle are equidistant. See also *circle*. (p. 404)

central angle An angle with its vertex at the center of a circle. (p. 589)

centroid The point at which the three medians of a triangle intersect. The centroid is also the center of balance of a triangle. The other points of concurrency studied in this course are the circumcenter and the incenter. (pp. 568, 604)

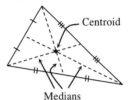

Centroid

Medians

chord A line segment with its endpoints on a circle. A chord that passes through the center of a circle is called a diameter. See also *circle*. (p. 583)

circle The set of all points on a flat surface that are the same distance from a fixed point. If the fixed point (center) is O, the symbol $\odot O$ represents a circle with center O. If r is the length of a circle's radius and d is the length of its diameter, the circumference of the circle is $C = 2\pi r$ or $C = \pi d$. The area of the circle is $A = \pi r^2$. The graphing form (also called "center-radius form" or standard form) of the equation of a circle with radius length r and center (h, k) is $(x - h)^2 + (y - k)^2 = r^2$. The general form (also called expanded form) is $ax^2 + ay^2 + bx + cy + d = 0$. (p. 404)

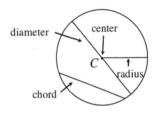

diameter   center

chord   radius

circular angle An angle with a measure of 360°. (p. 26)

360°

circumcenter The center of the circle that passes through the vertices of a triangle. It can be found by locating the point of intersection of the perpendicular bisectors of the sides of the triangle. The other points of concurrency studied in this course are the centroid and the incenter. (p. 604)

circumference The perimeter of (distance around) a circle. (p. 512)

circumscribed circle A circle circumscribes a polygon when it passes through all of the vertices of the polygon. (pp. 603, 604)

$C\bullet$

$\odot C$ circumscribes the pentagon.

clinometer A device used to measure angles of elevation and depression. (p. 231)

clockwise Clockwise identifies the direction of rotation shown in the diagram at right. The word literally means "in the direction of the rotating hands of a clock." The opposite of clockwise is *counter-clockwise*.

combination A combination is an arrangement of items that were selected without repeating items and without regard to order. The number of combinations that can be made by selecting r items from a set of n items can be found by dividing the total number of *permutations* by the number of arrangements of a single permutation, $_nC_r = \frac{_nP_r}{r!}$, which can be rewritten as $_nC_r = \frac{_nP_r}{r!} = \frac{n!}{r!(n-r)!}$. For instance, choosing a committee of 3 students from a group of 5 volunteers is a combination since the order in which committee members are selected does not matter: $_5C_3 = \frac{5!}{3!(5-3)!} = \frac{5\cdot4\cdot3\cdot2\cdot1}{3\cdot2\cdot1 \cdot 2\cdot1} = \frac{5\cdot4}{2} = 10$. See also *permutation*. (p. 643)

common difference The difference between consecutive terms of an arithmetic sequence, also known as the sequence generator of an arithmetic sequence. When the common difference is positive the sequence increases; when it is negative the sequence decreases. In the sequence $3,7,11,...$, the common difference is 4. See also *arithmetic sequence*. (p. 223)

common multiplier of a sequence Another name for *common ratio of a sequence*.

common ratio of corresponding sides Another name for the ratio of similarity. See *ratio of similarity*. (p. 154)

common ratio of a sequence Common ratio is another name for the multiplier or sequence generator of a geometric sequence. It is the number to multiply one term by to get the next one. In the sequence: $96, 48, 24, ...$, the common ratio is $\frac{1}{2}$. See also *geometric sequence*. (p. 223)

compass (a) A tool used to draw circles; (b) A tool used to navigate the Earth. A compass uses the Earth's magnetic field to determination which direction is north. (p. 554)

complement of an event The set of all the outcomes in the sample space that are not in the event. For example, if you randomly select one card from a deck of cards, the event {the card is a diamond} has a probability of $\frac{13}{52}$. The complement of the event is {the card is not a diamond}, or {the card is a heart, spade, or club}, and has a probability of $1-\frac{13}{52}$. (p. 255)

complementary angles Two angles whose measures add up to 90°. Angles T and V are complementary because $m\angle T + m\angle V = 90°$. Complementary angles may also be adjacent, like $\angle ABC$ and $\angle CBD$ in the diagram at far right. (p. 83)

completing the square A standard procedure for rewriting a quadratic equation from standard form into graphing form, or for rewriting the circle of an equation from general form into graphing form. For example, the first two terms in the equation $y = x^2 - 6x + 4$ look somewhat like $(x-3)^2$. But $(x-3)^2$ is 9 more than $x^2 - 6x$. That is, $x^2 - 6x = (x-3)^2 - 9$. We can rewrite $y = x^2 - 6x + 4$ in graphing form as follows: (p. 736)

$$y = x^2 - 6x \qquad + 4$$
$$y = (x-3)^2 - 9 \ + 4$$
$$y = (x-3)^2 - 5$$

concentric circles Circles that have the same center. For example, the circles shown in the diagram at right are concentric. (p. 554)

concurrency (point of) See *point of concurrency*.

conditional probability The probability of outcome A occurring, given that outcome B has already happened, is called the conditional probability of A given B. One way to calculate the conditional probability of A given B is to use the Multiplication Rule, $P(A \text{ given } B) = \frac{P(A \text{ and } B)}{P(B)}$. In many situations it is possible to calculate the conditional probability directly from the data by counting the number of outcomes (or computing the probabilities) of A that are within the outcomes (probabilities) for B. See also *Multiplication Rule for Probabilities*. (p. 624)

conditional statement A statement written in "If …, then …" form. For example, "*If a rectangle has four congruent sides, then it is a square*" is a conditional statement. (p. 119)

cone A three-dimensional figure that consists of a circular face, called the base, a point called the apex, that is not in the flat surface (plane) of the base, and the lateral surface that connects the apex to each point on the circular boundary of the base. The slant height of a cone is the distance from the circular boundary to the apex. See also *right pyramid (or cone)* and *oblique pyramid (or cone)*. (p. 690)

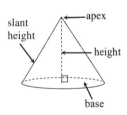

congruence conditions See *triangle congruence conditions*.

congruence statement A statement indicating that two figures are congruent. The order of the letters in the names of the shapes indicates which sides and angles are congruent to each other. For example, if $\triangle ABC \cong \triangle DEF$, then $\angle A \cong \angle D$, $\angle B \cong \angle E$, $\angle C \cong \angle F$, $\overline{AB} \cong \overline{DE}$, $\overline{BC} \cong \overline{EF}$, and $\overline{AC} \cong \overline{DF}$.

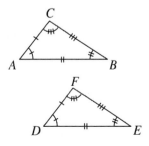

congruent Two shapes are congruent if they have exactly the same shape and size. Congruent shapes are similar and have a scale factor of 1. The symbol for congruence is $\cong$. (pp. 175, 345)

conic section A curve that is the intersection of a flat surface or plane with an infinite double cone. Conic sections include parabolas, ellipses, and hyperbolas. Circles, lines, and points are special cases of the conic sections. (p. 742)

conjecture An educated guess. Conjectures often result from noticing a pattern during an investigation. Conjectures are also often written in conditional ("If…, then…") form. Once a conjecture is proven, it becomes a theorem. (p. 11)

consecutive angles of a polygon The angles that occur at the two ends of any side of a polygon. For example, ∠B and ∠C are consecutive angles in the right trapezoid at right. (p. 443)

construction The process of using a straightedge and compass to solve a problem and/or create a geometric diagram. (p. 552)

converse The converse of a conditional statement can be found by switching the hypothesis (the "if" part) and the conclusion (the "then" part). For example, the converse of "*If P, then Q*" is "*If Q, then P.*" Knowing that a conditional statement is true does not tell you whether its converse is true. (p. 363)

convex polygon A polygon is convex if any pair of points inside the polygon can be connected by a segment without leaving the interior of the polygon. See also *non-convex polygon*. (p. 476)

coordinate geometry The study of geometry on a coordinate graph. (p. 454)

coordinate graph A method of specifying points (x, y) by their relationship to two perpendicular linear axes, often labeled the x-axis and y-axis. Also known as a rectangular coordinate graph or a Cartesian coordinate graph. See also *graph*.

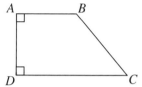

corresponding angles (a) When two lines are intersected by a third line (called a transversal), angles on the same side of the two lines and on the same side of the transversal are called corresponding angles. For example, the shaded angles in the diagram at right are corresponding angles. Note that if the two lines cut by the transversal are parallel, the corresponding angles are congruent. Conversely, if the corresponding angles are congruent, then the two lines intersected by the transversal are parallel; (b) Angles in two figures may also correspond, as shown in the figure in *corresponding parts*. See also *alternate interior angles* and *same-side interior angles*. (p. 100)

corresponding parts Points, sides, edges, or angles in two or more figures that are images of each other with respect to a sequence of transformations. If two figures are congruent, their corresponding parts are congruent to each other. (p. 410)

cosine ratio   In a right triangle, the cosine ratio of an acute angle, A, is $\cos A = \frac{\text{length of adjacent side}}{\text{length of hypotenuse}}$. In the triangle at right, $\cos A = \frac{AB}{AC} = \frac{4}{5}$. See also *sine ratio, tangent ratio,* and *inverse cosine.* (p. 285)

counter-clockwise   Counter-clockwise identifies the direction of rotation shown in the diagram at right. The opposite of counter-clockwise is clockwise.

counterexample   An example showing that a generalization has at least one exception; that is, a situation in which the statement is false. For example, the number 4 is a counterexample to the statement "*All even numbers are greater than 7.*" (p. 282)

cross-section   The intersection of a three-dimensional solid and a plane. The cross-sections of an infinite double cone are called conic sections. (p. 686)

cube   A polyhedron all of whose faces are squares. (p. 671)

cylinder (circular)   A three-dimensional figure that consists of two parallel congruent circular regions (called bases) and a lateral surface containing segments connecting each point on the circular boundary of one base to the corresponding point on the circular boundary of the other. See also *oblique prism (or cylinder)* and *right cylinder.* (p. 33)

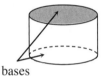

bases

decagon   A polygon with ten sides. (p. 52)

decision chart   A method for counting the number of outcomes (the size of the sample space) for a sequence of probabilistic situations, often in which the order of the items matters. A tree diagram could be used to count the number of outcomes, but if the number of outcomes is large a decision chart is more useful. For example, how many three-letter arrangements could be made by lining up any three blocks, chosen from a set of 26 alphabet blocks, if the first letter must be a vowel and the blocks are not reused? There are three decisions (three blocks to be chosen), with 5 choices for the first letter (a vowel), 25 for the second, and 24 for the third. According to the Fundamental Principle of Counting, the total number of possibilities is:

$$\underset{\text{1st decision}}{5} \cdot \underset{\text{2nd decision}}{25} \cdot \underset{\text{3rd decision}}{24} = 3000 \ .$$

This decision chart is a short way to represent a tree with 5 branches for the first alphabet block, followed by 25 branches for each of those branches; each of those 125 branches would then have 24 branches representing the possibilities for the third alphabet block. See also *Fundamental Principle or Counting.* (p. 631)

deck of cards   See *playing cards.*

degree   One degree is an angle measure that is $\frac{1}{360}$ of a full circle.

delta (Δ)   A Greek letter that is often used to represent a difference. Its uses include Δx and Δy, which represent the lengths of the horizontal and vertical legs of a slope triangle, respectively. (p. 59)

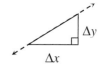

density   The quantity of something per unit measure, especially length, area, or volume. For example, the density of birds on a power wire may be 7 birds/meter, the population density of Singapore is 7301 people per square meter, or the mass density of iron is 7.874 $\frac{g}{cm^3}$. (p. 556)

diagonal   In a polygon, it is a segment that connects any two vertices of the polygon but is not a side of the polygon. (p. 481)

diameter   A line segment drawn through the center of a circle with both endpoints on the circle. The length of a diameter is usually denoted d. Note that the length of a circle's diameter is twice the length of its radius. See also *circle*. (p. 404)

dilation   A transformation which produces a figure similar to the original by proportionally shrinking or stretching the figure. In a dilation, a shape is stretched (or compressed) proportionally from a point, called the point of dilation. See also *point of dilation*. (p. 148)

dimension   (a) Flat figures have two dimensions (which can be labeled base and height); (b) Solids have three dimensions (such as "width," "height," and "depth"). (p. 107)

directrix   A line that, along with a point (called a focus), defines a conic section (such as a parabola). For any point on a parabola, the length of the segment between the focus and the point is equal to the length of the segment perpendicular from the directrix to point. (p. 743)

disjoint   Another name for *mutually exclusive*. (p. 610)

dissection   The process of dividing a flat shape or solid into parts that have no interior points in common.

dodecahedron   A polyhedron with twelve faces.

double cone   Two cones placed apex to apex so that their bases are parallel. Generally we think of double cones as extending to infinity beyond their bases.

double cone

edge   In three dimensions, a line segment formed by the intersection of two faces of a polyhedron. (p. 671)

ellipse   A conic section created by slicing a cone with a plane. In a future course it will be defined using a focus and a directrix. A typical algebraic equation of an ellipse in graphing form is $\frac{(x-h)^2}{a^2} + \frac{(y-k)^2}{b^2} = 1$ and in general form it is $ax^2 + by^2 + cx + dy + e = 0$.

foci

endpoint   See *line segment* and *ray*. (p. 749)

equator   If we represent the Earth as a sphere, the equator is the great circle equally distant between the North and South poles. The equator divides the Earth into two halves called the Northern and Southern hemispheres. The equator also marks a latitude of 0°. See also *latitude*. (p. 699)

equilateral   A polygon is equilateral if all its sides have equal length. The word equilateral comes from *equi* (meaning equal) and *lateral* (meaning side). Equilateral triangles not only have sides of equal length, but also angles of equal measure. However, a polygon with more than three sides can be equilateral without having congruent angles. For example, see the rhombus at right. (p. 416)

evaluate (an expression)   Substitute one or more numbers for the variables in a mathematical expression. Compare evaluating an expression, in which you know the value of a variable and use it to rewrite an expression, to solving an equation, in which you determine the value of a variable. For example, to evaluate $x^2 + 3$ for $x = -4$ means to rewrite $x^2 + 3$ as $(-4)^2 + 3$ or 19. See also *solve (an equation)*.

event   The set of one or more outcomes (or results) of a probabilistic situation. (p. 31)

exact answer   An answer that is precisely accurate and not approximate. For example, if the length of a side of a triangle is exactly $\sqrt{10}$, the exact answer to the question "*How long is that side of the triangle?*" would be $\sqrt{10}$, while 3.162 would be a decimal approximation of the answer. (p. 133)

expected value   For this course, the expected value of a game is the average amount expected to be won or lost on each play of the game if the game is played many times. Expected value can be found by summing the probability of each outcome multiplied by its value. For example, if you play a game where you roll a die and win one point for every dot on the face that comes up, the expected value of this game is $(\frac{1}{6})1 + (\frac{1}{6})2 + (\frac{1}{6})3 + (\frac{1}{6})4 + (\frac{1}{6})5 + (\frac{1}{6})6 = 3.5$ points for each play. The expected value need not be a value that a player could actually win on a single play of the game. (p. 304)

experimental probability   The probability based on data collected in experiments. The experimental probability of an event is defined to be $\frac{\text{number of successful outcomes in the experiment}}{\text{total number of outcomes in the experiment}}$. (p. 31)

exterior angle (of a polygon) When a side of a polygon is extended to form an angle with an adjacent side outside of the polygon, that angle is called an exterior angle. For example, the angles marked with letters in the diagram at right are exterior angles of the quadrilateral. Note that an exterior angle of a polygon is always adjacent and supplementary to an interior angle of that polygon. The sum of the exterior angles of a convex polygon is always 360°. See also *interior angle (of a polygon)*. (p. 484)

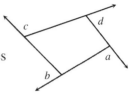

face of a polyhedron One of the flat surfaces of a polyhedron, including the base(s). (p. 671)

factor A factor of an expression is an integer or a polynomial, which when multiplied by one or more other factors, gives the expression. For example, $3, 6, (2x + 1)$, and $(4x + 2)$ are each factors of $12x + 6$, and factors of $x^2 + 3x + 2$ are $(x + 1)$ and $(x + 2)$.

factorial A shorthand notation for the product of a list of consecutive positive integers from the given number down to $1 : n! = n(n-1)(n-2)(n-3) \cdot ... \cdot 3 \cdot 2 \cdot 1$. For example, $5! = 5 \cdot 4 \cdot 3 \cdot 2 \cdot 1 = 120$. (p. 638)

fair game For the purposes of this course, a fair game has an expected value of 0 for all players. Therefore, over many plays, any player would expect to neither win nor lose points or money by playing a fair game. (p. 304)

flip See *reflection*.

flowchart A diagram showing an argument for a conclusion from certain evidence. A flowchart uses ovals connected by arrows to show the logical structure of the argument. When each oval has a reason stated next to it showing how the evidence leads to that conclusion, the flowchart represents a proof. See the example at right. (p. 187)

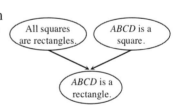

focus A point that, along with a line (called a directrix), can be used to define a conic section (like a parabola). For any point on a parabola, the length of the segment between the focus and the point is equal to the length of the segment perpendicular from the directrix to point. (p. 743)

Fraction Buster Fraction Busting is a method of simplifying equations involving fractions by using the Multiplicative Property of Equality to alter the equation so that no fractions remain. To use this method, multiply both sides of an equation by the common denominator of all the fractions in the equation. The result will be an equivalent equation with no fractions. For example, when given the equation $\frac{x}{7} + 2 = \frac{x}{3}$, we can multiply both sides by the Fraction Buster 21. The resulting equation, $3x + 42 = 7x$, is equivalent to the original but contains no fractions.

frequency table A two-way table that contains entries that are counts (as opposed to fractions or percents). See also *two-way table*.

function A relation in which for each input value there is one and only one output value. For example, the relation $f(x) = x + 4$ is a function; for each input value (x) there is exactly one output value. In terms of ordered pairs (x, y), no two ordered pairs of a function have the same first member (x). For example, a graph of a circle does not represent a function because for most x-values there are two y-values.

Fundamental Principle of Counting A method for counting the number of outcomes (the size of the sample space) of a probabilistic situation, often in which the order of the items matters. If event {A} has m outcomes, and event {B} has n outcomes after event {A} has occurred, then event {A} followed by event {B} has $m \cdot n$ outcomes. For a sequence of events, a tree diagram could be used to count the number of outcomes, but if the number of outcomes is large a decision chart is more useful. See also *decision chart*. (p. 631)

generic rectangle A type of diagram used to visualize multiplying expressions without algebra tiles. Each expression to be multiplied forms a side length of the rectangle, and the product is the sum of the areas of the sections of the rectangle. For example, the generic rectangle at right can be used to multiply $(2x + 5)$ by $(x + 3)$.

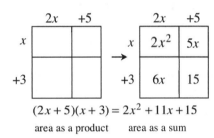

$(2x + 5)(x + 3) = 2x^2 + 11x + 15$

area as a product   area as a sum

geometric sequence An ordered sequence of mathematical terms in which each term is multiplied by a constant number to determine the next term in the sequence. The number each term is multiplied by to get the next term is called the multiplier, sequence generator, or common ratio. The equation for a geometric sequence is $t(n) = ab^n$ or $a_n = a_0 \cdot b^n$, where n is the term number, b is the multiplier, and a or a_0 is the zeroth (or initial) term of the sequence. Sequences are usually written starting with the first term, where $n = 1$. For example in the sequence, $5, 15, 45, \ldots$, the multiplier is 3, and the equation is $t(n) = \frac{5}{3} \cdot 3^n$. See also *arithmetic sequence*. (p. 223)

golden ratio The number $\frac{1 + \sqrt{5}}{2}$, which is often labeled with the Greek letter phi (ϕ), pronounced "fee." (p. 759)

golden rectangle A rectangle whose side lengths are in the proportion of the golden ratio. (p. 759)

graph   A graph represents numerical information spatially. The numbers may come from a table, situation (pattern), rule (equation or inequality), or figure. Most of the graphs in this course show points, lines, figures, and/or curves on a two-dimensional coordinate graph like the one below right.

A complete graph includes all the necessary information about a line or a curve. To be complete, a graph must have the following components: (1) the *x*-axis and *y*-axis labeled, clearly showing the scale; (2) the equation of the graph written near the line or curve; (3) the line or curve extended as far as possible on the graph with arrows if the line or curve continues beyond the axes; (4) the coordinates of all special points, such as *x*- and *y*-intercepts, shown in (*x*, *y*) form.

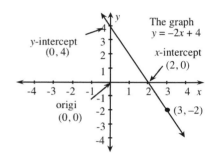

great circle   A cross-section of a sphere that has the same radius as the sphere. If the Earth is represented with a sphere, the equator is an example of a great circle. (p. 700)

height   (a) Triangle: the length of a segment that connects a vertex of the triangle to a line containing the opposite base (side) and is perpendicular to that line; (b) Trapezoid: the length of any segment that connects a point on one base of the trapezoid to the line containing the opposite base and is perpendicular to that line; (c) Parallelogram (includes rectangle, rhombus, and square): the length of any segment that connects a point on one base of the parallelogram to the line containing the opposite base and is perpendicular to that line; (d) Pyramid and cone: the length of the segment that connects the apex to a point in the plane containing the figure's base and is perpendicular to that plane; (e) Prism or cylinder: the length of a segment that connects one base of the figure to the plane containing the other base and is perpendicular to that plane. Some texts make a distinction between height and altitude, where the altitude is the segment described in the definition above and the height is its length. (p. 122)

hemisphere   Half of a sphere. A great circle of a sphere divides it into two congruent parts, each of which is called a hemisphere. Hemispheres can also be created by slicing a sphere with a plane passing through the sphere's center. If the Earth is represented as a sphere, the Northern hemisphere is the portion of the Earth north of (and including) the equator. Likewise, the Southern hemisphere is the portion of the Earth south of (and including) the equator. (p. 699)

heptagon   A polygon with seven sides. (p. 473)

heptahedron   A polyhedron with seven faces. (p. 674)

hexagon   A polygon with six sides. (p. 52)

hexahedron   A polyhedron with six faces. A regular hexahedron is a cube. (p.674)

Core Connections Geometry

HL ≅ (Triangle Shortcut) If the hypotenuse and one leg of one right triangle are congruent to the hypotenuse and corresponding leg of another right triangle, the two right triangles are congruent. Note that this congruence condition applies only to right triangles. (p. 358)

hyperbola A hyperbola looks like two curves (not parabolas) facing away from each other. A hyperbola is a conic section created by slicing a double cone with a plane. In a future course it will be defined using a focus and a directrix. A typical algebraic equation of a hyperbola is $\frac{(x-h)^2}{a^2} - \frac{(y-k)^2}{b^2} = 1$. (p. 749)

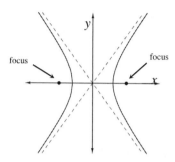

hypothesis A conjecture (or educated guess) in science.

hypotenuse The side of a right triangle opposite the right angle. Note that legs of a right triangle are always shorter than its hypotenuse. See also *legs*. (p. 128)

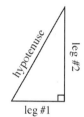

icosahedron A polyhedron with twenty faces. (p. 674)

"If ..., then ..." statement A statement written in the form "If ..., then ...." Also known as a conditional statement. (p. 119)

image The shape that results from a transformation, such as a translation, rotation, reflection, or dilation. (p. 37)

incenter The center of the circle inscribed in a triangle. It can be found by locating the point at which the angle bisectors of a triangle intersect. The other points of concurrency studied in this course are the centroid and the circumcenter. (p. 604)

independent events If the outcome of a probabilistic event does not affect the probability of another event, the events are independent. For example, assume you plan to roll a normal six-sided die twice and want to know the probability of rolling a 1 twice. The result of the first roll does not affect the probability of rolling a 1 on the second roll; the events are independent. If two events {A} and {B} are independent, then P(A given B) = P(A). The converse is also true. Alternatively, by rewriting the Multiplication Rule, if two events are independent, then P(A and B) = P(A) · P(B). Again, the converse is also true. (pp. 232, 624)

indirect proof See *proof by contradiction*. (p. 105)

inequality symbols The symbols < (less than), > (greater than), ≤ (less than or equal to), and ≥ (greater than or equal to).

inscribed angle An angle with its vertex on the circle and sides intersecting the circle at two distinct points. In the figure at right $\angle ABC$ is an inscribed angle. (p. 589)

Inscribed Angle Theorem The measure of an inscribed angle is half the measure of its intercepted arc. Likewise, the measure of an intercepted arc is twice the measure of an inscribed angle whose sides pass through the endpoints of the arc. In the figure at right, if $m\overset{\frown}{AC} = 60°$, then $m\angle ABC = 30°$. (p. 595)

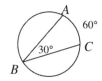

inscribed circle A circle is inscribed in a polygon if each side of the polygon intersects the circle at exactly one point. (p. 554)

$\odot B$ is inscribed in the pentagon.

The pentagon is inscribed in $\odot C$.

inscribed polygon A polygon is inscribed in a circle if each vertex of the polygon lies on the circle. (p. 555)

integers The set of numbers $\{ \ldots -3, -2, -1, 0, 1, 2, 3, \ldots \}$.

intercepted arc The arc of a circle bounded by the points where the two sides of an inscribed angle meet the circle. In the circle at right, $\angle ABC$ intercepts $\overset{\frown}{AC}$. (p. 588)

interior angle (of a polygon) An angle formed by two consecutive sides of the polygon. The vertex of the angle is a vertex (corner) of the polygon. The sum of the interior angles of a polygon with n-sides is $180°(n-2)$. (p. 479)

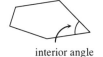

interior angle

intersection A point of intersection is a point that the graphs of two or more equations have in common. Graphs may intersect in one, two, several, many or no points. The set of coordinates of a point of intersection are a solution to the equation for each graph. The functions at right have two points of intersection. (p. 95)

intersection of two events The intersection of the two events {A} and {B} is a new event that includes all the outcomes in which both A *and* B will occur. For example, if event {A} is the thirteen diamond-suited cards in a deck of playing cards, and {B} is the four Aces, then the event {A intersection B} contains 1 outcome: {A♦}. See also *union of two events*. (p. 255)

inverse cosine ($\cos^{-1} x$), inverse sine ($\sin^{-1} x$), and inverse tangent ($\tan^{-1} x$)
The inverse of the cosine, sine, and tangent functions (the functions that "undo" cosine, sine, and tangent). When the ratio between the lengths of two sides of a right triangle is known, $\sin^{-1}$, $\cos^{-1}$, or $\tan^{-1}$ can be used to find the measure of one of the triangle's acute angles. For example, if $\cos\theta = \frac{\sqrt{3}}{2}$, to find θ, find the inverse cosine of both sides: (p.

$$\cos\theta = \frac{\sqrt{3}}{2}$$

$$\cos^{-1}(\cos\theta) = \cos^{-1}\left(\frac{\sqrt{3}}{2}\right)$$

$$\theta = 30°$$

294)

irrational numbers The set of numbers that cannot be expressed in the form $\frac{a}{b}$, where a and b are integers and $b \neq 0$. For example, π and $\sqrt{2}$ are irrational numbers.

isosceles trapezoid A trapezoid with a pair of equal base angles (from the same base). The base of a trapezoid is always one of the two parallel sides. Note that the non-parallel sides on an isosceles triangle are congruent. (p. 444)

isosceles triangle A triangle with two sides of equal length. (p. 46)

Isosceles Triangle Theorem If a triangle is isosceles, then the base angles (which are opposite the congruent sides) are congruent. For example, if $\triangle ABC$ is isosceles with $BA \cong BC$, then the angles opposite these sides are congruent; that is, $\angle A \cong \angle C$.

iteration The act of repeating an action over and over. (p. 760)

justify To give a logical reason supporting a statement or step in a proof. More generally, to use facts, definitions, rules, and/or previously proven conjectures in an organized sequence to convincingly demonstrate that your claim (or your answer) is valid (true).

kite A quadrilateral with two distinct pairs of consecutive congruent sides. (p. 431)

lateral edge See *pyramid*. (p. 680)

lateral face See *pyramid*. (pp. 537, 680)

lateral surface (a) All the faces of a prism or pyramid, with the exception of the base(s); (b) On a cone, the surface not including the circular base. The lateral surface connects the apex to each point on the circular boundary of the base.

lateral surface area The sum of the areas of all the lateral surfaces of a polyhedron or solid. See *lateral surface*. (p. 680)

latitude An angular measure (in degrees) that indicates how far north or south of the equator a position on the Earth is. All points on the equator have a latitude of $0°$. The North Pole has a latitude of $90°$, while the South Pole has a latitude of $-90°$. (p. 699)

Law of Cosines For any $\triangle ABC$ with sides a, b, and c opposite $\angle A$, $\angle B$, and $\angle C$ respectively, it is always true that $c^2 = a^2 + b^2 - 2ab \cdot \cos(C)$, $b^2 = a^2 + c^2 - 2ac \cdot \cos(B)$, and $a^2 = b^2 + c^2 - 2bc \cdot \cos(A)$. (p. 318)

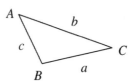

Law of Sines For any $\triangle ABC$ with sides $a, b,$ and c opposite $\angle A, \angle B,$ and $\angle C$ respectively, it is always true that $\frac{\sin A}{a} = \frac{\sin B}{b} = \frac{\sin C}{c}$. (p. 314)

legs The two sides of a right triangle that form the right angle. Note that the right triangle are always shorter than its hypotenuse. See also *hypotenuse*. (p. 128)

line A line is one-dimensional and extends without end in two directions. It is made up of points and has no thickness. A line can be named with a letter (such as *l*), but also can be labeled using two points on the line, such as $\overleftrightarrow{AB}$ below. A line is a mathematically undefined term in geometry. See also *ray* and *line segment*. (p. 88)

line of reflection Same as the *line of symmetry*. (pp. 37, 47)

line of symmetry A line that divides a shape into two congruent parts that are mirror images of each other. If you fold a shape over its line of symmetry, the shapes on both sides of the line will match each other perfectly. Some shapes have more than one line of symmetry, such as the example at right. Other shapes may only have one line of symmetry or no lines of symmetry. (p. 6)

line segment The portion of a line between two points. A line segment is named using its endpoints. For example, the line segment at right can be named either $\overline{AB}$ or $\overline{BA}$. See also *line*. (p. 46)

linear scale factor Same as *ratio of similarity*. (p. 499)

logical argument A logical sequence of statements and reasons that lead to a conclusion. A logical argument can be written in a paragraph, represented with a flowchart, or documented in a two-column proof. (p. 18)

longitude An angular measure (in degrees) that indicates how far west or east of the prime meridian a position on the Earth is. Lines of longitude (which are actually circles) are all great circles that pass through the North and South Poles. (p. 700)

major arc An arc with measure greater than 180°. Each major arc has a corresponding minor arc that has a measure that is less than 180°. A major arc is named with three letters on the arc. For example, the highlighted arc at right is the major arc $\overgroup{ABC}$. (p. 583)

mapping In general, the term mapping is synonymous with function, but in this course we restrict its meaning to refer to functions that take points on a line or in the plane, to other points on a line or in the plane. (p. 37)

mat plan A top (or bottom) view of a multiple cube solid. The number in each square is the number of cubes in that stack. For example, the mat plan at right represents the solid at the far right. (p. 531)

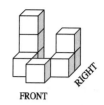

measurement For the purposes of this course, a measurement is an indication of the size or magnitude of a geometric figure. For example, an appropriate measurement of a line segment would be its length. Appropriate measurements of a square would include not only the length of a side, but also its area and perimeter. The measure of an angle represents the number of degrees of rotation from one ray to the other about the vertex.

median A line segment that connects a vertex of a triangle with the midpoint of <u>side</u> opposite to the vertex. For example, since D is a midpoint of $\overline{BC}$, then $\overline{AD}$ is a median of $\triangle ABC$. The three medians of a triangle intersect at a point called the centroid. (p. 568)

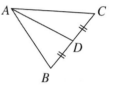

meridian A line of longitude. See *longitude* and *prime meridian*. (p. 700)

midpoint A point that divides a segment into two segments of equal length. For example, point D is the midpoint of $\overline{BC}$ in $\triangle ABC$ in the example for median. (p. 50)

midsegment A segment joining the midpoints of two sides of a triangle. (p. 444)

minor arc An arc with measure less than 180°. Each minor arc has a corresponding major arc that has a measure that is more than 180°. Minor arcs are named using the endpoints of the arc. For example, the highlighted arc at right is named $\overset{\frown}{AC}$. (p. 583)

Möbius strip A one-sided surface in a closed loop that can be formed by giving a rectangular strip of paper a half-twist and affixing its ends. (p. 9)

monomial An expression with only one term. It can be a number, a variable, or the product of a number and one or more variables. For example, 7, $3x$, $-4ab$, and $3x^2y$ are each monomials.

Multiplication Rule for Probabilities For two events, {A} and {B}, $P(A \text{ and } B) = P(A \text{ given } B) \cdot P(B)$, or equivalently, $P(A \text{ given } B) = \frac{P(A \text{ and } B)}{P(B)}$. When the two events are independent, then $P(A \text{ given } B) = P(A)$, and the Multiplication Rule can be rewritten as $P(A \text{ and } B) = P(A) \cdot P(B)$. See also *Addition Rule for Probability*. (p. 624)

multiplier in a geometric sequence The number by which one term in a geometric sequence is multiplied to generate the next term. The multiplier is also known as the common ratio or the sequence generator. In the sequence $5, 15, 45, \ldots$, the multiplier is 3. See also *geometric sequence*. (p. 223)

mutually exclusive   Two events {A} and {B} are mutually exclusive if they have no outcomes in common. That is, P(A and B) = 0. This situation is also called disjoint. (p. 610)

_n_-gon   A polygon with _n_ sides. A polygon is often referred to as an _n_-gon when we do not yet know the value of _n_. (p. 473)

net   A diagram that, when folded, forms the surface of a three-dimensional solid. A net is essentially the faces of a solid laid flat. It is one of several ways to represent a three-dimensional diagram. The diagram at right is a representation of the solid at the far right. Note that the shaded region of the net indicates the (bottom) base of the solid. (p. 535)

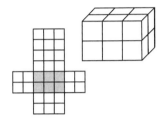

nonagon   A polygon with nine sides. (p. 473)

nonahedron   A polyhedron with nine faces. (p. 674)

non-convex polygon   A polygon that is not convex. An example of a non-convex polygon is shown at right. See also _convex polygon_. (p. 476)

oblique prism (or cylinder)   A prism (or cylinder) is oblique when its lateral surface(s) are not perpendicular to the base. See figure at right. See also _Cavalieri's Principle_. (p. 541)

oblique pyramid (or cone)   A pyramid (or cone) is oblique when its apex is not directly above the center of the base. (p. 684)

obtuse angle   Any angle that measures between (but not including) 90° and 180°. (p. 26)

octagon   A polygon with eight sides. (p. 52)

octahedron   A polyhedron with eight faces. In a regular octahedron, all of the faces are equilateral triangles. (p. 674)

opposite   In a figure, opposite means "across from." For example, in a triangle, an opposite side is the side that is across from a particular angle and is not a side that makes the angle. For example, the side $\overline{AB}$ in $\triangle ABC$ at right is opposite $\angle C$, while $\overline{AC}$ is opposite the right angle. (p. 285)

opposite interior angles   See _remote interior angles_.

orientation In this course, orientation refers to the placement and alignment of a figure in relation to others or an object of reference (such as coordinate axes). Unless it has rotation symmetry, the orientation of a figure changes when it is rotated (turned) less than 360°. Also, the orientation of a shape changes when it is reflected, except when reflected across a line of symmetry.

outcome The result of a probabilistic situation. The set of all possible outcomes of a probabilistic situation is called the sample space. See also *event*.

parabola A parabola is a conic section created by slicing a cone with a plane parallel to a lateral edge of the cone. Parabolas may also be generated geometrically: the set of all points that are equidistant from a single point (the focus) and a line (the directrix). The graph of a quadratic equation is a parabola. A quadratic equation can be given in standard form $y = ax^2 + bx + c$ or in graphing form $y = a(x-h)^2 + k$, with vertex at (h,k). (p. 749)

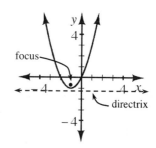

parallel lines Two lines on a flat surface are parallel if they never intersect. Two line segments on a flat surface are parallel if the lines they lie on never intersect. There is a constant distance between two parallel lines (or line segments). Identical arrow markings are used to note parallel lines or line segments as shown in the diagrams at right. (p. 59)

parallelogram A quadrilateral with two pairs of parallel sides. (p. 431)

pentagon A polygon with five sides. (p. 52)

pentagram A pentagram is created by connecting five equally-spaced points on the circumference of a circle. Note that all of the corresponding lengths and angles are equal to each other. (p. 738)

pentahedron A polyhedron with five faces. (p. 674)

perimeter The distance around the exterior of a figure on a flat surface. For a polygon, the perimeter is the sum of the lengths of its sides. The perimeter of a circle is also called the circumference. (p. 16)

permutation An arrangement of items in which items cannot be selected more than once and the order of selection matters. The number of permutations that can be made by selecting r items from a set of n total items can be represented with tree diagrams or decision charts, or calculated using the formula $_nP_r = \frac{n!}{(n-r)!}$. For example, if each of five letters, A, B, C, D, E, is printed on a card, the number of 3-letter sequences can you make by selecting three of the five cards is a permutation, $_5P_3 = \frac{5!}{2!} = \frac{5\cdot4\cdot3\cdot2\cdot1}{2\cdot1} = 5\cdot4\cdot3 = 60$. See also *combination*. (p. 638)

perpendicular   Two rays, line segments, or lines that meet (intersect) to form a right angle (90°) are called perpendicular. A line and a flat surface can also be perpendicular if the line does not lie on the flat surface, but intersects it and forms a right angle with every line on the flat surface passing through the point of intersection. A small square at the point of intersection of two lines or segments indicates that the lines are perpendicular. (p. 59)

perpendicular bisector   The perpendicular bisector of a line segment is a line segment perpendicular to the original segment, and passing through its midpoint. (p. 564)

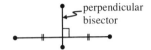

phi (φ)   A Greek letter, pronounced "fee," that represents the golden ratio. $\phi = \frac{1+\sqrt{5}}{2}$ (p. 761)

pi (π)   The ratio of the circumference (C) of the circle to its diameter (d). For every circle, $\pi = \frac{\text{circumference}}{\text{diameter}} = \frac{C}{d}$. Numbers such as $3.14, 3.14159$, or $\frac{22}{7}$ are approximations of π. (p. 512)

plane   A plane is an undefined term in geometry. It is a two-dimensional flat surface that extends without end. It is made up of points and has no thickness.
Platonic solid   A convex regular polyhedron. All faces of a platonic solid are congruent, regular polygons. There are only five possible Platonic solids: tetrahedron (with four faces of equilateral triangles), cube (with six faces of squares), octahedron (with eight faces of equilateral triangles), dodecahedron (with twelve faces of regular pentagons), and icosahedron (with twenty faces of equilateral triangles). (pp. 671, 674)

playing cards   A standard deck of playing cards contains the following 52 cards:
* 13 cards with red hearts (♥), numbered 2 through 10, Jack, Queen, King, and Ace
* 13 cards with red diamonds (♦), numbered 2 through 10, Jack, Queen, King, and Ace
* 13 cards with black spades (♠), numbered 2 through 10, Jack, Queen, King, and Ace
* 13 cards with black clubs (♣), numbered 2 through 10, Jack, Queen, King, and Ace
The face cards are the Jacks, Queens, and Kings (Aces are not considered face cards).

point of concurrency   The single point where two or more lines intersect on a plane. For the points of concurrency of a triangle, see *circumcenter, centroid,* and *incenter*. (pp. 568, 604)

point of dilation   The point from which a figure is stretched proportionally when the figure is dilated. For example, in the diagram at right, $\triangle ABC$ is dilated to form $\triangle A'B'C'$. Notice that while a dilation changes the size and location of the original figure, it does not rotate or reflect the original. While lengths can change, angles do not change under a dilation. (p. 148)

point of intersection   See *intersection*. (p. 95)

polygon   A two-dimensional closed figure of three or more line segments (sides) connected end to end. Each segment is a side and only intersects the endpoints of its two adjacent sides. Each point of intersection is a vertex. At right are two examples of polygons. See also *regular polygon*. (p. 52)

polyhedron (plural: polyhedra)   A three-dimensional object with no holes that is bounded by polygons. The polygons are joined at their sides, forming the edges of the polyhedron. Each polygon is a face of the polyhedron. See also *solid*. (p. 674)

polynomial   An algebraic expression that involves at most the operations of addition, subtraction, and/or multiplication. A polynomial in one variable is an expression that can be written as the sum of terms that have the form: (any number) $\cdot$ $x^{\text{(whole number)}}$. (p. 319)

postulates   Statements accepted as true without proof. Also known as axioms.

preimage   The original figure in a transformation.

prime meridian   The line of longitude on the Earth chosen to represent $0°$. It passes through Greenwich, England, on the eastern edge of London. (p. 700)

prism   A three-dimensional figure that consists of two parallel congruent polygons (called bases) and a lateral surface containing segments connecting each point on each side of one base to the corresponding point on the other base. The lateral surface of a prism consists of parallelograms. See also *right prism* and *oblique prism*. (p. 537)

probabilistic situation   A situation in which the outcomes are determined by random processes. See also *random*.

probability   A number that represents how likely an event is to happen. When a event has a finite number of equally-likely outcomes, the probability that one of those outcomes, called A, will occur is expressed as a ratio and written as:

$$P(A) = \frac{\text{number of successful outcomes}}{\text{total number of possible outcomes}}.$$

For example, when flipping a coin, the probability of getting tails, P(tails), is $\frac{1}{2}$ because there is only one tail (successful outcome) out of the two possible equally-likely outcomes (a head and a tail). Probability can be written as a ratio, decimal, or percent. A probability of 0 (or 0%) indicates that it is impossible for the event to occur, while a probability of 1 (or 100%) indicates that the event must occur. Events that "might happen" will have values somewhere between 0 and 1 (or between 0% and 100%). (p. 31)

probability table   Another name for *two-way table*.

proof A convincing logical argument that uses definitions and previously proven conjectures in an organized sequence to show that a conjecture is true. A proof can be written in a paragraph, represented with a flowchart, or documented in a formal two-column proof. (p. 11)

proof by contradiction A proof that begins by assuming that an assertion is true and then shows that this assumption leads to a contradiction of a known fact. This demonstrates that the assertion is false. Also known as an indirect proof. (p. 105)

proportional equation An equation stating that two ratios are equal. For example, the equation below is a proportion. A proportion is a useful type of equation to set up when solving problems involving proportional relationships. (p. 158)

$$\frac{68 \text{ votes for Mr. Mears}}{100 \text{ people surveyed}} = \frac{34 \text{ votes for Mr. Mears}}{50 \text{ people surveyed}}$$

protractor A geometric tool used for measuring the number of degrees in an angle. (p. 24)

pyramid A polyhedron with a polygonal base formed by connecting each vertex of the base to a single point (the apex) that is above the flat surface containing the base. The lateral faces of a pyramid are the triangles formed by connecting consecutive vertices of the base to the apex. Lateral edges are two of the sides of these lateral triangular faces. The slant height is the height of a lateral triangular face. See also *right pyramid* and *oblique pyramid*. (p. 679)

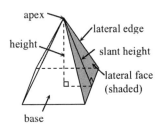

Pythagorean Theorem The statement relating the lengths of the legs of a right triangle to the length of the hypotenuse:
$(\text{leg } \#1)^2 + (\text{leg } \#2)^2 = \text{hypotenuse}^2$. The Pythagorean Theorem is powerful because if you know the lengths of any two sides of a right triangle, you can use this relationship to find the length of the third side. (p. 133)

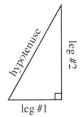

Pythagorean Triple Any three positive integers a, b, and c that make the relationship $a^2 + b^2 = c^2$ true. Commonly used Pythagorean Triples include 3, 4, 5 and 5, 12, 13. (p. 310)

quadratic function (equation) An equation that can be written in the form $ax^2 + bx + c = 0$, where a, b, and c are real numbers and a is nonzero. A quadratic equation written in this form is said to be in standard form. For example, $3x^2 - 4x + 7.5 = 0$ is a quadratic equation in standard form. The graph of a quadratic function is a parabola. (p. 319)

Quadratic Formula The Quadratic Formula states that if $ax^2 + bx + c = 0$ and $a \ne 0$, then $x = \frac{-b \pm \sqrt{b^2 - 4ac}}{2a}$. For example, if $5x^2 + 9x + 3 = 0$, then $x = \frac{-9 \pm \sqrt{9^2 - 4(5)(3)}}{2(5)} = \frac{-9 \pm \sqrt{21}}{10}$. (p. 238)

quadrilateral A polygon with four sides. (pp. 52, 431)

radians The ratio of the arc length to the radius for any sector of a circle. The ratio will be constant for a given central angle, regardless of the length of the radius of the circle. Along with degrees, radians are a very common method unit of measurement for the central angle of a circle. (p. 516)

radius (plural: radii) (a) Of a circle: A line segment drawn from the center of a circle to a point on the circle. Note that the length of a circle's radius is half the length of the circle's diameter. See also *circle*. (b) Of a regular polygon: A line segment that connects the center of a regular polygon with a vertex. The length of a radius is usually denoted r. (p. 404)

random An outcome is random if it happens by chance, that is, its result cannot be predicted from previous outcomes. A sequence of several random outcomes in a row will have no predictable order or pattern. For example, the outcome of rolling a die is random because the outcome cannot be predicted, and many rolls in a row will have no predictable pattern.

ratio A ratio compares two quantities by division. A ratio can be written using a colon, but is more often written as a fraction. For example, in the two similar triangles shown below, a ratio can be used to compare the length of $\overline{BC}$ in $\triangle ABC$ with the length of $\overline{EF}$ in $\triangle DEF$. This ratio can be written as 5:11 or as the fraction $\frac{5}{11}$. (p. 154)

ratios of similarity $r : r^2 : r^3$ (a) The ratio of any pair of corresponding sides of two similar figures. This means that once it is determined that two figures are similar, all of their pairs of corresponding sides have the same ratio. For example, for the similar triangles $\triangle ABC$ and $\triangle DEF$ above, the ratio of similarity is $\frac{5}{11}$. The ratio of similarity can also be called the linear scale factor. When the ratio is comparing a figure and its image after a dilation, this ratio can also be called the zoom factor.

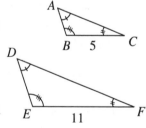

When a two-dimensional figure is enlarged (or reduced) proportionally, its lengths and area change. If the linear scale factor is r, then all lengths (such as sides, perimeter, and heights) of the original (preimage) figure is multiplied by a factor of r while the area is multiplied by a factor of r^2.

When a solid is enlarged (or reduced) proportionally, its lengths, surface area, and volume also change. If the linear scale factor is r, then the surface area is multiplied by a factor of r^2 and the volume is multiplied by a factor of r^3. Thus, if a solid is enlarged proportionally by a linear scale factor of r, then the new edge lengths, surface area, and volume can be found using the relationships below. (pp. 154, 499)

New edge length = $r \cdot$ (corresponding edge length of original polyhedron)

New surface area = $r^2 \cdot$ (original surface area)

New volume = $r^3 \cdot$ (original volume)

rationalizing the denominator   Rewriting a fractional expression that has radicals in the denominator, in order to eliminate the radicals from the denominator. For example, $\frac{2}{\sqrt{3}}$ can be rationalized as follows: $\frac{2}{\sqrt{3}} = \frac{2}{\sqrt{3}} \cdot \frac{\sqrt{3}}{\sqrt{3}} = \frac{2\sqrt{3}}{3}$. (p. 299)

ray   A ray is part of a line that starts at one endpoint and extends without end in one direction. In the example at right, ray $\overrightarrow{AB}$ is part of $\overleftrightarrow{AB}$ that starts at A and contains all of the points of $\overleftrightarrow{AB}$ that are on the same side of A as point B, including A. Point A is the endpoint of $\overrightarrow{AB}$. See also *line*.

reasoning   See *logical argument* and *proof*.

rectangle   A quadrilateral with four right angles. (p. 431)

reflection   A transformation across a line that produces a mirror image of the original (preimage) shape. The reflection is called the image of the original figure. The line is called a line of symmetry. See the example at right. Note that a reflection is also sometimes referred to as a "flip." (pp. 37, 47)

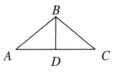

original   image

line of reflection

Reflexive Property   The Reflexive Property states that any expression is always equal to itself. That is, $a = a$. This property is often useful when proving that two triangles that share a side or an angle are congruent. For example, in the diagram at right, since $\triangle ABD$ and $\triangle CBD$ share a side ($\overline{BD}$), the Reflexive Property justifies that $BD = BD$. (p. 421)

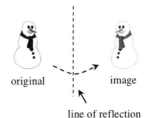

reflection symmetry   See *symmetry*.

regular polygon   A polygon is regular if it is a convex polygon with congruent angles and congruent sides. For example, the shape at right is a regular hexagon. (p. 416)

relation   An equation that relates two or more variables. For example, $y = 3x - 2$ and $x^2 + y^2 = 9$ are both relations. See also *function*.

relationship   For this course, a relationship is a way that two objects (such as two line segments or two triangles) are connected. When you know that the relationship holds between two objects, learning about one object can give you information about the other. Relationships can be described in two ways: a geometric relationship (such as a pair of vertical angles or two line segments that are parallel) and a relationship between the measures (such as two angles that are complementary or two sides of a triangle that have the same length). Common geometric relationships between two figures include being similar (when two figures have the shape, but not necessarily the same size) and being congruent (when two figures have the same shape and the same size).

relative frequency table A two-way table that contains entries that are fractions or percents (as opposed to counts). See also *two-way table*.

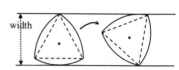

remote interior angles

remote interior angles If a triangle has an exterior angle, the remote interior angles are the two angles not adjacent to the exterior angle. Also called opposite interior angles. (p. 477)

Reuleaux curve The curve created by drawing arcs between two consecutive vertices (with a center at the opposite vertex) on a regular polygon with an odd number of sides. As the curve is "rolled," the width of the figure is constant. (p. 400)

rhombus A quadrilateral with four congruent sides. (p. 560)

right angle An angle that measures 90°. A small square is used to note a right angle, as shown in the example at right. (p. 26)

right prism (or cylinder) A prism (or cylinder) with lateral surface(s) that are perpendicular to the base. See the figure at right.

right pyramid (or cone) A pyramid (or cone) with its apex directly above the center of the base. (p. 684)

right triangle A triangle that has one right angle. The side of a right triangle opposite the right angle is called the hypotenuse, and the two sides adjacent to the right angle are called legs. Note that legs of a right triangle are always shorter than its hypotenuse. (p. 128)

rigid motions See *rigid transformations*.

rigid transformations Movements of figures that preserve their shape and size. Examples of rigid transformations are reflections, rotations, and translations. Also called rigid motions or "isometries." See also *similarity transformations*. (p. 37)

rotation A transformation that turns all of the points in the original (preimage) figure the same number of degrees around a fixed center point (such as the origin on a graph). The result is called the image of the original figure. The point that the shape is rotated about is called the center of rotation. To define a rotation, you need to state the measure of turn (in degrees), the direction the shape is turned (such as clockwise or counter-clockwise), and the center of rotation. See the example at right. Note that a rotation is also sometimes referred to as a "turn." (pp. 37, 47)

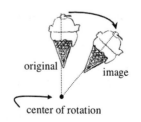

rotation symmetry   See *symmetry*. (p. 56)

same-side interior angles   Two angles between two lines and on the
same side of a third line that intersects them (called a transversal). The
shaded angles in the diagram at right are an example of a pair of same-
side interior angles. Note that if the two lines that are cut by the
transversal are parallel, then the two angles are supplementary (add up
to 180°). Conversely, if the two angles are supplementary, then the
two lines that are cut by the transversal are parallel. See also *alternate
interior angles* and *corresponding angles*. (p. 100)

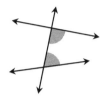

sample space   The set of all possible outcomes of a probabilistic situation. The sample
space for rolling a standard 6-sided die is the set $\{1, 2, 3, 4, 5, 6\}$ because those are all the
possible outcomes. (p. 31)

SAS ≅ (Triangle Congruence)   Two triangles are congruent if two sides and their
included angle of one triangle are congruent to the corresponding two sides and included
angle of another triangle. (p. 358)

SAS ~ (Triangle Similarity)   If two triangles have two pairs of corresponding sides that
are proportional and have congruent included angles, then the triangles are similar.
(pp. 170, 192)

scale   The ratio between a length of the representation (such as a map, model, or diagram)
and the corresponding length of the actual object. For example, the map of a city may use
one inch to represent one mile.

scalene triangle   A triangle with no congruent sides. (p. 68)

scatterplot   A way of displaying two-variable numerical data
where two measurements are taken for each subject (like
height and forearm length, or surface area of cardboard and
volume of cereal held in a cereal box). To create a scatterplot,
the two values for each subject are written as coordinate pairs
and graphed on a pair of coordinate axes (each axis
representing a variable). See also *association*.

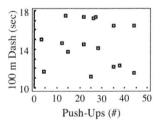

secant   A line that intersects a circle at two distinct points. (p. 598)

sector   A region formed by two radii of a central angle and the arc
between their endpoints on the circle. You can think of it as a portion of
a circle and its interior, resembling a piece of pizza. (p. 512)

sector

segment   See *line segment*. (p. 46)

semicircle   In a circle, a semicircle is an arc with endpoints that are endpoints of any diameter of the circle. It is a half circle and has a measure of 180°. (p. 592)

sequence   An ordered sequence of mathematical terms. A sequence is a function in which the independent variable is a positive integer (sometimes called the term number). The dependent variable is the term value. A sequence is usually written as a list of numbers, starting with the first term where $n = 1$. See also *arithmetic sequence* and *geometric sequence*. (p. 329)

sequence generator   The generator of a sequence tells what you do to each term to get the next term. Note that this is different from the function for the nth term of the sequence. The generator only tells you how to find the following term, when you already know one term. In an arithmetic sequence the generator is the common difference; in a geometric sequence it is the multiplier or common ratio. See also *arithmetic sequence* and *geometric sequence*.

side of an angle   One of the two rays that form an angle.

side of a polygon   See *polygon*.

similar figures   Two shapes are similar if they have exactly the same shape but are not necessarily the same size. Similar polygons have congruent angles, but not congruent sides – the corresponding sides are proportional. The symbol for similar is ~ . See also *ratio of similarity*. (p. 163)

similarity conditions   See *triangle similarity conditions*. (p. 166)

similarity statement   A statement that indicates that two figures are similar. The order of the letters in the names of the shapes in the similarity statement indicates which sides and angles correspond to each other. For example, $\triangle ABC \sim \triangle DEF$ is a similarity statement. It indicates that $\angle A$ corresponds to $\angle D$, and $\overline{AB}$ corresponds to $\overline{DE}$. (p. 163)

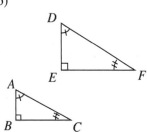

similarity transformations   Movements of figures that preserve their shape, but not necessarily their size. Examples of similarity transformations are reflections, rotations, translations, and dilations. See also *rigid transformations*. (p. 163)

sine ratio   In a right triangle, the sine ratio of an acute angle ($\angle A$) is $\sin A = \frac{\text{length of opposite side}}{\text{length of hypotenuse}}$. In the triangle at right, $\sin A = \frac{BC}{AC} = \frac{3}{5}$. See also *cosine ratio, tangent ratio,* and *inverse sine*. (p. 285)

skew lines   Lines that do not lie in the same flat surface (or plane).

slant height   See *pyramid* or *cone*. (p. 680)

slide   See *translation*.

slope   A ratio that describes how steep (or flat) a line is. Slope can be positive, negative, or even zero, but a straight line has only one slope. Slope is the ratio $\frac{\text{vertical change}}{\text{horizontal change}}$ or $\frac{\text{change in } y\text{-value}}{\text{change in } x\text{-value}}$, sometimes written $\frac{\Delta y}{\Delta x}$. When the equation of a line is written in $y = mx + b$ form, m is the slope of the line. A line has positive slope if it slopes upward from left to right on a graph, negative slope if it slopes downward from left to right, zero slope if it is horizontal, and undefined slope if it is vertical. Parallel lines have equal slopes, and the slopes of perpendicular lines are opposite reciprocals of each other (e.g., $\frac{3}{5}$ and $-\frac{5}{3}$). (p. 59)

slope angle   The acute angle a line forms with the *x*-axis on a coordinate graph. Also see *slope triangle*. (p. 214)

Slope-Intercept Form   A form of a linear equation: $y = mx + b$. In this form, m is the slope and the point $(0, b)$ is the *y*-intercept. (p. 129)

slope triangle   A right triangle with legs (parallel to the *x*- and *y*-axes) that meet the hypotenuse at two points on a given line or line segment. The lengths of the legs of the slope triangle can be used to find the slope of the line. The angle (θ) formed in a slope triangle by the hypotenuse and the horizontal leg is equivalent to the slope angle. See also *slope angle*.

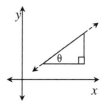

solid   A closed three-dimensional shape and all of its interior points. Examples include regions bounded by pyramids, cylinders, and spheres. (p. 537)

solve (an equation)   To find all the solutions to an equation or an inequality (or a system of equations or inequalities). Compare evaluating an expression, in which you know the value of a variable and use it to rewrite an expression, to solving an equation, in which you determine the value of a variable. For example, solving the equation $x^2 = 9$ gives the solutions $x = 3$ and $x = -3$. The solution(s) may be number(s), variable(s), or an expression.

space   The set of all points in three-dimensions.

special right triangle   A right triangle with particular notable features that can be used to solve problems. Sometimes, these triangles can be recognized by the angles, such as the 45°- 45°- 90° triangle (also known as an isosceles right triangle) and a 30°- 60°- 90° triangle. Some people also categorize triangles for which the sides are Pythagorean Triples as special triangles. (p. 310)

sphere   The set of all points in space that are the same distance from a fixed point. The fixed point is the center of the sphere and the distance is its radius. (p. 706)

square   A quadrilateral with four right angles and four congruent sides. (pp. 416, 431)

square root   A number a is a square root of b if $a^2 = b$. For example, the number 9 has two square roots, 3 and –3. A negative number has no real square roots; a positive number has two; and zero has just one square root, namely, itself. In a geometric context, the principal square root of a number x (written $\sqrt{x}$) represents the length of a side of a square with area x. For example, $\sqrt{16} = 4$. Therefore if the side of a square has a length of 4 units, then its area is 16 square units. (p. 299)

SSS ≅ (Triangle Congruence)   Two triangles are congruent if all three pairs of corresponding sides are congruent. (p. 358)

SSS ~ (Triangle Similarity)   If two triangles have all three pairs of corresponding sides that are proportional (this means that the ratios of corresponding sides are equal), then the triangles are similar. (p. 192)

straight angle   An angle that measures 180°. This occurs when the rays of the angle point in opposite directions, forming a line. (p. 26)

straightedge   A tool used as a guide to draw lines, rays, and segments. A ruler has measurement markings while a straightedge does not. (p. 552)

star polygon   A star polygon is created by connecting equally-spaced points on the circumference of a circle. The star polygon to the right is commonly called a pentagram. (p. 761)

statement   A recording of fact to present evidence in a logical argument (proof). (p. 119)

stretch point   See *point of dilation*. (p. 148)

Substitution Method   A method for solving a system of equations by replacing one variable with an expression involving the remaining variable(s). For example, in the system of equations at right the first equation tells you that y is equal to $-3x + 5$. We can substitute $-3x + 5$ in for y in the second equation to get $2(-3x + 5) + 10x = 18$, then solve this equation to find that $x = 2$. Once we have x, we substitute that value back into either of the original equations to find that $y = -1$. (p. 95)

$$y = -3x + 5$$
$$2y + 10x = 18$$

Substitution Property   The Substitution Property states that in an expression, one can replace a variable, number, or expression with something equal to it without altering the value of the whole. For example, if $x = 3$, then $5x - 7$ can be evaluated by replacing x with 3. This results in $5(3) - 7 = 8$.

supplementary angles   Two angles *a* and *b* for which
a + *b* = 180°. Each angle is called the supplement of the other.
In the example at right, angles *A* and *B* are supplementary.
Supplementary angles are often adjacent. For example, since
∠*LMN* is a straight angle, then ∠*LMP* and ∠*PMN* are
supplementary angles because *m*∠*LMP* + *m*∠*PMN* = 180°.
(p. 83)

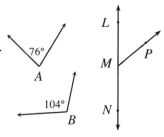

surface area   The sum of all the area(s) of the surface(s) of a three-dimensional solid.
For example, the surface area of a cylinder is the sum of the areas of its top base, its
bottom base, and its lateral surface. (p. 542)

symmetry   (a) Rotation symmetry: A shape has rotation symmetry when
it can be rotated for less than 360° and it appears not to change. For
example the hexagon at right appears not to change if it is rotated 60°
clockwise (or counter-clockwise); (b) Reflection symmetry: A shape has
reflection symmetry when it appears not to change after being reflected
across a line. The regular hexagon at right also has reflection symmetry
across any line drawn through opposite vertices, such as those shown in
the diagram. See *reflection, rotation,* and *line of symmetry.* (p. 55)

system of equations   A system of equations is a set of equations with
the same variables. Solving a system of equations means finding one or
more solutions that make each of the equations in the system true. A
solution to a system of equations gives a point of intersection of the
graphs of the equations in the system. There may be zero, one, or several solutions to a
system of equations. For example, (1.5, −3) is a solution to the system of linear equations
at right; x = 1.5 and *y* = −3 makes both of the equations true. Also, (1.5, −3) is a point of
intersection of the graphs of these two equations. (p. 95)

$$y = 2x - 6$$
$$y = -2x$$

systematic list   A list created by following a system (an orderly process).

tangent   A line on the same flat surface as a circle that intersects the circle
in exactly one point. A tangent of a circle is perpendicular to a radius of
the circle at their point of intersection (also called the point of tangency).
(p. 712)

tangent ratio   In a right triangle, the tangent ratio of an acute ∠*A* is
$\tan A = \frac{\text{length of opposite side}}{\text{length of adjacent side}}$. In the triangle at right, $\tan A = \frac{BC}{AB} = \frac{3}{4}$. See also
cosine ratio, sine ratio, and *inverse tangent.* (p. 228)

tetrahedron   A polyhedron with four faces. The faces of a tetrahedron are triangles. In a
regular tetrahedron, all of the faces are congruent equilateral triangles. Any of the faces of
a tetrahedron can be considered the base. (p. 404)

Core Connections Geometry

theorem A conjecture that has been proven to be true. Some examples of theorems are the Pythagorean Theorem and the Triangle Angle Sum Theorem. (p. 82)

theoretical probability A calculated probability based on the possible outcomes when each outcome has the same chance of occurring: (number of successful outcomes)/(total number of possible outcomes). (p. 31)

theta (θ) A Greek letter that is often used to represent the measure of an angle. Other Greek letters used to represent the measure of an angle include alpha (α) and beta (β). (p. 214)

three-dimensional An object that has length, width, and depth. (p. 403)

transformation This course studies four transformations: reflection, rotation, translation, and dilation. All of them preserve shape, and the first three preserve size. See each term for its particular definition. (p. 50)

translation A transformation that preserves the size, shape, and orientation of a figure while sliding (moving) it to a new location. The result is called the image of the original figure (preimage). Note that a translation is sometimes referred to as a "slide." (pp. 37, 47)

transversal A line that intersects two or more other lines on a flat surface (plane). In this course, we often work with a transversal that intersects two parallel lines. (p. 86)

trapezoid A quadrilateral with at least one pair of parallel sides. (p. 431)

tree diagram A model used to organize the possible outcomes, and the respective probabilities, of two or more events. For an example of a tree diagram, see the Math Notes box *Probability Models* in Lesson 4.2.3. (p. 241)

triangle A polygon with three sides. (p. 52)

Triangle Angle Sum Theorem The sum of the measures of the interior angles in any triangle is 180°. (p. 109)

triangle congruence conditions Conditions that use the minimum number of congruent corresponding parts to prove that two triangles are congruent. They are: SSS $\cong$, SAS $\cong$, AAS $\cong$, ASA $\cong$, and HL $\cong$. (p. 358)

Triangle Inequality In a triangle with side lengths a, b, and c, c must be less than the sum of a and b and greater than the difference of a and b. In the example at right, a is greater than b (that is, $a > b$), so the possible values for c are all numbers such that $c > a - b$ and $c < a + b$. (p. 128)

Triangle Midsegment Theorem   The segment that connects the midpoints of any two sides of a triangle measures half the length of the third side is and parallel to that side. (p. 444)

triangle similarity conditions   Conditions that use the minimum number of congruent and/or proportional corresponding parts to prove that two triangles are similar. They are: SSS ~, SAS ~, and AA ~. (p. 192)

trigonometry   Literally, the "measure of triangles." In this course, this word is used to refer to the development of triangle tools such as trigonometric ratios (sine, cosine, and tangent) and the Laws of Sines and Cosines. (p. 217)

turn   See *rotation*.

two-column proof   A form of proof in which statements are written in one column as a list and the reasons for the statements are written next to them in a second column. (p. 439)

two-dimensional   A figure that that lies on a flat surface and that has length and width. See also *plane*. (p. 403)

two-way table   A way to display categorical two-variable data. The categories of one of the variables is the header of the rows, the other variable is the header of the columns. The entries in the table can be counts (frequencies) or percents (relative frequencies). See also *relative frequency table*.

union of two events   The union of the two events {A} and {B} is a new event that includes all the outcomes that either A will occur *or* B will occur. For example, if event {A} is the thirteen diamond-suited cards in a deck of playing cards, and {B} is the four Aces, then the event {A union B} contains 16 outcomes: {all the diamonds (including the A♦), A♥, A♣, and A♠}. See also *intersection of two events*. (p. 255)

unit of measure   A standard quantity (such as a centimeter, second, square foot, or gallon) that is used to measure and describe an object. A single object can be measured using different units of measure, which will usually yield different results. For example, a pencil may be 80 mm long, meaning that it is 80 times as long as a unit of 1 mm. However, the same pencil is 8 cm long, so that it is the same length as 8 cm laid end-to-end. (This is because 1 cm is the same length as 10 mm.) (p. 107)

Venn diagram   A type of diagram used to classify objects. It is usually composed of two or more overlapping circles representing different conditions. An item is placed or represented in the Venn diagram in the appropriate position based on the conditions it meets. In the example of the Venn diagram at right, if an object meets one of two conditions, it is placed in region A or C but outside region B. If an object meets both conditions, it is placed in the intersection (B) of both circles. If an object does not meet either condition, it is placed outside of both circles (region D). (p. 64)

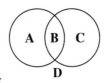

vertex (plural: vertices)   (a) For a two-dimensional geometric shape, a vertex is a point where two or more line segments or rays meet to form a "corner," such as in a polygon or angle. (b) For a three-dimensional polyhedron, a vertex is a point where the edges of the solid meet. See also *apex*. (c) On a graph, a vertex can be used to describe the highest or lowest point on the graph of a parabola or absolute value function (depending on the graph's orientation). (pp. 80, 671)

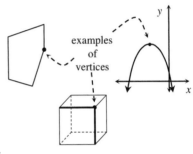

vertical angles   The two opposite (that is, non-adjacent) angles formed by two intersecting lines. "Vertical" is a relationship between pairs of angles, so one angle cannot be called vertical. Angles that form a vertical pair are always congruent. (p. 100)

volume   A measurement of the size of the three-dimensional region enclosed within an object. It is expressed as the number of $1 \times 1 \times 1$ unit cubes (or parts of cubes) that fit inside a solid. (p. 542)

x-intercept   A point where a graph crosses the x-axis. A graph may have several x-intercepts, no x-intercepts, or just one.

y-intercept   A point where a graph crosses the y-axis. A function has at most one y-intercept; a relation may have several.

Zero Product Property   The Zero Product Property states that when the product of two or more factors is zero, one of these factors must equal zero. That is, if $a \cdot b = 0$, then either $a = 0$ or $b = 0$ (or both). For example, if $(x + 4)(2x - 3) = 0$, then either $x + 4 = 0$ or $2x - 3 = 0$ (or both). The Zero Product Property can be used to solve factorable quadratic equations. (p. 238)

zoom factor   The amount each side of a figure is
multiplied by when the figure is proportionally enlarged
or reduced in size. It is written as the ratio of a length in
the new figure (image) to a length in the original figure
(preimage). For the triangles at right, the zoom factor is
$\frac{8}{6}$ or $\frac{4}{3}$. See also *ratio of similarity*. (p. 154)

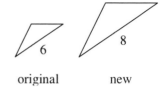

original   new

zero factorial   Zero factorial is $1, 0! = 1$. (p. 658)

Index
Student Version

Many of the pages referenced here contain a definition or an example of the topic listed, often within the body of a Math Notes box. Others contain problems that develop or demonstrate the topic. It may be necessary to read the text on several pages to fully understand the topic. Also, some problems listed here are good examples of the topic and may not offer any explanation. References to Math Notes boxes are bolded.

with Pythagorean Theorem, 195
   zoom factor, 151, **154**
$\sin^{-1}$, 288, **294**
Sine ratio (sin), 279, 280, 283, 289, **285**
Situation, proportional, 161
Slant height, **680**
Slide. *See* translation
Slope, 22, 39, **59**
   angle, **214**, 217, 231
   clinometer, 231
   horizontal change, **214**
   negative, **59**
   of parallel lines, **59**, **454**
   of perpendicular lines, 40, **59**, **454**
   positive, **59**
   ratio, **214**, 217, **228**
   triangle, **59**, 212, **214**, **228**
   undefined, **59**
   vertical change, **214**
   zero, **59**
Slope-intercept form, 129
Solid, 530, 531, **537**
   comparing, 684
   cone, 690
   cross-section, **686**
   cube, 671
   platonic, 671, 674
   polyhedron, **537**, 672
   prism, 535, 536
   ratios of similarity, **549**
   similar, 548
      volume of, 544
   sphere, 694
   surface area, 535
   total surface area, **542**
   views of, 532
   volume, 531
Solution of a system of equations, **95**
Solving
   equations
      Checkpoint 1, 69, 778
      linear, **21**
      Quadratic Formula, **238**
   persevere in, 202, 464, 719
   proportions
      Checkpoint 6, 365, 798
   Pythagorean Theorem
      Checkpoint 7, 456, 801
   quadratic equations
      Checkpoint 5A, 319, 791

systems of equations
   Checkpoint 2, 133, 780
   Substitution Method, **95**
trigonometry
   Checkpoint 7, 456, 801
Somebody's Watching Me, 79, 103
Spatial visualization, 28
Special right triangles, 296, **310**
   30°-60°-90°, 297
   45°-45°-90°, 297
Sphere, 29, 694, **706**
   center, **706**
   coordinates on, 699
   great circle, 700
   hemisphere, 699
   longitude lines, **700**
   radius, **706**
   surface area, 694, **706**
   volume, 694, **706**
Spiral, Fibonnaci, 762
Spiral, golden, 760
Square, **416**, **431**
   constructing, 563
Square root, rationalizing the denominator, **299**
SSA, 320, 321
SSS~, 185, **192**
SSS $\cong$, **358**
   proving, 354
Standard form of a quadratic, 735
Star polygon, 761
Statement, conditional, 87, **119**
Statue of Liberty, 231
Stoplight icon, 96
Straight angle, **26**
Straightedge, 552, 554
   perpendicular bisector, **564**
Stretch point, **148**
Strip, Möbius, 8, 9, 10
Structure, look for and make use of, 203, 465, 720
Study Team Expectations, 8
Substitution Method, **95**
Supplementary, 79, 80, **83**
Surface, lateral, **680**
   cone, **696**
   cylinder, 676

Surface area, 535, **542**
  cylinder
    Checkpoint 11, 708, 828
  lateral, **680**
    cone, **696**
  prism
    Checkpoint 11, 708, 828
  sphere, 694, **706**
Symbol, congruence, 343
Symmetry, 55
  line of, **6**, 54
  polygon, 414
  reflection, 3, **6**, 54, 55
  rotation, 54, 56
  translation, 56
  using, 381
Systems of equations, **95**, 96
  Checkpoint 2, 133, 780

T

Take A Shot, 409
Take It To The Bank, 366
$\tan^{-1}$, 288, **294**
Tangent, 704
  circle, 598, 709, **712**
    constructing, 705
Tangent ratio (tan), 227, **228**, 283, **285**, 289
  applications, 231
Task Manager, 5
Team Roles, 4
  Study Team Expectations, 8
Term zero, **223**
Tetrahedron, 402, 404
  triangular-based pyramid, 679
The Invention of the Wheel, 397
The Monty Hall Problem, 377
The Shape Bucket, 62
The Shape Factory, 50
Theorem, 82, 420, 439
  Inscribed Angle, 595
  Isoperimetric, 520
  Midsegment, 442
  Pythagorean, 131, 132, **133**
  Triangle Angle Sum, 98, **109**
  Triangle Midsegment, **444**
Theoretical probability, **31**
Theta (θ), **214**
Three-dimensional, 403
  solid, 531, 535
  volume, **542**

Tile pattern, 13
Tiling, 85
Time zones, **700**
Toolkit
  angle relationships, 94, 98, 104
  area, 123
  shapes, 67
  theorem, 420, 425, 439, 444
  triangle, 281
  trig table, 218
Tools, use appropriate, 203, 465, 720
Top view, 532
Transformation(s), 50
  defining, 44
  dilation, 145, 146, **148**
  prime notation, **88**
  reflection, 29, **37**, **47**
  rigid, 34, **37**
  rotation, **37**, **47**
  similarity, **163**
  translation, **37**, **47**
  using, 381
Translation, 34, **37**, **47**
  on a grid, 45
  symmetry, 56
Transversal, 85, 86, 91
Trapezoid, 118, **431**
  area, 116, 118, **124**
  base, 118
  isosceles, 84, 444, **481**
  right, 443
Tree diagram, 241
Trial of the Century, 18
Triangle, **52**, 473
  ambiguity, 320, 321
  Angle Sum Theorem, 98, **109**
  angles in, 98
  area, 112, 113, **124**
  centroid, 566, 567, **568**, **604**
  circumcenter, 603, **604**
  congruence, 178, 343
    conditions for, 348, **358**
    corresponding parts, **410**
    proving, 352, 429
  equilateral, 12, 24, **416**
  finding missing parts, 307
  incenter, 553, **604**
  inequality, 126, 128
  investigation, 370
  isosceles, 46, 84